Official CPC® Certification Study Guide

Second Edition

AAPC
Credentialing the Business Side of Medicine

DELMAR
CENGAGE Learning™

DELMAR
CENGAGE Learning™

Official CPC®
Certification Study Guide

Contributors:
Katherine Abel, CPC, CPMA, CPC-I, CRMS
Debra A. Apfel, RN, BA, CPC, CPMA
Carrie Bosela, CPC, CPC-I
Rhonda Buckholtz, CPC, CPC-I, CPMA, CGSC,
    CPEDC, COBGC, CENTC
Marcella Bucknam, CPC, CPC-H, CPC-P, CPC-I,
    CCC, COBGC
Shelly Cronin, CPC, CPMA, CANPC, CGIC, CGSC
Bill Dacey, MBA, MHA, CPC, CPC-I
Kelly Dennis, CPC, CPC-I, CANPC
Mary Divine, CPC, CPC-H, CPC-I, CUC
Brad Ericson, MPC, CPC, COSC
Raemarie Jimenez, CPC, CPMA, CPC-I CANPC, CRHC
Betty Johnson, CPC, CPC-H, CPC-I, CPCD
Dolly Perrine, CPC, CPMA, CPC-I, CUC
Jean Pryor, CPC, CPMA, CPC-I, CIMC
Dorothy Steed, CPC-H, CPMA, CPC-I, CEMC, CFPC
Kate Tierney, CPC, CPC-P, CEDC, CEMC, CGSC,
    COBGC
G. John Verhovshek, MA, CPC
Susan Ward, CPC, CPC-H, CPC-I, CEMC, CPCD, CPRC

Reviewers:
Lynn Anderanin, CPC, CPC-I, COSC
Nicole Benjamin, CPC, CPC-I, CEDC
Glade B. Curtis, MD, MPH, FACOG, CPC, CPC-I
    COBGC
Jennifer Hume, CPC, CPMA, CEMC
Lindsay-Anne McDonald Jenkins, CPC, CPC-H, CPC-I,
    CPMA, CANPC, CIRCC, RN, CRNA (retired)
Vandna Kejariwal, CPC, CPC-H, CPC-I, CEDC
Barbara Pross, CPC, CPMA, CPC-I, CEDC,
    CEMC, COBGC
Carrie Lynn Rawlings, CPC, CPMA, CPC-I,
    CCVTC, CEMC
Alice Reybitz, RN, BA, CPC, CPC-H, CPC-I, CHI
Carrie Severson, CPC, CPC-H, CPC-P, CPMA, CPC-I
Kathy Skolnick, CPC, CPC-I
Charleen Yamasato, CPC, CPC-I

Production:
Dianne Allred, Designer, Desktop Publisher
Michelle A. Dick, Copy Editor
Renee Dustman, Copy Editor
Tina M. Smith, Desktop Publisher

© 2012, Cengage Learning

For product information and technology assistance, contact us at **Cengage Learning Customer & Sales Support, 1-800-354-9706**.

For information about coding, the technical content of the book, and **AAPC**, contact us at **1-800-626-2633**.

For permission to use material from this text or product, submit all requests online at **www. cengage.com/permissions**. Further permissions questions can be emailed to **permissionrequest@cengage.com**.

ISBN: 978-1-133788-94-2

Cengage Learning is a leading provider of customized learning solutions with office locations around the globe, including Singapore, the United Kingdom, Australia, Mexico, Brazil and Japan. Locate your local office at: **international.cengage.com/region**

AAPC (**www.aapc.com**) is the nation's largest training and credentialing association for the business side of medicine with more than 110,000 members representing physician offices, outpatient facilities, and payer environments. AAPC certifications validate the knowledge and expertise of health care professionals in disciplines including medical coding, auditing and compliance. AAPC offers the industry-leading Certified Professional Coder (CPC®) and Certified Professional Medical Auditor (CPMA®) credentials, along with more than 20 specialty-specific coding credentials. AAPC also provides a wide variety of continuing education, resources and networking opportunities.

Contents

Appendix A
Answers and Rationales

Appendix B
Answers and Rationales

The 2012 *Official CPC® Certification Study Guide* is organized to help you prepare for the exam certifying you as a professional medical coder. The Certified Professional Coder (CPC®) credential is awarded by AAPC, the primary organization of around 110,000 medical coders, billers, and auditors.

This study guide, developed in cooperation with AAPC staff and members, can help you understand and practice the concepts, elements, and rules of medical coding. Throughout the 2012 *Official CPC® Certification Study Guide* are easy-to-understand explanations, examples, coding tips, and exercises meant to help you prepare for your exam.

Medical coding continues to grow and mature as a profession. Medical coders report the diagnoses, procedures, and supplies reported by physicians and other medical professionals to commercial and federal payers, such as Aetna or Medicare. They work closely with medical staff and must master medical terminology, anatomy, and physiology and apply this to health care providers' notes or operative reports.

As health care evolves so does medical coding. Medical coders perform in a variety of situations for physicians and facilities. They may participate in the actual billing process or audit claims sent to payers. They may code in independent billing companies. Medical coders often become the officers in charge of compliance with federal and state medical billing and coding regulations. They may work for the payers themselves as adjustors or auditors. Experienced coders often become consultants, serving clients who need coding, billing, auditing, or compliance assistance.

Medical coders will prove even more important as elements of health care reform, standardized electronic medical records, and the new ICD-10 code system are implemented. Coders will be instrumental as advisers, decision makers, technicians, medical coders, and auditors in the next year.

CPC® Confirms Credibility

The CPC® credential (and its derivative credentials: CPC-H®, CPC-P®, for example) illustrates to employers and colleagues that you understand the many facets of coding. A CPC® possesses the following:

- Knowledge of anatomy, physiology, and medical terminology necessary to correctly code provider diagnoses and services
- Skill in accurate medical coding for diagnoses, procedures and services in physician-based settings
- Proficiency across a wide range of services, which include evaluation and management, anesthesia, surgical services, radiology, pathology and medicine
- Sound knowledge of medical coding rules and regulations including compliance and reimbursement
- Understanding of issues such as medical necessity, claims denials, bundling, and charge capture
- Expertise of how to integrate medical coding and reimbursement rule changes into a practice's reimbursement processes

A CPC® successfully completes a 150 question examination in a 5 hour, 40 minute period. You should bring the latest CPT®, ICD-9-CM, and HCPCS Level II codebooks to the exam for code and guideline look-up. More information about the examination is available at www.aapc.com. A CPC® must hold membership in AAPC to sit for the exam and maintain a regimen of continuing education to keep the credential.

The Study Guide

The 2012 *Official CPC® Certification Study Guide* begins with a view of the business of medicine to help you understand the overall view of the medical office and how the coder fits in. After a review of anatomy, you will learn about ICD-9-CM guidelines with real life examples of how to apply them. Each body system is reviewed in its entirety, includes a review of the anatomy, related

ICD-9-CM diagnosis coding, CPT® coding, HCPCS Level II coding, and modifiers. End of chapter reviews provide certification questions similar to those you will find on the exam, along with operative notes for each section for you to code. The study guide concludes with testing techniques and a 35-question review to test your knowledge for the CPC® certification exam.

Unlike most coding certification study guides that focus on each code set, this one more realistically prepares the coder not only for the examination but for the field, where each case more likely will include at least two code sets and require the use of modifiers. Each chapter addresses specifically the particular issues associated with each body area or service offered by the health care provider.

Clinical Examples Used in this Book

AAPC believes it is important in training and testing to reflect as accurate a coding setting as possible to students and examinees. All examples and case studies used in our study guides and exams are actual, redacted office visit and procedure notes donated by AAPC members.

To preserve the real-world quality of these notes for educational purposes, we have not re-written or edited the notes to the stringent grammatical or stylistic standards found in the text of our products. Some minor changes have been made for clarity or to correct spelling errors originally in the notes, but essentially they are as one would find them in a coding setting.

Coding as a Profession

Each time an individual receives health care, a record is maintained of the resulting observations, medical or surgical interventions, diagnostic test and studies, and treatment outcomes. Coding is the process of translating this written or dictated medical record into a series of numeric or alpha-numeric codes. There are separate code sets to describe diagnoses, medical and surgical services/procedures, and supplies. These code sets serve as a common language to ease data collection (for example, to track disease), to evaluate the quality of care, and to determine costs and reimbursements.

Proper code assignment is determined both by the content (documentation) in the medical record and by the unique rules that govern each code set in that particular instance. Coding rules also may vary depending on who pays for the patient care.

Coding is typically performed by either the physician or a coder. When the physician performs the coding, the coder may take on the role of an auditor to verify that the documentation supports the codes the physician selected. In some practices, the coder will receive the documentation and code the services based on what is documented in the medical record.

If the medical record is inaccurate or incomplete, it will not translate properly to the language of codes. The coder must evaluate the medical record for completeness and accuracy, and communicate regularly with physicians and other health care professionals to clarify diagnoses or to obtain additional patient information.

Outpatient coding focuses on physician professional services and outpatient facility coding. Outpatient coders will focus on learning CPT®, HCPCS Level II, and ICD-9-CM codes volumes 1 and 2. They will work in physician offices, outpatient clinics, and facility outpatient departments. Outpatient facility coders will also work with Ambulatory Payment Classifications (APCs)

Hospital inpatient coding focuses on a different subset of skills, where coders will work with ICD-9-CM volumes 1, 2, and 3. These coders also will assign medical severity diagnosis related groups (MS-DRGs).

Regardless of the setting, code updates and insurance payment policies may change as often as quarterly. Coders require continuing education to stay abreast of these changes.

The Hierarchy of Providers

Physician offices and hospitals are staffed by a variety of medical providers, including physicians and mid-level providers (also known as physician extenders), such as physician assistants (PA) and nurse practitioners (NP). Mid-level providers often are reimbursed at a lower rate than physicians, and require physician oversight. Different providers have different levels of education, and each state has scope of practice guidelines for the various provider levels. Check your state health board's website for the scope of practice information.

The Different Types of Payers

Although some patients will pay in full for their own medical expenses, most patients will have some type of insurance coverage. There are two primary types of insurers: private insurance plans and government insurance plans.

Commercial carriers are private payers that may offer both group and individual plans. The contracts they provide vary, but may include hospitalization, basic, and major medical coverage.

The most significant government insurer is Medicare. Medicare is a federal health insurance program—administered by the Centers for Medicare & Medicaid Services (CMS)—that provides coverage for people over the age of 65, blind or disabled individuals, and people with permanent kidney failure or end-stage renal disease

(ESRD). CMS regulations determine the coding requirements for Medicare and non-Medicare payers alike. The Medicare program is made up of several parts:

◖ Medicare Part A helps to cover inpatient hospital care, as well as care provided in skilled nursing facilities, hospice care, and home health care.

◖ Medicare Part B helps to cover medically necessary physicians' services, outpatient care, and other medical services (including some preventive services) not covered under Medicare Part A. Medicare Part B is an optional benefit for which the patient must pay a premium, and which generally requires a yearly deductible and co-pay.

◖ Medicare Part C, also called Medicare Advantage, combines the benefits of Medicare Part A, Part B, and—sometimes—Part D. The plans are managed by private insurers approved by Medicare. The plans may charge different co-payments, coinsurance, or deductibles for services.

◖ Medicare Part D is a prescription drug coverage program available to all Medicare beneficiaries. Private companies approved by Medicare provide coverage.

Medicaid is a health insurance assistance program for some low-income people (especially children and pregnant women) sponsored by federal and state governments. It is administered on a state-by-state basis, but state programs must adhere to certain federal guidelines.

State-funded insurance programs that provide coverage for children up to 21 years of age may include Crippled Children's Services, Children's Medical Services, Children's Indigent Disability Services, and Children with Special Health Care Needs, among others.

Understanding RBRVS

Medicare payments for physician services are standardized using a resource-based relative value scale (RBRVS). Resource costs are divided into three components: physician work, practice expense, and professional liability insurance.

◖ The physician work component accounts for just over half (52 percent) of a procedure's/service's total relative value. Physician work is measured by the time it takes to perform the service; the technical skill and physical effort; the required mental effort and judgment; and stress due to the potential risk to the patient.

◖ Practice expense accounts for 44 percent of the total relative value for each service. Practice expense relative values are resource-based and differ by site of service because, for example, the expense of providing a service in the hospital may be different than the expense of providing the same service in a physician's office.

◖ The resource-based professional liability insurance (PLI) component accounts for 4 percent of the total relative value for each service.

Below is an excerpt from the 2011 National Medicare Physician Fee schedule, which lists the component values for each CPT® and HCPCS Level II code.

HCPCS CODE	MODIFIER	SHORT DESCRIPTION	PROC STAT	PCTC	NOT USED FOR MEDICARE	WORK RVU	NA FLAG FOR NON-FAC PE RVU	TRANSITIONED NON-FAC PE RVU	NA FLG FOR FULLY IMP NON-FAC PE RVU	FULLY IMPLEMENTED NON-FAC PE RVU	NA FLAG FOR TRANS FACILITY PE RVU	TRANSITIONED FACILITY PE RVU	NA FLAG FOR FULLY IMP FAC PE RVU	FULLY IMPLEMENTED FACILITY PE RVU	MP RVU
99214		Office /outpatient visit est	A	0		1.5		1.41		1.48		0.63		0.71	0.1

Table 1.1

CMS annually publishes Physician Fee Schedule (PFS) information on its website (www.cms.hhs.gov/Physician-FeeSched/) and posts the formula for calculating PFS payment amounts. The published formula for calculating the 2011 PFS payment amount is:

PE = Physician Expense

MP = Malpractice

GPCI = Geographic practice cost index (this is used to realize the varying cost based on geographic location)

CF = Conversion Factor (this is a fixed dollar amount used to translate the RVUs into fees)

Non-Facility Pricing Amount = [(Work RVU * Work GPCI) + (Transitioned Non-Facility PE RVU * PE GPCI) + (MP RVU * MP GPCI)] * (CF)

Facility Pricing Amount = [(Work RVU * Work GPCI) + (Transitioned Facility PE RVU * PE GPCI) + (MP RVU * MP GPCI)] * CF

The published conversion factor for CY 2011 is $33.9764. RVUs and the conversion factor may change from year to year and may be updated throughout the year based on legislative changes.

RVU table for E/M codes New Patient and Established Patients (99201–99215)

HCPCS	DESCRIPTION	WORK RVU	TRANSITIONED NON-FACILITY PE RVU	TRANSITIONED FACILITY PE RVU	MP RVU
99201	Office/outpatient visit, new	0.48	0.69	0.24	0.04
99202	Office/outpatient visit, new	0.93	1.09	0.44	0.07
99203	Office/outpatient visit, new	1.42	1.47	0.64	0.14
99204	Office/outpatient visit, new	2.43	2.00	1.06	0.23
99205	Office/outpatient visit, new	3.17	2.36	1.34	0.27
99211	Office/outpatient visit, est.	0.18	0.39	0.08	0.01
99212	Office/outpatient visit, est.	0.48	0.70	0.22	0.04
99213	Office/outpatient visit, est.	0.97	0.99	0.41	0.07
99214	Office/outpatient visit, est.	1.50	1.41	0.63	0.10
99215	Office/outpatient visit, est.	2.11	1.80	0.90	0.14

Table 1.2
Source: CMS (www.cms.gov); PPRVU11_082511_v2.

2011 Geographic Practice Cost Indices by State

Locality name (State)	Work** GPCI	PE GPCI	MP GPCI
Alabama	1.000	0.928	0.484
Alaska	1.500	1.092	0.648
Arizona	1.000	0.983	0.913
Arkansas	1.000	0.923	0.444
Delaware	1.012	1.041	0.678
Fort Lauderdale, FL	1.000	1.041	2.112
Miami, FL	1.000	1.072	2.984
Rest of Florida	1.000	0.976	1.635
Atlanta, GA	1.006	1.006	0.890
Rest of Georgia	1.000	0.943	0.876
Hawaii/Guam	1.000	1.198	0.685
Idaho	1.000	0.943	0.572

Table 1.3
Source: CMS PFS Relative Value Files, RVU11D, GPCI 11

Example 1: Non-Facility Pricing

Calculate the **Non-Facility Pricing Amount**, Medicare Payment for CPT® code 99212 for the state of Idaho.

Work RVUs x Work GPCI   0.48 x 1.000 = 0.48000
+Transitioned Non-Facility Practice
RVUs x Practice Expense GPCI   0.70 x 0.943 = 0.66010
+ MP RVUs x MP GPCI   0.04 x 0.572 = 0.02288
= Sum of geographic adjustment   1.16298

The sum of geographic adjustment x CF = 1.16298 x $33.9764 = $39.51 Non-Facility Pricing Amount (physician office, private practice)

Example 2: Facility Pricing

Calculate the **Facility Pricing Amount**, Medicare Payment for the CPT® code 99212 in Idaho.

Work RVU x Work GPCI   0.48 x 1.000 = 0.48000
+ Transitioned Facility PE
RVU x PE GPCI   0.22 x 0.943 = 0.20746
+ MP RVU x MP GPCI)] x CF   0.04 x 0.572 = 0.02288
= Sum of geographic adjustment   0.71034

Sum of geographic adjustment x CF = 0.71034 x $33.9764 = $24.13 Facility Pricing Amount (Medicare Part A facilities, eg, hospitals, skilled nursing facilities, nursing homes OR physician office if it is facility owned and billed for by a hospital)

Important: Health plans other than Medicare may not use the CMS calculations to determine provider reimbursement.

Medical Necessity

The term "medical necessity" refers to whether a procedure or service is considered appropriate in a given circumstance. Generally, a medically necessary service or procedure is the least radical service/procedure that allows for effective treatment of the patient's complaint or condition.

CMS has developed policies regarding medical necessity based on regulations found in title XVIII, §1862(a)(1) of the Social Security Act. When a physician provides services to a Medicare beneficiary, he or she should bill only those services that meet the Medicare standard of "reasonable and necessary" for the diagnosis and treatment of a patient.

National Coverage Determinations (NCD) explain when Medicare will pay for items or services. Each Medicare Administrative Contractor (MAC) is responsible for interpreting national policies into regional policies, called Local Coverage Determinations (LCD). LCDs explain when a given service is indicated or necessary, give guidance on coverage limitations, describe the specific CPT® codes to which the policy applies, and list ICD-9-CM codes that support medical necessity for the given service or procedure.

LCDs have jurisdiction only within their regional area. If an NCD doesn't exist for a particular item, it's up to the MAC to determine coverage.

If you are providing a service, and the Medicare patient's diagnosis does not support the medical necessity requirements per the LCD, the service may not be covered. In such a case, the practice would be responsible for obtaining an Advance Beneficiary Notice of Noncoverage (Advance Beneficiary Notice, or ABN), as explained below.

Commercial (non-Medicare) payers may develop their own medical policies. These policies may not follow Medicare guidelines, and are specified in private contracts between the payer and the practice or provider.

The Advance Beneficiary Notice (ABN)

The ABN is a standardized form that explains to the patient why Medicare may deny the particular service or procedure. An ABN protects the provider's financial interest by creating a paper trail that CMS requires before a provider can bill the patient for payment if Medicare denies coverage for the stated service or procedure.

The ABN form, entitled "Revised ABN CMS-R-131," along with a full set of instructions, is available as a free download on the CMS website: www.cms.gov/BNI/02_ABN.asp. CMS will accept the ABN CMS-R-131 for either a "potentially non-covered" service or for a statutorily excluded service.

Non-Medicare payers may not recognize an ABN. In some instances, health plan contracts may have a "hold harmless" clause found within the language that prohibits the billing to the patient for anything other than co-pays or deductibles.

The Need for Privacy and Security

The Health Insurance Portability and Accountability Act of 1996, or HIPAA, provides federal protections for personal health information when held by *covered entities*. Under federal guidelines (www.hhs.gov/ocr/privacy/hipaa/understanding/coveredentities/index.html), a covered entity may be:

- A Health Care Provider, such as:
  - Doctors
  - Clinics
  - Psychologists
  - Nursing Homes
  - Pharmacies

- A Health Plan, to include:
  - Health Insurance Companies
  - HMOs
  - Company Health Plans
  - Government programs that pay for health care, such as Medicare, Medicaid, and the military and veterans health care programs

- A Health Care Clearinghouse: This includes entities that process nonstandard health information they receive from another entity into a standard format (such as a standard electronic format or data content), or vice versa.

A key provision of HIPAA is the "Minimum Necessary" requirement. That is, *only the minimum necessary protected health information* (PHI) should be shared to satisfy a particular purpose. If information is not required to satisfy a particular purpose, it must be withheld.

Under the Privacy Rule, the minimum necessary standard does not apply to:

- Disclosures to or requests by a health care provider for treatment purposes.
- Disclosures to the individual who is the subject of the information.
- Uses or disclosures made pursuant to an individual's authorization.
- Uses or disclosures required for compliance with the HIPAA Administrative Simplification Rules.
- Disclosures to the U.S. Department of Health & Human Services (HHS) when disclosure of information is required under the Privacy Rule for enforcement purposes.
- Uses or disclosures that are required by other law.

It is the responsibility of a covered entity to develop and implement policies, best suited to its particular circumstances, to meet HIPAA requirements. As a policy requirement, only those individuals whose job requires it may have access to PHI.

More information on handling requests and disclosures for PHI may be found at: www.hhs.gov/ocr/privacy/hipaa/understanding/coveredentities/minimumnecessary.pdf.

HITECH and Its Impact on HIPAA

The Health Information Technology for Economic and Clinical Health Act, or HITECH, was enacted as part of the American Recovery and Reinvestment Act of 2009 (ARRA). Portions of HITECH strengthen HIPAA rules by addressing privacy and security concerns associated with the electronic transmission of health information.

HITECH allows patients to request an audit trail showing all disclosures of their health information made through an electronic record. HITECH also requires that an individual be notified if there is an unauthorized disclosure or use of his or her health information. Some samples of what may constitute breaches under HITECH can be found at www.hhs.gov/ocr/privacy/hipaa/enforcement/examples/allcases.html.

Fraud and Abuse

The OIG is mandated by public law to engage in activities to test the efficiency and economy of government programs to include investigation of suspected health care fraud or abuse. The definition of fraud is to purposely bill for services that were never given or to bill for a service that has a higher reimbursement than the service provided. As a part of Health Care Reform, the Affordable Care Act of 2010 amended the definition of fraud to remove the intent requirement. The person does not have to have knowledge of the violation in order for it to still be considered an offense. Abuse consists of payment for items or services that are billed by providers in error that should not be paid for by Medicare. The government continues to aggressively investigate fraud and abuse in every health care setting.

18 U.S.C. § 1347

(a) Whoever knowingly and willfully executes, or attempts to execute, a scheme or artifice—

(1) to defraud any health care benefit program; or

(2) to obtain, by means of false or fraudulent pretenses, representations, or promises, any of the money or property owned by, or under the custody or control of, any health care benefit program, in connection with the delivery of or payment for health care benefits, items, or services, shall be fined under this title or imprisoned not more than 10 years, or both. If the violation results in serious bodily injury (as defined in section 1365 of this title), such person shall be fined under this title or imprisoned not more than 20 years, or both; and if the violation results in death, such person shall be fined under this title, or imprisoned for any term of years or for life, or both.

"(b) With respect to violations of this section, a person need not have actual knowledge of this section or specific intent to commit a violation of this section."

The Need for Compliance Rules and Audits

All physician offices and health care facilities should have, and actively use, a *compliance plan*. The compliance plan is a written set of instructions outlining the process for coding and submitting accurate claims, and what to do if mistakes are found. These are especially critical as internal controls in the reimbursement, coding, and payment areas where claims and billing operations are often the source of fraud and abuse, and have been the focus of government regulation, scrutiny, and sanctions. A compliance plan may offer several benefits, among them:

- More accurate payment of claims
- Fewer billing mistakes
- Improved documentation and more accurate coding
- Less chance of violating self-referral and anti-kickback statutes

The increased accuracy of physician documentation that may result from a compliance program actually may assist in enhancing patient care. Voluntary compliance programs show the physician practice is making a good-faith effort to submit claims appropriately, and sends a signal to employees that compliance is a priority while providing a means to report erroneous or fraudulent conduct, so it may be corrected. The scope of a compliance program depends on the size and resources of the physician practice.

The Office of Inspector General (OIG) has provided compliance program guidance. This guidance can be used to form the basis of a voluntary compliance program for a physician practice. The OIG Compliance Program for Individual and Small Group Physician Practices can be found at www.oig.hhs.gov/authorities/docs/physician.pdf.

Key actions of the program include:

- Implement compliance and practice standards through the development of written standards and procedures
- Designate a compliance officer or contact(s) to monitor compliance efforts and enforce practice standards

- Conduct appropriate training and education on practice standards and procedures
- Conduct internal monitoring and auditing through the performance of periodic audits
- Respond appropriately to detected violations through the investigation of allegations and the disclosure of incidents to appropriate government entities
- Develop open lines of communication, such as: (1) discussions at staff meetings regarding how to avoid erroneous or fraudulent conduct; and (2) community bulletin boards, to keep practice employees updated regarding compliance activities
- Enforce disciplinary standards through well-publicized guidelines

The OIG Work Plan

Each year in October, the OIG releases a work plan outlining its priorities for the fiscal year ahead. Of special interest to health care, the work plan announces potential problem areas with claims submissions that it will target for special scrutiny. For example, here's an excerpt from the 2012 OIG Work Plan:

Evaluation and Management Services Provided During Global Surgery Periods

We will review industry practices related to the number of E/M services provided by physicians and reimbursed as part of the global surgery fee to determine whether the practices have changed since the global surgery fee concept was developed in 1992. Under the global surgery fee concept, physicians bill a single fee for all of their services that are usually associated with a surgical procedure and related E/M services provided during the global surgery period. The criteria for global surgery policy are in CMS's Medicare Claims Processing Manual, Pub. 100-4, ch. 12, § 40.

(OAS; W-00-09-35207; various reviews; expected issue date: FY 2012; work in progress)

Source: oig.hhs.gov/reports-and-publications/archives/workplan/2012/WP01-Mcare_A+B.pdf

What AAPC Will Do for You

AAPC was founded in 1988 to provide education and professional certification to physician-based medical coders, and to elevate the standards of medical coding by providing student training, certification, and ongoing education, networking, and job opportunities. AAPC has a membership base over 110,000 worldwide, of which more than 78,000 are certified.

AAPC credentialed coders have proven mastery of all code sets, evaluation and management principles, and documentation guidelines. Certified Professional Coders

(CPC®'s) and other AAPC-credentialed coders represent the best in outpatient coding.

AAPC offers over 450 local chapters across the United States and in the Bahamas. Through local chapters, AAPC members can obtain continuing education, gain leadership skills, and network.

AAPC specifies a Code of Ethics to promote and maintain the highest standard of professional service and conduct among its members.

AAPC Member Code of Ethics

Members of AAPC shall be dedicated to providing the highest standard of professional service for the betterment of health care to employers, clients, vendors, and patients. Professional and personal behavior of AAPC members must be exemplary.

AAPC members shall:

- Strive to maintain and enhance the dignity, status, competence, and standards of the health care industry.
- Maintain the highest standard of personal and professional conduct. Members shall respect the rights of patients, clients, employers, and all other colleagues.
- Use only legal and ethical means in all professional dealings and shall refuse to cooperate with, or condone by silence, the actions of those who engage in fraudulent, deceptive, or illegal acts.
- Respect and adhere to the laws and regulations of the land.
- Pursue excellence through continuing education in all areas applicable to our profession.
- Ensure that professional relationships with patients, employees, clients, or employers are not exploited for personal gain.

Adherence to these standards assures public confidence in the integrity and service of medical coding, auditing, compliance and practice management professionals who are AAPC members.

Failure to adhere to these standards, as determined by AAPC, will result in the loss of credentials and membership with AAPC.

The quality of AAPC certifications, along with the strength in its membership numbers, offers certified AAPC members credibility in the workforce—as well as higher wages. According to the 2011 AAPC Salary Survey, salaries for credentialed coders rose 3 percent from the previous year, to an average of $46,800. Even non-certified coders benefited from their affiliation with AAPC, with an average salary of $37,841.

Average Salaries by Region

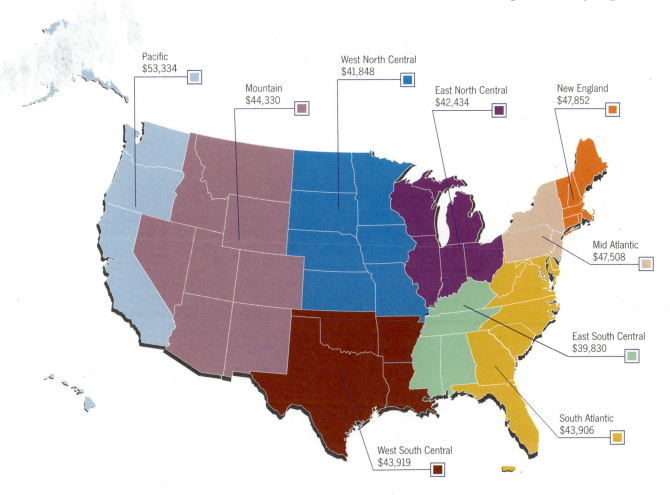

Pacific
$53,334

Mountain
$44,330

West North Central
$41,848

East North Central
$42,434

New England
$47,852

Mid Atlantic
$47,508

East South Central
$39,830

South Atlantic
$43,906

West South Central
$43,919

Source: AAPC

Acronyms

ABN	Advance Beneficiary Notification
AMA	American Medical Association
APC	Ambulatory Payment Classification
ARRA	American Recovery and Reinvestment Act of 2009
ASC	Ambulatory Surgical Centers
CF	Conversion Factor
CMS	Centers for Medicare & Medicaid Services
CPC®	Certified Professional Coder
CPT®	Current Procedural Terminology
DRG	Diagnosis Related Group
EHR	Electronic Health Record
E/M or E&M	Evaluation and Management
GPCI	Geographic Practice Cost Index
HCPCS	Healthcare Common Procedure Coding System
HHS	Department of Health & Human Services
HIPAA	Health Insurance Portability and Accountability Act of 1996
HITECH	Health Information Technology for Economic and Clinical Health Act
HMO	Health Maintenance Organization
ICD-9-CM	International Classification of Disease, 9th Clinical Modification
LCD	Local Coverage Determinations
MAC	Medicare Administrative Contractor
MP	Malpractice
MS-DRG	Medicare Severity—Diagnosis Related Group
NCD	National Coverage Determination
NP	Nurse Practitioner
OCR	Office for Civil Rights
OIG	Office of Inspector General
PA	Physician Assistant
PE	Physician Expense
PFS	Physician Fee Schedule
PHI	Protected Health Information
PLI	Professional Liability Insurance
RUC	Relative Value Update Committee
RVU	Relative Value Unit
RBRVS	Resource Based Relative Value System

Chapter Review Questions

1. A Medicare patient is receiving chemotherapy at her oncologist's office. While the patient is receiving chemotherapy, the oncologist calls in a prescription for pain medication to a pharmacy in the same building. The pharmacy delivers the medication to the patient in the oncologist's office for the patient to take home. What part of Medicare should be billed for the pain medication by the pharmacy?

    A. Part A

    B. Part B

    C. Part C

    D. Part D

2. What is medical coding?

    A. Reporting services on a CMS-1500

    B. Translating medical documentation into codes

    C. Programming an EHR

    D. Creating a 5010 electronic file for transmission

3. Using the table in the chapter, what would be the allowed amount for a level 5 new patient office visit in a provider's office for Miami, FL?

    A. $221.04

    B. $183.89

    C. $179.40

    D. $171.78

4. What is an NCD interpreted at the MAC level considered?

    A. MAC adjusted NCD

    B. ABN

    C. LCD

    D. MACs cannot interpret an NCD

5. When should an ABN be signed?

    A. When a service is considered medically necessary by Medicare.

    B. When a service is not expected to be covered by Medicare.

    C. Routinely for any services given to a Medicare patient.

    D. After a service is denied and the patient should be billed.

6. The amount on an ABN should be within how much of the cost to the patient?

   A. $250 of cost

   B. $100 or 25% of cost

   C. $10 or 10% of cost

   D. $100 or 10% of cost

7. An entity that processes nonstandard health information they receive from another entity into a standard format is considered what?

   A. Billing Company

   B. Electronic Health Record Vendor

   C. Clearinghouse

   D. Practice Management Vendor

8. What is PHI?

   A. Personal History Information

   B. Problem with History of Infection

   C. Partial Health Interaction

   D. Protected Health Information

9. Intentional billing of services not provided is considered _____.

   A. Deceptive Billing

   B. Fraud

   C. Abuse

   D. Common practice

10. What OIG document should a provider review for potential problem areas that will receive special scrutiny in the upcoming year?

    A. Compliance Program Guidance

    B. Safe Harbor Regulations

    C. Red Flag Rules

    D. OIG Work Plan

Chapter 2

Medical Terminology and Anatomy Review

Introduction

This chapter will introduce students to the basic elements of human anatomy and review medical vocabulary and terminology. Students may encounter terms not covered here within subsequent chapters. Objectives for this chapter include:

◖ Understand the language of medicine

◖ Review word elements such as combining forms, prefixes, and suffixes

◖ Acquire an understanding of procedural and diagnostic terms

◖ Understand anatomy as it relates to coding

Medical Terminology

The best way to learn medical terminology is by understanding word parts or elements of medical language—root words, prefixes, and suffixes—that serve as the foundation of the medical vocabulary.

The base of the word is considered the "root." Root words are terms that can stand alone as the main portion of a medical term. The root word is the word part that holds the fundamental meaning of the medical term. A word can have more than one root.

Examples may include:

Root word	Definition
Blephar/o	eyelid
Bucc/o	cheek
Cholecyst/o	gallbladder
Colp/o	vagina
Cyst/o	a fluid sac or pouch, urinary bladder
Derm/o	skin
Encephal/o	brain

Enter/o	intestine
Hem/o, hemat/o	blood
My/o	muscle
Myel/o	spinal cord, bone marrow
Onych/o	nail
Oste/o	bone
Phleb/o	vein
Pulm/o, pulmon/o	lungs
Synov/i	synovial fluid, joint, or membrane

A prefix typically is attached to the beginning of a word to modify or alter its meaning. Prefixes often indicate location, time, or number.

Some common prefixes include:

Prefix	Definition
Ab-	away from
Ad-	toward, near
Ante-	before
Ec-, ecto-	out, outside
End/o-	in, within
Mon/o-	one
Poly-	many, much
Post-	after, behind

A suffix is attached to the end of a word to modify or alter its meaning. In medical terms, suffixes frequently indicate the procedure, condition, disorder, or disease.

Some common suffixes include:

Suffix	Definition
-centesis	puncture, tap
-desis	binding, fusion
-ectomy	excision, surgical removal
-graphy	act of recording data
-pexy	surgical fixation
-plasty	plastic repair, plastic surgery, reconstruction
-tripsy	crushing

Due to Greek and Latin origins of medical terms, the conventions for changing from singular to plural endings are dictated by a specific set of guidelines, as demonstrated in the table below.

Plural Endings:

Word Ending	Plural Ending	Singular Example	Plural Example
a	ae	vertebra	vertebrae
en	ina	lumen	lumina
ex, ix, yx	ices	index	indices
is	es	prognosis	prognoses
ma	mata	stigma	stigmata
nx (anx, inx, ynx)	nges	phalanx	phalanges
on	a	phenomenon	phenomena
um	a	serum	sera
us	i	thrombus	thrombi

Using the word parts for translation, you will find the approximate meaning of the complete medical term.

Example:

The word "cardiomyopathy" can be broken down to find its meaning:

cardi/o—heart
my/o—muscle
pathy—disease

Cardiomyopathy is a diseased heart muscle.

Anatomic Positions and Planes

The standard body position is considered the "anatomic position." The anatomic position is an upright, face-forward position with the arms by the side and palms facing forward. The feet are parallel and slightly apart.

Anatomical Planes and Directions

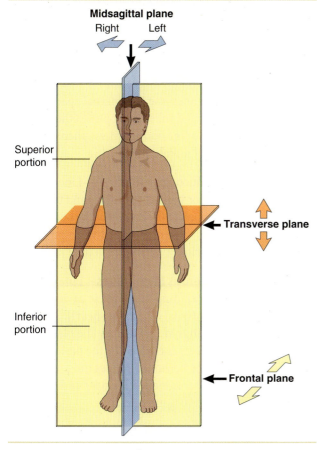

Source: Delmar/Cengage Learning.

Based on the anatomic position, the following directional terms are pertinent to understanding medical documentation:

Anterior (ventral)—Toward the front of the body.

Posterior (dorsal)—Toward the back of the body.

Medial—Toward the midline of the body.

Lateral—Toward the side of the body.

Proximal—Nearer to the point of attachment or to a given reference point.

Distal—Farther from the point of attachment or from a given reference point.

Superior (cranial)—Above; toward the head.

Inferior (caudal)—Below; toward the lower end of the spine.

Superficial (external)—Closer to the surface of the body.

Deep (internal)—Closer to the center of the body.

For radiological studies, the body is often virtually cut along a flat surface called a plane. The most frequently used planes include:

Sagittal—Cuts through the midline of the body from front to back, dividing the body into right and left sections.

Frontal (coronal)—Cuts at a right angle to the midline, from side to side, dividing the body into front (anterior) and back (posterior) sections.

Transverse (horizontal)—Cuts horizontally through the body, separating the body into upper (superior) and lower (inferior) sections.

Structure of the Human Body

The structure of the human body falls into four categories:

1. The cell is the basic unit of all living things. Human anatomy is composed of cells that vary in size and shape according to function.

2. Tissue is a group of similar cells performing a specific task; for instance, muscle tissue produces movement. Connective tissue is divided into four general groups: adipose tissue, cartilage, bone, and blood.

3. Organs are two or more kinds of tissue that together perform special body functions. As an example, the skin is an organ composed of epithelial, connective, and nerve tissue.

4. Systems are groups of organs that work together to perform complex body functions. For example, the nervous system is made up of the brain, spinal cord, and nerves. Its function is to coordinate and control other body parts.

Body Cavities

Source: Delmar/Cengage Learning.

Body Cavities

The body is not a solid structure as it appears on the outside. It has five cavities, each of which contains an orderly arrangement of internal organs.

1. The cranial cavity is a space inside the skull, or cranium, containing the brain.

2. The spinal (vertebral) cavity is the space inside the spinal column containing the spinal cord.

3. The thoracic, or chest, cavity is the space containing the heart, lungs, esophagus, trachea, bronchi, and thymus.

4. The abdominal cavity is the space containing the lowest portion of the esophagus, the stomach, intestines (excluding the sigmoid colon and rectum), kidneys, liver, gallbladder, pancreas, spleen, and ureters.

5. The pelvic cavity is the space containing the urinary bladder, certain reproductive organs, part of the large intestine, and the rectum.

Membranes

Membranes line the internal spaces of organs and tubes that open to the outside, and also line body cavities. There are five types of membranes:

1. **Mucous Membranes**—Line the interior walls of the organs and tubes that open to the outside of the body, such as those of the digestive, respiratory, urinary, and reproductive systems.

2. **Serous Membranes**—Line cavities, including the thoracic cavity and internal organs (eg, heart). The lungs are covered by the pleura; the heart is covered by the pericardium; the peritoneum lines the abdominopelvic cavity and covers the organs within.

3. **Synovial Membranes**—Line joint cavities and are composed of connective tissues. They secrete synovial fluid into the joint cavity so that bones can move freely.

4. **Meninges**—Are composed of three connective tissue membranes found within the dorsal cavity and serve as a protective covering of, for example, the brain and spinal cord.

5. **Cutaneous Membrane**—a.k.a., the skin—forms the outer covering of the body.

Integumentary System

The largest organ system in the body is comprised of the skin, hair, and nails. Together these structures protect from injury, fluid loss, and microorganisms (eg, bacteria, virus, fungus, yeasts); regulate body temperature and fluid balance; and provide sensation.

Skin

Two layers make up human skin:

1. The epidermis is composed of four to five layers (stratum):

   ◖ **Stratum Corneum**—Also called the horny layer; outermost layer.

   ◖ **Stratum Lucidum**—Clear layer. The stratum lucidum layer is normally found only on the palms of the hands and the soles of the feet.

   ◖ **Stratum Granulosum**—Granular layer of cells. They accumulate two types of granules; keratohyaline granules and lamellated granules.

   ◖ **Stratum Spinosum**—Composed of prickle cells.

   ◖ **Stratum Basale (Stratum Germinativum)**— Deepest of the five layers, made of basal cells.

2. The dermis is located just under the epidermis. It has two layers of stratum:

   ◖ **Stratum Papillare**—Thin superficial layer interlocked with the epidermis.

   ◖ **Stratum Reticulare**—Thick layer of dense, irregular connective tissue.

The dermis also contains vessels carrying blood and lymph, nerves and nerve endings, glands, and hair follicles.

The dermis lies on the subcutaneous (beneath the skin) layer. The subcutaneous layer is known as the hypodermis, but it is not considered to be a layer of the skin. The subcutaneous tissues are mostly composed of fatty or adipose tissue, plus some areolar tissue. The fibrous connective tissues referred to as superficial fascia are included in this layer.

Application to Documentation

NARRATIVE: After prone positioning and IV sedation, the left upper back was prepped and draped in a sterile manner. Local anesthesia 1% lidocaine and bicarbonate was used. A vertical incision was made over the mass and extended. **Deep in the subcutaneous tissue over muscle fascia** was an 8 cm lipoma with a lot of lobulations between skin ligaments, and these were all progressively divided to excise the entire mass **including a portion of the muscle fascia.** An oblique drain was positioned through an inferior stab wound and secured with Ethilon. All bleeding was controlled with cautery. The subcutaneous tissue was approximated with Vicryl, and the skin was approximated with intracuticular 4-0 Vicryl suture. Steri-Strips and dressings were applied. The patient was awakened and moved to the recovery room in satisfactory condition. There were no complications. Blood loss was minimal.

In the above documentation, understanding the depth of the procedure (eg, which skin tissue is involved) is necessary to select the appropriate procedure code.

Skin Layers

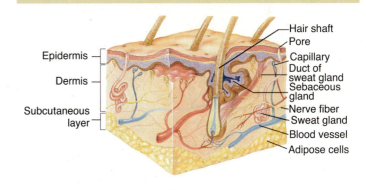

Source: Delmar/Cengage Learning.

Hair

Hair has two separate structures:

1. The follicle contains several layers. At the base is a bulb-like projection, called a papilla. Capillaries nourish the bulb. Inner and outer sheaths protect and mold the growing hair shaft surrounding the follicle. The inner sheath ends at the opening of the sebaceous gland, which secretes sebum that may pocket to cause benign lesions on the scalp. A muscle, called the erector pili, attaches to the outer sheath and causes the hair to stand up when it contracts.

2. The shaft is composed of keratin in three layers: the medulla, cortex, and cuticle. Pigment cells in the cortex and medulla give hair its characteristic color.

Nails

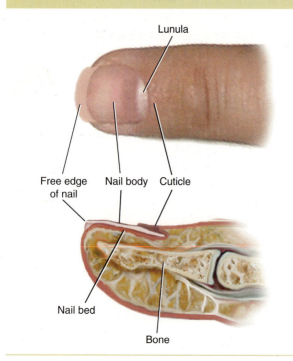

Source: Delmar/Cengage Learning.

Nails

The nail is divided into six specific parts:

1. The root, also known as the germinal matrix, lies beneath the skin behind the fingernail and extends several millimeters into the finger. The root produces most of the volume of the nail and the nail bed; and its edge is the white, crescent-shaped structure called the lunula.

2. The nail bed, called the sterile matrix, extends from the edge of the lunula to the hyponychium. The nail bed contains the blood vessels, nerves, and melanocytes (melanin-producing cells).

3. The nail plate is the actual fingernail, made of translucent keratin. Blood vessels underneath give the nail its pink appearance; the grooves along the inner length of the nail plate anchor the nail to the nail bed.

4. The cuticle, also called the eponychium, is between the skin of the finger and the nail plate that fuses the skin of the finger to the nail plate.

5. The perionychium, also known as the paronychial edge, is the skin that overlies the nail plate on its sides.

6. The hyponychium is the junction between the free edge of the nail and the skin.

Musculoskeletal System

The musculoskeletal system is a system of muscles, joints, tendons, and ligaments that provides movement, form, strength, and protection.

Bones

Bones form the skeleton, support the body, and protect vital organs, while also creating blood cells and storing calcium, phosphorus, and magnesium salts. Bones may be classified by shape:

Long or Tubular—Named for their elongated shape (eg, femur and humerus).

Short or Cuboidal—Cube-shaped bones found in the carpal bones of the wrist and tarsal bones of the ankle.

Sesamoid—A short bone formed within the tendons, such as the patella.

Flat—Consist of a layer of spongy bone between two thin layers of compact bone (eg, the skull and ribs).

Irregular—Examples include the zygoma and vertebrae.

Bone Classification

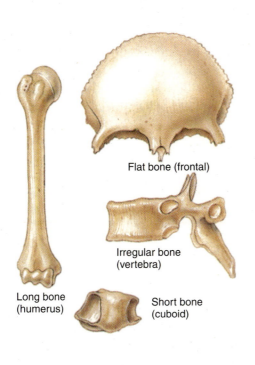

Flat bone (frontal)

Irregular bone (vertebra)

Long bone (humerus)

Short bone (cuboid)

Source: Delmar/Cengage Learning.

Bones may fracture in several ways: Understanding the type of fracture is essential to proper ICD-9-CM coding.

Closed Fracture—Does not involve a break in the skin.

Compound Fracture—Projects through the skin increasing the possibility of infection.

Comminuted Fracture—Shatters the affected part into bony fragments.

Transverse Fracture—Breaks the shaft of a bone across the longitudinal axis.

Greenstick Fracture—Where only one side of shaft is broken, and the other is bent; common in children.

Spiral Fracture—Spread along length of bone and produced by twisting stress.

Colles Fracture—Occurs in the wrist and affects the distal radius bone.

Compression Fracture—Occurs in vertebrae and is subject to extreme stress.

Epiphyseal Fracture—Occurs where the matrix is undergoing calcification and chondrocytes are dying; usually seen in children.

Cartilage and Joints

Cartilage is a non-vascular, flexible connective tissue matrix made of chondrocytes, collagen, and cells called proteoglycan. Joints (articulating surfaces) provide a connection between two or more skeletal parts. There are three types of joints: fibrous, cartilaginous, and synovial.

Most joints are synovial and have articular cartilage that covers the bone ends. The joint cavity is lined with a synovial membrane which secretes synovial fluid that cushions the joint and allows smooth motion. Fibrous connective tissue surrounds and provides stability of the joint, while accessory ligaments give reinforcement.

Human Skeleton

The human skeleton is divided into two parts:

1. Axial Skeleton, consisting of:

    o Skull
    o Hyoid and cervical spine (neck)
    o Ribs
    o Sternum
    o Vertebrae
    o Sacrum

2. Appendicular Skeleton, consisting of:

    o Shoulder girdle
    o Pelvic girdle
    o Extremities

Muscles

Types of Muscle

(A) Skeletal muscle

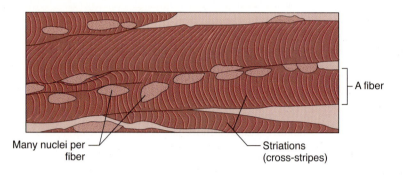

Many nuclei per fiber

Striations (cross-stripes)

A fiber

(B) Smooth muscle

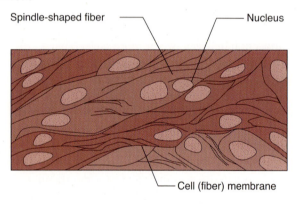

Spindle-shaped fiber

Nucleus

Cell (fiber) membrane

(C) Myocardial muscle

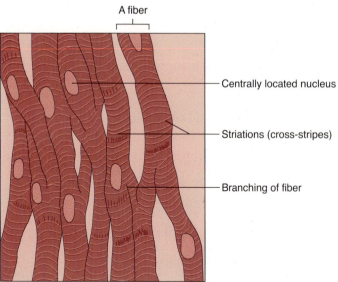

A fiber

Centrally located nucleus

Striations (cross-stripes)

Branching of fiber

Source: Delmar/Cengage Learning.

There are three types of muscles found in the body:

Skeletal Muscle—Also called striated muscle, it is attached to the skeleton; contraction of skeletal muscle is under voluntary control.

Cardiac Muscle—Also called heart muscle; makes up the wall of the heart.

Smooth Muscle—Found in the walls of all the hollow organs of the body (except the heart). Its contraction reduces the size of these structures; movement generally is considered involuntary (not under voluntary control).

Cardiovascular System

The heart and the blood vessels work together to move blood throughout the body.

Blood Vessels

Vessels–Arterial Circulation

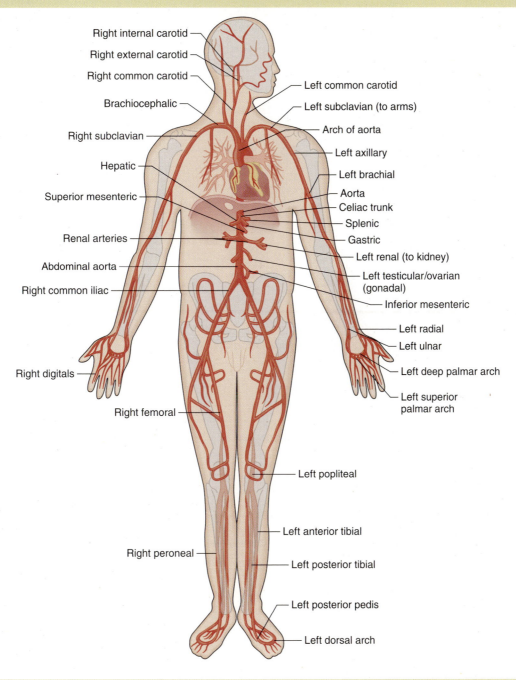

Source: Delmar/Cengage Learning.

Vessels—Venous Circulation

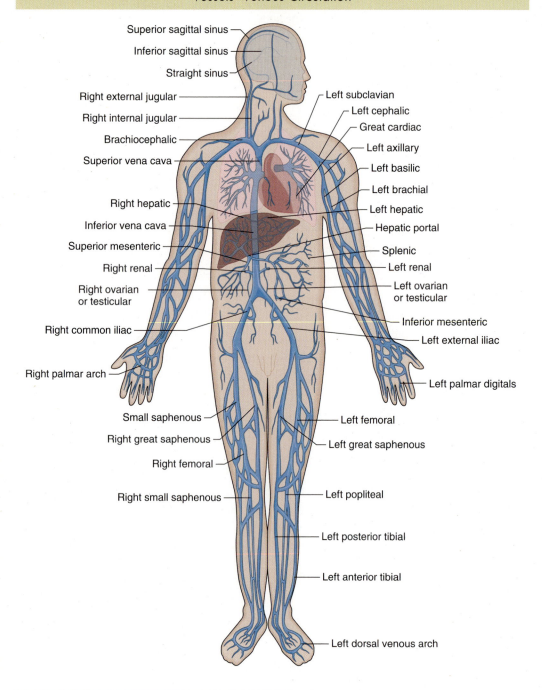

Superior sagittal sinus
Inferior sagittal sinus
Straight sinus
Right external jugular
Right internal jugular
Brachiocephalic
Superior vena cava
Right hepatic
Inferior vena cava
Superior mesenteric
Right renal
Right ovarian or testicular
Right common iliac
Right palmar arch
Small saphenous
Right great saphenous
Right femoral
Right small saphenous

Left subclavian
Left cephalic
Great cardiac
Left axillary
Left basilic
Left brachial
Left hepatic
Hepatic portal
Splenic
Left renal
Left ovarian or testicular
Inferior mesenteric
Left external iliac
Left palmar digitals
Left femoral
Left great saphenous
Left popliteal
Left posterior tibial
Left anterior tibial
Left dorsal venous arch

Source: Delmar/Cengage Learning.

The human body contains three types of blood vessels:

1. The arteries carry oxygenated blood away from the heart. These vessels get smaller and turn into arterioles as they go into the extremities. Eventually they comprise the arterial side of the capillary bed.

2. Most veins carry deoxygenated blood back to the heart. The venous side of the circulation begins in the venous side of the capillary bed, enlarging to form venules and eventually forming veins.

3. Capillaries are tiny vessels, usually a single cell layer thick. They are semi-permeable and facilitate the exchange of fluids, oxygen, nutrients, and waste between local tissues and the blood stream.

Heart

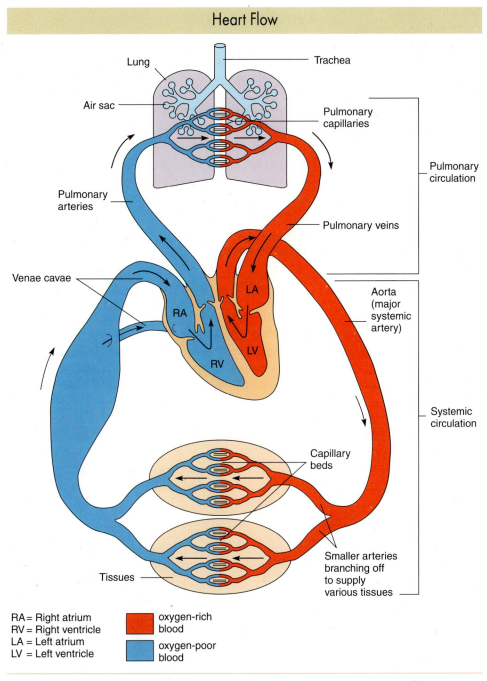

Heart Flow

RA = Right atrium
RV = Right ventricle
LA = Left atrium
LV = Left ventricle

🟥 oxygen-rich blood
🟦 oxygen-poor blood

Source: Delmar/Cengage Learning.

The heart pumps blood to two distinct systems for circulation:

1. The pulmonary circulation receives deoxygenated blood from the right ventricle via the right and left pulmonary artery. The blood is circulated through the pulmonary vascular tree in the lungs and sent back into the left atrium of the heart through the right and left pulmonary veins.

2. Oxygenated blood is pumped from the left side of the heart out to the systemic circulation from the left ventricle to the aorta. Because the left side of the heart is responsible for pumping the blood throughout the entire body, the muscle surrounding the left ventricle is stronger and larger than that of the right ventricle.

The heart is composed of three layers:

1. The epicardium is the outer layer of the heart.

2. The main muscle of the heart is the myocardium. The myocardial tissues allow electrical impulses to pass quickly across the muscle fibers as part of the heart's unique electrical conduction system.

3. The inner lining of the heart is the endocardium.

The heart is enclosed in a double-wall lining called the pericardial sac, which prevents the heart from rubbing against other organs or body structures as it beats.

Note: Physicians often will dictate using medical abbreviations to indicate which artery or vein they are operating on—eg, right subclavian artery (RSCA), right carotid artery (RCA), left carotid artery (LCA).

Application to Documentation

The **LAD** was then dissected out. Arteriotomy was performed and the **IMA** was anastomosed in an end-to-side fashion to the **LAD** using running 7-0 Prolene around the heel of the anastomosis. The toe of the anastomosis was closed using interrupted 7-0 Prolene. Rewarming was begun during this anastomosis. The **IMA** pedicle clamp was released. Rapid resuscitation of the heart was seen as well as rapid distal filling of the **LAD**. The **IMA** pedicle was affixed to the epicardium using 5-0 silk suture. The aortic cross-clamp was removed. A partial occlusion clamp was placed on the aorta and three punch arteriotomies were made on the aorta. The vein grafts were measured to length, cut, and spatulated and anastomosed in an end-to-side fashion to the aorta using running 6-0 Prolene. All three proximal vein graft anastomoses were marked with titanium clips. The most distal graft on the aorta is that to the posterolateral branch of the circumflex, more proximal is that to the ramus, and the vein graft to the **PDA** was brought to the right side of the aorta. Partial occlusion clamp was removed.

In the documentation above, "IMA" indicates the internal mammary artery; "LAD" indicates the left anterior descending artery; and "PDA" indicates the posterior descending artery.

Lymphatic System

The lymphatic system is comprised of lymph vessels and nodes. This system serves to collect excess fluid from the interstitial spaces and returns it to the heart. The venous end of the capillaries reabsorb fluid pushed from the arterial capillaries into the interstitial space; the lymph picks up any excess fluid. This system operates without a pump by using a series of valves to ensure the fluid travels in one direction back to the heart. The lymphoid organs scattered throughout the body house phagocytic cells and lymphocytes that are essential to the body's defense system and its resistance to disease. Lymphoid organs include the spleen, thymus, tonsils, and Peyer's patches of the intestine.

Lymphatic Vessels

Lymphatic capillaries are closed off at one end. After the lymph fluid is picked up, it is circulated to increasingly larger lymph vessels called lymphatic vessels. The lymphatic vessels empty their contents into either the right lymphatic duct or the thoracic duct, situated in the thoracic cavity.

Spleen

The spleen filters and destroys red blood cells that are no longer efficient. It serves as a blood-forming organ early in life, and later as a storage unit for extra red blood cells and platelets.

Thymus

The thymus is a bi-lobed organ located in the neck and extends into the thorax. After puberty, the thymus starts to atrophy gradually. The thymus is responsible for T-lymphocyte maturation, enabling them to function against specific pathogens in the immune response.

Tonsils

The tonsils are partially encapsulated lymph nodes in the throat. They are named according to their location: palatine tonsils, lingual tonsils, and pharyngeal tonsil (referred to as the adenoids if enlarged).

Lymphatic System

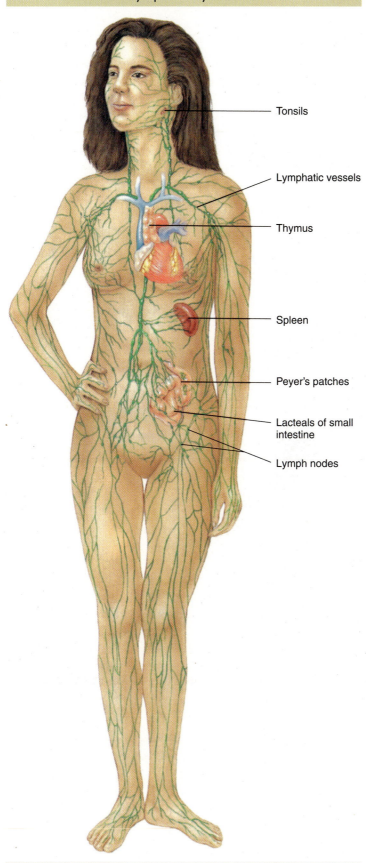

- Tonsils
- Lymphatic vessels
- Thymus
- Spleen
- Peyer's patches
- Lacteals of small intestine
- Lymph nodes

Source: Delmar/Cengage Learning.

Peyer's Patches & Appendix

Peyer's patches are found in the lining of the intestine and contain high levels of white blood cells, which help in fighting infection and disease. The appendix is a mass of lymphoid tissue attached to the first part of the large intestine. Both help to protect against invading microorganisms.

Respiratory System (Pulmonary System)

Pulmonary System

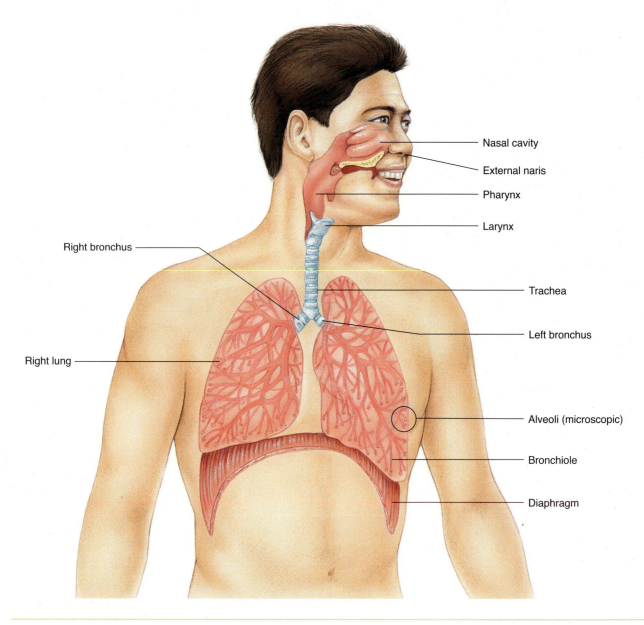

Nasal cavity

External naris

Pharynx

Larynx

Right bronchus

Trachea

Left bronchus

Right lung

Alveoli (microscopic)

Bronchiole

Diaphragm

Source: Delmar/Cengage Learning.

The respiratory system includes the nose and nasal cavity, pharynx, larynx, trachea, and bronchi and their smaller branches, the lungs, and alveoli.

The nose provides an airway to breathe (moistening, warming, and filtering inspired air), serves as a resonating chamber for speech, and houses the smell receptors.

The pharynx is divided into three regions: nasopharynx (air passageway), oropharynx (air and food passageway), and laryngopharynx (air and food passageway).

The larynx is your voicebox. In addition to voice production, it also helps provide an open (patent) airway and to act as a switching mechanism to route air and food into the proper channels.

The trachea is in the mediastinal region and splits into two bronchi (at the carina) which enter the lungs. The lungs are divided into lobes; the right lung has three lobes and the left lung has two lobes.

At the smallest branch of the bronchial tree, the airways are called bronchioles. Each of these bronchioles narrow further until they end in a tiny pouch called an alveolar sac. Gases are exchanged across the single-cell layer of tissue comprising the alveolar sac into the pulmonary circulation. Capillaries from the pulmonary circulation form a bed around each alveoli; gas is exchanged between the alveoli and the capillaries via diffusion.

Application to Documentation

TECHNIQUE: After induction of satisfactory general anesthesia, flexible fiberoptic bronchoscopy was performed. Airways were essentially normal with minimal secretions. No endobronchial lesions. The patient was kept supine and the neck was prepared with DuraPrep and draped in the sterile fashion. A transverse incision was used and deepened with cautery. The pretracheal fascial plane was entered and the mediastinoscope easily passed. Samples of nodes from three different stations were taken from the **subcarinal area**, the **right tracheobronchial angle area**, and the **low pretracheal area**. All were negative for neoplasm. The wound was irrigated, checked for hemostasis, closed with absorbable sutures, and a dry sterile dressing was placed. A double-lumen lube was placed and its proper position confirmed bronchoscopically.

In the sample documentation above, it is important to understand anatomy to determine from where the biopsies were taken.

Digestive System

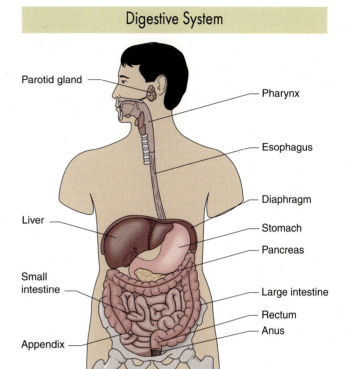

Digestive System

Parotid gland — Pharynx — Esophagus — Diaphragm — Stomach — Pancreas — Liver — Small intestine — Large intestine — Rectum — Anus — Appendix

Source: Delmar/Cengage Learning.

The feeding tube begins in the mouth and ends at the anus. The system mechanically and chemically breaks down food into minuscule or molecular size for absorption into the blood stream and use at the cellular level.

Food enters the digestive system via the mouth. The teeth and tongue mechanically break food into small particles to provide greater exposure/surface area for the chemical processes that follow. The salivary glands that surround the mouth secrete saliva, which aids in early phases of chemical digestion and liquefaction of the food. The food is swallowed and peristalsis in the esophagus moves food down through the upper thoracic cavity into the stomach.

The opening is the cardiac orifice. The fundus is the rounded upper portion of the stomach. The main portion of the stomach is considered the body. The lower portion of the stomach is the pyloric antrum. The pyloric sphincter leads to the duodenum (the first one-third of the small intestine). The second one-third of the small intestine is the jejunum, and the distal one-third is the ileum (not ilium, a bone in the pelvis).

The large intestine begins after the ileocecal valve at the cecum, with the appendix attached at the bottom. There are four portions to the colon: The ascending colon proceeds from the ileocecal valve upward to the hepatic flexure, becomes the transverse colon, and then turns downward to become the descending colon at the splenic flexure; the descending colon gives way to the sigmoid colon and ends at the rectum; and, the internal and external anal sphincters terminate the rectum.

Ancillary organs such as the pancreas, liver, and gallbladder also are considered parts of the digestive system. The digestive (or exocrine) pancreas produces digestive enzymes that are secreted into the intestines. The gallbladder stores bile (which helps digest fats) that is produced in the liver.

Application to Documentation

The patient first was placed into occlusion using Karlis bolts of 8 mm in length. The jaws were put in proper occlusion using 24-gauge stainless steel wires. A buccal incision was made just above the sulcus, carried down through the subcutaneous tissues with the electrocautery. Xylocaine 0.5% with epinephrine had been injected for hemostasis. The periosteum was elevated, and the patient was noted to have a comminuted fracture of the maxilla that created a Le Fort I fracture. Placement into occlusion had placed the patient in good reduction.

In the documentation above, understanding that "buccal" refers to the cheek provides an understanding of where the incision occurred.

Urinary System

The excretion of metabolic wastes, along with fluid and electrolyte balance, is the main function of the urinary system. Key structures are the kidneys, ureters, urinary bladder, and urethra. The male and female urethras are different anatomically but perform the same functions. Urine is formed in the kidneys, conveyed through ureters to the bladder for temporary storage, and drained out of the body by the urethra.

Source: Delmar/Cengage Learning.

Reproductive Systems

The organs of the reproductive system differ greatly between male and female. Reproduction is achieved through production of a 23-chromosome gamete called a sperm (male), and a 23-chromosome gamete called an egg (female). The female houses, feeds, and protects the growing fetus through the gestational period.

Male Genitalia

External genitalia for the male include the testes, epididymis, scrotum, and penis. Internal organs for the male genital system include the prostate gland, seminal vesicle, and Cowper's glands. The system of tubes and ducts that sperm travel through to leave the body is comprised of the vas deferens, ejaculatory duct, and the urethra.

Female Genitalia

External genitalia for the female includes the vulva, labia majora and minora, clitoris, external opening of the vagina (introitus), opening of the urethra (urinary meatus), Skene's glands (found on either side of the urinary meatus), and Bartholin's glands (found on either side of the introitus). Internal organs for the female genital system include the vagina, uterus, two fallopian tubes, and two ovaries.

Nervous System

The nervous system functions as both the central operator and central intelligence for the body. It regulates bodily functions, provides for an internal method of communication between the brain and other organs as well as between the organism and the environment. The brain and spinal cord are the components of the central nervous system (CNS). The peripheral nervous system (PNS) includes the cranial and spinal nerves. The CNS is the command center and the PNS serves as the communication lines that link all parts of the body to the CNS. Injuries to the nervous system can often result in paralysis (paraplegia, quadriplegia, and hemiplegia).

Application to Documentation

The skin incision was marked at the sagittal linear incision extending from the external occipital protuberance to approximately C2. The incision was infiltrated with 0.5% Marcaine with 1:200,000 epinephrine and opened with a scalpel. The **midline fascia between the suboccipital muscles** was used as a plane of dissection. The dorsal arch of CI was exposed, and the **muscle was dissected off the suboccipital bone bilaterally**.

The term "suboccipital" assists in selecting the correct CPT® code for this craniectomy. Another location for a craniectomy could have been "subtemporal."

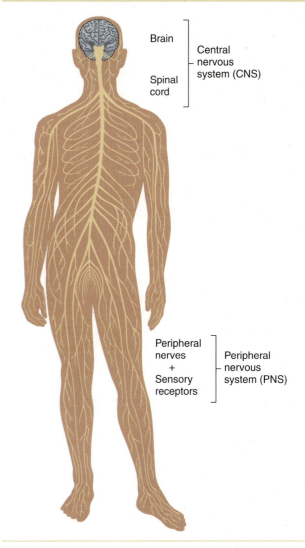

Nervous System

Source: Delmar/Cengage Learning.

Organs of Sense—Eye

Organs of sense are classified to the nervous system because they coalesce in nerve endings called sensory receptors.

The eye is a complex structure situated in the bony orbit or socket formed by seven bones: frontal, maxillary, sphenoid, lacrimal, malar bone, ethmoid, and palatine bones. The eyeball has three layers: the retina (innermost), choroid (middle), and sclera (outermost). It is separated into an anterior segment filled with aqueous humor and a posterior segment filled with vitreous humor. The crystalline lens separates the two segments and refracts light as it enters the eye.

There are many adnexal or accessory structures to the eye, such as the eyelids, eyelashes, and the lacrimal system. There are six ocular muscles that work in opposition to move the eye in multiple directions to facilitate a wide field of vision.

Ophthalmology has its own vocabulary and is a very specialized field of medicine and coding. There are two types of services that pertain to the eye: vision services and surgical services. Vision services can be found in the 92002–92499 range of CPT® codes. Surgical services on the eye can be found in the 65091–68899 range of CPT® codes.

Organs of Sense—Ear

The ear works in tandem with the auditory nerves to send auditory impulses to the temporal lobes of the cerebrum. These structures, working together, form the auditory apparatus. The ear has three distinct and separate anatomic divisions: the outer ear (external ear), middle ear (tympanic cavity), and inner ear (labyrinth).

Otology (the study of the ear) also is a very specialized field of medicine and coding. There are two types of services that pertain to the ear: audiometry services (hearing testing) and surgical services. Surgical services on the ear can be found in the 69000–69979 range of CPT® codes. Special otorhinolaryngologic services can be found in the 92502–92700 range.

Endocrine System

Endocrine Glands

Pineal

Pituitary

Thyroid

Parathyroid glands

Posterior view

Thymus

Cortex

Medulla

Adrenal

Pancreas (Islets of Langerhans)

Testis

Ovary

Source: Delmar/Cengage Learning.

The endocrine system is comprised of glands, which secrete or excrete chemicals called hormones. Each gland and its associated hormones have a cause and effect that is unique.

Adrenal Glands—Ductless, pyramid-shaped glands are situated near the top of each kidney. There are two structural parts of the adrenal gland. The inner portion is called the medulla and the outer portion is the cortex. The medulla secretes epinephrine and norepinephrine. The cortex secretes several steroids (eg, glucocorticoids, mineral corticoids, and adrenal estrogens and androgens).

Carotid Body—Located on each side at the bifurcation (division) of the common carotid arteries. Although not a true endocrine structure, it is made of both glandular and nonglandular cells. The carotid body detects changes in pH, temperature, and partial pressure of oxygen and carbon dioxide.

Parathyroid Gland—Small round bodies are located on the posterior side of the thyroid gland and imbedded in the connective tissue surrounding it. These glands regulate calcium and phosphorus metabolism.

Pituitary Gland (hypophysis cerebri)—This single gland has two separate parts located in an area of the brain just under the hypothalamus. The posterior pituitary or neurohypophysis secretes oxytocin, a hormone responsible for uterine contractions and the "let down" reflex of milk in response to a baby's suckling; and vasopressin, an antidiuretic. The anterior pituitary manufactures the adrenocorticotrophic hormone (ACTH), thyroid stimulating hormone (TSH), follicle stimulating hormone (FSH), luteinizing hormone (LH), growth hormone (GH) (somatotrophin), melanocyte stimulating hormone (MSH), and prolactin (PRL).

Thymus Gland—Located in the mediastinum of the chest. This gland helps to regulate humoral immune functions, and is most active in early childhood. By puberty, it may be replaced by fat.

Thyroid Gland—Located in the neck just below the thyroid cartilage of the trachea, it regulates metabolism and serum calcium levels through the secretion of thyroid hormone and Calcitonin, respectively.

Hematologic (Hemic) System

The hemic system involves the blood. Red cells, white cells, and platelets are made in the marrow of bones. Red cells (erythrocytes) contain hemoglobin that enables the cells to pick up and deliver oxygen to all parts of the body. White cells (leukocytes) are the body's primary defense against infection. Types of leukocytes include neutrophils, lymphocytes, monocytes, eosinophils, and basophils. Platelets form clusters to plug small holes in blood vessels and assist in the clotting process.

Plasma is a pale yellow mixture of water, proteins, and salts, and acts as a carrier for blood cells, nutrients, enzymes, and hormones.

Components of the Blood

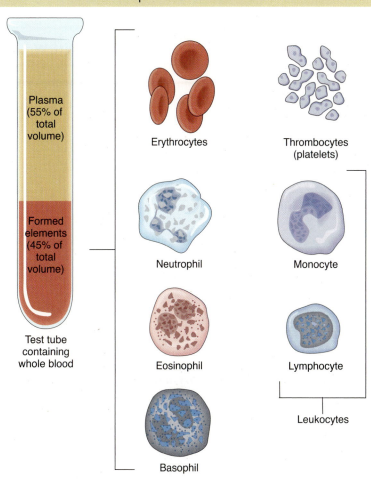

Plasma (55% of total volume)

Formed elements (45% of total volume)

Test tube containing whole blood

Erythrocytes

Thrombocytes (platelets)

Neutrophil

Monocyte

Eosinophil

Lymphocyte

Basophil

Leukocytes

Source: Delmar/Cengage Learning.

Immune System

Most immune cells have their origins in the hematologic system. In medicine, the study of the immune system (immunology) and the study of allergies often go hand in hand because an allergic response is, in fact, an immune response. The human immune system is the body's final line of defense against invading microorganisms, harmful chemicals, and foreign bodies. There are two kinds of immune cells: B-cells and T-cells. Several types of cells protect the body from infection (eg, neutrophils, lymphocytes, monocytes, eosinophils, and basophils). Neutrophils are the body's main defense against infection and antigens. High levels may indicate an active infection; a low count may indicate a compromised immune system or depressed bone marrow (low neutrophil production).

Lymphocytes are involved in protection of the body from viral infections such as measles, rubella, chickenpox, or infectious mononucleosis. Elevated levels may indicate an active viral infection and a depressed level may indicate an exhausted immune system; or, if the neutrophils are elevated, an active infection.

Monocytes fight severe infections and are considered the body's second line of defense against infection. Elevated levels are seen in tissue breakdown, chronic infections, carcinomas, leukemia (monocytic), or lymphomas. Low levels indicate a good state of health.

The body uses eosinophils to protect against allergic reactions and parasites; elevated levels may indicate an allergic response. A low count is normal. Basophilic activity is not understood fully, but it is known to carry histamine, heparin, and serotonin. High levels are found in allergic reactions; low levels are normal.

Antibodies are immune system-related proteins called immunoglobulins. Some antibodies destroy antigens directly; others indirectly by making it easier for white blood cells to destroy the antigen.

Chapter Review Questions

1. **A patient sustaining an injury to her great saphenous vein would have sustained an injury to which of the following anatomical sites?**

    A. Neck

    B. Arm

    C. Leg

    D. Abdomen

2. **Which of the following is a function of the pancreas?**

    A. Supplies digestive enzymes

    B. Manufactures melatonin

    C. Stimulates growth

    D. Secretes vasopressin

3. **Sebaceous glands are a part of which anatomic system?**

    A. Circulatory

    B. Endocrine

    C. Genitourinary

    D. Integumentary

4. **Which of the following has a refraction function in the eye?**

   A. Macula

   B. Retina

   C. Lens

   D. Iris

5. **The myocardium is thickest around which chamber of the heart?**

   A. Right atrium

   B. Left atrium

   C. Right ventricle

   D. Left ventricle

6. **The tunica vaginalis is part of which system?**

   A. Male reproductive

   B. Female reproductive

   C. Urinary

   D. Musculoskeletal

7. **Complete this series: Incus, stapes, _____.**

   A. Radius

   B. Isthmus

   C. Meatus

   D. Malleus

8. **Hemiplegia is a disorder caused by a defect in which anatomic system?**

   A. Musculoskeletal

   B. Nervous

   C. Digestive

   D. Integumentary

9. **What is the result of a ureteral blockage?**

   A. Urine will not be able to flow from the kidney to the bladder.

   B. Urine will not be able to flow from the bladder to the urethra.

   C. Urine will not be able to flow from the bladder to the kidney.

   D. Urine will not be able to be voided, but will be trapped in the bladder.

10. **Which of the following is a renal calculus?**

    A. Pyelectasia

    B. Hydroureter

    C. Nephrolithiasis

    D. Pyonephrosis

Introduction

The ICD-9-CM coding system used in the United States to translate medical terminology for diseases and procedures into numeric codes originated in 17th century England. The statistical data was gathered through a system known as the London Bills of Mortality to collect information on the most frequent causes of death. By 1937, this ongoing statistical study of diseases evolved into the International List of Causes of Death. Over the years, the World Health Organization (WHO) used this information to assist in tracking morbidity and mortality for making statistical assessments of international health and disease trends. This led the way for the International Classification of Diseases, Ninth Revision (ICD-9).

By 1977, the worldwide recognition of ICD-9-CM prompted the federal National Centers for Health Statistics (NCHS) to expand and modify the statistical study with clinical information. In addition to providing statistics on basic health care, the modifications provided a way to index medical records, facilitate medical case reviews and provide ambulatory and other medical care programs. The final changes resulted in the current International Classification of Diseases, Ninth Revision, Clinical Modification (ICD-9-CM). The ICD-9-CM is currently the national standard coding language (with some international application) used to define the patient's condition, diagnosis, disease, injury, anomaly, or other reason for medical services, procedures, and supplies.

The ICD-9-CM Coordination and Maintenance Committee, which is co-chaired by the NCHS and the Centers for Medicare & Medicaid Services (CMS), performs maintenance on ICD-9-CM. This committee meets twice a year in a public forum to discuss changes and revisions. After the final decisions are made, the changes are published in the *Federal Register* and become effective October 1 of each year.

The United States made the transition in 1999 to the 10th revision of the International Classification of

Diseases for coding mortality (death statistics); and will migrate to ICD-10-CM for reporting of diseases on Oct. 1, 2013. WHO published the 10th revision in 1994, and maintains this revision for international reporting of death and disease. ICD-10 accommodates advances in medical knowledge of disease and disease processes, where ICD-9-CM has become outdated and insufficient.

During this chapter, we will discuss:

◖ Overview of the ICD-9-CM layout

◖ ICD-9-CM conventions

◖ How to look up an ICD-9-CM code

◖ Official ICD-9-CM coding guidelines

Overview of ICD-9-CM Layout

ICD-9-CM is published in three volumes:

Volume 1—Tabular List: Diagnosis codes organized in order by code

Volume 2—Index to Diseases: Diagnosis codes organized in an alphabetic index

Volume 3—Alphabetic Index and Tabular List of Procedures: Procedures performed in the inpatient setting

Volumes 1 and 2 are used by all coders to assign diagnosis codes that establish medical necessity for services rendered. In other words, diagnosis codes support "why" a service was rendered. For example, a patient has a bad cough and congestion. The provider performs a chest X-ray. On the claim form, the coder assigns diagnosis codes for the documented cough and congestion, which support the service. We will discuss the proper selection of ICD-9-CM codes later in this chapter.

Establishing medical necessity is the first step in third-party reimbursement. Payers require the following information to determine the need for care:

1. Knowledge of the emergent nature or severity of the patient's complaint or condition.

2. All signs, symptoms, complaints, or background facts describing the reason for care, such as required follow-up care.

These facts must be substantiated by the patient's medical record, which must be available to payers on request.

Volume 3 includes procedure codes and is typically used by facilities for inpatient services. Hospitals use Volume 3 in the outpatient facility for tracking purposes only and do not submit claims using Volume 3. Historically, annual updates to ICD-9-CM Volume 3 are published each October. ICD-10-PCS (Procedural Coding System) will be implemented concurrent to ICD-10-CM diagnostic codes in October of 2013.

We will focus on the proper use of Volume 1 and Volume 2 in this chapter.

Volume 1: Tabular List

The Tabular List is a numerical listing of disease and injury. There are 17 chapters for the classification of diseases and injury, grouped by etiology (cause) or anatomical (body) site. There are two additional chapters for supplementary classifications. The Tabular List is organized in three-digit codes and their titles, called category codes. Some three-digit codes are very specific and are not subdivided. These three-digit codes can stand alone to describe the condition being coded.

Most three-digit categories (rubrics) have been subdivided with the addition of a decimal point, followed by either one or two additional digits. The fourth digit provides specificity or more information regarding etiology, site, or manifestation. Fourth digit subcategory codes take precedence over three-digit category codes. Fourth and fifth digits are required where indicated; they are not optional. A valid diagnosis code can have three, four, or five digits, depending on the disease.

There are symbols throughout the Tabular List to identify when a code requires a fourth or fifth digit:

√ 4th   This symbol alerts the coder a fourth digit is required to report the diagnosis in the category accurately.

√ 5th   This symbol alerts the coder a fifth digit is required to report the diagnosis in the category accurately.

When fourth and fifth digits are required, the additional digit options may be presented as sub terms, or at the beginning of the three-digit category.

Examples:

√ 5th 575.1   Other cholecystitis

  575.10   Cholecystitis, unspecified
  575.11   Chronic cholecystitis
  575.12   Acute and chronic cholecystitis

√ 5th 718.9   Unspecified derangement of joint
       [0–5, 7–9]

The digits in the brackets instruct the coder that the only valid fifth-digit code ends in 0–5 or 7–9. To select the correct fifth digit, refer to the beginning of category 718 for the subclassification designation.

The following fifth-digit subclassification is for use with category 718; valid digits are in [brackets] under each code. See list at beginning of chapter for definitions.

  0 site unspecified

  1 shoulder region

  2 upper arm

  3 forearm

  4 hand

  5 pelvic region and thigh

  6 lower leg

  7 ankle and foot

  8 other specified sites

  9 multiple sites

Supplementary Classification in Volume 1

1. Classification of Factors Influencing Health Status and Contact with Health Services, V01–V91

Codes from category V01–V91 are known as V codes. V codes are commonly used when the patient presents for treatment with no complaints. Common reasons to report V codes are for screening tests (eg, mammogram to screen for breast cancer), routine physicals (eg, well-child checkup), and when a patient has a personal history or family history of a disease or disorder (eg, family history of colon cancer). In order for a V code to be listed first, it must meet the definition of a principal or first-listed diagnosis code. A list of codes meeting these requirements can be located in the ICD-9-CM Guidelines, Section I.C.18.e.

2. Classification of External Causes of Injury, E000–E999

Codes from category E000–E999 are known as E codes. E codes are used to report how an injury occurred (eg, motor vehicle accident), and where the injury occurred (eg, injury occurred in the workplace).

Volume 2: Index to Diseases

Main terms in the Index to Diseases in Volume 2 usually reference the disease, condition, or symptom. Sub terms modify the main term to describe differences in site, etiology, or clinical type. Sub terms add further modification to the main term.

Example:

Pain(s) (*see also* Painful) 780.96

√ 5th   abdominal 789.0

    acute 338.19

      due to trauma 338.11

      postoperative 338.18

In this example, the sub terms further define the location of pain and type of pain.

Appendices

Appendix A—Morphology of Neoplasms: This list is from an adapted version of the International Classification of Diseases for Oncology (ICD-O). It consists of coded descriptions for morphology, which is the science of the form and structure of organisms. The morphology codes consist of five digits. The first four digits identify the histological type of the neoplasm and the fifth digit indicates the behavior. Tumor registries utilize these codes for statistical purposes. Coders use these codes infrequently, but the appendix can be useful in determining whether a neoplasm, documented with its scientific name, is classified as a malignant, benign, or other type of neoplasm.

Appendix B—Deleted effective October 1, 2004. It contained the Glossary of Mental Disorders. The code descriptions in chapter 5 of the ICD-9-CM were updated to coincide with the *Diagnostic and Statistical Manual of Mental Disorders, Fourth Edition* (DSM-IV) which is the patient classification system used in the mental health field.

Appendix C—Classification of Drugs by American Hospital Formulary Service List Number and Their ICD-9-CM Equivalents: This appendix is available to assist in the coding of adverse effects.

Appendix D—Classification of Industrial Accidents According to Agency: This list is used primarily for statistical purposes. It provides information about employment injuries.

Appendix E—List of Three Digit Categories: This list contains the three-digit categories in ICD-9-CM and provides an alternative view of the contents of ICD-9-CM.

Conventions

To apply the diagnosis coding system correctly, coders need to understand the various conventions and terms. Section I of the official guidelines includes conventions, general coding guidelines, and chapter specific guidelines.

NEC Not elsewhere classifiable

This abbreviation is used when the ICD-9-CM system does not provide a code specific for the patient's condition. Selecting a code with the NEC classification means the provider documented more specific information regarding the patient's condition, but there is not a code in ICD-9-CM that reports the condition accurately.

NOS Not otherwise specified

This abbreviation is the equivalent of "unspecified" and is used only when the coder lacks the information necessary to code to a more specific fourth- or fifth-digit subcategory.

[ ] Brackets are used to enclose synonyms, alternate wording, or explanatory phrases.

Example:

 008.0 Escherichia coli [E. coli]

[ ] Slanted brackets are used to indicate multiple codes are required.

Example:

Diabetes, diabetic 250.0
    cataract 250.5 *[366.41]*

In this example, two codes are required: 250.5x *Diabetes with ophthalmic manifestations*, which requires a fifth digit to indicate the type of diabetes and whether it is controlled or uncontrolled; and 366.41 *Diabetic cataract.*

( ) Parentheses are used to enclose supplementary words that may be present or absent in the statement of a disease or procedure without affecting the code number to which it is assigned.

Example:

Cyst (mucus) (retention) (serous) (simple)

: The colon is used in Volume 1 (Tabular List) after an incomplete term requiring one or more of the descriptions that follow to make it assignable to a given category.

Example:

553.21 Incisional
    Hernia:
        postoperative
        recurrent, ventral

Other Conventions

Boldface Boldface type is used for all codes and titles in the Tabular List.

Italicized Italicized type is used for all exclusion notes and to identify codes that should not be used for describing the primary diagnosis.

EXCLUDES Terms following "excludes" notes are to be reported with a code from another category. The use of "excludes" in the Tabular List guides the coder to a more appropriate code for a specific condition than is listed in the current category.

Example:

599.0 Urinary tract infection, site not specified
EXCLUDES   candidiasis of urinary tract (112.2)
        urinary tract infection of newborn (771.82)

In this example, we see that if the patient has candidiasis of the urinary tract, the correct code is 112.2.

Testing Technique

Highlight conditions following "excludes" notes. This will help draw your eye to the excluded conditions while you are taking your exam.

INCLUDES The "includes" note appears immediately after a three-digit code title to further define or clarify the category.

Example:

280 Iron deficiency anemias

anemia:

INCLUDES	asiderotic
	hypochromic-microcytic
	sideropenic

Use additional code

This instruction signals the coder an additional code should be used, if the information is available, to provide a more complete picture of the diagnosis.

Example:

282.42 Sickle-cell thalassemia with crisis

Sickle-cell thalassemia with vaso-occlusive pain

Thalassemia Hb-S disease with crisis

Use additional code for the type of crisis, such as:

acute chest syndrome (517.3)

splenic sequestration (289.52)

In this example, an additional code is reported to identify the type of crisis. When sequencing codes, the codes listed under the "use additional code" are secondary to code 282.42. If a patient has a sickle-cell thalassemia crisis with acute chest syndrome, the proper codes in the correct sequence are 282.42, 517.3.

Code first

This instruction is used in categories not intended to be the principal diagnosis. These codes are also written in italics with a note. The note requires the underlying disease (etiology) be recorded first and the particular manifestation be recorded second. This note appears only in the Tabular List.

Example:

284.2 Myelophthisis

Leukoerythroblastic anemia

Myelophthisic anemia

Code first the underlying disorder, such as:

malignant neoplasm of breast (174.0–174.9, 175.0–175.9)

tuberculosis (015.0–015.9)

The "code first" indicates the codes listed should be sequenced first. If a female patient with breast cancer is diagnosed with myelophthisis, the proper codes and sequencing are 174.9, 284.2.

Use additional code, if applicable

The causal condition note indicates this code may be assigned as a diagnosis when the causal condition is unknown or not applicable. If a causal condition is known, the code should be sequenced as the principal diagnosis.

Example:

416.2 Chronic pulmonary embolism

Use additional code, if applicable, for associated long-term (current) use of anticoagulants (V58.61)

In this example, report code V58.61 in addition to 416.2 only if it is documented that the patient has been taking anticoagulants for an extended period.

Combination code

This note indicates a single code is used to classify two diagnoses, a diagnosis with an associated secondary process (manifestation), or a diagnosis with an associated complication.

Example:

If a patient has nausea and vomiting, it is reported with one code that describes both symptoms.

Vomiting 787.03

with nausea 787.01

In this example, 787.01 is reported for a patient who has symptoms of nausea and vomiting. It would be inappropriate to report two codes when one code describes the patient's signs and symptoms.

Eponym

This term indicates the code describes a disease or syndrome named after a person. An example is Lou Gehrig's disease. Lou Gehrig was a famous baseball player who was diagnosed with what is also known as amyotrophic lateral sclerosis (ALS).

Modifiers

Essential modifiers are subterms listed below the main term in alphabetical order, and are indented two spaces. Nonessential modifiers are sub terms that follow the main term and are enclosed in parentheses; they can clarify the diagnosis, but are not required.

Notes

Notes are used to define terms, clarify information, or list choices for additional digits.

Other

"Other" or "other unspecified" codes (usually with fourth digit 8 or fifth digit 9) are used when the information in the medical record provides detail for which a specific code does not exist. Index entries with NEC in the line designate "other" codes in the Tabular List. These index entries represent specific disease entities for which no specific code exists, so the term is included within the "other code."

See

This instruction directs you to a more specific term under which the correct code can be found.

See also

This indicates additional information is available that may provide an additional diagnosis code.

See category

The "see category" indicates that you should review the category specified before assigning a code.

Unspecified

"Unspecified" codes (usually with a fourth digit 9 or fifth digit 0) are used when the information in the medical record is not available for coding more specifically. Unspecified codes should be selected only when there is no other option. For example, if the provider documents hypertension without additional information as to the cause or type of hypertension, the only option is an unspecified code (401.9).

Steps to Look Up a Diagnosis Code

Determine the main term of the diagnosis documented in the medical record. It is important for a coder to have a solid foundation in medical terminology and anatomy so he or she can review the medical record and determine the documented diseases/conditions that should be reported.

Look up the main term in the Index to Diseases (Volume 2). Review all sub terms to determine the most specific code. Review all "see" and "see also" notes.

Refer to the code referenced in the Index to Diseases in the Tabular List (Volume 1). Review all "includes," "excludes," and "use additional code" notations to verify the accuracy of the code. The notations and conventions in the ICD-9-CM codebook provide hints to the coder when a more appropriate code should be reported. Throughout the chapter, we will discuss the coding guidelines that include rules for proper ICD-9-CM code selection and sequencing.

Example:

A patient is diagnosed with an acute asthma exacerbation. In this example, the key word is "asthma." Refer to asthma in the Index to Diseases. There is a symbol next to code 493.9 alerting the coder that a fifth digit is required.

Note: Use the following fifth-digit subclassification with codes 493.0–493.2, 493.9:

   0 without mention of status asthmaticus or acute exacerbation or unspecified

   1 with status asthmaticus

   2 with acute exacerbation

In this example, the Index to Diseases refers to 493.9 with a fifth digit of "2" to report the acute exacerbation. Refer to code 493.92 in the Tabular List. The provider did not indicate if the asthma is extrinsic, intrinsic, or chronic obstructive. We know the asthma is exacerbated, but no other information is provided. For this example, the correct code is 493.92 *Asthma, unspecified, with (acute) exacerbation*.

Highlight the fifth digit sub classifications for each code category where they apply.

Following the steps to look up diagnosis codes is extremely important to verify accuracy.

ICD-9-CM Official Guidelines for Coding and Reporting

CMS and the NCHS provide the official coding and reporting guidelines for ICD-9-CM. These guidelines are found in the front of the ICD-9-CM codebook. The guidelines provide instructions for proper code selection and code sequencing rules. Section I of the official guidelines is broken down into three subsections:

- Subsection A includes the conventions and punctuation discussed in the beginning of this chapter;
- Subsection B includes general coding concepts; and
- Subsection C includes chapter-specific coding guidelines.

Section I.B General Coding Guidelines

Use Both Alphabetic Index and Tabular List

Always use both Volume 1 (Tabular List) and Volume 2 (Index to Diseases). Verify the code number in the Tabular List. Never code directly from the Index to Diseases because important instructions often appear in the Tabular List.

Locate Each Term in the Alphabetic Index

Locate the main term in the Index to Diseases, Volume 2:

- Refer to any notes under the main term.
- Read any terms enclosed in parentheses following the main term.
- Refer to any modifiers of the main term.
- Do not skip over any sub terms indented under the main term.

- Follow any cross-reference instructions such as "see also."

Use of a medical dictionary can help you identify main terms and understand the disease process to assist with accurate coding.

Level of Detail in Coding

Code to the highest degree of specificity. A three-digit code may be used only when the category is not subdivided further. When a three-digit code has subdivisions, the appropriate subdivision must be coded. Fourth- and fifth-digit symbols (discussed above) alert the coder when a fourth or fifth digit is required.

Signs and Symptoms

In the outpatient setting, do not code a diagnosis unless it is certain. Examples of language seen in the medical record that identify uncertain diagnoses include: probable, suspected, questionable, working, differential and rule out.

When a definitive diagnosis has not been determined, code the signs, symptoms, and abnormal test result(s) or other reasons for the visit.

Example: Fatigue, suspect iron deficiency anemia. In this instance, it is only necessary to code fatigue because the physician has not confirmed a diagnosis for iron deficiency anemia.

In the inpatient setting for facility diagnosis coding, it is appropriate to report suspected or "rule out" diagnoses as if the condition exists. HIV is the only condition that must be confirmed to report it in the inpatient setting.

Conditions That Are an Integral Part of a Disease Process

Codes for symptoms, signs, and ill-defined conditions are not to be used as first-listed diagnoses when a related definitive diagnosis is established.

For example, a patient presents with severe abdominal pain, nausea, and vomiting. The provider diagnoses the patient with appendicitis. In this case, only a code for the appendicitis is sequenced because the abdominal pain, nausea, and vomiting are symptoms of appendicitis.

To locate the code, refer to appendicitis in the Index to Diseases. No sub terms apply in this example. The code referred to in the index is 541, which must be confirmed by reviewing the code in the Tabular List (Vol. 1).

Conditions That Are Not an Integral Part of the Disease Process

Codes for signs and symptoms that are not routinely associated with other definite diagnoses should be reported.

For example, a patient presents with a runny nose and cough. The provider diagnosed the patient with a URI (Upper Respiratory Infection). The patient also complains of right knee pain. In this example, a code is selected for the URI and the knee pain. The runny nose and cough are symptoms of the URI (465.9) and should not be reported. Knee pain (719.46) is not related to the URI, and should be coded separately.

Multiple Coding for a Single Condition

Multiple coding of diagnoses is required for certain conditions not subject to the rules for combination codes.

a. Index to Diseases: Codes for both etiology and manifestation of a disease appear following the subentry term, with the second code italicized and in slanted brackets. Assign both codes in the same sequence in which they appear in the Index to Diseases.

b. Tabular List: Instructional notes that indicate when to use more than one code:
   o Code first underlying condition
   o Code also
   o Use additional code

For example, endocarditis due to typhoid: In the Index to Diseases, two codes are listed on the same line—002.0 [421.1]. This indicates both codes are required to describe this diagnosis. In verifying 421.1 in the Tabular List, notice the statement "code first underlying disease." This statement indicates that 421.1 is a "manifestation code" and should be coded second.

Combination Code

A combination code is used to identify fully an instance in which two diagnoses, or a diagnosis with an associated secondary process (manifestation) or complication, are included in the description of a single code. Assign a combination code only when that code fully identifies the diagnostic conditions involved or when instructed in the alphabetic index.

Acute and Chronic

When an acute and chronic condition is documented, and there is a separate code for each, code both. The acute code is sequenced first.

An acute condition is one that is severe and with a sudden onset. Chronic conditions treated on an ongoing basis may be coded as many times as required for treatment and care of the patient, or when applicable to the patient's care plan. Do not code conditions previously treated or those that no longer exist. History of previous conditions should be coded using V codes only if they affect patient care or support the need for a patient to seek medical attention.

Late Effects

A late effect is "usually an inactive, residual effect or condition produced after the acute portion of an injury or illness has passed." Key phrases such as "due to an old injury" or "due to previous illness" are indicators the problem or condition may be a late effect. If these indicators are not present in the diagnostic statement, the injury or condition may be considered a late effect if sufficient time has elapsed between the original condition and the late effect.

When a patient is being treated for a condition that is a "late effect" of an earlier injury or disease, the reference "late" from Volume 2 is used.

1. A "late effect" is the residual effect that remains after the acute phase of an illness or injury has terminated.

2. The residual effect may be apparent early after an acute phase of an illness, as in a cerebrovascular accident, or it may occur much later (one year or more), as with a previous injury or illness (eg, following an auto accident).

3. The residual effect is coded first and is followed by the "late effect" code to show the cause of the late effect condition.

Late effects should be coded according to the nature of the residual condition of the late effect. Two codes usually are required when coding late effects. The residual condition is coded first and the code(s) for the cause of the late effect (905.0–909.9) are coded as a secondary diagnosis. It may be necessary for the coder to assign an E code to identify an external cause. The documentation in the medical record should support the manifestation or residual effect as well as the cause.

The code for the cause of the late effect may be used as a principal diagnosis when no residual diagnosis is identified. The following terminology may be used to document a late effect: due to an old injury, due to a previous illness, due to an illness or injury that occurred one year or more before the current encounter.

The code for the acute phase of an illness or injury that leads to the late effect is never used with a code for the cause of the late effect.

Impending or Threatened Condition

When a patient is discharged with a condition described as "impending" or "threatened," review the alphabetic index for the sub term of "impending" or "threatened" under the main term of the condition. If a sub term does not exist, reference "impending" or "threatened" as the main term with the condition as a sub term. If there is not a listing there either, report the signs and symptoms that led the provider to suspect an impending or threatened condition.

Reporting Same Diagnosis Code More Than Once

Do not report the same diagnosis code more than once. There will be instances when a provider will document a bilateral condition, or two different conditions that are reported with the same diagnosis code. When either situation occurs, only report the unique ICD-9-CM code once.

For example, if a patient complains of pain in his right and left leg. There is not a code to distinguish between the right and left leg. Code 729.5 *Pain in limb* is reported for leg pain. This code is only reported once.

ICD-10-CM will allow for the reporting for bilateral conditions. Until its implementation October 1, 2013, we use the ICD-9-CM codes, which do not have bilateral reporting capabilities.

Admissions/Encounters for Rehabilitation

When the purpose of the encounter is rehabilitation, the first listed code is a V code from category V57 Care involving use of rehabilitation procedures. The second listed code is the condition for which the patient requires the rehabilitation services. For example, if a provider orders physical therapy for a patient with sciatica, report V57.1 *Other physical therapy* followed by 724.3 *Sciatica*.

Documentation for BMI and Pressure Ulcer Stages

Codes for BMI (Body Mass Index) and pressure ulcer stage codes can be reported based on documentation from any clinician involved in the patient's case. For example, a nurse caring for the patient's pressure ulcer will provide documentation needed to determine the proper stage of a pressure ulcer. The underlying condition, such as diabetes or obesity, must be documented by the patient's provider.

Syndromes

When coding syndromes, if the syndrome is not located in the alphabetic index, code the patient's signs and symptoms. For example, a patient is diagnosed with Alstrom syndrome (a rare genetic disease). From the alphabetic index, look up syndrome, Alstrom, which does not have a listing. There also is no listing for Alstrom in the index. Review the documentation to report the patient's signs and symptoms.

Documentation of Complications of Care

Not all conditions that occur during or following surgery or other medical care are classified as complications of care. In order to code a complication of care, there must be a cause-and-effect relationship between the care provided and the condition. The provider must also document that it is a complication.

Section I.C
Chapter-Specific Coding Guidelines

The Tabular List is organized into seventeen chapters that are categorized by etiology or anatomic site. Section I.C of the official coding guidelines includes instructions for the correct code selection and sequencing specific to each chapter. There are no official guidelines for each category within each chapter. Coders must know all the official coding guidelines in addition to the conventions discussed to code diagnoses accurately.

Chapter 1: Infectious and Parasitic Diseases (Codes 001–139)

This chapter includes infectious and parasitic diseases that can be transmitted easily. When selecting codes from this category two codes may be required. There are a few different ways codes from this category can be reported.

- Two codes: one for the organism and one for the condition
- A combination code for the organism and condition
- A single code

The chapter-specific coding guidelines for this chapter include HIV (Human Immunodeficiency Virus), septicemia, systemic inflammatory response syndrome (SIRS), sepsis, severe sepsis, septic shock and MRSA (Methicillin Resistant Staphylococcus Aureus) conditions.

HIV (Human Immunodeficiency Virus)

Code only confirmed cases of HIV infection/illness. Confirmation does not require documentation of positive serology or culture for HIV; the physician's diagnostic statement that the patient is HIV positive or has an HIV-related illness is sufficient.

Selection and Sequencing

When a patient is admitted for an HIV-related condition, 042 is sequenced first followed by additional diagnosis codes for all reported HIV-related conditions.

If a patient with HIV disease is admitted for an unrelated condition (eg, Fracture), the code for the unrelated condition is sequenced first. Code 042 is reported

as an additional diagnosis, as are any HIV-related conditions.

V08 *Asymptomatic human immunodeficiency virus (HIV) infection* is applied when the patient is HIV positive and does not have any documented symptoms of an HIV-related illness. Do not use this code if the term AIDS is used or if the patient is treated for any HIV-related illness or is described as having any condition resulting from HIV positive status; use 042 in these cases.

Patients with inconclusive HIV serology, but not definitive diagnosis or manifestations of the illness, may be assigned code 795.71 *Inconclusive serologic test for Human Immunodeficiency Virus (HIV).*

Previously Diagnosed HIV-Related Illness

Known prior diagnosis of an HIV-related illness should be coded to 042. After a patient has developed an HIV-related illness, the patient's condition should be assigned code 042 on every subsequent admission/encounter. Never assign 795.71 or V08 to a patient with an earlier diagnosis of HIV-related illness (042).

HIV Infection in Pregnancy, Childbirth, and the Puerperium

Asymptomatic HIV infection status during pregnancy, childbirth, or the puerperium should be coded using 647.6x *Other viral diseases* followed by V08. If the patient develops an HIV-related illness during pregnancy, report 647.6x, 042 and the code for the HIV-related illness. Codes from chapter 11 always take sequencing priority.

Encounters for HIV Testing

If a patient is being seen to determine HIV status, use code V73.89 *Screening for other specified viral disease.* Use code V69.8 *Other problems related to lifestyle* as a secondary code if an asymptomatic patient is in a known high-risk group for HIV. Should a patient with signs, symptoms or illness, or a confirmed HIV-related diagnosis be tested for HIV, code the signs and symptoms or the diagnosis. If the results are positive and the patient is symptomatic, use code 042 *HIV infection*, with codes for the HIV-related symptoms or diagnosis. The HIV counseling code (V65.44) may be used as an additional diagnosis if counseling is provided for patients with positive test results.

Example:

A patient with AIDS has developed acute myocarditis as a manifestation of AIDS and is being seen in the office for the myocarditis. The appropriate ICD-9-CM codes are 042 as primary and 422.0 *Acute myocarditis in diseases classified elsewhere* as the secondary diagnosis code.

Septicemia, SIRS, Sepsis, Severe Sepsis, and Septic Shock

These diagnoses are defined similarly. Sometimes providers will document them interchangeably. Query the provider if a diagnosis is questionable.

When reporting SIRS, sepsis, and severe sepsis, a minimum of two codes are required. The documentation must include sepsis or SIRS to code from this category. First, report the code that identifies the underlying condition (infection), followed by a code from category 995.9 *Systemic inflammatory response syndrome (SIRS)*.

Sepsis and severe sepsis require a code to indentify the systemic infection. If the documentation does not include the causal organism, report 038.9 *Unspecified septicemia*. The second listed code reported is 995.91 *Sepsis* or 995.92 *Severe Sepsis* depending on what is documented.

Severe sepsis is associated with acute organ dysfunction. Select an additional code to report each appropriate organ dysfunction. If the patient has sepsis with multiple organ dysfunctions, follow the same coding rules as with severe sepsis.

When coding septic shock, first code the systemic infection followed by 995.92 and 785.52.

Methicillin Resistant Staphlococcus Aureus (MRSA) Conditions

MRSA is any strain of Staphylococcus aureus that has developed a resistance to antibiotics. It is a difficult infection to treat. There are combination codes that report the infection and the causal agent. For example, a patient with methicillin resistant pneumonia due to Staphylococcus aureus is reported with combination code

482.42. If there is not a combination code, select a code for the condition with the code for MRSA.

If the patient is a carrier of MRSA and does not have an active infection, report a personal history code V02.54 *Methicillin resistant Staphylococcus aureus.*

Chapter 2: Neoplasms (Codes 140–239)

A Neoplasm is an abnormal growth of new tissue. There are two ways to begin the search for neoplasm codes. If the histology is documented, look up the term in the Index to Diseases. For example, if the patient is diagnosed with basal cell carcinoma on the forehead, look up Carcinoma, basal-squamous cell, mixed. You are referred to see also Neoplasm, skin, malignant. This statement is referring you to the Neoplasm Table, which is found under Neoplasm in Index to Diseases.

Information in the table is organized alphabetically by site. Using the table, each site is broken into four main categories: malignant, benign, uncertain behavior, and unspecified. Under the heading of malignant, there are three categories to describe the types of malignancy: primary, secondary, and carcinoma *in situ*.

A primary malignancy is where the cancer originates. A secondary malignancy results from metastasis and forms a new focus of malignancy elsewhere (such as the lymph nodes, liver, lungs, or brain), or develops when the primary cancer has invaded adjacent structures. For example, a patient has lung cancer that metastasizes to the spinal cord. In this case, the primary location is the lung, and the secondary location is the spinal cord.

In situ describes a malignancy confined to the origin site, without invading neighboring tissues. That is, the neoplasm is encapsulated (think of the yolk within the shell of an egg). This type of neoplasm may grow large enough to cause major problems.

The fourth column of the Neoplasm Table identifies benign neoplasms that do not contain precancerous or cancerous cells.

If the pathology report returns with indications of atypia or dysplasia, the neoplasm is in transition from benign to malignant (precancerous). This is a neoplasm of uncertain behavior. It is not benign because benign has no precancerous cells, and it is not malignant because it has not become cancer yet. If the process continues and the mass is left untreated, the neoplasm could eventually become malignant.

"Unspecified" indicates that you cannot, or have not, determined the neoplasm's nature. If the provider excises a neoplasm, but does not wait for the pathology report, you should select an unspecified code. It is recommended that you wait for the pathology report to select the most specific code.

Testing Technique

Do not confuse "uncertain" with "unspecified." A pathologist makes an "uncertain" determination based on analysis. "Unspecified" indicates that no analysis was done, or the neoplasm's behavior is not indicated. Do not use an "uncertain" diagnosis for a neoplasm that has not been determined as such by pathology.

Many kinds of neoplasms are excluded from the Neoplasm Table. For example, lipomas, melanomas, neuroendocrine tumors, and Merkel cell carcinomas are not included in the Neoplasm Table, but are addressed in the Index to Diseases. Some polyps and other conditions are indexed to benign neoplasms—but you would know this only by starting in the index. The Index to Diseases and the Neoplasm Table each have instructions very useful to coders. Do not skip these steps.

For malignant neoplasms, determine the primary and secondary sites and then code first the site requiring patient care.

If the initial or primary cancer is still active and represents the reason for the service, list the code for the primary site first. If a secondary growth is the primary reason for the patient care, choose a code from the secondary column of the table, which is listed first.

When coding an encounter for chemotherapy (V58.11) and radiotherapy (V58.0), report the V code first, followed by the active code for the malignant neoplasm, even if that neoplasm has already been removed. As long as the neoplasm is being treated as adjunctive therapy following a surgical removal of the cancer, you can code that neoplasm as if it still exists.

After a neoplasm has been treated successfully, it is inappropriate to use the neoplasm codes for treatment of follow-up care. Offices should be using codes V10–V19 for the following situations:

- The primary malignancy has been removed.
- The patient is not receiving chemotherapy or radiotherapy associated with an active neoplasm.
- There is no evidence of any remaining malignancy.

Admission/Encounters Involving Chemotherapy and Radiation Therapy

When an episode of care involves the surgical removal of a neoplasm followed by chemotherapy or radiation treatment, the neoplasm code should be assigned as the principal or first-listed diagnosis, followed by the code for the therapy.

When the patient develops anemia because of the neoplasm and presents for treatment of the anemia, the code for the anemia is listed first, followed by the code to identify the neoplasm. If the anemia is caused by the chemotherapy, report the code for antineoplastic chemotherapy induced anemia. If the reason for the visit is to treat the malignancy, first sequence the malignancy code followed by the appropriate anemia code.

When a patient becomes dehydrated because of the malignancy, first sequence the code for dehydration, followed by the code to report the malignancy.

A malignant neoplasm of a transplanted organ requires three codes. First, code the transplant complication from category 996.8. Next, report 199.2 *Malignant neoplasm associated with transplanted organ*. Then, the code to specify the malignancy.

Chapter 3: Endocrine, Nutritional and Metabolic Diseases and Immunity Disorders (240–279)

Diabetes mellitus is one of the most frequently used category codes in chapter 3 (Endocrine, Nutritional, and Metabolic Disease and Immunity Disorders) of ICD-9-CM.

Manifestations that may appear with diabetes are identified by the fourth digit and include renal, ophthalmic, neurological, peripheral, circulatory, and other manifestations, such as diabetic hypoglycemia and hypoglycemic shock. The diabetes mellitus code with the specified manifestation should be listed as a primary diagnosis and the specific manifestation reported as a secondary diagnosis.

There are two types of diabetes: Type I and Type II. A Type I diabetic requires insulin to survive. This type of diabetes usually occurs early in life, typically in childhood or before the patient reaches the age of 30. Type II diabetics still produce insulin, but because of obesity, age, or genetic weakness, the insulin produced is not enough to keep their blood sugar levels within normal limits.

When coding for diabetes, choose between diabetes mellitus, secondary diabetes, or gestational diabetes. For diabetes mellitus and secondary diabetes, the fourth digit identifies any complication associated with the disease. For diabetes mellitus, the fifth digit indicates the type of diabetes (Type I or Type II) and whether a diabetic condition is in an uncontrolled state. This information must be documented by the provider; it cannot be assumed or implied.

If the type of diabetes mellitus is not documented in the medical record, the default is Type II. All Type I diabetics must use insulin to replace what their bodies do not produce. The use of insulin does not mean a patient is a Type I diabetic. Some patients with Type II diabetes mellitus are unable to control their blood sugar through diet/exercise and oral medication alone, and require insulin. If the documentation in a medical record does not indicate the type of diabetes but does indicate the patient uses insulin, the appropriate fifth digit for Type II must be used.

For Type II patients who routinely use insulin, code V58.67 *Long-term (current) use of insulin* also should be assigned to indicate that the patient uses insulin. Code V58.67 should not be assigned if insulin is given temporarily to bring a Type II patient's blood sugar under control during an encounter.

When assigning codes for diabetes and its associated conditions, the following applies:

1. The code(s) from category 250 must be sequenced before the codes for the associated conditions.

2. The diabetes codes and the secondary codes that correspond to them are paired codes that follow the etiology/manifestation convention of the classification.

3. Assign as many codes from category 250 as needed to identify all of the associated conditions the patient has.

4. The corresponding secondary codes are listed under each of the diabetes codes.

Three Digit Subclassification: 250 Diabetes Mellitus

The fourth digit indicates any conditions or manifestations present (an additional code may be required to identify the specific manifestation; see below). The fifth digit indicates whether the patient is Type I, Type II, or whether the diabetes is documented as controlled or uncontrolled.

In the Index to Diseases, you will note that many of the subterms have two codes listed; the 250.x code will be followed by an italicized code in brackets. Multiple coding is common with the diabetes code because both the manifestation (symptom) and the etiology (cause) must be reported. The first code indicates the etiology (diabetes) and the second code indicates the manifestation.

Example:

Uncontrolled type I diabetic with associated glaucoma (ophthalmic manifestations): The fourth digit "5" indicates "diabetes with ophthalmic manifestations" and the fifth digit "3" indicates "Type I (juvenile type), uncontrolled" under category 250. When looking at the description associated with 250.5, the coder will see, "Use additional code to identify manifestation, as diabetic...glaucoma (365.44)." The correct codes are 250.53 *Type I (juvenile type) diabetes mellitus with ophthalmic manifestations, uncontrolled* and 365.44 *Glaucoma associated with systemic syndromes (secondary diagnosis)*.

To code a disease or condition as a manifestation of diabetes mellitus, it must be stated that the disease or condition is diabetic or due to the diabetes. A cause-and-effect relationship must be evident. If you are unsure of the relationship, you must clarify this with the physician. If a cause-and-effect relationship is not evident, do not code as a manifestation of the diabetes.

Secondary Diabetes

Secondary diabetes is coded to category 249. A fifth digit is required to identify whether the diabetes is controlled or uncontrolled.

Secondary diabetes is always caused by another condition or event. When assigning codes for secondary diabetes and its associated conditions (eg, renal manifestations), code(s) from category 249 must be sequenced before the codes for the associated conditions. The secondary diabetes codes and the diabetic manifestation codes that correspond to them are paired codes that follow the etiology/manifestation convention of the classification.

The sequencing of the secondary diabetes codes in relationship to codes for the cause of the diabetes is based on the reason for the encounter, applicable ICD-9-CM sequencing conventions, and chapter-specific guidelines.

If the type of diabetes mellitus is not documented in the medical record, the default is Type II, unless the patient has diabetic ketoacidosis, in which case the default is Type I.

You may assign as many codes from category 249 as needed to identify all of the associated conditions the patient has. All corresponding codes for the associated conditions are listed under each of the secondary diabetes codes.

If the patient is treated for the condition causing the secondary diabetes, the code for the cause of the secondary diabetes is reported as the first-listed diagnosis, followed by the secondary diagnosis code in category 249.

Chapter 4: Diseases of Blood and Blood Forming Organs (280–289)

This chapter includes guidelines for reporting anemia. As discussed earlier, there is a code to report anemia caused by neoplastic disease. There also is a code for anemia in chronic kidney disease. These codes are sequenced first if the reason for the encounter is to treat

the anemia. If the reason for the encounter is to treat the other chronic illness, report the code for the malignancy or chronic kidney disease first, followed by the code for the anemia.

Chapter 5: Mental Disorders (290–319)

There are no chapter-specific coding guidelines for this chapter. Coding mental disorders is complicated by the availability of another set of widely-used codes in the *Diagnostic and Statistical Manual, Fourth Edition* (DSM-IV), published by the American Psychiatric Association. The DSM-IV should be used as a reference to assist in the determination of a diagnosis. DSM-IV lists the specific DSM-IV code along with a description of the problem, and any diagnostic or associated features.

Chapter 6: Diseases of Nervous System and Sense Organs (320–389)

The official coding guidelines for this chapter are for the proper code selection and sequencing for pain and glaucoma.

The instructions for pain include acute and chronic pain, pain associated with neoplasms, postoperative pain, and central pain syndrome. When selecting a pain code, you need to know if the pain is acute or chronic. Unless the patient presents for pain management, code the underlying condition that is causing the pain instead of a code from category 338. If the encounter is for pain management, select a code from category 338 followed by the code that identifies the underlying condition. An additional code can also be reported to identify the site of the pain.

When the encounter is to treat the underlying disease and to insert a neurostimulator, two codes are required. First select the code for the underlying condition, followed by the pain code.

Codes for glaucoma are based on the type of glaucoma. If the patient has a different type of glaucoma in each eye, both types should be reported. When codes for glaucoma are reported, a code for the highest stage of glaucoma should be reported as an additional diagnosis. Only one glaucoma stage code should be reported, even if the glaucoma exists in both eyes with different stages.

Chapter 7: Diseases of Circulatory System (390-459)

Hypertension codes are located in the Hypertension Table in the Index to Diseases. This table contains a complete listing of all conditions due to, or associated with, hypertension. At the top of the heading are the following words:

- Malignant—An accelerated, severe form of hypertension, manifested by headaches, blurred vision, dyspnea, and uremia; this type of hypertension usually causes permanent organ damage.
- Benign—Is a continuous, mild blood pressure elevation.
- Unspecified—Has not been specified as either benign or malignant.

Some descriptions in the Hypertension Table have a code listed under each category, while other descriptions have only one code listed under just one column. Not every type of hypertension applies in every case. The information is found only in the Hypertension Table; the table replaces the index entries for hypertension. By initially looking for a code in the table, the coder will be able to choose the correct code from the Tabular List in Volume 1.

Example:

Hypertension due to brain tumor. In the Hypertension Table, recognize that "due to" is a modifier. The type of hypertension was not stated so it is "unspecified." The correct code is 405.99 *Other secondary hypertension, unspecified.*

Hypertension with Heart Disease

High blood pressure can lead to heart disease and heart failure. Heart conditions (429.0–429.3, 429.8, and 429.9) are assigned a code from category 402 when a causal relationship is stated as due to hypertension or implied as hypertensive. Use an additional code from category 428 to identify the type of heart failure. More than one code from category 428 may be assigned if the patient has systolic or diastolic failure and congestive heart failure. If the causal relationship between the hypertension and the heart disease is not documented, each condition is coded separately.

Hypertensive Disease with Chronic Kidney Disease

Chronic kidney conditions and hypertension go hand in hand. Assign codes from category 403 Hypertensive Renal Disease when conditions classified to categories 585 are present. Unlike hypertension with heart disease, ICD-9-CM presumes a cause-and-effect relationship and classifies renal failure with hypertension as hypertensive renal disease. Fourth and fifth digits for category 403 should be assigned.

The appropriate code from category 585 Chronic Kidney Disease (CKD) should be reported as a secondary diagnosis with a code from category 403 to identify the stage of CKD.

Hypertensive Heart and Chronic Kidney Disease

Sometimes, the hypertensive patient has both heart disease and kidney disease. Assign codes from combination category 404 Hypertensive Heart and Chronic Kidney Disease when both hypertensive kidney disease and hypertensive heart disease are stated in the diagnosis. Assume a relationship between the hypertension and the chronic kidney disease, regardless of whether the condition is so designated. Assign an additional code from category 428 to identify the type of heart failure. More than one code from category 428 may be assigned if the patient has systolic or diastolic failure and congestive heart failure.

The appropriate code from category 585 Chronic Kidney Disease should be used as a secondary code with a code from category 404 to identify the stage of chronic kidney disease.

Hypertensive Cerebrovascular Disease

Assign categories codes from 430–438 Cerebrovascular Disease and the appropriate hypertension code from categories 401–405.

Hypertensive Retinopathy

Hypertension in the small vessel of the eyes can cause serious damage, and even lead to blindness. In retinopathy, the increased pressure leads to the growth of unstable vessels in the eye. These vessels can fracture and bleed, causing complications to vision and to eye circulation. Two codes are necessary to identify the condition. First, assign the eye code from subcategory 362.11 *Hypertensive retinopathy*; then, select an appropriate code from the circulatory categories 401–405 to indicate the type of hypertension.

Hypertension, Secondary

Just as hypertension can cause disorders, disorders can cause hypertension. Two codes are required to report secondary hypertension: one to identify the underlying etiology and one from category 405 to identify the hypertension. The reason for the encounter determines code sequencing.

Hypertension, Transient

Sometimes, a fleeting bout of high blood pressure readings can occur. One example of this is called "white coat syndrome"—the stress of being in the doctor's office causes a temporary increase in blood pressure. One elevated reading does not constitute a diagnosis of hypertension. Assign code 796.2 *Elevated blood pressure reading without diagnosis of hypertension* unless the patient has an established diagnosis of hypertension. Assign code 642.3x for *transient hypertension of pregnancy*.

Elevated Blood Pressure

For a statement of elevated blood pressure without further specificity, assign code 796.2 *Elevated blood pressure reading without diagnosis of hypertension*.

Chapter 8: Diseases of Respiratory System (460–519)

COPD (chronic obstructive pulmonary disease) is chronic bronchitis and emphysema that causes the respiratory passages to narrow.

Asthma is a chronic inflammatory disease of the airway. It can be due to allergies. Acute exacerbation of asthma is an increased severity of asthma. Status asthmaticus indicates the patient is not responding to treatment. When a patient has status asthmaticus and COPD, sequence the code for the status asthmaticus first.

Report 491.22 *Obstructive chronic bronchitis with acute bronchitis* when acute bronchitis with COPD is diagnosed. There is no need to report an additional code.

The sequencing of acute respiratory failure is determined by the reason for the encounter. If a patient is admitted for acute respiratory failure, 518.81 is sequenced first. If the patient is admitted for multiple reasons, select the condition that required the most care.

Chapter 9: Diseases of Digestive System (520–579)

There are no chapter-specific coding guidelines for this chapter. Common diagnoses in this chapter include cholelithiasis and cholecystitis. The codes describe a calculus of the gallbladder with different types of cholecystitis (eg, acute, chronic, or both, or without cholecystitis, and with or without an obstruction). The obstruction is usually a calculus lodged in the neck of the gallbladder or cystic duct. A fifth digit indicates the presence or absence of obstruction.

Chapter 10: Diseases of Genitourinary System (580–629)

When reporting chronic kidney disease (CKD), select the code with the proper fourth digit to identify the stage of CKD. Sometimes providers will document CKD and end stage renal disease (ESRD) for the same patient. Report 585.6 *End stage renal disease* only. Do not assume a patient who has had a kidney transplant and chronic kidney disease developed the CKD because of the transplant. Select the code to report the stage of CKD and V42.0 to report kidney transplant status.

Chapter 11: Complications of Pregnancy, Childbirth, and the Puerperium (630–679)

For routine care, supervision of normal first pregnancy (V22.0) or supervision of other normal pregnancy (V22.1) is coded. If the patient is seen for an unrelated condition, such as a fracture, incidental to pregnancy (V22.2) you may report this as an additional diagnosis.

Prenatal complications may range from pregnancy, related conditions, such as preeclampsia or hyperemesis gravidarum, to other conditions that can be coded elsewhere but are complicating the pregnancy. If the patient's current pregnancy appears normal but the patient is considered high risk because of a history of complications, a code from category V23 for supervision of high-risk pregnancy may be used.

Complications relating to pregnancy can occur early, during delivery, or during the follow-up period. The puerperium, or follow-up period, is the period from the termination of labor to complete involution of the uterus, usually defined as 42 days in length.

Fifth-digit subclassification is for use with categories 640–649 and 651–676 to denote the current episode of care. Valid fifth digits are in [brackets] under each code.

Chapter 11 codes have sequencing priority over all other codes. A code from another category can be reported as an additional diagnosis, but not as a first-listed diagnosis.

Example:

A patient with controlled Type II diabetes is five months pregnant. Report 648.03 *Other current conditions in the mother classifiable elsewhere, but complicating pregnancy, childbirth, or the puerperium, diabetes mellitus* and a separate ICD-9-CM code to identify the diabetic condition. The proper sequence is 648.03, 250.00.

Chapter 12: Diseases Skin & Subcutaneous Tissue (680–709)

Pressure ulcers are also known as bed sores and decubitus ulcers. Two codes are required to identify the location of the ulcer and the stage of the ulcer. If the pressure ulcer is documented as unstageable, assign 707.25 *Pressure ulcer, unstageable*. This diagnosis is determined based on the clinical documentation. This code should not be used if the stage is not documented. In that instance, report the unspecified code, 707.20.

Bilateral ulcers with the same stage are reported with one code for the location and one code for the stage. Bilateral ulcers with different stages require a code to identify the site and codes to identify each stage documented. When multiple sites are documented, select a code for each anatomic site and each stage.

Chapter 13: Diseases of Musculoskeletal and Connective Tissue (710–739)

A pathologic fracture is a broken bone that occurs in an area of weakened bone. These codes are not reported for a traumatic fracture (which will be discussed later in this chapter). A code from category 733.1 is reported for a new fracture. When the patient has completed the active phase of treatment, report the appropriate after-care code (V code). Aftercare codes can be found in the Index to Diseases under "aftercare."

Chapter 14: Congenital Anomalies (740–759)

Assign an appropriate code(s) from categories 740–759 Congenital Anomalies when an anomaly is documented. A congenital anomaly may be the first-listed diagnosis on record or a secondary diagnosis.

Codes from chapter 14 may be used throughout the life of the patient. If a congenital anomaly has been corrected, a personal history code should be used to identify the history of the anomaly.

For the birth admission, the appropriate code from category V30 *Single liveborn infants according to type of birth* should be sequenced as the principal diagnosis, followed by any congenital anomaly codes 740–759.

Chapter 15: Newborn (Perinatal) Guidelines (760–779)

For coding and reporting purposes, the perinatal period is defined as birth through day 28 following birth. The following guidelines are provided for reporting purposes:

◖ General Perinatal Rule: All clinically significant conditions noted on routine newborn exam should be coded.

◖ When coding the birth of an infant, assign a code from categories V30–V39 according to the type of birth. A code from this series is assigned as a principal diagnosis and assigned only once to a newborn at the time of birth.

- Assign a code from category V29 *Observation and evaluation of newborns and infants for suspected conditions not found* when a healthy newborn is evaluated for a suspected condition determined not to be present. When the patient has identified signs or symptoms of a suspected problem, code the sign or symptom and not V29.

- Codes from categories 760–763 *Maternal causes of perinatal morbidity and mortality* are assigned only when the maternal condition has affected the fetus or newborn.

- Assign a code for newborn conditions originating in the perinatal period (categories 760–779), as well as complications arising during the current episode of care classified in other chapters, only if the diagnoses have been documented by the physician at the time of transfer or discharge as having affected the fetus or newborn.

- Codes from category 764 *Slow fetal growth and fetal malnutrition* and subcategories 765.0 and 765.1 should not be assigned based solely on recorded birth weight or estimated gestational age, but on the attending physician's clinical assessment of maturity of the infant.

Chapter 16: Symptoms, Signs, and Ill-defined Conditions (780–799)

Symptoms, Signs, and Ill-defined Conditions in the Tabular List also include abnormal results of investigations and other ill-defined conditions. Use codes from this section when:

- No more-specific diagnoses can be made after investigation.

- Signs and symptoms existing at the time of the initial encounter proved to be transient, or the cause could not be determined.

- A patient fails to return and a provisional diagnosis is the only thing recorded.

- A case is referred elsewhere before a definitive diagnosis could be made.

- A more precise diagnosis is not available for any other reason.

- Certain symptoms, which represent important problems in medical care, exist and might be classified in addition to a known cause.

Do not use the codes from Symptoms, Signs and Ill-defined Conditions when:

- A definitive diagnosis is available.

Example

The diagnostic statement is right lower quadrant abdominal pain due to acute appendicitis. Because the reason for the pain is acute appendicitis, the symptom of abdominal pain is not coded. The only code assigned is for the acute appendicitis (540.9).

- The symptom is considered an integral part of the disease process.

Example

The diagnostic statement reads, "cough and fever with pneumonia." Both fever and cough are symptoms of the pneumonia; therefore, codes are not assigned for either symptom. The only code assigned is the code for the pneumonia (486).

Chapter 17: Injury and Poisoning (800–999)

This chapter includes the diagnosis codes for injuries, fractures, burns, adverse effects, poisonings, toxic effects and complications of care.

Injuries

Injuries are classified according to the type and site of injury (eg, fracture, burn). Look in the Index to Diseases for the main term describing the injury and then for a subterm identifying the site. When coding multiple injuries, assign separate codes for each injury unless a specific combination code is provided.

- List first the code for the most serious injury, as determined by the physician.

- Superficial injuries such as abrasions or contusions are not coded when associated with more severe injuries of the same site (for example, a contusion at the site of a closed fracture).

◖ When a primary injury results in minor damage to peripheral nerves or blood vessels, the primary injury is sequenced first with additional code(s) from categories 950–957 injury to nerves and spinal cord, and/or 900–904 injury to blood vessels sequenced secondarily.

◖ The cause of the injury should be identified with an E code. E codes are coded in addition to primary and secondary diagnoses. E codes are never sequenced first.

◖ An open wound is identified by site and complexity. E codes are used to identify the cause of the wound. The code for an open wound is located under the main term "Wound, open" in the Index to Diseases.

Traumatic Fractures

Category 800–829 contains the codes assigned for fractures caused by trauma. A fracture not indicated as closed or open should be classified as closed. A dislocation and fracture of the same bone is coded to the fracture site only.

The codes are classified according to particular bone(s) involved, the type of fracture, and whether it is opened or closed.

Fractures are coded as long as active treatment is rendered. Aftercare categories V54.0, V54.1, V54.8 or V54.9 are reported after the patient ends active treatment of the fracture and is receiving routine care for the fracture during healing or the recovery phase.

Complication codes are reported if a complication occurs during healing or recovery phase using the appropriate complication code(s). Malunion of a fracture is reported with 733.81, and a nonunion of a fracture is reported with 733.82.

Multiple fractures are sequenced according to the severity of the fracture.

To locate codes for fractures, look up the main term "fracture," then look for the bone that is fractured. There are sub terms to identify if the fracture is open or closed.

Example

Fractured hip with dislocation. Because the fracture is not defined as open or closed, it is classified as closed. Code only for the fracture because the diagnosis includes both fracture and dislocation. The correct code is 820.8 *Closed fracture of unspecified part of neck of femur.*

Burns

ICD-9-CM coding for a burn is a situation when a single code cannot describe adequately an entire condition. A burn is coded by site, severity or degree of burn, and total body surface area (TBSA).

Always code to the greatest depth of the burn in a given category/anatomical area. Sequence first the diagnosis that reflects the highest degree of burn when multiple burns are present. Classify burns of the same local site (940–947) but of different degrees to the subcategory identifying the highest degree of burn.

Example:

When there are both second and third degree burns on the back, report code 942.34. Code 942.24 would not be reported. It would not be appropriate to report both codes from the same category because the deepest level of burn in a given anatomical area or category is sufficient.

Always list the code for the deepest level of burn first when there are burns to multiple areas. Non-healing burns are coded as acute burns. Necrosis of burned skin is coded as a non-healed burn. When coding burns, assign separate codes for each burn site. Category 946 for burns of multiple specified sites should only be used if the locations of the burns are not documented.

Assign codes from category 948, which classifies burns according to extent of body surface involved, when the site of the burn is not specified or when there is need for additional data. Use category 948 as an additional code for reporting purposes when there is a third degree burn involving 20 percent or more of the body surface. In assigning codes from category 948:

- Fourth-digit codes are used to identify the percentage of total body surface involved in a burn (all degrees).
- Fifth-digits are assigned to identify the percentage of body surface involved in a third degree burn.
- Fifth-digit zero (0) is assigned when less than 10 percent or when the body surface is involved in a third degree burn.

Complications such as infections, associated injuries, and comorbid conditions should be coded in addition to the burn code(s). Examples of comorbid conditions are diabetes mellitus, cardiovascular disorders, alcoholism, peptic ulcers, and asthma. These comorbid conditions may influence the healing process.

Category 946 Burns of Multiple Specified Sites is used when multiple burns have been identified across multiple three digit categories in the 940–945 range. Coders should sequence the burn code for the highest degree of burn first when coding multiple burns. If a patient has a third degree burn of the palm of the left hand and a second degree burn on the right forearm, the codes are 944.35 and 943.21.

Unless space is of issue, the recommendation is to list each burn site individually from most severe to least severe.

Category 948 signifies the extent of the body surface involved. The fourth digit in this category described the percentage of TBSA burned, while the fifth digit classification indicates the TBSA with third degree burns only. The fourth digit assignment represents the percentage of total body surface involved in the burn injury regardless of degree and the fifth digit represents the percentage of body surface with third degree burn. To determine the TBSA, the rule of nines is used.

Adverse Effects, Poisoning and Toxic Effects

The Table of Drugs and Chemicals is used to identify the substances and causes for adverse effects and poisonings. The Table of Drugs and Chemicals organizes codes associated with specific substances. Use of the Table of Drugs can be substituted for the index. Within the table

is an alphabetic list of generic and brand name agents that may cause a reaction or poisoning if taken in the wrong dosage, or if taken in error. It is also for intoxication or poisoning by a drug or other chemical substance. The table contains an extensive list of drugs, set in a six-column format, including industrial solvents, corrosive gases, noxious plants, pesticides, and other toxic agents. The first column provides the codes for the substance involved. The next five columns are grouped under the heading External Causes (E codes) and identify the circumstances of poisoning.

More than one code is required to report an adverse effect of a drug or chemical. One code reports the circumstance of the substance's adverse effect and the second code identifies whether the substance was in therapeutic use, or a suicide attempt, assault, or accident. Codes in the table must be verified in the Tabular List.

Index to External Causes of Injuries and Poisonings

The Index to External Causes of Injuries and Poisonings in Volume 2, section 3 contains the codes for classifying environmental events, circumstances, and other conditions as the cause of injury or adverse effects, as listed below:

The E codes in this table are defined as follows:

- Accidental Poisoning Codes [E850–E869]—Identify accidental ingestion of drugs for incorrect use in medical or surgical procedures, incorrect administration for ingestion of the drug, or inadvertent or accidental overdose. This category also includes accidental poisoning by other solid and liquid substances, gases and vapors.
- Therapeutic Use Codes [E930–E949]—Indicate an adverse effect or reaction to a drug that was administered correctly, either therapeutically or prophylactically.
- Suicide Attempt Codes [E950–E952]—Identify the effects of the drugs or substances taken to cause self-inflicted injury or to attempt suicide.
- Assault Codes [E961–E962]—Indicates drugs or substances are "purposely inflicted" by another person with the intent to cause bodily harm, injury, or death.
- Undetermined Codes [E980–E982]—Apply when the cause of poisoning or injury is unknown.

Adverse Reaction

Adverse reaction occurs when a prescription medicine or drug is taken according to physician instruction and the patient develops a reaction to the medication. Adverse reactions happen in spite of proper administration.

When coding adverse reactions to a correct substance properly administered, you will use two or more codes:

1. Use the first code to identify the manifestation(s).

2. The second code identifies the drug causing the reaction (use "Therapeutic Use" column in the Table of Drugs and Chemicals). This is reported with an E code.

Poisoning

Poisoning occurs when the wrong drug or an incorrect dosage of a correct drug is ingested. Poisoning by drugs can be accidental (given in error during a procedure, given in error by one person to another, or taken in error by self) or purposeful (suicide or homicide attempt). To code poisoning correctly:

1. The first code, from the poisoning column, identifies the drug.

2. The second code indicates the condition(s), manifestation(s) that resulted from the poisoning.

3. An E code from the Table of Drugs and Chemicals indicates the circumstance (accidental, suicide attempt, assault, or undetermined).

Complications

If a complication from medical or surgical care initiates a visit to the provider's office or an admission to the hospital, a complication code would be reported as the primary diagnosis. Complication codes are found in the 996–999 series of ICD-9-CM codes. When available, the code for the specific complication also should be listed. There must be a cause-and-effect relationship between the care provided and the condition documented in the medical record. If the documentation does not indicate it is a complication, query the provider.

Example

A patient is discharged from the hospital after internal fixation of an open fracture. Four days after surgery, the patient's surgical wound is red, swollen, and draining fluid. The patient presents to the orthopaedic clinic. The provider determines the patient has a postoperative infection due to the implant and takes a culture. The culture comes back from the laboratory positive for a Streptococcus B infection. The appropriate codes are 996.67 to describe the complication due to implant of the internal fixation device and 041.02 to describe the Streptococcus B infection.

Diagnosis Coding Guidelines for Outpatient Reporting

Diagnostic Coding and Reporting Guidelines for Outpatient Services is described in section IV of the *ICD-9-CM Official Guidelines for Coding and Reporting*. These coding guidelines for outpatient diagnoses have been approved for use by hospitals/physicians in coding and reporting hospital based outpatient services and physician office visits. Review the following guideline sections for coding and reporting outpatient services.

Selection of First-Listed Condition

◖ In the outpatient setting, the first-listed diagnosis is used in lieu of principal diagnosis.

◖ In determining the first-listed diagnosis, the coding conventions of ICD-9-CM, as well as the general and disease specific guidelines, take precedence over the outpatient guidelines.

Diagnoses often are not established at the time of the initial encounter/visit. It may take two or more visits before the diagnosis is confirmed.

The most critical rule involves beginning the search for the correct code assignment through the Index to Diseases. Never begin searching initially in the Tabular List because this will lead to coding errors.

Example

A middle-aged male presents with a complaint of constant facial pain. The physician orders diagnostic tests to determine the source of the pain. The initial patient visit is completed with the diagnosis of facial pain (diagnosis code 784.0) because a definitive diagnosis has not yet been determined.

Example

Patient presents to the outpatient clinic complaining of abdominal cramps. The physician performs a complete history and physical examination but does not determine the cause of the cramps. The diagnosis code reported for this encounter is based on the symptom of abdominal cramps (789.00).

Codes From 001.0 Through V91

The appropriate code or codes from 001.0 through V91.99 must be used to identify diagnoses, signs, symptoms, conditions, problems, complaints, or other reason(s) for the encounter/visit.

Accurate Reporting of ICD-9-CM Diagnosis Codes

For accurate reporting of ICD-9-CM diagnosis codes, the documentation should describe the patient's condition, using terminology that includes specific diagnoses as well as symptoms, problems, or reasons for the encounter. There are ICD-9-CM codes to describe all of these situations.

Selection of Codes 001.0 Through 999.9

The selection of codes 001.0 through 999.9 frequently will be used to describe the reason for the encounter. These codes are from the section of ICD-9-CM for the classification of diseases and injuries (eg, infectious and parasitic diseases; neoplasms; symptoms, signs, and ill-defined conditions).

Codes that Describe Symptoms and Signs

Codes that describe symptoms and signs, as opposed to diagnoses, are acceptable for reporting purposes when a diagnosis has not been established (confirmed) by the physician. Chapter 16 of ICD-9-CM, Symptoms, Signs, and Ill-defined Conditions (codes 780.0–799.9) contain many, but not all codes for symptoms.

Encounters for Circumstances Other Than a Disease or Injury

ICD-9-CM provides codes to deal with encounters for circumstances other than a disease or injury. The Supplementary Classification of Factors Influencing Health Status and Contact with Health Services codes (V01.0–V91.9) are provided to deal with occasions when circumstances other than a disease or injury are recorded as diagnosis or problems.

Level of Detail in Coding

Where fourth-digit subcategories and/or fifth-digit subclassifications are provided, they must be assigned. A code is invalid if it has not been coded to the full number of digits (highest level of specificity) required for that code. See also the discussion under Section I, General Coding Guidelines, level of detail.

ICD-9-CM Code for the Diagnosis, Condition, Problem or Other Reason for the Encounter

List first the ICD-9-CM code for the diagnosis, condition, problem, or other reason for encounter/visit shown in the medical record to be chiefly responsible for the services provided. List additional codes that describe any co-existing conditions.

Example

The patient presents for evaluation and generalized osteoarthrosis, multiple sites. During the encounter, the physician also evaluates the patient's constipation and recommends a change in diet. Diagnosis codes for this encounter are 715.09 *Generalized osteoarthrosis, involving multiple sites* and 564.00 *Unspecified constipation*.

Uncertain Diagnosis

Do not code diagnoses documented as "probable," "suspected," "questionable," "rule out," or "working diagnosis." Rather, code the condition(s) to the highest degree of certainty for that encounter/visit, such as symptoms, signs, abnormal test results, or other reason for the visit.

Chronic Diseases

Chronic diseases treated on an ongoing basis may be coded and reported as many times as the patient receives treatment and care for the condition(s).

Code All Documented Conditions that Coexist

Code all documented conditions that co-exist at the time of the encounter/visit, and require or affect patient care, treatment, or management. Do not code conditions treated prior to this encounter/visit that no longer exist. History codes (V10–V19) may be used as secondary codes if the historical condition or family history has an impact on current care or influences treatment.

Example

The patient presents with chest pain and has a father with a prior diagnosis of ischemic heart disease. Diagnosis codes for this encounter include 786.50 *Unspecified chest pain* and V17.3 *Family history of ischemic heart disease*.

Patients Receiving Diagnostic Services Only

For patients receiving diagnostic services only during an encounter/visit, sequence first the diagnosis, condition, problem, or other reason for encounter/visit shown in the medical record to be chiefly responsible for the outpatient services provided during the encounter/visit. Codes for other diagnoses (eg, chronic conditions) may be sequenced as additional diagnoses.

The findings from diagnostic tests can be coded for outpatient services if they are interpreted by a physician and the final report is available at the time of coding. Do not code related signs and symptoms as additional diagnoses. See section: Diagnostic Tests with Signs and Symptoms. This differs from the coding practice in the hospital inpatient setting regarding abnormal findings on test results.

Example

A patient presents for an MRI of the brain with the complaint of dizziness. This patient has been previously diagnosed with a malignant neoplasm of the bladder. The diagnosis code 780.4 *Dizziness and giddiness* is sequenced first because it is the primary reason for the outpatient diagnostic service. Diagnosis code 188.9 *Bladder malignancy, unspecified* may be sequenced as the secondary diagnosis code.

Patients Receiving Therapeutic Services Only

For patients receiving therapeutic services only during an encounter/visit, sequence first the diagnosis, condition, problem, or other reason for encounter/visit shown in the medical record to be chiefly responsible for the outpatient services provided during the encounter/visit. Codes for other diagnoses (eg, chronic conditions) may be sequenced as additional diagnoses.

Patients Receiving Preoperative Evaluations Only

For patients receiving preoperative evaluations only, sequence a code from category V72.8 *Other specified examinations* to describe the preoperative consultations. Assign a code for the condition to describe the reason for the surgery as an additional diagnosis. Code also any findings related to the preoperative evaluation.

Example

A patient presents for a preoperative screening chest X-ray prior to surgery for a unilateral inguinal hernia. The X-ray detects an undefined abnormality in the right lower lobe, and the radiologist recommends additional imaging studies. Diagnosis sequencing for this encounter includes:

- V72.83   Other specified preoperative examination
- 550.90   Unilateral inguinal hernia
- 793.19   Other nonspecific abnormal finding of lung field.

Ambulatory Surgery

For ambulatory surgery, code the diagnosis for which the surgery was performed. If the postoperative diagnosis is known to be different from the preoperative diagnosis at the time the diagnosis is confirmed, select the postoperative diagnosis for coding because it is the most definitive.

Routine Outpatient Prenatal Visits

For routine outpatient prenatal visits when no complications are present, report codes V22.0 *Supervision of normal first pregnancy* and V22.1 *Supervision of other normal pregnancy* as principal diagnoses.

Glossary

Acute—A condition with a rapid onset with a short course.

Chronic—A condition that develops slowly and lasts a long period of time.

Closed Fracture—A fractured bone that does not pierce the skin.

E Codes—Codes reported to indentify how an injury occurred and the location when it occurred. E codes are never sequenced first.

First-Degree Burn—Superficial burns through only the epidermis.

Late Effect—An inactive, residual effect or condition produced after the acute portion of an injury or illness has passed.

Open Fracture—A fractured bone that pierces the skin.

Second-Degree Burn—A partial-thickness burn involving the epidermis and the dermis.

Septicemia—A systemic disease that is associated with microorganisms or toxins in the blood. These toxins are caused by bacteria, viruses, fungi, or other organisms.

Systemic Inflammatory Response Syndrome (SIRS)—Systemic response to infection, burns, trauma, or cancer.

Sepsis—Whole body inflammatory state. It generally refers to SIRS that is due to an infection.

Severe Sepsis—Sepsis with associated acute organ dysfunction.

Third-Degree Burn—A full-thickness burn that involves the epidermis, dermis, and varying levels of the subcutaneous and underlying structures.

V Codes—Codes used to describe circumstances or conditions that could influence patient care.

Chapter Review Questions

1. Which of the following V codes can be reported as a first listed code?

    A. V27.0

    B. V07.4

    C. V13.61

    D. V20.2

2. **When coding for a patient who has had a primary malignancy of the thyroid cartilage that was completely excised a year ago, and no current treatment, which of the following statements is TRUE?**

   A. When no further treatment is provided and there is no evidence of any existing primary malignancy, code V10.87.

   B. When further treatment is provided and there is evidence of an existing metastasis, code first V10.87 and then 161.3.

   C. Any mention of extension, invasion, or metastasis to another site is coded as a 239.1.

   D. When further treatment is provided and there is evidence of an existing metastasis, code first 197.3

3. **The patient has acute, gangrenous tonsillitis. Code his condition.**

   A. 474.00, 785.4

   B. 474.00

   C. 463, 785.4

   D. 463

4. **The patient has a history of symptomatic HIV. What is the ICD-9-CM code reported?**

   A. V08

   B. 042

   C. V12.2

   D. 795.71

5. **Patient presents with sternal chest pain, possible angina. Physician rules out angina and documents probable costochondritis. Code the diagnosis.**

   A. 786.50

   B. 733.6

   C. 786.51

   D. 413.9

6. **Following the MUGA scan, the physician documents the patient has developed congestive heart failure as an adverse affect of the trastuzumab she received as a treatment for her breast cancer. The trastuzumab antineoplastic antibiotic therapy is being discontinued while he attempts to manage the heart failure pharmaceutically. Code the patient's condition.**

   A. 428.0, 960.7, V10.3, E930.7

   B. 428.0, 963.1, 174.9, E930.7

   C. 428.0, 174.9, E930.7

   D. 428.0, 174.9, E933.1

7. Mr. Jones is here today to receive an intercostal nerve block to mitigate the debilitating pain of his malignancy. His cancer has metastatized to his lungs. Code the patient's condition.

   A. 338.3, 197.0

   B. 338.3, 162.9

   C. 338.12, 162.9

   D. 338.12, 197.0

8. Four years post hepatic transplant, the patient is diagnosed with combined hepatocellular carcinoma and cholangiocarcinoma of the liver. Code the patient's condition.

   A. 996.82, 199.2, 155.0

   B. 199.2, 155.2, V45.87

   C. 996.82, 199.2, 155.2

   D. 996.82, 199.2, 155.0, V45.87

9. Mrs. Bixby, 83, is being admitted for dehydration and anorexia, probable cause, dementia. She was brought in by her daughter who is visiting from out of town. Her daughter will take her from our office to St. Mary's. The gerontology unit will evaluate her mental condition tomorrow after she is stabilized. How would you code the diagnoses?

   A. 307.1, 276.51

   B. 783.0, 276.51

   C. 307.1, 276.51, 294.8

   D. 783.0, 276.51, 294.8

10. A 27-year-old man with a 25-year history of juvenile diabetes is admitted to the ICU with diabetic keto-acidosis brought on the H1N1 influenza virus which includes respiratory symptoms. Which codes best report how his consulting endocrinologist will report his condition?

   A. 250.11, 488.12

   B. 487.8, 250.10

   C. 488.11, 250.13

   D. 249.10, 487.8

Chapter 4

Introduction to CPT®, Surgery Guidelines, HCPCS Level II, and Modifiers

Introduction to CPT®

The Current Procedural Terminology (CPT®) codebook is a compilation of guidelines, codes, and descriptions used to report health care services. The CPT® code set, Healthcare Common Procedure Coding System (HCPCS) Level I, is copyrighted and maintained by the American Medical Association (AMA). In 1983, the Health Care Financing Administration (now the Centers for Medicare & Medicaid Services, or CMS) adopted CPT®, and its own HCPCS Level II, mandating these code sets be used for billing Medicare. In August 2000, the Transactions and Code Sets Final Rule (45 CFR 160.103) additionally named CPT®, HCPCS Level II, and their respective modifiers as standard code sets for national use.

The CPT® code set includes three categories of medical nomenclature and descriptors:

- Category I CPT® codes utilize a five-digit numerical code (eg, 12345). The codes are reviewed and updated annually by an AMA panel. It is mandatory to use Category I CPT® codes for reporting and reimbursement. For Medicare, a HCPCS Level II code may be used instead of HCPCS Level I CPT® code if available.
- Category II CPT® codes are optional "performance measurement" tracking codes. They are used for the Physician Quality Reporting System (PQRS), an incentive-based program developed by CMS to record evidence-based measures, discussed later in this chapter. The format for Category II codes is alphanumeric, with the letter F in the last position (eg, 0001F).

Category II codes are reported in addition to evaluation and management (E/M) services or clinical services CPT® Category I codes.

Example

A physician examines a patient currently taking Statin therapy for coronary artery disease during an E/M visit. Report 4002F *Statin therapy, prescribed or currently being taken (CAD)* and an appropriate-level office visit code (99201–99215).

- Category III CPT® codes are temporary codes assigned by the AMA for emerging technology, services, and procedures. Category III codes are alphanumeric, with the letter **T** in the last position, eg, 0075T. Unlike the Category II CPT® codes, Category III codes can be reported alone, without an additional Category I code.

The AMA updates the CPT® codebook annually.

The Organization of the CPT® Codebook

The CPT® codebook is organized by:

- CPT® sections—Category I has six sections that include services and surgical procedures separated into subsections.
- Section Guidelines
- Section Table of Contents
- Notes
- Category II Codes (0001F–7025F)
- Category III Codes (0019T–0290T)
- Appendices A–N
- Alphabetized Index

The CPT® subsections also include:

- Indicator icons
- Boldfaced type
- Italicized type
- Cross-referenced terms

◀ Anatomy illustrations

◀ Procedural reviews that aid with medical terminology and anatomy

Introduction Guidelines

CPT® guidelines introduce each section/subsection of the CPT® codebook. Guidelines apply only for the section/subsection in which they appear.

Testing Technique

Review every guideline in your codebook. Underline or highlight specific coding information within the guidelines.

CPT® Conventions and Iconography

An established set of conventions and symbols is used throughout the CPT® codebook, as follows:

; Semicolon and Indented Procedure—A CPT® procedure or service code that contains a semicolon is divided into two parts:

a) The words before the semi-colon are considered the "common procedure" in the code descriptor.

b) The indented descriptor is dependent on the preceding "common procedure" code descriptor.

c) It is not necessary to report the main code (eg, 00160) when reporting the indented codes (eg, 00162 or 00164).

Example:

00160 *Anesthesia for procedures on nose and accessory sinuses; not otherwise specified*
00162 *radical surgery*
00164 *biopsy, soft tissue*

The full descriptor for 00162 and 00164 includes the text before the semicolon in 00160. For instance, the full descriptor for 00162 is *Anesthesia for procedures on nose and accessory sinuses; radical surgery.*

+ Add-on Codes (see CPT® Appendix D)—Some procedures, identified with a "+" symbol, are commonly carried out in addition to a primary procedure. Add-on codes must be used with their specified primary procedure.

Example:

+ 11201 *each additional ten lesions, or part thereof. (List separately in addition to code for primary procedure) (Use 11201 in conjunction with 11200)*

● A bullet placed before the code number indicates new procedures and services added to the CPT® codebook.

Example:

● 33227 *Removal of permanent pacemaker pulse generator with replacement of pacemaker pulse generator; single lead system*

▲ A triangle indicates that a code descriptor has been revised.

Example:

▲ 39200 *Resection of mediastinal cyst*

▶◀ Opposing horizontal triangles (bowties) indicate new or revised guidelines or instructions.

Example:

29880 *Arthroscopy, knee, surgical; with meniscectomy (medial AND lateral, including any meniscal shaving)* ▶ **including debridement/shaving of articular cartilage (chondroplasty), same or separate compartment(s), when performed** ◀

⊘ The "forbidden" symbol identifies codes that are modifier 51 exempt (CPT® Appendix E).

Example:

⊘ **20974** *Electrical stimulation to aid bone healing; noninvasive (nonoperative)*

⊙ A bull's-eye identifies codes that include moderate sedation (CPT® Appendix G).

Example:

⊙ **43200** *Esophagoscopy, rigid or flexible; diagnostic, with or without collection of specimen(s) by brushing or washing (separate procedure)*

⚡ A lightning bolt identifies vaccines pending Food and Drug Administration (FDA) approval. If a vaccine is approved by the FDA a revision notation is provided on the AMA CPT® "Category I Vaccine Codes" website: www.ama-assn.org/ama/pub/physician-resources/solutions-managing-your-practice/coding-billing-insurance/cpt/about-cpt/category-i-vaccine-codes.page (see Appendix K for Products Pending FDA Approval).

Example:

⚡ **90661** *Influenza virus vaccine, derived from cell cultures, subunit, preservative and antibiotic free, for intramuscular use*

\# The pound sign identifies CPT® codes that have been resequenced and are out of numerical order.

Example:

\# **46947** Hemorrhoidopexy (eg, for prolapsing internal hemorrhoids) by stapling

Category I CPT® Section Numbers

CPT® Category I codes are divided into six main sections:

Evaluation and Management (99201–99499)

Anesthesiology (00100–01999, 99100–99140)

Surgery (10021–69990)

Radiology (70010–79999)

Pathology and Laboratory (80047–89398)

Medicine (90281–99199, 99500–99607)

Sections are organized by anatomic location, procedure, condition, or descriptor subheadings. Be sure to follow parenthetical instructions and other coding guidelines provided.

Example:

Section: **Surgery** (10021–69990)
Subsection: **Integumentary System**
Subheading: **Skin, Subcutaneous and Accessory Structures**
Category: **Debridement**

    (For dermabrasions, see 15780–15783)
    (For nail debridement, see 11720–11721)
    (For burn(s), see 16000–16036)
    (For pressure ulcers, see 15920–15999)

11000	Debridement of extensive eczematous or infected skin; up to 10% of body surface
+ 11001	each additional 10% of the body surface (List separately in addition to code for primary procedure)

    (Use 11001 in conjunction with 11000)

Section Guidelines

Follow guidelines at the beginning of each section; these identify correct coding protocols.

Example:

Section, **Surgery**
Subsection: **Cardiovascular System** (33010–37799)
Guideline:

Selective vascular catheterizations should be coded to include introduction and all lesser order selective catheterizations used in the approach (eg, the description for a selective right middle cerebral artery catheterization includes the introduction and placement catheterization of the right common and internal carotid arteries).

Additional second and/or third order arterial catheterizations within the same family of arteries supplied by a single first order artery should be expressed by 36218 or 36248. Additional first order or higher catheterizations in vascular families supplied by a first order vessel different from a previously selected and coded family should be separately coded using the conventions described above.

(For monitoring, operation of pump and other nonsurgical services, see 99190–99192, 99291, 99292, 99354–99360)

(For other medical or laboratory related services, see appropriate section)

(For radiological supervision and interpretation, see 75600–75978)

CPT® Code Basics

The CPT® Index is alphabetized with main terms organized by:

1) A condition (eg, Cerumen, Cyst, Angle Deformity)

2) The name of the procedure or medical service documented (eg, Removal, Suture, Fasciotomy)

3) The name of the anatomic site or organ (eg, Neck, Skin, Femur)

4) Synonyms, eponyms and abbreviations (eg, toe/interphalangeal joint, Watson-Jones Procedure, EEG)

Subterms clarify the main term by noting a condition, procedure, or anatomic site. To clarify and ensure selection of the correct CPT® code, the code or code range

from the alphabetical index is located in the CPT® numeric index. Do not select a CPT® code using only the alphabetical index.

Example:

The condition and procedure for earwax (cerumen) removal seems straightforward.

Cerumen

Removal 69210

In the numeric index, you'll find additional information to assign 69210 correctly.

Section: **Surgery**
Subsection: **Auditory System** (69000–69979)
Subheading: **External Ear (69000–69399)**
Category: **Removal (69200–69222)**

69210   Removal impacted cerumen (separate procedure), one or both ears

➲ *CPT® Assistant* Apr 03:9, Jul 05:14

Important considerations found in the example's descriptor include:

* Separate Procedure—A designated "separate procedure" should be reported only when performed alone, or when the service or procedure is unrelated to other services/procedures provided on the same day; in the latter case, modifier 59 *Distinct procedural service* may be required (this will be discussed further below).

* The descriptor specifies, "*one or both ears;*" modifier 50 *Bilateral procedure* is not necessary if both ears are treated.

* ➲ *CPT® Assistant*—This example cites two references: the April 2003 issue, page 9, and the July 2005 issue, page 14. The latter instructs that a simple lavage to remove impacted cerumen does not constitute billing 69210. The impacted cerumen has to be removed by a physician using instrumentation.

Testing Technique

Make notes in your CPT® codebook for easy reference to information found in *CPT® Assistant.*

Some health plans have specific billing instructions and coverage issue clarifications posted on their websites. For example, CMS publishes the Internet-Only Manuals (IOMs) (www.cms.gov/Manuals/) and provides a Medicare Coverage Center (www.cms.gov/center/coverage.asp). Each Medicaid agency maintains its website and program requirements.

National Correct Coding Initiative (NCCI)

CMS implemented the National Correct Coding Initiative (NCCI) to promote accurate and appropriate coding. NCCI identifies codes considered by CMS to be bundled, or not reported separately, because one code is included in the work of another code. Repeated unbundling may be characterized as fraudulent coding.

The NCCI includes two types of indicator edits:

- "1" Comprehensive/component edits describe code pairs that should not be billed together because one service inherently includes the other.
- "2" Mutually exclusive edits describe code pairs that are unlikely to be performed on the same patient on the same day (eg, two approaches to perform the same surgery).

Column1/Column 2 Edits					
Column 1	Column 2	* = In existence prior to 1996	Effective Date	Deletion Date *=no data	Modifier 0=not allowed 1=allowed 9=not applicable
11042	0213T		20100701	*	0
11042	0216T		20100701	*	0
11042	0228T		20101001	*	0
11042	0230T		20101001	*	0
11042	10060		19960101	*	1
11042	11000		19960101	*	1
11042	11001		19960101	19960101	9
11042	11040	*	19960101	20101231	1
11042	11041	*	19960101	20102331	1

A Correct Coding Modifier (CCM) indicator determines whether, under appropriate conditions, you may override a code pair edit. This indicator will be either a "0," a "1," or a "9."

   0 = A CCM is not allowed and will not bypass the edits.

   1 = A CCM is allowed and will bypass the edits.

   9 = Modifier use is not specified. This indicator is used for all code pairs that have a deletion date that is the same as the effective date. This indicator was created so that no blank spaces would be in the indicator field.

Sequencing CPT® Codes

CPT® code sequencing is crucial to appropriate claims submission and appropriate reimbursement. When reporting claims with multiple CPT® codes, sequence the codes from highest to lowest relative value.

Example:

Using RVUs for the sequencing of CPT® codes, while maintaining correct coding guidelines, is seen in this example:

Two polyps are identified during a colonoscopy. The physician performs a biopsy on one polyp and removes a second polyp at a different site, during the same procedure. CPT® codes 45380 and 45385 are reported.

Referencing the 2011 RVU lookup function on the CMS website (www.cms.gov/PFSlookup), we find the following information:

HCPCS	Short Description	WORK RVU	Transitioned Non-Facility PE RVU	Transitioned Facility PE RVU	MP RVU
45380	Colonoscopy and biopsy	4.43	8.82	2.69	0.67
45385	Lesion removal colonoscopy	5.30	9.59	3.14	0.80

For this example, the professional coder may use the information provided by CMS for establishing the sequence of treatment charges. The sequence of the CPT® coding for this example is 45385, 45380-59. CPT® 45385 has the highest total RVU value, and is sequenced first. Review NCCI modifier 59 article for proper use of modifier 59.

An additional resource available for coding reference is the *Medicare RBRVS: The Physician's Guide*. The guide is a reference for physicians, professional coders, and their staff to use for detailed background information and explanations of the physician payment system.

CPT® Assistant

The ➲ symbol posted after many CPT® codes indicates that the AMA has published reference material in *CPT® Assistant* regarding that particular code. *CPT® Assistant* is available by subscription. It provides additional information, clarification and guidance for proper use of codes which cannot be found in the CPT® codebook.

CPT® Category II Codes and a Brief Overview of the PQRS

CPT® Category II Codes

CPT® Category II codes and some HCPCS Level II G codes are used voluntarily to report performance measures, and to make up the Quality Data Codes (QDCs) for the Physician Quality Reporting System (PQRS), established by CMS. The codes typically describe clinical components included in E/M services, and are not assigned RVUs. Category II codes also may describe results from tests and other procedures identified as measurable data for quality patient care. CPT® Category II codes are updated throughout the year and are posted on the AMA website (www.ama-assn.org).

Physician Quality Reporting System (PQRS)

PQRS was implemented in 2007. Physicians who successfully report specified quality measures for Medicare Part B beneficiaries (including Railroad Retirement Board and Medicare Secondary Payer) may be eligible to receive an incentive payment equaling 1 percent of their Medicare Physician Fee Schedule (PFS) total estimated allowed charges furnished during the reporting period for CY 2011. The CMS PQRS Measures Groups Specifications Manual explains methods for reporting measure groups and coding information required for measure submissions. It also instructs how to report the Quality Data Codes (QDCs). The manual is posted annually on the CMS website; to download the manual, go to www.

cms.gov/PQRS and click on the Measures Codes link on the left side of the page.

When billing for medical charges and reporting QDCs for performance measures on the CMS 1500 form, only one diagnosis from the claim should be referenced in the diagnosis pointer field (field #24e) even though all diagnoses reported on the claim will be included in PQRS analysis. Depending on the billing system software used for claim submissions, a line item charge of $0.00 should be entered for the QDC. If the billing system software does not allow for a $0.00 line item charge, a nominal charge of $0.01 may be entered. The claim will be denied with remark code N365, which means, "This procedure code is not payable. It is for reporting/information purposes only" (www.cms.gov/MLNMattersArticles/downloads/MM6514.pdf).

CPT® Category III Codes

Category III CPT® code set contains temporary codes used for data collection in the FDA approval process regarding new and emerging technology, services, and procedures. Reimbursement may be available through health plans, although no RVU is assigned.

Codes are updated twice a year, January 1 and July 1. Updates are published on AMA's website (www.ama-assn.org). When FDA approval is obtained for a Category III CPT® Code, it becomes a Category I CPT® code. If the Category III code is not FDA approved within five years, the code is either renewed for another five years or removed from the CPT® codebook.

Category III codes describe services or procedures with more specificity than Category I unlisted codes. If a Category III code is available, it must be reported instead of a Category I "unlisted procedure" code.

Stay Current

Medical practices should be aware the AMA updates and publishes the CPT® code set each year. Submission of outdated codes may negatively affect reimbursement and claim denials.

1) CPT® Category I is published in the late summer or early fall in two available formats: electronic files and books. The updated CPT® code set is effective January 1 of the next calendar year.

2) CPT® Category II codes are released three times a year and are effective three months after the publication date.

3) CPT® Category III and vaccine product codes are updated twice a year and released January 1 and July 1, with effective dates for use six months after they are published.

CPT® Appendices

Appendices A through N reference topics that are important for coding specificity and provide examples.

Appendix A
Modifiers—This appendix lists modifiers categorized as:

1. CPT® Level 1 Modifiers—lists all of the modifiers applicable to CPT® codes

2. Anesthesia Physical Status Modifiers

3. CPT® Level I Modifiers approved for Ambulatory Surgery Center (ASC) Hospital Outpatient Use

4. Commonly used Level II (HCPCS/National) Modifiers

Appendix B
Summary of Additions, Deletions, and Revisions—Appendix B contains the actual changes and additions to the CPT® codes from the previous year to the current publication.

Appendix C
Clinical Examples—Limited to E/M services, the AMA has provided clinical examples for different specialties. These clinical examples do not encompass the entire scope of medical practice, and guides professional coders to follow E/M patient encounter rules for level of service.

Appendix D
Summary of CPT® Add-on Codes—These codes are not reported as single or stand-alone codes. The

codes listed are identified throughout CPT® with the + symbol.

Appendix E
Summary of CPT® codes Exempt from Modifier 51—This listing is a summary of CPT® codes that are exempt from the use of modifier 51. The codes are identified in the CPT® codebook with the ⊘ symbol.

Appendix F
Summary of CPT® codes Exempt from Modifier 63—This listing is a summary of CPT® codes that are exempt from the use of modifier 63. The listed codes will also be identified by the CPT® convention of parenthetical instruction "(Do not report modifier 63 in conjunction with…)."

Appendix G
Summary of CPT® codes that Include Moderate (Conscious) Sedation— CPT® codes identified by the ⊙ symbol include conscious sedation; it is not appropriate to report sedation codes 99143–99145 separately.

Appendix H
Alphabetic Index of Performance Measures by Clinical Condition or Topic—Appendix H is now available only on the AMA website (www.ama-assn.org) due to the performance measures constantly being updated.

Appendix I
Genetic Testing Code Modifiers—These modifiers are reported with molecular laboratory procedures related to genetic testing.

Appendix J
Electrodiagnostic Medicine Listing of Sensory, Motor, and Mixed Nerves—This appendix provides a summary that assigns each sensory, motor, and mixed nerve with its appropriate nerve conduction study code to enhance accurate reporting of 95900–95904.

Appendix K
Product Pending FDA Approval—Some vaccine products listed as CPT® Category I codes are still pending FDA approval. A lightning bolt symbol identifies the pending codes throughout CPT®. For updated vaccine approvals by the FDA, visit the AMA CPT® Category I Vaccine Codes website (www.ama-assn.org).

Appendix L
Vascular Families—Based on the assumption that a vascular catheterization has a starting point of the aorta, Appendix L illustrates vascular "families" and identifies the "order" of vessels. The largest "First Order Branch" emerges from the aorta. The "Second Order Branch" emerges from the "First Order Branch," and so on to include the vessel's "Third Order Branch" and "Beyond Third Order Branches." If the starting point of the catheterization is other than the aorta, the orders might change.

Appendix M
Crosswalk to Deleted CPT® codes—This listing is a summary of the crosswalks noting the deleted CPT® codes and descriptors from the previous year to the current year. This is an essential tool when updating charge masters, charge capture documents, and any system or process using CPT® codes.

Appendix N
Summary of Resequenced CPT® codes—This listing is a summary of CPT® codes not appearing in numeric sequence (This allows existing codes to be relocated to an appropriate location.).

Surgery Guidelines

The following services are included in a given CPT® surgical code, and not separately billable:

- Local infiltration, metacarpal/metatarsal/digital block or topical anesthesia
- Subsequent to the decision for surgery, one related E/M encounter on the date immediately prior to or on the date of procedure (including history and physical)
- Immediate postoperative care, including dictating operative notes, talking with the family and other physicians
- Writing orders
- Evaluating the patient in the post-anesthesia recovery area
- Typical postoperative follow-up care

Global Package as Defined by CPT®

Payment for surgical procedures includes a standard package of preoperative, intraoperative, and postoperative services. Preoperative and postoperative periods will differ based on the classifications of the service as a major or minor surgery. The services included in the global surgical package may be furnished in any service location (eg, a hospital, an ASC, or physician office). Visits to a patient in an intensive care or critical care unit are also included when made by the surgeon. Under some circumstances, critical care services (99291–99292) are not considered part of the global package and are reimbursed separately.

According to CPT®, follow-up care only includes services that are usually a part of the surgical services. Additional services required for care, such as complications, recurrence, or other diseases should be reported separately.

Global Package—Non-Medicare Health Plans

Most health plans have adopted the CMS global package concept, and assign postoperative periods of 0, 10, or 90 days. Third-party payers have the option to establish different guidelines, so check with the individual payer for specifics.

Global Days for Surgery as Defined by Medicare

Medicare has classified major and minor surgeries and has determined what services are included and not included with the global package. Medicare has also determined the preoperative and postoperative days allowed for each type of surgery.

The preoperative period included in the global fee for major surgery is 1 day with 90 days for the postoperative period. The preoperative period for minor surgery is the day of the procedure with a postoperative period of either 0 or 10 days, depending on the procedure. For endoscopic procedures (except procedures requiring an incision), there is no postoperative period. Global period days may be accessed on the CMS website: www.cms.gov/PhysicianFeeSched/01_overview.asp.

Testing Technique

Add a note to your CPT® codebook surgical guidelines of the Medicare Global Periods:

Major Surgery—90 days

Minor Surgery—10 days

Status Indicators

Each CPT® is assigned a global period status indicator per the CMS payment policies:

000 Endoscopies or minor procedures with preoperative and postoperative relative values on the day of the procedure only are reimbursable. Evaluation and management services on the same day of the procedure are generally not payable (for example, CPT® 43256, 53020, 67346).

010 Minor procedures with preoperative relative values on the day of the procedure and postoperative relative values during a 10-day postoperative period are reimbursable services. Evaluation and management services on the day of the procedure and during the 10-day postoperative period are not reimbursable (for example, CPT® 17261, 40800, 64612).

090 Major procedures with a one-day preoperative period or a 90-day postoperative period are considered to be a component of the global package of the major procedure. Evaluation and management services on the day prior to the procedure, the day of the procedure, and during the 90-day postoperative period are not reimbursable (for example, CPT® 21048, 32664, 49582).

MMM Maternity codes; the usual global period concept does not apply (for example, CPT® 59400, 59612).

XXX The global concept does not apply to this code (for example, CPT® 10021, 36593, 38220, 44720).

YYY Unlisted codes; and subject to individual pricing (for example, CPT® 19499, 20999, 44979).

ZZZ Add-on codes. These codes are related to other services and are always included in the global period of the primary service (for example, CPT® 27358, 44955, 67335).

Services Included in the Global Package

1) Preoperative Visits—Preoperative visits after the decision is made to operate beginning with the day before the day of surgery for major procedures, and the day of surgery for minor procedures.

2) Intraoperative Services—Intraoperative services that are normally a usual and necessary part of a surgical procedure.

3) Complications Following Surgery—All additional medical or surgical services required of the surgeon during the postoperative period of the surgery because of complications which do not require additional trips to the operating room.

4) Postoperative Visits—Follow-up visits within the postoperative period of the surgery that are related to recovery from the surgery.

5) Postsurgical Pain Management—By the surgeon.

6) Supplies and Miscellaneous Services—Items such as dressing changes; local incisional care; removal of operative pack; removal of cutaneous sutures and staples, lines, wires, tubes, drains, casts, and splints; insertion, irrigation and removal of urinary catheters, routine peripheral intravenous lines, nasogastric, and rectal tubes; and changes and removal of tracheostomy tubes.

Services Not Included in the Global Package

1) The initial consultation or evaluation of the problem by the surgeon to determine the need for surgery.

2) Visits unrelated to the diagnosis for which the surgical procedure is performed, unless the visits occur due to complication of the surgery.

3) Treatment for the underlying condition or an added course of treatment that is not part of the normal recovery from surgery.

4) Diagnostic tests and procedures, including diagnostic radiological procedures.

5) Clearly distinct surgical procedures during the postoperative period that are not re-operations or treatment for complications. (A new postoperative period begins with the subsequent procedure.) This includes procedures performed in two or more parts for which the decision to stage the procedure is made prospectively or at the time of the first procedure.

6) Treatment for postoperative complications which requires a return trip to the operating room (OR). The term "operating room" includes a cardiac catheterization suite, a laser suite, and an endoscopy suite. It does not include a patient's room, a minor treatment room, a recovery room, or an intensive care unit (unless the patient's condition is so critical there would be insufficient time for transportation to an OR).

7) If a less extensive procedure fails, and a more extensive procedure is required, the second procedure is separately reportable.

8) For certain services performed in a physician's office.

9) Immunotherapy management for organ transplants.

10) Critical care services (codes 99291 and 99292) unrelated to the surgery where a seriously injured or burned patient is critically ill and requires constant attendance of the physician.

11) For minor surgeries and endoscopies, the Medicare program will not pay separately for an E/M service on the same day as a minor surgery or endoscopy, unless a significant, separately identifiable service is also performed, for example, an initial consultation or initial new patient visit.

HCPCS Level II

The Healthcare Common Procedure Coding System (HCPCS) Level II codebook is the national procedure code set for health care practitioners, providers, and medical equipment suppliers when filing health plan claims for medical devices, medications, transportation services, and other items and services. Medical supplies may be covered when used outside a physician's office and may be coded using the HCPCS Level II codes. The existence of a HCPCS Level II code does not determine coverage or non-coverage for an item or service. Neither manufacturers nor brand/trade names are specified when reporting HCPCS Level II.

HCPCS Level II Basics

The HCPCS Level II codebook consists of an alphabetical index used for locating HCPCS Level II codes within the sections/chapters with the alphanumeric nomenclature. The HCPCS Level II appendices reference topics important to HCPCS Level II coding.

The main body of the HCPCS Level II codebook is divided by types of services and products, and includes a number of code types:

Permanent National Codes—National codes are updated annually and describe products and services grouped in alphanumeric sections. Examples of permanent codes are found in the J code section and are used to report drugs administered by other than oral means.

Miscellaneous Codes—not otherwise classified—Used when there is no existing national code that describes the item or service being billed. Miscellaneous codes allow suppliers to bill for items or services as they are FDA-approved. When there is no assigned code to describe the item or service, verify with the health plan if there is a specific code (rather than the miscellaneous code) for use. If the claim is to be submitted to Medicare, it may be beneficial to contact your Medicare representative for coding advice.

Dental Codes—The Current Dental Terminology (CDT®), copyrighted by the American Dental Association (ADA), is the listing for codes used for billing dental procedures and supplies. The CDT® is included in the HCPCS Level II codebook.

Temporary National Codes—These codes are used at the discretion of CMS and are developed as a means to meet specific operating needs, such as newly issued coverage policies or legislative requirements. Temporary codes allow health plans to establish codes prior to the annual update on

January 1. If a temporary code becomes a permanent national code, the temporary code is deleted and is cross-referenced to the new permanent code. Temporary codes can be added, changed, or deleted on a quarterly basis. Newly established temporary codes effective dates are posted on the HCPCS Level II website: www.cms.gov/HCPCSReleaseCodeSets/02_HCPCS_Quarterly_Update.asp.

Types of temporary HCPCS Level II codes:

1. **C codes** are required under the Medicare Outpatient Prospective Payment System (OPPS) for use by hospitals. Other facilities may report C codes at their discretion.

2. **G codes** are national codes assigned by CMS to identify professional health care procedures and services, that may not have assigned CPT® codes.

3. **H codes** establish unique temporary codes to identify mental health services for state Medicaid agencies mandated by state law to establish separate codes for those services.

4. **K codes** are used by Durable Medical Equipment Medicare Administrative Contractors (DME MACs). DME MACs develop new K codes when existing national codes for supplies and certain product categories do not include the codes needed to implement a DME MAC medical review policy.

5. **Q codes** identify services that would not be given a CPT® code or are not identified by national level II codes but are needed by CMS to facilitate claims processing. Such services include drugs, biologicals, and other types of medical equipment or services.

6. **S codes** meet various business needs of commercial and Medicaid agency health plans. S codes report drugs, services, and supplies for which national codes do not exist but are needed to implement policies, programs, or support claims processing. They are not payable by Medicare.

7. **T codes** are designated for use by Medicaid agencies to establish codes for items for which there are no permanent national codes, and for which codes are necessary to meet Medicaid program operating needs. T codes are not used by Medicare, but may be used by commercial health plans.

HCPCS Level II Appendices

HCPCS Level II appendices can vary depending on the publisher of the HCPCS Level II book used. A representation of appendices which can be included in a typical HCPCS Level II book include:

Appendix 1—Table of Drugs—Generic and brand or trade names are alphabetically listed with unit information

Appendix 2—Alphabetized HCPCS Level II modifiers and descriptors

Appendix 3—Abbreviations and acronyms, as listed in the *Federal Register*

Appendix 4—PUB 100 references

Appendix 5—New, changed, deleted, and reinstated HCPCS Level II codes

Appendix 6—Place of service and type of service codes

Appendix 7—National Average Payment Table for HCPCS Level II

HCPCS Level II Modifiers

In some instances, health plans instruct suppliers to append a HCPCS Level II modifier to the HCPCS Level II code to provide additional information regarding the service or item. HCPCS Level II modifiers are either alphanumeric or two alphabetic characters.

Example

E1130 Standard Wheelchair; fixed full-length arms, fixed or swing-away, detachable footrests

This DME may have modifier UE identifying "used equipment" or modifier NU to identify "new equipment."

Testing Technique

Use brackets to identify and label similar modifiers in the HCPCS Level II codebook. For example:

Eyelids
- E1—Upper left, eyelid
- E2—Lower left, eyelid
- E3—Upper right, eyelid
- E4—Lower right, eyelid

Medicare and HCPCS Level II

CMS maintains and distributes HCPCS Level II codes. CMS maintains HCPCS Level II quarterly updates, release information, and transaction/code set standards on its website.

The Medicare Improvements for Patients and Providers Act of 2008 (MIPPA) requires CMS to review HCPCS Level II codes for coding changes to ensure accurate reporting and billing for medical items and services. Providers may acquire the HCPCS Level II application form and instructions for submitting a recommendation to establish, revise or discontinue a code on the CMS website: www.cms.gov/MedHCPCSGenInfo/.

When a CPT® code and HCPCS Level II code exist for the same service, Medicare requires the HCPCS Level II code be reported. Other payers may have similar instruction.

Modifiers

Modifiers are appended to CPT® and HCPCS Level II codes to report specific circumstances or alterations to a procedure, service, or medical equipment without changing the definition of the code. Both CPT® and HCPCS Level II codebooks list modifiers and their descriptions.

Appendix A lists CPT® modifiers, and includes a wide range of modifiers, including those used for anesthesia and modifiers reported by ASCs. HCPCS Level II modifiers are located in Appendix 2 of the HCPCS Level II codebook.

When reporting codes with more than one modifier, always list functional, or pricing modifiers in the first position. Payers consider functional modifiers when determining reimbursement. Next, report the informational modifiers; these modifiers clarify certain aspects of the procedure or service provided for the payer (eg, procedures performed on the left or right side of the patient's body).

CPT® Code Modifiers:

CPT® modifiers are two-digit, numeric codes.

22	**Increased Procedural Services:** When the service(s) provided is greater than that usually required for the listed procedure, it may be identified by adding modifier 22 to the usual procedure code number. Documentation must support the substantial additional work and the reason for the additional work. *(Append modifier 22 to a procedure code when the physician describes "above and beyond" circumstances within his operative report, and there is no other procedure code to describe the extensive services.)* *Example: A surgeon spends an extra 1-1/2 hours removing adhesions that are extremely vascular. This increased the technical difficulty during a laparoscopic cholecystectomy with cholangiograms: CPT® 47563-22* *Example of Inappropriate Use: A surgeon performs the lysis of adhesions in the process of a partial colectomy. Rationale: Just because a surgeon performs adhesiolysis does not mean it qualifies for modifier 22.* *Keywords: extended time, took longer than normal, extenuating circumstances, etc.*
23	**Unusual Anesthesia:** When a procedure that usually requires either no anesthesia or local anesthesia must be performed under general anesthesia due to unusual circumstances. Modifier 23 is only used by anesthesiologists and CRNAs with anesthesia codes 00100–01999. *Appropriate example: A patient requires general anesthesia for an ERCP: CPT® 00740-23.* *Example of Inappropriate Use: General anesthesia is performed on a patient for the convenience of the surgeon. Unless the patient has a medical reason for the anesthesia, it would be inappropriate to report it to the patient's insurance carrier.* *Keywords: Unable to tolerate without general anesthesia, etc.*
24	**Unrelated E/M by the Same Physician During a Postoperative Period:** The physician may need to indicate an E/M service was performed during a postoperative period for reason(s) unrelated to the original procedure. This circumstance may be reported by adding modifier 24 to the appropriate level of E/M service. *Appropriate Example: Append modifier 24 to an E/M code if a physician treats a patient for migraines during a postoperative period, and they are unrelated to the surgical procedure.* *Keywords: unrelated, outside of, not related to, etc.*

25	**Significant, Separately Identifiable Evaluation and Management Service by the Same Physician on the Same Day of the Procedure or Other Service:** It may be necessary to indicate that on the day a procedure or service identified by a CPT® code was performed, the patient's condition required a significant, separately identifiable E/M service above and beyond the other service provided or beyond the usual preoperative and postoperative care associated with the procedure performed. *Example: Append modifier 25 to an E/M code when an established male patient is treated by the physician for hypertension and then asks the physician to biopsy a soft tissue lump located on his back: CPT® 99213-25, 21920* *Keywords: unrelated, outside of, not related to, etc.*	**32**	**Mandated Services:** Services related to mandated consultation and/or related services. *Append modifier 32 to an E/M code if an insurance company requests a patient to receive a second opinion, before additional services/procedures are authorized.* *Keywords: second opinion, required by insurance, etc.*
		47	**Anesthesia by Surgeon:** Regional or general anesthesia provided by the surgeon may be reported by adding modifier 47 to the basic service. *Appropriate example: Patient in a remote area required exploration of a deep penetrating wound of the thigh. The surgeon gave the patient an epidural and then explored the leg. 20103-47.* *Keywords: surgeon administered anesthesia, anesthesiologist not available, etc.*
26	**Professional Component:** Certain procedures are a combination of a professional component and a technical component. When the professional component is reported separately, identify it as such by adding modifier 26 to the usual procedure code. *Appropriate Example: Append modifier 26 to a procedure code (77001–77003) if a physician provides the professional component of fluoroscopy use during a surgical procedure when the facility owns the equipment and employs the staff operating the equipment.* *Example of Inappropriate Use: Appending modifier 26 to services that do not have a professional and technical component, such as an E/M visit.* *Keywords: independent radiologist, performed in a hospital, physician owns, etc.*	**50**	**Bilateral Procedure:** Bilateral procedures performed at the same operative session code. *Appropriate example: Append modifier 50 to the procedure code when a patient undergoes surgery for a bilateral laparoscopic inguinal hernia repair: CPT® 49650-50. It is inappropriate to report this modifier in addition to modifier Right (RT) and/or Left (LT), because modifier 50 already indicates this information* *Example of Inappropriate Use: Do not use modifier 50 for trigger point injections for muscles on the right and left side of the body. Code 20553 represents trigger point injections for 3 or more muscles, and laterality does not come into play.* *Keywords: bilateral, both sides, left and right, etc.*

51	**Multiple Procedures:** When multiple procedures, other than E/M services are performed at the same session by the same provider. *Appropriate Example: Excision of a benign lesion of the arm (11402), and excision of a benign lesion of the face (11422) during the same session—11422, 11402-51,* *Example of Inappropriate use: Assignment of modifier 51 to an add-on code, such as destruction of two lesions, 17000, 17003-51* *Keywords: a different procedure, separate from, etc.*	**54**	**Surgical Care Only:** When one physician performs the surgical procedure and another provides preoperative and/or postoperative management, surgical services may be identified by adding modifier 54 to the surgical procedure code. *Keywords: only performed the surgical procedure, no pre or post-op management, etc.*
52	**Reduced Services:** Under certain circumstances a service or procedure is partially reduced or eliminated at the physician's discretion. Under these circumstances, the service provided can be identified by its usual procedure code and the addition of modifier 52. *Appropriate Example: Debridement of an ischial pressure ulcer without ostectomy in preparation for myocutaneous flap, 15946-52* *Keywords: partially, to be reduced, part of procedure not completed, etc.*	**55**	**Postoperative Management Only:** When one physician performs the surgical procedure and another physician performs postoperative management, the postoperative component is identified by adding modifier 55 to the surgical procedure code. *Keywords: post-op follow-up only, postoperative care turned over to, transfer of care, etc.*
		56	**Preoperative Management Only:** When one physician performs the preoperative care and evaluation and another physician performs the surgical procedure, the preoperative component is identified by adding modifier 56 to the surgical procedure code. *Keywords: pre-op evaluation only, covering for surgeon, etc.*
53	**Discontinued Procedure:** Under certain circumstances, the physician may elect to terminate a surgical or diagnostic procedure. Due to extenuating circumstances, or those that threaten the well-being of the patient, it may be necessary to indicate that a surgical or diagnostic procedure was started but discontinued. *Appropriate Example: A percutaneous biopsy of the liver is discontinued mid-procedure, because of dense adhesions, 47000-53.* *Keywords: procedure stopped before completion, aborted the procedure, etc.*	**57**	**Decision for Surgery:** When an E/M service provided the day before or the day of a surgery results in the decision to perform surgery, append modifier 57 to the appropriate level of E/M service. *Appropriate Example: Append modifier 57 to an E/M code if a physician exams a patient in the ER and makes the decision to admit the patient and perform an appendectomy the same day: CPT® 99221-57, 44950.* *Keywords: decision to perform surgery, will need to go to OR, etc.*

58	**Staged or Related Procedure or Service by the Same Physician During the Postoperative Period:** It may be necessary to indicate the performance of a procedure or service during the postoperative period was: a) planned prospectively at the time of the original procedure (staged); b) more extensive than the original procedure; or c) for therapy following a diagnostic surgical procedure. Report the circumstance by adding modifier 58 to the staged or related procedure. *Appropriate Example: Debridement of skin, muscle and fascia for necrotizing infection of the abdominal wall without fascial closure. Five days later, the abdominal wall was closed, 13160-58.* *Keywords: return to OR, will proceed with additional services in next procedure, etc.*
59	**Distinct Procedural Service:** Under certain circumstances, it may be necessary to indicate a procedure or service was distinct or independent from other non-E/M services performed on the same day. Modifier 59 is used to identify services not normally reported together, but are appropriate under the reported circumstances. CMS NCCI documentation has specific examples for the correct use of modifier 59. *Keywords: separate procedure, needed additional services, etc.*

62	**Two Surgeons:** Append modifier 62 when two surgeons work together as primary surgeons performing distinct part(s) of a procedure. Each surgeon must provide an operative report that describes his or her portion of the surgery. Each surgeon must report the same CPT® code with modifier 62. *Appropriate Example: An Ivor Lewis procedure is performed (partial esophagectomy, distal two-thirds, with thoracotomy and separate abdominal incision, with proximal gastrectomy with thoracic esophagogastrostomy, with pyloroplasty). A thoracic surgeon performs the thoracic approach and thoracic procedures, and a general surgeon performs the abdominal procedures. Each surgeon reports 43117-62.* *Keywords: co-surgeon, shared procedure with, etc.*
63	**Procedures Performed on Infants Less Than 4 kg:** Procedures performed on neonates and infants up to a present body weight of 4 kg may involve significantly increased complexity and physician work commonly associated with these patients. *Keywords: weight, incubator, neonate, newborn, etc.*
66	**Surgical Team:** Under some circumstances, highly complex procedures are carried out under the "surgical team" concept. *Keywords: surgical team working together, presence of other surgeons, etc.*
76	**Repeat Procedure or Service by Same Physician:** The physician may need to indicate a procedure or service was repeated. This may be reported by adding modifier 76 to the repeated service. *Appropriate Example: Chest X-ray taken in the morning which revealed pneumothorax was repeated and read by the same physician after the placement of a chest tube, 71010-26, 71010-26-76.* *Keywords: repeated, again, previous, etc.*

77	**Repeat Procedure by Another Physician**: The physician may need to indicate a procedure or service performed by another physician had to be repeated. Modifier 77 is then added to the repeated procedure/service. *Keywords: repeated by another physician, etc.*
78	**Unplanned Return to the Operating/Procedure Room by the Same Physician Following Initial Procedure for a Related Procedure During the Postoperative Period**: It may be necessary to indicate that another procedure was performed during the postoperative period of the initial procedure. Modifier 78 describes a return to the operating room for a complication during the global period of another procedure. *Appropriate Example: A CABG procedure was performed and later in the day the patient was brought back to the OR for control of postoperative hemorrhage, 35820-78.* *Keywords: complications, had to return to OR, etc.*
79	**Unrelated Procedure or Service by the Same Physician During the Postoperative Period**: The physician may need to indicate the performance of a procedure or service during the postoperative period was unrelated to the original procedure. This circumstance may be reported by using modifier 79. *Keywords: not related to previous care, etc.*
80	**Assistant Surgeon**: Surgical surgeon assistant services may be identified by adding modifier 80 to the usual procedure code(s). *Keywords: assisted, surgeon called in to help, etc.*
81	**Minimum Assistant Surgeon**: Minimum assistant surgeon services are identified by adding modifier 81 to the procedure code(s). Another surgeon is called in to assist for a limited time. *Keywords: assisted partially, helped with part of procedure, etc.*

82	**Assistant Surgeon (when qualified resident surgeon not available)**: The unavailability of a qualified resident surgeon is a prerequisite for use of modifier 82 appended to the usual procedure code(s). *Keywords: surgical resident not available, etc.*
90	**Reference (Outside) Laboratory**: Identify laboratory procedures performed by a party other than the treating or reporting physician by appending modifier 90 to the procedure codes. *Keyword: independent lab, separate from physician, etc.*
91	**Repeat Clinical Diagnostic Laboratory Test**: Reporting modifier 91 is appropriate when it is necessary to repeat the same laboratory test on the same day to obtain subsequent test result(s). It is not appropriate to use this modifier to repeat a laboratory test due to a lost specimen, equipment failure, or lost results. *Keywords: sequenced lab tests, repeat lab after 4 hours, etc.*
92	**Alternative Laboratory Platform Testing**: Reporting modifier 92 is appropriate when laboratory testing is being performed using a kit or transportable instrument that wholly or in part consists of a single use, disposable analytical chamber. *Keywords: portable, kit, disposable, etc.*
99	**Multiple Modifiers**: Under certain circumstances, two or more modifiers may be necessary to delineate a service completely. Append modifier 99 to the basic procedure. Other applicable modifiers may be listed as part of the service description. *Appropriate Example: A payer can only accept one modifier on the claim. Three modifiers are required to report the service. The service is reported with modifier 99. The three modifiers are added in box 19 of the claim, or in another location specified by the payer.*

HCPCS Level II Modifiers

There are numerous HCPCS Level II modifiers—many more than CPT® modifiers. HCPCS Level II modifiers are two-digit codes that may be two alphabetic characters (AA) or one alphabetic and one numeric character (U4).

HCPCS Level II modifiers are required to add specificity to CPT® procedure codes performed on eyelids, fingers, toes, and coronary arteries. They are specific to HCPCS Level II codes.

Listed are a few of the HCPCS Level II modifiers with coding examples:

BO	**Orally Administered Nutrition, Not By Feeding Tube** *Example: Append modifier BO to enteral nutrients (B4149–B4162) when administered orally [by mouth].*
E2	**Lower Left Eyelid** *Example: Append E2 to CPT® code 67700 when a blepharotomy, drainage of abscess, of the left lower eyelid is performed.*
F1	**Left Hand, Second Digit** *Example: Append F1 to CPT® code 26340 when manipulation, finger joint, under anesthesia, each joint is performed on the second digit of the left hand.*
LT	**Left Side** *Example: Append LT to CPT® code 24000 when an arthrotomy, elbow, including exploration, drainage, or removal of foreign body is performed on the left elbow.*
NU	**New Equipment** *Example: Append NU to HCPCS Level II code E0143 when a new walker, folding, wheeled, adjustable or fixed height is sold to a patient.*

TC	**Technical Component** *Example: Append TC to CPT® code 92081 when a visual field examination, unilateral or bilateral, is performed by a technician in a hospital and the report is performed by an independent physician. The physician would report 92081 with modifier 26. The hospital would report the technical component of 92081.*

Glossary

Add-on Code—CPT® code used to report a supplemental or additional procedure appended to a primary procedure (stand-alone) code. Add-on codes are recognized by the CPT® symbol "+" used throughout the CPT® codebook.

The Centers for Medicare & Medicaid Services (CMS)—The agency within the U.S. Department of Health & Human Services (HHS) that administers the Medicare program and works in partnership with state governments to administer Medicaid and state Children's Health Insurance Programs (CHIP).

Current Procedural Terminology (CPT®)—A code set copyrighted and maintained by the AMA.

Global Package—The period (0–10 days, or 0–90 days as determined by the health plan) and services provided for a surgery inclusive of preoperative visits, intraoperative services, post-surgical complications, postoperative visits, post-surgical pain management by the surgeon, and several miscellaneous services as defined by the health plan, regardless of setting (eg, in a hospital, an ASC, or physician office).

Global Surgery Status Indicator—An assigned payment indicator, which determines classification for a minor or major surgery, based on RVU calculations.

Healthcare Common Procedure Coding System (HCPCS) Level II—HCPCS Level II is the national procedure code set for health care practitioners, providers, and medical equipment suppliers when filing insurance claims for medical devices, medications, transportation services, and other items and services.

Major Surgery—Surgeries classified as major have a global surgical period that includes the day before the surgery, the day of surgery, and any related follow-up visits with the physician 90 days after the procedure.

Minor Surgery—Surgeries classified as minor have a global surgical period that includes the preoperative service the day of surgery, surgery, and any related follow-up visits with the physician 0–10 days after the surgery.

Resource-Based Relative Value Scale (RBRVS)—The physician payment schedule established by Medicare.

Relative Value Units (RVU)—CMS reimburses physicians for Medicare services using a national payment schedule based on the resources used in furnishing physician services. RVUs are configured using work based on specialties, practice expense, and physician liability insurance.

Chapter Review Questions

1. **Which anatomic site would you look under in the CPT® index to find carinal reconstruction?**

    A. Breast

    B. Chest

    C. Esophagus

    D. Trachea

2. **When the entry point for a catheterization is the aorta, what order would the right brachial artery be considered?**

    A. First Order

    B. Second Order Branch

    C. Third Order Branch

    D. Beyond Third Order Branch

3. **Which option below would be the appropriate way to report the removal of 30 skin tags?**

    A. 11201 x 3

    B. 11200, 11201

    C. 11200, 11201 x 2

    D. 11200, 11201-51 x 2

4. **According to the National Correct Coding Initiative, what edit is placed on codes 11042 and 10060?**

    A. Mutually Exclusive; a modifier will not bypass the edit

    B. Mutually Exclusive; a modifier will bypass the edit

    C. Comprehensive/Component; a modifier will not bypass the edit

    D. Comprehensive/Component; a modifier will bypass the edit

5. The provider performed debridement of an open leg wound. Two days later, the provider performed a more extensive debridement of the same wound. What modifier would be reported for the second service?

    A. 58

    B. 78

    C. 79

    D. No modifier is required

6. When coding for a surgical service, which of the following is not included in the global surgical package?

    A. Digital block

    B. General anesthesia

    C. Talking with the family

    D. E/M encounter on the date immediately prior to a major procedure

7. How often does CMS release updates for HCPCS Level II codes?

    A. Monthly

    B. Quarterly

    C. Semi-Annually

    D. Annually

8. When a service having both a technical and professional component (eg, X-ray) is performed in the hospital, which modifier would be used by the physician?

    A. 26

    B. 47

    C. TC

    D. AM

9. Excision of the inferior turbinate is reported with CPT® code 30130. What CPT® code is reported for excision of the middle turbinate?

    A. 30117

    B. 30130

    C. 30130-52

    D. 30999

10. The separate reporting for use of mesh (+49568) during a hernia repair can be reported with which code?

   A. 49507

   B. 49520

   C. 49560

   D. 49587

Introduction

The Integumentary System is made up of the skin, hair, nails, and breasts. Objectives for this chapter include:

◖ Understand the key components of the skin, hair, nails, and breasts

◖ Define key terms

◖ Understand the most common pathologies affecting the skin, hair, nails, and breasts

◖ Understand procedures and surgeries as they relate to the skin, hair, nails, and breasts

◖ Recognize common eponyms and acronyms for this section

◖ Identify when other sections of CPT® or ICD-9-CM should be accessed

◖ Know when HCPCS Level II codes or modifiers are appropriate

Skin Anatomy

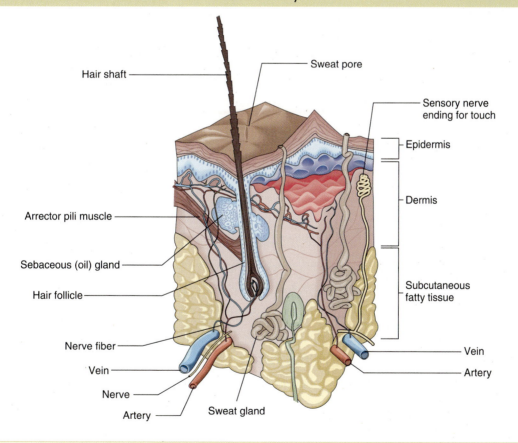

Source: Delmar/Cengage Learning.

Anatomy and Medical Terminology

The skin is the largest organ system in the body. It is made up of two primary layers. The epidermis is the outermost portion of skin. It contains different types of cells; the most common are squamous cells (flat, scaly cells on the surface of the skin), basal cells (round cells) and melanocytes (which give the skin color). There are four to five layers of the skin: Stratum Corneum, Stratum Lucidum (palms and soles), Stratum Spinosum, and Stratum Basale (Germinativum).

The dermis is under the epidermis and performs most of the skin's functions. The dermis consists of blood vessels, connective tissue, nerves, lymph vessels, glands, receptors and hair shafts. The dermis is made up of two layers, the upper papillary layer and the lower reticular layer.

The subcutaneous tissue is primarily fat cells that smooth the skin and act as a cushion. The subcutaneous tissue is not a layer of the skin, but is just below the dermis.

The protein keratin stiffens epidermal tissue to form fingernails. Nails grow from a thin area called the nail matrix at an average rate of about 1 mm per week.

ICD-9-CM Coding

Diagnostic codes for the skin are found primarily in three chapters in the ICD-9-CM codebook:

◖ Chapter 2—Neoplasms
◖ Chapter 12—Diseases of the Skin and Subcutaneous Tissue
◖ Chapter 17—Injury and Poisoning

In addition to codes found in these chapters, we also will discuss codes for disorders of the breast (categories 610–612). Diagnoses for the breast are typically found in ICD-9-CM chapter 10, Diseases of the Genitourinary System.

Neoplasms

The neoplasm table is broken down into six columns. The first three columns indicate malignancies, which are classified as Primary, Secondary and Ca *in situ*; after the malignancies are columns for Benign, Uncertain Behavior, and Unspecified.

◖ Primary Malignancy—The first location of the cancer (carcinoma) (eg, Skin; eyebrow 173.30).
◖ Secondary Malignancy— The cancer has spread to a secondary location (metastases) (eg, Skin; eyebrow 198.2).
◖ Ca *in Situ*—The cancer is encapsulated and has not spread (eg, Skin; eyebrow 232.3).
◖ Benign—The pathology report indicates no cancer or pre-cancerous cells associated with the lesion (eg, Skin; eyebrow 216.3).
◖ Uncertain Behavior—The pathology report indicates pre-cancerous cells or dysplastic cells associated with the lesion (eg, Skin; eyebrow 238.2).
◖ Unspecified—There is no pathology report indicating the nature of the lesion (eg, Skin; eyebrow 239.2).

| | Malignant | | | | | |
	Primary	Secondary	Ca in situ	Benign	Uncertain Behavior	Unspecified
Neoplasm, neoplastic						
Skin NOS	173.90	198.2	232.9	216.9	238.2	239.2
ear (external)	173.20	198.2	232.2	216.2	238.2	239.2
basal cell carcinoma	173.21					
specified type NEC	173.29					
squamous cell						
carcinoma	173.22					
elbow (*see also* Neoplasm, skin, upper limb)	173.60	198.2	232.6	216.6	238.2	239.2
eyebrow (*see also* Neoplasm, skin, face)	173.30	198.2	232.3	216.3	238.2	239.2
eyelid	173.10	198.2	232.1		238.2	239.2
basal cell carcinoma	173.11					
specified type NEC	173.19					
squamous cell						
carcinoma	173.12					

Example

1. Squamous Cell Carcinoma of Right Arm

   To find the appropriate diagnosis code for squamous cell carcinoma of the right arm, using the Index to Diseases, Carcinoma/skin appendage" directs you to "see Neoplasm, skin, malignant." In the neoplasm table under "arm NEC*", there is an asterisk that indicates NEC (not elsewhere classified). Because you are dealing with the skin of the arm, you should look up Skin/arm. Under Malignant/Primary, you will find 173.60. Verify your code selection in the Tabular List to be sure you have the correct diagnosis code.

2. Melanoma of the Lip.

   Your first thought might be to go directly to the neoplasm table. In the case of melanoma, that would be incorrect. Find "Melanoma" in the Index to Diseases, and then find "lip." The Index will guide you to 172.0 as the diagnosis.

Diseases of the Skin and Subcutaneous Tissue

Common skin infection and disorder diagnosis codes are found in chapter 12 of the ICD-9-CM codebook under Skin and Subcutaneous Tissue, which includes codes for:

◖ Skin infections (bacterial and fungal)

◖ Inflammatory conditions of the skin including dermatitis, erythema, rosacea, and psoriasis

◖ Other disorders of the skin, including corns and calluses, keloid scars, keratosis, diseases of the hair (eg, alopecia), diseases of sweat glands (eg, hidradenitis), diseases of the sebaceous glands (eg, acne), and ulcers

Infections of the Skin and Subcutaneous Tissue

Skin infections can be bacterial or fungal. Carbuncles and furuncles (boils) typically are caused by a staphylococcal infection. Several furuncles together make up a carbuncle and often involve a group of hair follicles. The fourth digit of the diagnosis code will depend on the location of the furuncle or carbuncle.

Cellulitis and abscess of the skin are coded using the same subset of ICD-9-CM codes; category 681 is cellulitis and abscess of finger and toe, and category 682 is other cellulitis and abscess. Cellulitis is a bacterial infection in the deeper subcutaneous tissues. The selection of the diagnosis code will be dependent on the location of the cellulitis or abscess. In addition to the cellulitis code, you also will need to code the organism causing the infection, such as staphylococcus.

Impetigo (684) is caused by group A streptococci or Staphylococcus aureus bacteria entering the skin, typically through cuts or insect bites.

A pilonidal cyst is a cyst, fistula, or sinus on the skin located at the bottom of the tailbone, near the natal cleft of the buttocks. The cyst can contain hair, skin debris, and other abnormal tissue. If it becomes infected, it is considered abscessed. Coding for pilonidal cyst depends on whether an abscess is present.

Inflammatory Conditions of the Skin

Inflammatory conditions of the skin include dermatitis, erythema, rosacea, and psoriasis.

There are different types of dermatitis, such as seborrheic, atopic, and contact dermatitis. Code selection for contact dermatitis depends on the irritant causing the reaction. When the irritant is a drug, the appropriate E code should be coded in addition to 692.3. If the rash is identified only as a rash, with no other description or qualification, it is coded as 782.1.

Erythema is redness of the skin due to capillary dilation. Types of erythema include rosacea, erythema multiforme, and erythema nodosum. When erythema multiforme is documented, you will report:

1. The code for erythema multiforme (695.10–695.19);

2. The associated manifestation;

3. An additional code from 695.50–695.59 to identify the percent of skin exfoliation; and

4. An additional E code to identify the drug, if drug induced.

Other Diseases of Skin and Subcutaneous Tissue

Other disorders of the skin include corns and calluses, keloid scars, keratosis, diseases of the hair (eg, alopecia), diseases of sweat glands (eg, hidradenitis), diseases of the sebaceous glands (eg, acne), and ulcers.

A keloid scar (701.4) is excess growth of the connective tissue during the healing process.

Keratosis is an overgrowth of the horny layer of the skin. Actinic keratosis (AK), also known as solar keratosis, is caused by sun exposure. Actinic keratosis is known as precancerous, because it can be the first step leading to squamous cell carcinoma. Seborrheic keratosis is a benign growth that typically is not cancerous. Warts, also a growth on the skin, are typically caused by human papilloma virus (HPV). Keratosis is coded from category 702, while warts are mainly coded from category 078.

Alopecia is loss of hair. Alopecia areata is an autoimmune disease where the immune system mistakenly attacks the hair follicles causing hair loss. Telogen effluvium is alopecia caused by a metabolic or hormonal stress or by medications.

An ulcer is a lesion on the skin caused by superficial loss of tissue. In ICD-9-CM, skin ulcers are selected based on whether the ulcer is a pressure ulcer and by location. A pressure ulcer, also known as a bedsore or decubitis ulcer, occurs when there is loss of tissue due to pressure on the skin. When a pressure ulcer code is reported from subcategory 707.0, an additional code from subcategory 707.2 must be reported to identify the stage of the ulcer.

Testing Technique

Highlight the statement, "Use additional code to identify pressure ulcer stage (707.20–707.25)" in your ICD-9-CM codebook.

ICD-9-CM code 707.25 is used for unstageable pressure ulcers. Unstageable is not the same as unspecified. "Unstageable" means the base of the ulcer is covered in eschar or slough and the depth cannot be determined. "Unspecified" means the physician has not specified the stage of the ulcer. Be sure to review your ICD-9-CM chapter guidelines regarding pressure ulcers.

Urticaria (hives) show on the skin as raised, red, itchy wheals. Urticaria can be caused by an allergy to food or medications, external factors such as heat or friction, or can be idiopathic. The ICD-9-CM code is selected based on the cause of the urticaria.

Injury and Poisoning

The main subsections for the integumentary system in ICD-9-CM chapter 17: Injury and Poisoning are Open Wound (870–897), Superficial Injury (910–919), Contusion with Intact Skin Surface (920–924), and Burns (940–949).

Lacerations to the skin are coded as open wounds. In the ICD-9-CM index, look for "Wound/open". The code is based on the location of the laceration and whether it is complicated. Complicated wounds are those that have delayed healing, delayed treatment, foreign body, or infection.

Superficial injuries are injuries occurring to the outer layers of the skin. This includes abrasions, blisters, insect bites, and splinters. Contusions are bruises or hematomas. Superficial injuries and hematomas should not be coded when they are part of a more serious injury to the same site.

Burns are coded based on several factors:

- **Location**—A separate code should be reported for each burn site.
- **Degree of the burn (first, second, or third)**—When there are multiple degrees of burns in the same location (same three

digit category), code the highest degree burn for that location. When coding multiple degrees of burns in different locations, sequence the code for the burn of the highest degree first.

Degree of Burns

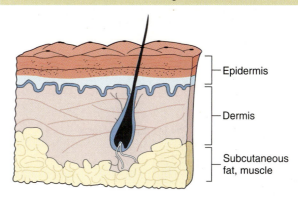

Skin red, dry

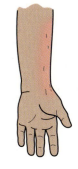
First-degree (superficial)

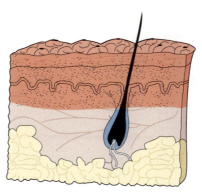
Blistered, skin moist, pink or red

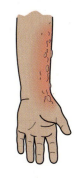
Second-degree (partial thickness)

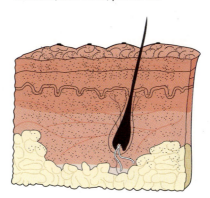
Charring, skin black, brown, red

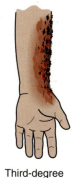
Third-degree (full thickness)

Source: Delmar/Cengage Learning.

- **Total body surface area (TBSA)**—The total body surface area affected by the burn. A code from category 948 should be used to record burn mortality, or when there is mention of a third-degree burn involving 20 percent or more of the body surface. The Rule of Nines assigns percentages to each body area to assist you coding the TBSA of burns. Note for 948.xx, the fourth digit denotes TBSA burned, and the fifth digit denotes, the TBSA with third-degree burns.

Rule of Nines

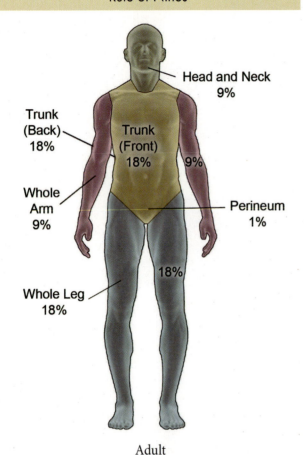

Adult

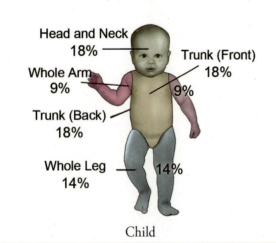

Child

Source: AAPC.

Disorders of the Breast

Category 610 *Benign mammary dysplasia* notates abnormal tissue. The most common mammary dysplasia is fibrocystic disease or mammary cysts. Fibrocystic changes in the breasts typically would be a diagnosis associated with an E/M code or breast exam.

Category 611 *Other disorders of the breast* contains common signs and symptoms such as 611.71 *Mastodynia* (pain in the breast), and 611.72 *Lump or mass in breast*. Also in this section is 611.5 *Galactocele*, which is a milk-fed cyst often cured by aspiration.

The final category 612 *Deformity and disproportion of reconstructed breast*, is used when a correction to a breast is required after reconstructive surgery.

CPT® Coding

CPT® codes found in the Integumentary System section include procedures performed on the skin and nails, as well as those performed on the breasts.

Fine Needle Aspiration

Fine needle aspiration (FNA) is used to sample fluid or tissue from a cyst or mass. When the mass or cyst is difficult to find by palpation, ultrasound or fluoroscopic guidance (referred to as imaging guidance) may be used.

Incision and Drainage

An incision and drainage (I&D) may be performed for an abscess, cyst, or hematoma by opening the abscess or cyst with a surgical instrument and allowing the contents to drain. The surgical opening is often left open to allow for continued drainage. For complicated or multiple cysts, the physician may place a drain or gauze packing strip to permit continued drainage. A complicated cyst may require surgical closure at a later date. When an I&D is performed below the subcutaneous layer, it is reported from other sections in CPT® (eg, I&D of the arm in the Musculoskeletal System is 23930–23931).

When the patient presents with a pilonidal cyst, the physician makes an incision to allow drainage and to remove the epithelial lining by curettage (10080). The wound heals secondarily, relying on local wound care. To report a complicated I&D of pilonidal cyst (10081), the procedure must be documented as complicated and will require primary closure, excision of tissue, or a Z-plasty.

To remove a foreign body embedded beneath the epidermis, the physician makes a simple incision directly above it and uses forceps or other instruments to remove the foreign body. Primary closure is common and included with this procedure. If the foreign body is embedded deep in the subcutaneous tissue, and requires dissection of underlying tissues, report 10121.

CPT® 10160 describes the puncture aspiration of an abscess, hematoma, bulla, or cyst. The physician uses a large needle attached to a syringe and guides it into the site and aspirates the fluid. This differs from the incision and drainage codes, because the abscess, hematoma, bulla, or cyst is drained by puncturing a hole, instead of the physician making an incision. If necessary, a pressure dressing is applied.

When a patient presents with a post-operative wound infection, the physician may perform an I&D. The infected wound is reopened and drained. Necrotic or dead tissues are removed, and the site is irrigated with saline and either re-sutured or packed with gauze to allow additional drainage. This is reported with CPT® code 10180. In some cases, the wound is left open and may require sutures at a later date, referred to as a secondary closure.

Debridement

Debridement is defined as the removal of dead tissue. The debridement codes in the Integumentary System section are used more often for friction burns, frost bite, abrasions, pressure ulcers and more, but not are used for second- and third-degree burns of the skin. Pay close attention to the body area, and the level of debridement in square centimeters (eg, skin, subcutaneous tissue, muscle, or bone). Debridement is coded to the deepest level of tissue removed. When multiple wounds are debrided, the wounds of the same depth should be added together for correct code selection.

For necrotizing soft tissue infection (NSTI), the physician removes the necrotic eschar tissue to allow for

proper healing of the site. Codes 11000–11008 are based on key components, such as percentage of body surface area and location of the wound. In some cases, prosthetic material or mesh of the abdominal wall becomes infected and also needs to be removed. The removal of the mesh is reported with add-on code 11008.

When reporting 11010–11012, documentation for debridement including removal of foreign matter at the site of an open fracture, must include the depth (eg, skin and subcutaneous, muscle fascia, muscle and bone) of the debridement. Codes 11042–11047 include partial thickness or full thickness debridement of the skin, as well as debridement of muscle fascia, muscle, and bone.

Paring or Cutting

The codes in this category are used for the removal of hyperkeratotic lesions, such as corns and calluses. Local anesthetic may be used. Code selection is based on the number of lesions removed.

Biopsy CPT® Code Range

Punch biopsy is performed by a tool to obtain a circular sample of the lesion. Sutures often are needed to close the defect. A shave biopsy occurs when the provider uses a sharp instrument, such as a scalpel, and slices the suspicious lesion in a horizontal fashion as close to the base of the lesion as possible. When the provider chooses to do a shave biopsy, the wound often is covered by a bandage and does not require suturing. Skin biopsies are coded based on the number of lesions. Obtaining tissue for biopsy during excision, destruction, or shave removal of lesions is not reported. Biopsy for pathological examination must be unrelated to other procedures provided at the same time.

Removal of Skin Tags

Skin tags are defined as an outgrowth of both the epidermis and dermal fibrovascular tissue. CPT® states that skin tag removal often is done by scissoring or any sharp method. Code selection is determined based on how many skin tags are removed. Payers may consider this to be cosmetic, so check for coverage details.

Shaving of Epidermal or Dermal Lesions

Shave removal often is confused with biopsy. A shave removal is the removal of the lesion without taking a full thickness excision, and does not require suture closure. Shave removals are coded by body area and lesion size. Physicians will determine the medical necessity of a shave removal of a lesion versus the excision removal of the lesion.

Removal of Lesions by Excision

Excision is defined as a full thickness removal of a lesion of the skin. Pathology will determine which code set (benign or malignant) is used for the proper coding. If possible, the coding of the procedure should wait until the pathology report has been received. Code selection also is based on the size of the lesion (prior to excision) and anatomic location of the lesion excised. Per CPT®, the excised diameter is the lesion's diameter plus the narrowest margins required (refer to CPT® *Professional Edition* for examples of measuring lesions). If the lesion size is not listed, consult the physician for an addendum to the report. If not provided, report the smallest lesion for the correct category.

Testing Technique

Highlight the guidelines in each section of Excisions (Benign and Malignant), reminding you to code each lesion separately.

All excised lesions include simple repair. In the case where the removal of the lesion calls for an intermediate or complex closure, the closure is reported separately.

Nails

Nails are plates of tightly packed, hard, keratinized epidermal cells. The nail unit consists of:

◀ Nail plate—the hard part of the nail

◀ Nail bed—skin underneath the nail

◀ Nail matrix—portion of the nail extending under the skin

◀ Hyponychium—secures the nail to the finger;

◀ Nail folds—the proximal and later skin overlapping the nail

◀ Eponychium—cuticle

◀ Free edge—the white end extending past the finger

(Refer to figures for Lateral Nail View and the Dorsal Nail View in CPT® *Professional Edition*.)

Report 11719 for trimming of the nondystrophic nail(s); any number. A nondystrophic nail is essentially a normal nail that is unaffected by abnormal development or changes in structure or appearance due to disease, injury, or aging.

Avulsion of a nail plate is described with 11730 for partial or complete; simple; single. This procedure involves the removal of part of or the entire fingernail or toenail. After local anesthetic is administered the physician separates the nail plate from the nail bed to remove the nail. If the physician is removing more than one nail from the fingers or toes, +11732 is used for each additional nail.

When a patient presents with a hematoma (collection of blood) of the fingernail or toenail the physician removes the collection of blood using an electrocautery unit to pierce the nail plate and drain the fluid (11740). When more than one nail is involved, report each additional procedure with the appropriate FA–F9 modifier to indicate which fingernail or TA–T9 modifier to indicate which toenail is involved.

Common procedures involving the nail relate to ingrown nails or deformed nails. The nail is removed using blunt dissection with the assistance of electrocautery to minimize bleeding. Report 11750 for partial or complete removal.

Pilonidal Cysts

A pilonidal cyst is a sac under the skin at the base of the spine that can become infected. Code selection is based on whether the excision of the cyst is simple, extensive, or complicated. A simple excision (11770) is closed in only one layer. If several layers of closure are required, and the documentation indicates extensive or complicated, code selection is directed to 11771 or 11772. Extensive is superficial to the underlying fascia, greater than 2 cm or the cyst has multiple sinuses. A complicated pilonidal cyst may be infected with multiple sinuses.

Introduction

In some cases, the physician will choose to inject a lesion (such as a wart, erythemas, hordeolums, or keloid scars), typically with a steroid material. Code 11900 describes injection of up to and including seven lesions; 11901 describes more than seven lesions being injected.

Injection of filling material, such as collagen, is used in many facets of reconstructive and cosmetic surgery. The physician will inject filling material subcutaneously to treat acne scars, facial wrinkles, and abnormality of the breast due to reconstruction. Codes for injections of filling material are selected based on the amount of material injected in cubic centimeters (cc). For example, 11950 describes 1 cc or less, whereas 11954 describes over 10.0 cc.

Tissue expanders are used in a number of ways, such as for burn victims and breast cancer patients. Insertion of the tissue expander for other than breast reconstruction is reported with 11960. When the tissue expander is removed and replaced with a permanent prosthesis for breast reconstruction, report 11970. In certain instances, considerable capsular adjustments are necessary to allow proper placement of the prosthesis within the fibrous capsule that has formed around the expander, and with appropriate documentation, code 19342 *Delayed insertion of breast prosthesis following mastopexy, mastectomy or in reconstruction*, is sometimes used instead of 11970.

Codes for insertion and removal of implantable contraceptive devices (11976–11983) are selected based on the procedure (insertion, removal, or both) and the substance (implantable contraceptive capsule, subcutaneous hormone pellet or non-biodegradable drug delivery implant).

Repair (Closure)

Repair of wounds are divided into simple, intermediate, or complex. Simple repair is used when the wound is superficial and requires a simple one-layer closure. This also includes the use of Dermabond® to close a wound.

Intermediate repair includes the repair as described in simple repair, but also requires a layered closure of one or more of the deeper structures, such as the deeper level of the dermis. It also includes single-layered closure of heavily contaminated wounds that require extensive cleaning or removal of particulate matter.

Complex repair includes the repair as described in intermediate repair, but also includes wounds that require more than a layered repair, such as scar revision, debridement, or extensive undermining. Necessary preparation includes creation of a defect for repairs or the debridement of complicated lacerations or avulsions.

If repairs include deeper structures, such as nerves, blood vessels, or tendons, refer to the appropriate anatomic system section for correct coding. The repair of these associated wounds is included in the primary procedure unless it qualifies as a complex repair, in which case modifier 59 applies.

CPT® divides repairs by total repair and body area. When multiple wounds are repaired, add together the lengths of those in same anatomic location with the same type of repair.

Example

1. Simple repairs of the scalp measuring 0.5 cm, neck measuring 0.6 cm, trunk measuring 2.0 cm, and cheek measuring 0.6 cm.

   The repairs for the scalp, neck, and trunk are added together to report 12002, and the repair of the cheek is reported separately with 12011.

2. A complex repair measuring 2.7 cm is performed on the left arm, and an intermediate repair measuring 8.2 cm is performed on the right arm.

   The repairs are different complexities (intermediate and complex), so they are reported separately with:

   13121 for the complex repair (2.7 cm) on the left arm; and

   12034-59 for the intermediate repair (8.2 cm) on the right arm

   Modifier 59 is required to indicate it is two separate locations (right and left arms).

Adjacent Tissue Transfer or Rearrangement

Some wounds require more than just a simple, intermediate, or complex closure. The physician may choose to close the wound with an adjacent tissue transfer (Y-plasty, Z-plasty, advancement flap, or rotation flap), taking a full thickness portion of the skin and rotating or advancing the skin into the defect. In this scenario, the codes are divided into body areas and square centimeters. Refer to the figures in the *CPT® Professional Edition* for Adjacent Tissue Repairs.

If a lesion is excised and the defect is closed with a flap, the excision is included in the flap reconstruction.

Tissue transferred from an area adjacent to the defect is known as a local flap. It may be described based on its shape (such as V-Y flap), or as an advancement or pivotal flap. Tissue transferred from a noncontiguous anatomic site—a different part of the body—is referred to as a distant flap.

Skin Replacement Surgery and Skin Substitutes

Skin grafts are identified by size and location of the defect (recipient site), and the type of graft or skin substitute used. Therefore, codes will be selected based on the recipient site, where the graft is going, not from where the graft came.

An autograft is a graft obtained from the patient, such as a split-thickness or full thickness graft. An allograft is a graft obtained from another human donor, such as a cadaver. A xenograft is obtained from an animal, such as a pig. Cultured tissue is man-made skin substitutes created in a laboratory (for example, Alloderm®, Apligraft® and Integra®).

A split-thickness skin graft includes a full layer of the epidermis and part of the dermis. A full thickness skin graft includes a full layer of the epidermis and dermis. Split-thickness and full thickness skin grafts are reported by square centimeters for adults or 1 percent of the body area of infants and children.

Surgical preparation (15002–15005) is performed when the wound or recipient site requires initial preparation prior to application of a skin graft. The codes are selected based on the location and size of the resultant

defect. Sum the surface area of all wounds from all anatomic sites that are grouped together into the same code descriptor (eg, sum surface area of all wounds on the trunk and arms).

Flaps (Skin and/or Deep Tissues)

Flaps (Skin and/or Deep Tissue) describe a section of skin that is transferred to the recipient site while still remaining attached to a blood supply source. Most of the procedures in this section describe pedicle flaps.

Although this process sounds similar to an adjacent tissue replacement, there are important differences to keep in mind when distinguishing between the two services:

1. The pedicle (base) of the pedicle flap is eventually cut or severed from its original blood supply after the skin transfer establishes independent blood supply. In an adjacent tissue transfer, the base remains intact permanently.

2. Pedicle flaps are formed on an area distant from the defect where it is being transferred. In an adjacent tissue transfer, the transfer is made from a local flap.

3. Pedicle flaps are often completed in multiple stages but can be formed and transferred in one stage. Adjacent tissue transfers are completed in a single stage.

Muscle flaps are coded with CPT® codes 15732–15738. These codes are listed based on the donor site of the flap. Each of these codes refers to a more general anatomic area than may be listed in an operative note. If the muscle flap is created from the gracilis, the CPT® code 15738 is used (Plastic Surgery News, April 1994, Raymond Janevicius, MD).

Pressure Ulcers (Decubitus Ulcers)

Pressure ulcer, decubitus ulcer and bedsore are synonyms referring to ulcerations of the skin and the underlying tissues. They are usually confined to one area and are commonly found over the bony projections, such as the sacrum, coccyx, ischium, knee, and heel, just to name a few areas. Pressure sores may be superficial, that is, confined to the skin, or they may go deep, extending below the skin into layers of tissue under it. Pressure sores are commonly found in patients confined to bed.

When using a code with the descriptor "in preparation for muscle or myocutaneous flap," such as CPT® code 15936, use the appropriate code for reporting the muscle flap or myocutaneous flap procedure in addition to the pressure sore excision code (Flaps [Skin and/or Deep Tissues]). When coding for pressure sore procedures that include an adjacent tissue transfer, flap closure, or skin flap closure, choose the appropriate code under the Pressure Ulcers section of the CPT®.

Burns, Local Treatment

The origin of a burn may be thermal, produced by chemicals, radiation, or friction. Depth and the percentage of total body surface area (TBSA) determine code selection. Codes are also available for escharotomy, an incision into necrotic tissue to relieve pressure.

When the services involve dressings and/or debridement, use codes 16020–16030. Any local infiltration, metacarpal/digital block, or topical anesthesia, when used, is not reported separately.

Other Procedures

The Integumentary System section also contains the code sets for procedures that may be considered cosmetic. Keep in mind, although the codes describe something we may consider cosmetic, there could be medical necessity, allowing payers to reimburse for these procedures. These procedures include:

- dermabrasion
- chemical peel
- cervicoplasty (neck lift)
- blepharoplasty (eyelid lift)
- rhytidectomy (brow lift)
- abdominoplasty (tummy tuck)
- liposuction (suction assisted lipectomy)

Destruction

Per CPT®, destruction means ablation of benign, premalignant, or malignant tissues by any method, with or without curettement, including local anesthesia, and not usually requiring any closure. These methods include electrosurgery, cryosurgery, laser, and chemical treatment.

Code selection is based on pathology. CPT® codes 17000–17004 are used for the destruction of benign or pre-malignant lesions, such as actinic keratoses. CPT® 17000 describes the destruction for the first lesion, and add-on code 17003 describes the destruction of the 2nd through 14th lesion, and is assigned per lesion. If there is an occasion that the physician is destroying 15 or more lesions, CPT® code 17004 is reported. In coding for wart destruction, report 17110–17111, depending on the number of warts destroyed.

There are occasions where the physician and patient will choose to have a skin cancer destroyed (as opposed to excised). In this situation, it is important first to have the pathology report that indicates the lesion is malignant, and also the location and size of the lesion prior to destruction.

Mohs Micrographic Surgery

Mohs micrographic surgery is a unique procedure performed by a surgeon who also performs as the pathologist. The surgeon removes the tumor tissue, and maps and divides the tumor specimen into pieces. These pieces are examined under a microscope to check for positive margins. If positive margins are present, the surgeon returns to excise additional margins. This procedure is repeated until the margins are clear. It is very important to understand this process, as the CPT® codes directly apply to each step. Simply put, each time the surgeon removes a portion of the tumor, it is referred to as a stage; each stage is mapped and divided into tissue blocks. CPT® breaks Mohs micrographic surgery down by body site, and by each stage and up to five tissue blocks. Add-on codes are available for additional stages and up to five tissue blocks, and additional tissue blocks beyond the initial five blocks.

Breast

When a patient presents with what appears to be a breast cyst, the physician may perform a puncture aspiration. Pay attention to the parenthetical instructions and remember to code for imaging guidance when applicable.

A mastotomy is performed when the abscess is deep in the breast tissue, forcing the physician to create an incision into the breast over the tissue or abscess. If the tissue is normal, the physician will close the site with sutures. If an abscess is found, the physician commonly will pack the wound with gauze to assist in draining of the abscess.

Breast biopsies can be performed as percutaneous or open. The procedures are performed based on the approach (percutaneous or open) and whether imaging guidance is used. These procedures are performed for suspicious masses found in the breast.

Depending on what is found during a biopsy, the patient may undergo open breast procedures to remove the mass or, in the case of breast cancer, the patient may undergo a mastectomy.

Mastectomy for gynecomastia (19300) is a surgery performed only on male patients for enlarged breasts. This surgery is very similar in approach to the mastopexy and reduction mammoplasty performed for women.

A partial mastectomy (19301) is described as a lumpectomy, tylectomy, quadrantectomy, or segmentectomy. If the surgeon also removes axillary lymph nodes, both portions of the surgery are reported with a single code (19302).

The remaining mastectomy codes describe the extent of the surgery. Simple complete (19303) is the removal of just the breast; radical (19305) includes the pectoral muscles and axillary lymph nodes. Radical mastectomy (19306) includes the breast, pectoralis muscles, and axillary and internal mammary lymph nodes (Urban type). A modified radical mastectomy (19307) includes axillary lymph nodes, with or without pectoralis minor muscle, but excludes pectoralis major muscle.

A mastopexy is performed to lift the breast. A reduction mammoplasty is performed for patients with an abundance of breast tissue; and due to the enlargement of the breasts, have back, neck, and shoulder pain in addition to shoulder grooving. Another breast surgery is a breast augmentation, which is performed in breast reconstruc-

tion or cosmetically for patients who are unhappy with their current breast size.

There are times when a patient will present after undergoing a breast augmentation or implant placement in reconstruction where the implant has ruptured. In these cases, the implant and possibly the implant material must be removed. Not all cases will allow for the implant to be replaced.

Reconstruction options for the mastectomy patient can start immediately or be delayed. CPT® 19340 describes immediate insertion of breast prosthesis following mastopexy, mastectomy or in reconstruction. This means the implant is placed during the same surgical session as the mastectomy. CPT® 19342 describes delayed insertion of breast prosthesis following mastopexy, mastectomy, or in reconstruction. This means the implant is placed after the mastectomy surgery has had time to heal or after the patient has completed chemotherapy and/or radiation therapy.

Another breast reconstruction option is the immediate or delayed insertion of a tissue expander (19357), which allows the skin to be stretched to allow for the placement of the breast prosthesis. These procedures typically are performed in two stages: Placement of the tissue expander is first, followed by removal of the tissue expander with placement of the permanent prosthesis.

CPT® 19361 is breast reconstruction with latissimus dorsi flap, without prosthetic implant. Another common breast reconstruction is the TRAM (transverse rectus abdominis myocutaneous flap) (19367). This surgery is similar to the latissimus dorsi flap in that it takes a muscle and moves it from one location to the chest wall for breast reconstruction. TRAM with supercharging refers to a TRAM procedure with microvascular anastomosis (19368).

Capsulotomy is when the physician makes an incision over the previous scar and creates a larger pocket by cutting the scar tissue surrounding the implant. The capsulectomy is when the surgeon actually removes the scar tissue around the implant.

Glossary

Actinic Keratosis—A premalignant warty lesion occurring on the sun-exposed skin of the face or hands in aged light-skinned people.

Alopecia—Lack of hair, especially on the scalp, which may be partial or total, and can occur at any age.

Basal Cell Carcinoma—A slow-growing malignant neoplasm.

Benign Lesion—A tumor that does not form metastases, and does not invade and destroy adjacent normal tissue.

Biopsy—A process of removing tissue from a patient for microscopic diagnostic examination.

Congenital Nevus—A melanocytic nevus visible at birth, often larger than an acquired nevus.

Contact Dermatitis—Acute or chronic dermatitis caused by initial irritant effect of a substance that comes in contact with the skin.

Debridement—Removal of foreign materials, necrotic matter, and devitalized tissue from a wound or burn.

Decubitis Ulcer—Focal ischemic necrosis of skin and underlying tissues at sites of constant pressure or recurring friction.

Dermabrasion—Procedure used to remove acne scars or pits, performed with sandpaper or other abrasive materials.

Dermatofibroma—A slow-growing, benign skin nodule consisting of poorly demarcated cellular fibrous tissue.

Dermatologist—A physician who specializes in diagnosing and treating cutaneous and related systemic diseases.

Dermatone—An instrument for cutting thin slices of skin for grafting or excising small lesions.

Dermis—Directly below the epidermis, the dermis is the second layer of the skin.

Dysplastic Nevus—Cutaneous pigmented lesions with notched, irregular borders, considered pre-malignant.

Epidermis—The outer layer of the skin.

Eschar—A thick, crusty covering or slough that develops after thermal or chemical burn or cauterization of the skin.

Gynecomastia—Excessive development of the male mammary glands.

Impetigo—A contagious superficial pyoderma, caused by Staphylococcus aureus (staph) or Streptococcus pyogenes (strep).

Intradermal Nevus—A nevus in which nests of melanocytes are found in the dermis, but not at the epidermal-dermal junction.

Keloid—A nodular, firm, often linear mass of hyperplastic, thick scar tissue.

Mycoses—Any disease caused by a fungus.

Necrosis—Pathologic death of one or more cells, or of a portion of tissue or organ, resulting from irreversible damage.

Nevus—A circumscribed malformation of the skin, especially one colored by hyperpigmentation.

Pilonidal Cyst—Hair-containing cyst or sinus in the tissues of the sacrococcygeal area.

Pruritis—Relating to itching.

Psoriasis—A common autoimmune condition characterized by the eruption of reddish, silvery-scaled maculopapules.

Sebaceous Cyst—A common cyst of the skin and sucutis containing sebum and keratin.

Seborrhea—Over activity of the sebaceous gland, resulting in an excessive amount of sebum.

Official CPC® Certification Study Guide   **95**

Chapter Review Questions

1. Melonocytes exist in which layer of the skin?

    A. Stratum Lucidum

    B. Stratum Granulosum

    C. Stratum Spinosum

    D. Stratum Basale (Stratum Germinativum)

2. Which of the following best describes psoriasis?

    A. An inflammatory conditions characterized by redness, pustular and vesicular lesions, crusts, and scales.

    B. A contagious infection of the skin generally caused by the Staphylococcus bacterium.

    C. A chronic condition characterized by lesions that are red, dry, elevated, and covered by silvery scales.

    D. An allergic reaction characterized by wheals and generally accompanied by pruritus.

3. A four-year-old presents with an upper arm abscess in the subcutaneous tissue. An incision and drainage technique is performed. Pus is expressed and dry gauze dressing is applied. The procedure should be coded as:

    A. 10060

    B. 10061

    C. 23930

    D. 10180

4. Mohs surgery is to be performed on a 56-year-old with basal cell carcinoma on the neck. The gross tumor is completely excised. Tissue is divided into two tissue blocks which are mapped and color coded at their margins; frozen sectioning is performed. A full thickness graft is used to harvest skin from the patient's left axillae for an area of 5 sq cm. The appropriate CPT® codes are:

    A. 26115, 15260

    B. 11600, 15240

    C. 17311, 15240

    D. 17313, 15260

5. A 32-year-old male presents to the physician's office for a follow-up debridement of a dragging injury that occurred when he fell from his horse. Both palms were affected. The injury occurred a week ago. Today, minimal dead skin is removed with a scalpel from the epidermis of the right palm. Dead tissue is removed from the subcutaneous layer of the left palm. Topical ointment and a gauze dressing were placed over the surgical sites. The procedure(s) should be coded as:

    A. 11042, 97597-59

    B. 97602

    C. 16020-50

    D. 11043, 11042-59

6. An 11-year-old female presents to the doctor's office with two dark lesions and a skin tag on her back. The two lesions on her right upper back are punch biopsied. The skin tag on her back is removed by electrocauterization. The procedures should be coded as:

    A. 11100, 11200-59, 11201

    B. 11100, 11101, 11200-59

    C. 11056, 11200-59

    D. 11100 x 2, 11200-59

7. A 3-year-old pulls a pot of hot water off the stove and it splashes on his face and arms. When examined, the infant has first-degree burns on his lower face and second-degree burns on both arms. The physician treats the burn on the face, approximately 3 percent of the total area, with Silvadene dressing. For the second-degree burns, both arms (approximately 11% TBSA) have no infection and the blisters are intact. The burn is cleansed and Silvadene dressing is applied. The procedures and diagnoses should be coded as:

    A. 16025, 16020-59, 943.20, 941.10, E924.2

    B. 16030, 16020-59, 942.23, 941.17, E924.0

    C. 16025, 16000-59, 943.24, 941.14, E924.2

    D. 16030, 16000-59, 943.20, 941.10, E924.0

8. A patient has a 4.3 cm x 2 cm lesion on the left thigh excised. Due to the size and location of the lesion, the decision was made to harvest a full thickness skin graft from his left lower leg. An excision of 5 cm x 5 cm full thickness graft was obtained and grafted onto the defect and sewn. The pathology finding confirmed that the lesion was basal cell carcinoma. The CPT® code(s) to report is (are):

    A. 14021

    B. 11406, 15100-51

    C. 11606, 15220-51, 15221

    D. 11606, 15150-51

Official CPC® Certification Study Guide   **97**

9. **Operative Note #1.**

Procedure(s) Performed: Excision of a melanoma *in situ* on left dorsal forearm;
Excision with Layered closure right lower leg

Preoperative Diagnosis: Melanoma *in situ*, left dorsal forearm and basal cell carcinoma right lower leg.

Postoperative Diagnosis: Melanoma *in situ*, left dorsal forearm and basal cell carcinoma right lower leg.

Indications: Well-marginated, erythematous, slightly scaly, plaque(s): posterior right lower leg.

Biopsy revealed a superficial BCC (basal cell carcinoma). The patient is allergic to Codeine. The patient takes the following medication(s): Hydroxyurea, alegralide, Boniva. Informed consent was obtained from the patient. Risks of the procedure including, bleeding, infection, scarring, and recurrence were explained, and the patient acknowledged understanding of these potential complications.

Procedure: The preoperative measurement of the lesion on the right lower leg was 0.9 cm. The proposed excision lines were drawn. Anesthesia was delivered locally with 12.0 cc of 1% Xylocaine with epinephrine buffered 1:10. The site was cleansed with Betadine. The site was prepped and draped in the usual sterile fashion. An incision was performed with a number 15 blade 0.5 cm outside the margin of the identified neoplasm extending deep, through the dermis and into the subcutaneous fat. The excised diameter (total pre-operative dimensions including margins) measured 1.9 cm. The specimen was tagged at the superior tip. This tissue was dissected from the patient with care to preserve histologic features. The surgical site was undermined to a distance of 2.0 cm. Hemostasis was obtained by electrocautery and vessels ligated as necessary. The specimen was placed in a bottle of Formalin labeled with the patient's identifying information. The specimen was sent for pathologic and/or margin analysis. In order to prevent dehiscence due to wound tension, an intermediate layered closure was performed. Seven 4-0 Polysorb™ sutures were placed subcuticularly utilizing a simple inverted interrupted stitch. Seven 4-0 nylon sutures were placed cutaneously utilizing a simple interrupted stitch. The final length of the surgical repair was 2.5 cm. The surgical site was cleansed with saline. A sterile dressing was applied utilizing the following: sterile petrolatum, gauze, and taped into place to form a pressure bandage. The patient tolerated the procedure well. Postoperative instructions were given to the patient. The patient was instructed to return in nine days for suture removal.

Lesion Treatment: The lesion on the left dorsal forearm was cleansed with alcohol and anesthetized with lidocaine with epinephrine. Electrodesiccated and curetted x 3. Appropriate dressing was applied and post-op instructions were given. The final defect measures 0.9 cm in size.

The patient tolerated both procedures well. Recommend routine skin examination in three months. The patient was released in good condition.

What are the CPT® and ICD-9-CM codes for this procedure?

10. **Operative Note #2**

Indications: The patient has an excision of a painful cyst on midline upper back. The lesion has previously ruptured and has significant scarring. The patient also has a painful cyst on the left upper back. The patient is allergic to penicillin and takes aspirin and Micardis for blood pressure. Informed consent was obtained from the patient. Risks of the procedure, including bleeding, infection, scarring and recurrence, were explained, and the patient acknowledged understanding of these potential complications.

Procedure 1-Excision cyst midline upper back:

The preoperative measurement of the lesion was 1.1 cm. The proposed excision lines were drawn. Anesthesia was delivered locally with 5.0 cc of 1% Xylocaine with epinephrine buffered 1:10. The site was cleansed with Betadine. The site was prepped and draped in the usual sterile fashion. An incision was performed with a number 15 blade extending deep, through the dermis and into the subcutaneous fat. This tissue was dissected from the patient with care to preserve histologic features. The cyst was not enucleated intact, but the contents and cyst wall remnants were extracted. The specimen was placed in a bottle of Formalin, labeled with the patient's identifying information. The specimen was sent for pathologic and/or margin analysis. The surgical site was undermined to a distance of 1.5 cm. Hemostasis was obtained by electrocautery and vessels ligated as necessary. In order to prevent dehiscence due to wound tension, an intermediate layered closure was performed. Three 4-0 Vicryl sutures were placed subcuticularly utilizing a simple inverted interrupted stitch. Four 4-0 nylon sutures were placed cutaneously utilizing a simple interrupted stitch. The final length of the surgical repair was 2.5 cm. The surgical site was cleansed with saline. A sterile dressing was applied utilizing the following: sterile petrolatum, gauze, and taped into place to form a pressure bandage. The patient tolerated the procedure well. Postoperative instructions were given to the patient. The patient was instructed to return in nine days for suture removal. Because the cyst ruptured during the surgery, we will have him take a course of Cipro, which cleared the secondary infection after the cyst ruptured several weeks ago.

Procedure 2-Excision cyst left upper back:

The preoperative measurement of the lesion was 1.5 cm. The proposed excision lines were drawn. Anesthesia was delivered locally with 6.0 cc of 1% Xylocaine with epinephrine buffered 1:10. The site was cleansed with Betadine. The site was prepped and draped in the usual sterile fashion. An incision was performed with a number 15 blade extending deep, through the dermis and into the subcutaneous fat. This tissue was dissected from the patient with care to preserve histologic features. The cyst was enucleated intact via sharp and blunt dissection. The specimen was placed in a bottle of Formalin, labeled with the patient's identifying information. The specimen was sent for pathologic and/or margin analysis. The surgical site was undermined to a distance of 1.0 cm. Hemostasis was obtained by electrocautery and vessels ligated as necessary. In order to prevent dehiscence due to wound tension, an intermediate layered closure was performed. Three 4-0 Vicryl sutures were placed subcuticularly utilizing a simple inverted interrupted stitch. Four 4-0 nylon sutures were placed cutaneously utilizing a simple interrupted stitch. The final length of the surgical repair was 2.9 cm. The surgical site was cleansed with saline. A sterile dressing was applied utilizing the following: sterile petrolatum, gauze, and taped into place to form a pressure bandage. The patient tolerated the procedure well. Postoperative instructions were given to the patient. The patient was instructed to return in nine days for suture removal. Prescribed Cipro 500 mg 1 tab b.i.d. (Oral) (Quantity: 20 Refills: 0). The patient was released in good condition.

Pathology:

Specimen #1: Ruptured epidermoid cyst. Slide interpreted by ABC laboratory. No further treatment needed. The patient will be notified of the results via letter.

Specimen #2: Epidermoid cyst. Slide interpreted by. No further treatment needed. The patient will be notified of the results via letter.

What are the CPT® and ICD-9-CM codes for this procedure?

Introduction

In this chapter, we will look at how muscles and bones work together to form the framework for the body, and the many procedures used to keep this system in shape. Objectives for this chapter include:

◖ Understand the components of the musculoskeletal system

◖ Define key terms

◖ Understand the most common pathologies affecting these organs

◖ Understand orthopaedic surgeries and how they relate to pathological conditions

◖ Recognize common eponyms and acronyms

◖ Identify when other sections of CPT® or ICD-9-CM should be accessed

◖ Know when HCPCS Level II codes and modifiers are appropriate

Anatomy and Medical Terminology

The musculoskeletal system contains 206 bones, more than 600 muscles, and ligaments, tendons, and cartilage.

The skeleton is divided into two parts: the axial skeleton and the appendicular skeleton. The axial skeleton consists of the bones of the skull, the hyoid bone, the chest and the spine. The appendicular skeleton includes the remaining bones of the upper and lower limbs, shoulders, and pelvis.

The primary functions of the musculoskeletal system are to provide protection for the internal organs and to assist with movement. The skeleton is the basic framework for the entire body, and the bones store calcium and produce blood cells.

Each type of bone has a specific function. Long bones such as the femur, tibia, and fibula in the legs and the humerus, radius, and ulna in the arms have large surface areas for muscle attachment. Short bones are found in

the wrists and ankles. Flat bones are found covering soft body parts. These are the shoulder blades, pelvic bones, and ribs. Sesamoid bones are shaped like sesame seeds and are found near a joint, such as the patella (kneecap). Irregular bones—for instance, the vertebrae or mandible (jaw bone)—are other various shapes.

The muscles assist with heat production, locomotion, and posture. There are three basic muscle types: striated (skeletal) muscle, smooth (visceral) muscle, and cardiac muscle. The musculoskeletal system includes mostly striated (voluntary) muscle. Cardiac muscle is found in the heart and smooth muscle is involuntary muscle found in the internal organs, such as the bowel and blood vessels.

Ligaments attach bones to other bones, and tendons attach muscles to bones. Cartilage acts as a cushion between bones in a joint.

Skeletal System

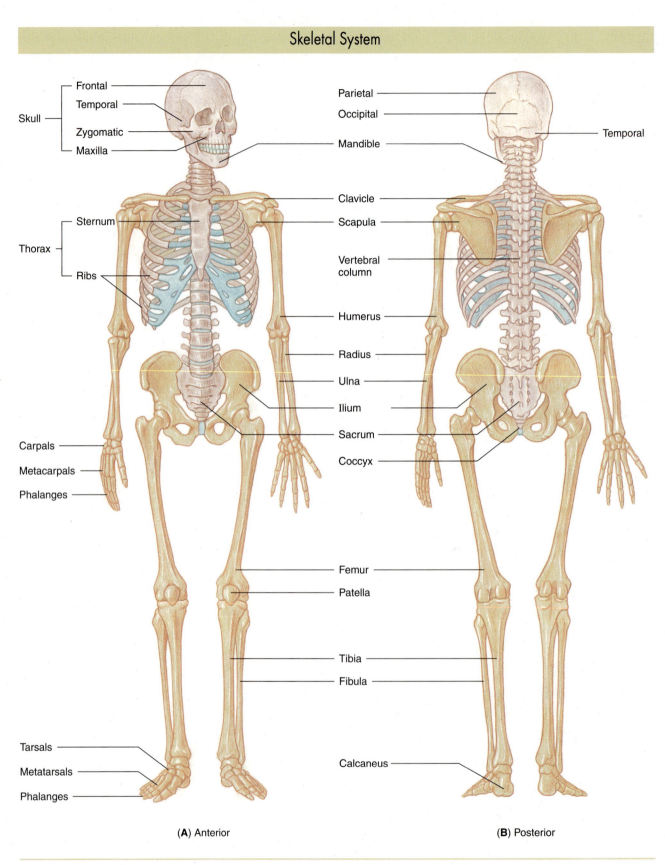

Skull
- Frontal
- Temporal
- Zygomatic
- Maxilla

Parietal
Occipital
Temporal
Mandible

Clavicle
Scapula

Thorax
- Sternum
- Ribs

Vertebral column

Humerus
Radius
Ulna
Ilium
Sacrum
Coccyx

Carpals
Metacarpals
Phalanges

Femur
Patella

Tibia
Fibula

Tarsals
Metatarsals
Phalanges

Calcaneus

(**A**) Anterior

(**B**) Posterior

Source: Delmar/Cengage Learning.

Muscles—Anterior

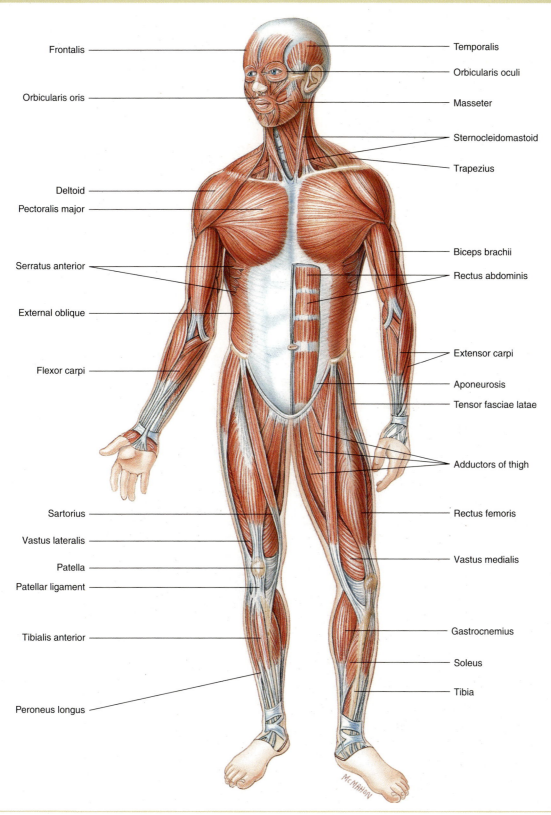

Frontalis

Orbicularis oris

Deltoid

Pectoralis major

Serratus anterior

External oblique

Flexor carpi

Sartorius

Vastus lateralis

Patella

Patellar ligament

Tibialis anterior

Peroneus longus

Temporalis

Orbicularis oculi

Masseter

Sternocleidomastoid

Trapezius

Biceps brachii

Rectus abdominis

Extensor carpi

Aponeurosis

Tensor fasciae latae

Adductors of thigh

Rectus femoris

Vastus medialis

Gastrocnemius

Soleus

Tibia

Source: Delmar/Cengage Learning.

Muscles—Posterior

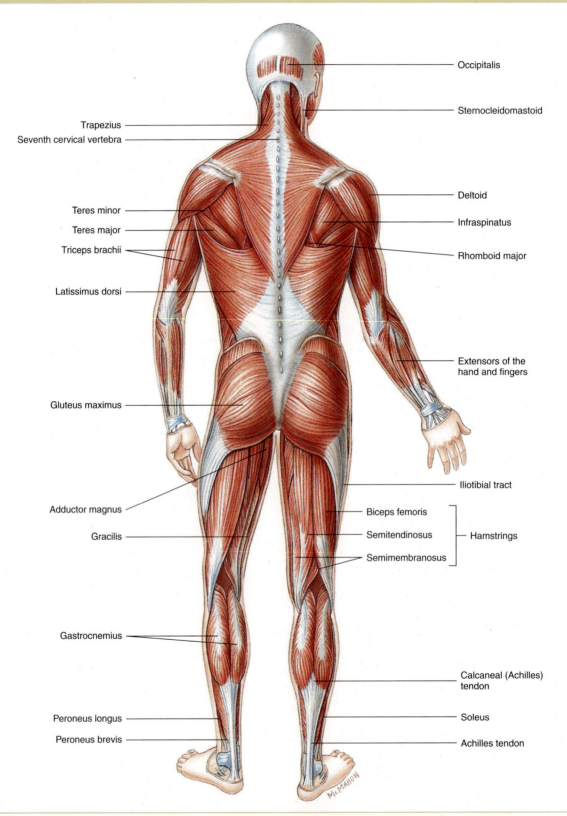

Occipitalis

Sternocleidomastoid

Trapezius

Seventh cervical vertebra

Deltoid

Teres minor

Infraspinatus

Teres major

Rhomboid major

Triceps brachii

Latissimus dorsi

Extensors of the hand and fingers

Gluteus maximus

Iliotibial tract

Biceps femoris

Adductor magnus

Semitendinosus

Hamstrings

Gracilis

Semimembranosus

Gastrocnemius

Calcaneal (Achilles) tendon

Peroneus longus

Soleus

Peroneus brevis

Achilles tendon

Source: Delmar/Cengage Learning.

Key Terms and Concepts

Axilla (Mass of Axilla): The armpit. There are numerous lymph nodes in this area, as well as muscles and tissue. There are times when the axilla may refer to the upper arm, back, or flank area. It is important to understand the anatomy in the medical record to determine the correct location for coding. If you are unable to determine the location based on anatomy within the medical documentation, you will need to query the provider.

Manipulation: Returning a fracture or dislocation to its normal anatomical position.

Reduction: Treatment of a fracture or dislocation by returning the part to its normal position. Reduction of a fracture can also mean surgical restoration.

Decompression: Removing scar tissue or bone from an area, most commonly the spine, to relieve pressure on nerves or nerve roots. It is often performed with placement of a bone graft, screws, plates, or rods to maintain the alignment of the bones. Another common decompression is of the median nerve in the wrist, also known as carpal tunnel.

Internal/External Fixation: Some fractures are treated with fixation, either internal or external, to maintain the alignment of the bone while it heals, or to reinforce the bone permanently. Internal fixation can be done with pins, screws, plates, or wires placed directly in the bone to immobilize it. External fixation is primarily on the outside of the body, and can include a cage-like structure, as well as pins and rods.

Approach: When coding orthopaedic surgeries, it is vital first to determine the approach—the method and direction the surgeon uses to access the part of the body that needs to be repaired. An approach can be from the front of the body (anterior), from the back (posterior), or from the side (lateral). An endoscopic or arthroscopic approach accesses a body area with a scope instrument.

Instrumentation: Used primarily in the spinal area to permanently align the vertebrae. Segmental instrumentation is defined as a spinal rod or device placed with three or more areas anchored by screws or wires. With non-segmental instrumentation, rods or wires are anchored at the top and bottom of the device only.

Sprain Nomenclature: A sprain or strain is the twisting or stretching of a joint in a way that causes pain and damage to a ligament. A sprain involves the non-contractile tissue (the ligament), and a strain involves the contractile tissue (muscle or tendon).

Scapula: The scapula is a flat, triangular-shaped bone on the dorsal thorax or back. The acromion is an extension of this bone that joins with the clavicle at the shoulder to form the acromioclavicular joint.

Fracture Eponyms: These often are named after the physician who first documented or described the fracture or the treatment. Common eponyms are:

Colles fracture: A fracture of the wrist at the distal radius. Sometimes the ulnar styloid also is involved.

Smith's fracture: Similar to a Colles fracture except the bones are displaced toward the palm.

Jones fracture: A stress fracture of the fifth metatarsal of the foot.

Salter-Harris fracture: An epiphyseal plate fracture; a common injury seen in children.

Dupuytren's fracture: Fracture of the distal fibula with rupture of the distal tibiofibular ligaments and lateral displacement of the talus.

Monteggia fracture: Fracture of the proximal third of the ulna with associated dislocation of the radial head.

Osteomyelitis: An inflammation of the bone and/or bone marrow caused by infection.

Curettage: Use of a curette to remove tissue by scraping.

Curette: A spoon-shaped instrument used to cut or scoop away (currettage) tissue.

Bunion Terms: A bunion, or hallux valgus, is the swelling and deformity of the metatarsophalangeal joint, usually at the base of the big toe. There are numerous ways to repair a bunion:

A *Silver* type procedure is a simple resection of the medial eminence of the metatarsal bone.

A *Keller, McBride,* or *Mayo* type procedure is a removal of the medial eminence of the metatarsal bone and the base of the proximal phalanx. Sometimes a wire holder or implant is used to stabilize the joint.

A *Joplin* procedure includes the transplant of the extensor tendon to the head of the metatarsal bone.

The *Mitchell* procedure is a double step-cut, biplanar osteotomy through the metatarsal bone.

The *Lapidus* type procedure is a fusion of the first metatarsal and first cuneiform joint, and the first and second metatarsal bases.

No Man's Land: The term for the fibrous sheath of the flexor tendons of the hand, specifically in the zone from the distal palmar crease to the proximal interphalangeal joint. Stiffness following injury is a common problem in this area.

Flexor: A muscle that causes flexion or bending of a limb or body part.

Extensor: A muscle that causes straightening of a limb or body part.

Adductor: A muscle that moves a part of the body towards the midline of the body.

Abductor: A muscle that moves a part of the body away from the midline of the body.

Polydactylous Digit: An extra digit on the hand or the foot. This digit may be soft tissue, or may contain bones and tendons.

Cheilectomy: Removal of a large portion of the dorsal metatarsal head and associated bone spurs.

ICD-9-CM Coding

Many of the codes in ICD-9-CM used for the musculoskeletal system are found in chapter 13: Diseases of the Musculoskeletal System and Connective Tissue. There are also numerous codes used from other chapters, including chapter 16: Symptoms Signs, and Ill-Defined Conditions, and chapter 17: Injury and Poisoning. Many codes in this section require a fifth digit.

The first conditions listed under Diseases of the Musculoskeletal System and Connective Tissue (710–719) are arthropathies and related disorders.

Systemic lupus erythematosus (710.0), or "lupus," is an autoimmune inflammatory connective tissue disease. It is most common in women, and the cause is unknown.

An arthropathy is a pathology or abnormality of a joint; arthritic conditions are classified in this section. Many of the arthropathy codes require use of another code first to specify an underlying disease. Rheumatoid arthritis (714.x) and osteoarthritis (715.xx) are listed here.

Also found in this classification are joint derangement codes, which include tears or damage to cartilage and ligaments. A common example is chronic bucket handle tear of the lateral meniscus, 717.41.

Dorsopathies (720–724) are disorders affecting the spinal column. The fourth digit classifies the type of disorder, and the fifth classifies the area of the spine. It is also important to note if the disorder is affecting the vertebrae or the intervertebral discs, because these are listed separately.

Rheumatism is a non-specific term for any painful disorder of the joints, muscles, or connective tissues.

Enthesopathies are disorders of peripheral ligamentous or muscular attachments. Synovitis and tenosynovitis (disorders of the synovium and/or tendons) are also listed here.

Bursitis is inflammation of the bursae, which are small fluid-filled sacs located between movable parts of the body, especially at the joints.

Osteopathies, chondropathies, and acquired musculoskeletal deformities (730–739) include codes for osteomyelitis (730.xx), osteoporosis (733.0x) and pathologic fractures (733.1x) (bone fractures caused by disease, not accident or injury).

The codes for hallux valgus, or bunion, can be found here (735.0). A congenital bunion would be coded from chapter 14: Congenital Anomalies (740–759).

How to Code Acute Vs. Chronic, Acute and Chronic

An acute condition is one of rapid onset with severe symptoms, and usually is of brief duration. A chronic condition develops and worsens over time. The acute condition is always listed first.

When a condition is documented as acute and chronic, select both codes if the sub terms in the ICD-9-CM index exist. If a sub term for "acute and chronic" is available, review that code in the Tabular List instead of reporting acute and chronic codes separately.

Coding Injuries

Closed fractures can be treated open and open fractures can be treated closed.

Fracture types are classified differently than fracture treatments. It is important to distinguish between the fracture type and the treatment type.

A closed fracture is one that has not broken the skin. The treatment for a closed fracture can be "closed," for example placing a cast, manipulating the bone without surgery, or applying traction to reduce the fracture. The treatment for a closed fracture can be "open," in which the fracture site is opened surgically to reduce the fracture, and pins, wires, screws, or plates are applied to stabilize the fracture.

An open fracture is one where the bone is protruding through the skin. The treatment for an open fracture may be an "open" treatment, in which surgery is required to re-align the bones, or "closed," in which traction is applied to re-align the bones and the wound is sutured.

Injuries are Usually the Cause of Compartment Syndrome

Compartment syndrome is the compression of nerves and blood vessels within an enclosed space. This leads to muscle and nerve damage, and problems with blood flow. To find compartment syndrome in ICD-9-CM Index to Diseases, look for Syndrome/compartment. Codes are grouped by cause (whether non-traumatic, post-surgical, or traumatic) and anatomical site.

Rotator Cuff Tears in Sports

The four muscles of the rotator cuff (supraspinatus, infraspinatus, subscapularis, and teres minor muscles) are attached to the scapula on the back through a single tendon unit. The rotator cuff holds the head of the humerus into the scapula at the shoulder. Chronic inflammation or injury can cause the tendons of the rotator cuff to tear.

If the rotator cuff is torn, surgery may be necessary. Arthroscopic surgery can remove bone spurs and inflamed tissue around the area. Small tears can be treated with arthroscopic surgery. Larger tears require open surgery to repair the torn tendon.

Physical therapy can help strengthen the muscles of the rotator cuff. If therapy is not possible because of pain, a steroid injection may reduce pain and inflammation enough to allow effective therapy.

Rotator cuff problems are indexed in ICD-9-CM by the type of problem: sprain, tear, or injury.

Toddlers Who Present with Nursemaid's Elbow

Nursemaid's elbow is a partial dislocation of the elbow, or proximal radial head dislocation. It is most common in small children, caused by a sudden pull on the child's arm or hand. It is found in ICD-9-CM under Nursemaid's/elbow.

Bone Fractures and Their Classification

A fracture is the traumatic or pathologic breaking of a bone or cartilage. ICD-9-CM usually classifies fractures as either open or closed.

Comminuted Fracture—The bone is crushed or splintered into several pieces.

Impacted Fracture—One part of a bone is forcefully driven into another.

Simple Fracture—The bone is broken in only one place.

Greenstick Fracture—The bone is broken on one surface and bent on the other (think of the way a "green" twig will break when bent too far); this fracture occurs in children before the bones have hardened.

Pathologic Fracture—Caused by disease, such as an infection or a tumor.

Compression Fracture—The bone is compressed onto another bone; caused by trauma or osteoporosis, and common in vertebrae.

Torus or Incomplete Fracture—One side of the bone buckles; mostly common in children because of their softer bones.

Further documentation in the medical record will aid code selection for the fracture (eg, pathological, compression, the site, etc.). Many fractures are listed as eponyms: Smith's fracture, deQuervain's fracture, Bennett's fracture, etc.

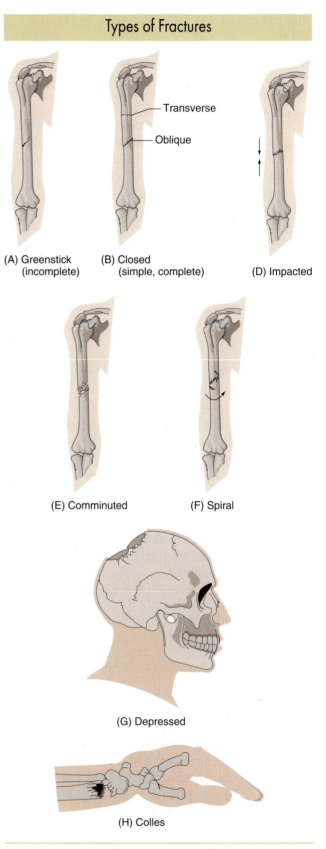

Types of Fractures

(A) Greenstick (incomplete)   (B) Closed (simple, complete)   (D) Impacted

— Transverse
— Oblique

(E) Comminuted   (F) Spiral

(G) Depressed

(H) Colles

Source: Delmar/Cengage Learning.

E Codes

E codes are used for supplementary classification of external causes of injury and poisoning. Many payers require E codes to explain how the patient was injured.

An index of the E codes is listed after the Table of Drugs and Chemicals. It is important to be as specific as possible when using these codes. Look carefully for the cause of the injury. Never select an E code as the first-listed diagnosis. E codes help payers determine liability. For example, if the injury is work related, the claim is paid by the worker's compensation carrier. Without an E code identifying a work-related injury, the claim may be denied inappropriately.

CPT® Coding

Codes 20005 to 29999 are specific to the musculoskeletal system; you also may select codes from the Radiology and Medicine sections to describe musculoskeletal services and procedures.

Wound exploration is listed first in the CPT® chapter on the Musculoskeletal System. Penetrating gunshot or stab wound trauma has its own category. The codes in this category are selected based on the anatomic site explored. Treatment includes the exploration and enlargement of the wound.

The next section covers excision and biopsy of muscle and bone. When coding excision procedures in the musculoskeletal system, carefully read the medical report to determine the depth of the wound or tissue excised. A muscle biopsy is considered superficial, for example, if it involves a muscle close to the surface of the skin; a deep biopsy involves underlying muscle.

Introduction or removal includes codes for injections, foreign body removal, and placement of catheters for radioelement application. Surgical injections involve direct insertion of a needle into a tendon, muscle, or joint for the aspiration of fluid and/or the administration of medication. When coding injections, watch for bundled procedures. For example, trigger point injections (20552–20553) are selected based on the number of muscles injected, not the number of injections performed.

Testing Technique

Highlight the number of muscles in the code descriptions for 20552 and 20553. Write a note that states "Select code according to number of muscles, not the number of injections."

An arthrocentesis of a joint includes the aspiration of fluid and/or the injection of an anesthetic agent and/or steroid. The codes are selected based on the size of the joint. When a joint aspiration and injection are performed on the same joint, only report the procedure once. If the procedures are performed on more than one joint, list each procedure separately.

Injection of a substance does not include the drug itself; the drug supply may be billed separately using a HCPCS Level II code.

Example:

The provider removes 3 cc of fluid from the left knee. He injects 40 mg of Kenalog into the right knee. The knee is a major joint. The proper codes are 20610-LT and 20610-RT for the procedures. The Kenalog is reported with HCPCS Level II code J3301 with four units because the code is for 10 mg.

Removal of foreign body procedures are coded by the depth of tissue the surgeon must incise to reach the foreign body.

External fixation codes are used when coding the stabilization of a fracture or protecting the skull, as in the application of a halo. Uniplane fixation is defined as pins, wires, rods or screws applied in one plane or direction, and multiplane fixation is the application of "hardware" in two or more planes or directions.

Replantation codes are used when the surgeon is replanting a digit or a limb after a complete amputation. If the digit or limb is amputated partially, use specific codes for repair of bones, ligaments, tendons, nerves, or blood vessels.

Grafts (or implant) codes are used when obtaining bone, cartilage, tendon or fascia lata grafts, or other tissue.

An autograft is a graft of tissue or bone harvested from the patient. In coding orthopaedic surgery, an autograft can be bone, cartilage, muscle or tendon. If the material being grafted is from a donor, it is known as an allograft. Bone grafting to stabilize the spine is common. Codes 20930–20938 report the grafting procedures, and usually are coded separately.

Testing Technique

If the procedure code description includes the harvesting of the graft, do not report the graft code separately. Add a notation in this section to indicate graft is only reported if not include in the procedure note description. For example, 21194 includes obtaining the graft.

The next few sections of the CPT® book are listed anatomically. The first of these anatomical sections is the head. This area includes procedures on the skull, facial bones, and temporomandibular joint (TMJ).

TMJ is the "hinge" of the jaw between the mandible and temporal bones. There are many procedures listed in CPT® for repair, reconstruction, and manipulation of this joint. The most common problem is displacement of the articular disc, which can require manipulation or reconstruction. An arthrotomy of the TMJ is coded with 21010; codes 21050–21070 and 21240–21243 are other reconstructive surgical procedures. Treatment of a TMJ dislocation is coded with 21480, 21485 or 21490, depending on whether the surgery is open or closed.

The vertical part of the lower jaw extends from the TMJ to the angle where it curves into the mandibular body, called the mandibular rami. Surgery on the mandibular rami is performed for reconstruction after a fracture, or to move the lower part of the jaw forward or back to correct an orthognathic defect. CPT® codes for reconstruction of the mandibular rami are 21193–21196. If a bone graft is performed, it is included with 21194.

The spine is divided into three main sections: the cervical spine, the thoracic spine, and the lumbar spine.

A vertebral segment describes the basic constituent part into which the spine may be divided. It represents a single complete vertebral bone with its associated articular processes and laminae. A vertebral interspace is the non-bony compartment between two adjacent vertebral bodies that contains the intervertebral disc, and includes the nucleus pulposus, annulus fibrosus, and two cartilagenous endplates.

Spinal surgery often requires the skills of more than one surgeon. When these surgeons work together as primary surgeons performing a portion of the same procedure, modifier 62 should be appended to report the service. Each surgeon dictates an operative report for his or herr portion of the surgery, and each surgeon reports the same code with modifier 62.

Spinal instrumentation codes are add-on codes; they are to be coded in addition to the primary surgery (eg, arthrodesis 22800–22812).

Diagnostic arthroscopy is always included in a therapeutic or surgical arthroscopy.

When coding an injection of contrast material for an X-ray of a joint (arthrography), use the code for the injection in addition to the code for the radiologic service itself.

During mosaicplasty, cylindrical osteochondral (bone and cartilage) grafts are removed from a donor site and transplanted to holes prepared at the recipient site. A mosaicplasty is coded with CPT® 27416 if performed via an open incision; if performed via arthroscopy, use 29866 or 29867. Mosaicplasty includes harvesting of the bone and cartilage.

Arthrodesis is the surgical immobilization of a joint, which is intended to result in bone fusion. This procedure is often documented in the operative note as a fusion. A physician may implant pins, plates, screws, wires, or rods to position the bones together until they fuse. Bone grafts may be needed if there is significant bone loss. When selecting codes for spinal arthrodesis, you need to know the approach (anterior, posterior, posterolateral or lateral transverse). You also need to know the vertebral segment (cervical, thoracic or lumbar).

Disarticulation is the separation of two bones at the joint, either traumatically or by surgical amputation. CPT® has codes for disarticulation of the ankle, hip, knee, and wrist. Shoulder disarticulation is coded with

23920 or 23921, depending on whether it is the initial surgery, or a secondary closure or scar revision.

There are three compartments in the knee: medial, lateral, and patellofemoral. When coding surgeries on the knee joint, each compartment is considered a separate area.

CPT® usually defines compartments in the shoulder as anterior or posterior. The American Academy of Orthopaedic Surgeons (AAOS) recognizes three "areas" or "regions" of the shoulder: the glenohumeral joint, the acromioclavicular joint, and the subacromial bursal space. These "areas" are clearly separate; procedures performed in one area should not influence coding in a different area.

Fracture code selection is based on type of treatment (open or closed), whether manipulation is performed and, in some cases, the use of internal fixation.

Test Technique

Highlight key words in the fracture care codes, such as "with manipulation," "without manipulation" and "with internal fixation."

"Articular" refers to a moveable joint. When a code refers to a fracture that is "extra-articular," the fracture does not extend into the joint. "Intra-articular" refers to a fracture that extends into the joint. In certain fracture coding subsections, these key words are important for proper code selection. For example, one of the differences between codes 25607 and 25608 is whether the distal radial fracture is extra-articular or intra-articular.

Non-union or malunion of a fracture occurs when a fracture does not heal properly. Surgery to correct this problem is not coded with fracture codes; use codes from Repair, Revision, and/or Reconstruction. For a nonunion/malunion of the femur, there are codes for repairing the defect with a graft (27472) or without a graft (27470).

The term "radical," when referring to surgery of the musculoskeletal system, is used to describe removal of an extensive area of tissue surrounding an area of infection or malignancy. For example, 21620 *Ostectomy*

of sternum, partial reports the removal of a portion of the sternum, and 21630 *Radical resection of sternum* is reported for excision of most or all of the sternum and some of the surrounding tissue.

When a physician reports a treatment of a fracture and then applies a cast or strapping, the cast or strapping is included in the procedure. A physician may code for a cast or strapping when the cast or strapping is the only treatment given at the first visit and no surgical treatment is planned. Each replacement cast or strapping can be reported.

Modifier 58 is reported with a cast or strapping procedure performed in the post-operative period. The removal of a cast or strapping is not reported separately unless the service is provided by a physician who did not apply the cast.

A bunion is also known as a *hallux valgus* deformity. There are many types of surgeries described in CPT® for repair of a bunion. Pins, rods, wires, and/or screws are used to stabilize the bones of the foot. Removal of the pins after the bones have healed is coded separately.

HCPCS Level II

HCPCS Level II L codes are for orthotic and prosthetic procedures and supplies. Many HCPCS Level II E codes are also used with musculoskeletal and orthopaedic services, such as canes, crutches, walkers, traction devices, wheelchairs, and other orthopaedic devices. Some physicians will provide basic orthopaedic supplies, but most of them are supplied by a durable medical equipment (DME) provider fulfilling the physician's order. J codes are used to report the supply of medications given by injection, IV, or intrathecally.

Modifiers

Modifiers often are used in orthopaedic surgery to indicate on which side of the body the surgery was performed; which finger or toe was repaired; or to show identical procedures were performed on both sides of the body. These modifiers are critical to indicate a procedure was performed twice, or to a certain part of the body, so the payer won't inappropriately deny the claim as a duplicate or bundled procedure.

The most common modifiers used in orthopaedic surgery are:

50 *Bilateral procedure*—Before using this modifier, consult with the payer. Some payers prefer RT and LT instead of modifier 50.

54 *Surgical care only*

57 *Decision for surgery*

58 *Staged or related procedure or service by the same physician during the postoperative period*—This modifier is used when a physician performs an additional procedure(s) that was planned or related to the initial procedure. This often happens in the case of staged, reconstructive surgeries, and a second or third surgery must be performed (eg, cleft lip and palate surgery or removal of hardware after stabilization of a fracture).

59 *Distinct procedural service*—This modifier is used to indicate a service should not be considered a bundled service when it normally might be bundled (eg, service performed on a repair of a laceration in the foot and a treatment of a fracture of the distal radius).

62 *Two surgeons*—This modifier is used when two surgeons work together to perform distinct portions of the same service (using the same CPT® code), this modifier is appended.

66 *Surgical team*—This modifier is used when a surgical team (three or more surgeons) is required for complex procedures (for example, some spine surgeries or complicated repairs).

78 *Unplanned return to the operating/procedure room by the same physician following initial procedure for a related procedure during the postoperative period (complication).*

80 *Assistant surgeon*—Modifier AS is used for a surgical assistant who is a physician assistant.

LT *Left side of the body*

RT *Right side of the body*

FA *Left hand, thumb*

F1 *Left hand, second digit*

F2 *Left hand, third digit*

F3 *Left hand, fourth digit*

F4 *Left hand, fifth digit*

F5 *Right hand, thumb*

F6 *Right hand, second digit*

F7 *Right hand, third digit*

F8 *Right hand, fourth digit*

F9 *Right hand, fifth digit*

TA *Left foot, great toe*

T1 *Left foot, second digit*

T2 *Left foot, third digit*

T3 *Left foot, fourth digit*

T4 *Left foot, fifth digit*

T5 *Right foot, great toe*

T6 *Right foot, second digit*

T7 *Right foot, third digit*

T8 *Right foot, fourth digit*

T9 *Right foot, fifth digit*

Chapter Review Questions

1. **Muscle is attached to bone by what method?**

   A. Tendons, ligaments, and directly to bone

   B. Tendons and aponeuroses

   C. Tendons, aponeuroses and directly to bone

   D. Tendons, ligaments, aponeuroses, and directly to bone

2. **What is affected by myasthenia gravis?**

   A. Neuromuscular junction

   B. Muscle belly

   C. Muscle/bone connection

   D. Bone

3. **A patient is given Xylocaine, a local anesthetic, by injection into the thigh above the site to be biopsied. A small bore needle is then introduced through the skin into the muscle, about 3 inches deep, and a muscle biopsy is taken. What is the CPT® code for this service?**

   A. 20205

   B. 20206

   C. 20225

   D. 27324

4. **This 45-year-old male presents to the operating room with a painful mass of the right upper arm. General anesthesia is induced. Soft tissue dissection is carried down through the proximal aspect of the teres minor. Upon further dissection a large mass is noted just distal of the IGHL, which appears to be benign in nature. With blunt dissection and electrocautery, the 4 cm mass is removed en bloc and sent to pathology. Wound is irrigated, repair of the teres minor with subcutaneous tissue is then closed with triple-0 Vicryl. Skin is closed with double-0 Prolene in a subcuticular fashion. What is the correct CPT® code for this service?**

   A. 23076-RT

   B. 23066-RT

   C. 23075-RT

   D. 11406-RT

5. The patient has a torn medial meniscus. An arthroscope was placed through the anterolateral portal for the diagnostic procedure. The patellofemoral joint showed some grade 2 chondromalacia on the patella side of the joint only, and this was debrided with the 4.0 mm shaver. The medial compartment was also entered and a complex posterior horn tear of the medial meniscus was noted. It was probed to define its borders. A meniscectomy was carried out back to a stable rim. Select the appropriate CPT® code(s) for this service.

   A. 29880, 29879-59

   B. 29881, 29877-59

   C. 29880

   D. 29881

6. A 3-year-old is brought into the ER crying. He cannot bend his left arm after his older brother pulled it. The physician looks at the X-ray and makes a diagnosis of dislocated nursemaid's elbow. The ER physician reduces the elbow successfully. The patient is able to move his arm again. The patient is referred to an orthopaedist for follow-up care. What CPT® and ICD-9-CM codes should be reported?

   A. 24640-54, 832.2, E927.0

   B. 24565-54, 832.2, E929.8

   C. 24640-54, 832.10, E927.0

   D. 24600-54, 832.00, E928.8

7. A 50-year-old male had surgery on his upper leg one day ago and is presenting with serous drainage from the wound. He is scheduled back to the operating room for an evaluation of the hematoma. His wound is explored and there is a hematoma at the base of the wound, which is very carefully evacuated, and the wound irrigated with antibacterial solution. The correct CPT® and ICD-9-CM codes are?

   A. 10140-79, 998.12

   B. 27603-78, 998.59

   C. 10140-76, 998.9

   D. 27301-78, 998.12

8. A 45-year-old presents to the operating room with a right index trigger finger and left shoulder bursitis. The left shoulder is injected with 1 cc of Xylocaine, 1 cc of Celestone, and 1 cc of Marcaine. An incision was made over the A1 pulley in the right distal transverse palmar crease, about an inch in length. This is taken through skin and subcutaneous tissue. The A1 pulley is identified and released in its entirety. The wound is irrigated with antibiotic saline solution. The subcutaneous tissue is injected with Marcaine without epinephrine. The skin is closed with 4-0 Ethilon suture. Clean dressing is applied. What are the codes for these procedures?

   A. 26055-F6, 20610-76-LT

   B. 20552-F6, 20605-52-LT

   C. 26055-F6, 20610-51-LT

   D. 20553-F6, 20610-59-LT

9. **Operative Report**

Preoperative Diagnosis: Unstable left distal radius fracture.

Postoperative Diagnosis: Unstable left distal radius fracture.

Procedure: Closed reduction and percutaneous pinning with manipulation of left distal radius fracture.

Anesthesia: General

Indications: Patient is a very pleasant 14-year-old young man who is here for evaluation. I had seen him in clinic earlier today and he had a bike wreck with an unstable distal radial ulnar joint and unstable fracture. I discussed with him and his mother, preoperatively, the risks and benefits, and they wish to proceed with surgery.

Description of Procedure: The patient was brought to the operating room and placed in the supine position on the operating table. General anesthesia was induced. Antibiotics were given preoperatively. The left arm was prepped and draped in the usual standard orthopaedic fashion. Landmarks were identified; closed reduction maneuver was performed with traction and reproduction of the deformity and then reduction. A near anatomic reduction was afforded, visualized with multiplanar C-arm fluoroscopic imaging. I then placed two 6.2 K-wires percutaneously, one through the radial styloid and one through the Lister's tubercle, which gave us adjunctive fixation of this manipulated fracture. Multiplanar C-arm fluoroscopic imaging confirmed good placement of the implants and a near anatomic reduction. A sterile dressing and sugar-tong splint was applied. The patient was awakened from anesthesia and taken to the Recovery Room in stable condition postoperatively. There were no operative complications. Estimated blood loss was minimal. All counts were correct.

What are the CPT® and ICD-9-CM codes for this procedure?

10. **Operative Report:**

Preoperative Diagnosis: Right clavicle retained deep hardware.

Postoperative Diagnosis: Right clavicle retained deep hardware.

Procedure Performed: Removal of hardware, clavicle, deep.

Anesthesia: General.

Indications for Procedure: The patient had a previous clavicle ORIF and is now here for hardware removal from symptomatic problems. We discussed the above-mentioned surgery, along with the potential risks and complications, and the patient understood and wished to proceed.

Description of Procedure: The patient was taken to the operating suite and placed on the operating table in supine position. He was administered preoperative antibiotics, general anesthetic followed by intubation by the anesthesia team. Extremity was positioned, prepped and draped in typical sterile fashion. The previous incision was re-opened down to the clavicle. The plate was found where it was freed up both medially and laterally. All the screws were removed, including the interfrag screws. Plate was taken out. We then used a rongeur to clean up the edges of the soft tissue. There were no prominent bone areas. We then irrigated the wound thoroughly, closed the deep tissue with 2-0 Vicryl, followed by closure of the superficial layer using 2-0 Monocryl and a running 3-0 Monocryl stitch. Sterile dressing was placed. A 0.25% Marcaine with epinephrine was injected around the incision site. A sterile dressing was placed. The patient was awakened and taken to the recovery room in stable condition.

What are the CPT® and ICD-9-CM codes for this procedure?

Chapter 7

Respiratory, Hemic, Lymphatic, Mediastinum, and Diaphragm

Introduction

This chapter reviews CPT®, ICD-9-CM, and HCPCS Level II coding for the respiratory system, the hemic and lymphatic systems, and the mediastinum and diaphragm. Objectives for this chapter include:

◖ Highlight basic anatomy and functions relevant to these systems

◖ Define key terms

◖ Provide practical advice to apply CPT® codes and modifiers relevant to these systems

◖ Review common diagnoses

◖ Introduce HCPCS Level II codes and coding guidelines as they apply to these systems

Anatomy and Medical Terminology

The Respiratory System

The human respiratory system begins with air entering the nostrils. The cilia are microscopic filaments bathed in nasal mucus that cover the inside surface of the nose. A sticky layer of mucus and the cilia draws particles to the back of the throat, into the esophagus for swallowing.

The larynx (voice box) connects the pharynx with the trachea. The larynx is formed by nine cartilages connected by muscles and ligaments. The epiglottis covers the larynx to protect the trachea from inhaled food or liquid. The larynx also contains vocal cords separated by a triangular opening, called the glottis, through which air flows. The hyoid bone provides attachment to the muscles of the floor of the mouth and the tongue above, the larynx below, and the epiglottis and pharynx behind.

The trachea (windpipe) connects the nose and mouth to the lungs. If the epiglottis fails to cover the larynx, and food or liquid enter the trachea, the body's natural defense is to cough. For boys, the largest cartilage of the larynx, the thyroid cartilage, grows larger and protrudes at the bottom of the throat. This is the "Adam's Apple."

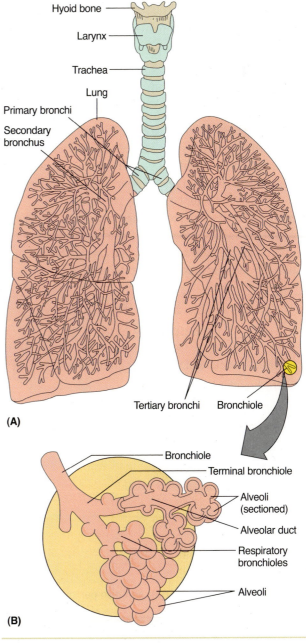

Trachea, Bronchi, and Bronchioles

(A)

Hyoid bone
Larynx
Trachea
Lung
Primary bronchi
Secondary bronchus
Tertiary bronchi
Bronchiole

(B)

Bronchiole
Terminal bronchiole
Alveoli (sectioned)
Alveolar duct
Respiratory bronchioles
Alveoli

Source: Delmar/Cengage Learning.

The trachea branches into the right and left bronchi. The carina is the ridge that separates the opening of the right and left bronchi. The right bronchus branches into three bronchi that provide airways to the three lobes of the right lung. The left bronchus branches into two bronchi to the two lobes of the left lung. The lobar bronchi branch into tertiary or segmental bronchi, and into smaller bronchioles. Bronchioles branch into alveolar ducts and sacs. The alveoli, or air sacs, are the primary units for the exchange of oxygen and carbon dioxide in the lungs. The exchange occurs by diffusion across the alveoli and the walls of the capillaries that surrounds the alveoli.

The lungs are located in the thoracic cavity. The right lung is divided into three lobes and the left lung is divided into two lobes. The lobes are divided by fissures. The individual lobes are divided further into segments and lobules.

The lungs are protected by the pleura, a dual-layered serous membrane. The space between the pleural layers is the pleural cavity. It contains pleural fluid that allows the membranes to slide past one another as the lungs expand and contract. The outer layer of the pleural (parietal pleura) attaches the lung to the chest wall. The inner pleura (visceral pleura) cover the lungs. There is no connection between the right and left pleural cavities; disease or trauma to one lung may not affect the other lung.

Key Roots, Suffixes, Prefixes for the Respiratory System

---

centesis—puncture of a cavity or organ to remove fluid

pnea—breathing

peri—surrounding

phonia—voice

rhino/naso—nose

broncho/bronchi—bronchus

pharyngo—pharynx

trachea—trachea

pleura—pleura

pulmono/pulmo—lung

phreno—diaphragm

pneumo/pneumato—air, gas; can also pertain to lung, respiration

spiro—breathing

Mediastinum and Diaphragm

The mediastinum is the space containing the heart, aorta, esophagus, trachea, and thymus gland, as well as blood vessels and nerves.

The diaphragm is a muscle that divides the thoracic (chest) cavity from the abdominal cavity. Inhalation occurs when the diaphragm contracts or moves down: Air pressure in the thoracic cavity is reduced, allowing air to flow into the lungs. During exhalation, the diaphragm is relaxed and pushes air out of the chest.

Contraction of the external and internal intercostal muscles of the rib cage elevate the ribs and push the sternum forward to increase the diameter of the thoracic cavity. These muscles are necessary for respiration. The parasternal, scalene, sternocleidomastoid, trapezius, and pectoral muscles are engaged typically only when a respiratory disorder—such as chronic obstructive pulmonary disease (COPD) or asthma—is present.

The Hemic and Lymphatic Systems

The hemic system pertains to the production of blood. The primary structures of the hemic system are the spleen (which is also a component of the lymphatic system) and bone marrow.

The spleen is located in the upper-left quadrant of the abdomen, and serves several functions:

- Creates and stores new red blood cells
- Phagocytizes (leukocytes eat/destroy) bacteria and worn-out platelets and red blood cells
- Holds a reserve of blood in case of hemorrhagic shock
- Recycles iron
- Synthesizes antibodies
- Holds in reserve monocytes and other bodies crucial to immune and restorative function

Bone marrow is the flexible tissue found in the center of many bones, primarily in the cancellous tissue of the ribs, vertebrae, sternum, and bones of the pelvis. It produces the majority of red blood cells (for oxygen distribution), most white blood cells (for immune function), and platelets (for blood clotting, among other functions). Bone marrow also contains so-called "stem cells" that can develop into several cell types.

Lymph nodes are glands located throughout the body. There are aggregations of lymph nodes in the neck, under the arms, and in the groin. Lymph nodes filter the lymph fluid to remove harmful bacteria, viruses, and other foreign material. The lymphatic system includes four organs: the spleen, tonsils, thymus gland, and Peyer's patches. The tonsils are immune tissue located on the back of the throat, one per side. They are an initial "line of defense" against inhaled or ingested pathogens, and as such are a common site of infection (especially in children). The thymus is located in the mediastinum. It is responsible for the production of T cells, which are crucial to function of the adaptive immune system. The thymus also plays a role in autoimmunity (preventing the body from attacking its own tissue). Peyer's patches are found in the wall of the small intestine. Bacteria are always present in large numbers in the intestine, and the macrophages in Peyer's patches prevent the bacteria from infecting and penetrating the walls of the intestine.

ICD-9-CM Coding

The Respiratory System

ICD-9-CM contains a dedicated chapter for the respiratory system, although relevant codes may be found outside this range. As always, begin your search for a diagnosis code from the index, and verify code selection using the Tabular List.

Acute Respiratory Infections (460–466)

Infection may be caused by a virus or bacteria. Viral infections usually are self-limiting. Bacterial acute respiratory infections (ARIs) typically are treated with antibiotics (viral infections are not). ICD-9-CM codes for ARIs are separated by the anatomy: nose, pharynx, larynx, bronchus, and bronchioles.

Laryngitis is caused by irritation and inflammation of the vocal cords. Codes for acute laryngitis describe with obstruction (464.01) or without obstruction (464.00).

Croup (464.4) is a common, high-pitched, barking cough found in infants and children with nasal-type symptoms. Croup usually is caused by parainfluenza viruses; however, respiratory syncytial virus (RSV), measles, adenovirus, and influenza all can cause croup.

A milder form of croup, stridulous croup, also known as laryngismus stridulous or false croup, is a sudden onset of spasmodic laryngeal closure with crowing inspiration. RSV (466.11) is the leading cause of respiratory infections in children. Bronchitis (466.0) and bronchiolitis (466.11, 466.19) commonly are diagnosed when a patient presents with symptoms of a severe and/or productive cough.

Other Disease of the Upper Respiratory System (470–478)

Most codes in this section pertain to chronic conditions and include code 470 for an acquired deviated septum of the nose. This condition is commonly caused by trauma. The septum is the bone and cartilage that separates the right and left nostrils. Note the congenital code for deviated septum is 754.0. Nasal polyps (471.0–471.9) are sac-like growths inside the nose and are often associated with chronic sinusitis (473.0–473.9). Code selection will depend on which sinus is infected and inflamed.

Pneumonia and Influenza (480–488)

Pneumonia, like ARI, can be caused by a virus, fungi, or bacteria. An acute respiratory infection can lead to pneumonia if not treated. ICD-9-CM codes for pneumonia are based on the causative agent, and may require you to report an additional code to describe the underlying disease.

Influenza is a viral infection that can be very serious. ICD-9-CM coding is based on the influenza strain: Avian (488.0x), H1N1 (488.1x), or unspecified with pneumonia or other respiratory manifestations (487.x). Code only confirmed cases of avian flu (see Coding Guidelines 1.C.8.d in the ICD-9-CM codebook).

Chronic Obstructive Pulmonary Disease and Allied Conditions (490–496)

Chronic obstructive pulmonary disease (COPD) is a progressive disease that causes coughing, wheezing, shortness of breath, and difficulty breathing. The number one cause of COPD is smoking. According to ICD-9-CM Coding Guidelines (1.C.8), when the patient has conditions related to COPD, those conditions determine which ICD-9-CM codes are appropriate.

Asthma associated with COPD is reported using one of the following:

- 493.20 Chronic obstructive asthma
- 493.21 Chronic obstructive asthma with status asthmaticus
- 493.22 Chronic obstructive asthma with (acute) exacerbation

Acute exacerbation of asthma is an increase in the severity of symptoms, such as wheezing and shortness of breath. Status asthmaticus means the patient fails to respond to therapy during an asthmatic episode; this is a life-threatening complication. If the provider documents status asthmaticus with any type of COPD, list 493.21 as the first diagnosis. A status asthmaticus diagnosis supersedes any type of COPD, including COPD with acute exacerbation or acute bronchitis (see Coding Guidelines 1.C.8.a.4 in the ICD-9-CM codebook).

Testing Technique

Highlight guideline 1.C.8.a.4 in your ICD-9-CM codebook: Acute exacerbation of asthma and status asthmaticus.

Bronchitis (chronic 491.9, acute 466.0) also is commonly associated with COPD. If the provider documents both COPD and acute bronchitis, report 491.22 *Obstructive chronic bronchitis, with (acute) bronchitis*. For acute bronchitis with COPD causing an acute exacerbation, the bronchitis supersedes the exacerbation and you should report 491.22. If documentation states the patient has COPD with acute exacerbation, but doesn't mention acute bronchitis, report 491.21 *Obstructive chronic bronchitis, with (acute) exacerbation* (see Coding Guidelines 1.C.8.b.1).

Testing Technique

Highlight guideline 1.C.8.b.1: Acute bronchitis with COPD in your Official ICD-9-CM Guidelines for Coding and Reporting.

If the provider diagnoses COPD without associated manifestations or conditions (chronic bronchitis or emphysema), report COPD alone using 496 *Chronic airway obstruction, not elsewhere classified*. Whenever possible, avoid assigning an unspecified code.

In emphysema (reported alone using 492.0, 492.8), the walls between the air sacs are damaged, causing them to lose their shape and elasticity. Most people who have COPD have both emphysema and chronic obstructive bronchitis. Mediastinal emphysema is reported with code 518.1.

Pneumoconiosis and Other Lung Diseases Due to External Agents (500–508)

Pneumoconiosis (500–505) is a restrictive lung disease caused by inhalation of dust, causing irreversible scarring of the lungs. Other ICD-9-CM codes in this section include exposure to chemicals such as fumes, vapors, solids, and liquids.

Other Diseases of the Respiratory System:

Empyema (510.0, 510.9) is collection of pus between the lung and the lining of the lung. It is caused by a lung infection that spreads to the pleural space. Pleurisy (511.0–511.9) is an inflammation of the pleura, and also is caused by a lung infection such as pneumonia or tuberculosis.

Pneumothorax (512.0–512.89) is the collapse of the lung. Spontaneous tension pneumothorax (512.0) has no traumatic cause. Pneumothorax also can occur postoperatively (512.1); this may be referred to as iatrogenic pneumothorax. Traumatic pneumothorax is not coded in this section; it is found in the injury section and is coded with 860.0–860.5.

Interstitial lung disease (ILD), or diffuse parenchymal lung disease (DPLD), refers to a group of lung diseases affecting the interstitium (the tissue and space around the air sacs of the lungs). ILD (515) often is the result of pulmonary fibrosis from exposure to contaminants like asbestos.

Pulmonary edema is indexed in ICD-9-CM as "Edema, lung." Many codes are available, ranging from 514 *Chronic pulmonary edema* to 518.4 *Acute pulmonary edema*.

Cystic fibrosis (subcategory 277.0) is a genetic disease that causes sticky mucus to build up in the lungs and digestive tract. The code is listed in the Immunity Disorders section of ICD-9-CM. An additional code to identify any infectious organism should also be reported.

Symptoms, V Codes

When a definitive diagnosis cannot be coded, it is appropriate to code symptoms. This excludes symptoms that are an integral part of the disease process. Signs and symptoms not typically associated with a disease process may be reported separately. Chapter 16: Symptoms, Signs, and Ill-Defined Conditions (780–799) contains many codes for symptoms. For example, respiratory system symptom codes 786.00–786.4 describe symptoms such as shortness of breath, wheezing, and cough.

V codes may be reported for personal or family history of conditions of respiratory disease. These codes should not be used as the primary code, but can be used as a supplementary code. Screenings and status codes are also found among the V codes. As an example, code V81.3 is the special screening for chronic bronchitis and emphysema.

Mediastinum and Diaphragm

Herniation of the diaphragm can occur due to weakening and is reported using 553.3. If herniation is due to a congenital or gross defect of the diaphragm, report 756.6. Diaphragmatic hernia with obstruction is reported with 552.3.

With bilateral diaphragmatic paralysis (519.4), respiration accessory muscles assume some or all of the work of breathing by contracting more intensely. If the paralysis is due to severance of the phrenic nerve during a procedure, report 998.2.

Thymic hyperplasia (254.0) is abnormal growth of the thymus gland. Thymoma is a benign (212.6) or malignant (164.0) tumor in the thymus.

Hemic and Lymphatic Systems

Lymphoma (200.0–202.9) is a cancer of the lymphatic system, which can spread to the bone marrow.

Lymphadenitis (289.1–289.3) is an infection of a lymph node, often associated with bacterial disease.

Lymphedema (acquired 457.0, 457.1, or congenital 757.0) is lymphatic system obstruction, which leads to localized fluid retention and tissue swelling. Left untreated, lymphedema may cause severe deformity.

Disorders involving the immune mechanism are coded to category 279. Lymphoproliferative disorders pertain to several disorders that are marked by increased lymphocyte production. Typically, these disorders occur in patients with suppressed immune systems; examples include autoimmune lymphoproliferative syndrome (ALPS) (279.41) and Wiskott-Aldrich syndrome (279.12).

Hypersplenism (289.4) describes an enlarged, overactive spleen. This can cause a decrease in the blood cells circulating throughout the body.

Splenic rupture has several codes, depending on the cause. Code 767.8 is assigned for rupture during birth; 865.04 and 865.14 are for traumatic ruptures. For all other causes, assign 289.59.

The most familiar disease of the blood and bone marrow is leukemia; leukemia is a broad term encompassing a number of disorders. It is a form of cancer characterized by an abnormal increase of (usually white) blood cells. Codes for leukemia are found in code range 203–208. All codes in this section require a fifth-digit classification:

- 0—Without mention of having achieved remission or failed remission
- 1—In remission
- 2—In relapse

Review and carefully apply all "includes" and "excludes" notes that accompany categories 203–208. These will assist you greatly when assigning a code.

CPT® Coding

Respiratory System

Nose

Rhinotomy codes report draining an abscess in the nasal cavity (30000) or on the nasal septum (30020).

Excisional codes include biopsy, and the removal of lesions, cysts, and/or polyps. Follow CPT® parenthetical instructions to help you differentiate among the codes. For example, a parenthetical reference instructs that simple excision of nasal polyp (30110) normally would be completed in an office; whereas extensive excision of a nasal polyp (30115) normally would require the facilities available in a hospital. Codes differ for excision of intranasal lesion (30117–30118) based on the approach and dermoid cyst (30124–30125) based on whether it is simple or complex.

Testing Technique

Highlight parenthetical instructions. Overlooking these instructions may cause incorrect code selection.

Turbinates are bony structures in the nose. There are three turbinates on each side of the nose: superior, middle, and inferior. These may become swollen and require surgery to restore airflow. Methods to reduce the turbinates include excision (30130–30140) or ablation (30801–30802). Sometimes, the superior or middle turbinate are excised. In this instance, 30999 would be appropriate based on CPT® parenthetical instructions.

If a rhinectomy—total (30160) or partial (30150) removal of the nose—is performed, closure or reconstruction can be coded from the skin/repair section of CPT®. A bone graft (20900–20912) may also be reported separately if performed.

Codes 30300–30320 report the removal of a foreign body from the nasal cavity; 30300 describes removal of a foreign body from a single nostril and is typically performed in an office setting. More invasive procedures are 30310, requiring general anesthesia and 30320,

requiring the nostril be incised or cut to remove the foreign body.

Rhinoplasty (repair) procedures may be medically necessary when a patient has difficulty breathing through the nose. Septoplasty often is performed for a (congenital or traumatic) deviated septum. Vestibular stenosis is a narrowing of the nasal inlet resulting in airway obstruction; repair may be reported with 30465. Note that 30465 is bilateral, and applies to procedures performed on both sides of the nose. If it is performed unilateraly, modifier 52 is appended to 30465. Choanal atresia is a congenital disorder where the back of the nasal passage (choana) is blocked by abnormal tissue. Repair of this condition may be performed by intranasal (30540) or transpalatine (30545) approach. Intranasal synechiae are lesions, often resulting from trauma or prior surgery. These lesions may be lysed (destroyed), as reported with 30560.

Control-of-nosebleeds codes can be found in the "Other Procedures" section. Nosebleeds typically are unilateral and the use of RT or LT modifier would be appropriate. A bilateral nosebleed will require the addition of modifier 50 as indicated in the parenthetical instructions. Fracture of inferior turbinates may be performed as a therapeutic procedure to reduce the turbinates and improve airflow through the nose. This is reported as 30930; do not report 30930 in addition to excision (30130) or resection (30140) of inferior turbinates. For fracture of the superior or middle turbinates, report 30999.

Accessory Sinuses

There are four pairs of sinuses in the respiratory system, located in and around the nasal-oral cavities. Incisional procedures (sinustomy) can be obliterative or non-obliterative. Obliterative procedures are a radical treatment for chronic conditions of the sinuses. The entire mucosa of the sinus is removed and the sinus is filled with "fat," typically taken from the patient's own belly or thigh. Non-obliterative procedures preserve the cavity. Coders must choose the correct sinus and approach. Approach can be from the front or transorbital (through the eye).

Sinuses

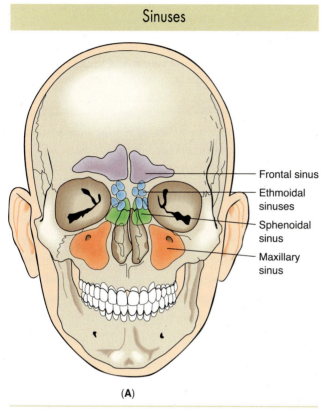

(A)

Source: Delmar/Cengage Learning.

Codes 31231–31235 describe diagnostic endoscopies; these "refer to employing a nasal/sinus endoscope to inspect the interior of the nasal cavity and the middle and superior meatus, the turbinates, and the spheno-ethmoid recess. Any time a diagnostic evaluation is performed, all the areas would be inspected and a separate code is not reported for each area," according to CPT®. **Diagnostic endoscopy always is included in surgical endoscopy.**

Codes 31237–31297 describe surgical endoscopies to treat an already diagnosed condition. CPT® provides extensive parenthetical instruction in this section. Read and apply these guidelines carefully. The endoscope may be used for biopsy, polypectomy, or debridement (31237), or for more extensive procedures ranging from control of hemorrhage (31238) to ethmoidectomy (31254–31255), and more. Highlights in this section include:

● Dacryocystorhinostomy (31239) restores the flow of tears into the nose from the lacrimal sac when the nasolacrimal duct does not function.

● Concha bullosa is enlargement of the nasal turbinate; it may be resected (31240) to improve airflow.

● Maxillary antrostomy (31256) involves making an opening in the maxillary sinus to improve drainage.

● Sphenoidotomy (31288) is the creation of an opening into the anterior (front) wall of the sphenoid sinus.

● Decompression (31292–31294), depending on the structure(s) treated, relieves pressure on the optic nerve or other structures of the eye, to treat a various optic neuropathies.

Larynx

Laryngotomy (31300) is an incision **into** the larynx to remove a tumor. Laryngectomy is excision **of** the larynx, and may be total (31360–31365), subtotal (31367–31368), or partial (31370–31382). Watch for related procedures, such as neck dissection, when selecting a code. Radical neck dissection is the removal of not only the larynx but also the lymph glands and/or surrounding tissue. This is to ensure all cancerous tissue is removed. For partial laryngectomy, the surgical approach (eg, laterovertical vs. anterovertical) affects code selection.

Pharyngolaryngectomy is removal of the pharynx and larynx. For procedures with reconstruction, report 31395; and without reconstruction, report 31390. Arytenoidectomy is the excision of laryngeal cartilage to which the vocal cords attach. Code 31400 is used to report an open arytenoidectomy; code 31560 is used to report the endoscopic procedure.

Code 31500 describes emergency endotracheal intubation, which may be performed for maxillofacial injuries, acute inflammation of the head or neck, or severe facial burns. Tracheostomies also may be performed when there is need for long-term mechanical ventilation, such as for a comatose patient.

Tracheotomy tube placement involves a fistula tract from the skin of the anterior neck to the trachea. If the tracheotomy tube must be changed before the tract is established fully (usually after about seven days), report 31502. Any tube changes after the tract is established cannot be billed and become a component of the appropriate E/M service billed for the visit. A planned tracheostomy (31600) is a "separate procedure" that usually should not be billed if performed at the same time as a more extensive, related procedure. Planned tracheostomies on children under age two should be reported using 31601. Codes 31603 and 31605, which differ according to the area of access, are reported rarely because of the risk involved.

Indirect laryngoscopy involves the use of mirrors and lights to view the larynx. The physician views, biopsies or removes a lesion by visualizing the larynx through the reflection in a mirror.

> 31505 Laryngoscopy, indirect; diagnostic (separate procedure)
>
> 31510   with biopsy
>
> 31511   with removal of foreign body
>
> 31512   with removal of lesion
>
> 31513   with vocal cord injection

Direct laryngoscopy is an examination of the back of the throat and vocal cords using a laryngoscope. The physician can see the vocal cords directly. Direct laryngoscopy almost always takes place in the operating room under general anesthesia or conscious sedation. This laryngoscopy category contains over a dozen codes and involves the most complex procedures. The most commonly performed direct laryngoscopies are:

> 31535 Laryngoscopy, direct, operative, with biopsy;
>
> 31536   with operating microscope or telescope
>
> 31541 Laryngoscopy, direct, operative, with excision of tumor and/or stripping of vocal cords or epiglottis; with operating microscope or telescope

Many of the endoscopy codes include use of a microscope or telescope. For example, 31531 is a direct laryngoscopy for removal of a foreign body with operating microscope or telescope. Add-on code 69990 would not be coded with 31531 because the operating microscope is included with the code. When a CPT® code does not include an operating microscope, but an operating microscope was used, 69990 should be coded in addition to the procedure code.

Testing Technique

Reference the guidelines for Operating Microscope (+69990) for a listing of codes where the use of the operating microscope is an inclusive component.

Endoscopic stroboscopy (31579) allows an examiner to gather information on the vibratory nature of the vocal cords.

A laryngeal web is a congenital malformation of the larynx. Via horizontal neck incision, the surgeon exposes the laryngeal web between the vocal cords, excises the web, and inserts a laryngeal keel (spacer) between the vocal cords. At a later operative session, the surgeon removes the keel. In 31582, the stenosis (web) involves the arytenoid cartilages. The surgeon excises the affected area and places a graft to allow for support of the larynx.

A cricoid split is a break in the circular cartilage of the larynx. This may be restored via laryngoplasty (31587).

Trachea and Bronchi

Tracheostoma revision may be simple (31613 *Tracheostoma revision; simple, without flap rotation*) or complex (31614 … complex, with flap rotation). Insertion of a laryngeal speech prosthesis (such as a voice button) is reported using 31611.

The primary codes in the Trachea/Bronchi section are the endoscopic codes. **Surgical bronchoscopy always includes diagnostic bronchoscopy when performed by the same surgeon**. Code the appropriate endoscopy of each anatomical site examined. If multiple bronchoscopies are performed, modifier 51 may apply. Additional highlights in this section include:

- Codes 31622–31646 include fluoroscopic guidance, when performed. Do not report fluoroscopic guidance separately with these procedures.
- Bronchial alveolar lavage (31624) allows sampling of lung tissue by irrigating with saline followed by suctioning the fluid.

◗ For a fiducial marker delivered via the airway using bronchoscope, report 31626; this code may be appropriate when physicians place fiducial markers used to guide a thoracoscopy, or to improve visualization for lung wedge biopsy.

◗ Code 31627 describes computer-assisted, image-guided navigation during bronchoscopy. It includes 3-D reconstruction (do not separately report 76376, 76377). This add-on code should only be reported with 31615, 31622–31631, 31635, and 31638–31643.

◗ **CPT® provides extensive parenthetical notes throughout this section. Read and apply these guidelines carefully for best code selection. Note additionally that many codes in this section are add-on codes (indicated with a "+"); others include moderate sedation, when provided, as indicated by the "bull's-eye" symbol.**

Endotracheal ultrasound (EBUS) allows physicians to perform a technique known as transbronchial needle aspiration to obtain tissue or fluid samples from the lungs and surrounding lymph nodes. The samples can be used for diagnosing and staging lung cancer, detecting infections, and identifying inflammatory diseases that affect the lungs. EBUS can be performed during a bronchoscopy (31620).

A transtracheal injection for bronchography (31715) is performed to examine the structures of the lower respiratory tract, including the trachea and bronchi.

Code 31656 describes a bronchoscope introduced through the nose or mouth after a local anesthetic is sprayed in the back of the throat. The bronchoscope is advanced into the bronchial segment to be studied, and contrast is injected. The contrast media coats the lining of the interior walls of the lower respiratory tract, allowing the physician to examine the anatomy radiographically.

Excision and repair codes primarily describe reconstructive procedures, such as tracheoplasty (31750–31760, according to location) and bronchoplasty (31770–31775, by method of repair). Also included in this section are suture of tracheal wound (31785–31786, by location) and closure of tracheostomy or fistula, with (31825) or without (31820) plastic repair.

Lungs and Pleura

Open thoracotomy procedures are coded based on the procedure performed. Open thoracotomy biopsies are further defined based on the location of the biopsy. Additional thoracotomy procedures include hemorrhage control, removal of a foreign body, intrapleural pneumolysis, etc. If thoracotomy is part of the approach to perform a more extensive surgery, the thoracotomy is included in the surgical procedure. For example, when reporting removal of lung (32440), you would not code separately for the thoracotomy. Add-on procedures are available to report additional wedge resections. When a chest wall tumor is resected along with a lung resection, both procedures are reported separately.

"Open" decortication (32200, 32225) is performed to remove fibrous or scarred pleura adhered to the lungs.

Excision and removal codes describe open procedures to remove portions of the lung and pleura. A pleurectomy is excision of the pleura; this is a "separate procedure" and reported separately only when it is the only procedure performed, or is unrelated to any major procedures performed on the same day. Thoracentesis involves inserting a needle into the pleural space and aspirating fluid (32421), or placing a tube for drainage via a water-seal, suction device (32422).

A pneumonectomy (32440) is the removal of the lung. Partial removal of a lobe, two lobes, segment, wedge, or other resections, requires a code from 32480–32507.

Chest tube insertion (32551) is bundled into all thoracotomy and chest endoscopic procedures. Chest tubes are required to re-expand the lungs following these procedures.

Code 32560 describes pleurodesis for recurring pneumothorax (collapsed lung). The instilled agent (talc) causes adhesion of the surface of the lung to the inside surface of the chest. Codes 32561 (initial day) and 32562 (each subsequent day) describe fibrinolysis to break up effusions (excess fluid that accumulates in space surrounding the lungs) and facilitate drainage. Report a single unit of 32561 on the initial day and one unit of 32562 for each subsequent treatment day.

Video-Assisted Thoracoscopic Surgery, or VATS, is a minimally invasive procedure for lung disorders.

CPT® guidelines specify that surgical VATS (32650–32674) always includes same-session diagnostic VATS (32601–32609).

Additional highlights in this section include:

- Diagnostic thoracoscopy of the lungs, pericardial sac, mediastinal or pleural space, without biopsy (for visualization only) is reported 32601; this is a separate procedure and should be reported if it is the only procedure performed, or is unrelated to more extensive procedures performed at the same session. Biopsy procedures (32604–32609) are specific to the location of the biopsy (eg, pericardial sac, mediastinal space, pleura etc.).

- Surgical codes describe a wide range of services, from endoscopic pulmonary decortication (32651–32652) (the open procedure 32200–32225 was discussed above) to lung wedge resection (32666–32668) to a single lobectomy (32663). Additional codes describe control of traumatic hemorrhage (32654) total pericardiectomy (excision of pericardial sac, usually to remove malignancy) or excision of a pericardial cyst, tumor, or mass (32661) or mediastinal cyst, tumor, or mass (32662).

- Add-on code 32674 is reported when mediastinal lymph nodes are removed in addition to the primary procedure.

Testing Technique

Highlight the names of the right mediastinal lymph nodes in one color and the names of the left mediastinal lymph nodes in another color. The lists of mediastinal lymph nodes are found under CPT® codes +32674 and +38746.

Lung Transplant codes 32850–32856 include three separate areas of work:

1. Donor pneumonectomy
2. Benchwork to prepare the donor lung
3. Recipient lung transplant

These codes typically are reported by separate providers at different facilities. CPT® provides explanatory guidelines preceding the code listings.

Thoracoplasty is a treatment for chronic empyema. After extensive unroofing of the empyema space by resecting overlying ribs and partial removal of the lining of the chest cavity, the area is packed with gauze. This procedure takes place over many days and is staged. All stages are included in 32905 *Thoracoplasy, Schede type or extrapleural (all stages)*. Because the code descriptor identifies this as a staged procedure, you would not need to add modifier 58.

Pneumonolysis (32940) separates the chest wall from the lungs to prevent collapse.

Respiratory/Medicine Codes

A ventilator is a machine used to assist with the ventilation of a patient who is unable to breathe sufficiently. Management of the ventilator settings usually is reported with codes 94002–94005.

Pulmonary function tests (PFTs) are a series of different breathing tests led by a trained pulmonary function technologist. Spirometry measures inhale and exhale airflow and volume, and assists providers in the treatment of asthma. Forced vital capacity (FVC) measures the amount of air exhaled from full inspiration to full expiration. All of the codes in this section can be used alone or with each other, depending on what the provider is trying to diagnose.

Codes 94011–94013 are for infant PFTs. The tests are performed only for children up through age two and include moderate sedation.

Mediastinum and Diaphragm

Mediastinum

Mediastinum codes include a mediastinotomy via a cervical approach (39000) or a thoracic approach (39010). Resection codes are to remove a cyst (39200) or to remove a tumor (39220). An endoscopic approach would be reported with 39400 and a thoracoscopic approach would be reported with 32662.

Diaphragm

Hernia repair codes for the diaphragm are divided based on the age of the patient. Codes are also divided by traumatic acute or traumatic chronic. Resections of the diaphragm are based on whether it is a simple or complex procedure.

Hemic and Lymphatic Systems

Spleen

Splenectomy may be total (38100), partial (38101), or total at the time of another procedure (+38102). This last code refers to "en bloc" removal, meaning the spleen was removed as a whole or in total; 38102 is an add-on code, which should be reported in addition to the code for the "other procedure." Repair of the spleen (splenorrhaphy) is reported with code 38115.

Surgical laparoscopic procedures on the spleen are reported with code 38120. If an X-ray of the spleen and portal system is needed, a splenoportography (38200, 75810) would be performed.

General

Additional codes describe bone marrow or stem cell procedures. Codes 38204–38206 support the work of donor search and actual harvesting of the hematopoietic progenitor cells for transplant. Transplant preparation codes are found in code range 38207–38215. Bone marrow aspiration or biopsy is coded with 38220 or 38221. Codes 38220 and 38221 should not be reported for the same session unless the procedures are performed on two separate anatomic sites (eg, right iliac and left iliac). When the procedures are performed on the same anatomic site, only report 38221. For patients covered by Medicare, if the provider performs an aspiration and biopsy at the same anatomic site, report 38221 and G0364 *Bone marrow aspiration performed with bone marrow biopsy through the same incision on the same date of service.*

Bone marrow or blood derived peripheral stem cell transplant can be obtained by three different sources: Allogenic (genetically different but obtained from the same species), 38240; Autologous (obtained from the patient), 38241; or Allogenic donor lymphocyte infusions, 38242.

Lymph Nodes and Lymphatic Channels

Lymph nodes may need to be incised to drain an abscess, by either simple approach (38300), or an extensive procedure (38305); query the provider if documentation of the extent of the procedure is unclear.

Lymph nodes may be excised to remove malignant tissue (therapeutic), or for a definitive diagnosis (diagnostic). The extent of the biopsy or excision, along with the location, determines the code (CPT® code range 38700–38780).

Laparoscopic procedures of the lymph nodes are for biopsies (38570), pelvic lymphadenectomy (38571), or pelvic lymphadenectomy and periaortic lymph node sampling (38572).

Lymphangiography is an imaging technique in which a radiopaque contrast medium is injected (38790) and an X-ray picture is taken to visualize the lymph vessels (75801–75807). The same procedure may be used to identify sentinel nodes (38792). A sentinel node is the first lymph node (or group of nodes) reached by metastasizing cancer cells from a primary tumor.

HCPCS Level II

The Medicare pulmonary rehab codes are found in HCPCS Level II. Commercial payers may allow different codes such as G0424 or S9473. You will want to check your contracts.

G0237 Therapeutic procedures to increase strength or endurance of respiratory muscles, face-to-face, one-on-one, each 15 minutes

G0238 Therapeutic procedures to improve respiratory function, other than described by G0237, one-on-one, face-to-face, per 15 minutes

G0239 Therapeutic procedures to improve respiratory function or increase strength or endurance of respiratory muscles, two or more individuals (includes monitoring)

Supplies used during pulmonary rehabilitation are reported separately (for example, A4614 for a peak flow meter, or A7003 for a disposable nebulizer circuit).

Modifiers

CPT® modifiers may be used when coding for respiratory, hemic/lymphatic, or mediastinum/diaphragm procedures and services. Several specific instances of modifier use have been illustrated throughout this chapter. Rules for applying modifiers are consistent throughout all portions of the CPT® codebook.

Glossary

Allogenic—Genetically different, but obtained from the same species.

Alveoli (air sacs)—The primary units for the exchange of oxygen and carbon dioxide in the lungs.

Apheresis—Filtering of blood to remove stem cells.

Autologous—Obtained from the patient.

Bone Marrow—The flexible tissue found in the center of many bones, primarily in cancellous tissue of the ribs, vertebrae, sternum, and bones of the pelvis.

Bronchi—Bottom portion of the trachea that splits into airways to the right and left lung; the right is shorter and wider than the left.

Carina—The ridge that separates the opening of the right and left bronchi.

Chronic Obstructive Pulmonary Disease (COPD)—A progressive disease that causes coughing, wheezing, shortness of breath, and difficulty breathing. The primary cause is smoking.

Cilia—Microscopic filaments bathed in nasal mucus that cover the surface of the tissue in the nose.

Concha Bullosa—Enlargement of the nasal turbinate.

Croup—A common, high-pitched, barking cough found in infants and children with nasal-type symptoms.

Diaphragm—Muscle separating the abdominal cavity from the thoracic cavity; assists in respiration by contracting (inflating) and relaxing (deflating) the lungs.

Dacryocystorhinostomy—Surgical procedure that restores the flow of tears into the nose from the lacrimal sac when the nasolacrimal duct does not function.

Decortication—Separating the pleura adhering to lungs to assist with expansion of the lungs.

Direct Endoscopy—Use of an endoscope to look directly at the larynx.

Empyema—Collection of pus between the lung and the lining of the lung (pleural space).

En bloc—In total or in full; as a single piece.

Epiglottis—A lid or flap that covers the larynx to protect the trachea from inhaled food or liquid.

Glottis—Vocal cords separated by a triangular opening, through which air flows. The glottis narrows, controlling the flow of air, which causes the vocal cords to vibrate and create sound.

Hemic—Pertaining to blood.

Hyoid Bone—A horseshoe-shaped bone in the anterior midline of the neck. It is not part of the trachea and does not articulate with any other bone. It provides attachment to the muscles of the floor of the mouth and the tongue above, the larynx below, and the epiglottis and pharynx behind.

Indirect Endoscopy—Use of mirrors with a rigid laryngoscope to view the larynx.

Instill—To introduce gradually.

Larynx (Voice Box)—Connects the nasopharynx to the trachea, covered by the epiglottis during swallowing to prevent aspiration.

Lungs—The right lung has three lobes and the left lung has two lobes.

Mediastinum—The portion of the thoracic cavity between the lungs containing the heart, aorta, esophagus, trachea, and thymus gland, as well as blood vessels and nerves.

Pleura—A serous membrane that folds back onto itself to form a two-layered structure.

Pleural Cavity—The space between the two pleural layers.

Pneumonectomy—Removal of a lung.

Pneumonolysis—A procedure that separates the chest wall from the lungs to prevent collapse.

Pneumothorax—Collapse of the lung.

Pulmonary Function Tests—Tests to diagnosis breathing problems.

Trachea (windpipe)—Cartilaginous structure that carries air from the nasopharynx to the lungs via the bronchi.

Turbinates—Superior, middle, and inferior bony structures found in each right and left nasal cavity to assist with air movement.

Septum—Bony structure that separates the left nasal cavity from the right nasal cavity.

Splenoportography—A method of using X-ray imaging to view the portal system via the spleen.

Video-Assisted Thoracoscopic Surgery (VATS)—Use of endoscope and video to perform diagnostic and surgical procedures.

Vital Capacity (VC)—The maximum volume of air a person can exhale after maximum inhalation. The measure is used in diagnostic pulmonary testing.

Chapter Review Questions

1. The term "pneumomediastinum" describes what condition?

   A. Inflammation of the mediastinum

   B. Puncture of the alveoli of the lungs

   C. Presence of a cyst or tumor in the mediastinum

   D. The presence of air in the mediastinum

2. A respiratory disease characterized by overexpansion and destruction of the alveoli is identified as:

   A. Cystic fibrosis

   B. Pneumoconiosis

   C. Emphysema

   D. Respiratory distress syndrome

3. A 35-year-old was diagnosed with stage I ductal carcinoma *in situ* in her right breast. She underwent a localized biopsy of sentinel lymph and axillary nodes in her right breast. An incision was made with the scalpel, once the glandular tissue of the breast was intercepted; dissection was carried down through the skin and subcutaneous tissue. One to two centimeters of the breast tissue was dissected free to the lymph node. The incision was carried deep to the right axilla and two sentinel and non-sentinel lymph nodes were identified and excised. What CPT® code should be used to report this procedure?

   A. 38525

   B. 38570

   C. 38500

   D. 38505

4. A 29-year-old female in the hospital who has AIDS has been put on a ventilator due to her weakness and dyspnea. The physician suspects she has pneumonia and performs a thoracoscopy. The contents of the chest cavity are inspected with an endoscope and multiple nodules are seen in the right lung and biopsied. Pneumocystis carinii pneumonia is diagnosed. What are the correct CPT® and ICD-9-CM codes?

    A. 32601, 486, 042

    B. 32608, 042, 136.3

    C. 32606, 042, 136.3, V08

    D. 32650, 136.3, 042

5. A 45-year-old male with Stage III non-Hodgkin's lymphoma showed pathologic cervical nodes on the PET scan. A biopsy was recommended. A supraclavicular incision was made, deepened down through the platysmal muscle. Ligation of the external jugular vein was performed and, deep to this structure, numerous large nodes—approximately 3 to 3.5 cm in greatest dimension—were seen. Once elevated, the hilar aspect of one of the nodes was serially clipped with hemoclips to remove it. What code would accurately report this procedure?

    A. 38720

    B. 38520

    C. 21550

    D. 38510

6. A patient with chronic maxillary sinusitis underwent a prior ethmoid surgery. A recent CT scan reveals mucous membrane thickening, and an opaque sinus. An endoscope and scalpel are used to surgically remove the diseased tissue, and an antrostomy is performed. What code accurately describes this procedure?

    A. 31233

    B. 31020

    C. 31000

    D. 31256

7. A 22-year-old was in a motor vehicle accident and has a broken nose. An X-ray shows a deviated septum causing airway obstruction. The deviated portion of the bony and cartilaginous septum is excised by grafting the septum. The septum is noted to be straight in the midline. What CPT® code(s) should be used to report this service?

    A. 30420

    B. 30462

    C. 30520

    D. 30620, 15120

8. A patient with a life-threatening diaphragmatic laceration requires resection and complex prosthetic repair. Which procedure code should the general surgeon handling the case use to report this treatment?

    A. 39501

    B. 39540

    C. 39560

    D. 39561

9. **Operative Report #1**

    Preoperative Diagnosis:

    1. Inferior turbinate hypertrophy

    2. Deviated nasal septum with nasal obstruction

    Postoperative Diagnosis:

    1. Inferior turbinate hypertrophy

    2. Deviated nasal septum with nasal obstruction

    Procedure: Septoplasty with inferior turbinate reduction

    Complications: None

    Estimated Blood Loss: 20 cc

    History: This is a 17-year-old young man who came to see me in the office with difficulty breathing through his nose. He states he used to breathe fine through his nose until about three years ago when he broke it. Since then he has had a lot of problems with nasal obstruction.

    Physical exam did reveal a severely deviated nasal septum to the left and this, coupled with inferior turbinate hypertrophy, is giving him 100 percent on the left side. It was my recommendation that he undergo a septoplasty with inferior turbinate reduction. The procedure, risks, and benefits were discussed with him and his aunt in the office. They were agreeable to the surgery.

    Description of Procedure: The patient was identified in the preoperative waiting area and taken back to the operating room where he underwent general anesthesia. Approximately 6 cc of 1% Lidocaine with epinephrine were injected into the septum and the inferior turbinates bilaterally. Afrin-soaked pledgets were placed in each side of the nose and left there for about five minutes. These were then removed. A right-sided hemitransfixion incision was made in the anterior septum and a mucoperichondrial and mucoperiosteal flap was then raised on the left side. I came back to the bony-cartilaginous junction and raised a mucoperichondrial flap on the right side. I removed the deviated portions of the bony septum which were quite extensive mainly to the left and then coming more anterior. He had a severe deflection of the left side of the cartilaginous septum. This was removed. He also had a very prominent maxillary crest on the left side which I needed a hammer and chisel to remove. After doing all of this, the patient did have a straight nasal septum, so a 4-0 chromic was then sewn in a mattress-type fashion back and forth a across the septal flap to eventually close the hemitransfixion incision. The Boies elevator was used to medialize and lateralize the inferior turbinates. The turbinate bipolar was used to reduce the size of the inferior turbinates bilaterally. Once that was done, the patient had a nice open nasal airway. Doyle splints with antibiotic ointment were placed in each side of the nose and sewn in place using a single nylon stitch anteriorly. A small amount of blood was suctioned from the nasopharynx. The patient was awakened and taken to the postoperative recovery room in stable condition.

The patient was awakened and taken to the postoperative recovery room in stable condition.

What are the CPT® and ICD-9-CM codes for this service?

10. **Operative Report #2**

   Preoperative Diagnosis: Recurrent right-sided epistaxis

   Postoperative Diagnosis: Recurrent right-sided epistaxis

   Procedure: Right maxillary antrostomy with biopsy and right internal maxillary artery ligation

   Complications: None

   Estimated Blood Loss: 5 cc

   History: This is a 71-year-old male with a problem with recurrent epistaxis. He did have a widely deviated nasal septum which I did repair about a month ago, but despite that he is still having one to two nosebleeds a week, which are fairly severe. Because of that I did recommend to him that he undergo an internal maxillary artery ligation. The procedure, risks, and benefits were discussed with him in the office and he is agreeable to the surgery.

   Description of Procedure: The patient was identified in the preoperative waiting area and taken back to the operating room where he underwent anesthesia. Approximately 3 cc of 1% Lidocaine with epinephrine were injected into the right inferior turbinate, the right middle turbinate, and the uncinate process on the right. Afrin-soaked pledgets were then placed on that side of the nose and left there for about five minutes. These were then removed and a 0 degree nasal endoscope was placed on the right side of the nose. I used a Freer to medialize the middle turbinate and then I was able to locate the maxillary ostia on the right side. Following this posterior, I did end up using a thru-cut forceps to widen the opening slightly to get me closer to the posterior wall of the maxillary sinus on the right side. Tissue was sent away for pathology. It did appear to be inflamed. I then used the Freer to raise a mucosal flap from the lateral wall. Once I was able to get to the posterior portion of the maxillary sinus, I was immediately able to see the right internal maxillary artery. I did isolate this both in front of, above, and below the artery itself. I was able to place three clips on the vessel itself. There appeared to be good hemostasis. The 0 degree nasal endoscope was removed. I did inspect the rest of the right side of the nose and left side of the nose. There appeared to be a few prominent blood vessels, namely on the lateral side of the nose, involving the inferior turbinate. I did cauterize these areas giving them good hemostasis. Again, just a small amount of blood was suctioned from the nasopharynx.

   The patient was awakened and taken to the postoperative recovery room in stable condition.

   What are the CPT® and ICD-9-CM codes for this service?

Introduction

This chapter will review the cardiovascular system. Codes relevant to this system are found in several sections of the CPT® codebook (specifically surgery, radiology, and medicine), and throughout the ICD-9-CM (primarily chapter 7) and HCPCS Level II codebooks. Objectives for this chapter are:

- Provide an overview of cardiovascular system anatomical concepts
- Define key terms, and recognize common eponyms and acronyms
- Explain the most common pathologies that effect this system
- Highlight relevant procedures and how to apply CPT® codes that represent them
- Introduce ICD-9-CM and HCPCS Level II codes and guidelines as they apply to this system

Anatomy and Medical Terminology

The cardiovascular system is comprised of the heart, arteries, and veins.

The Heart

The Heart

Aorta
Superior vena cava
Right pulmonary veins
Right atrium
Right atrio-ventricular (tricuspid) valve
Chordae tendineae
Inferior vena cava
Papillary muscles
Right ventricle
Septum (interventricular)

Left pulmonary artery
Left pulmonary veins
Left atrium
Left atrio-ventricular (bicuspid) valve
Semilunar valves
Left ventricle

(A)

Pulmonary semilunar valve
Bicuspid valve
Fibrous connective tissue

Aortic semilunar valve
Tricuspid valve

(B)

Source: Delmar/Cengage Learning.

The heart is a fist-sized, cone-shaped muscle (the myocardium) that beats, on average, 80 times per minute. It is divided into right and left sides by a muscular wall, the septum. A two-layered, protective membrane, the pericardium, surrounds the heart and the roots of the great vessels (the aorta, pulmonary trunk, and superior and inferior vena cava).

The heart contains four chambers. The upper chambers are the atria (singular = atrium), which receive blood as it comes into the heart. The lower chambers are the ventricles, which pump blood out of the heart. The left ventricle, which forces oxygen-rich blood into the body, is the most muscular chamber of the heart (see "Oxygenation Process" below).

To ensure that the blood moves through the heart in one direction, the ventricles have inlet and outlet valves. The heart valves are flaps (cusps/leaflets) that operate like one-way swinging doors. The atrioventricular valves (tricuspid on the right and mitral on the left) are inlet valves that open from the atrium to the ventricles. The semilunar valves (pulmonary or pulmonic on the right and aortic on the left) are outlet valves.

The inlet valves are supported by chordea tendinae, string-like tendons (heart-strings) linking the papillary muscles of the inferior wall of the ventricles to the tricuspid valve in the right ventricle and the mitral valve in the left ventricle. When the atria contract, the valves open, and blood flows into the ventricles during diastole (ventricles relaxed). When the ventricles contract, the valves close. The contraction of the papillary muscles prevents inversion or prolapse of these valves during ventricular contraction (systole), which forces the blood out of the ventricles.

Oxygenation Process

Oxygen-deficient blood enters the right atrium through the venae cavae. The tricuspid valve opens, and the blood flows into the right ventricle. The blood is pumped from the right ventricle, through the pulmonary valve, and into the pulmonary artery to the lungs. Oxygen-rich blood returns to the left atrium through the pulmonary veins. The mitral valve opens, and the blood flows into the left ventricle, which forces the blood through the aortic valve, into the aorta, and out to the body.

Conduction System

The heart is controlled by an electrical conduction system containing pacemaker cells, nodes, the bundle of His (AV bundle), and the Purkinje fibers. The pacemaker cells generate an electrical impulse and pass that impulse to other cells. The impulse causes muscle fibers to shorten (contract), causing the heart to "beat."

The sinoatrial (SA) node is located in the right atrium by the superior vena cava. It is the normal pacemaker of the heart. The atrioventricular (AV) node is located lower in the septal wall of the right atrium. It slows the impulse between the atria, and the ventricles to allow time for the atria to fill with blood before the ventricles contract. The impulse then travels to the bundle of His, which are muscle fibers that branch off to the right and left. The impulse arrives at the Purkinje fibers at the end of the bundle branches. These fibers lie across the surface of the ventricles and give the final signal for the ventricles to contract.

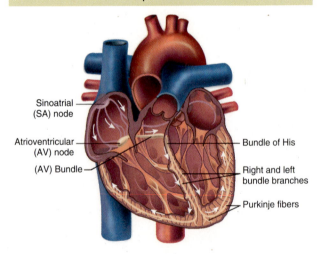

Electrical Impulses in the Heart

Source: Delmar/Cengage Learning.

Coronary Arteries

To work effectively, the heart must have a constant supply of oxygen and nutrients. The coronary arteries are the network of blood vessels that carry oxygen- and nutrient-rich blood to the cardiac muscle tissue. The left and right coronary arteries, which supply the heart, emerge from the beginning of the aorta, near the top of the heart. The initial segment of the left coronary artery is called the left main coronary. It branches into the left anterior descending coronary artery and the left circumflex coronary artery. The arteries continue to branch into progressively smaller vessels. The smallest branches are the capillaries, in which red blood cells provide oxygen and nutrients to the cardiac muscle tissue and bond with carbon dioxide and other metabolic waste products, taking them away from the heart for disposal through the lungs, kidneys, and liver.

Blood Vessels

During blood circulation, the arteries carry blood away from the heart (remember: "A" = artery = away). The capillaries connect the arteries to veins. Veins carry blood back to the heart. To withstand the pumping pressure of the heart, an artery is composed of three layers: a tough outer layer of tissue, a muscular middle, and an inner layer of epithelial cells. The muscle in the middle is strong and elastic. The inner layer is very smooth so that the blood can flow easily.

Veins are similar to arteries, but because they transport blood at a lower pressure, they are not as strong. Like arteries, veins have three layers: An outer layer of tissue, muscle in the middle, and a smooth inner layer of epithelial cells. These layers are thinner and contain less elastic tissue and smooth muscle than arterial layers; however, there is more fibrous connective tissue in the outer layer.

Unlike arteries and veins, capillaries are very thin and fragile. The capillaries are a single epithelial cell thick—so thin that blood cells can pass through them only in single file. The exchange of oxygen and carbon dioxide takes place through the thin capillary wall.

Circulation

Three methods of circulation carry blood throughout the body: systemic, pulmonary, and coronary. Systemic circulation supplies nourishment to all of the tissue located throughout the body, with the exception of the heart and lungs. Pulmonary circulation is the movement of blood from the heart, to the lungs, and back to the heart again. Pulmonary circulation can be heard through a stethoscope. Coronary circulation refers to the movement of blood through the tissues of the heart.

Key roots, suffixes and prefixes for the cardiovascular system

Combining forms

angi/o; vas/o; vascul/o	vessel
arter/o; arteri/o	artery
arteriol/o	arteriole
ather/o	yellowish, fatty plaque
atri/o	atrium
cardi/o	heart
ech/o; son/o	sound
electr/o	electrical
my/o	muscle
ox/i	oxygen
phleb/o; ven/o	vein
pulmon/o	lung
scler/o	hard
sept/o	septum
sin/o	sinus
steth/o; thorac/o	chest
venul/o	venule

Prefixes

brady-	slow
de-	down; from
epi-	upon; above
peri-	around
poly-	many
tachy-	fast

Suffixes

-ary	pertaining to
-edema	swelling
-graph	instrument used to record
-graphy	process of recording
-gram	record

Suffixes (continued)

-ium	membrane
-megaly	enlarged
-ole	small
-oma	tumor
-sclerosis	hardening
-stenosis	narrowing; stricture
-stomy	artificial opening
-tome	cutting instrument

ICD-9-CM Coding

Most diagnostic codes for the cardiovascular system can be found in ICD-9-CM chapter 7: Diseases of the Circulatory System (390–459).

Arrhythmias/Conduction Disorders

An arrhythmia (dysrhythmia) is any disorder of the heart rate or rhythm. Common types include: premature atrial contractions (PACs), premature ventricular contractions (PVCs), atrial fibrillation (AF), atrial flutter, paroxysmal supraventricular tachycardia (PSVT), ventricular tachycardia (V-tach), ventricular fibrillation (V-fib), and bradyarrhythmias. Some arrhythmias arise from conduction disorders (abnormal electrical impulses in the heart). Common conduction disorders include atrioventricular block, right and left bundle branch block (BBB), and Long Q-T Syndrome. Most ICD-9-CM codes for arrhythmias and conduction disorders are found in the range 426–427. There are separate codes for postoperative arrhythmia (997.1), psychogenic arrhythmia (306.2), and vagal arrhythmia (780.2).

Hypertension

Hypertension (HTN), or high blood pressure, is classified as either primary (essential) or secondary. About 90–95 percent of cases are termed "primary hypertension," for which no medical cause can be found. The remaining 5–10 percent of cases (secondary hypertension) are caused by other conditions affecting the kidneys, arteries, heart, or endocrine system. There is a Hypertension Table in the Index to Diseases, and the Official ICD-9-CM Guidelines for Coding and Reporting gives extensive direction on code assignment.

Hypertension is assigned to category 401, with the necessity to assign a fourth digit to indicate malignant (0), benign (1), or unspecified (9). The medical record must indicate malignant or benign to assign the 0 or 1 fourth digit. In the absence of specific documentation, an unspecified fourth digit (9) must be assigned.

Hypertension with Heart Disease

Heart conditions are assigned to category 402 if a causal relationship with hypertension is stated or implied. You would look for words such "hypertensive," or phrases, such as "due to hypertension," to support this choice. Report also an additional code from category 428 to identify the type of heart failure, if present. More than one code from category 428 may be assigned if necessary to describe fully the patient's condition. The same heart condition with hypertension, but without the causal relationship documented, must be coded separately (that is, the heart condition and hypertension are separate and unrelated). Sequence them in the order of importance for the patient admission or encounter, according to the documentation.

Hypertensive Chronic Kidney Disease

There is a presumed cause-and-effect relationship between hypertension and chronic kidney disease (CKD). When conditions classifiable to 585 *Chronic kidney disease* are present, assign codes from category 403 *Hypertensive chronic kidney disease*. Assign a fifth digit to subcategory 403.x: 0 for CKD stage I–IV or unspecified, or 1 for CKD stage V or end stage renal disease. Use an additional code to identify the stage of CKD from category 585.

Testing Technique
Make a note next to the *Hypertensive chronic kidney disease* category in your ICD-9-CM codebook that there is a presumed cause-and-effect relationship between hypertension and CKD.

Hypertensive Heart and Chronic Kidney Disease

When a patient has both hypertensive heart disease and CKD, assign a code from category 404 *Hypertensive heart and chronic kidney disease*. A relationship is assumed between the hypertension and the CKD. An additional code or codes should be assigned from category 428 *Heart failure* to indicate the type of heart failure. Fifth digits for category 404 are:

- 0 without heart failure and with CKD stage I–IV, or unspecified
- 1 with heart failure and with CKD stage I–IV, or unspecified
- 2 without heart failure and with CKD stage V or end stage renal disease
- 3 with heart failure and CKD stage V or end stage renal disease

An additional code from category 585 is necessary to identify the stage of kidney disease.

Hypertensive Cerebrovascular Disease

When a patient has hypertensive cerebrovascular disease (430–438), code that condition first. List second the appropriate hypertension code from categories 401–405.

Hypertensive Retinopathy

Two codes are necessary to identify this condition. Assign first the code 362.11 *Hypertensive retinopathy*, followed by the appropriate code from categories 401–405 to show the type of hypertension.

Secondary Hypertension

Two codes are required to report secondary hypertension. Assign one code to show the underlying etiology and another code from category 405 to identify the type of hypertension. Sequencing order is determined by the reason for the admission or encounter.

Transient Hypertension and Elevated Blood Pressure

Assign 796.2 *Elevated blood pressure reading without diagnosis of hypertension*, unless the patient has an established diagnosis of hypertension. For transient hypertension complicating pregnancy, assign 642.3x.

Hypertension, Controlled or Uncontrolled

Controlled hypertension usually refers to an existing state of hypertension under control by therapy. Uncontrolled hypertension may refer to untreated hypertension or hypertension not responding to therapy. Assign the appropriate code from categories 401–405.

Arteriosclerosis

Arteriosclerosis is hardening of the arteries. If it is arteriosclerosis of the coronary arteries, assign a code from category 414 *Other forms of chronic ischemic heart disease*. A fifth digit describes whether the atherosclerosis is of native artery, bypassed artery, or transplanted heart.

Overuse of 414.00 *Coronary atherosclerosis; of unspecified type of vessel, native or graft* is a common error. Report 414.00 when documentation indicates status post coronary artery bypass graft (CABG) and the physician does not specify the coronary artery disease (CAD), and whether it is of a native vessel or a replaced vessel.

If documentation specifies CAD of a native coronary artery, and the patient is not a heart transplant patient, select 414.01 *Coronary atherosclerosis; of native coronary artery*. Also apply 414.01 if:

- the patient has CAD with no history of CABG.
- the patient had a prior percutaneous transluminal coronary angioplasty (PTCA) of a native artery, and the patient is admitted with reocclusion of this lesion.

Report 414.2 *Chronic total occlusion of coronary artery* when the patient has a coronary artery 100 percent occluded for several months. Code first coronary atherosclerosis (414.00–414.07). Report 440.4 *Chronic total occlusion of artery of the extremities* when a patient has 100 percent chronic occlusion of an artery that supplies the arms or legs. Code first atherosclerosis of the extremities (440.20–440.29, 440.30–440.32).

Note: Report 411.81 *Acute coronary occlusion without myocardial infarction* if documentation shows debris causes an acute blockage of a coronary artery. If documentation shows calcium and plaque have built up over time in the coronary artery (atherosclerosis), choose an appropriate fifth-digit code from subcategory 414.0.

Codes for arteriosclerosis of the non-coronary arteries are found mostly in category 440 *Atheroslerosis*.

Endocarditis

Endocarditis is inflammation or infection of the inner lining of the heart (endocardium). Left untreated, it can damage or destroy the heart valves. Bacterial infection is the most common source, but the cause may be fungi, or it may be unidentified. Most codes for endocarditis are found in the categories 421–424. Rheumatic endocarditis is an exception: Acute rheumatic endocarditis is coded as 391.1, and chronic rheumatic endocarditis is 397.9.

Sometimes multiple codes are necessary to report acute endocarditis when the infectious organism is known or when the underlying disease is known. The order will depend on the type of endocarditis. For example, acute streptococcal endocarditis is coded 421.0, 041.0x; acute influenzal endocarditis is coded 487.8, 421.1.

Heart Failure

Heart failure (also, congestive heart failure) occurs when the heart cannot pump enough blood to supply the body's other organs. Multiple codes may be necessary to describe the condition. At other times, combination codes may be used. For example, hypertensive heart failure (explained above) requires at least two codes. In contrast, acute systolic and diastolic heart failure are reported with combination code 428.4x.

Pericarditis

Pericarditis is inflammation of the sac surrounding the heart (pericardium), caused by infection. Most codes for pericarditis are in found in categories 420 and 423. Multiple codes may be necessary to describe the patient condition if the underlying disease is documented. Observe ICD-9-CM guidelines for sequencing.

Peripheral Arterial Disease (PAD)

PAD affects the arteries outside the heart and brain. It is the most common type of peripheral vascular disease (PVD). If the only diagnosis given is PAD or PVD, report unspecified code 443.9. If the PVD is due to diabetes, report 249.7x or 250.7x (fifth digit as appropriate) and 443.81.

Valve Disorders

The most prominent heart valve disorders are stenosis, regurgitation, and prolapse. Valve stenosis occurs when one or more of the heart valve openings narrows and restricts blood flow through the heart. Valve regurgitation occurs when the valve does not close properly. Valve prolapse occurs when valve leaflets prolapse into the heart chamber. Code selection is driven by which valve(s) is affected and whether the condition is congenital or acquired. For congenital heart valve stenosis, look to category 746. For non-congenital disorders, you must know if the condition is rheumatic, acute, or involves multiple valves.

Myocardial Infarction (MI)

An MI, or heart attack, is a sudden decrease in the coronary artery blood flow that results in death of the heart muscle. When an MI is suspected, the provider may order lab tests to determine the levels of creatinine phosphokinase (CPK) and troponin in the patient's blood. Elevated levels of CPK and troponin may indicate damage to the heart muscle. If there is a diagnosis of elevated CPK or elevated troponin, the elevated lab result is coded from Nonspecific Abnormal Findings (790–796) in the ICD-9-CM codebook.

When an MI has been diagnosed, it is classified based on the affected heart tissue. The fourth digit describes the location of the infarction (for example, subcategory 410.5 *Of other lateral wall*), and the fifth digit identifies the episode of care being provided.

A subsequent episode of care must be provided within eight weeks of the initial episode of care. After eight weeks, the MI is considered "old." If the patient has another infarct during the initial eight weeks, and it is an extension of the same site, it is part of the original infarct. A different site is considered a new infarct.

Acute MI (AMI)

For an acute MI, select from category 410 according to site. Subcategories 410.0–410.6 and 410.8 are used for STEMI, or ST elevation myocardial infarction. In a STEMI, the coronary artery is completely blocked, and virtually all the heart muscle being supplied by the affected artery starts to die. Subcategory 410.7 *Subendocardial infarction* is used for NSTEMI (non-ST elevation myocardial infarction) and nontransmural MIs. In an NSTEMI, the blood clot partly occludes the artery, and only a portion of the heart muscle being supplied by the affected artery dies.

The fifth-digit subclassification for acute MI is used to show the episode of care. A fifth digit of 0 is used when the episode of care is not specified. A fifth digit of 1 is used to show an initial episode of care. This is appropriate when the patient first presents for treatment of the newly diagnosed MI. It is assigned no matter how many times the patient may be transferred during the initial episode. A fifth digit of 2 is used to show a subsequent episode of care, such as when the patient is presenting for further observation, evaluation, or treatment following the initial episode of care, but the MI is still less than eight weeks old.

Chronic MI and Old MI

There is only one code for a chronic MI, 414.8. There is only one code for an old MI, 412. With a chronic MI, the patient is still symptomatic after eight weeks. With an old MI, the patient is asymptomatic. Code 414.8 is also assigned for chronic insufficiency.

In cases where the documentation does not state whether the MI is acute or chronic, you can follow the "eight-week rule." If a patient presents with symptoms less than eight weeks post-MI, it is considered acute. If the patient presents with symptoms after eight weeks, select chronic.

CPT® Coding

Codes throughout the CPT® codebook may report procedures and diagnostic tests of the heart. For example, a coronary artery bypass graft (CABG) is coded from the 30000 section of CPT®; ECGs are coded from the 90000 section; and the radiologic portion of an interventional procedure is coded from the 70000 section.

Surgery (33010–33999)

Pacemaker or Pacing Cardioverter-Defibrillator (33202–33249)

A pacemaker or defibrillator system is made up of a pulse generator (battery and electronics) and one or more electrodes (leads). When reading descriptors for pacer/defibrillator codes, the first word generally defines the procedure; for example, 33202 is an insertion code and 33218 is a repair code.

Next, you will need to know the type of system. A pacemaker uses low-energy electronic pulses to overcome conduction disorders of the heart. An implantable cardioverter-defibrillator delivers electrical shocks and sometimes paces the heart, if needed. CPT® separates some of the codes by the type of system, such as 33222 *Revision or relocation of skin pocket for pacemaker*, and 33223 *Revision of skin pocket for cardioverter-defibrillator*.

For pacemakers, you will need to know if it is a temporary or permanent pacemaker. Temporary pacemaker placement codes are 33210–33211.

For pacemakers, there also are different codes if the system is a single or dual chamber. CPT® codes 33206 and 33207 are for single chamber pacemaker system insertion or placements. CPT® code 33208 is for a dual chamber pacemaker system placement. These codes are for entire systems. If only the generator is inserted, look to 33212 and 33213.

Electrodes can be placed transvenously, or epicardially. Epicardial electrode placement is further differentiated by approach—open or endoscopic. You may need to use multiple codes to "build" the placement of the system when epicardial placement of electrodes occurs. For example, a dual chamber pacemaker system inserted with epicardial placement of electrodes is coded 33202, 33213-51.

The codes in this section are used "a la carte." More than one code is usually required to describe the full procedure. If a new system is placed after removal of an old system, for instance, code the removal of the parts, and the insertion of the new system. The removal of a dual system with replacement is reported with 33235, 33208–51, 33233–51.

Cardiac Valve Procedures (33400–33478)

Cardiac valve procedure codes are assigned by valve (aortic, mitral, tricuspid, or pulmonary) and procedure. Valvuloplasty (repair) may be accomplished by sutures, patches, or rings. It involves work on the whole valve, including the leaflets of the valve and the ring or the annulus. Annuloplasty involves work solely on the ring (annulus). Replacement of the valve can be performed using either a mechanical or a biologic prosthesis. If more than one valve is operated on, report separate codes for each procedure.

Most aortic valve surgery is performed while the patient is on cardiopulmonary bypass, because the heart cannot pump blood during surgery. Codes 0256T–0259T report implantation of a catheter-delivered prosthetic heart valve. Code 33401 (aortic valve) and codes 33463–33464 (surgeries for tricuspid valvuloplasty) do not include cardiopulmonary bypass. Percutaneous valvoplasty of the mitral valve is reported 92987; the same procedure for the pulmonary valve is reported 92990.

Coronary Artery Bypass Grafts (CABG) (33510–33536)

CABG is performed to bypass blockages in the coronary arteries to improve blood flow. Arterial or venous grafts are harvested from the patient to be used as conduits to the coronary arteries. CPT® divides codes by venous, arterial, and combination arterial-venous. If only venous grafting is performed, 33510–33516 *Coronary Artery Bypass: Venous Grafts* is applicable. If arterial grafting is performed, 33533–33536 *Coronary Artery Bypass: Arterial Grafts* is applicable. If both arterial and venous grafting are performed, two codes must be reported from code ranges 33517–33523 *Coronary Artery Bypass Venous AND Arterial Grafts* (these are add-on codes) and 33533–33536 *Coronary Artery Bypass: Arterial Grafts*. The codes indicate the number of the specific type of graft. For example, CPT® code 33512 describes a three-venous-graft CABG, and CPT® code 33534 describes a two-arterial-graft CABG.

You must know which arteries and veins were procured for the grafts; some procurements are reported separately and some are bundled. According to CPT®, procurement of most arteries and the saphenous vein is bundled into the code set. Harvesting may be reported separately for the following:

◖ upper extremity artery (eg, radial): 35600
◖ upper extremity vein: 35500
◖ femoropopliteal vein: 35572

How the vein was harvested also is important. Endoscopic harvesting of veins for coronary artery bypass grafting is reported separately with add-on code 33508.

Whether the patient has had a previous CABG is important for several reasons:

◖ ICD-9-CM coding may be different if the patient has atherosclerosis of native coronary arteries (414.00–414.01) versus previous bypass grafts (414.02–414.04).
◖ Add-on code 33530 should be coded for additional reimbursement for reoperation CABG or valve procedures performed more than one month after the original procedure.

Do not use HCPCS Level II coronary artery modifiers (LC, LD and RC) to identify the bypass graft placement. These modifiers are used to indicate the specific vessel involved in percutanous coronary artery procedures 92980, 92981, 92984, 92995, and 92996.

Transluminal Angioplasty (35450–35476)

Angioplasty opens narrow or blocked vessels. When done percutaneously, it is called a percutaneous transluminal angioplasty (PTA). Balloon angioplasty involves inserting a balloon catheter into a narrow or occluded blood vessel to dilate the vessel by inflating the balloon.

Codes for angioplasty and artherectomy are chosen by vessel and method. For example, an open aortic angioplasty is 35452, but a percutaneous aortic angioplasty is 35472.

Bypass Graft (35500–35683)

These grafts are performed on non-coronary vessels. There are three sections: Vein, *In Situ* Vein, and Other

Than Vein. You must know the anastomosis sites (where the graft is connected on the ends). For example, if a synthetic bypass graft is placed from the femoral artery to the popliteal artery, report 35656.

"*In situ*" graft is used for revascularization of lower and upper extremities to avoid amputation. Codes 35583–35587 are for use of venous material alone, and are reported for the lower extremities. The saphenous vein is isolated, but left in its original position and vessel clamps are affixed above and below the site of the anastomosis. All side branches are tied off. The valves inside the vein are stripped to allow arterial blood flow toward the foot. The upper and lower ends of the saphenous vein are connected to the arteries (eg, femoral artery and popliteal artery), thereby creating a new circulatory pathway.

Codes 35601–35671 are reported for bypass performed on the upper and lower extremities with the use of synthetic vein (prosthetic) material for the grafting.

Add-on code 35681 is reported when the graft is composed of autogenous vein and prosthetic graft. Add-on codes 35682–35683 report harvest and anastomosis of two or more vein segments from distant sites, from a limb other than that undergoing bypass.

Any venipuncture, arterial punctures, and closures of surgical wounds are considered inherent to these procedures. Any additional procedures performed to improve blood flow (toward or away from the graft site), as well as intraoperative angiograms, are considered inherent. Procurement of the saphenous vein is included in the description of the 35501–35587. To report harvesting of femoropopliteal vein segment use add-on code 35572. For multiple vein segments from distant sites, use add-on codes 35682–35683.

Central Venous Access Procedures (36555–36598)

Central venous access devices (CVAD) are catheters placed in large veins for patients who require frequent access to the bloodstream. The tip of the catheter must terminate in the subclavian, brachiocephalic, or iliac veins to qualify as a CVAD.

There are five code categories: insertions, repairs, partial replacements, complete replacements, and removals. The devices may be inserted centrally or peripherally.

Central insertion is into the jugular, subclavian, or femoral vein. Peripheral insertion is into the basilic, cephalic, or other peripheral vein. The devices may be tunneled or non-tunneled, and may be accessed via an exposed catheter or a subcutaneous port or pump.

If an existing CVAD is removed and a new one placed via a separate venous access site, report both the removal of the old device and insertion of the new device. Any imaging procedures used to gain access to the venous entry site, or to manipulate the catheter into the final central position, should be reported using 76937 or 77001, as appropriate.

Interventional Procedures

Interventional cardiology/radiology (IVR) is used to diagnose and/or treat diseases using minimally-invasive techniques under imaging guidance (fluoroscopy, ultrasound, etc.). A catheter threaded through the vessels, rather than an open technique, is used to perform the procedure(s). To report such procedures in full, you may need to report multiple codes from different sections of CPT® (eg, Surgery and Radiology). We will discuss each of these separately, and use a two-part example to illustrate proper coding principles.

Vascular Injection Procedures (36000–36598)

CPT® guidelines listed under the Vascular Injection Procedure section address proper application of these codes. All "necessary local anesthesia, introduction of contrast media with or without automatic power injection, and/or necessary pre- and post-injection care specifically related to the injection procedure" are included. Catheters, drugs, and contrast material are not included. Additional guidelines for interventional procedures include:

- Selective catheterizations are coded to the highest level accessed within a vascular family.
- The highest level accessed when coded includes all of the lesser order selective catheterizations used in the approach (if a second order vessel is catheterized, the first order vessel and nonselective catheterization are bundled).

- Additional second and/or third order arterial catheterization within a vascular family of arteries or veins supplied by a single first order are expressed by 36012, 36218, or 36248, as appropriate.
- Additional first order or higher catheterizations in vascular families supplied by a first order vessel different from a previously selected and coded family are coded separately (you may code separately for catheterizations within each new vascular family).

To code an interventional radiology procedure, you must consider:

- The number of catheter access sites (each access site is coded as a separate procedure).
- The number of catheter end points. This will tell you how many vascular families and how many vessel orders were accessed.
- The number of vessels visualized. This will tell you how many radiology supervision and interpretation codes you need (radiology codes will be discussed separately after the surgical codes).

Vascular Family Order

Think of the vessel order like highway off ramps. The main trunk (nonselective) is the main highway. If you take an off ramp to get gas, you have taken one turn off the main highway (first order vessel). Two turns off the main highway is a second order vessel. Now, assume you get back on the main highway and need to stop again. When you get off the main highway the next time, you have taken a new turn off the main highway (first order of new vascular family). Always "drive back" to the main trunk when coding vascular families and vascular order. Appendix L of the CPT® codebook contains the vascular families and their orders, which you may find helpful when trying to determine order and families for coding. The appendix makes the assumption that the starting point is catheterization from the aorta. If the starting point is different, the orders may be different.

Example: Part 1 (Surgical)

In the hospital, a catheter was placed in the aortic arch, and right and left common carotid, with imaging performed in all locations from a right femoral artery puncture (access).

The aorta is the main trunk. CPT® Appendix L defines the right common carotid as a second order vessel from the innominate (brachiocephalic) family, and the left common carotid as a first order vessel off the left common carotid family. There are two different vascular families accessed in this example. We will code the highest order accessed first; this is the right common carotid as a second order vessel.

Report 36216 for the initial second order vessel. The innominate had to be passed through to get to the right common carotid, and is included (bundled) into 36216. The left common carotid is the first order vessel. Because it is a separate family from the innominate, it can be coded in addition to the right common carotid. The code for the left common carotid is 36215.

The complete coding for the surgical portion of the case is 36216-RT (right common carotid) and 36215-59-LT (left common carotid). Modifier 59 is appended to show that we accessed a different family and were not unbundling the first and second order vessels from one another.

Vascular Procedures Radiology (75600–75893)

If the physician provides both portions of an interventional service, the radiology codes—in addition to the surgery codes—also must be reported. Remember that modifier 26 *Professional component* may be required when reporting radiology procedures performed in a facility/hospital setting, or when using equipment that does not belong to the provider. The following radiology guidelines apply to interventional procedures:

- Diagnostic angiography radiologic supervision and interpretation (S&I) codes should *not* be used with interventional procedures for:
  - contrast injections, angiography, roadmapping, and/or fluoroscopic guidance for the intervention
  - vessel measurement; or
  - post-angioplasty/stent/atherectomy angiography as this work is captured in the S&I codes.

- Diagnostic angiography performed at the time of an interventional procedure is separately reportable if:

  o no prior catheter-based angiographic study is available, and a full diagnostic study is performed, and the decision to intervene is based on the diagnostic study, OR

  o a prior study is available, but as documented in the medical record:

    a. the patient's condition with respect to the clinical indication has changed since the prior study, OR

    b. there is inadequate visualization of the anatomy and/or pathology, OR

    c. there is a clinical change during the procedure that requires new evaluation outside the target area of intervention

- Diagnostic angiography performed at a separate setting from an interventional procedure is separately reportable.

- If diagnostic angiography is necessary, is performed at the same session as the interventional procedure, and meets the above criteria, modifier 59 must be appended to the diagnostic radiological supervision and interpretation code(s) to denote that diagnostic was done following these guidelines.

- Diagnostic angiography performed at the time of an interventional procedure is NOT separately reportable if it is specifically included in the interventional code descriptor.

In the Radiology section of CPT®, when a code descriptor states *selective*, the catheter must be placed in that vessel to report the code. If the code does not state *selective*, the vessel must be visualized and an interpretation must be documented to report the code.

Some codes are unilateral, and some codes are bilateral; pay careful attention to the code descriptors and CPT® parenthetical notes. Unlike with the surgical codes, you may report a nonselective S&I if it is documented.

Example: Part 2 (Radiology)

In the hospital, a catheter was placed in the aortic arch, and right and left common carotid, with imaging performed in all locations from a right femoral artery puncture.

Because imaging was performed in all locations (with a report), we can code the nonselective S&I, 75650-26. Possible S&I codes for the common carotids include 75676 and 75680-26; because both the right and the left common carotid were visualized, the correct choice is 75680-26.

By combining parts 1 (surgical) and 2 (radiologic) of this example, complete coding for this case is: 36216-RT, 36215-59-LT, 75680-26, 75650-26.

Testing Technique

Make an entry in your CPT® Index for Aortic Arch Imaging and list code 75650 next to it.

Endovascular Revascularization (37220–37235)

Atherectomy is a procedure used to remove plaque (atheroma) from arteries. It involves inserting a catheter with a cutting device into a narrow blood vessel to enlarge the lumen by mechanical removal of the intima and the plaque. Atherectomy, as well as angioplasty, and stent procedures of the lower extremities are reported with codes 37220–37235. Carefully read the notes for Endovascular Revascularization (Open or Percutaneous, Transcatheter). The codes in this section include the work of accessing and selectively catheterizing the vessel, traversing the lesion, radiological supervision and interpretation directly related to the intervention(s) performed, embolic protection if used, closure of the arteriotomy by pressure and application of an arterial closure device or standard closure of the puncture by suture, and imaging performed to document completion of the intervention in addition to the intervention(s) performed.

Radiology

Radiology codes were discussed for interventional coding above. We will now look at some other tests that fall under the Radiology section.

Heart (75557–75574)

This section contains codes for cardiac magnetic resonance imaging (MRI) and computed tomography (CT). Cardiac MRI differs from traditional MRI in its ability to provide a physiologic evaluation of cardiac function. Only one procedure from code range 75557–75563 may be reported per session. Only one add-on code for flow velocity (75565) may be reported per session. Cardiac MRI can be performed at rest and/or during pharmacologic stress. Stress test codes (93015–93018) also may be reported, if appropriate.

Cardiac CT and coronary computed tomographic angiography (CTA) are described by 75571–75574. Contrast-enhanced cardiac CT and coronary CTA include any quantitative assessment when performed as part of the same encounter. Only one CT heart service may be reported per encounter.

Cardiovascular System (78414–78499)

Cardiac SPECT (single photon emission computed tomography) scans, or myocardial perfusion imaging, are non-invasive tests used to assess the heart's structure and function. SPECT scans use small amounts of radioactive substances injected into a vein and a special camera to produce images of the heart. A computer measures blood flow through the heart and detects areas of abnormal heart muscle. Myocardial perfusion imaging studies are reported 78451–78454.

Cardiac blood pool imaging is performed when a radioactive solution is introduced into the bloodstream and monitored as it travels through the heart; these are coded from 78472–78483 and 78494–78496. This study will provide an ejection fraction, the percentage of blood pumped out of the heart with each heartbeat.

Myocardial perfusion and cardiac blood pool imaging studies can be performed at rest and/or during stress. When performed during exercise and/or pharmacologic stress, the appropriate stress testing codes (93015–93018) should be reported.

Positron Emission Tomography (PET) is a type of nuclear imaging that can evaluate heart function after administration of a natural biochemical substance, such as glucose or fatty acids. PET scans can be used to look for coronary artery disease by examining how blood flows through the heart. PET is reported with 78459 and 78491–78492.

Medicine (92950–93799)

Therapeutic Services and Procedures (92950–92998)

Cardiopulmonary resuscitation (CPR) is reported with 92950. It is not bundled into critical care E/M codes.

Cardioversion is the use of defibrillator paddles to restore effective normal sinus rhythm of the heart by electrical shock. Code 92960 is for external placement of the paddles; 92961 is for internal placement. A parenthetical note with 92961 instructs, "do not report 92961 in conjunction with 93282–93284, 93287, 93289, 93295, 93296, 93618–93624, 93631, 93640–93642, 93650–93652, 93662." Codes 92960–92961 are used only for elective cardioversion.

Testing Technique
Pay attention to parenthetical notes. Following code 92961, there is a parenthetical note that includes the codes that should not be reported in addition to this code. If you report the codes listed in the parenthetical, you will be unbundling services.

Thrombolysis (destruction of a blood clot) is coded by method of administration: 92975 is for intracoronary infusion including selective coronary angiography, and 92977 is for IV infusion.

Add-on codes 92978 and 92979 describe intravascular ultrasound (IVUS) when performed during a diagnostic or therapeutic intervention. During IVUS, a catheter with a transducer at its tip is inserted and threaded through a selected coronary artery(s) or coronary bypass graft(s). These procedures are coded per vessel and include all transducer manipulations and repositioning within the specific vessel being examined both before and after therapeutic intervention.

Percutaneous transluminal coronary angioplasty, or PTCA (92982–92984), is a non-surgical procedure that relieves narrowing and obstruction of the coronary arteries. PTCA is accomplished with a small balloon catheter inserted into an artery in the groin or arm and advanced to the narrowing in the coronary artery. The balloon is then inflated to enlarge the narrowing in the artery.

Intracoronary stent placement (92980–92981) is a procedure in which a perforated stainless tube is mounted on a balloon catheter in a "crimped" or collapsed state and inserted into the coronary artery. When the balloon is inflated, the stent expands and pushes against the inner wall of the coronary artery. This holds the artery open when the balloon is deflated and removed.

PTCA, intracoronary stent placement, percutaneous transluminal coronary atherectomy, percutaneous transluminal pulmonary artery balloon angioplasty, and IVUS are coded per vessel. Look for the specific artery when applying these codes because there are specific bundling issues:

◖ Coronary angioplasty (92982–92984) or atherectomy (92995–92996) in the same artery is considered part of the stenting procedure, and is not reported separately.

◖ For stent placement following completion of angioplasty or atherectomy, report 92980 or 92981.

◖ To report transcatheter placement of radiation delivery device for coronary intravascular brachytherapy, report 92974.

One vessel may have a stent placed, while another vessel may have a PTCA performed. Special modifiers are used with coronary interventions to indicate the vessel treated. Only three coronary vessels are recognized and they are identified with modifiers LC (left circumflex), LD (left anterior descending) and RC (right coronary). Only one primary procedure can be performed in any of the three coronary arteries. The hierarchy for procedures from lowest to highest is angioplasty, atherectomy, stent. Therefore, the primary procedure would always be stent placement if a stent is placed. All other procedures performed in the other two coronary arteries must be add-on codes for additional procedures.

Testing Technique

Make sure to pay attention to the parenthetical statements. For example, parenthetical instruction following add-on code 92984 states, "Use 92984 in conjunction with 92980, 92982, 92995." As such, if a stent is placed in the left coronary artery and PTCA is performed in the right coronary artery, report 92980-LC, 92984-RC. If the stent placement follows the PTCA in the left coronary artery, report only 92980-LC.

Cardiography (93000–93278)

The electrocardiogram (ECG or EKG) measures and records the electrical activity of the heart. ECG codes 93000–93010 are differentiated by which part of the procedure the provider is reporting. Code 93000 is for the complete global procedure—both the professional (interpretation and report) and technical (machine ownership, etc.) components. Because the codes are separated in this manner, modifiers 26 and TC are not necessary when reporting these services. If the physician owns the ECG machine and performs the official interpretation and report, 93000 is reported. If the physician performs the official interpretation and report only, report 93010. If the physician's ECG machine is used, but someone else performs the interpretation and report, 93005 is reported by the provider who owns the ECG machine.

Cardiovascular stress tests are defined in a similar manner. Code 93015 *Cardiovascular stress test using maximal or submaximal treadmill or bicycle exercise, continuous electrocardiographic monitoring, and/or pharmacological stress with physician supervision, with interpretation and report* is for the global procedure. Physician monitoring during the test is required. If a physician monitors the test only, report 93016. If a physician interprets the study and writes the official report, report 93018. If a physician performs both services, report both 93016 and 93018.

The Holter monitor (93224–93227) records the heart rhythm continuously for 48 hours. Coding is similar to that for ECGs and stress tests; you may report the complete service, or portions thereof, as appropriate. For less than 12 hours of continuous recording, use modifier 52.

Implantable and Wearable Cardiac Device Evaluations (93279–93299)

Cardiac device evaluation services are diagnostic medical procedures using in person and remote technology to assess device therapy and cardiovascular physiologic data. Read all CPT® notes before coding from this section. Important coding concepts include:

- Codes 93279–93292 are reported per procedure.
- Codes 93293–93296 are reported no more than once every 90 days, and cannot be reported if the monitoring period is less than 30 days.
- Codes 93297–93298 are reported no more than once up to every 30 days, and cannot be reported if the monitoring period is less than 10 days.
- A physician may not report an in person and remote interrogation of the same device during the same period. Report only remote services when an in person interrogation device evaluation is performed during a period of remote interrogation device evaluation.
- Programming device evaluation and in person interrogation device evaluations may not be reported on the same date by the same physician.
- CPT® 93296 or 93299 is for reporting by a service center during a period in which a physician performs an in person interrogation device evaluation. They are technical component only codes.
- Do not report 93268–93272 when performing 93279–93289, 93291–93296 or 93298–93299.
- Do not report 93040–93042 when performing 93279–93289, 93291–93296, or 93298–93299.

Echocardiography (93303–93352)

Echocardiography records the position and motion of the heart walls or the internal structures of the heart and neighboring tissue, using echoes obtained from ultrasonic waves directed through the chest wall. There are transesophageal echoes (TEE, 93312–93318) and transthoracic echoes (TTE, 93303–93308). Within each group, codes are separated by whether a congenital cardiac anomaly exists; there are codes for complete and follow-up (or limited) studies for TTE.

According to CPT®, a complete TTE without spectral or color flow Doppler (93307) is a comprehensive procedure that includes 2-D, and when performed, selected M-mode examination of the left and right atria, left and right ventricles, the aortic, mitral, and tricuspid valves, the pericardium, and adjacent portions of the aorta. Despite significant effort, identification and measurement of some structures may not always be possible. In such instances, the reason that an element could not be visualized must be documented.

A complete TTE with spectral and color flow Doppler (93306) is a comprehensive procedure that includes spectral Doppler and color flow Doppler in addition to the 2-D documentation and selected M-mode examinations, when performed. Complete, bundled TTE (93306) includes the TTE, spectral Doppler, and color flow Doppler (93307 + 93320 or 93321 + 93325). Watch for parenthetical notes following the codes to ensure proper code selection.

There is also a grouping of codes (93350–93351) for TTE with cardiovascular stress testing. In addition to these codes, the stress test codes 93016–93018 also would be reported.

Add-on code 93352 is for contrast agent used during stress echo. The code may be reported only once per stress echo.

Cardiac Catheterization (93451–93581)

Cardiac catheterization provides information relating to overall function of the heart and may reveal a stenotic lesion (hardening or narrowing) of the coronary artery or cardiac valve. It may be performed on the right heart, left heart, or as a combined (right heart and left heart) procedure. Left heart catheterization requires arterial access; right heart catheterization requires venous access. The following procedures are considered inclusive components of cardiac catheterization and not separately billed: local anesthesia or sedation, introduction of catheters, positioning and/or repositioning of catheters, recording of pressures, obtaining blood samples for measurement of blood gases or dilution curves and cardiac output measurements, final evaluation and report of procedure.

Cardiac catheterization involves placement of the catheter, injection of contrast, and supervision and interpretation imaging. Congenital cardiac catheterization requires injection procedures, which include imaging. For congenital cardiac catheterizations, separate injection procedures can also be reported. Refer to your guidelines in this section for correct coding.

Intracardiac Electrophysiological Procedures/Studies (93600–93662)

Electrophysiological studies (EPS) are invasive tests of the electrical conduction system of the heart (the system that generates the heart beat).

Comprehensive studies are reported with 93619–93622. If less than a comprehensive study is performed, the portions performed are coded separately. Many codes in this section are add-on codes, and/or are modifier 51 exempt. All codes in this section contain both a professional and technical component, and you will need to apply modifiers 26/TC if the global service is not provided.

Intracardiac catheter ablation procedures use radiofrequency energy to destroy cardiac tissue selectively. Code 93650 is for ablation of AV node function/AV conduction to create complete heart block; code 93651 is for ablation for treatment of supraventricular tachycardia (SVT); and code 93652 is for ablation for treatment of ventricular tachycardia (V-tach).

Modifiers

The cardiology section uses the same modifiers as the other sections, with the exception of the LC, LD, and RC modifiers already discussed. What follows is a quick review of recommended use for many of the most often accessed modifiers in cardiology.

Modifier 22

Consider appending modifier 22 *Increased procedural services* when the service(s) is "greater than that usually required for the listed procedure," according to CPT® Appendix A (Modifiers). Truly "unusual" circumstances occur in only a small minority of cases. Provider documentation must demonstrate the special circumstances,

such as extra time or highly complex trauma, that warrant modifier 22.

Modifier 26 and Modifier TC

When a physician conducts diagnostic tests or other services using equipment he or she doesn't own, modifier 26 *Professional component* may be used to indicate that the physician provided only the professional component (the administration or interpretation) of the service. The facility providing the equipment may receive reimbursement for the service's technical component (the cost of equipment, supplies, technician salaries, etc.) by reporting the appropriate CPT® code with modifier TC *Technical component* appended. The physician may report the appropriate CPT® code without either modifier 26 or modifier TC if he or she provides both components of the service (for instance, the service is provided in the physician's office using his or her own equipment).

Modifier 51

Modifier 51 *Multiple procedures* indicates that more than one (non-E/M) procedure was provided during the same session. Many payers now use software that automatically detects second and subsequent procedures, thereby making modifier 51 unnecessary. Check with your individual payer for guidelines, and request the payer's instructions in writing.

Modifier 58

Append modifier 58 to a procedure or service during the postoperative period when the procedure or service is:

◖ Planned prospectively at the time of the original procedure

◖ More extensive than the original procedure

◖ For therapy following a diagnostic surgical procedure

Do not use modifier 58 when the patient requires a follow-up procedure for surgical complications or unexpected postoperative findings that arise from the initial surgery. For complications that require a return to the operating room, append modifier 78.

Official CPC® Certification Study Guide   **147**

Modifier 59

Use modifier 59 *Distinct procedural* service to identify procedures that typically would be considered bundled, but that under the circumstances are distinctly separate from any other procedure provided on the same date. Do not append modifier 59 to E/M codes; and do not use modifier 59 if another, more specific modifier is available.

Modifiers 76 and 77

Modifiers 76 and 77, which describe repeat procedures, often are used with serial ECGs and chest X-rays when performed on the same date.

Modifier 78

Apply modifier 78 *Unplanned return to the operating room for a related procedure during the postoperative period* when the same physician must undertake a subsequent surgery because of conditions (complications) arising from an initial surgery.

Modifier 79

Modifier 79 *Unrelated procedure or service by the same physician during the postoperative period* may be appended when an unrelated surgery by the same physician occurs during the global period of a previous surgery.

HCPCS Level II

HCPCS Level II codes that may be applicable to cardiology include drug codes such as J1245 for Persantine, which may be needed for testing. When reporting drug codes, pay careful attention to dosage to be sure that you are reporting the proper number of units.

Additional HCPCS Level II codes relevant to this section include:

G0275 Renal angiography, nonselective, one or both kidneys, performed at the same time as cardiac catheterization and/or coronary angiography, includes positioning or placement of any catheter in the abdominal aorta at or near the origins (ostia) of the renal arteries, injection

of dye, flush aortogram, production of permanent images, and radiologic supervision and interpretation (List separately in addition to primary procedure)

G0278 Iliac and/or femoral artery angiography, nonselective, bilateral or ipsilateral to catheter insertion, performed at the same time as cardiac catheterization and/or coronary angiography, includes positioning or placement of the catheter in the distal aorta or ipsilateral femoral or iliac artery, injection of dye, production of permanent images, and radiologic supervision and interpretation (List separately in addition to primary procedure)

G0389 Ultrasound B-scan and/or real time with image documentation; for abdominal aortic aneurysm (AAA) screening

G0422 Intensive cardiac rehabilitation; with or without continuous ECG monitoring with exercise, per session

G0423 Intensive cardiac rehabilitation; with or without continuous ECG monitoring; without exercise, per session

M0300 IV chelation therapy (chemical endarterectomy)

Other codes may apply to the specialties of cardiology, cardiothoracic surgery, cardiovascular surgery, and interventional cardiology/radiology. Check with CMS and/or the individual payer for requirements.

Glossary

Anastomosis—Joining of two or more blood vessels.

Angiography—Radiographic visualization of blood vessels following introduction of contrast material.

Angioplasty—Procedure to open narrow or blocked vessels.

Annuloplasty—Surgical reconstruction of the ring (annulus) of the heart valve.

Antegrade—Moving forward or with the usual direction of flow.

Arrhythmias—Disorder of the heart rate or rhythm.

Arteriosclerosis—Hardening of the arteries.

Atherectomy—Procedure to remove plaque from the arteries.

Atherosclerosis—Build up of plaque on artery walls.

Atria—Upper chambers of the heart.

Atrioventricular (AV)—Relating to both the atria and the ventricles of the heart.

Bifurcation—Division into two branches.

Bundle of His (AV bundle)—Muscle fibers in the heart's conduction system that branch off to the right and left.

Capillaries—Smallest branches of the coronary arteries.

Cardioversion—The use of defibrillator paddles to restore normal rhythm of the heart by electrical shock.

Cardioverter-Defibrillator—Implantable device that delivers an electrical shock to restore a normal heart rhythm.

Chordae Tendineae—String-like tendons linking the papillary muscles to the tricuspid valve in the right ventricle and the mitral valve in the left ventricle.

Conduction System—Generates electrical impulses over the heart to stimulate contraction, allowing blood to move throughout the body.

Contralateral—Situated on, pertaining to, or affecting the opposite side (as opposed to ipsilateral).

Coronary Circulation—The movement of blood through the tissues of the heart.

Endocarditis—Inflammation or infection of the inner lining of the heart (endocardium).

Epicardial—Relating to the innermost layer of the heart wall.

Infarction—Death of tissues.

Intracoronary—Within the heart.

Ipsilateral—Situated on, pertaining to, or affecting the same side (as opposed to contralateral).

Myocardial—Relating to the myocardium (second layer of the wall of the heart).

Nonselective Catheterization—A catheter is placed in the main trunk; contrast may be injected and images may be taken, but the catheter is not moved into any other branches.

Non-tunneled Catheter—A catheter that is inserted through the skin directly into a central vessel.

Occlusion—Closure.

Papillary Muscles—Muscles that attach to the lower portion of the interior wall of the ventricles and connect to the chordae tendineae.

Prolapse—An organ or part of an organ falling out of place.

Pulmonary circulation—The movement of blood from the heart, to the lungs, and back to the heart again.

Purkinje Fibers—Conduction myofibers branching off of the right and left bundle branches into the cells of the myocardium.

Regurgitation—Flowing backwards.

Retrograde—Moving backward or against the usual direction of flow.

Revascularization—Reestablishment of blood supply to a part.

Selective Catheterization—A catheter is placed into the branches further off the main trunk (second, third or higher order).

Sinoatrial Node—Modified cardiac cells positioned on the wall of the right atrium, near the entrance of the superior vena cava.

Stenosis—Narrowing, stricture.

Subendocardial—Under the inner layer of the heart.

Syncope—Transient loss of consciousness (fainting).

Systemic Circulation—Supplies nourishment to all of the tissue located throughout the body, with the exception of the heart and lungs.

Thrombolysis—Destruction of a blood clot.

Transluminal—Through or across the lumen (tube) of an artery.

Transvenous—Through or across a vein.

Trifurcation—Division into three branches or parts.

Tunneled Catheter—A catheter that is tunneled through the skin and subcutaneous tissue to a central vessel; the entrance point of the catheter is distant from the entrance to the vascular system.

Valvular Prolapse—Valve leaflets fall backward into the heart chamber.

Valvuloplasty—Surgical reconstruction of a valve.

Ventricle—Lower chamber of the heart.

Chapter Review Questions

1. **Which vessel can be accessed for the insertion of a central venous catheter?**

   A. Basilic vein

   B. Subclavian vein

   C. Aorta

   D. Pulmonary artery

2. **Which chamber of the heart is the most muscular?**

   A. Right atria

   B. Left atria

   C. Right ventricle

   D. Left ventricle

3. **A patient with malignant cardiovascular hypertension is admitted by his primary care physician. What are the ICD-9-CM code(s) for this encounter?**

   A. 401.0, 429.2

   B. 402.00, 429.2

   C. 402.90

   D. 402.00

4. **The patient is a 69-year-old white female with 10-year status post dual chamber pacemaker where the generator is at its end of life. The pacemaker generator is explanted and the leads are then attached to the new generator. What are the CPT® code(s) for this encounter?**

   A. 33213

   B. 33208

   C. 33213, 33233

   D. 33228

5. A 38-year-old's blood pressure was progressively trending downward, and it was determined that an emergent central venous access was needed for fluid resuscitation. A non-tunneled catheter was used to access the subclavian vein and secured into place to infuse medication. Due to the patient's low blood pressure and anticipated need for vasopressor agents, a radial arterial line was also desired. The left radial artery pulse was easily palpable, and the skin was punctured by a needle, and the Angiocatheter was placed in the left wrist. What are the CPT® code(s) for this encounter?

    A. 36555, 36625-51

    B. 36556, 36620

    C. 36558, 36640-51

    D. 36569, 36620

6. Mrs. Doelle goes to the procedure room to have a permanent pacemaker implanted. She is given a mild sedative, and the area just under the right clavicle is prepped and draped in a sterile manor. An incision is made to create a pocket for the pulse generator. A venogram is shot through an indwelling antecubital IV, and a catheter is threaded from the pocket into the right subclavian vein. The catheter is then advanced into the right atrium under fluoroscopic guidance. Using the Seldinger technique the catheter is withdrawn over a guide wire, and a 32 FR Medtronic pacing wire is threaded back over the guide wire and into the right atrium under fluoroscopy. The guide wire is removed, and the pacing tip is screwed into the myocardium. Thresholds are tested for sensing and capture. The lead is then attached to the pulse generator and placed into the pocket. The pocket is closed with interrupted 4-0 Prolene. What are the CPT® code(s) for this encounter?

    A. 93288-26, 33249

    B. 33206, 36140-51, 93288-26, 75820-26

    C. 33206

    D. 33206, 33212-51

7. Using Xylocaine local anesthesia, aseptic technique and ultrasound guidance for vascular access, a 21-gauge needle was used to aspirate the right cephalic vein of a 72-year-old patient. When blood was obtained, a 0.018 inch platinum tip guidewire was advanced to the central venous circulation. A 6-French dual lumen PICC was introduced through a 6-French peel-away sheath to the superior vena cava and right atrium junction, and after removal of the sheath, the catheter was attached to the skin with a STAT-LOCK device and flushed with 500 units of Heparin in each lumen. A sterile dressing was applied, and the patient was discharged in improved condition. What are the CPT® code(s) for this encounter?

    A. 36569, 76937-26

    B. 36556, 76942-26

    C. 36561

    D. 36569

8. After obtaining an aortogram and CT scan, a 45-year-old woman was found to have an infrarenal abdominal aortic aneurysm measuring at least 4.5 cm in size. It was felt that with the rapid recent expansion, she should have this aneurysm repaired. The infrarenal artery aneurysm was repaired using a modular bifurcated prosthesis with one docking limb without incident. What are CPT® code(s) for this procedure?

   A. 34800, 34806

   B. 34802

   C. 34825

   D. 35081

9. **Operative Report #1**

   Preoperative Diagnosis: Sick sinus syndrome with bradycardia/tachycardia

   Postoperative Diagnosis: Permanent DDDR pacemaker insertion

   Operation Performed: Pacemaker insertion

   Anesthesia: Local with conscious sedation

   Complications: None

   Estimated Blood Loss: Minimal

   Adjunctive Procedures: Fluoroscopy

   Description of Procedure: Following informed consent, the left subclavian artery was prepped and draped in the usual sterile manner. Following local, administration of 1% Xylocaine anesthesia, the left subclavian vein was entered with an 18-gauge, thin-wall needle. J-wire was placed. Transverse incision was created and dissected at the pectoral fascia. A subcutaneous pocket was created and one gauze sponge was placed in the pocket. A 7-French sheath introducer was placed leaving a J-wire in place. A Medtronic 5076 (serial number PJNZZZZXXX) bipolar lead was placed in right ventricle apex and measurements taken. This lead screwed into position. A second 7-French introducer was placed. A Medtronic 5076 (serial number PJNZZZZXXX) atrial lead positioned in the right atrial appendage using fluoroscopic guidance. Measurements were taken and lead screwed into position. Both leads were then suture-ligated in position. The gauze sponge was extracted from the pocket. The pocket was irrigated with bacitracin solution. The leads were connected to a Medtronic Adapta (serial number PWBXXXXYYY) device. The device was placed in the pocket. The subcutaneous tissue was closed with one row of running 3-0 suture. Subcutaneous tissue was closed with one row of running 4-0 suture. A sterile dressing was applied. The patient tolerated the procedure well. Dermabond dressing was also applied. At the end of the procedure, the patient was returned to a room in good condition. Initial measures include an R-wave of 10.9 mV with threshold 0.9 volts and resistance of 810 ohms of the V-lead. The atrial lead had a P-wave of 2.0 mV, threshold 0.5 volts, resistance 1184 ohms. Initial settings include the AAIR-DDDR mode with a lower rate of 60, upper rate limit of 130, Paced AV intervals 150 and sensed 120 milliseconds. Pulse amplitude on both leads is 3.5 volts with a pulse width of 0.4 milliseconds. Atrial sensitivity is 0.5 mV. Ventricular, 2.8 mV.

   What are the CPT® and ICD-9-CM codes for this procedure?

10. **Operative Report #2**

   Preoperative Diagnosis: Angina

   Postoperative Diagnosis: Angina

   Procedure: Coronary artery bypass x2 with left internal mammary artery bypass to the left anterior descending; saphenous vein graft to the posterior descending branch of the right coronary artery; harvesting of saphenous vein.

   Anesthesia: General endotracheal anesthesia.

   Indications: As described in admission note.

   Description of Procedure: Mr. Williams was taken to the operating room. After general endotracheal anesthesia, his entire chest and abdomen were prepped and draped and exposed in a sterile field. A midline sternotomy was performed. The left internal mammary artery was taken down from its retrosternal location. It proved to be a suitable conduit with the bypass. The saphenous vein was harvested. Once both conduits were felt to be suitable, the pericardium was opened, incised, and sutured to the skin edges. The patient was heparinized and appropriate cannulas were placed. The patient was then placed on cardiopulmonary bypass at approximately 5.0 L per minute. The heart was then mechanically arrested with a combination of antegrade and retrograde cold cardioplegia and topical saline.

   With cardiac arrest now stable, the midportion of the left anterior descending was identified and dissected free. In the epicardial fat, the posterior descending branch of the right coronary artery was also dissected free. Longitudinal arteriotomy was made in the posterior descending, and a segment of saphenous vein was sutured without difficulty. In like fashion the left internal mammary artery was sutured to the left anterior descending at its midposition. The single proximal end of the right coronary graft was placed around the ascending aorta.

   Once completed, the aortic cross-clamp was removed. The air was evacuated from the graft. The patient regained sinus rhythm immediately and appropriate ejection. A single set of pacing wires was placed on the inferior surface of the left ventricular wall. Two chest tubes were positioned. The patient was subsequently decannulated and hemodynamically remained stable, and eventually closure was accomplished with heavy stainless steel sternal wires in a figure-of-eight fashion. All wounds were covered with a dressing.

   The patient was returned to the intensive care unit in satisfactory condition. He appeared to have tolerated the procedure without event.

   What are the CPT® and ICD-9-CM codes for this procedure?

Introduction

The digestive system consists of the alimentary or digestive tract and its accessory organs. The major function of the digestive system is to digest or break down foods taken into the body.

The objectives of this chapter are:

◖ Define and understand key terms associated with the digestive tract and the procedures performed in this section

◖ Understand the anatomy associated with Digestive System procedures

◖ Explain the organization and content of the CPT® Surgery/Digestive System subsections

◖ Learn to appropriately assign CPT® surgery codes from the Digestive System subsection

Anatomy and Medical Terminology

Digestive System

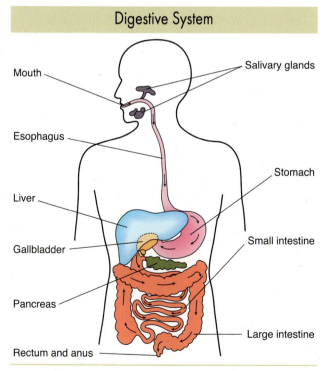

Mouth
Salivary glands
Esophagus
Stomach
Liver
Small intestine
Gallbladder
Pancreas
Large intestine
Rectum and anus

Source: Delmar/Cengage Learning.

Lips/Mouth

The lips form the entrance to the digestive tract. The oral cavity includes the mouth and its associated structures; the soft and hard palates, teeth, gums, tongue, and salivary glands. The teeth and tongue break the food into small particles. The salivary glands secrete saliva and enzymes to aid in digestion. The tongue mixes saliva with food and keeps the food pressed between the teeth for chewing before it pushes the food backward for swallowing.

There are three categories of teeth:

* Incisors—These are the teeth in the front of the mouth. They are shaped like chisels and are useful in biting off large pieces of food. Each person has eight (four on top and four on bottom).

* Cuspids—These are the pointy teeth immediately behind the incisors. Also called the canines, these teeth are used for grasping or tearing food. Each person has four of these (two on top and two on bottom).

* Molars—These are flat teeth used for grinding food. They are the furthest back in the mouth, and their number varies among people.

Pharynx

The pharynx is a five-inch tube located immediately behind the mouth. It aids in closure of the nasopharynx and larynx when swallowing, keeping food out of the respiratory tract and in the digestive tract.

Esophagus

The esophagus is a tube about 10 inches long that arises from the pharynx, passes through the diaphragm (a muscular and membranous partition that separates the chest cavity from the abdominal cavity), and continues into the stomach. The esophagus moves food into the stomach by peristalsis.

Stomach

The stomach has four parts: cardia, fundus, body, and antrum (pylorus). It further digests food received from the esophagus and passes partially digested food, known as chime, into the duodenum.

Small Intestine

The small intestine occupies the central and lower abdomen. The duodenum is the first portion of the small intestine and is connected to the stomach. It is about 10 inches long. Small ducts from the liver (hepatic ducts) and gallbladder (cystic duct) merge together to form the bile duct. The bile duct and the pancreatic duct join together and open into the duodenum via the hepato-pancreatic ampulla (ampulla of Vater). The jejunum, the middle third of the small intestine, is about 7 ½ feet long. Vigorous, peristaltic waves move fluid contents to the ileum. The ileum, approximately 12 feet in length, is the last and longest section of the small intestine. Most food absorption takes place in the ileum, which connects to the large intestine.

Large Intestine

The large intestine is about five feet long. It is divided into the cecum, appendix, ascending colon, hepatic (right colic) flexure, transverse colon, splenic (left colic) flexure, descending colon, sigmoid colon, rectum, and anus. Most of the colon is retroperitoneal, except the transverse colon and sigmoid colon, which are intraperitoneal. Water is reabsorbed as food material travels through the large intestine and eventually is eliminated from the body.

Pancreas

The pancreas is a soft, oblong gland located beneath the great curvature of the stomach. It consists of five parts: the head, neck, body, tail, and uncinate process. The pancreas empties digestive fluid (mixture of enzymes) into the duodenum and insulin into the bloodstream. Insulin is a hormone produced in the pancreas by the islands of Langerhans. Lack of insulin causes diabetes mellitus.

Liver

The liver lies in the upper abdomen on the right side under the diaphragm and above the duodenum. The human liver has four lobes: the right lobe and left lobe, which may be seen in an anterior view, plus the quadrate lobe and caudate lobe on the visceral surface. The liver converts ammonia into urea, which is then excreted by the kidney or the sweat glands. The liver also converts excess glucose into glycogen or fat. Bile salts are produced by the liver. When bile is secreted into the duodenum, fat is emulsified and absorbed by the intestines. The liver is the only organ in the human body that can regenerate itself.

Gallbladder/Biliary System

The gallbladder is a sac-like structure that serves as a reservoir for bile. Bile is produced by the liver and aids in the digestive process. It periodically empties into the duodenum by way of the cystic ducts.

ICD-9-CM Coding

Diagnoses for diseases of the digestive system are found throughout ICD-9-CM: chapter 9, Diseases of the Digestive System (520–579); chapter 1, Infectious and Parasitic Diseases (001–139); chapter 2, Neoplasms (140–239); chapter 14, Congenital Anomalies (740–759); and chapter 16, Signs, Symptoms, and Ill-Defined Conditions (780–799). Additional codes also may be found in the Supplemental Classification of Factors Influencing Health Status and Contact with Health Services (V01–V91) section.

Esophageal and Swallowing Disorders

Barrett's Esophagus—An abnormal growth of stomach or intestinal cells at the distal end of the esophagus, which may develop because of chronic gastroesophageal reflux disease.

Esophagitis—An inflammation of the lining of the esophagus; can be caused by an infection or irritation in the esophagus.

Esophageal Varices—Extremely dilated sub-mucosal veins in the lower end of the esophagus.

Mallory-Weiss Tear—Occurs in the mucous membrane of the esophagus, where it connects to the stomach; usually caused by forceful or long-term vomiting, coughing, or epileptic convulsions.

Hiatal Hernia—Part of the stomach protrudes or herniates through the opening of the diaphragm, into the chest.

Swallowing Disorders/Dysphagia—Any conditions that cause impaired movement of solids or fluids from the mouth, down the throat, and into the stomach.

Gastritis and Peptic Ulcer Disease

Gastritis is an acute or chronic inflammation of the stomach. A common cause of gastritis is a bacterium named helicobacter pylori, or H. pylori.

Peptic ulcer disease is a sore or opening in the inner lining of the stomach or duodenum. The two most common causes of peptic ulcers are H. pylori infections and prolonged use of NSAIDS.

Gastrointestinal (GI) Bleeding

GI bleeding can range from microscopic bleeding, only detectable by a lab test, to massive bleeding. It may be caused by esophageal varices, Mallory-Weiss tears, peptic ulcer disease, etc.

Gastroenteritis

Gastroenteritis is an infection or irritation of the digestive tract, particularly the stomach and intestines. Symptoms include nausea and vomiting, diarrhea, and abdominal cramps.

Inflammatory Bowel Disease (IBD)

Inflammatory bowel disease (IBD) is a group of inflammatory conditions of the colon and small intestine. The major types of IBD are Crohn's disease and ulcerative colitis. Crohn's disease (regional enteritis) is a chronic, inflammatory bowel process that often leads to fibrosis and obstructive symptoms. Ulcerative colitis is a chronic inflammatory disorder limited to the colon. It causes inflammation and sores in the lining of the colon and rectum.

Irritable Bowel Syndrome (IBS)

When irritable bowel syndrome (IBS)—also known as spastic colon, spastic colitis, and nervous or functional bowel—occurs, the colon contracts in a disorganized, violent manner. These abnormal contractions result in changing bowel patterns, commonly with constipation and pain.

Foreign Bodies

Foreign bodies in the GI tract are typically swallowed, and may cause perforation or obstruction. Foreign bodies in the esophagus may be removed or manipulated endoscopically into the stomach.

Diverticular Disease

Diverticulosis describes pockets or projections (diverticula) extending from the colon, which develop through weaknesses of muscle layers in the colon wall. It can cause changes in bowel function, such as discomfort, diarrhea, and/or constipation. Bacteria in the colon can cause infection of the diverticular pockets, referred to as diverticulitis.

Anorectal Disorders

Rectal prolapse can be partial or complete. Partial rectal prolapse occurs when the mucous membrane lining the anal canal protrudes through the anus. Complete rectal prolapse occurs when the whole thickness of the bowel protrudes though the anus.

Abscess is a localized pocket of pus caused by infection.

Hemorrhoids are dilated or enlarged varicose veins that occur in and around the anus and rectum. They may be external (distal end of the anal canal) or internal (in the rectum) and slip to the outside of the anus (prolapsed).

Anal fissure is a tear in the mucosa and skin of the anal canal due to passing a large stool, straining during childbirth, and laceration from passing a foreign body.

Anal fistula is a tiny channel or tract that develops because of an infection, inflammation, or abscess. The channel has one opening in the anal canal and runs to the perianal skin, rectum, bladder, or vagina.

Pancreatitis

Pancreatitis is an (acute or chronic) inflammation of the pancreas. The digestive enzymes of the pancreas break out into the tissues of the organ rather than staying within the tubes (ducts), which damages the pancreas.

Benign and Malignant Neoplasms of the GI Tract

Benign and malignant neoplasms can occur throughout the digestive tract. Coding for neoplasms requires specific physician documentation regarding neoplasm behavior and exact location within the GI tract. Be sure to confirm the code found in the Index to Diseases in the Tabular List.

Polyps are defined as an abnormal tissue growth projecting from a mucous membrane. Coding for polyps can be accomplished by using the Index to Diseases and confirming the code choice in the Tabular List. The Neoplasm Table can be used, but is not always necessary.

Personal history and/or family history of neoplasm are significant and should be coded in addition to the reason for treatment. Personal history of a malignant neoplasm of the GI tract is coded using V10.00–V10.09. Family history of a malignant neoplasm of the GI tract is coded using V16.0.

Use code V76.41 when screening for a malignant neoplasm of the rectum, V76.42 when screening for a malignant neoplasm of the oral cavity, and a code from subcategory V76.5 when screening for a malignant neoplasm of the intestine.

Congenital Disorders

ICD-9-CM codes for a congenital disorder are found in chapter 14: Congenital Anomalies (740–759).

Cleft lip and palate are congenital conditions that result due to abnormal facial development during gestation. The deformity can affect the lip, soft palate, hard palate, and even the nasal cavities.

Meckel's diverticulum is a remnant of the connection from the yolk sac to the small intestine present during embryonic development; it normally remains asymptomatic.

Congenital megacolon is an abnormal dilation of the colon, often accompanied by paralysis of peristaltic bowel movements.

Redundant colon means the colon is longer than normal.

Imperforate anus or anal atresia is a malformed rectum. These defects need to be corrected surgically very soon after birth.

CPT® Coding

The digestive system subsection is arranged first by anatomic region, and then by the procedure.

Lips

The lips are composed of skin, muscle, and mucosa, which are then divided into three main regions: cutaneous, vermilion, and mucosal. If a procedure is performed on the skin of the lips, do not code from this section; choose a code from the Integumentary System instead.

Biopsy of the lip (40490) is performed on any portion of the lip. A biopsy would be performed when there is a concern for malignancy.

Vermilionectomy (40500) is shaving or excision of the vermilion border of the lip, including repair of the excisional area by mucosal advancement. If more tissue is excised or removed from the lip area, choose a code from range 40510–40530. Wedge resections or full thickness excisional codes include reconstructions.

Cheiloplasty (40650–40761) is plastic surgery of the lips. These procedures can be cosmetic, or to repair congenital conditions (eg, cleft lip), injury, or disease.

Mouth

The space between the cheek, lips, and teeth is referred to as the vestibule of the mouth, or buccal cavity. Vestibuloplasty is a repair in the vestibule of the mouth.

Glossectomy (41120–41155) is surgical removal of all or part of the tongue. Codes are selected based on the extent of the procedure performed.

Palatoplasty is a surgical procedure to reconstruct the palate or roof of the mouth. A palatoplasty with bone graft to alveolar ridge includes obtaining the bone graft.

There are three salivary glands (parotid, submandibular, and sublingual). Codes 42300–42699 describe treatment of abscesses, cysts, tumors, fistulas, and stones of the salivary glands and ducts.

Pharynx, Adenoids, and Tonsils

Tonsillectomy is removal of the tonsils (located at the back of the throat); adenoidectomy is removal of the adenoids (located at the back of the nose). Coding is based on the tissue removed, patient age, and whether the procedure is primary (first excision) or secondary (previously-excised tissue has grown back).

Esophagus

Codes 43100–43135 report the removal of all or part of the esophagus, according to approach (cervical, thoracic or thoracic with abdominal incision) and if reconstruction is performed.

Endoscopic procedures (43200–43273) visualize the digestive organs, via either a flexible fiber-optic tube or ridged instruments. Select and report an appropriate code for each anatomic site examined.

Esophagoscopy (43200–43232) is direct visualization of the esophagus that does not extend into the stomach. Code 43200 *Esophagoscopy, rigid or flexible* is the parent code for this series; other codes in this series include the parent code.

Upper GI endoscopic (EGD) procedures (43234–43259) include visualization of the esophagus, stomach, and proximal duodenum or jejunum. If the physician does not report an exam of the proximal duodenum or jejunum, append modifier 52 *Reduced procedure* to the appropriate code.

Endoscopic retrograde cholangiopancreatography (ERCP), 43260–43273, uses a combination of endoscopy and fluoroscopy to diagnose and/or treat the biliary or pancreatic ductal systems for problems such as gallstones, inflammatory strictures (scars), leaks (from trauma and surgery), and malignancies.

Laparoscopy (43279–43289) includes surgical esophagogastric fundoplasty, paraesophageal herniorrhaphy, and esophageal lengthening procedures.

Repair (43300–43425) includes open procedures similar to the laparoscopic procedures listed above.

Manipulation (43450–43460) includes various types of esophageal dilation procedures, and esophagogastric tamponade.

Testing Technique

Highlight codes 43200, 43235, and 43260 in this section to indicate these are separate procedures that should not be billed with a surgical endoscopy. When both are performed at the same time, only report the surgical endoscopy.

Stomach

Gastrectomy (43620–43635) is removal of all or part of the stomach. Code according to the amount of stomach removed and reconstruction type.

Several different surgical techniques can be used to attach the remaining portion of the stomach to the small intestine. These range from a simple anastomosis of the duodenum (43631) or the jejunum (43632) to more complex reconstructions such as a Roux-en-Y (43633). Code 43634 *Gastrectomy, partial, distal; with formation of intestinal pouch* describes reconstruction where the distal end of the jejunum is folded in upon itself to form a pouch, the bottom of which is connected to the remaining portion of the small intestine. If the surgeon performs these procedures laparoscopically, report 43659 *Unlisted laparoscopy procedure, stomach*.

Bariatric surgery and gastric bypass are performed to treat morbid obesity. There are several procedures (Roux-en-Y, banding, etc.) and approaches. Laparoscopic gastric restrictive procedures are reported using 43644–43645 and 43770–43775. Open gastric restrictive procedures and bypass surgeries are reported using 43842–43848.

The endoscopic procedures of the stomach are reported using 43234–43259.

Nasogastric and Gastrostomy Tubes

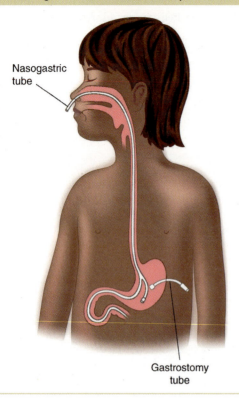

Nasogastric tube

Gastrostomy tube

Source: Delmar/Cengage Learning.

For nasogastric/orogastric intubation that *requires the skill of a surgeon* **and** *fluoroscopic guidance*, report 43752. Gastric intubation and aspiration procedures are reported with a code from range 43753–43755.

Intestines

Incision procedures for the intestines include enterolysis (44005, freeing of intestinal adhesions) and exploratory procedures for biopsy(s) or foreign body removal (44010, 44020, etc.).

Endoscopic procedures are divided by small intestines (44360–44379), beyond the second portion of the duodenum, and stomal endoscopy (44380–44383), where the scope is inserted through an existing ileostomy. Colonoscopies performed via the stoma can be found in this section, as well, with codes 44388–44397.

Enterostomy is the creation of external stomas, or openings in the body for the discharge of body waste. Codes are chosen by the portion of the digestive tract brought

to the surface of the abdomen (this assumes the ostomy is not included in a more extensive procedure).

Appendectomies may be open (44950–44960) or laparoscopic (44970). Unless performed by itself, or for an indicated purpose (rupture, fecalith, and intussusception), an appendectomy is incidental to other intra-abdominal procedures.

Rectum

Proctosigmoidoscopy (45300–45327) examines the rectum and sigmoid colon. Sigmoidoscopy (45330–45345) involves the entire rectum and sigmoid colon, and may include the descending colon. Colonoscopy (45355–45392) visualizes the entire colon from the rectum to cecum and might include the terminal ileum.

Techniques via scope to remove lesions, polyps, or tumors include bipolar cautery (an electric current that flows from one tip of the forceps to the other), hot biopsy forceps (tweezer-like forceps connected to a monopolar electrocautery unit and a grounding pad), cold biopsy forceps (the provider simply grasps the polyp and pulls it from the colon wall), electrocautery snare (a wire loop encircles the specimen), or laser.

NOTE—When multiple specimens are removed during the same proctosigmoidoscopy, report procedure code 45315. For sigmoidoscopies and colonoscopies, report each removal procedure with different methods and sequence codes from highest to lowest value.

Anus

Hemorrhoids are common diagnoses for anal procedures. There are two types: internal (occur above the anal verge) and external (occur below the anal verge). If left untreated, hemorrhoids can become prolapsed and/or strangulated. Thrombosis of an external hemorrhoid occurs when a vein ruptures and/or a blood clot develops.

Treatments for hemorrhoids range from hemorrhoidectomy by banding or ligation via a rubber band (46221) to complete hemorrhoid excisions with treatment for anal fissures and/or fistulas (46945–46946 and 46320–46262).When multiple methods are used to remove multiple hemorrhoids, use a separate code for each removal method.

Liver, Biliary Tract, and Pancreas

Hepatectomy is removal of a portion of the liver. A partial lobectomy (47120) removes a single tumor from a lobe of the liver. The liver is made up of four lobes, the left, right, caudate, and quadrate lobes. It is also separated into eight segments, the caudate (1), lateral (2, 3), medial (4a, 4b) and right (5, 6, 7, 8). Code 47120 should be reported for each tumor, if removed from different lobes of the liver.

Liver injuries can result from trauma, such as stabbing, gunshot wounds, and blunt traumas. To report repairs, choose 47350–47362, depending on the extent of the wound and hemorrhaging involved.

The biliary tract includes the liver, gallbladder, and pancreas. The most common procedure performed on the biliary tract is a cholecystectomy (removal of gallbladder), which can be performed laparoscopically (47562–47564) or open (47600–47620). Additional procedures can be performed during a cholecystectomy, such as a cholangiography and/or an exploration of the common bile duct.

Pancreas procedures are coded from range 48000–48999. A Whipple procedure (pancreaticoduodenectomy or pancreatoduodenectomy) is performed to treat malignancies in the head of the pancreas, or malignant tumors involving the common bile duct or duodenum near the pancreas. Coding depends on how much of the duodenum is removed, whether a partial gastrectomy is performed, and whether pancreatojejunostomy is performed.

Abdomen, Peritoneum, and Omentum

Hernia repairs, reported with 49491–49659, are performed due to a protrusion of internal organs (eg, intestines or omentum) through a weakening in the abdominal wall. Code according to the hernia site (lumber, inguinal, or ventral); the patient's age; the type of hernia (initial or recurrent); the hernia's clinical presentation (eg, reducible, incarcerated, strangulated, or recurrent); and the approach (eg, open or laparoscopic).

Herniorrhaphies can include the placement of reinforcing mesh (eg, Marlex or Prolene), which in some cases may be coded separately using add-on code +49568.

Radiology Section

Digestive radiology codes include 74210–74363 (GI tract, gastric emptying, colon), 76700–76776 (diagnostic ultrasound studies of the abdomen and retroperitoneum), 78201–78299 (nuclear medicine studies of the GI tract).

Diagnostic ultrasound is an imaging technique that uses sound waves to display real-time scanning images and movement; for example, a patient undergoing an ultrasound, real time, of a transplanted kidney with duplex Doppler scan including image documentation (76776 Ultrasound, transplanted kidney, real time and duplex Doppler with image documentation).

Nuclear medicine makes use of radioactive elements for diagnostic imaging and radiopharmaceutical therapy to destroy diseased tissue, and can diagnose other diseases and/or anomalies. Gastric emptying is a radiologic exam to aid in diagnosing neoplasms, ulcers, obstructions, and other diseases. Several of these procedures include kidneys, ureter, and bladder (KUB).

Computed tomographic (CT) colonography or virtual colonoscopy (74261) provides detailed, cross-sectional views of the colon using an X-ray machine linked to a computer. CT pneumocolon is a variation that uses thicker collimation and intravenous contrast without 3-D reconstruction.

Radiology procedures often include both a technical and professional component. To report only the professional component, append modifier 26. To report only the technical component, append modifier TC. To report the complete procedure, submit the claim without a modifier. All permanent images must be saved in the patient's medical record.

Testing Technique

Make sure to read all parenthetical notes in this section, to know what codes should or should not be reported with radiology codes.

Medicine Section

Codes 91010–91013 are used to report esophageal motility or manometry studies to determine how well the esophagus and/or gastroestophageal junction are functioning. Code 91020 describes gastric motility study, and 91022 reports duodenal motility study. Code 91117 describes a colon motility study.

HCPCS Level II Coding

Use codes G0104–G0106 and G0120–G0122 when performing a sigmoidoscopy, colonoscopy, or barium enema when screening for GI malignancies for Medicare patients.

Modifiers

Common modifiers to the digestive system include:

- Modifier 22 *Increased procedural service*—Use when significant additional work is required for extensive lysis of adhesions, or due to obesity.
- Modifier 51 *Multiple procedures*—Use when multiple procedures are performed during the same session by the same provider.

- Modifier 53 *Discontinued procedure*—Use when there is too much undigested food in the area to work effectively.
- Modifier 58 *Staged or related procedure or service by the same physician during the postoperative period*—Use when the procedure can only be accomplished in staged fashion during the global period of another procedure performed by the same provider.
- Modifier 78 *Unplanned return to the operating room by the same physician*—Use when the patient is returned to the operating room for a related procedure (especially work on the intestines) such as internal bleeding, or repair of a suture that rips apart internally (complications).

Other less commonly used modifiers are 80 *Assistant surgeon*, 62 *Two surgeons* (two surgeons of equal stature and responsibility perform the procedure), and 66 *Surgical team*, generally used with liver and pancreatic transplants.

Glossary

Anastomosis—Surgical connection of two tubular structures.

Anoscopy—Procedure using a scope to examine the anus.

Bariatric Surgery—Gastric restrictive procedures that are used to treat morbid obesity.

Barium Enema—Radiographic contrast medium enhanced examination of the colon.

Biliary—Gallbladder, bile, or bile duct.

Bypass—To go around.

Calculus—Concretion of mineral salts, also known as a stone.

Cholangiography—Radiographic recording of the bile ducts.

Cholangiopancreatography—Radiographic recording of the biliary system and pancreas.

Cholecystectomy—Surgical removal of the gallbladder.

Cholecystoenterostomy—Creating a connection between the gallbladder and intestine.

Cholecystography—Radiographic recording of the gallbladder.

Colonoscopy—Fiberscopic examination of the entire colon that may include part of the terminal ileum.

Colostomy—Artificial opening between the colon and the abdominal wall.

Congenital—Existing from birth.

Conscious (moderate) Sedation—A decreased level of consciousness in which the patient is not completely asleep.

Crohn's Disease—Regional enteritis.

Diaphragm—Muscular wall that separates the thoracic and abdominal cavities.

Diaphragmatic Hernia—Hernia of the diaphragm.

Dilatation—Expansion.

Diverticulum—Protrusion of the intestinal wall.

Duodenography—Radiographic recording of the duodenum, or the first part of the small intestine.

Dysphagia—Difficulty swallowing.

Endoscopy—Inspection of body organs or cavities through an existing opening or through a small incision.

Enterolysis—Releasing of adhesions of intestine.

Epiglottidectomy—Excising the covering of the larynx.

Eventration of Intestines—Intestinal protrusion of the intestines through the abdominal wall.

Evisceration—Pulling the viscera outside of the body through an incision.

Exenteration—Major operation during which an organ and its adjacent structures are removed.

Exstrophy—Condition in which an organ is turned inside out.

Exteriorization—Exposing an internal structure outside the body for observation, surgery, or experimentation, such as creating a passage from the bladder to the abdominal wall.

Fistula—Abnormal opening from one area to another area in the body or outside of the body.

Fluoroscopy—Procedure for viewing the interior of the body using X-rays and projecting the image onto a television screen.

Fulguration—Use of electric current to destroy tissue.

Fundoplasty—Repair of the bottom of an organ or muscle.

Gastrointestinal—Pertaining to the stomach and the intestine.

Gastroplasty—Stomach operation for repair or reconfiguration.

Gastrostomy—Artificial opening between the stomach and the abdominal wall.

Hepatography—Radiographic recording of the liver.

Hernia—Organ or tissue protruding through the wall or cavity that usually contains it.

Hypogastric—Lowest middle abdominal area.

Ileostomy—Artificial opening between the ileum and the abdominal wall.

Incarcerated—Constricted, irreducible hernia that may cause obstruction of the organ contained within the hernia.

Intussusception—Slipping of one part of intestine into another part.

Jejunostomy—A procedure to create an artificial opening between the jejunum and the abdominal wall.

Laparoscopy—Exploring the abdomen and pelvic cavities using a scope placed through a small incision in the abdominal wall.

Lavage—Washing out an organ.

Marsupialization—Surgical procedure to create an exterior pouch from an internal abscess.

Omentum—Peritoneal connection between the stomach and other internal organs.

Peritoneal—Within the lining of the abdominal cavity.

Peritoneoscopy—Visualization of the abdominal cavity using a scope placed through a small incision in the abdominal wall.

Polyp—Tumor on a pedicle that bleeds easily and may become malignant.

Proctosigmoidoscopy—Fiberscopic examination of the sigmoid colon and rectum.

Reanastomosis—Reconnecting a previous connection between two places organs or spaces.

Rectocele—Herniation of the rectal wall through the posterior wall of the vagina.

Reducible—Able to be corrected or put back into a normal position.

Sialolithotomy—Surgical removal of a stone located in the salivary gland or duct.

Varices—Varicose veins.

Volvulus—Twisted section of intestine.

Chapter Review Questions

1. The Splenic (left colic) flexure lies in the upper-left quadrant, between what two portions of the large intestine?

   A. The cecum and ascending colon

   B. The descending and sigmoid colon

   C. The transverse and descending colon

   D. The ascending and transverse colon

2. A surgical procedure that creates an opening into the jejunum is defined as a:

   A. Colostomy

   B. Gastrojejunostomy

   C. Gastroenterostomy

   D. Jejunostomy

3. A 50-year-old male with a body mass index of 45 has uncontrolled diabetes and hypertension. Failing non-operative obesity interventions the decision has been made to perform gastric banding. A laparoscope along with four to six trocar ports are sited through the anterior abdominal wall above the umbilicus. The silicone gastric band is placed and secured around the upper stomach to form a smaller stomach pouch with a narrowed outlet. Tubing is attached to the band and tunneled through the abdominal wall connecting it to an access port. What CPT® code should be used for this procedure?

   A. 43634

   B. 43645

   C. 43770

   D. 43848

4. A CT scan of a 68-year-old female shows a large ventral incisional hernia in the epigastric midline just superior to the umbilicus. The skin of the abdomen is prepped and the physician makes an incision over the hernia. Attention is turned to the midline hernia and an ellipse of skin is excised over the hernia, deepened down through subcutaneous tissue. There is a very large fatty sac and the hernia has very poor quality tissue on all sides of the defect. This area of the anterior abdominal wall and rectus sheath are reinforced. The posterior rectus sheath is then sutured from side to side, to itself, to close the midline defect. The correct CPT® code is:

    A. 49652

    B. 49654

    C. 49565

    D. 49560

5. A 35-year-old male has internal hemorrhoids and has elected to have them removed. The ligator and alligator forceps have been inserted though an anoscope. The physician identifies the most prominent hemorrhoid and ligates it at the base with a rubber band. Which CPT® code should be used?

    A. 46250

    B. 46945

    C. 46255

    D. 46221

6. An 81-year-old woman underwent a radical right hemicolectomy for carcinoma of the ascending colon. She returns at this time as advised for a follow-up colonoscopy. The physician inserts the video colonoscope into the anus and starts to advance the scope through the colon past the splenic flexure when the patient's blood pressure drops. The physician elects to terminate the procedure and the scope is withdrawn. The correct CPT® code and modifier are:

    A. 45378-53

    B. 45391-22

    C. 44360-52

    D. 45355-59

7. A 79-year-old male has acute cholecystitis and abnormal liver function test. He has elected to go in for surgery. A laparoscope is placed through an epigastric incision with the insertion of two lateral 5 mm ports. The gallbladder is elevated and the cystic duct is located and dissected out. In the process of transecting the duct, the gallbladder tears and several gallstones were released. These are removed with a gallstone retriever along with removal of the gallbladder. The cystic duct stump is tied off and the common bile duct is incised. A large stone is seen and removed. The common bile duct is closed over a t-tube catheter which is brought out through the abdominal wall and connected to a drainage bag. What are the codes for this procedure?

    A. 47564

    B. 47480, 47564-51

    C. 47420, 47562-51

    D. 47480, 47562-51

8. An elderly gentleman presents with a high-grade small bowel obstruction. A midline abdominal incision is performed encountering fairly dense adhesions. Using a combination of sharp dissection and electrocautery, a full adhesiolysis is performed on several adhesions up to the anterior abdominal wall, which appears to be the culprit for this patient's small bowel obstruction. In dissecting out this mat of adhesions, an enterotomy is made and a limited small bowel resection and a double-stapled anastomosis is performed. What CPT® code(s) describe(s) the procedure?

    A. 44120, 44005-51

    B. 44125

    C. 44120

    D. 44130, 44005-51

9. **Operative Note #1:**

Procedure: Colonoscopy

Extent of Examination: Terminal ileum

Reason(s) for Examination: Hx of rectal cancer s/p LAR and colonic J pouch for closure of loop ileostomy

Description of Procedure:
Informed consent was obtained with the benefits, risks, and alternatives to colonoscopy explained, including the risk of perforation. The patient agreed to proceed. No contraindications were noted on physical exam. Monitored anesthesia care (MAC) was administered. The bowel was prepared with Fleets enemas. The quality of prep was fair. Prior to the exam a digital exam was performed and was unremarkable. The procedure was performed with the patient in left lateral decubitus position. The cecum was identified by the ileocecal valve. The withdrawal time from the cecum was 7 minutes. The patient tolerated the procedure well. There were no complications. The exam was limited by poor preparation.

Findings:
At the splenic flexure, moderate inflammation with erythema, granularity, friability, and hypervascularity was seen. There was no mucosal bleeding. In the proximal descending colon, moderate segmental inflammation with erythema, granularity, friability, and hypervascularity was seen. In the rectum, an abnormality was noted: Anastomosis -patent and normal. No evidence of polyp. Just proximal to anastomosis—significant diffuse colitis.

Endoscopic Diagnoses (see above description):
Colitis

What are the CPT® and ICD-9-CM codes for the operative report?

10. **Operative Report #2:**

Extent of Examination: Upper GI Endoscopy

Reason(s) for Examination: GERD

Description of Procedure:
Informed consent was obtained with benefits, risks, and alternatives to upper GI endoscopy explained, including the risk of perforation. The patient agreed to proceed. No contraindications were noted on physical exam. Anesthesia administered by CRNA (see anesthesia report). MAC was administered. The procedure was performed with the patient in left lateral decubitus position. The instrument was inserted to the second part of the duodenum. The patient tolerated the procedure well. There were no complications. The heart rate was normal. The oxygen saturation and skin color were normal. Upon discharge from the endoscopy area, the patient will be recovered per established procedures and protocols.

Findings:
The esophagus was examined and no abnormalities were seen. The gastroesophageal junction (upper level of gastric folds) was located 40 cm from the incisors. The stomach was examined and no abnormalities were seen. The small bowel was examined and no abnormalities were seen.

What are the CPT® and ICD-9-CM codes for the operative report?

Chapter 10

Urinary System and Male Genital System

Introduction

In this chapter, we will explore the kidneys, ureters, bladder, and urethra. Objectives for this chapter include:

◖ Describe the anatomy of the urinary system and male reproductive system

◖ Identify and locate diseases specific to the urinary system within ICD-9-CM

◖ Review the components of the CPT® codebook specific to the genitourinary system and male genital system

◖ Determine when and how to apply modifier(s)

◖ Discover which HCPCS Level II codes are significant for the genitourinary system

Anatomy and Medical Terminology

The Urinary System

The urinary system removes the waste product urea from the blood. The human urinary system consists of two kidneys, two ureters, one bladder, and one urethra. In ICD-9-CM and CPT® coding, terms such as "renal" and "nephro" usually are interchangeable. The definition of renal is "pertinent to the kidney," whereas the meaning of "nephro" is "kidney."

Urinary System

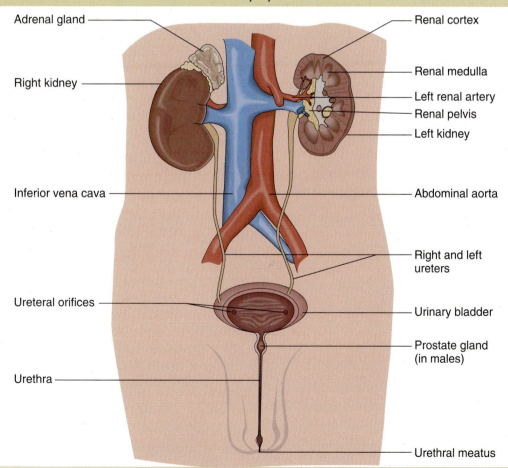

Source: Delmar/Cengage Learning.

Within the renal sinus of the kidney is the renal pelvis. The renal pelvis ("pyelo-") is the expanded proximal end of the ureter (where the ureter attaches to the kidney). It receives urine through the major calyces. The primary function of the renal pelvis is to act as a funnel for urine flowing to the ureter. Urine passes through the ureters and flows into the bladder, where it is stored.

At the time of urination, the bladder muscles tighten and squeeze urine from the bladder into the urethra (the outlet for the urine to exit the body). The proximal opening of the urethra is called the bladder neck; in men, it is adjacent to the prostate gland. If the bladder neck does not open completely during voiding, the bladder neck may become obstructed. This can be caused in men by an enlarged prostate. In women, vaginal or pelvic prolapse is the most common cause of bladder neck obstruction.

The kidneys are bean-shaped organs approximately the size of your fist, located near the middle of the back. The kidneys remove urea from blood through tiny filtering units called nephrons. Each nephron consists of a ball formed of small capillaries, called a glomerulus, and a small tube called a renal tubule. Urea, together with water and other waste substances, form urine as it passes through the nephrons and down the renal tubules of the kidney.

The ureters are muscular tubes that carry urine from the kidneys to the bladder. The ureters originate in the renal pelvis and end in the bladder. The muscles in the ureter walls constantly tighten and relax (peristalsis) to force urine downward away from the kidneys. If urine is allowed to stand still, or back up, a kidney infection (pyelonephritis) can develop.

The urinary bladder is a hollow, muscular, expandable organ that collects urine. It can be referred to as "vesical" or "cyst" in coding of procedures. When you urinate, the brain signals the bladder muscles to tighten, squeezing urine out of the bladder. At the same time, the brain signals the sphincter muscles to relax. As these muscles relax, urine exits through the urethra.

The urethra is a tube that connects the urinary bladder to the outside of the body. In the male, the portion of the urethra passing through the prostate gland is known as the prostatic urethra. This section of the urethra is designed to accept the drainage from the tiny ducts within the prostate and is equipped with two ejaculatory tubes. The female urethra leads out of the body via the urethral orifice.

Male Reproductive System

The male reproductive system consists of the testicles (or testes), the duct system (which includes the epididymis and vas deferens), and the accessory glands (which include the seminal vesicles, prostate gland, and the penis).

The testes produce and store sperm cells. They are surrounded on the front and sides by a serous membrane called the tunica vaginalis. The testicles are part of the endocrine system because they secrete hormones. As a male develops, the pituitary gland—which is located near the brain—induces the testicles to produce testosterone.

The epididymis and vas deferens (deferent duct) make up the duct system. The epididymis is a coiled tube within the scrotum connecting the testicles to the vas deferens. The vas deferens are muscular tubes that transport semen from the epidiymis into the pelvis, and then connect to the prostatic urethra.

The scrotum holds testicles outside the body. The testicles need to be kept cooler than body temperature to create sperm.

Seminal vesicles are a pair of tubular glands located behind the bladder and above the prostate gland that contribute fluid to the ejaculate. The seminal vesicles and prostate gland, also known as the accessory glands, provide fluids that lubricate the duct system and nourish the sperm.

Sperm develops in the testicles within a system of tiny tubes called the seminiferous tubules. Testosterone and other hormones cause the cells to transform into sperm cells. These cells push themselves into the epididymis, where they complete their development. The sperm then move to the vas deferens, or sperm duct.

The prostate gland surrounds the neck of a man's bladder and urethra. It is approximately the size of a walnut. The function of the prostate gland is to secrete fluid that forms part of the seminal fluid, which carries sperm. During orgasm, the muscular glands of the prostate help propel the prostate fluid and sperm (produced in the testicles) into the urethra. Semen leaves through the tip of the penis during ejaculation.

The penis is made up of two parts: the shaft and the glans (or head). At the end of the glans is a small slit or opening called the meatus, where semen and urine exit the body through the urethra. The foreskin, or prepuce, is the loose skin covering the end of the penis. Excision of the prepuce is called circumcision.

Key Root Words, Suffixes and Prefixes

-cele	herniation, or prolapse
cyst/o	relating to a bladder
dys-	painful, bad, disordered, difficult
ex/o	outside of, without
hydr/o	relating to fluid, water or hydrogen
-ia/sis	condition of
lith/o	calcification, stone
nephr/o	relating to the kidney
-oma	tumor
orchi/o	relating to the testicles
-orrhaphy	suturing
osche/o	relating to the scrotum
-osis	condition, process
-pexy	fixation or suspension
pyel/o	relating to the renal pelvis
vesic/o	relating to the urinary bladder

ICD-9-CM Coding

Diseases specific to the kidney, ureters, bladder, and urethra are covered primarily in chapter 10: Diseases of the Genitourinary System (580–629). This chapter also includes Diseases of the Male Genital Organs (600–608). Diagnoses for the genitourinary system also can be found in chapter 14: Congenital Anomalies (740–759),

chapter 2: Neoplasms (140–239), and chapter 16: Signs, Symptoms, and Ill-Defined Conditions.

Diseases of the Genitourinary System (580–629)

Nephritis (category 583) is inflammation of the kidneys, usually caused by bacteria or their toxins. Glomerulonephritis (categories 580 & 582) is a form of nephritis in which the lesions involve primarily the glomeruli. This condition may be acute, subacute, or chronic. Nephrotic syndrome (category 581) is a condition marked by increased glomerular permeability to proteins, usually caused by glomerular injury.

Renal (kidney) failure (categories 584–586) is the inability of the kidneys to function. There are many causes. The condition may be partial, temporary, acute, chronic, or complete. In chronic kidney disease (CKD) (585), the kidneys' ability to filter waste from the blood declines slowly. CKD has five stages, based on the patient's glomerular filtration rate (GFR):

Stage	GFR
Stage I	> 90
Stage II	60–89
Stage III	30–59
Stage IV	15–29
Stage V	0–14

End stage renal disease (ESRD-585.6) is the stage of chronic renal failure that requires renal replacement therapies. These may include dialysis or transplantation.

Encounters for patients presenting with hypertension and chronic kidney disease (CKD) are coded from range 403–405. Although coders rarely are allowed to assume information that is not documented specifically, whenever a patient has both chronic kidney disease and hypertension, you should code primary hypertension unless secondary hypertension is specified in the documentation. Secondary hypertension is defined as "high arterial blood pressure due to or with a variety of primary diseases, such as renal disorders, CNS disorders, endocrine, and vascular diseases."

Renovascular disease is a progressive condition caused by narrowing or blockage of the renal arteries or veins. It can be coded as malignant, benign, or unspecified. Generally, this term describes three disorders:

1. Renal artery occlusion: The arteries carrying blood to the kidneys are blocked. This condition can affect one or both of the arteries. Renal veins carry the filtered blood away from the kidneys to the rest of the body.

2. Renal vein thrombosis: A rare condition that occurs when one or both of these veins develop clots.

3. Renal atheroembolism: Fatty materials build up and block the renal arterioles (the smallest arteries leading to the capillaries).

Impaired renal function resulting from other conditions is coded from category 588. Conditions that can cause impaired renal function include renal osteodystrophy, nephrogenic diabetes insipidus, and secondary hyperparathyroidism. The physician must document that the condition was caused by the impaired renal function.

Diabetes insipidus causes renal impairment through excessive urination, due either to inadequate amounts of the antidiuretic hormone in the body (central diabetes insipidus, 253.5) or by failure of the kidney to respond to the antidiuretic hormone (nephrogenic diabetes insipidus, 588.1).

Hyperparathyroidism is an excessive level of the parathyroid hormone level in the body. When parathyroid hormone levels are elevated, increased bone reabsorption, decreased new bone formation, and decreased bone mass result (renal osteodystrophy).

Small kidney (category 589) may be unilateral or bilateral. It can result from several conditions. Congenital dysplasia occurs when the kidney does not grow with the rest of the body, or is small at birth. The kidney also can be damaged because of a blockage in drainage (reflux nephropathy), severe kidney infection (pyelonephritis), decreased blood supply to the kidney, or glomerulonephritis. If both kidneys are small, there may be inadequate excretion. One small kidney can cause problems such as high blood pressure, even if the other kidney is normal.

Other Diseases of Urinary System (590–599)

Kidney

Pyelonephritis (category 590) is an infection of the kidney. It differs from nephritis in that pyelonephritis is usually the result of a bacterial infection that has ascended from the urinary bladder. If the organism causing the infection is known, use an additional code to identify the organism. In most cases, Escherichia coli (E. coli) is the responsible microbe (041.41–041.49).

Testing Technique
It is important to follow sequencing rules in the ICD-9-CM codebook. The instruction to "use additional code" alerts the coder to sequence the additional code secondarily. The proper order in this example is 590, 041.4x.

Hydronephrosis (591) is the accumulation of fluid in the renal pelvis and kidney due to a urinary obstruction. If the obstruction is not treated, the urine may cause infection. Some causes of obstruction are kidney or ureteral stones, neurogenic bladder, and hyperplasia of the prostate (BPH) or enlargement of the prostate. Neurogenic bladder is a dysfunction of the urinary bladder caused by the nerves supplying the bladder, or lesions of the central nervous system.

Calculi (stones) are reported by location: kidney (592.0) and ureter (592.1) or lower urinary tract (category 594). Although the male patient may have a diagnosis of prostatic calcification (stone within the prostate, 602.0), most calculi are located in the urinary system. If the stone is small, the patient may pass it without surgical intervention. If the stone cannot be passed, additional treatment—including surgery or procedures to break up the stone so that it can be passed—may be necessary.

Kidney disorders coded in category 593 include: nephroptosis, hypertrophy of the kidney, kidney cysts, strictures of the kidney and ureter, hydroureter, postural proteinuria, vesicoureteral reflux (backflow of urine from the bladder into ureter), vascular disorders of the kidney, ureteral fistula, and other unspecified disorders of the kidney and ureter.

Bladder

Cystitis (category 595) is an inflammation of the bladder, usually because of a urinary tract infection (UTI). There are many forms of cystitis; they are classified as acute, chronic, interstitial, and trigonitis. Interstitial cystitis, also known as painful bladder syndrome, is a chronic inflammation of the bladder, usually with an unknown etiology (cause). People with interstitial cystitis usually cannot hold much urine in their bladders and may experience urinary frequency.

Voiding disorders (category 596) are conditions that affect the normal functions of urinating and can include bladder neck obstruction, bladder diverticulum, neurogenic bladder, and detrusor instability. Urinary incontinence is probably the most common voiding disorder. These codes can be found in Signs and Symptoms subcategory 788.3.

Types of incontinence include:

◖ Urge incontinence—Leakage of urine that occurs immediately after an urgent, irrepressible need to void

◖ Stress incontinence—Leakage of urine due to abrupt increases in intra-abdominal pressure caused by coughing, sneezing—laughing, bending, or lifting

◖ Overflow incontinence—Dribbling of urine from an overly full bladder

◖ Functional incontinence—Urine loss due to cognitive or physical impairments such as stroke or dementia

◖ Mixed incontinence—Any combination of the above types of incontinence

With the exception of stress incontinence, these ICD-9-CM codes are not gender specific.

Infections of the Urinary Tract

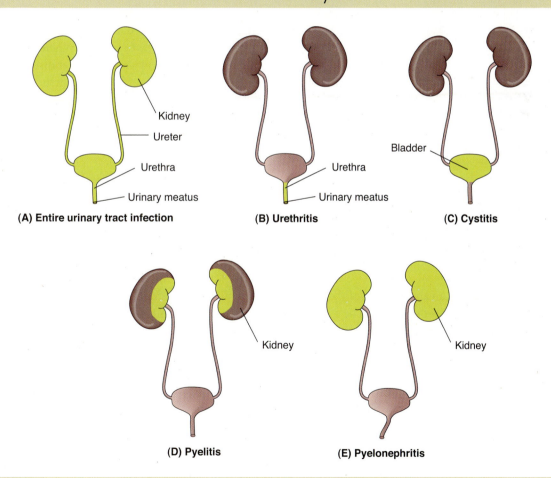

(A) Entire urinary tract infection

(B) Urethritis

(C) Cystitis

(D) Pyelitis

(E) Pyelonephritis

Source: Delmar/Cengage Learning.

Urinary tract infection (UTI) (599.0) is a bacterial infection that affects any part of the urinary tract. UTI usually presents with dysuria (burning on urination), frequency of urination, urgency, painful urination, and cloudy urine. When the organism causing the UTI is known, such as E. Coli, use an additional code to report the organism.

Diseases of the Male Genital Organs (600–608)

Prostate

One of the most common prostatic disorders is benign hyperplasia of the prostate (BPH), coded in category 600. BPH is a benign enlargement of the prostate gland caused by excessive growth of prostatic nodules.

If the prostate gland becomes enlarged, the urethra may become compressed, resulting in partial or complete obstruction, and causing symptoms of urinary hesitancy, frequency, dysuria (painful urination), urinary retention, and an increased risk of urinary tract infections. These symptoms commonly are referred to as LUTS (lower urinary tract symptoms). There is no specific code for LUTS; you will need to code each symptom individually.

Prostatitis (category 601) is an inflammation of the prostate gland, usually because of infection. It can be either acute or chronic. A patient presenting with prostatitis may have an elevated prostate specific antigen (PSA). If this is the case, the patient will need to be monitored closely because an elevated PSA may be an indicator of prostate cancer. Elevated PSA without a diagnosis of cancer should be coded as an abnormal finding (790.93).

Dysplasia of the prostate is an abnormality of shape and size of the tissues of the prostate. It can be a pre-malignant condition. If the documentation states prostatic intraepithelial neoplasia III (PIN III), ICD-9-CM code 233.4 *Carcinoma in situ of prostate* should be used. PIN I and PIN II are coded to 602.3 for dysplasia of the prostate.

Testing Technique

It is important to understand the malignant classifications in the Neoplasm Table. Carcinoma *in situ* means the cancer is contained and has not spread to another location.

Spermatic cord, Testis, Tunica Vaginalis, Epididymis

Hydrocele (category 603) is an accumulation of serous fluid in a sac-like cavity, especially the spermatic cord, testis, or tunica vaginalis. Encysted hydrocele describes a cyst above the testis. When an infection is noted in a hydrocele, an additional code should be used to report the infecting organism, if known.

Orchitis (category 604) is an inflammation of the testis, which can be caused by trauma, ischemia, metastasis, mumps, or a secondary infection. Epididymitis is an inflammation of the epididymis, usually because of infection, or rarely due to trauma. When orchitis or epididymitis is present due to another disease, the underlying disease should be coded first.

Penis

Phimosis is a stricture, stenosis, or narrowing of the preputial orifice so that the foreskin cannot be pushed back over the glans penis. Phimosis (605) and balanitis (607.1) are the most common diagnosis codes reported when a circumcision is performed on an adult. When a routine circumcision is performed on an infant, use diagnosis code V50.2 *Ritual circumcision*, unless there is a medical reason to perform the procedure.

Male infertility codes are listed within category 606 and include Azoospermia (absence of spermatozoa in the semen), oligospemia (insufficient number of sperm in the semen), and extratesticular causes of infertility.

Penile disorders coded in category 607 include: leukoplakia of penis (white, thickened patches on glans penis), balanoposthitis (inflammation of glans penis and prepuce), other inflammatory disorders of penis and priapism (prolonged penile erection), vascular disorders, edema, impotence, and Peyronie's disease (curvature of the erect penis).

Congenital Anomalies (752–753)

The most common congenital problems of the penis are hypospadias and epispadias. These conditions are abnormal urethra meati. In hypospadias, the urethra meatus is on the underside of the penis instead of at the end. Epispadias is when the meatus is on the upper side of the penis.

Neoplasms

Genitourinary cancer diagnoses are found within the Neoplasm chapter of ICD-9-CM and are specific to the anatomy of the organ. The Table of Neoplasms is used to select codes to describe primary and secondary (metastatic) tumors, benign tumors, and tissue of uncertain behavior. "Uncertain behavior" neoplasm codes should only be reported when the pathologist has documented the tissue has characteristics of several different diseases, or when it is described as hypoplasia or pre-cancerous. It should also be coded when the specific morphology indicates that the neoplasm is of uncertain behavior.

Renal cell carcinoma (RCC) is the most common type of kidney cancer. RCC includes clear cell, papillary, chromophobe, and collecting duct carcinomas, and is difficult to detect in its early stages. Classic symptoms are blood in the urine (hematuria), flank pain, palpable mass, recurrent fever, rapid weight loss, abdominal or lower back pain, or fatigue.

Bladder cancer is more common in men than women. Types of bladder cancer include:

◖ Transitional cell bladder cancer begins in the cells lining the bladder; cancers confined to the lining of the bladder are superficial bladder cancers.

◖ Squamous cell bladder cancer begins in squamous cells, which are thin, flat cells that may form in the bladder after long-term infection or irritation.

◖ Adenocarcinoma develops in the inner lining of the bladder, usually because of chronic irritation and inflammation.

Prostate cancer is the second most common cause of cancer-related death in men in the United States. Age is the most significant risk factor; screening for prostate cancer is recommended for men over the age of 50.

Testicular cancer most often occurs in young men. Types of testicular cancer include:

◖ Germ cell tumors, which occur in the cells that produce sperm

◖ Stromal tumors occur in the testicular tissue where hormones are produced

Penile cancer is rare. The most common types of penile cancer are squamous cell carcinoma, adenocarcinoma, melanoma, basal cell penile cancer, and sarcoma.

Injuries

Injuries to the genitourinary organs are located in the Injury and Poisoning section (866–867). This section includes Complications of Surgical and Medical Care, Not Elsewhere Classified (996–999), such as inflammation and infection and mechanical complications of genitourinary devices.

Signs, Symptoms, and Ill-Defined Conditions

Symptoms, Signs and Ill-defined Conditions (780–799), which include the subcategories Symptoms Involving the Urinary System (category 788) and Other Symptoms Involving Abdomen and Pelvis (category 789), often are used when a final diagnosis is not documented.

At times, a patient will be referred to a urologist for an abnormal digital rectal exam. Although there is no specific diagnosis, 796.4 would be an appropriate diagnosis. Diagnosis code V76.44 *Screening for malignant neoplasm of the prostate* may also be documented. Let the physician's documentation be your guide when choosing not only these codes, but also all diagnosis and procedure codes.

CPT® Coding

Urinary System (50010–53899)

The Urinary System section of CPT® includes procedures on the kidneys, ureters, bladder, and urethra. Some code descriptors specifically state unilateral or bilateral. If procedures do not state "bilateral," and the procedure is performed on both the right and left sides, modifier 50, or RT and LT modifiers, depending upon the carrier, will need to be added. Within the Urinary System, bilateral services may be billed for procedures on the kidneys and ureters only. The bladder and urethra are singular structures.

Testing Technique

Be careful when selecting codes for the ureters versus the urethra. These structures are similar in spelling. Make sure to read the procedure description carefully and select the correct code for the structure involved.

Use of an operating microscope is not included with many of these codes and should be reported separately using CPT® 69990. Reading the description of each code and the associated information noted below each code will assist you when choosing the correct and complete code(s).

A surgical endoscopy (eg, laparoscopy, cystoscopy) always includes any diagnostic endoscopy performed at the same session; diagnostic endoscopy should not be reported with a surgical endoscopy.

Kidney Diseases and Disorders

Incision

Procedures described as "-otomy" (eg, pylonephrotomy) typically are coded with incision codes for the specific location. Incision codes include stent and catheter insertions.

Treatment for renal abscess or renal stone extraction may require a nephrostomy tube to be placed. This is often performed under CT guidance not only to place the tube, but also to perform the abscess drainage or stone removal. If this is the case, report CPT® 75989 in addition to the appropriate code for the tube placement. Percutaneous removal of stones is coded by the size of the stone, and usually will require fluoroscopic guidance and an existing nephrostomy tube or tract. In most cases, the nephrostomy tube has been placed during a previous surgical setting; if this is not the case, a nephrostomy tract must be created and reported using CPT® 50395.

Testing Technique

Append modifier 26 to imaging guidance codes when a procedure is performed by a provider in a facility setting. If the procedure is performed in the physician's office, modifier 26 is not required.

Nephrotomy is an incision into the kidney, sometimes performed for exploration (50045). Pyelotomy and nephrotomy are not the same procedure. Nephrotomy relates to the kidney proper and pyelotomy relates to the renal pelvis, which is the larger portion of the ureter. When renal stones are removed from the renal pelvis, codes 50130–50135 are reported.

When reporting incision procedures of the ureter, 50610–50630 are location specific regarding the ureterolithotomy (eg, 50610 upper one-third of the ureter; 50620 middle one-third of the ureter; and 50630 lower one-third of the ureter). Stent insertion codes within this category are "open" procedures and do not include cystoscope for stent placement. When stents are inserted via cystoscopy, report 52332.

Excision

Care should be used when reporting 50650 *Ureterectomy with bladder cuff (separate procedure)*. Services listed as "separate procedures" are an integral component of another service or procedure and should not be reported in addition to the code for which it is considered an integral component.

Bladder aspiration codes (51100–51102) are reported under the heading "removal," and include aspiration by needle, trocar, or catheter. Also included in this section are the codes for insertion of a suprapubic catheter (51102). The difference between using 51102 for suprapubic catheter insertion and 51040 is the technique. In 51040, the physician places the catheter through an open incision in the bladder. In 51102, a suprapubic catheter is placed in the bladder through the skin, but without an open incision into the bladder.

A urachal cyst is the remnant of bladder development that attaches from the bladder to the umbilicus. Excision of urachal cyst or sinus, with or without umbilical hernia repair, is reported with 51500.

Cystectomy (bladder removal) is described using 51550–51596. The codes are designated as partial or complete. During these procedures, it is necessary to divert urine from the ureters to either an opening in the skin (ureterostomy), or to a sigmoid or neobladder. When the bladder is removed and the urine diverted to the skin via a stoma, the urine is collected in an appliance (bag) attached to the outside of the patient's abdomen. A sigmoid bladder can be catheterized from the skin, but does not require an appliance attached to the patient's skin to collect the urine. The opening in the skin for patients with a sigmoid bladder (51590) can be covered by a Band-Aid. A neobladder is constructed using a segment of the small and/or large intestine and the patient will void through his or her urethra if a neobladder is created (51596). A bilateral pelvic lymph node dissection is included with all of the cystectomy procedures except creation of the neobladder. If bilateral pelvic lymph node dissection is performed with creation of the neobladder, it should be reported separately (38770).

CPT® 51597 is a procedure where the physician removes the bladder, lower ureters, lymph nodes, urethra, prostate (if applicable), colon, and rectum due to a vesical, prostatic or urethral malignancy. This code is used only when the need for the excision is related to a lower urinary tract or male genital malignancy, and not for gynecological or intestinal malignancy.

Urethral procedures noted in CPT® 53000–53520 are performed using an "open" approach. When reviewing the operative report, ascertain the approach to assign the correct code, either via cystoscope (52000–52318) or open.

Repair

Ureteral repair often is performed for stricture (obstruction), inflammatory disease, injury, or for repositioning or reconnection (anastomosis). It may be necessary for the surgeon to divide and reconnect the ureter to bypass a defect or obstruction. When the ureter is divided and repositioned, the description will state "-ostomy" as a suffix (eg, ureterureterostomy (end-to-end anastomosis of two parts of the ureter), ureterocalycostomy (anastomosis of ureter to renal calyx).

Creation of a ureteral conduit (50820) is a procedure that diverts the flow of urine through an opening of the

skin. Urinary diversion is usually required for cancer or obstruction. When creation of a diversion is performed with removal of the bladder (cystectomy), see code 51596. Continent diversion codes include harvesting a piece of intestine to create the diversion and reconnection of the remaining bowel (intestinal anastomosis); intestinal anastomosis should not be coded separately.

Introduction

Ureteral stents are either indwelling or externally accessible. There are separate CPT® codes for placement of indwelling stents or externally accessible stents, and for stent removal or removal with replacement. Services are reported with different codes based on the approach (percutaneous or transurethral). The codes in this series are for stent placement without cystoscopy.

Injection or insertion procedures of the bladder often are performed in an office or minor procedure suite. These codes include catheter changes (51702–51703), suprapubic catheter changes (51705–51710), and bladder irrigation and/or instillation procedures (51700). If a separately, identifiable evaluation and management (E/M) service is performed on the same day as one of these procedures, append modifier 25 to the E/M code.

Laparoscopy

Laparoscopic surgery is a minimally invasive surgical technique performed through small incisions. Trocars, or cannulas, are placed through these incisions and used to access the structures to be treated. The abdomen usually is insufflated with carbon dioxide gas. This lifts the abdominal wall away from the internal organs, improving visualization and access to the surgical field. Instruments are then placed through the trocars to perform the surgical procedure. CPT® laparoscopy codes are reported for procedures performed on the kidney, ureter, and bladder.

Endoscopy

Endoscopy includes a rigid or flexible tube, a light delivery system, a lens system to transmit the image from the scope, and an additional channel to allow entry of medical instruments. Although most endoscopic procedures are performed through a natural opening (eg, urethra or anus), some are performed through an established nephrostomy or pyelostomy (surgically created artificial opening), or through a nephrotomy or pyelotomy (small incision made in the organ).

Other Procedures of Kidney

Renal transplantation codes (50300–50380) are divided into renal autotransplantation (tissue transplanted from one part of the body to another in the same individual, also known as an autograft) and renal allotransplantation. When coding a renal allotransplantation, at least three CPT® codes must be reported: cadaver or living donor nephrectomy, backbench work, and recipient renal allotransplantation.

Lithotripsy, extracorporeal shock wave (ESWL) (50590) is used to break up kidney stones by directing shock waves through a liquid surrounding the patient. A series of shock waves (each lasting only a fraction of a second) are directed at the stone. These shock waves pulverize the stone, breaking it into tiny fragments that pass through the patient's urinary system. A ureteral stent may be placed to assist with the evacuation of the stones.

Percutaneous ablation of renal tumor(s) (50592) uses radiofrequencies under CT, MRI, or ultrasound guidance. An internally cooled radiofrequency needle is placed into a renal tumor through a small incision. The tumor tissue is then heated until there is sufficient and permanent cell damage and tumor necrosis.

Percutaneous cryotherapy ablation of renal tumor(s) (50593) also is performed using CT, MRI, or ultrasound guidance, but differs from the radiofrequency ablation in that a cryoprobe is placed in the tumor and cycles of freezing and thawing are used to cover the tumor tissue in an ice ball, which destroys the tumor.

Urodynamics

Urodynamics (51725–51798) codes have both a professional and technical component. If the equipment is owned by and the service performed in a facility location, append modifier 26. Urodynamics studies assess the bladder, urethra, and associated nerves and muscles for appropriate functioning. These studies usually are performed for incontinence, frequent urination, problems emptying the bladder, and urinary tract infections. The studies help to define the cause of the urinary

dysfunction so that it can be treated through surgical repair, injection, or medication.

A cystometrogram (CMG) measures how much fluid the bladder can hold, how much pressure builds up inside the bladder, how full it is when you feel the urge to urinate, and whether the bladder can be emptied completely. Catheters placed in the bladder contain a pressure-measuring device called a manometer. Another catheter may be placed in the rectum or vagina to record intra-abdominal pressures. As the bladder slowly is filled with warm water, the manometer records the volume of water and bladder pressure. If the bladder contracts suddenly while being filled, the manometer records the leakage. When the bladder is filled, the patient is asked to void while the manometer measures the neurologic activity and pressures, as well as any residual urine. CMG procedures are described using CPT® codes 51725–51729. The code for voiding pressure studies is 51797. It is an add-on code and can only be used with code 51728 or 51729. Uroflometry (51736–51741), commonly called uroflow, measures the amount of urine and the flow rate.

Electromyography (EMG) studies (51784–51785) measure the electrical activity associated with the bladder during filling and emptying. In stimulus evoked response studies (51792), the head of the penis is stimulated and equipment measures the delay time for travel of stimulation through the pelvic nerves to the pudenal nerve. This procedure usually is not performed with CMGs. Measurement of post-void residual is described in CPT® 51798. This procedure is performed using non-imaging ultrasound.

Endoscopy—Cystoscopy, Urethroscopy, Cystourethroscopy (52000–52700)

Codes in this section also include procedures of the ureter, pelvis, vesical neck, and prostate. These procedures are performed using a cystoscope inserted transurethrally (through the urethra).

Cystoscopy procedures are organized according to urethra and bladder, ureter and renal pelvis, and bladder neck and prostate. Radiological services are reported separately. Read code descriptions carefully to identify the specific procedure performed and area treated. Watch for codes that reference the urethra or ureters because the words look quite similar, particularly in their combining forms.

Cystourethroscopy (52000) is a separate procedure. Cystourethroscopy codes that include endoscopy of the ureter (ureteroscopy) are found in 52320–52355. Non-endoscopic ureteral catherization is described with 52005, which does not include visualization of the ureter, but only placement of a catheter(s) into the ureter(s) without any instillation of medication or other procedure. The insertion of a ureteral catheter should not be confused with the insertion of an indwelling ureteral stent(s) (52332). If a catheter(s) is inserted into the ureter, it usually is removed at the end of the case, whereas a stent will remain afterward. Stents are used to provide support for healing or to hold tissue in place. If a stent remains in the ureter for an extended time, it will need to be replaced. A stent exchange is coded 52332. If a stent exchange is performed, the removal of the initial stent (52310) is not coded.

Testing Technique

The provider performs a cystoscopy and a ureteral stent removal. There is a parenthetical note following the code for cystoscopy (52000), which states it is a separate procedure. Cystoscopy is not reported separately, when it is an integral component of another procedure performed. Only the stent removal should be coded (52310).

Vesical neck and prostate procedures include the transurethral resection of the prostate (TURP) and laser procedures of the prostate. For instance, GreenLight laser of the prostate is reported with 52648. Transurethral microwave therapy (TUMT) is reported with 53850.

Procedures of the Urethra

Treatments for urethral strictures are listed as manipulation codes (53600–53665). These codes are selected based upon the type of dilation, patient's gender, and if anesthesia was used. Most of the codes within this category are gender specific. Initial or subsequent dilation is described separately.

Male Genital System (54000–55899)

The Male Genital System section of CPT® includes procedures on the penis, testis, epididymis, tunica vaginalis, scrotum, vas deferens, spermatic cord, seminal vesicles, and prostate.

Incision

There are no "incision" codes for the testis. These services are described in the Epididymis subsection.

Incision of the vas deferens (55200) usually is performed to obtain a sample of semen or to test the patency of the tubes. This is a separate procedure, and should not be reported when a more complex service is performed at the same site.

A prostate biopsy (needle or punch, single or multiple, any approach) is reported using 55700, and may require imaging guidance. If imaging guidance is used, report 76942 in addition. Code 76942 has both professional and technical components; modifier 26 should be applied if the procedure is performed in a facility location. No modifier is needed if the physician provides the equipment and writes an interpretation of the service.

Excision

Vasectomy usually is performed for birth control and is reported with 55250. This code is reported once, whether performed unilaterally or bilaterally. The code also includes post-operative semen examination.

The codes for prostatectomy procedures, which usually are performed for cancer of the prostate, are determined by the approach and whether lymph node biopsy or dissection was performed (55801–55845). If a lymph node dissection is performed at a different surgical session than the initial removal of the prostate, report 38770 and append modifier 50 if the dissection was bilateral. When the prostate is exposed for insertion of a radioactive substance, select from 55860–55865, depending on whether a lymph node biopsy or dissection was also performed.

Repair

Transplantation of testis(es) to the thigh (54680) is performed because of scrotal destruction. In this procedure, the testicle(s) is placed under the skin of the thigh to preserve function and viability. This usually is a temporary location until scrotal reconstruction is complete.

Plastic operations performed on the penis for straightening or hypospadias repair are reported with 54300–54440. The description of many of these codes begins with "urethroplasty," but it is appropriate that the services are reported here because they refer to the portion of the urethra that passes through the penis.

Codes 54400–54417 describe services for insertion or removal of penile prostheses. A penile prosthesis is used to treat organic erectile dysfunction (ICD-9-CM 607.84). The code for removal or repair is determined by the type of prosthesis involved.

Vasectomy reversal procedures are reported with 55400; if performed bilaterally, modifier 50 should be appended.

Epididymovasostomy, or anastomosis of epididymis to vas deferens (54900), is performed when an obstruction of the flow of spermatozoa from the epididymis to the vas deferens occurs. This procedure usually is performed because of stricture, congenital defect, or insufficient production of sperm in semen.

Other Procedures of Male Genital System

Services for excision or destruction of lesions on the skin generally are coded in the Integumentary System; in the penis section of CPT®, there are codes for lesion excision under the Destruction of Penis Lesions: Multiple Methods subsection (54050–54065). These include chemical, electrodesiccation, cryosurgery, laser surgery, and surgical destruction of penile lesions. The codes are differentiated as "simple" or "extensive" and technique (simple only). Foreskin manipulation is reported with 54450. This procedure is used when adhesions between the uncircumcised foreskin and the head of the penis prevent retraction of the foreskin. By stretching the foreskin back over the head of the penis, these adhesions are broken.

Radiation treatment for prostate cancer may require the surgeon to place needles, catheters, or interstitial devices (such as fiducial markers) for radiation therapy (55875–

55876). Ultrasonic guidance or imaging is not included and is reported separately, when performed.

HCPCS Level II

HCPCS Level II codes used for urological procedures primarily describe supplies and drugs, including catheters, irrigation trays, and drugs to treat prostate cancer and decreased testosterone levels. Many carriers consider catheterization supplies included with the procedure. The most common HCPCS Level II codes used for urological procedures include codes for catheter supplies (A4310–A4360), chemotherapy injections for prostate cancer (J3315, J9217–J9218), and testosterone injections for decreased testosterone (J1070–J1080).

Modifiers

Modifiers are used to report or indicate that a service or procedure has been altered by some specific circumstance. Listed below are common modifiers used when coding urological procedures.

Modifier 22 *Increased procedural services*: For example, the operative report states the procedure took over two hours longer than it typically would. Many carriers will require documentation of claims submitted with modifier 22.

Modifier 26 *Professional component*: As discussed previously, this code is used when the physician interprets the study but does not provide the equipment.

Modifiers 50 *Bilateral procedure*, RT *Right Side*, and LT *Left Side*: Depending upon the carrier, modifiers RT and LT can be used instead of modifier 50.

Modifier 51 *Multiple procedures*: This modifier should not be appended to designated "add-on" codes. CMS does not recognize modifier 51 and many carriers are following this recommendation.

Modifier 52 *Reduced services*: For instance, if the physician performs a urethroscopy, but is unable to view the bladder, modifier 52 would be appended to 52000.

Modifier 53 *Discontinued procedure*: For instance, during an operative procedure the patient's blood pressure cannot be controlled and continuation with the surgical procedure may threaten the well-being of the patient. Modifier 53 should be appended to the CPT® code.

Modifier 58 *Staged or related procedure or service by the same physician during the postoperative period*: For instance, the patient has a TURP and returns to the clinic to confirm that his bladder is emptying appropriately. Modifier 58 would be added to 51798.

Modifier 59 *Distinct procedural service*: Documentation must support a different session, different procedure or surgery, different site or organ system, separate incision/excision, separate lesion, or separate injury (or area of injury in extensive injuries) not ordinarily encountered or performed on the same day by the same individual.

Modifier 76 *Repeat procedure or service by the same physician*: For instance, a patient has a cystoscopy to control bleeding from a bladder diverticulum but he continues to have bleeding after the procedure and the procedure must be repeated. Modifier 76 would be added to the second cystoscopy procedure.

Modifier 78 *Unplanned return to the operating/procedure room by the same physician following the initial procedure for a related procedure during the postoperative period*: For instance, a status-post radical retropubic prostatectomy with bilateral lymph node dissection patient is found to have post-operative bleeding and must be returned to the operating room. Modifier 78 would be added to the procedure used to control the post-operative bleeding.

Modifier 79 *Unrelated procedure or service by the same physician during the postoperative period*: For instance, an ESWL is performed on the right kidney. During the global period of the initial surgery, the patient returns to the operating room for a second ESWL procedure, but on the left kidney. Modifier 79 would be reported on the ESWL procedure performed on the left kidney.

Glossary

Anuria—Suppression, cessation, or failure of the kidneys to secrete urine.

Azoospermia—Failure of the development of sperm or the absence of sperm in semen; one of the most common factors in male infertility.

Balanoposthitis—Inflammation and/or infection of the glans penis and prepuce.

Brachytherapy—Form of radiation therapy in which radioactive pellets or seeds are implanted directly into the tissue being treated to deliver their dose of radiation in a more directed fashion.

Calculus—Abnormal, stone-like concretion of calcium, cholesterol, mineral salts, or other substances that forms in any part of the body.

Chordee—Ventral (downward) curvature of the penis due to a fibrous band along the corpus spongiosum seen congenitally with hypospadias, or a downward curvature seen on erection in disease conditions causing a lack of distensibility in the tissues.

Chronic Interstitial Cystitis—Persistently inflamed lesion of the bladder wall, usually accompanied by urinary frequency, pain, nocturia, and a distended bladder.

Circumcise—Circular cutting around the genitals to remove the prepuce or foreskin.

Condyloma—Infectious tumor-like growth caused by the human papilloma virus, with a branding connective tissue core and epithelial covering that occurs on the skin and mucous membranes of the perianal region and external genitalia.

Cystitis—Inflammation of the urinary bladder.

Cystitis Cystica—Inflammation of the bladder characterized by the formation of multiple cysts.

Cystocele—Herniation of the bladder into the vagina.

Cystostomy—Formation of an opening through the abdominal wall into the bladder.

Cystotomy—Surgical incision into the urinary bladder or gallbladder.

Dysuria—Painful urination.

Epididymis—Coiled tube on the back of the testis that is the site of sperm maturation and storage and where spermatozoa are propelled into the vas deferens toward the ejaculatory duct by contraction of smooth muscle.

Epididymo-orchitis—Inflammation of the testes and epididymis.

Epispadias—Male anomaly in which the urethral opening is abnormally located on the dorsum of the penis, appearing as a groove with no upper urethral wall covering.

Extrophy of Bladder—Congenital anomaly occurring when the bladder everts itself, or turns inside out, through an absent part of the lower abdominal and anterior bladder walls with incomplete closure of the pubic bone.

Foley Catheter—Temporary indwelling urethral catheter held in place in the bladder by an inflated balloon containing fluid or air.

Hematospermia—Blood in the seminal fluid, often caused by inflammation of the prostate or seminal vesicles, or prostate cancer.

Hematuria—Blood in the urine, which may present as gross visible blood or as the presence of red blood cells visible only under a microscope.

Horseshoe Kidney—Congenital anomaly in which the kidneys are fused together at the lower end during fetal development, resulting in one large, horseshoe-shaped kidney, often associated with cardiovascular, central nervous system, or genitourinary anomalies.

Hydronephrosis—Distention of the kidney caused by an accumulation of urine that cannot flow out due to an obstruction. It may be caused by conditions such as kidney stones or vesicoureteral reflux.

Hydroureter—Abnormal enlargement or distension of the ureter with water or urine caused by an obstruction.

Hyperplasia—Abnormal proliferation in the number of normal cells in regular tissue arrangement.

Hypospadias—Fairly common birth defect in males in which the meatus, or urinary opening, is abnormally positioned on the underside of the penile shaft or in the perineum, requiring early surgical correction.

Incontinence—Involuntary escape of urine.

Impotence—Psychosexual or organic dysfunction in which there is partial or complete failure to attain or maintain erection until completion of the sexual act.

Lithotripsy—Destruction of calcified substances in the gallbladder or urinary system by smashing the concretion into small particles to be washed out. This may be done by surgical or noninvasive methods, such as ultrasound.

Lumen—The space within an artery, vein, intestine or tube.

Meatus—Opening or passage into the body.

Nephrostomy—Placement of a stent, tube, or catheter to form a passage from the exterior of the body into the renal pelvis or calyx, often for drainage of urine or an abscess, for exploration, or calculus extraction.

Neurogenic Bladder—Dysfunctional bladder due to a central or peripheral nervous system lesion that may result in incontinence, residual urine retention, infection, stones, and renal failure.

Nocturnal Enuresis—Bed wetting.

Oligospemia—Insufficient production of sperm in semen, a common factor in male infertility.

Orchiectomy—Surgical removal of one or both testicles via a scrotal or groin incision, indicated in cases of cancer, traumatic injury, and sex reassignment surgery.

Patency—State of a tube-like structure or conduit being open and unobstructed.

Perineal—Pertaining to the pelvic floor area between the thighs: the diamond-shaped area bordered by the pubic symphysis in front, the ischial tuberosities on the sides and the coccyx in the back.

Peritoneum—Strong, continuous membrane that forms the lining of the abdominal and pelvic cavities.

Peyronie's Disease—Development of fibrotic hardened tissue or plaque in the cavernosal sheaths in the penis. This causes pain and a severe chordee or curvature in the penis, typically during erection.

Phimosis—Condition in which the foreskin is contracted and cannot be drawn back behind the glans penis.

Priapism—Persistent, painful erection lasting more than four hours and unrelated to sexual stimulation, causing pain and tenderness.

Prepuce—Fold of penile skin covering the glans.

Prolapse—Falling, sliding, or sinking of an organ from its normal location in the body.

Prostate—Male gland surrounding the bladder neck and urethra, which secretes a substance into the seminal fluid.

Retroperitoneal—Located behind the peritoneum.

Scrotum—Skin pouch that holds the testes and supporting reproductive structures.

Seminal Vesicles—Paired glands located at the base of the bladder in males that release the majority of fluid into semen through ducts that join with the vas deferens forming the ejaculatory duct.

Skene's Gland—Paraurethral ducts that drain a group of the female urethral glands into the vestibule.

Spermatic Cord—Structure of the male reproductive organs that consists of the ductus deferens, testicular artery, nerves and veins that drain the testes.

Stricture—Narrowing of an anatomical structure.

Testes—Male gonadal paired glands located in the scrotum that secrete testosterone and contain the seminiferous tubules where sperm is produced.

Torsion of Testis—Twisting, turning, or rotation of the testicle upon itself.

Trigone—Triangular, smooth area of mucous membrane at the base of the bladder, located between the ureteric openings in back and the urethral opening in front.

Tunica Vaginalis—Serous membrane that partially covers the testes formed by an outpocketing of the peritoneum when the testes descend.

Urachus—Embryonic tube connecting the urinary bladder to the umbilicus during development of the fetus that normally closes before birth, generally in the fourth or fifth month of gestation.

Urethra—Small tube lined with mucous membrane that leads from the bladder to the exterior of the body.

Ureterocele—Saccular formation of the lower part of the ureter, protruding into the bladder.

Urethral Caruncle—Small, polyp-like growth of a deep red color found in women on the mucous membrane of the urethral opening.

Urostomy—Creation of an opening from the ureter to the abdominal surface to divert urine flow.

Vas deferens—Duct that arises in the tail of the epididymis that stores and carries sperm from the epididymis toward the urethra.

Vesical fistula—Abnormal communication between the bladder and another stricture.

Vesicoureteral reflux—Urine passage from the bladder back up into the ureter and kidneys that can lead to bacterial infection and an increase in hydrostatic pressure, causing kidney damage.

Chapter Review Questions

1. **Urine is transported from the kidneys to the urinary bladder by which structure?**

    A. Urethra

    B. Ureter

    C. Kidney pelvis

    D. Urinary vein

2. The loop of Henle is located in which structure?

     A. Bladder

     B. Kidney

     C. Urethra

     D. Prostate

3. A 17-year-old male presents to the ED. He was playing football when a large line backer tackled him, falling onto his groin area with all his weight. A urologist is called in for consult. There is a 3 cm laceration to the left scrotum. Through this opening the urologist explores the testis for damage and finds some tearing of the testicular tissue that needs suturing. The only other apparent injury is swelling and bruising. The urologist repairs the testicle, which requires a layered closure. The patient is released to go home with instructions to stay in bed for a couple of days, icing the area as needed. Which code should be used to report the procedure performed by the urologist?

     A. 54600-LT

     B. 54670-LT

     C. 12001

     D. 12042

4. A 55-year-old female presents with right hydronephrosis. A 23-French cystoscope is introduced into the urethra and passed into the bladder. The bladder is carefully inspected, and no tumors or stones are visualized. The first effluxed urine from the bladder is sent for urine cytology. Then a 6-French access catheter is passed into the right ureteral orifice, requiring a 0.35 guidewire to help cannulate the right ureteral orifice because of the angulation. There is some stiffness in the intramural portion of the ureter, and then the catheter pops through into a more dilated ureter. Contrast is injected and there are no filling defects, fixed tumors, or stones noted. There is mild hydroureteral nephrosis against the bladder. The renal pelvis is barbotaged with saline and the renal pelvis urine is drained and sent to pathology for urine cytology. After the retrograde pyelogram is performed, the access catheter is removed and there is brisk efflux of the contrast and it drains very well. The bladder is then drained and the patient is awakened and transferred in stable condition to the recovery room. Which CPT® codes should be reported?

     A. 52005, 74420-26

     B. 52327, 74420-26

     C. 52010, 74420-26

     D. 52281, 74420-26

9. **Operative Report:**

Preoperative Diagnosis: Left distal ureteral stone, 7–8 mm

Postoperative Diagnosis: Left distal ureteral stone, 7–8 mm

Procedure: Cystoscopy; left retrograde pyeloureterogram; left ureteroscopy with Holmium lithotripsy; and stone basketing

Estimated Blood Loss: Minimal

Specimens Removed: Left ureteral stone

Description of Procedure:
After obtaining informed consent and properly identifying the patient, he was taken to the operating room where general anesthesia was induced without difficulty. He was placed in the dorsal lithotomy position with the adjustable stirrups. The genital area was prepped and draped in the usual sterile fashion.

A 12-degree cystoscope was used to enter the urethra and the bladder. The entire length of the urethra was normal. The prostatic urethra is short and unobstructed. The bladder was entered. A systematic cystoscopy was then performed with the 70-degree lens. Both ureteral orifices were identified in normal anatomic position. There was no evidence of stones, malignancies, or foreign bodies in the bladder. Next, using the cone-tipped 8-French ureteral catheter, in which contrast material was injected and left retrograde pyeloureterogram was performed. The patient had a filling defect, 2 to 3 cm above the UVJ consistent with stone, which was seen on the preoperative KUB. The ureter above the stone was dilated. The cone-tipped catheter was removed. A .035-sensor guidewire was then advanced in the UO past the stone and was seen curling on the renal pelvis nicely under fluoroscopy. Next, the ureteral balloon dilator was used to dilate the ureteral orifice. Next, the rigid ureteroscope was advanced alongside the wire into the ureteral orifice. The stone was well-visualized.

A 200 micron fiber for the Holmium laser was then passed through the ureteroscope and brought into the surgical field. The stone was then lithotripsied until they were just only very small fragments. Multiple fragments were removed with a 43 Segura basket to be sent for pathologic stone analysis.

Ureteroscopy was performed at the level of the crossing of the iliac vessels. There were no remaining stones, only very small sand particles. The distal ureter was free of any significant stone. Certainly, there was nothing larger than the tip of the Holmium fiber remaining. The ureteroscope was removed. The cystoscope was back loaded over the wire and a temporary ureteral stent was positioned appropriately with proximal curl in the renal pelvis and distal curl in the bladder. The bladder was emptied and left with 50 cc of irrigant for voiding trial.

The patient tolerated the procedure well. He was taken to the recovery room in stable condition.

What are the CPT® and ICD-9-CM codes for this procedure?

5. A 45-year-old female has a stricture of the left ureter with ileal conduit at the ureteroileal anastomosis. She has had this chronic stricture and she receives scheduled stent changes on this side. She is here for her regularly scheduled stent change. What CPT® and ICD-9-CM codes should be reported?

    A. 50688, 997.5, V55.6

    B. 50605, 569.3, V44.6

    C. 50688, V55.6

    D. 52332, 997.5

6. A 65-year-old male presents with a medium size bladder tumor on the posterior wall of the bladder behind the trigone and has an elevated PSA. Six needle biopsies of the right and left lobe of the prostate are performed. Each biopsy core is performed under transrectal ultrasound guidance and sent for pathologic review. Then the instrument is inserted through a sheath, and using the cutting mode of the Bovie through the loop, a resection is performed on the bladder tumor. The procedure is performed in an ASC. Which CPT® codes should be reported for the physician's services?

    A. 55700, 52234-51, 76942-26

    B. 55706, 52310-51

    C. 55706, 52315-51

    D. 55700, 52235-51, 76942-26

7. A 43-year-old male undergoing a cystoscopy has a 1.5 cm mass on the left posterior bladder wall, which cannot be definitively classified as malignant, and an area of velvety, peach-colored tissue less than 1 cm on the bilateral ureteral orifices. Using cold-cup biopsy forceps, biopsies are performed and all areas of suspicion that are not biopsied are fulgurated. What CPT® code(s) describe this procedure?

    A. 52204, 52234-51

    B. 52214, 51020-51

    C. 52007, 52354-51

    D. 52234

8. A neonatal male has an elective circumcision before home discharge from the newborn nursery. The physician uses a ring block for the local anesthetic and the foreskin is placed over the glans. A clamp is selected for the size of the glans and a constricting circular ring is placed over the foreskin to compress and devascularize the foreskin. The devascularized foreskin is excised with a scalpel, the ring device is removed, and the penis is dressed. Which CPT® code is reported?

    A. 54150

    B. 54160

    C. 54161

    D. 54150-52

10. Operative Report #2

Preoperative Diagnosis:

1. Scrotal swelling which was suggestive of bilateral spermatocelectomy bilateral hydroceles and the patient had requested bilateral vasectomy at the same time.

Postoperative Diagnoses:

1. Bilateral small hydroceles, significant amount of adhesions and scarring from previous surgery on the right side.

2. Large 6–7 cm diameter spermatocele on the right side and 4 small spermatoceles on the left side.

3. Vasectomy was carried out as requested.

Anesthesia: Spinal anesthesia and IV antibiotic coverage

Title of Operation:

1. Bilateral hydrocelectomy

2. Bilateral spermatocelectomy

3. Bilateral vasectomy

Description: The patient was prepared and draped in the usual fashion in the supine position. Under spinal anesthesia, through midline raphe incision, exploration of the scrotal sac was carried out. It was noted that the patient had a significant amount of adhesions into the scrotal sac and the testis on the right side, and the left testis was pushed laterally as a result of the large spermatocele. On exploration, the testis was noted to be separated from the spermatocele, and adhesions were removed; the spermatocele sac was removed and sent for histological examination. There was a significant amount of scarring noted around the scrotal area on the right side and hence it was difficult to identify vas on the right side. There was a small area of hydrocele around the testicle, which was also opened, drained, and the sac was sutured behind the testicle to prevent further occurrence of hydrocele. Exploration was carried out for vas and it was felt that the only place that the vas could be easily identified was higher up into the scrotal sac near the inguinal region. The identification of the vas was done, double 11 gated, divided and replaced back. Excised tissue was sent for histologic examination to confirm the presence of vas as this was difficult palpation and identification due to thickening, scarring and edema. On the left side, exploration was then carried out and it was noted that the patient had 3–4 small spermatoceles near the epididymal region. There was a small amount of hydrocele also noted on the left side, which was drained. The sac was then sutured behind the testis and the spermatoceles were excised and drained. The left vas was identified and vasectomy was carried out on the left side. The tissue was sent for histologic examination to confirm that the vasectomy is satisfactory. Both testes were replaced back into the scrotal sac and good hemostasis was obtained. A quarter-inch Penrose drain was infiltrated through separate stab wound incisions into the right side for drainage for an initial 24 to 48 hours. The wound was closed with 2 layers #2-0 Vicryl into the deeper part of the scrotal tissue and the skin was closed with #2-0 chromic catgut sutures in interrupted suture fashion. Total blood loss was about 100 mL. The patient tolerated the procedure well. There were no complications and there was no pain associated with the surgery as this was done under spinal anesthesia. The wound was infiltrated by about 8 mL of 0.53% Marcaine for postoperative pain relief, and pressure dressing was applied to the wound. The patient was transferred to the recovery room in satisfactory condition; he will be admitted for postoperative care.

What are the CPT® and ICD-9-CM codes for this procedure?

Introduction

In this chapter, we will discuss CPT®, ICD-9-CM, and HCPCS Level II coding for the female reproductive system. This chapter includes coding for labor, delivery, abortions, and infertility. The objectives for this chapter include:

◖ Describing the structures associated with the female reproductive system

◖ Using appropriate medical terminology to identify services and select codes

◖ Applying ICD-9-CM guidelines for assigning codes and special guidelines for coding complications of pregnancy, childbirth, and the puerperium

◖ Selecting CPT® and HCPCS Level II codes and modifiers to describe the services and procedures related to the female reproductive system

Anatomy and Medical Terminology

Female Reproductive System

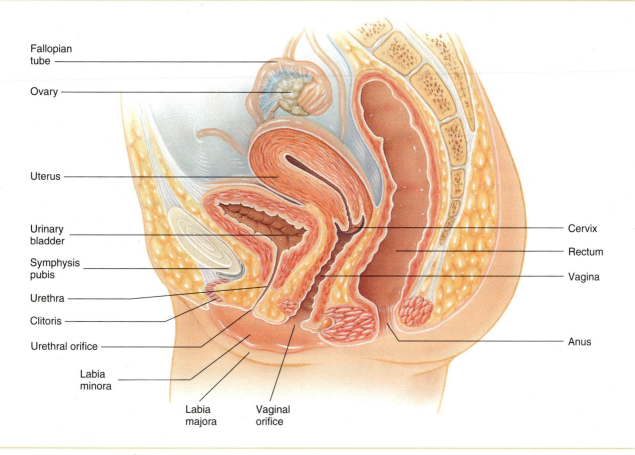

Fallopian tube
Ovary
Uterus
Urinary bladder
Symphysis pubis
Urethra
Clitoris
Urethral orifice
Labia minora
Labia majora
Vaginal orifice
Cervix
Rectum
Vagina
Anus

Source: Delmar/Cengage Learning.

The central organ of the female reproductive system is the uterus. The *cervix uteri*, or neck of the uterus, is the lower portion of the uterus that tapers to connect to the vagina. The opening in the cervix is known as the *os* or external *os*. The body, or fundus, of the uterus is known as the *corpus uteri*.

The *fallopian tubes* are two tubes, one on either side of the uterus, leading from the bilateral ovaries into the uterus. They also are called oviducts, uterine tubes, and salpinges (*singular* salpinx). The distal ends of the fallopian tubes are called the infundibulum. The fimbriae, or fingers, are near the ovaries and help to capture the ovum (eggs or oocytes) as they make their way into the tubes, and to the uterus. The ovaries are the egg-producing reproductive organs. They also produce hormones related to the female reproductive cycles, and are part of both the female reproductive and the endocrine systems. Together, the fallopian tubes and ovaries are the uterine adnexa.

The vagina is a tubular, muscular canal. The anterior vagina surrounds part of the cervix. The distal vagina opens to the vulva. The vagina may contain a congenital partition, or vaginal septum. This septum may be either longitudinal, essentially creating a double vagina, or transverse.

The vulva contains many structures, including the labia majora and minora, mon pubis, clitoris, and the vestibule or vagina introitus. The vagina introitus is also the location of the hymen that surrounds or partially covers the external vaginal opening.

Several glands also are found in the vulva. The Bartholin's glands (also called the greater vestibular glands) are located slightly inferior and to either side of the vaginal introitus. The Skene's glands (also called the lesser vestibular glands, or periurethral glands) are located on the anterior wall of the vagina around the lower end of the urethra.

The perineum is the area between the pubic symphysis and the coccyx, between the legs. This word can refer to only the superficial structures in this region, or it can be used to include both superficial and deep structures.

ICD-9-CM Coding

Diagnosis codes related to the female reproductive system are found primarily in two chapters of ICD-9-CM: chapter 10, Diseases of the Genitourinary System, and chapter 11, Complications of Pregnancy, Childbirth, and the Puerperium. Codes from chapter 2, Neoplasms, and from the Supplementary Classification of Factors Influencing Health Status and Contact with Health Services (V codes), are frequently important, as well.

Neoplasms

Neoplasms, or tumors, can originate in the ovaries, uterus, cervix, and vulva. After a specific neoplasm has been confirmed by biopsy, it should be coded from the Table of Neoplasms by looking up the specific structure that is the origin of the cancer.

There are many tests to identify cancers of the female reproductive system. These tests are indicative of disease, but not conclusive. An abnormal CA-125, Pap smear, or other test should *not* be coded as cancer. chapter 16, Signs, Symptoms, and Ill-defined Conditions, has codes for abnormal findings that should be used until a biopsy proves whether cancer is present. Find these codes in the alphabetic index under "Findings, abnormal." Then, look for the specific test or the type of substance tested.

A number of hyperplastic conditions occur in the female reproductive system. These are unusual growths that have some characteristics of malignancies, but are not malignant. These types of tissues often are referred to as pre-cancerous. Two of the most common are cervical intraepithelial neoplasia (CIN) and vulvar intraepithelial neoplasia (VIN). Both can be found under Dysplasia in the ICD-9-CM index. These hyperplastic conditions are staged as I, II, or III (eg, CIN II or VIN I). Stages I and II are coded as hyperplasia of the cervix or vulva, stage III is coded as cancer *in situ*.

Leiomyoma (fibroid) are benign tumors often found on or embedded in the musculature of the uterus.

Female Genitourinary System

Chapter 10 of ICD-9-CM has the codes for non-neoplastic conditions of the reproductive organs for women who are not pregnant. Conditions arising during pregnancy are coded in chapter 11 Complications of Pregnancy, Childbirth, and the Puerperium. Care should be taken when coding for bleeding to differentiate between excessive or frequent menstrual bleeding (626.2) and Metrorrhagia (bleeding unrelated to menstruation) (626.6), *Premenopausal menorrhagia* (627.0) and *Postmenopausal bleeding* (627.1).

Complications of Pregnancy, Childbirth, and the Peurperium

Chapter 11 codes have sequencing priority over codes from other chapters. Any condition a woman has during pregnancy, childbirth, or post-partum encounters that impacts the pregnancy or the pregnancy impacts the condition's treatment—whether pre-existing or new—should be coded from chapter 11. Only if the physician states the condition is unrelated to the pregnancy, should a code from one of the other chapters be chosen with reporting V22.2 as an additional code. Codes can be added to describe further condition(s) during pregnancy. For example, a woman with well-controlled type II diabetes (250.00) gets pregnant. Now her diabetes is coded 648.0x with 250.00 as a second code to describe the condition further.

Note: Gestational diabetes is coded 648.8x and is only reported when the patient has developed diabetes during the pregnancy until the pregnancy ends. Do not report category codes 249 and 250 with the gestational diabetes code. Code 648.0x is reported when the patient had pre-existing diabetes or already had diabetes before the pregnancy.

ICD-9-CM and CPT® recognize three types of abortions: spontaneous (also called a miscarriage), induced (caused by a deliberate procedure), or missed. A missed abortion is when the fetus dies before completion of 22 weeks of gestation but the products of conception are retained.

Codes for complications of pregnancy start with category 640. There are five possible fifth digits (0–4) for virtually all of the codes in this part of the chapter. The use of the fifth digit in this chapter tells the insurer when during the pregnancy the service was provided.

- ◖ 0—Use fifth digit "0" when the coder does not know whether the patient is still pregnant, delivered during this episode of care, or during a previous episode of care. This rarely applies to professional services and more often is used for poorly-documented services in facility billing.

- ◖ 1—Use fifth digit "1" when the woman delivered during this episode of care has a prior or new condition occurring with the delivery.

- ◖ 2—Use fifth digit "2" when the woman delivered during this episode of care and there was a postpartum problem, or an antenatal problem continued after delivery.

- ◖ 3—Use fifth digit "3" when the woman had not delivered by the end of the episode of care being described.

- ◖ 4—Use fifth digit "4" when the woman delivered during a previous episode of care and now has a postpartum problem.

Testing Technique

Chapter 11—Complications of Pregnancy, Childbirth, and the Puerperium, has many definitions and color-prompted notes of which to be aware in the Tabular List. Under the codes, there is also information about how many weeks a pregnant woman should be to report the code. For example, code 643.0x is to be reported when the hyperemesis starts before the end of week 22 of gestation.

Each code in this chapter also has only specified fifth digits that can be used with it. They are shown in square brackets [ ] under the code itself. You may not assign a fifth digit to that code unless it is in brackets under the code. For example, code 653.6 may use [0, 1, 3]. You may not assign 2 or 4 as a fifth digit with this code.

Code 650 is the exception to the rules above. Code 650 is *only* used for a normal delivery. Normal delivery is defined as requiring minimal or no assistance, with or without episiotomy, without fetal manipulation or instrumentation or spontaneous, cephalic, vaginal, full-term, single, live-born infant. It is always used with code

V27.0 indicating a single live-born outcome of delivery. It may never be used with any other code from chapter 11.

There are a number of V codes that describe the reason for the encounter or the outcome of delivery. Codes from category V27 describe the number and survival status of the baby after delivery. Codes V22.0 and V22.1 describe encounters to manage a normal pregnancy. Code V22.2 is used in the rare circumstances when a patient is pregnant and receives some unrelated health care service. Category V23 describes monitoring of a high-risk patient who has not developed a problem. There are also a number of V codes that describe encounters for birth control, normal well-woman encounters, and other situations where the patient encounters health care but has no problems.

Testing Technique

Make a note: Code V22.2 is never coded with Complication Pregnancy codes (630–649).

CPT® Coding

Codes for surgical treatment of the female genital system can be found in the range 56405–59899. This section contains gynecologic procedures, as well as codes for maternity care, delivery, and abortion treatment.

Vulva

The most common surgically treated vulva problems are infections and cancers. Infections tend to be localized abscesses and cysts, or manifestations of sexually-transmitted disease. Abscesses usually are treated with incision and drainage. Occasionally, abscesses do not clear up after incision and drainage. When this happens, the physician may decide to perform a marsupialization, during which a scalpel is used to cut an opening in the top of the abscess pocket. The leaflets created by this procedure are pulled away from the pocket and attached to the surrounding skin with stitches or glue. In more radical treatments, or for very large abscesses, the abscess and surrounding tissue may have to be excised.

Testing Technique

Treatment of abscesses and cysts of the Skene's glands are coded in the Urinary subsection using codes 53060 or 53270. Make a note in this section of your CPT® for easy reference.

For other types of infectious lesions, such as genital warts, or when there is widespread infection, the area may be treated with cryotherapy (freezing), laser surgery, or other methods.

Excision of the vulva typically is performed for cancer. Excisions may be simple or complete, radical or partial, in various combinations (eg, partial simple or partial radical). Simple vulvectomies include only the skin and superficial subcutaneous tissues. Radical vulvectomies include removal of deep subcutaneous tissue. To code a radical vulvectomy, documentation must specify removal of deep tissue. Partial vulvectomies remove less than 80 percent of the vulvar area; complete vulvectomies remove 80 percent or more.

The vulva has two sides, so a procedure described as a complete unilateral vulvectomy is a partial vulvectomy because 50 percent of the tissue has been removed.

Repair codes in the vulva section refer primarily to repairs related to congenital anomalies, except code 56810, which is used for repair of traumatic injuries. Note that any repairs related to delivery are coded in the section on labor and delivery.

There are also two endoscopy codes in this section. These procedures refer to inspection of the vulva and describe examination and biopsy alone.

Vagina

Vagina incision and excision codes are similar to those for the vulva, with a few exceptions. Code 57022 is the only code related to treatment of post-obstetric problems that is not in the labor and delivery section. Use code 57023 for incision and drainage of non-obstetric hematoma.

A frequent problem that occurs as women age, and is particularly a problem for women who have had multiple children, is prolapse of the uterus and/or vagina. A minimally invasive treatment option is using a pessary. A pessary is a flexible ring that can be inserted into the vagina where it provides additional support for the uterus, bladder, and rectum. For older women who are not sexually active, colpocleisis may be performed. In this procedure, the vaginal walls are sewn together, eliminating prolapse from the vagina.

A colpopexy can be performed via various approaches (abdominal, laparoscopic, or vaginal). In this procedure, suture material and/or mesh may be used to suspend the vagina from the boney structures in the pelvis. This may be performed with a hysterectomy for severe prolapse. If the patient has a rectocele, it may be necessary to perform a posterior colporrhaphy, or posterior repair. If the bladder and/or urethra are involved, an anterior colporrhaphy or anterior repair may be needed. The vaginal wall may also be reinforced with mesh material (57267).

If the tendons that support the urethra have also been stretched, an additional procedure may be needed to create a sling to support the bladder (coded from the vagina section if performed transvaginally. Use code 51992 if performed laparoscopically).

Other codes found in this section include 57170 for fitting of diaphragm or cervical cap for contraception, 57300–57330 for vaginal fistulae repair, 57415 for impacted foreign body removal from the vagina under anesthesia (frequently performed when the patient presents to the emergency department [ED]), and 57420–57421 for colposcopy of the entire vagina and distal cervix, if present.

Cervix

The section on the cervix (cervix uteri) primarily includes various biopsy procedures performed via endoscope or transvaginally. One procedure that can be performed by either approach is conization of the cervix. In this procedure, a cone-shaped sample of tissue is removed from the cervix by either cold knife method (57520, or 57455 if performed colposcopically) or loop excision, also referred to as loop electrode excision procedure (LEEP) (57522, or 57461, colposcopically). The procedure can be either a biopsy or treatment for dysplasia following an abnormal Pap smear.

The code for cervical cerclage (57700) is also noted in this section. This is a treatment for a non-pregnant women with a history of miscarriage due to an incompetent cervix, and should not be used for obstetrical cerclage.

Uterus

In the section we find a number of codes related to the endometrium (lining of the uterus), including endometrial sampling (biopsy), and dilation and curettage (D&C).

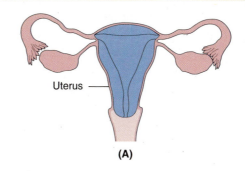

Types of Hysterectomies

Uterus

(A)

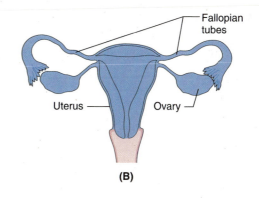

Fallopian tubes

Uterus   Ovary

(B)

Source: Delmar/Cengage Learning.

Other significant procedures in this section include hysterectomies. The basic hysterectomy is 58150. This is a total abdominal hysterectomy with or without bilateral salpingo-oophorectomy (TAH-BSO). The service is coded the same way whether none of the tubes and ovaries, or either or both tubes and ovaries are removed.

The more extensive procedures are only performed for cancer, including the most extensive (58240), which is removal of essentially the entire pelvic contents. These procedures also can be performed vaginally, vaginal with laparoscopic assistance, or entirely laparoscopically. Note the differences in coding when procedures are performed vaginally; and tubes and ovaries are not automatically included. Also, the size of the uterus, by weight, affects code selection.

Testing Technique

When selecting the code involving the size of the uterus and the size is not documented, code for the uterus 250g or less.

Another set of codes unique to the uterus section are hysteroscopies. In these procedures, a scope is placed into the uterus via the vagina. Procedures are to treat conditions of the endometrium, and also to assess and treat blockages of the fallopian tubes.

Oviducts and Ovaries

Laparoscopic procedures are prominent in this section. These procedures include laparoscopic lysis of adhesions, partial and total removal of adnexa (which includes ovarian cystectomies), treatment of lesions on the ovaries, pelvic viscera or peritoneal surfaces and other procedures.

Ovary

Most of the codes in the ovary subsection describe open procedures that are often bundled when performed with other procedures; however, there is also a group of radical hysterectomies for ovarian cancer treatment. They include debulking procedures performed to reduce the size and number of tumors prior to chemotherapy and radiation therapy, as well as other radical excisions.

The last three codes in this section are for implantation of fertilized embryos.

Maternity Care and Delivery

The codes in the Maternity Care and Delivery section are used to describe services related to antepartum, delivery, and postpartum care. All typical care—including initial and subsequent history and physical

exam and routine labs throughout the normal antepartum period (usually about 13 visits), delivery, and postpartum care—is part of the global OB package. Extra visits related to complicated maternity care, or any other unrelated problems treated by the physician, are billed separately.

There are four codes for the global delivery package:

- 59400 is for the entire global package including vaginal delivery.
- 59510 is for the global package including cesarean delivery.
- 59610 and 59618 are for global delivery when the patient has had a previous cesarean delivery but now labors to delivery vaginally. Use 59610 if the baby is delivered vaginally, and 59618 if delivered by cesarean after trying to deliver vaginally. Do not use these codes if the woman does not labor prior to delivery.

There are additional codes to use if the package must be broken because of a payer or doctor change. Antepartum care, delivery, and postpartum care can be billed separately when needed.

If twins are delivered vaginally, 59400 should be coded along with 59409 for an additional vaginal delivery only. Nothing extra is coded for twin deliveries by cesarean section; however, if one baby is delivered vaginally and one baby is delivered by cesarean, code 59510 and 59409.

A number of services may be performed during the antenatal period that are not part of the package. Amniocenteses, fetal stress and non-stress tests, and several services coded in the Radiology section of CPT® are included in this group.

The most common radiologic service is the limited ultrasound (76815). This procedure is performed so routinely that many payers include one ultrasound in the typical delivery reimbursement. Other ultrasounds in the obstetrical section require additional specific documentation, as outlined in the CPT® codebook.

Non-obstetrical ultrasounds also have specified documentation requirements. All billable ultrasound services require an image of the service to be captured and stored either on paper or electronically.

Abortions

Abortion codes are chosen based on the type of abortion involved: spontaneous, induced, or missed. It's important to note that if a patient has a spontaneous abortion (eg, miscarriage), but does not require surgical completion, management of this is coded using evaluation and management (E/M) codes, including prolonged services when appropriate. A missed abortion treated non-surgically is coded with E/M codes only. Administration of pitocin only to speed the process of expelling the products of conception is not considered surgical treatment.

Testing Technique

The ICD-9-CM codebook describes missed abortions, spontaneous abortions, and induced abortions. These are important to know to properly assign with the CPT® abortion codes.

When documentation reflects a patient had a complete abortion initially, and then returned with pain and bleeding at a later time and was found to have retained products of conception, the abortion is incomplete.

Related Coding

Just before the female reproductive system codes start, there is a small subsection called Reproductive System Procedures. The single code (55920) is for placement of needles or catheters into pelvic organs and/or genitalia for subsequent interstitial radioelement application. This code can be used for either males or females and should be used when a more specific code (for example, placement of needles into the prostate, 55875, or placement of uterine tandems or vaginal ovoids, 57155) is not appropriate.

There are also two codes for intersex surgery: one for male to female (55970) and one for female to male (55980).

In the Medicine Section, there is a single time-based code (96040) for one-on-one medical genetics counseling. This code is used only by non-physicians. Physicians who provide one-on-one genetics counseling should use E/M codes to describe the service. For group counseling by a non-physician, use 98960–98962; by a physician, use 99401–99412.

HCPCS Level II Coding

Two important HCPCS Level II codes with special importance in the female reproductive system coding are: G0101 and Q0091. G0101 is for the Medicare breast and pelvic exam. Medicare expects at least seven of the 11 elements described in this code will be documented to bill the service. The 11 elements can be found in the 1997 Documentation guidelines.

Code Q0091 is used for obtaining a Pap smear. In CPT®, code 99000 is used to describe this service, but is rarely paid as it is considered to be bundled into an E/M service performed on that date.

Modifiers

The standard CPT® E/M modifiers apply to the female reproductive coding, including modifier 25 when an E/M service is performed on the date of another separate service. Of note, no modifiers are required on E/M services performed and billed separately during the antenatal period. Although there is a global period involved, the global concept does not attach until after the delivery is billed. Modifier 24 is inappropriate to use unless the insurer requires it (or some other modifier) to indicate the service was not part of the global care.

Chapter Review Questions

1. The term "episiotomy" best describes a procedure of what type?

   A. An incision made in the perineum to enlarge the passage for the fetus during delivery

   B. A procedure to initiate cervical ripening prior to labor

   C. Surgical removal of an oviduct

   D. Removal of lining from the cervix

2. If a woman has a Pap smear performed by her gynecologist, what part of the female anatomy would that involve?

   A. Cervix

   B. Corpus uteri

   C. Endometrium

   D. Fallopian tube

3. A VBAC is performed on a 30-year-old woman who received routine OB care for nine office visits from physician A and postpartum care and delivery from physician B from a different practice. What would be the correct CPT® code(s) for physician B's services?

   A. 59614

   B. 59610

   C. 59426, 59612

   D. 59400, 59614

4. A vulvectomy is performed on a female patient diagnosed with vulvar malignancy. The gynecologist oncology surgeon takes skin and deep subcutaneous tissue from approximately half of the patient's vulva as well as her inguinofemoral lymph nodes bilaterally. What are the CPT® and ICD-9-CM codes for this scenario?

   A. 56620-50, 184.0

   B. 56630, 233.32

   C. 56631-50, 239.5

   D. 56632, 184.4

5. A 22-year-old presents in the ED with menorrhagia that she has had since her contraceptive device, an IUD, was put in. The decision is made to remove the device. Going through the cervix, the physician sees the string for the IUD and grasps it for removal. What CPT® and ICD-9-CM codes should be reported?

   A. 11981, 626.2, V45.51

   B. 58301, 996.76, 626.2, V25.12

   C. 11976, 626.2, V25.42

   D. 58301, 996.65, 626.2, V45.42

6. A 48-year-old female presents with vaginal bleeding for the last 15 days. Upon examination there is a mass approximately 3 x 4 cm, hard and irregular on the right upper vaginal wall. A small amount of tissue is obtained from the vaginal mass and sent to pathology. Which CPT® code should be used?

   A. 58100

   B. 57100

   C. 57500

   D. 56605

7. A 30-year-old disabled Medicare patient is scheduled for surgery due to what looks like an ovarian mass on the right ovary. On entering the abdomen, the surgeon finds an enlarged ovarian cyst on the right, but the ovary is otherwise normal. The left ovary is necrotic looking. The decision is made, based on the patient's age, to remove the cyst from the right ovary. He also performs a left salpingo-oophorectomy. Select the codes.

   A. 58720-RT, 58925-LT

   B. 58925, 58720-51

   C. 58925, 58700-51

   D. 58720, 58920-51

8. A pregnant patient delivers twins at 30 weeks gestation. The first baby is delivered vaginally, but during this delivery, the second baby turned into the transverse position during labor. The decision is made to perform a cesarean to deliver the second baby. Both babies are healthy. The physician performing the deliveries also performed the prenatal and postpartum care. Code the procedure and diagnosis codes.

   A. 59400, 59514, 651.01, 652.31, V27.2

   B. 59510, 59409-51, 651.01, 652.31, V27.2

   C. 59510-22, 651.01, 660.01, 652.31, V27.2

   D. 59510, 59409-51, 651.01, 660.30, V27.2

9.   **Operative Case 1:**

Preoperative Diagnoses: 1. Menometrorrhagia

2. Uterine mass

Postoperative Diagnoses: 1. Menometrorrhagia

2. Irregular endometrium

Anesthesia: General

Name of Operation: 1. Hysteroscopic-directed biopsy

2. Fractional D&C

Estimated Blood Loss: Minimal

Urine Output: 60 milliliters

Hysteroscopic Deficit: 100 milliliters normal saline

Intravenous Fluids: 1400 milliliters crystalloid

Findings: Uterus sounds to 8 centimeters. Irregular shedding, ragged endometrium. No discrete polyp or fibroid. No mass.

Brief History: This is a 45-year-old female with abnormal uterine bleeding, almost continuous bleeding since November. Sonohystogram showed and endometrial stripe of 14 millimeters with a 1.6 x 2.2 centimeter fungating mass filling the endometrial cavity with a residual endometrium thickness of 1 millimeter. Recommendation was to proceed with hysteroscopic evaluation prior to proceeding with any more definitive therapy such as endometrial ablation, IUD, or hysterectomy. She does have a history of infertility. No other increased risk factors for endometrial cancer. We are, therefore, proceeding with a hysteroscopy, possible polypectomy, possible myomectomy, directed biopsy and D&C. Risks include bleeding, infection, uterine perforation, with injury to surrounding organs, fluid overload, thromboembolism, and anesthesia. Risks were discussed. She took Cytotec 200 micrograms the night prior to surgery.

Description of Procedure:

With the patient in the dorsal lithotomy position, under adequate general anesthesia and after confirmation of appropriate procedure and patient identification, bimanual exam was performed. The uterus was midposition, 8 weeks' size, mobile. Cervix was soft. Bivalve speculum was placed in the vagina. The anterior lip of the cervix was grasped with an Allis clamp and the cervix was very soft. It did not require any significant dilatation. The uterus sounded to 8 centimeters. The 10 millimeter hysteroscope was placed into the uterine cavity. The endocervix was evaluated. There were no masses or polyps in the endocervix. The uterine cavity was evaluated with a finding of irregular shedding endometrium but no discrete mass or polyp. The entire upper portion of the uterus was involved with the irregular shedding, and indeed the lower portion had less irregularity of the endometrium. The volume of irregular endometrium was grasped at the base and removed repetitively until a clear view of the entire endometrial cavity was obtained. Due to the irregular endometrium at the bilateral uterine cornua, I was able to discretely identify the tubal ostia, however, I do feel that I had excellent visualization of the entire uterine cavity. With the directed biopsy being complete, the hysteroscope was removed from the uterine cavity, sharp curettage was performed of the endocervix, and specimen was also collected with a cytobrush. Sharp curettage of the uterine cavity was then performed beginning at 12 o'clock and proceeded in a clockwise manner. The tissue was collected. There were three specimens. The first is a directed biopsy of the irregularly shedding endometrium. The second is endocervical curettage, and the third is sharp curetting of the endometrium. All of the instruments were removed from the vagina. There was minimal bleeding noted at the end of the procedure. Final sponge, needle, and instrument count were reported as correct. There were no known complications. The patient was transferred to recovery in good condition.

What are the procedure and diagnosis codes?

10. **Operative Case #2**

Preoperative Diagnosis:	Uterine prolapse, cystocele
Postoperative Diagnosis:	Same
Operation:	Vaginal hysterectomy (uterus 235 g), bilateral salpingo-oophorectomy, anterior repair cystocele

Anesthesia: General endotrachal

Estimated Blood Loss: 100 cc

Fluids: 1500 cc lactated Ringer's

Urine Output: 400 cc via Foley, to gravity

Specimen: Uterus, tubes and ovaries bilaterally, portion of anterior vagina x 2, sent to pathology

Complications: None

Disposition: Patient was extubated and brought to recovery room in stable condition

Findings: Uterine prolapse and incomplete cystocele

Procedure: The patient was brought to the operating room and, after induction of general endotracheal anesthesia she was placed in dorsolithotomy position. The vagina was prepped and draped in the usual normal sterile fashion. A weighted speculum was placed in the vagina, and the cervix was grasped, with two single tooth tenaculum and grabbing the anterior and posterior surface of the cervix. The cervix was retracted anteriorly, and the Bovie cautery was used to separate the vaginal reflection on the cervix from the peritoneum below. This was done circumferentially around the cervix and it was retracted with the suction. Subsequent to this, posteriorly two forceps were used to tent up the posterior portion of the dissected cervix and the Metzenbaum scissors were used to incise an area through the peritoneum posteriorly. At this time, a #0 Vicryl suture was placed from the perineum through the posterior cervix to retract the separation created along the cervix, leading into the abdominal cavity.

The Heaney clamps were then used to clamp on both sides of the uterosacral ligaments, and #0 Vicryl suture was used to tie the pedicle on both sides. Subsequent to this, the weighted speculum was replaced inside this area to expose the intraperitoneal cavity posteriorly. Again the Heaney clamps were used on both sides to isolate the cardinal ligaments that were clamped and transected with Mayo scissors. The pedicles were sutured with #0 Vicryl.

Attention was turned to the anterior surface of the cervix, where smooth forceps were used to tent the area, and an incision was made into the peritoneum, again opening the vagina to the intraperitoneal cavity anteriorly. At this time, from below, Heaney clamps were used to isolate the uterine vessels, and again Mayo scissors were used after clamping both uterine vessels on both sides. Heaney clamps were used and these were suture ligated as well on both sides bilaterally.

Subsequent to this, the single tooth tenaculum was used to grasp the fundus of the uterus that was then retracted toward the vaginal vault. The Heaney clamps were used to transect the final portion of uterus including the round ligaments. Again, these pedicles were also tied with #0 Vicryl suture. The uterus and cervix were removed, and a Babcock clamp was used on both sides bilaterally to isolate the ovaries. At this time, a Heaney clamp was placed on the infundibulopelvic ligaments and vessels on both sides to transect this area and to suture ligate this area, as well. Both ovaries and tubes were handed to the scrub nurse as specimens.

Subsequent to this, all pedicles were evaluated and found to be hemostatic. A 2-0 Vicryl suture was used to close the inferior portion of the vaginal cuff that was created, and then anteriorly attention was tuned to the cystocele repair. Using the Mayo scissors to dissect, an incision was made in the midline extending posteriorly to anteriorly to transect the vaginal area covering the bladder. This area was separated from the bladder below using retraction and the Bovie cautery. The incision with the Metzenbaum scissors created two flaps of vagina that were then held with T clamps. With the Bovie on cut mode, the excess portion of vagina was transected bilaterally.

Subsequent to this, the fascia was grasped with interrupted 2-0 Vicryl sutures and brought together over the exposed bladder surface with three interrupted sutures in a continuous locked fashion anteriorly. Subsequent to this, the area was irrigated and found to be completely hemostatic. The vagina was then packed with gauze, with lubrication surrounding it. All instruments were removed from the vagina. The instrument counts were correct x 2. The patient was brought to the recovery room in stable condition.

What are the procedure and diagnosis codes?

Endocrine and Nervous System

Introduction

This chapter includes CPT®, ICD-9-CM, and HCPCS Level II coding for the endocrine and nervous systems. Objectives for this chapter are:

◖ Review anatomical concepts to understand the endocrine and nervous systems

◖ Highlight relevant terminology

◖ Discuss application of most-frequently used CPT® modifiers

◖ Provide an overview of ICD-9-CM and HCPCS Level II codes and coding guidelines as they apply to these systems

Anatomy and Medical Terminology

The Endocrine System

The endocrine system is comprised of ductless glands that produce various hormones and secrete them directly into the blood circulatory system. Hormones regulate many body functions, including growth and development, mood, metabolism, and tissue function.

The thyroid controls how quickly the body uses energy, makes proteins, and determines how sensitive the body will be to other hormones. This butterfly-shaped gland is composed of two wings, or lobes, on either side of the trachea, connected by an isthmus located over the trachea.

There are four parathyroid glands, embedded in the posterior surface of the thyroid gland, that maintain the body's calcium level for proper functioning of the nervous and muscular systems.

The thymus produces thymosin, which stimulates T-lymphocytes, or T cells, and produces and secretes hormones to control immune function. The gland is composed of two identical lobes, and usually shrinks after puberty. By adulthood, it is replaced by fat, but continues to produce T cells.

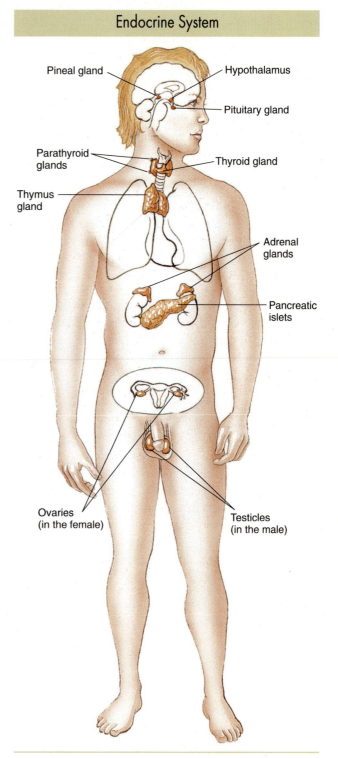

Endocrine System

Source: Delmar/Cengage Learning.

Each adrenal gland is comprised of two portions: the cortex (outer portion), and the medulla (inner portion). The cortex secretes glucocorticoids, mineral corticoids, and adrenal estrogen and progesterone. The medulla secretes epinephrine and norepinephrine (catecholamines). Pheochromocytomas are benign tumors of the chromaffin cells of the medulla, which produce extra catecholamines (fight or flight hormones). These tumors are sometimes extra-adrenal.

The pancreas performs both endocrine and exocrine (digestive) functions. The islets of Langerhans (pancreatic islets) of the pancreas produce the hormones insulin and glucagon that regulate blood glucose levels. As a digestive organ, the pancreas secretes digestive enzymes that flow into the pancreatic duct to the small intestine. CPT® subheading Parathyroid, Thymus, Adrenal Glands, Pancreas, and Carotid Body includes the pancreas; however, there are no codes for the pancreas listed. Codes pertaining to the pancreas are listed in the Digestive System subsection.

The carotid body, located at the bifurcation of the common carotid artery, contains some glandular tissue, and serves primarily as an "oxygen sensor" to help regulate breathing and blood pressure.

CPT® groups the pituitary gland and pineal gland into the nervous system codes (61000–64999), due to the glands' location within the brain. The pituitary gland has two lobes (anterior and posterior). This "master gland" regulates a wide variety of functions, from growth, to metabolism, to milk production and uterine contractions in pregnant woman. The pineal gland (also pineal body, epiphysis cerebri, or epiphysis) produces the hormone melatonin, which modulates wake/sleep patterns and seasonal functions, and serotonin that acts as a neurotransmitter and vasoconstrictor.

The testes and ovaries also secrete sex hormones as endocrine glands. CPT® includes procedures for these organs in the Male Genital System (54000–55899) and the Female Genital System (56405–58999) sections.

The Nervous System

The nervous system is comprised of two parts:

1. The brain and spinal cord (the central nervous system, or CNS)

2. The remaining network of nerves running throughout the body (the peripheral nervous system, or PNS)

Nerves

Individual nerves come in a variety of sizes and specialized functions. At its most basic, however, a single nerve, or neuron, is comprised of a soma (or cell body, which contains the cell nucleus), several dendrites, and an axon.

Dendrites resemble tree branches, and increase the number of possible connections among nerve cells. Signals picked up by dendrites travel through the cell and continue along the axon, and are transmitted to the next cell. Axon terminals (synaptic bulbs) of a transmitting neuron and dendrites of a receiving neuron do not touch; they are separated by a small space, called a synapses. Across a synapses, minute electrical impulses are passed from one nerve to another via chemical messengers called neurotransmitters (such as serotonin). Any disruption of normal production or function of neurotransmitters may cause problems, including mood and attention disorders.

A nerve plexus is a network of intersecting nerves that combines spinal nerves serving the same body area. There are several plexuses in the body, including:

Cervical Plexus—Serves the head, neck, and shoulders

Brachial Plexus—Serves the chest, shoulders, arms, and hands

Lumbar Plexus—Serves the back, abdomen, groin, thighs, knees, and calves

Sacral Plexus—Serves the pelvis, buttocks, genitals, thighs, calves, and feet

Solar or Coccygeal Plexus—Serves internal organs

Because the lumbar and sacral plexus are interconnected, they sometimes are referred to as the lumbosacral plexus.

The Spinal Cord (and Spine)

The spinal cord has three main functions:

1. To serve as a conduit for motor information that travels down the spinal cord (to the muscles)

2. To serve as a conduit for sensory information that travels up the spinal cord (to the brain)

3. To serve as a center for coordinating a number of reflexes

The spinal cord lies within the vertebral column, which protects it. Procedures of the spine and spinal column (62263–63746) may differentiate among vertebral segments and vertebral interspaces.

◖ A vertebral segment describes the basic constituent part into which the spine may be divided. It represents a single, complete vertebral bone with its associated articular processes and laminae.

◖ A vertebral interspace is the non-bony compartment between two adjacent vertebral bodies that contains the intervertebral disc, and includes the nucleus pulposus, annulus fibrosus, and two cartilagenous endplates.

The main portion of the vertebra is the body (corpus). The vertebral foramen is the opening through which the spinal cord passes. The posterior projection of the vertebra is the spinous process. The projections on either side of the vertebra are the transverse processes. Between the spinous process and each transverse process are the laminae.

Facet joints—also known as paravertebral facet joints and/or zygapophyseal or "Z" joints—are located on the posterior spine on each side of the vertebra where it overlaps the neighboring vertebra. They are made up of two surfaces of the adjacent vertebrae separated by a thin layer of cartilage.

The brain is divided into distinct regions. The cerebrum contains the frontal, temporal, parietal, and occipital lobes. The frontal lobe is the front part of the brain. There are two temporal lobes located on either side of the brain. The parietal lobes lie just behind the frontal lobe and above the temporal lobes at the top of the brain. The occipital lobe is in the back of the brain.

The cerebellum is located at the "bottom" of the brain, below the occipital lobe. The brainstem is the low extension of the brain where it connects to the spinal cord. Most of the cranial nerves come from the brainstem. The ventricles of the brain are structures containing

cerebrospinal fluid (CSF), which bathes and cushions the brain and spinal cord. The ventricles are continuous with the central canal of the spinal cord. The brain and spinal cord are covered by a series of tough membranes known as meninges. The meninges include the pia mater (inner), arachnoid mater (middle), and dura mater (outer).

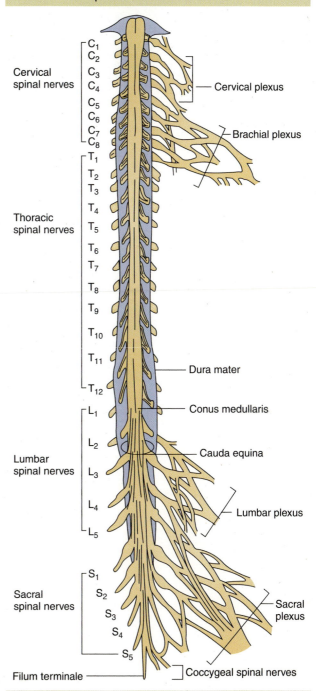

Spinal Cord and Nerves

Cervical spinal nerves — C_1, C_2, C_3, C_4, C_5, C_6, C_7, C_8

Cervical plexus

Brachial plexus

Thoracic spinal nerves — T_1, T_2, T_3, T_4, T_5, T_6, T_7, T_8, T_9, T_{10}, T_{11}, T_{12}

Dura mater

Conus medullaris

Cauda equina

Lumbar spinal nerves — L_1, L_2, L_3, L_4, L_5

Lumbar plexus

Sacral spinal nerves — S_1, S_2, S_3, S_4, S_5

Sacral plexus

Filum terminale

Coccygeal spinal nerves

Source: Delmar/Cengage Learning.

The Brain

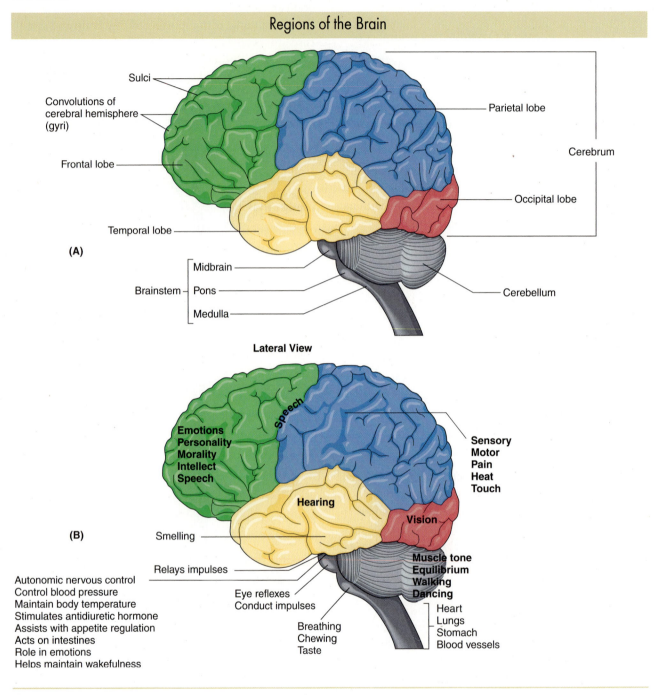

Regions of the Brain

(A)

Sulci

Convolutions of cerebral hemisphere (gyri)

Frontal lobe

Temporal lobe

Midbrain
Pons
Medulla

Brainstem

Parietal lobe

Cerebrum

Occipital lobe

Cerebellum

Lateral View

(B)

Speech

Emotions
Personality
Morality
Intellect
Speech

Hearing

Smelling

Relays impulses

Autonomic nervous control
Control blood pressure
Maintain body temperature
Stimulates antidiuretic hormone
Assists with appetite regulation
Acts on intestines
Role in emotions
Helps maintain wakefulness

Eye reflexes
Conduct impulses

Breathing
Chewing
Taste

Sensory
Motor
Pain
Heat
Touch

Vision

Muscle tone
Equilibrium
Walking
Dancing

Heart
Lungs
Stomach
Blood vessels

Source: Delmar/Cengage Learning.

ICD-9-CM Coding

The Endocrine System

ICD-9-CM codes related to the endocrine system are concentrated in chapter 3: Endocrine, Nutritional and Metabolic Diseases, and Immunity Disorders (240–279). Disorders of the individual glands are ordered by location (eg, disorders of the thyroid gland [240–246], disorders of parathyroid gland [252], diseases of thymus gland [254], etc.).

Use the Index to Diseases (Vol. 2) to find the disorder/disease, and confirm code selection in the Tabular List (Vol. 1). Be sure to heed all "includes" and "excludes" information, as well as required fourth- or fifth-digit specificity. Some codes may require an additional code be cited; for instance, instruction with 242.8x Thyrotoxicosis of other specified origin indicates, "Use additional E code to identify cause, if drug-induced."

ICD-9-CM instructions in the Tabular List of chapter 3 specify: "All neoplasms, whether functionally active or not, are classified in chapter 2." Codes in the Endocrine, Nutritional and Metabolic Diseases, and Immunity Disorders chapter "may be used to identify such functional activity associated with any neoplasm, or by ectopic endocrine tissue." That is, the neoplasm should be reported first, and any functional activity caused by the neoplasm should be reported as a secondary code.

Diabetes Mellitus

The *ICD-9-CM Official Guidelines for Coding and Reporting* provides extensive notes and instruction for coding diabetes and its manifestations. You should review these guidelines in full. The following summary identifies key points.

All diabetic codes fall into categories 249 and 250. The fourth digit indicates whether there are any complications or manifestations. If the patient has a documented manifestation, assign the diabetic code from categories 249–250, followed by the associated condition. For many diabetic codes there is a "use additional code" note for the manifestation specific for that diabetic code. Assign as many codes from categories 249 and 250 as necessary to identify all of the patient's associated conditions.

The fifth digit in category 250 indicates the type of diabetes (type I or type II) and if it is controlled.

If the documentation doesn't specify the type, or whether it is controlled or uncontrolled, assign code 250.00 *Diabetes mellitus without mention of complication type II or unspecified type, not stated as uncontrolled.*

Secondary diabetes (category 249) identifies complications/manifestations associated with secondary diabetes mellitus. Secondary diabetes always is caused by another condition or event, such as cystic fibrosis, neoplasm of pancreas, poisoning, etc. The fifth digit in category 249 indicates whether the secondary diabetes is controlled, unspecified "0," or uncontrolled "1."

The Nervous System

ICD-9-CM codes specific to the nervous system are listed primarily in chapter 6: Diseases of the Nervous System and Sense Organs (320–389). Use the Index to Diseases to find the disorder/disease, and confirm code selection by referring to the Tabular List. Be sure to heed all "includes" and "excludes" information, as well as required fourth- or fifth-digit specificity.

Meningitis

Meningitis is inflammation of the lining of the brain and/or spinal cord, which also causes changes in the cerebrospinal fluid. When coding for meningitis, you must know the agent responsible (for example, pneumococcal, streptococcal, gram-negative anaerobes, arbovirus, etc.). In some cases (eg, 321.3 *Meningitis due to trypanosomiasis*), you must code first the underlying disease (eg, 086.1 *Trypanosomiasis with involvement of organ other than heart*). For unspecified meningitis, report 322.9.

Encephalitis, Myelitis, and Encephalomyelitis

Encephalitis is swelling or inflammation of the brain. Myelitis is swelling or inflammation of the spinal cord. Encephalomyelitis is combined brain and spinal cord inflammation. When coding for these disorders, check ICD-9-CM notation as to whether you should code first the underlying disease, and whether additional E codes are necessary.

Organic Sleep Disorders

Organic sleep disorders, including organic insomnia (inability to sleep), hypersomnia (excessive sleep), sleep apnea (pauses in breathing during sleep), parasomnia (night terrors, sleepwalking, and related abnormal movement during sleep), and others, are found in category 327. See subcategory 307.4 for sleep disorders not documented as organic.

Hereditary and Degenerative Diseases of the Central Nervous System

Codes 330–337 describe hereditary and degenerative diseases of the CNS. Diagnoses in this range include Alzheimer's disease (331.0), Reye's syndrome (331.81), Parkinson's disease (332.0–332.1), and abnormal movement disorders—such as blepharospasm (uncontrolled winking, 333.81) and restless legs syndrome (RLS) (333.94)—among others.

Follow ICD-9-CM instruction regarding the use of additional codes to identify associated conditions, or to report underlying diseases as primary. Watch also for "excludes" notes.

Pain (not elsewhere classified)

The *ICD-9-CM Official Guidelines for Coding and Reporting* provides extensive notes and instruction for coding pain (category 338). The following summary identifies key points.

When reporting a pain diagnosis, identify as precisely as possible the location and/or source of the pain. If pain is the primary symptom, and you know the location, the Index to Diseases will generally provide the information you need.

If the patient has a documented, more-comprehensive diagnosis that causes the documented acute or chronic pain, but the documentation indicates the primary reason for the visit/service is management or control of the pain, report a diagnosis code from category 338 as the primary or first-listed ICD-9-CM code. Next, report the specific site of pain. The underlying cause is reported as an additional diagnosis, if known.

If the encounter is for any reason other than pain control or pain management, and a related differential

diagnosis has not been established, assign the code for the specific site of pain first, followed by the appropriate code from category 338.

The ICD-9-CM official guidelines specify not to report a diagnosis from category 338 "if the pain is not specified as acute or chronic, except for post-thoracotomy pain, postoperative pain, or neoplasm related pain."

Note that chronic pain syndrome is not the same as chronic pain. Report chronic pain syndrome (338.4) only when the provider has documented that exact condition.

Testing Technique

Know where to find the ICD-9-CM guidelines for pain. They begin with 1.C.6.a.1–1.C.6.a.6.

Other Disorders of the Central Nervous System

Other disorders of the CNS are found in codes 340–349. Examples include multiple sclerosis (an autoimmune disease of the brain and spinal cord), some types of myelitis, and hemiplegia or hemiparesis (weakness on a single side of the body). Code selection is straightforward; be sure to abide by ICD-9-CM instruction regarding the use of additional codes to identify associated conditions and/or cause. Watch also for "excludes" and "includes" notes.

Migraine

Category 346 describes migraines. Per ICD-9-CM instruction, migraine does not include headache not otherwise specified (784.0) or various syndromes as described by 339.00–339.89. For each code in the 346.xx set, you must include a fifth digit to indicate the presence of status migrainosus:

◖ 0—Without mention of intractable migraine without mention of status migrainosus

◖ 1—With intractable migraine, so stated, without mention of status migrainosus

◖ 2—Without mention of intractable migraine with status migrainosus

◖ 3—With intractable migraine, so stated, with status migrainosus

Status migrainosus is an unrelenting, debilitating headache of severe intensity lasting more than 72 hours, with less than an hour of pain-free period. The fifth digits also specify whether a migraine is "tractable" or "intractable." An intractable migraine is sustained and continual and does not respond to normal treatment.

A persistent migraine may occur with (346.6x) or without (346.5x) cerebral infarction. Migraine related to menstruation is reported with 346.4x.

Disorders of the Peripheral Nervous System

Disorders of the PNS are found in code sets 350–359. Examples include trigeminal nerve disorders (pain resulting in disorder of the nerve connecting part of the face to the brain), lesions of the nerve roots and plexus, nerve inflammation (neuritis—the most prominent of these is carpel tunnel syndrome, 354.0), and hereditary and idiopathic peripheral nerve disease (neuropathy).

Neoplasms

Neoplasms may occur throughout the endocrine and nervous systems. Selecting a neoplasm diagnosis is the same as for any other system. Go to the ICD-9-CM Index to Diseases, and look up the main term that describes the neoplasm type. Don't skip to the Neoplasm Table: Although the Index to Diseases often directs you to the Neoplasm Table, checking the index is not a wasted step. You won't find all the codes you need in the Neoplasm Table. ICD-9-CM lists certain conditions only in the Index to Diseases; in other cases, using the index saves time and reduces confusion. If the Index to Diseases doesn't provide the information you need, consult the Neoplasm Table.

CPT® Coding

CPT® codes relevant to the endocrine and nervous system will come primarily from the 60000 series, with some additional services in the 90000 series.

The Endocrine System

The Thyroid Gland

Procedures include incision and drainage, biopsy, and excision or aspiration of a thyroid cyst. The majority of codes describe excision procedures, including total or partial removal of the thyroid that may include related procedures, such as neck dissection. Lobectomy describes removal of a single lobe of the thyroid, and isthmusectomy (eg, 60210–60225) describes excision of the isthmus, or central portion, of the thyroid.

Parathyroid, Thymus, Adrenal Glands, Pancreas, and Carotid Body

Procedures in this section describe primarily excisions of the parathyroid, thymus, adrenal glands, and carotid body. An adrenalectomy may be either open (60540–60545) or laparoscopic (60650).

Unlisted Procedure

Unlisted procedures of the endocrine system are reported using 60699. Use an unlisted procedure code only when no CPT® code or Category III code properly describes the procedure the provider performs. When filing a claim using an unlisted procedure code, submit a cover letter of explanation and full documentation of services.

Endocrinology

Endocrinology services in the medicine portion of CPT® are limited to 95250–95251 for continuous monitoring of glucose (CGM) for a minimum of 72 hours. CGM is indicated for patients with type 1, type 2, or gestational diabetes who require better regulation of blood glucose levels.

The Nervous System

Many codes within this portion of CPT® may be performed with radiologic imaging, and often radiological supervision and interpretation may be reported separately. Pay attention to CPT® parenthetical notes following code descriptors, as well as instructions in section headings.

Skull, Meninges, and Brain

Twist Drill, Burr Holes or Trephine, Craniectomy or Craniotomy

Various methods may be used to pierce the skull and access the brain. These include twist drill holes for puncture (eg, 61105–61108) and burr holes (eg, 61120–61210). A trephine is a surgical instrument with a cylindrical blade, used to create an opening in the skull. The reason for access and location (for instance, for aspiration of hematoma or cyst, intracerebral) determine code selection.

Craniectomy or craniotomy (61304–61576) is more extensive than twist drill holes or burr holes. A section of skull, or bone flap, is removed to access the brain underneath. If the bone flap is not replaced, the procedure is called a craniectomy. Code according to the reason for the procedure and its location.

Skull Base Surgery

CPT® provides extensive notes for skull base surgery codes 61580–61619. These procedures are performed to treat lesions involving the skull base, and consist usually of three distinct parts:

1. To find the appropriate skull-base surgery approach code, look to the surgeon's documentation to determine the fossa targeted and whether the incision was through the dura. Confer with the surgeon to verify the exact structures he or she moved or removed to select the code that best describes the procedure. Documentation in the medical record may not always match CPT® code descriptor language.

2. The definitive portion of the procedure is determined according to the area of the skull base (anterior, middle, or posterior cranial fossa) from which the surgeon performs the procedure. When coding for skull-base surgeries, the approach and definitive procedure codes should match. An anterior approach (such as 61586) should accompany a code describing, for instance, removal of a lesion in the same portion of the skull (the anterior cranial fossa). Other factors, such as whether the dura is entered, also will factor into code selection.

3. Often, the surgeon must perform a secondary repair following skull-base surgery. Report repair/reconstruction codes (61618–61619) separately "if extensive dural grafting, cranioplasty, local or regional myocutaneous pedicle flaps or extensive skin grafts are required," according to CPT®

guidelines. Such secondary repairs will occur during a later operative session, which may require application of modifier 58 (the repair was planned) or modifier 78 (the repair was unplanned), as appropriate. According to CPT®, refer to the appropriate codes for primary closure, such as 15732, or a code from 15756–15758.

Endovascular Therapy

Endovascular treatment of arterial disease of the nervous system involves the use of balloons or stents to treat a diseased artery. Procedures described by 61623–61642 generally include selective catheterization of the target vessel only, and radiological supervision and interpretation often are reported separately. Look to parenthetical references in CPT® for instruction. Diagnostic procedures performed prior to the intervention during the same session are reported separately with modifier 59. Report also the nonselective or selective catheterization for the diagnostic procedure with modifier 59 when performed with 61623–61642. Remember to use 75898, *Angiography through existing catheter for follow-up study for transcatheter therapy, embolization or infusion* when applicable.

Surgery for Aneurysm, Arteriovenous (AV) Malformation, or Vascular Disease

Codes 61680–61692 specify surgery of intracranial arteriovenous malformation. The malformation may be supratentorial (above the tentorium cerebella, or in the cerebrum), infratentorial (in the lower part of the brain or cerebellum), or dural (within the dura). These procedures may be coded as simple or complex, determined by accessibility and difficulty of repair.

Codes 61697–61703 describe repair of intracranial (within the skull) aneurysms. An aneurysm is a bulge or abnormal dilation caused by weakened blood vessel walls. These repairs are classified as either simple or complex. According to CPT®, a repair is complex when the aneurysm(s) is larger than 15 mm, involves calcification of the aneurysm neck (the constricted portion at the "base" of the aneurysm), incorporates normal vessels into the aneurysm neck, or requires temporary vessel occlusion, trapping, or cardiopulmonary bypass to complete the repair.

The carotid circulation supplies blood to the anterior (front) and middle portions of the brain (via the carotid artery), and the vertebrobasilar circulation supplies the cerebellum and brain stem via vessels coming up the vertebral arteries. Code 61703 *Surgery of intracranial aneurysm, cervical approach by application of occluding clamp to cervical carotid artery (Selverstone-Crutchfield type)* describes a unique procedure involving an approach through the neck to occlude the carotid artery to control bleeding. The surgeon performs a craniotomy and locates the aneurysm. The ipsilateral carotid artery is then occluded while the surgeon occludes the aneurysm with a clip. Once bleeding is controlled, the carotid clamp is removed, the dura is closed, and the bone flap is repositioned and secured. The scalp and neck incisions are closed.

Codes 61705–61710 describe other techniques or approaches for repairing intracranial vascular abnormalities:

- A combined approach through the neck and skull; the surgeon interrupts blood flow to the abnormality in both directions (61705)
- Intracranial electrothrombosis (cautery) to obliterate the lesion (61708)
- Intra-arterial embolization, injection procedure, or balloon catheter (61710)

Code 61711 *Anastomosis, arterial, extracranial-intracranial (eg, middle cerebral/cortical) arteries* describes the joining of arteries to bypass an aneurysm or other defect.

Cranial Stereotaxis and Stereotactic Radiosurgery

CPT® provides extensive explanation and instruction preceding stereotactic radiosurgery codes 61796–61800. Familiarize yourself with these guidelines prior to attempting code selection.

When treating cranial lesions by stereotactic radiosurgery (61796–61799), the number and type of lesions treated differentiate the codes. Complex lesions include those adjacent (5 mm or less) to the optic nerve/optic chasm/optic tract, or within the brain stem. Certain types of lesions automatically are considered complex—including lesions 3.5 cm in maximum dimension or greater, schwannomas, arterio-venous malformations,

pituitary tumors, glomus tumors, pineal region tumors, and cavernous sinus/parasellar/petroclival tumors. Simple cranial lesions are less than 3.5 cm in maximum dimension and do not otherwise meet the definition of a complex lesion.

Codes 61797 and 61799 are "each additional codes" that may be reported as add-on codes after the initial lesion. For a frame-based stereotactic system, report +61800 *Application of stereotactic headframe for stereotactic radiosurgery (List separately in addition to code for primary procedure)* as an add-on code in conjunction with 61796 and 61798.

Cranial Neurostimulators

Placement of intracranial neurostimulators is reported using 61850–61888. These procedures include access by burr hole, craniectomy, craniotomy, etc., and apply to any type of intracranial neurostimulator (simple or complex). The code descriptors are straightforward. Follow CPT® instruction preceding the codes, as well as parenthetical notes, for proper code selection.

Repair

Codes 62000–62148 describe repairs to the skull. The code descriptors are straightforward. Follow CPT® parenthetical notes, when applicable, for proper code selection.

Neuroendoscopy

Codes 62160–62165 describe procedures performed by neuroendoscopy. The code descriptors are straightforward. Follow CPT® parenthetical notes, when applicable, for proper code selection.

Do not report an endoscopy code in addition to the code that describes the identical open procedure. If the surgeon must "convert" an endoscopic procedure to an open procedure because of complications, report only the successful (open) procedure. A surgical endoscopy always includes diagnostic endoscopy.

Cerebrospinal Fluid (CSF) Shunt

Standard surgical treatment for hydrocephalus (an accumulation of cerebrospinal fluid) includes placement of an extracranial shunt, or tube, to divert excess CSF from the ventricles of the brain to another body area (most often the abdominal cavity). Coding for these procedures depends on the location of both the proximal portion of the shunt and the drain site.

Intracranial shunts are created by means of ventriculo-cisternostomy, or ventriculocisternal shunting (62180). Stereotactic endoscopic third ventriculostomy (62201) involves the use of a laser under neuroendoscopic guidance to create a duct from the third lateral ventricle to the cisterna magna without need for a shunt.

Extracranial shunts may require periodic revisions, including irrigation and complete or partial replacement (eg, 62194, 62225, 62230, and 62258).

The reprogrammable shunt allows noninvasive pressure adjustments to correct over- or under-drainage of CSF; reprogramming is reported with 62252.

Spine and Spinal Cord

Injection, Drainage, or Aspiration

CPT® supplies extensive notes prior to the subsection for Injection, Drainage, or Aspiration, as well as numerous parenthetical instructions. Read and understand these guidelines prior to selecting a code. Highlights in this section include:

- During epidural lysis of spinal adhesions (Racz catheter procedure or epidural adhesiolysis), 62263–62264, the surgeon inserts a needle near the patient's tailbone and threads a catheter through the needle to inject medication into adhesions. These codes include the injection of contrast and fluoroscopic guidance and localization. Code 62263 describes treatments spanning two or more days, and is only reported once for the entire series.

- Diagnostic spinal puncture (spinal tap) is reported with 62270; therapeutic procedure for drainage of CSF is reported with 62272.

- Report 62280 for all neurolytic injections or infusions to the subarachnoid space, regardless of the spinal level. For neurolytic injection or infusion into the epidural space, choose between 62281 and 62282.

- For non-neurolytic substances (anesthetic, antispasmodic, opioid, steroid, etc.) administered

through single injection or via a continuous infusion or intermittent bolus by indwelling catheter into the epidural or subarachnoid space, select a code from range 62310–62319, depending on the location. These codes include use of contrast material for localization or epidurography.

Testing Technique

The region of the spine injected will determine code selection. Highlight words such as "cervical," "thoracic," and "lumbar" to help you select the correct code.

- For transforaminal epidural injection of a non-neurolytic substance, select from 64479–64484.

- For anesthetic injection of an anesthetic agent for autonomic nerves, see 64505–64530.

- For paravertebral facet (zygapophyseal) joint injections, report 64490–64495. Imaging guidance and localization are required for these procedures, and are inclusive components. If imaging is not used, report 20552–20553. If ultrasound guidance is used, report 0213T–0218T.

Catheter, Reservoir/Pump Implantation

Procedures for "pain pumps" (for pain management or spasticity treatment) are reported with 62350–62370. Available codes distinguish between programmable and non-programmable pumps. CPT® parenthetical instructions provide guidance on coding for associated procedures, such as refilling and maintenance of implantable infusion pump. Codes 62369 and 62370 report analysis with reprogramming and refill, without or requiring physician's skill.

Laminotomy, Laminectomy

Laminectomy (excision of lamina and spinous process) and laminotomy (partial excision of lamina) are performed primarily for nerve decompression. Read code descriptors carefully to determine if related procedures, such as facetectomy, foraminotomy, excision of herniated intervertebral discs, etc., are included.

These procedures are grouped according to spinal region (cervical, thoracic, lumbar). Some of these procedures are reported per segment (eg, 63015–63017), while others are reported per interspace (eg, 63020–63044). Generally, a single code is reported for the first segment or interspace, with add-on codes used to report additional segments or interspaces.

Codes 63040–63044 specifically describe re-exploration, or a repeat procedure.

Follow CPT® parenthetical instruction regarding proper reporting of bilateral procedures and allowable code combinations.

Excision by laminectomy of lesion other than herniated disk is reported using 63250–63290, as appropriate to the type of lesion and its location. Add-on code 63295 describes reconstruction of dorsal spinal elements following an intraspinal procedure. CPT® provides parenthetical notes outlining correct use of this code.

Extradural Exploration/Decompression

Exploration and Decompression codes 63055–63103 are grouped according to approach, which also determines whether the procedure includes removal of bone (for instance, vertebral corpectomy). Read code descriptors carefully to determine if related procedures, such as osteophytectomy, etc., are included.

CPT® provides instructional guidance for this section (for instance, regarding the proper use of modifier 62 with discectomy procedures), as well as numerous parenthetical notes. Read and understand these guidelines prior to selecting a code.

Excision of Intraspinal Lesion, Anterior or Anterolateral Approach

These codes (63300–63308) are selected according to spinal region (cervical, thoracic, lumbar), whether intra- or extradural, and (in some cases) by specific approach. CPT® provides instructional guidance regarding the proper use of modifier 62 for this section.

Spinal Stereotaxis and Stereotactic Radiosurgery

Stereotaxis may include lesion creation (63600), stimulation not followed by other surgery (63610), and biopsy, aspiration, or excision of lesion (63615). CPT® provides extensive explanation and instruction preceding

63620–63621 for stereotactic radiosurgery. Familiarize yourself with these guidelines prior to attempting code selection.

Spinal Neurostimulators

Spinal cord stimulation delivers low voltage electrical stimulation to the dorsal columns of the spinal cord to block the sensation of pain. The systems consist of electrodes implanted along the spine, which are connected to a programmable pulse generator or receiver. The electrodes may be either a catheter electrode array, or arranged on a "paddle."

Implantation of electrodes is reported with 63650 or 63655, according to method. Two codes (63661, 63662) describe removal of spinal neurostimulator electrodes, according to type (electrode array or plate/paddles) and approach (percutaneous or via laminotomy/laminectomy). Two additional codes describe revision (63663, 63664)—including replacement when performed—of spinal neurostimulator electrodes according to approach. All of the above include fluoroscopy if performed.

Implantation or replacement of pulse generator or receiver is reported 63685; revision or removal of the same is reported 63688. Programming may be reported separately.

Extracranial Nerves, Peripheral Nerves, and Autonomic Nervous System

This code section (64400–64495) applies to extracranial nerves only; for intracranial surgery on cranial nerves, see 61450, 61460, or 61790.

Diagnostic or Therapeutic Nerve Block

Nerve blocks are reported according to the nerve/plexus targeted. CPT® provides extensive parenthetical notes in this section to guide code selection, and indicates when associated procedures (such as image guidance) may be reported separately.

The term "facet joint injection" may describe either a nerve block or more extensive nerve destruction. When reporting nerve blocks (64490–64495), focus on the "joint"—the area between adjacent nerves—the provider targets; therefore, one nerve block "level" will involve two nerves. For example, if the physician provides diagnostic nerve blocks for C2, C3, and C4, he or she is addressing three nerves but only two levels (the joint at C2–C3 and the joint at C3–C4). Be sure to apply 64490–64495 per level, rather than per injection (the physician may provide more than one injection per level).

Codes 64490–64495 include imaging guidance and describe unilateral procedures. If the provider addresses both the left and right side at the same level, CPT® guidelines allow modifier 50 to report a bilateral procedure.

Peripheral Neurostimulators

Placement and revision/replacement of peripheral nerve neurostimulators (simple or complex) are reported using 64550–64595, depending on the nerve targeted and type of neurostimulator. The code descriptors are straightforward. Follow CPT® instruction preceding the codes, as well as parenthetical notes, for proper code selection.

Destruction by Neurolytic Agent

Neurolytic agents for nerve destruction may include chemical, thermal, electrical, or radiofrequency methods. Codes in this range (64600–64681) are specific as to the nerve(s)/plexus, muscle(s), or glands targeted. CPT® instructions that precede these codes, as well as all parenthetical references, provide necessary guidance to report these procedures with accuracy.

When coding for nerve destruction, count the facet joints treated by the destruction of nerves. For codes 64633–64636, one facet joint may mean multiple nerves. Multiple injections in the same facet joint count as a single facet joint. Nerve destruction codes, like nerve block codes, describe unilateral procedures; report bilateral procedures using modifier 50 or modifiers LT and RT, as appropriate.

The use of fluoroscopic guidance for needle placement with either nerve block or nerve destruction procedures is considered inclusive. Note that paravertebral facet joint injections (64490–64495) include image guidance (fluoroscopy or CT). If imaging is not used, report 20550–20553. If ultrasound guidance is used, report 0213T–0218T.

Neuroplasty

Neuroplasty (64702–64727) describes decompression and freeing of intact nerve(s) from scar tissue. The codes are applied according to the nerve targeted.

Transection and Avulsion

Codes for transection (to divide by transverse incision) and avulsion (tearing away) of nerves codes are selected according to the nerve targeted. CPT® parenthetical notes provide guidance for proper reporting of bilateral procedures.

Excision

Excision of nerves is coded according to the nerve targeted. Biopsy of a somatic nerve is reported with 64795.

Neurorrhaphy

Neurorrhaphy is the surgical suturing of a divided nerve. Codes in the range 64831–64876 describe suturing only; the appropriate code is selected according to the nerve(s) targeted.

Codes 64885–64911 describe neurorrhaphy with nerve graft, vein graft, or conduit. Most codes are selected according to location (head or neck, hand or foot, etc.) and nerve length (more or less than 4 cm). Add-on codes 64901 and 64902 describe each additional nerve graft, single and multiple strands, respectively. If the surgeon repairs two or more nerves using grafts, report 64901–64902, as appropriate.

Unlisted Procedures

Unlisted procedures of the nervous system are to be reported using 64999. Call on an unlisted procedure code only when no CPT® code or Category III code properly describes the procedure the provider performed.

Operating Microscope

Report +69990 only for procedures requiring microsurgery or microdissection, and only when the primary surgery does not include microdissection as an integral part of the operation. Do not report 69990 if the surgeon uses the microscope only for magnification or corrective vision. Do not report 69990 for magnifying loupes.

CPT® provides instructions for when you may report 69990 in addition to other procedures, but be aware not all payers abide by American Medical Association (AMA) rules. The National Correct Coding Initiative (NCCI) bundles 69990 extensively, where CPT® otherwise allows separate coding.

Neurology and Neuromuscular Procedures

Neurology and neuromuscular procedures include a wide range of services, and may be found in the Medicine chapter (90000-series) of CPT®.

Sleep Studies

Polysomnography includes sleep staging with varying "parameters of sleep" (as defined by CPT®) studied. CPT® defines sleep staging to include a 3-lead electro-encephalogram (EEG) (frontal, central, and occipital), a right and left electro-oculogram (EOG), a submental electromyogram (EMG), and 4 or more additional parameters.

Testing Technique

Underline or highlight the additional parameters in the Sleep Testing guidelines.

These studies (and other sleep studies described in CPT®) require continuous monitoring and recording for six or more hours. If fewer than six hours of recording takes place, modifier 52 should be appended to identify a reduced service.

CPT® codes 95808 and 95810 identify diagnostic polysomnograms, depending on the parameters of sleep recorded. Code 95811 requires sleep staging with four or more additional parameters of sleep and further includes initiation of treatment.

A multiple sleep latency test (95805) is a daytime sleep study that measures how sleepy the patient is and how long it takes the patient to fall asleep.

Actigraphy testing (95803) is done to study a patient's circadian rhythms and sleep schedule.

Electroencephalography (EEG)/Special EEG

Routine EEG codes 95816–95822 include 20–40 minutes of recording. Extended EEG codes 95812–95813 include reporting times longer than 40 minutes.

Code 95819 is appropriate when an awake/asleep study was intended even if the patient did not sleep. Report 95819 (rather than 95816) if an awake-only study is planned, but the patient falls asleep.

EEG monitoring as describe by 95953 more precisely localizes certain types of seizures; when employed, it often follows monitoring as described by 95950 or 95951.

The descriptors for 95950–95953 specify "each 24 hours;" if fewer than 12 hours of monitoring are provided, report the appropriate CPT® code with modifier 52 appended.

Digital analysis as described by 95957 requires analysis using quantitative analytical techniques, such as data selection, quantitative software processing, and dipole source analysis. This kind of analysis entails additional work to process the data, as well as extra time to review the data.

Muscle and Range of Motion Testing

Manual muscle testing codes (95831–95834) are specific to the area tested: extremity (excluding hand), or trunk, hand, total body with/without hands). All codes include physician report.

Range of motion measurement codes are reported per extremity or each trunk section (95851), or for the hand (95852). Included with these codes is 95857 *Cholinesterase inhibitor challenge test for myasthenia gravis*.

Electromyography

EMG is used to evaluate the cause of weakness, paralysis, involuntary muscle twitching, or other symptoms.

To report EMG limb testing (95860–95864), the provider must evaluate extremity muscles innervated by at least three nerves (for example, radial, ulnar, median, tibial, peroneal or femoral—but not sub branches) or four spinal levels, with a minimum of five muscles studied per limb.

"Related paraspinal areas" include all paraspinals except those of the thoracic (T1 or T12) region. If the provider studies the paraspinals from T2–T11, report 95869; report only one unit of 95869, regardless of the number of levels studied or whether bilateral.

For fewer than five muscles tested, report limited EMG code 95870 or 95885. Non-extremity muscle EMG (cranial nerve supplied or axial) is reported with code 95887.

Guidance for Chemodenervation

For EMG when administering chemodenervation, report the guidance separately using 95873–95874. Use 95873/95874 only with injection codes 64612–64614.

Nerve Conduction

All nerves can contain motor fibers, sensory fibers, or a mixture of the two. Codes 95900–95903 describe motor fiber testing (without F-wave study/with F-wave study); code 95904 describes sensory or mixed fiber testing. For each separately reportable nerve tested, report one unit of service of the corresponding NCS code. Refer to CPT® Appendix J for a list of separately billable sensory, motor, and mixed nerves.

Code 95905 describes studies conducted using preconfigured electrode arrays, such as the NeuroMetrix NC-stat® System.

Intraoperative Neurophysiology Monitoring

Intraoperative monitoring (IOM) is reported using 95920. Report one unit of 95920 for each hour of monitoring. A minimum of 31 minutes of monitoring must be documented to bill an hour of service. Do not count "standby time" in the operating room or the time spent conducting any baseline studies. Only a dedicated physician, with the sole task of monitoring the patient during the surgery, should separately claim IOM services.

Prior to IOM, the monitoring physician may first conduct one or more studies to establish a patient's "baseline" responses. Report these baseline studies separately. CPT® provides a list of approved baseline studies/primary procedures for use with IOM.

Evoked Potentials and Reflex Testing

A comprehensive auditory evoked response (AER) exam (92585) measures middle latency and late cortical responses, and evaluates brainstem response. A limited audiometry examination (92586) describes limited auditory brainstem response (ABR) testing.

For stimulation of peripheral nerves or skin sites, report from 95925–95926, 95983, 95927. Regardless of the number of skin sites (dermatomes) tested, report only a single unit.

Report 95928 (upper limbs), 95929 (lower limbs), or 95939 (upper and lower limbs) as appropriate, for central motor (rather than sensory) EP study.

Analysis and Programming of Neurostimulators

A neurostimulator pulse generator system is a surgically implanted, pacemaker-like device that delivers preprogrammed intermittent electrical pulses to a particular nerve(s) or brain structure(s). Codes 95970–95982 are specific to location: spinal cord or peripheral nerve (95970–95973), cranial nerve (95974–95975), deep brain (95978–95979), and gastric (95980–95982).

Neurostimulators may be either simple or complex. A simple neurostimulator is capable of affecting three or fewer of the following, while a complex neurostimulator is capable of affecting more than three:

- Rate
- Pulse amplitude
- Pulse duration
- Pulse frequency
- Eight or more electrode contacts
- Cycling
- Stimulation train duration
- Train spacing
- Number of programs
- Number of channels
- Alternating electrode polarities
- Dose time (stimulation parameters changing in the time periods of minutes including dose lockout times)
- More than one clinical feature (eg, rigidity, dyskinesia, tremor)

Coding for complex neurostimulator programming is always time-based.

Unlisted Neurological or Neuromuscular Diagnostic Procedure

Unlisted neurological or neuromuscular diagnostic procedures are to be reported using 95999. Call on an unlisted procedure code only when no CPT® code or Category III code properly describes the procedure the provider performs.

Category III

Category III codes are temporary codes for emerging technologies, services, and procedures. If a Category III code is available, this code must be reported instead of a Category I unlisted code.

HCPCS Level II

Endocrine and nervous system codes can be found throughout the HCPCS Level II codebook. These codes are primarily used to report drug supplies (often using J codes, for example J0585 *Injection, onabotulinumtoxinA, 1 unit for Botox®*); some supply codes (such as L8680 *Implantable neurostimulator electrode (with any number of contact points), each)*; and temporary national codes (S-codes) for emerging procedures or technology (for instance, S2348 *Decompression procedure, percutaneous, of nucleus pulposus of intervertebral disc, using radiofrequency energy, single or multiple levels, lumbar)*.

Check the HCPCS index or Table of Drugs for easy code location and assignment.

Modifiers

Reporting endocrine and nervous-system-related services and procedures requires a familiarity with the full gamut of CPT® modifiers, as well as several HCPCS Level II modifiers.

Modifier 22

Consider appending modifier 22 *Increased procedural services* when the service(s) is "greater than that usually required for the listed procedure," according to CPT®

Appendix A ("Modifiers"). Provider documentation must demonstrate the special circumstances, such as extra time or highly complex trauma, that warrant modifier 22.

Modifier 24

Apply modifier 24 *Unrelated evaluation and management service by the same physician during a postoperative period to describe an unrelated E/M service* during the global period of another procedure. Modifier 24 designates that the physician is evaluating the patient for a new problem, and the evaluation is not included in a previous procedure's global surgical package.

Modifier 25

To apply modifier 25 *Significant, separately identifiable evaluation and management service by the same physician on the same day of the procedure or other service appropriately,* for an E/M service at the same time as another minor procedure or service, documentation must substantiate that the E/M is both significant and separately identifiable. Any E/M service separately reported must be "above and beyond" the minimal E/M normally included in a procedure or other service.

Modifier 26 and Modifier TC

When a physician conducts diagnostic tests or other services using equipment he or she doesn't own, modifier 26 *Professional component* may be used to indicate that the physician provided only the professional component (the administration or interpretation) of the service. The facility providing the equipment may receive reimbursement for the service's technical component (the cost of equipment, supplies, technician salaries, etc.) by reporting the appropriate CPT® code with modifier TC *Technical component* appended.

Apply modifiers 26 and TC only to those codes that have both a professional and a technical component. The professional portion of the service includes the physician interpretation and report; the technical component pays for operation and maintenance of equipment, necessary supplies, etc. The CMS National Physician Fee Schedule Relative Value File separately lists code values with modifier 26, with modifier TC, and with no modifier appended.

If the physician provides both components of the service (for instance, by providing the service in his or her own office), he or she may report the appropriate CPT® code without either modifier 26 or modifier TC.

Modifier 50

Append modifier 50 *Bilateral procedure* when the provider performs a procedure bilaterally (on both sides of the body), and no available CPT® code otherwise describes the procedure as bilateral. Not every code is eligible to receive modifier 50, because not all procedures may be performed bilaterally. For Medicare payers, guidance on when to append modifier 50 can be found in the CMS National Physician Fee Schedule Relative Value File.

Modifier 52

Apply modifier 52 *Reduced services* when the physician plans or expects a reduction in the service, or the physician electively cancels the procedure prior to completion. The reduction of services must have occurred by choice (either the surgeon's or the patient's), rather than necessity.

Modifier 53

Modifier 53 *Discontinued services* describes an unexpected problem, beyond the physician's or patient's control, that necessitates terminating the procedure.

Modifier 54, Modifier 55, and Modifier 56

All procedures with a global surgical package have three parts: pre-operative services (for example, pre-operative exam), the surgery itself, and postoperative care (follow-up visits, minor complications). In some circumstances, a physician (or physician group billing under the same provider number) will furnish only part of the total surgical service as described by the global surgical package. When this occurs, modifiers 54 *Surgical care only,* 55 *Postoperative management only,* and 56 *Preoperative management only* may be appropriate.

For example, most patients seen in the ED require follow-up by another physician. In such cases, the ED physician should report any applicable procedures using modifier 54, and the physician providing follow-up reports the same codes with modifier 55.

Modifier 57

To append modifier 57, the E/M service must meet four conditions:

1. The E/M service must occur on the same day of or the day before the surgical procedure.

2. The E/M service must directly lead to the surgeon's decision to perform surgery.

3. The surgical procedure following the E/M must have a 90-day global period. For a separate and significantly identifiable E/M service on the same day as a minor procedure, append modifier 25.

4. The same physician (or one with the same tax ID) provides the E/M service and the surgical procedure.

Modifier 58

Append modifier 58 to a procedure or service during the postoperative period if the procedure or service was:

◖ Planned prospectively at the time of the original procedure.

◖ More extensive than the original procedure.

◖ For therapy following a diagnostic surgical procedure.

The subsequent procedure or service either is related to the underlying problem/diagnosis that prompted the initial surgery, or anticipated at the time the surgeon performs the initial surgery, according to CPT® instruction. For complications that require a return to the operating room, append modifier 78.

Modifier 59

Use modifier 59 *Distinct procedural* service to identify procedures that are distinctly separate from any other procedure provided on the same date. According to CPT® instruction, you may append modifier 59 when the provider:

◖ Performs a procedure which is usually bundled with another procedure, when performed at the same session; however, one procedure was performed at another session on the same day (eg, biopsy of a lesion, then removal of the lesion later in the day).

- Tends to a different lesion of the same site and size.
- Do not append modifier 59 to E/M codes and do not use modifier 59 if another, more specific modifier is available.

Do not append modifier 59 to E/M codes, and do not use modifier 59 if another, more specific modifier is available.

Modifier 62

Append modifier 62 *Two surgeons* when two primary surgeons work together to complete a procedure described by a single CPT® code. Each physician should document his or her own operative notes. Not all CPT® codes allow modifier 62. For Medicare payers, guidance on when modifier 62 may apply can be found in the CMS National Physician Fee Schedule Relative Value File.

Modifier 78

Apply modifier 78 *Unplanned return to the operating room for a related procedure during the postoperative period* when all of the following conditions are met:

- The physician must undertake the subsequent surgery because of conditions (complications) arising from an initial surgery during the global period;
- The subsequent surgery occurs during the global period of the initial surgery; and
- The subsequent surgery requires a return to the operating room.

Modifier 79

Modifier 79 *Unrelated procedure or service by the same physician during the postoperative period* may be appended when an unrelated surgery by the same physician occurs during the global period of a previous surgery.

Modifier LT and Modifier RT

Modifiers LT *Left side* and RT *Right side* differentiate procedures performed on paired structures (such as eyes, lungs, arms, breasts, knees, etc.). Finally, modifiers LT and RT may be used to provide location-specific information for those services defined either as unilateral or bilateral.

Glossary

Actigraphy Testing—Measures the movement of a limb; the term actigraphy refers to methods utilizing miniaturized sensors that translate physical motion into a numeric presentation.

Anastomosis—A surgical connection between two (usually hollow) structures.

Chemodenervation—An interruption of messages sent between nerves and muscles by administration of a chemical substance.

Chemonucleolysis—Injection of an enzyme to dissolve the gelatinous cushioning material in an intervertebral disk.

Cranioplasty—Surgical repair of a defect or deformity of a skull.

Decompression—When referring to nerves of the spine: The freeing of a pinched nerve, for instance, from between adjacent vertebrae.

Encephalocele (cephalocele, meningoencephalocele)—A rare disorder in which the bones of the skull do not close completely, creating a gap through which cerebral spinal fluid, brain tissue, and the meninges can protrude into a sac-like formation.

Fossa—Any one of three hollows (anterior, middle, and posterior) in the base of the cranium for the lobes of the brain.

F-wave—A voltage change observed after electrical stimulation is applied to the skin surface above the distal region of a nerve; often used to measure nerve conduction velocity.

Ligation—To tie off.

Meninges—Collective name for the membranes that envelop the central nervous system. The meninges consist of three layers: the dura mater, the arachnoid mater, and the pia mater. Its primary function (along with that of the cerebrospinal fluid) is to protect the brain and spinal cord.

Meningocele—Protrusion, through a bone defect in the vertebral column, of the meninges that cover the spinal cord.

Myelomeningocele—A birth defect in which the backbone and spinal canal do not close before birth; a type of spina bifida (a developmental birth defect caused by the incomplete closure of the embryonic neural tube). The spinal cord and the meninges protrude.

Neurolytic Agent—Agent used to destroy nerves; for instance alcohol, phenol, etc.

Osteomyelitis—An acute or chronic bone infection.

Spinal Tap—A procedure to withdraw cerebrospinal fluid, such as spinal puncture (CPT® 62270–62272).

Stereotactic Head Frame—A guiding device that positions the head for precise treatment during stereotactic radiosurgery.

Transection—To divide by cutting transversely; a cross section along the long axis.

Trephination (Trepanning, Trephining, Burr Hole)—Drilling a hole in the skull to expose the dura mater.

Vasospasm—A condition in which blood vessels spasm, leading to vasoconstriction and possible stroke or other injury; may arise in the context of subarachnoid hemorrhage.

Zygapophyseal Joint (Z Joint, Paravertebral Facet Joint, Facet Joint)—Located on the posterior spine on each side of the vertebra where it overlaps the neighboring vertebra; the facet joints provide stability and give the spine the ability to bend and twist. A facet joint includes the two surfaces of the adjacent vertebrae that are separated by a thin layer of cartilage.

Chapter Review Questions

1. **Which cells produce hormones to regulate blood sugar?**

    A. Eosinophils

    B. Pancreatic islets

    C. Hemoglobin

    D. Target cells

2. **What are chemicals which relay, amplify, and modulate signals between a neuron and another cell?**

    A. Neurotransmitters

    B. Hormones

    C. Interneurons

    D. Myelin

3. A 35-year-old has neuroplasty performed in the wrist for carpal tunnel syndrome. The palm is opened
    through a curved incision, and further skin flaps are developed. The ulnar origin of the transverse
    carpal ligament is divided, decompressing the carpal tunnel. Tension of the nerve is released, and the
    incision is sutured in layers. What CPT® code describes this procedure?

    A. 64721

    B. 64719

    C. 64708

    D. 64704

4. A 30-year-old male has lumbar facet syndrome. The affected nerve in the facet joints of the lumbar
    region is destroyed by a neurolytic agent in the right segmental medial branches innervating facet joints
    L3–L4, and L4–L5. What CPT® codes are reported?

    A. 64493, 64494

    B. 64635, 64636

    C. 64483, 64484

    D. 64633, 64634-50

5. A patient has spinal stenosis and disk displacement in the L3–L4 and L4–L5 and underwent a removal of
    the posterior arch of a vertebra to provide additional space for the nerves and to widen the spinal canal.
    The back was prepped, and an incision was made down to the deep fascia and the spinous processes of
    L5, L4 and L3 were identified performing the laminectomy of L4 up to L3 and a resection of the flavum
    ligament. There was resection of the facet and decompression was carried out laterally to the level of the
    medial border of the pedicle. Foraminotomies of L3–L4 and L4–L5 were performed with the Kerrison
    punch and there was plenty of room for the nerve roots to exit in these regions with no further stenosis
    above or below this area. What procedure code(s) are reported?

    A. 63047, 63048

    B. 63042, 63044

    C. 63017

    D. 63005

6. A six-week-old infant has hydrocephalus, and the parents have consented to have surgery to drain the cerebrospinal fluid. The infant's scalp is incised, and a burr hole is drilled. A catheter is inserted through the brain tissue into the enlarged lateral ventricle. A valve is attached to the ventricular catheter. A periumbilical incision is made dissecting through until the peritoneum is identified and incised. The shunt is tunneled, passing over from the belly up to the cranial incision with a small counter incision in the neck. The shunt tubing is passed through and then cut and attached to the strata valve. Free flow of cerebrospinal fluid is obtained from the distal shunt tubing and is placed into the peritoneum. What code is reported for this procedure?

   A. 61070

   B. 61210

   C. 62192

   D. 62223

7. A 43-year-old female patient diagnosed with papillary carcinoma of the thyroid is admitted for a total thyroidectomy. The neck and anterior chest are prepped, and an incision is made two fingerbreadths above the sternal notch and deepened down through the platysma muscle, where flaps are created both superior and inferior to the incision. The left side of the interior, inferior, and superior poles vessels are serially clamped, cut, and ligated, on the thyroid side dividing the isthmus on the right lobe side of the midline removing the left lobe and several enlarged lymph nodes. Then dissection is performed on the right side, removing the right lobe from the trachea. Which CPT® code is reported?

   A. 60240

   B. 60252

   C. 60260

   D. 60220

8. Biochemical and imaging evaluations reveals a 3.0 cm pheochromocytoma of the left adrenal gland on a 25-year-old female consenting to have it removed. The physician uses a sharp instrument to puncture the proximal area of the back to the retroperitoneal space superior to the kidney, adjacent to the adrenal gland. Then a laparoscope was used in excising the adrenal gland. The correct CPT® code is:

   A. 60500

   B. 60520

   C. 60540

   D. 60650

9. **Operative Note #1**

    Preoperative Diagnoses: 1.   Low back pain

                                  2.   Degenerative lumbar disc

    Postoperative Diagnoses: 1.   Low back pain

                                  2.   Degenerative lumbar disc

    Procedure Performed: 1.   Bilateral facet joint injections of steroid at the L4–L5 and L5–S1 with fluoro-
                                       scopic guidance

    Description of Procedure: The patient was transferred to the operative suite at the hospital and placed in
    the prone position with a pillow under the abdomen. A smooth IV sedation was given with midazolam and
    fentanyl. The patient's back was prepped with Betadine in a sterile fashion, and we used lidocaine, 1% plain as
    a local anesthetic at the injection site. With the use of fluoroscopy assistance, first to the right and then to the
    left 20-degree, the scotty-dog view was identified, and we were able to place the spinal 22-gauge needle first
    to the right L4–L5, then right L5–S1, then to the left L4–L5, and then to left L5–S1. We used a lateral X-ray
    to assess the proper placement of the needle. We proceeded to inject a mixture of 4 mL of 0.25% Marcaine
    plain plus 80 mg of methylprednisolone and divided between the four joints. The needles were removed. The
    patient's back was cleaned, and a Band-Aid® was applied. The patient was transferred to the recovery area with
    no apparent procedural complications.

    What are the CPT® and ICD-9-CM codes for this procedure?

10. **Operative Note #2**

    Preoperative Diagnosis: Papillary carcinoma of the thyroid by needle biopsy

    Postoperative Diagnosis: Multinodular goiter of the thyroid

    Operative Procedure: Near total thyroidectomy, left lobe isthmus and 80+% of the right lobe

    Indications: The patient is a 72-year-old white male who was being evaluated for hypopituitarism and had
    been referred to one of the local endocrinologists. An evaluation was also done of his thyroid which showed a
    mass in the left lobe of the thyroid and subsequent needle biopsy was performed and revealed the presence of
    papillary carcinoma of the thyroid.

    Procedure: The patient was placed on the operating room table in the supine position, and neck placed in a
    somewhat hyperextended position with a padded support beneath his scapula bilaterally, allowing his head
    to tilt posteriorly. It was supported by a small pillow. This was done and intubation was carried out via a glide
    scope. However he was a very difficult intubation and cords were extremely difficult to visualize. They did,
    however, function symmetrically.

    The skin of the anterior neck and chest was prepped and draped in the usual sterile fashion. A transverse inci-
    sion was made within one of his skin folds, approximately two fingerbreadths above the sternal notch.

    Following this skin wrinkle, the incision was deepened through the platysmus muscle and the midline was
    opened between the strap muscles. Then exposure was gained to the left lobe of the thyroid. The inferior pole of

the left lobe of the thyroid was very distal and actually was below the head of the clavicle, in the superior portion of the mediastinum. This was carefully mobilized and the inferior thyroidal veins were serially clamped, cut, and ligated with ligature of 3-0 silk. As the gland was able to be rolled medially, we stayed within or just outside the capsule of the thyroid during the course of the dissection. Multiple branches of the middle thyroidal vessels were clamped, cut, and ligated. The recurrent laryngeal nerve was actually deep to this portion of the dissection. The superior pole was then also dissected out, vessels clamped, cut, and ligated with suture of 3-0 silk.

Once the gland had been rolled medially, the isthmus was then mobilized and this specimen amputated at the junction of the isthmus and the right lobe. This was submitted for frozen section diagnosis, which we did not base further surgery on the frozen section. We went ahead, but the eventual frozen section diagnosis returned with so far benign tissue. The right lobe of the thyroid was mobilized from medial to lateral. The inferior thyroidal veins were ligated but none of the other vasculature was in fact divided. Once the gland was mobilized away from the trachea, the anterior portion of the right lobe was removed, leaving intact the entire posterior wall of the right lobe of the thyroid from the inferior to the superior pole. The cross-clamped thyroid gland was controlled hemostatically with figure-of-eight sutures of 3-0 silk.

Following this, hemostasis was secure. A 10 mm Jackson Pratt drain was placed through all layers and brought out through a separate stab wound on the anterior surface of the chest. The drain was secured with 0 silk. The wound was then closed in layers, closing the midline strap muscles and then the platysmus with 2-0 Vicryl. The skin was closed with 3-0 Monocryl and Dermabond. Prior to extubation, the video bronchoscope was inserted per the right naris. The scope was advanced to the level of the larynx where the vocal cords could in fact be visualized. They both moved symmetrically around the endotracheal tube. The endotracheal tube was removed and, again, all observers were able to see that both cords moved symmetrically. The procedure was then concluded, scope withdrawn. The patient tolerated the procedure and was transferred to the recovery area in stable condition. Estimated blood loss was 75 to 100 cc. Sponge and needle counts were correct times two.

What are the CPT® and ICD-9-CM codes for this procedure?

Eye: Introduction and Anatomy

Eye Structures

- Ciliary body and muscle
- Suspensory ligament
- Conjunctiva
- Iris
- Pupil
- Path of light
- Cornea
- Lens
- Retina
- Retinal arteries and veins
- Fovea centralis
- Optic nerve
- Choroid
- Sclera

Source: Delmar/Cengage Learning.

The eyeball is composed of a tough membrane called sclera. This white outer skin of the eye is covered with a thin protective layer of conjunctiva. Light first enters the eye through the cornea. The cornea has five layers; sometimes corneal defects will be managed by removing one or two layers, rather than full-thickness cornea. The cornea meets the sclera in a ring called the limbus, also known as the sclerocorneal junction. Behind the cornea is the anterior segment of the eye, which is filled with a clear, salty fluid called aqueous humor.

The eyeball's shape affects the way light is focused and directed (refraction). Any reduction in fluid within the eye will affect the eye's shape and refraction. For instance, if the eyeball is too oblong, the patient will be near-sighted. In far-sightedness, the eyeball is foreshortened, and close-up vision is impaired.

Next, light from the aqueous humor enters the crystalline lens, a convex disc suspended on threads just behind the iris. The iris is a muscle that expands and contracts to regulate the amount of light entering the posterior chamber of the eye through the pupil. If the light is too bright, the iris expands so the size of the pupil shrinks. If there is too little light, the iris contracts to enlarge the pupil and allow more light into the eye. The threads holding the lens and the ciliary body to which they are connected automatically tug at the lens to change its shape to help focus on items near or far.

After the light has been bent by the crystalline lens, it enters the vitreous humor, a gel-like mass that fills the large posterior chamber of the eye. The vitreous humor presses against the inner layer of the eye, maintaining the eyeball's shape and keeping the blood-rich choroid layer in contact with the retina. The light is placed upon the retina's rods and cones like a projected image at a movie theater, and these images are transmitted via the optic nerve to the brain.

Each eye has six muscles that direct the gaze up and down and from side to side.

To trace again the refraction path: Light travels from the cornea to the aqueous humor to the lens to the vitreous humor to the retina. The eyeball's stability and the refractive elements must all be perfect for vision to be 20-20.

The lacrimal system produces tears in glands behind the eyebrows. These tears flow through ducts into the eyes where they drain out the lacrimal puncta, or flow into the nose.

The visual field can be affected by many things: Blood, foreign bodies (FBs), or other tissue can obstruct the pathway to the retina. Examples include: excessive skin on the eyelids, shielding a portion of the eye from light, a cloudy condition in any of the refractive properties of the eye, or damage to the retina.

Ear: Introduction and Anatomy

Ear Structures

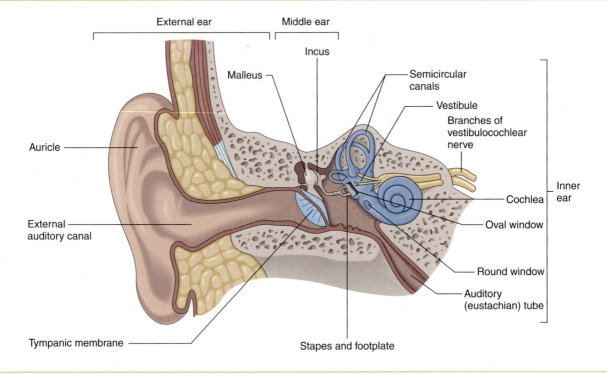

Source: Delmar/Cengage Learning.

In the context of the ear, conduction refers to the transfer of sound waves. Sound waves take two paths in humans:

1. The waves can be captured by the pinna, or outer ear, and travel by air along the external auditory meatus to the tympanic membrane. The tympanic membrane vibrates to telegraph its message to the middle ear, where the malleus picks up the vibration, and transfers it to the incus and stapes. These three tiny bones, the ossicles, carry the message to the oval window and round window in the vestibule of the inner ear and into the cochlea, where perilymph fluid vibrates and creates nerve impulses to the cochlear nerve.

2. Bone conduction is secondary to air conduction (above). The mastoid bones contain tiny air cells that also form a conductive path for sound.

The ear is also a center for balance. Information within the vestibule and the three semicircular canals is sent to the brain, signaling the body to compensate by making adjustments to posture or movement as appropriate for the orientation of the body.

The entry to the ear is well protected by the meaty exterior, and the ear canal is lined with hairs and lubricated with cerumen to filter out out FBs. To equalize the pressure between the middle ear and the outer world, the Eustachian tubes link the middle ear to the nasopharynx.

Key Roots, Suffixes, Prefixes for Eye and Ear

- acous/o — hearing
- blephar/o — eyelid
- canth/o — corner of eyelid
- cochle/o — cochlear
- conjunctiv/o — conjunctival
- dacry/o — relating to lacrimal system
- dipl/o — two
- goni/o — angle
- irid/o — iris
- kerat/o — corneal
- myring/o — tympanic membrane
- -opia — vision
- ot/o — ear
- phak/o — lens
- phot/o — light
- -ptosis — droop
- retin/o — retinal
- rhin/o — nose
- scler/o — ocular sclera
- staped/o — stapes
- tars/o — margin of eyelid
- trabecul/o — relating to meshwork for drainage of aqueous humor
- uve/o — uveal
- vitre/o — vitreous

ICD-9-CM Coding

Eye

Most eye disorders fall into these general categories:

- Infection and inflammation
- Neoplastic disease
- Injury
- Glaucoma
- Cataracts
- Retinopathy
- Retinal detachment
- Strabismus

Infection and inflammation—When the patient has an infection or inflammation, first determine the location. The codes within Disorders of the Eye and Adnexa (360–379) are organized according to anatomic site, beginning with globe, then moving from the posterior segment forward to the anterior segment of the eye and finishing with the adnexa: eyelids, lacrimal system, and musculature. Some eye infections (for instance herpes zoster, 053.2x or trachoma, 076.x) are found in the Infectious and Parasitic Diseases chapter. Remember to report secondarily the infectious agent, if known (for example, 041.12 for Methicillin-resistant Staphylococcus aureus [MRSA]).

Neoplastic disease—Codes for neoplasms are straightforward for the eye. Remember to begin in the index and move to the Table of Neoplasms, as directed. Do not look up "Eye" in the Table of Neoplasms. Instead, look up the specific organ. For example, there are separate entries for lacrimal canaliculi, duct, gland, punctum, and sac.

The retina is delicate and blood-rich, making it difficult to biopsy. Instead of a biopsy, the physician will monitor the spot, sometimes called a retinal freckle. Report 239.81 for this condition.

Remember: Melanoma is reported with different codes than other malignant neoplasms of the skin.

Injury—Most eye injury codes are found in the Injury and Poisoning chapter of ICD-9-CM; however, acute chemical conjunctivitis (372.06) and corneal disorder due to a contact lens (371.24) are among the exceptions. Superficial injury to the eye is reported with codes from category 918, or in the case of FBs, 930. Penetrating wounds of the eye are addressed in category 870 and 871. By definition, a wound is complicated only if there is delayed healing, infection, delayed treatment, or a FB, according to ICD-9-CM. For penetrating FBs, the classification distinguishes between metallic FBs and nonmetallic FBs. Eye burns are handled with categories 940 and 941, with an additional code from 948 to identify the extent of the burn.

Injuries also can occur during eye surgery. Seek codes in the 996–999 section if there is a mechanical complication, for example, 996.51 for corneal graft, or 996.53 for intraocular lens (IOL). If fragments remain in the eye following cataract surgery, see 998.82.

Glaucoma—Too much pressure from fluid can lead to a hypertensive condition in the eye called glaucoma. Glaucoma codes are covered in category 365, except for congenital glaucoma, which is found in subcategory 743.2x.

Glaucoma is classified according to the type of angle closure. Acute angle closure would occur quickly, for example, in the minutes or hours following an injury to the eye. Chronic angle closure can be due to a defect that could be the result of illness or age. Glaucoma can occur with an open angle, as well.

Cataracts—Cataracts describe flaws or clouds that develop in the crystalline lens, and are reported with codes from category 366, unless congenital in origin (743.3x). The lens has many layers, and specific ICD-9-CM codes can be selected to identify cataracts by their layer.

Often, when a cataract is removed from the eye, the physician opts to retain the posterior outermost shell so there remains an organic separation between the posterior and anterior chambers. Later, this remaining shell may develop opacities as well, and this is called an "after-cataract."

Retinopathy—Retinopathy describes changes that occur in the blood vessels within the retina. These aneurysms, hemorrhages, and proliferation of small vessels damage the retina and put the patient's vision at risk.

Retinal detachment—Injury or anatomic defect can cause the retina to be freed from the blood-rich choroid at the back of the eye. Corrective action might include the injection of fluid, air, or external eye pressure to push the retina back into place, or bursts of laser to burn the retina to the choroid.

Strabismus—Coordinated eye movement is essential to depth perception, single vision, and other aspects of sight. When the eyes do not move in synchrony, it is often because of misalignment of mismatched strength in the eye muscles. Variations in strabismus are called "tropias." In esotropia, the eye deviates inward; in exotropia, it deviates outward. In hypertropia, the eye deviates upward; and in hypotropia, it deviates downward. Balance is restored to the eyes by lengthening or shortening muscle.

Ear

Most disorders of the ear fall into the following categories:

- Infection and inflammation
- Neoplastic disease
- Injury
- Vertigo
- Hearing loss
- Congenital disorders

Infection and inflammation—When the patient has an infection or inflammation, first determine the location. The codes within Diseases of the Ear and Mastoid Process (380–389) are organized according to anatomic site, beginning with the external ear, moving to the middle and inner ear, and ending with codes describing hearing loss.

By far, the most common codes used in this chapter are the codes for otitis media (OM), or middle ear infection.

Neoplastic disease—Acoustic neuroma, also called a vestibular schwannoma, is likely the most common neoplasm related to the ear. The Table of Neoplasms has a fairly complete listing of subcategory sites under "Ear," but always begin in the index to ensure your code is listed in the table.

Injury—Most ear injury codes are found in the Injury and Poisoning chapter of ICD-9-CM.

Vertigo—Vertigo usually is classified as being peripheral or central. Peripheral vertigo is caused by disease in the inner ear. Central vertigo arises from brain pathology. Vertigo can be a symptom (780.4) or, if the cause is known, reported with a code from category 386. Ménière's disease is the most common form of peripheral vertigo, and often is accompanied by hearing loss and tinnitus, or ringing in the ears. Vertigo also can cause nystagmus, or reflexive jerky eye movements.

Hearing loss—Conductive hearing loss originates in the continuity sound transmission. Sensorineural hearing loss occurs along the nerve conduction that begins in the cochlear nerve and travels to the brain. Sometimes, there are mixed reasons for hearing loss.

Congenital disorders—Many chromosomal syndromes have ear anomalies as a component. Typically, the individual anomaly being treated is reported in addition to the code for the syndrome itself. Other syndromes occur with microtia, or less visible defects. A combination of codes from Diseases of the Ear and Mastoid Process (380–389) and the congenital section for the ear (category 744) may be necessary to capture the clinical picture completely.

Symptoms and V Codes

V codes specific to the eye and ear include codes for family histories for blindness, deafness and other anomalies, and personal histories of cornea, globe, and lens replacements. There are codes identifying the reason for the encounter encounter, such as fitting and adjustment of glasses, contacts or hearing aids, issuance of prescriptions, or aftercare following plastic reconstruction. Other codes report eye vision and hearing screening exams. Read the guidelines and notes carefully and refer to the index as well for sequencing advice.

ACRONYMS

AACG	acute angle closure glaucoma
AC	anterior chamber
AMD	age related macular degeneration
CACG	chronic angle closure glaucoma
CE	cataract extraction
DA	dark adaptation
FA	fluorocein angiography
FB	foreign body
FTG	fulltime glasses
GDD	glaucoma drainage device
GP	gas permeable
IOL	intraocular lens
LL	lower lid
NLD	nasal lacrimal duct
OAG	open angle glaucoma
OD	right eye
OS	left eye
OU	both eyes
PCIOL	posterior chamber IOL
PMMA	polymethylmetacrylate
PSC	posterior subcapsular cataract
RD	retinal detachment
RK	radial keratotomy
ROP	retinopathy of prematurity
TM	trabecular meshwork
VALE	visual acuity, left eye
VARE	visual acuity, right eye
WNL	within normal limits

CPT® Coding

Codes throughout the CPT® codebook may be used to report procedures on the eye and ear. The codes specific to Eye and Ocular Adnexa (65091–68899) and Auditory

System (69000–69979), with a few exceptions, are reported almost exclusively by specialists.

Eye

An eye typically is removed for one of three reasons: the eye has a malignancy; the eye is blind and very painful, or the eye is blind and disfiguring.

There are three types of removals (65091–65114):

1. **Evisceration**—The contents of the eyeball are scooped out but the sclera shell remains connected to the eye muscles, so the prosthesis, fitted into the globe, will have natural movement.

2. **Enucleation**—The connections (muscles, vessels, and optic nerve) are severed and the entire eyeball is removed en mass.

3. **Exenteration**—Surrounding skin, fat, muscle and bone is removed.

In any removal, a temporary implant may be placed to protect the void that may later hold a permanent implant. This temporary implant is included in the procedure and not reported separately. The implant codes reference permanent implants with aesthetic properties.

Today, whenever a laser can be used to surgically cauterize, cut, destroy, or repair the eye, it will be used instead of a knife. When you are reviewing the codes in CPT®'s Eye and Ocular Adnexa section, assume any procedure with a laser approach is preferred to an open approach.

Some surgeries require incisions. Removal of a lens with a cataract requires an incision, so the lens can be extracted and an IOL inserted. Even so, cataract surgery is done microscopically today, and tiny incisions in the limbus are all that is required.

Injections are sometimes required to numb the eye. A retrobulbar or Tenon's capsule injection are two common approaches for delivery of anesthetic. These nerve blocks are bundled into the procedures and not reported separately.

The majority of procedures performed on the anterior segment of the eye are microsurgeries performed using an operating microscope. The scope, otherwise reported with 69990, would not be reported separately.

Surgeries on the iris and trabecular meshwork, including goniotomy, are usually a therapeutic treatment for glaucoma, to improve the flow of aqueous in the eye. Sometimes aqueous is removed for therapy in paracentesis. This procedure also can be performed diagnostically.

There are many procedures performed on the ocular adnexa. The extraocular muscles may be lengthened or shortened. In some cases, the procedure is not completed until the patient is awakened and lengthy sutures extruding from the back of the eye adjusted to ensure perfect binocular vision. These adjustable sutures are reported with add-on code +67335.

The eyelids and conjunctiva are included in the adnexal codes. In prosthetics following evisceration, the conjunctiva may traverse an artificial cornea. When conjunctiva is damaged, buccal mucosa may be harvested and used as a graft (68325). Procedures to remove excess skin from the eyelid (blepharoplasty) are found in the integumentary chapter. Blepharoplasty codes in the Eye and Adnexa section involve more complex structures within the eye.

Medicine Codes

Ophthalmology office visit codes focus entirely upon the eye. Follow closely the guidelines appearing with these codes, 92002–92014, to determine whether evaluation and management (E/M) or ophthalmology office visits are more appropriate.

In addition to the office visit codes, the Medicine section contains dozens of codes for special ophthalmology tests and for services associated with dispensing contacts and spectacles.

Ear

Procedures for the ear are organized anatomically. Many of the external ear procedures are simple procedures; for example, 69200 *Removal foreign body from external auditory canal; without anesthesia.* The repair codes for external ear often are performed by plastic surgeons, and relate to plastic defects that may be due to congenital defects or injury.

The middle ear begins at the tympanic membrane, and procedures from this point and beyond usually are limited to specialists. The most common tympanic procedure is the placement of ventilating tubes (69433 and 69436) to mitigate frequent middle ear infections that occur because the immature Eustachian tube is inadequate for draining fluid that builds up behind the eardrum. These tubes typically fall out as the child grows, but in some cases must be removed surgically. Another approach to Eustachian inadequacy is inflation or catheterization of this tube.

The mastoid process is also included in the middle ear. Mastoiditis can occur if a middle ear infection goes untreated. Mastoidectomies may be performed, for instance, if the patient develops cholesteatoma from chronic infection. The mastoid bone also may be removed to make room for a cochlear implant. The middle ear also contains the ossicles, and surgeries may be performed to repair the ossicular chain or address defects in the oval and round windows. None of the codes in the Auditory System represent services that include use of an operating microscope, so 69990 would be reported in addition to any procedure, if an operating microscope is used.

As with the eye, a section for auditory and vestibular testing is presented in the Medicine chapter of CPT®. Most of the services represented in the Medicine chapter could be performed by ancillary providers such as audiologists.

HCPCS Level II

HCPCS Level II codes report injectible or implantable drug supplies used in the treatment of ear and eye disorders, as well as supplies of prostheses, visual aids, contact lenses, glasses, and hearing aids.

Glaucoma screening codes for ophthalmologists or optometrists participating in the Physician Quality Reporting System (PQRS) are found in the temporary G codes (G0117 and G0118).

Many of the prosthetics and durable medical equipment (DME) reported through HCPCS Level II are no longer distributed by physicians. Instead, they write prescriptions for these items. The most important codes to consider as you study the HCPCS Level II codes for

ophthalmic and ear, nose, and throat (ENT) procedures are drug injection supplies. The Table of Drugs in your HCPCS Level II book will list these alphabetically, so they are easy to locate. Always confirm your code choice in the tabular section of your HCPCS Level II book.

Modifiers

Because the eyes and ears are bilateral organs, identifying a procedure as bilateral (50) or identifying laterality (RT and LT) becomes very important to payment processes.

Another issue for payers is whether the patient has his own lens (phakic), an artificial lens (pseudophakic), or no lens (aphakic). Aphakic patients may be eligible for benefits not available to others; hence modifier VP.

Commonly used modifiers:

50	Bilateral procedure
E1	Upper left, eyelid
E2	Lower left, eyelid
E3	Upper right, eyelid
E4	Lower right, eyelid
LS	FDA—monitored intraocular lens (IOL) implant
LT	Left
PL	Progressive addition lenses
RT	Right
VP	Aphakic patient

Glossary

Acoustic Neuroma—Benign tumor arising from cells of the auditory nerve, also called a vestibular schwannoma.

After-cataract—Following cataract removal, the physician opts to retain the posterior outermost shell, so an organic separation remains between the posterior and anterior chambers. This remaining shell later may develop opacities called "after-cataract."

Anterior Segment—Cornea up to the vitreous body, including the aqueous humor, iris, and lens.

Aqueous Humor—Clear fluid filling the area behind the cornea, in front of the iris.

Blepharoplasty—Surgical repair of the eyelid.

Cholesteatoma—Benign growth of skin in the middle ear; usually caused by chronic otitis media.

Cataract—Flaws or clouding in the crystalline lens.

Cerumen—Ear wax.

Choroid—Middle layer between the retina and the sclera in the eye's posterior segment. The choroid nourishes the retina.

Ciliary Body—Thickened layer of the vascular tunic. It contains the muscle that controls the shape of the lens.

Cochlea—Inner ear structure shaped like a snail shell. It is divided into two canals and the organ of Corti.

Conduction—Receptions or conveyance of sound, heat, or electricity. Sound waves are conducted to the inner ear through bones in the skull.

Conjunctiva—Thin protective layer lining the eyelid and covering the sclera.

Cornea—"Bay window" of the eye. The cornea has five layers and they act to refract the light entering the eye.

Crystalline Lens—Convex disc suspended on threads just behind the iris.

Dacryolith—Calculus on the lacrima.

Enucleation—Removal of a structure, such as the eyeball.

Esotropia—Ward deviation of the eye.

Eustachian Tube—Tube in the ear linking the middle ear to the nasopharynx. This tube equalizes pressure between the middle ear and the outer atmosphere.

Evisceration—Procedure where the contents of the eyeball are removed, but the sclera shell remains connected to the eye muscles so a prosthesis fitted into the globe will have natural movement.

Exenteration—Removal of a complete structure. Surrounding skin, fat, muscle, and bone are removed.

External Auditory Meatus—Pathway from the pinna (outer ear) to the tympanic membrane.

Exotropia—Outward deviation of the eye.

Glaucoma—Hypertensive condition of the eye caused by too much pressure from fluid.

Goniotomy—Procedure where an opening is made in the trabecular meshwork of the front part of the eye. The provider uses a goniolens during the procedure.

Hypertropia—Upward deviation of the eye.

Incus—Tiny bone (ossicle) in the middle ear.

Iris—Muscular ring around the pupil that regulates the amount of light that enters the pupil; it is the source of eye color.

Limbus—Ring where the cornea meets the sclera; also known as the sclerocorneal junction.

Malleus—Tiny bone (ossicle) in the middle ear that picks up vibration from the tympanic membrane.

Mastoiditis—Inflammation or infection of the mastoid bone.

Ménière's Disease—Most common form of peripheral vertigo, caused by dilation of the lymphatic channel of the cochlea and accompanied by hearing loss and tinnitus.

Nystagmus—Reflexive jerky eye movements as a response to the messages of the inner ear.

Microtia—Congenital deformity of the ear.

Optic Nerve—Nerve that transmits images from the eye to the brain. Damage to the optic nerve can result is loss of or impaired vision.

Ossicles—Three tiny bones of the middle ear.

Otitis Media—Middle ear infection.

Oval Window—Membrane-covered window from the inner ear to the middle ear.

Perilymph—Fluid in the cochlea that vibrates and creates nerve impulses to the cochlear nerve.

Puncta—Tiny openings of the tear ducts.

Pupil—Opening of the eye's center where light enters.

Mastoid—Bone in the skull just behind the ear containing tiny air cells that also form a conductive path for sound.

Refraction—Focus and direction of light.

Retina—Layer of tissue in the back of the eye that is light sensitive.

Retinal Detachment—Retina is freed from the blood-rich choroid at the back of the eye. When the retinal layer floats away, it loses its supply of nutrients. Nutrients must return or vision is lost.

Retrobulbar—Space behind the eye.

Round Window—Membrane-covered window from the inner ear to the middle ear.

Sclera—White outer skin of the eye that's covered with a thin protective layer of conjunctiva.

Sclerocorneal Junction—Ring where the cornea meets the sclera, also known as the limbus.

Semicircular Canals—Three tiny tubes in the inner ear, filled with fluid to assist in balance.

Stapes—Tiny bone (ossicle) in the middle ear.

Strabismus—Improper alignment of the eyes.

Tenon's Capsule—Connective tissue surrounding the posterior eyeball.

Trachoma—Bacterial infection of the eyes.

Tympanic Membrane—Thin, delicate tissue separating the outer ear from the inner ear.

Vestibule—Inner part of the ear that connects the semi-circular canals and the cochlea. The vestibule contains the sense organs responsible for balance.

Vestibular Schwannoma—Benign tumor arising from nerve cells of the auditory nerve, also called acoustic neuroma.

Vertigo—Dizziness resulting in the loss of balance.

Visual Field—Total area that can be seen by peripheral vision.

Vitreous Humor—Gel-like mass that fills the large posterior chamber of the eye.

Chapter Review Questions

1. **Where is a retrobulbar injection delivered?**

   A. Testis

   B. Eye

   C. Ovary

   D. Ear

2. **What are cataracts?**

   A. A defect in the management of intraocular pressure

   B. Opacities or other defects in the lens of the eye

   C. Proliferation of abnormal vessels at the back of the eye

   D. A drooping of eyelids that occurs with age

3. The patient has a significant visual impairment due to astigmatism in the left eye. It is corrected with glasses. The right eye has normal vision. Code the patient's diagnosis based on this information.

   A. 367.20, 369.76

   B. 367.20

   C. 367.21, 369.76

   D. 369.70, 367.20

4. A patient with a left tympanic membrane tear arrives for a left lateral graft tympanoplasty with the use of an operating microscope. What procedure and diagnosis code(s) would be reported?

   A. 69631, 384.25

   B. 69641, 384.25

   C. 69631, 69990, 384.20

   D. 69641, 69990, 384.20

5. A 2-year-old arrives at the emergency department (ED) crying and tugging and holding her ear. After examination, the physician determines there is a small plastic toy piece lodged in the external auditory canal and removes it using small forceps. What is the procedure code for this service?

   A. 69105

   B. 69110

   C. 69200

   D. 69205

6. After multiple orbital operations, fibrous adhesions formed between the extraocular muscle and the orbital contents on the walls of the orbital cavity itself. When the surgeon releases extensive scar tissue without detaching the extraocular muscle. What is the CPT® code(s) for the procedure?

   A. 67311, 67340

   B. 67311, 67331

   C. 67343

   D. 67343, 67332

7. A patient with a history of persistent serous otitis media presents to have tubes placed in her ears. The patient was brought to the operating room (OR), given a general anesthetic with a bag and mask. The ear canals were inspected. A tympanostomy incision was made in the anterior inferior quadrant in a radial incision. A small amount of serous fluid was found in the middle ear space on both sides. An Armstrong grommet ventilation tube was placed in both ears with alligator forceps and suctioned clear. TobraDex drops were placed through the PE tube in each ear.

    The correct coding for this procedure is:

    A. 69631-50

    B. 69433-50

    C. 69641-50

    D. 69436-50

8. A patient with bilateral, upper-eyelid ptosis and bilateral, upper-eyelid blepharochalasis arrives for upper-eyelid ptosis repair, via external approach using the levator aponeurosis plication technique, both eyes, and upper-eyelid blepharoplasties, both eyes. The upper eyelids were injected with approximately 3 cc each of a ½ and ½ mixture of Xylocaine 2 percent with epinephrine and Marcaine 0.5 percent with epinephrine. The physician then cut along the pre-marked lines and excised a skin/muscle flap. The orbital septum was identified and opened and any herniating orbital fat was removed. The levator aponeurosis was identified and two horizontal mattress 6-0 silk sutures were placed through the mid-upper tarsus and the levator aponeurosis. The patient was sat upright to elevate the lid height and contour. The patient was then repositioned, and re-approximation of the skin and orbicularis was accomplished using interrupted 6-0 silk sutures, bilaterally.

    What are the procedure codes for this procedure?

    A. 67904-E1, 67904-E3, 15822-E1, 15822-E3

    B. 67904-E1, 67901-E3, 15823

    C. 67903-50

    D. 67904-E1, 67904-E3, 15823-E1, 15823-E3

9. **Operative Report**

Preoperative Diagnosis: Ruptured globe, full thickness corneal laceration, right eye

Postoperative Diagnosis: Ruptured globe, full thickness corneal laceration, right eye

Operation: Surgical repair of ruptured globe, surgical repair of full thickness corneal laceration, right eye

Operative Procedure: The patient was brought to the operating theater and properly positioned. The patient was subsequently prepped and draped in the usual sterile fashion. A lid speculum was placed in the patient's operative right eye. Fluorescein was used to delineate the evidence of the patient's wound leakage. A diamond blade and 0.12 forceps were used to make a temporal paracentesis port. Nonpreserved lidocaine was injected into the anterior chamber as well as BSS. Two interrupted 10-0 nylon sutures were used to close the corneal laceration. Fluorescein was used to test the wound which showed no evidence of wound leak. Gentamicin 0.5 mL and Dexamethasone 0.5 mL were injected subconjunctivally. Tobradex ointment was placed in the patient's operative eye. The lid speculum was removed from the patient's operative eye. The patient tolerated the procedure well without apparent complications and went to the recovery room in good condition.

Prognosis: Immediate and remote good specimen sent to lab: None

Complications: None

What are the CPT® and ICD-9-CM codes for this procedure?

10. **Operative Report**

Preoperative Diagnosis: Bilateral serous otitis media

Postoperative Diagnosis: Bilateral serous otitis media

Operative Technique: The patient has a history of persistent chronic serous otitis media, unimproved with aggressive antibiotic therapy over the past six months.

The patient was brought to the OR, given a general anesthetic with a bag and mask. The ear canals were inspected. A tympanostomy incision was made in the anterior inferior quadrant in a radial incision. A small amount of serous fluid was found in the middle ear space on both sides. An Armstrong grommet ventilation tube was placed in both ears with alligator forceps and suctioned clear. TobraDex drops were placed through the PE tube in each ear.

The patient was sent to the recovery room in good condition, discharged with a TobraDex drop prescription for two days and will follow-up in the office in two weeks.

What are the CPT® and ICD-9-CM codes for this procedure?

Introduction

Anesthesia codes are grouped anatomically, beginning with the head. Many anesthesia codes indicate "not otherwise specified." This allows the code to be reported for the anatomic area, unless a more specific code exists. For example, code 00920 describes anesthesia for procedures on male genitalia (including open urethral procedures); not otherwise specified.

Selecting an anesthesia code follows the same basic steps as assigning procedure codes for other specialties. Coders either look for the Anesthesia in the CPT® index to locate the correct anatomic area, or turn to the Anesthesia 00100–00210 section in CPT® and look under the appropriate anatomic heading.

Until the new anesthesia coder becomes familiar with anesthesia codes, it is best to use the Anesthesia section to learn this area of coding. Keep in mind, codes are not always found under the surgical description and the coder may need to default backward to find the most accurate description. For example, code ranges for anesthesia for a simple "mastectomy" are not listed under "mastectomy," but rather under "breast."

Testing Technique

Although the liver is located in the upper abdomen, the harvesting of a liver is reported with code 01990 *Physiological support for harvesting of organ(s) from a brain-dead patient*, which is listed under "Other procedures."

Anesthesia "crosswalk" books assist coders by "crosswalking" the known surgical code to an appropriate anesthesia code. When more than one code is suggested by the crosswalk, the coder must determine the code with the highest base unit, which is the most applicable code to report.

Types of Anesthesia

There are three primary types of anesthesia: General, Regional, and Monitored Anesthesia Care (MAC):

General Anesthesia—Drug-induced loss of consciousness.

Regional Anesthesia—Loss of sensation in a region of the body, using technique such as:

◖ Spinal Anesthesia
◖ Epidural Anesthesia
◖ Nerve Block or Local Nerve Block

Monitored Anesthesia Care—Anesthesia service where the patient may be sedated. The anesthesia provider must be qualified to convert to general anesthesia, if necessary.

Testing Technique

Local anesthesia is not reported using anesthesia codes. Local anesthesia is included in the surgical package and not reported separately.

Anesthesia Providers

The anesthesiologist is a physician licensed to practice medicine and who has completed an accredited anesthesiology program. These physicians may personally perform, medically direct, or medically supervise members of an anesthesia care team.

A certified registered nurse anesthetist (CRNA) is a registered nurse who has completed an accredited nurse anesthesia training program. The CRNA may be either medically directed by an anesthesiologist or non-medically directed.

An anesthesiologist assistant (AA) is a health care professional who has completed an accredited

Anesthesia Assistant training program. The AA may only be medically directed by an anesthesiologist.

An anesthesia resident is a physician who has completed his medical degree and is currently in a residency program specifically for anesthesiology training.

A student registered nurse anesthetist (SRNA) is a registered nurse training in an accredited nurse anesthesia program.

Anesthesia Coding Terminology

One-Lung Ventilation (OLV)—one lung is ventilated and the other lung is collapsed temporarily to improve surgical access to the lung. Several anesthesia codes separately identify utilization of one-lung ventilation.

Pump Oxygenator—When a cardiopulmonary bypass (CPB) machine is used to function as the heart and lungs during heart or great vessel surgery.

Intraperitoneal—Within the peritoneum; organs in the upper abdomen include the stomach, liver, gallbladder, spleen, jejunum, ascending, and transverse colon. Intraperitoneal organs in the lower abdomen include the appendix, cecum, ileum, and sigmoid colon.

Extraperitoneal or **Retroperitoneal**—Indicates outside or behind the peritoneum or peritoneal cavity. Extraperitoneal organs in the lower abdomen include the ureter and urinary tract. The kidneys and adrenal glands and lower esophagus are extraperitoneal organs of the upper abdomen. Also located in the retroperitoneum are the aorta and inferior vena cava. The appendix and colon are examples of intraperitoneal organs.

Radical—Extensive and complex surgery intended to correct a severe health threat such as cancer.

Diagnostic or **Surgical Arthroscopic Procedures**—Performed on the temporormandibular joint, shoulder, elbow, wrist, hip, knee, and ankle. Coders assign a diagnostic code only, if no surgical procedure is performed (eg, if a knee arthroscopy is listed as "diagnostic" and a meniscectomy is performed, a surgical arthroscopic code is assigned).

Postoperative Pain Management

Postoperative pain management may be requested by the surgeon and billed separately by the anesthesiologist if anesthesia for the surgical procedure is not dependent on the efficacy of the regional anesthetic technique.

Nerve block codes, for example 64415 (brachial plexus block), are used as an adjunct to general anesthesia if placement is for postoperative pain management. Nerve block codes are not reported separately if the block is the mode of anesthesia for a procedure being performed. For example, if a carpal tunnel procedure is performed with an axillary block, a code from the anesthesia section (01810 + related anesthesia time) is reported. No separate code is reported for the axillary block.

Coding depends on the medication injected, the site of the injection, and placement of either a single injection block or a continuous block by catheter. The CPT® code reported is appended with modifier 59 *Distinct procedural services* to signify the service is separate and distinct from the anesthesia care provided for the surgery.

When ultrasound or fluoroscopic guidance is utilized for pain management procedures and appropriately documented, codes are reported separately with modifier 26 *Professional component*, unless the code selected includes image guidance (fluoroscopy, ultrasound or CT).

Acute pain diagnosis codes are separately identified in category 338 of the ICD-9-CM codebook.

Continuous catheter codes, for example 64448 *Injection, anesthetic agent; femoral nerve, continuous infusion by catheter (including catheter placement)*, are reported for continuous administration of anesthesia for postoperative pain management. If the infusion catheter is placed for operative anesthesia, the appropriate anesthesia code plus time is reported. If the continuous infusion catheter is placed for postoperative pain management, the daily postoperative management of the catheter is included in 64448.

Code 01996 *Daily hospital management of epidural or subarachnoid continuous drug administration* is assigned for daily hospital management of epidural or subarachnoid continuous drug administration. Continuous infusion by catheter, such as femoral (64448) or sciatic nerve

(64446), is not an epidural catheter; therefore, 01996 is not reported with these codes. Anesthesiologists report an appropriate E/M service to re-evaluate postoperative pain if documentation supports the level of service reported and billed.

As with the nerve blocks, the epidural/subarachnoid injection is either a single injection or a continuous catheter. For example, a continuous infusion in the thoracic area is reported as 62318 *Injection, including indwelling catheter placement, continuous infusion or intermittent bolus, of diagnostic or therapeutic substance(s) (including anesthetic, antispasmodic, opioid, steroid, other solution), not including neurolytic substances, includes contrast for localization when performed, epidural or subarachnoid; cervical or thoracic.* When these techniques are used for postoperative pain management, the same rules apply.

When an epidural or subarachnoid catheter is placed for a laboring patient, injection codes typically are not reported. CPT® codes to describe labor epidural/subarachnoid services are listed under the Anesthesia for Obstetrics subsection.

Daily hospital management of continuous epidural or subarachnoid drug administration (01996) cannot be reported on the day of the epidural or subarachnoid catheter placement. It may be reported starting with the first *postoperative* day.

ICD-9-CM Coding

The majority of anesthesia services are provided to patients during surgery. The postoperative diagnosis should be coded because the preoperative diagnosis may change intra-operatively. For example, if a patient is admitted with pain in the right lower quadrant and subsequently has an appendectomy, the postoperative diagnosis may be acute appendicitis.

Supporting diagnosis codes are reported if relevant to either substantiate medical necessity or support physical status modifiers, which will be discussed in the next section.

With few exceptions, diagnosis codes for anesthesia are assigned in the same manner as any other diagnosis:

- Identify reason for anesthesia service

- Review for other pertinent information and supporting diagnosis codes
- Check the Index to Diseases and then check the code in the Tabular List
- Locate main entry term
- Pay attention to notes listed in main terms
- Understand coding conventions (See ICD Official and Additional Conventions)
- Look for additional instructions in the Tabular (numeric) List
- Make sure code is to highest level of specificity
- Assign pertinent related ICD-9-CM code(s)

CPT® Coding

Services included with the base unit value of anesthesia codes reported are:

- All usual preoperative and postoperative visits
- Anesthesia care during the procedure
- Administration of fluids and/or blood products during the surgery
- Non-invasive monitoring (ECG, temperature, blood pressure, pulse oximetry, capnography, and mass spectrometry)

Unusual forms of monitoring—for example, arterial lines, central venous (CV) catheters and pulmonary artery catheters (eg, Swan Ganz)—are not included in the base unit value of the anesthesia code.

Base unit values are not listed separately in CPT®. The American Society of Anesthesiologists (ASA) determines the base unit values for anesthesia codes, based on the difficulty of the procedure performed. The ASA and Medicare each publish a list of base unit values.

Determining the base value is the first step in calculating anesthesia charges and payment expected. Time reporting is the second step.

Anesthesia time begins when the anesthesiologist begins to prepare the patient for anesthesia in either the operating room or an equivalent area. Pre-anesthesia assessment time is not part of reportable anesthesia time. Anesthesia time ends when the anesthesiologist is no longer in personal attendance, and generally is reported when the patient is safely placed under postoperative supervision. Time reporting on claims may vary, and there is no national guideline. Time units are added to the base unit value as is "customary in the local area."

Medicare requires exact time reporting without rounding to the nearest five minutes. For example, if anesthesia time starts at 11:02 and the patient is turned over to PACU at 11:59, the reported anesthesia time is 57 minutes. Medicare divides the 57 minutes by 15-minute increments for a total value of 3.8 units. If the procedure has a base value of six units, adding 3.8 units gives a total of 9.8 units, which is then multiplied by the Anesthesia Conversion Factor for the geographic location where the services are provided.

Other insurance companies may process the anesthesia time reported in increments—from exact time (like Medicare), to 10, 12, and 15 minutes, or some other time increment.

Multiple (surgical) procedures may be performed on one patient during anesthesia administration. When this occurs, the surgery representing the most complex procedure is reported because this service carries a higher base unit value. Anesthesia time is reported as usual, from the time the anesthesiologist begins to prepare the patient until the patient is safely placed under postoperative supervision.

Testing Technique

The surgical time does not play a role in determining the anesthesia time.

Example:

A patient has an inguinal hernia repair (00830, base 4) and a ventral hernia repair (00832, base 6) —only the ventral herniorrhaphy (00832) is reported because it is more complex and has a higher base value than the inguinal hernia surgery. The total time for both procedures is reported as anesthesia time. The diagnosis code related to the ventral hernia is reported in the primary position. Reporting the inguinal hernia diagnosis as secondary helps explain why the reported anesthesia time is longer than normally expected for the procedure reported.

Only one anesthesia code is reported during anesthesia administration, except in the case where there is an anesthesia add-on code. For example, the anesthesia section of CPT® has add-on codes listed under Burn Excision or Debridement and Obstetric. These add-on procedures may not be reported alone; they must be reported with the applicable primary anesthesia code referenced in parentheses.

For example, add-on code +01953 *Anesthesia for second- and third-degree burn excision or debridement with or without skin grafting, any site, for total body surface area (TBSA) treated during anesthesia and surgery; each additional 9% total body surface area or part thereof (List separately in addition to code for primary procedure)* is reported if the total body surface area (TBSA) treated during surgery exceeds 9 percent. This add-on code is reported in addition to 01952 *Anesthesia for second- and third-degree burn excision or debridement with or without skin grafting, any site, for total body surface area (TBSA) treated during anesthesia and surgery; between 4% and 9% of total body surface area* for each additional 9% or part thereof of the TBSA treated. Therefore, a TBSA of 40% is reported as follows:

01952 + Time units   First 4 to 9% of TBSA

+01953 x 4   Represents the remaining 31% of TBSA in increments of 9% (the remaining 4% is considered a "part thereof")

Note the first anesthesia code, 01952, is reported with time units. The add-on code 01953 is reported in units only.

Physical Status Modifiers

Physical status modifiers are anesthesia modifiers describing the physical status of the patient. These modifiers are not recognized by Medicare for additional payment, and no base values are listed in CPT®. Because insurance companies are familiar with anesthesia coding guidelines in CPT®, non-Medicare payers typically pay additional base units.

The following modifiers are assigned to patients based on their individual physical status:

◖ P1—A normal healthy patient—No extra value added

◖ P2—A patient with mild systemic disease—No extra value added

- P3—A patient with severe systemic disease—1 extra unit
- P4—A patient with severe systemic disease that is a constant threat to life—2 extra units
- P5—A moribund patient who is not expected to survive without the operation—3 extra units
- P6—A declared brain-dead patient whose organs are being removed for donor purposes—No extra value added

For example, a non-Medicare patient has a severe systemic disease, which is a constant threat to life and is undergoing a direct coronary artery bypass graft (CABG) with a pump oxygenator is reported as 00567-P4.

Qualifying Circumstances

Qualifying circumstances (QC) are anesthesia add-on codes assigned to report anesthesia services performed under difficult circumstances affecting significantly the character of an anesthesia service. ASA assigns base unit values for the qualifying circumstances. The base values are not listed in CPT®. These add-on codes are not recognized by Medicare for additional payment.

+99100—Anesthesia for patient of extreme age, younger than one (1) year and older than 70—1 extra unit

+99116—Anesthesia complicated by utilization of total body hypothermia—5 extra units

+99135—Anesthesia complicated by utilization of controlled hypotension—5 extra units

+99140—Anesthesia complicated by emergency conditions (specify)—2 extra units

Documentation must support the qualifying circumstance code(s) reported. An emergency is defined as existing when a delay in the treatment of the patient would lead to a significant increase in a threat to the patient's life or body parts.

Testing Technique

Highlight parenthetical notes pertaining to use of qualifying circumstance codes with the CPT® code for the anesthesia service. For example, following code 00326, it states "Do not report 00326 in conjunction with 99100."

Coders should understand the calculation for anesthesia services is BASE + TIME + PHYSICAL STATUS MODIFERS + QUALIFYING CIRCUMSTANCES multiplied by the CONVERSION FACTOR for non-Medicare payers. For Medicare, the calculation for anesthesia services is BASE + TIME multiplied by the Medicare conversion factor for the region.

Additional Billable Items by Anesthesiologist

When the anesthesia provider places invasive monitoring devices, an additional code is reported. Monitoring is included in the base value, so if another provider—such as the surgeon or a perfusionist—places the line or catheter, no additional information is reported by the anesthesia provider on the claim form. The anesthesia provider only reports service(s) he or she performs.

Time is not reported separately for "flat fee" procedures. Unlike anesthesia codes that *require* anesthesia time be documented and reported, these codes are found in the surgery section of the CPT® and no time is associated for reporting or payment.

The most common codes reported in addition to the anesthesia service are:

31500—*Intubation, endotracheal, emergency procedure*: Emergency intubation may be reported separately when an anesthesia provider is requested to intubate a patient who is NOT undergoing anesthesia. Normal intubation for patients undergoing anesthesia is included in the base value of the anesthesia code.

36620—*Arterial Catheterization or cannulation for sampling, monitoring or transfusion (separate procedure); percutaneous:* (placed in a radial artery "through" needle puncture of the skin).

36555 or 36556—*Insertion of non-tunneled central venous catheter*: Because these codes are age-related, appropriate code assignment is based on whether the patient is under five years of age or over.

93503—*Insertion and placement of flow directed catheter (eg, Swan-Ganz) for monitoring purposes*

For example, anesthesia coders look for documentation to support placement of a pulmonary artery catheter by the anesthesia provider. It is identified as either a PAC (pulmonary artery catheter) or SG (Swan-Ganz), and should have procedure notes documented in either the comments section of the anesthesia record, in progress notes, or on a separate procedure form.

Moderate Sedation

Moderate sedation can be provided by a physician other than the surgeon; and an anesthesiologist may provide moderate sedation in these circumstances. Moderate sedation is provided without an anesthesia machine and backup for general anesthesia. In addition, moderate sedation codes do not include minimal sedation, deep sedation, or monitored anesthesia care. Coders are directed to the anesthesia section of CPT® to report services. Only anesthesia providers report anesthesia codes.

Monitored Anesthesia Care (MAC) is distinctly different from moderate sedation. MAC may vary from "light" to "deep" sedation, based on each patient's health status. The patient's anesthesia plan is determined on a case-by-case basis. When using MAC, the anesthesia provider must be qualified and prepared at all times to convert to general anesthesia, if necessary. MAC services are paid in the same way as general or regional anesthesia services—although, many insurance companies request special modifiers to identify the service as monitored anesthesia care. We will discuss MAC and these modifiers more completely in the Healthcare Common Procedure Coding System (HCPCS) section.

CPT® Modifiers

Modifier 23 *Unusual anesthesia*—reported to describe a procedure usually not requiring anesthesia, but, due to unusual circumstances, is performed under general anesthesia. For example, a pediatric patient may require general anesthesia for the surgeon to perform a procedure not requiring anesthesia under usual circumstances.

Modifier 47 *Anesthesia by surgeon*—reported by the surgeon when he or she also provides regional or general anesthesia for the surgical service. Anesthesia providers do not report this modifier. Modifier 47 should not be appended to anesthesia codes (00100–01999).

Modifier 53 *Discontinued procedure*—is reported to describe a procedure started and, due to extenuating circumstances, discontinued.

Modifier 59 *Distinct procedural service*—used to indicate a procedure or service is distinct or independent from other non-evaluation and management procedures. Documentation must support a different session, procedure, surgery, site, organ system, incision/excision, or injury. This modifier is often appended to post-operative pain management services to indicate it is separate from the anesthesia administered during the surgery.

Modifier 73 *Discontinued outpatient hospital/ambulatory surgery center (ASC) procedure prior to the administration of anesthesia*—approved for ASC and hospital outpatient use; carrier policy often identifies this as the modifier to report when anesthesia services are discontinued prior to administration of anesthesia. Note: physician reporting of discontinued procedures is referred to modifier 53.

Modifier 74 *Discontinued outpatient hospital/ambulatory surgery center (ASC) procedure after administration of anesthesia*—approved for ASC and hospital outpatient use. Although this modifier is not strictly anesthesia related, carrier policy often identifies this as the modifier to report when anesthesia services are discontinued after administration of anesthesia. Note: physician reporting of discontinued procedures is referred to modifier 53.

Direction, Supervision, and Monitoring

Medical direction occurs when an anesthesiologist is involved in two, three, or four anesthesia procedures at the same time; or a single anesthesia procedure with a qualified CRNA or anesthesiologist assistant.

According to the Centers for Medicare & Medicaid Services (CMS), when an anesthesiologist is medically directing, he or she must:

1. Perform a pre-anesthetic examination and evaluation;

2. Prescribe the anesthesia plan;

3. Personally participate in the most demanding procedures of the anesthesia plan including, if applicable, induction and emergence;

4. Ensure that any procedures in the anesthesia plan that he or she does not perform are performed by a qualified anesthetist;

5. Monitor the course of anesthesia administration at frequent intervals;

6. Remain physically present and available for immediate diagnosis and treatment of emergencies; and

7. Provide the indicated post anesthesia care.

If one (or more) of the above services is not performed by the anesthesiologist, the service is not considered medical direction.

While medically directing, anesthesiologists should not provide services to other patients. However, anesthesiologists are allowed to provide the following to other patients without affecting their ability to provide medical direction:

◖ Addressing an emergency of short duration in the immediate area

◖ Administering an epidural or caudal anesthetic to ease labor pain

◖ Periodic rather than continuous monitoring of an obstetrical patient

◖ Receiving patients entering the operating suite for the next surgery

◖ Checking on or discharging patients from the post anesthesia care unit

◖ Coordinating scheduling matters

Medical supervision occurs when an anesthesiologist is involved in five or more anesthesia procedures at the same time, or when the required services listed under

the medical direction above are not performed by the anesthesiologist.

Non-medically directed CRNAs are working without medical direction.

MAC is the intraoperative monitoring by an anesthesiologist or qualified individual under the direction of an anesthesiologist of a patient's vital physiological signs, in anticipation of:

◖ The need for administration of general anesthesia; or

◖ The development of an adverse physiological patient reaction to the surgical procedure.

Monitored anesthesia care includes the performance of the following by the anesthesiologist or qualified individual under the direction of an anesthesiologist:

◖ Pre-anesthetic examination and evaluation

◖ Prescription of the anesthesia care required

◖ Completion of an anesthesia record

◖ Administration of any necessary oral or parenteral medication

◖ Provision of indicated postoperative anesthesia care

The anesthesiologist, CRNA or a qualified individual under the medical direction of an anesthesiologist, must be continuously present to monitor the patient and provide anesthesia care.

Medical direction modifiers from HCPCS Level II (discussed below) allow reporting of the appropriate medical direction/supervision/non-medically directed status.

HCPCS Level II Modifiers

The following personally performing, medical supervision and medical direction modifiers are reported only with anesthesia CPT® codes:

◖ AA—Anesthesia services performed personally by anesthesiologist

◖ AD—Medical supervision by a physician: More than four concurrent anesthesia procedures

Note: "Concurrency" refers to all current ongoing anesthesia cases during the same time under the direction or supervision of the same anesthesiologist.

◖ QK—Medical direction of two, three, or four concurrent anesthesia procedures involving qualified individuals

◖ QY—Medical direction of one certified registered nurse anesthetist (CRNA) by an anesthesiologist

◖ GC—This service has been performed in part by a resident under the direction of a teaching physician

The following medical supervision/direction modifiers are reported with CRNA or Anesthesiologist Assistant services:

◖ QX—CRNA service: With medical direction by a physician

◖ QZ—CRNA service: Without medical direction by a physician

The state "scope of practice" may prohibit an anesthesiologist assistant (AA) from reporting claims with a non-medical direction modifier. The AD modifier only applies to the anesthesiologist. The CRNA reports QX if medical direction is broken by the anesthesiologist because the CRNA would not know the status of other cases.

Medical direction modifiers are associated with specific providers and are reported in the first position after the anesthesia CPT® code because payment often is related to the modifier reported.

Additional anesthesia-related modifiers usually are reported in the second position after any related medical direction modifiers; they are considered informational or statistical. Modifiers affecting payment are reported in the position before information/statistical modifiers.

Physical status modifiers (already discussed) are also reported in the second or third position, as applicable.

Example:

1. 00910-AA-P3 (to report a personally performed physician service with a physical status 3 patient)

2. 00142 QK-QS-P3 and 00142 QX-QS-P3 (to report the medically directing physician and CRNA service with a physical status 3 patient under monitored anesthesia care)

When reporting MAC services, CMS and other insurance carriers may require the use of one of the following:

◖ QS—Monitored anesthesia care service

◖ G8—Monitored anesthesia care for deep complex, complicated, or markedly invasive surgical procedure

◖ G9—Monitored anesthesia care for patient who has a history of severe cardiopulmonary disease

When reporting modifier G8 or G9, it is not necessary to report a QS modifier separately because the description of these modifiers includes MAC.

Testing Technique

Most anesthesia modifiers are reported *only* with anesthesia codes; they are not listed with other CPT® code categories.

Anesthesia-Related Teaching Rules

To interpret Medicare's teaching rules for anesthesia correctly, the following italicized teaching information is taken directly from chapter 12, section 50 in the Medicare Internet-only Manual at www.cms.gov/manuals/downloads/clm104c12.pdf. The chapter should be reviewed in its entirety before billing anesthesia services to Medicare.

Payment at Personally Performed Rate

The Part B contractor must determine the fee schedule payment, recognizing the base unit for the anesthesia code and one time unit per 15 minutes of anesthesia time if:

- The physician personally performed the entire anesthesia service alone;
- The physician is involved with one anesthesia case with a resident, the physician is a teaching physician as defined in §100, and the service is furnished on or after January 1, 1996;
- The physician is involved in the training of physician residents in a single anesthesia case, two concurrent anesthesia cases involving residents or a single anesthesia case involving a resident that is concurrent to another case paid under the medical direction rules. The physician meets the teaching physician criteria in §100.1.4 and the service is furnished on or after January 1, 2010;
- The physician is continuously involved in a single case involving a student nurse anesthetist;
- The physician is continuously involved in one anesthesia case involving a CRNA (or AA) and the service was furnished prior to January 1, 1998. If the physician is involved with a single case with a CRNA (or AA) and the service was furnished on or after January 1, 1998, carriers may pay the physician service and the CRNA (or AA) service in accordance with the medical direction payment policy; or
- The physician and the CRNA (or AA) are involved in one anesthesia case and the services of each are found to be medically necessary. Documentation must be submitted by both the CRNA and the physician to support payment of the full fee for each of the two providers. The physician reports the "AA" modifier and the CRNA reports the "QZ" modifier for a nonmedically directed case.

Payment at the Medically Directed Rate

For services furnished on or after January 1, 1994, the physician can medically direct two, three, or four concurrent procedures involving qualified individuals, all of whom could be CRNAs, AAs, interns, residents or combinations of these individuals. The medical direction rules apply to cases involving student nurse anesthetists if the physician directs two concurrent cases, each of which involves a student nurse anesthetist, or the physician directs one case involving a student nurse anesthetist and another involving a CRNA, AA, intern, or resident.

For services furnished on or after January 1, 2010, the medical direction rules do not apply to a single resident case that is concurrent to another anesthesia case paid under the medical direction rules or to two concurrent anesthesia cases involving residents.

The GC modifier is reported by the teaching physician to indicate he rendered the service in compliance with the teaching physician requirements in §100.1.2. One of the payment modifiers must be used in conjunction with the GC modifier.

Glossary

Add-on Codes—Procedures commonly carried out in addition to the primary procedure performed. Add-on codes may *not* be reported alone, and are identified with a + sign.

Anesthesiologist Assistant—A health professional who has completed an accredited anesthesia assistant training program.

Anesthesiologist—A physician licensed to practice medicine and has completed an accredited anesthesiology program.

Anesthesia Time—Begins when the anesthesiologist (or anesthesia provider) begins to prepare the patient for the induction of anesthesia and ends when the anesthesiologist (or anesthesia provider) is no longer in personal attendance.

Arterial Line—A catheter inserted into an artery, used most commonly to measure real-time blood pressure and obtain samples for arterial blood gas.

Base Unit Value—Value assigned to anesthesia codes for anesthetic management of surgery and diagnostic tests. Base unit values vary depending on the difficulty of the surgery, and thus the administration of anesthesia.

Cardiopulmonary Bypass (CPB)—A technique used during heart surgery to take over temporarily the function of the heart and lungs.

CRNA (Certified Registered Nurse Anesthetist)—A registered nurse who has completed an accredited nurse anesthesia training program.

Controlled Hypotension—A technique used in general anesthesia to reduce blood pressure to control bleeding during surgery. Watch anesthesia record for notes regarding deliberate or controlled hypotension.

Conversion Factor—A unit multiplier to convert anesthesia units into a dollar amount for anesthesia services. Conversion factors are reviewed annually by CMS. Conversion factors also may be negotiated with insurance companies.

Central Venous Catheter—A catheter placed in a large vein such as the internal jugular, subclavian, or femoral vein with the tip of the catheter close to the atrium, or in the right atrium of the heart.

CVP (Central Venous Pressure)—A direct measurement of the blood pressure in the right atrium and vena cava. CVP reflects the amount of blood returning to the heart and the ability of the heart to pump blood from the right heart into the pulmonary system.

Emergency—A delay in treatment would lead to significant increase in the threat to life or body part.

Flat Fee—A flat fee is based on the physician fee schedule. Payments are made under the relative value unit (RVU). Time is not a consideration for payment. Examples are arterial lines, CVP lines, emergency intubation, and Swan-Ganz catheter insertion.

General Anesthesia—Drug-induced loss of consciousness during which patients cannot be aroused.

Hypothermic Circulatory Arrest—Implies a temperature of 20 degrees centigrade or less.

Medical Direction—Occurs when an anesthesiologist is involved in two, three, or four concurrent anesthesia procedures, or a single anesthesia procedure with a qualified anesthetist. CMS and other carriers publish criteria to be met to report medical direction.

Medical Supervision—Occurs when an anesthesiologist is involved in five or more concurrent anesthesia procedures, or fails to meet required medical direction criteria.

Monitored Anesthesia Care—Refers to a continuum of sedation ranging from light to deep. Anesthesia provider must be prepared to convert to general anesthesia, if necessary.

PAC—Pulmonary Artery Catheter (eg, Swan-Ganz)—A flow-directed catheter inserted into the pulmonary artery. PACs are used to measure pressures and flows within the cardiovascular system.

Physical Status Modifier—A modifier used to report the physical status assigned to each patient undergoing anesthesia. Patients are ranked by their individual health status.

Pump Oxygenator—Term used when a cardiopulmonary bypass (CPB) machine is used to function as the heart and lungs during heart surgery.

Qualifying Circumstances—Circumstances significantly affecting the character of an anesthesia service. These add-on procedures are reported only with anesthesia codes. More than one may be reported, if applicable. Qualifying circumstances may not be reported separately when a code descriptor already indicates the circumstance.

Regional Anesthesia—Loss of sensation in a region of the body, produced by application of an anesthetic agent.

Relative Value Unit—Unit measure used to assign a value to services. Determined by assigning weight to factors such as physician work, practice expense and malpractice expense.

Resident—A physician who has completed his or her medical degree and entered a residency program specifically for anesthesiology training.

SRNA (Student Registered Nurse Anesthetist)—A registered nurse training in an accredited nurse anesthesia program.

Surgical Field Avoidance—Anesthesia provider avoids an area where the surgeon is working (usually on procedures around the head, neck or shoulder girdle). The ASA assigned a minimum base unit value of "5" for procedures requiring field avoidance.

Total Body Hypothermia—Deliberate reduction of a patient's total body temperature, reducing the general metabolism of the tissues. Watch anesthesia record for notes regarding total body hypothermia. Generally, temperature is reduced 20 percent to 30 percent below a patient's normal temperature. This may not be reported separately when the code indicates it is included.

Chapter Review Questions

1. An epidural is considered which type of anesthesia?

    A. Local

    B. MAC

    C. Regional

    D. General

2. Which of the following is separately billable and is NOT included in anesthesia services?

    A. Pre-operative visits

    B. Blood pressure monitoring

    C. Blood transfusion

    D. Introduction of an arterial line

3. A healthy 79-year-old male patient with communicating hydrocephalus undergoes creation of a ventriculo-peritoneal shunt. What is the correct anesthesia code selection for this procedure?

    A. 00220-P1, 99100

    B. 00220-P1

    C. 00210-P1

    D. 00210-P1, 99100

4. A 42-year-old with renal pelvis cancer receives general anesthesia for a laparoscopic radical nephrectomy. The patient has controlled type II diabetes with no other co-morbidities. What are the correct CPT® and ICD-9-CM codes for the anesthesia services?

    A. 00860-P1, 189.0, 250.00

    B. 00840-P3, 189.1, 250.00

    C. 00862-P2, 189.1, 250.00

    D. 00868-P2, 198.0, 250.00

5. A healthy 32-year-old with a closed distal radius fracture received monitored anesthesia care for an ORIF of the distal radius. What is the code for the anesthesia service?

    A. 01830-P1

    B. 01860-QS-P1

    C. 01830-QS-P1

    D. 01860-QS-G9-P1

6. A 10-month-old child is taken to the operating room for removal of a laryngeal mass. What anesthesia code(s) is/are reported?

    A. 00320

    B. 00326

    C. 00320, 99100

    D. 00326, 99100

7. A patient receiving radiation therapy for a brain tumor requires anesthesia. What is the correct anesthesia code?

    A. 01922

    B. 01924

    C. 01930

    D. 01933

8. A 50-year-old female had a left subcutaneous mastectomy for cancer. She now returns for reconstruction which is done with a single TRAM flap. Right mastopexy is done for asymmetry. Code the anesthesia for this procedure.

    A. 00404

    B. 00402

    C. 00406

    D. 00400

9. **Case 1**

Anesthesiologist: DD, MD

Dr. D placed a CVP in the right internal jugular and a Swan-Ganz in the left internal jugular.

Time: 15:37 to 17:51

Physical Status Modifier: P5

Preoperative Diagnosis: Severe coronary artery occlusive disease with failed stent insertion requiring emergency bypass grafting.

Postoperative Diagnosis: Severe coronary artery occlusive disease with failed stent insertion requiring emergency bypass grafting.

Name of Procedure: Emergency coronary artery bypass graft x2, (saphenous vein graft to proximal obtuse marginal circumflex, saphenous vein graft to distal right coronary artery).

Anesthesia: General endotracheal anesthesia. Cardiopulmonary bypass was instituted.

History: This patient is a 58-year-old female with known peripheral vascular disease, who recently was found to have high-grade two vessel occlusive disease with an ostial 70 to 75 percent lesion of the right coronary artery and a 90 percent mid body lesion of the proximal obtuse marginal branch of the circumflex. She came in and underwent attempted percutaneous transluminal coronary angioplasty with stent placement earlier today. Apparently the lesion could not be crossed with a stent and she developed chest pain. The lesion was maintained with a wire across it. We were called to see the patient to perform emergency bypass grafting. After assessing the situation, we agreed to proceed.

What are the CPT® and ICD-9-CM codes for this service?

10. **Case 2**

Anes Start: 7:50   **Anes End:** 16:54

Anesthesiology: DD, MD   **CRNA:** JS, CRNA

PS III

Attending was immediately available, present at all critical points, present during positioning, present at induction, reviewed patient chart and performed the preoperative assessment. Dr. D was medically directing two other anesthesia cases during this case.

Dr. D performed placement of the A line and CVP. After the area was prepped and draped, Dr. D inserted the arterial line in the right radial artery. The line was secured with tape. Dr. D also inserted the central line in the right internal jugular vein of this 56-year-old patient.

Operative Report

Preoperative Diagnosis:

Primary pancreatic neoplasm of the head of the pancreas

Postoperative Diagnosis:

1. Adenocarcinoma of the uncinate process of the pancreas

2. Liver cirrhosis

3. Pancreatitis

Procedure:

1. Pyloric-sparing Whipple procedure

2. Liver wedge biopsy

Anesthesia:

General endotracheal anesthesia

What are the CPT® and ICD-9-CM codes for the Anesthesiologist and the CRNA?

Introduction

Radiology is a branch of medicine which uses radiation to diagnose and treat disease. Using radiography (X-rays), physicians may navigate within the body to visualize and identify internal structures. Imaging technology includes a variety of advanced applications, such as computerized axial tomography (CAT or CT scanning), magnetic resonance imaging (MRI), ultrasound technology, nuclear medicine, radiation oncology, and positron emission tomography (PET).

Anatomy and Medical Terminology

Planes are ways in which the body can be divided. The most common planes are the frontal (coronal) plane, which divides the body into front (anterior) and back (posterior) halves, the sagittal plane, which divides the body into right and left portions, and the transverse (axial) (horizontal) plane, which divides the body into upper (superior) and lower (inferior) halves. The midsaggital plane divides the body into equal portions of right and left.

Main positional terms include:

Anatomic Position—Erect, facing forward, hands open with thumbs pointed out, and feet together.

Supine—Lying down on the back with face up; also known as dorsal recumbent.

Prone Position—Lying face down on the front of the body; also known as ventral recumbent.

Lateral Position—The side of the subject is next to the film; can be performed as erect lateral (standing side) or lateral decubitus (lying down side).

Oblique Position—Patient is lying at an angle neither prone nor supine; for example: right anterior oblique (RAO), left anterior oblique (LAO), right posterior oblique (RPO), or left posterior oblique (LPO). The anterior or posterior terminology indicates the part of the body closer to the film.

Radiological projections refer to the path in which the X-ray beam flows through the body. Common projections include:

Anteroposterior (AP)—The X-ray beam enters the front of the body (anterior) and exits the back of the body (posterior).

Posteroanterior (PA)—The X-ray beam enters the back of the body (posterior) and exits the front of the body (anterior).

Lateral—The X-ray beam enters one side of the body and exits the other side. Lateral projections are named by the side of the body which is placed next to the film.

Oblique—The X-ray beam enters at an angle which is neither frontal (AP or PA) nor lateral.

Radiographic Projection Positions

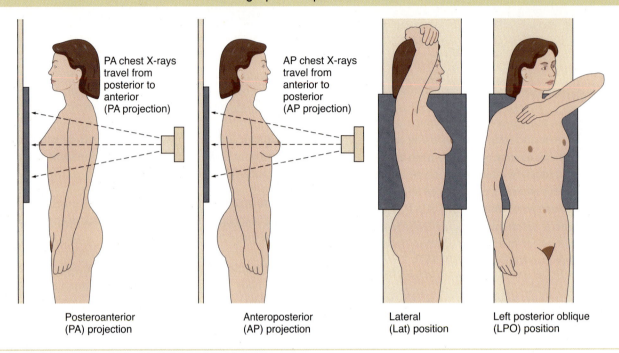

Posteroanterior
(PA) projection

Anteroposterior
(AP) projection

Lateral
(Lat) position

Left posterior oblique
(LPO) position

Source: Delmar/Cengage Learning.

ICD-9-CM Coding

A radiology service can be performed as routine, as a screening, or for a sign or symptom. A routine screening might be performed with a preventive medicine exam, such as a routine chest X-ray. If a chest X-ray is performed as part of a preventive medicine exam, report diagnosis code V72.5 *Radiological examination, not elsewhere classified*.

Screening examinations are performed when there are no signs or symptoms, but the provider is looking for a specific disease or illness. When the radiological service is part of a screening for a particular disease or illness, such as mammography to screen for breast cancer, use the appropriate screening diagnosis from the V codes (eg, V76.11 *Screening mammogram for high-risk patient*, or V76.12 *Other screening mammogram*).

Another screening reported is when a patient is being cleared for surgery. When an X-ray is performed as part of a pre-operative examination, select a code from V72.81–V72.84.

If the sign or symptom is the only documented diagnosis, use the sign or symptom as the diagnosis for the

radiological service. Similarly, when a test is ordered for a sign or symptom, and the outcome of the test is a normal result with no confirmed diagnosis, report the sign or symptom that prompted the physician to order the test. An example might be when a physician orders a mammography for breast pain. The findings on the mammography were normal. In this instance, you would report 611.71 *Pain in breast* for the mammography.

If the radiologist has interpreted the radiology test, and the final report is available at the time of coding, report the confirmed diagnosis based on the report. This is specified in ICD-9-CM Official *Guidelines for Coding and Reporting*, section IV:

> For outpatient encounters for diagnostic tests that have been interpreted by a physician, and the final report is available at the time of coding, code any confirmed or definitive diagnosis(es) documented in the interpretation. Do not code related signs and symptoms as additional diagnoses.

Sometimes, providers will order a radiological examination with a "rule out" or "questionable" diagnosis. In this instance, if the report has not been read and a final diagnosis given, communicate with the physician to obtain the sign or symptom for which the test was ordered. Each payer may have varying guidelines on how this communication needs to be documented.

According to the Medicare *Claims Processing Manual*, chapter 23, §10.1.2, an order may include:

◖ A written document signed by the treating physician/practitioner, which is hand-delivered, mailed, or faxed to the testing facility;

◖ A telephone call by the treating physician/practitioner or his or her office to the testing facility; or

◖ An electronic mail by the treating physician/practitioner or his or her office to the testing facility.

Occasionally, when a radiologist reads an X-ray, he or she will find something on the X-ray for which he or she was not looking. This is considered an incidental finding and reported as an additional diagnosis. Do not report an incidental finding as a primary diagnosis.

CPT® Coding

Radiological procedures may be performed on any part of the body. They sometimes are performed as standalone services (such as a chest or ankle X-ray), or in addition to other services (such as MRI guidance for needle placement during a biopsy). To code radiological services correctly, a coder should be able to recognize the types of radiology equipment, determine which equipment is used for the evaluation, and understand the applicable guidelines in the Radiology section.

Radiology Guidelines

Separate Procedures

Designated "separate procedures" may be performed as an integral part to another procedure, or alone. Separate procedures should be coded only if performed alone, or performed with an unrelated service. There are very few separate procedure codes in the Radiology section.

Unlisted Procedures

Radiological services not covered by a specific CPT® code should be coded with an unlisted code. Anytime an unlisted service code is reported, the claim should be

accompanied by a special report describing the procedure, and the reason the procedure was medically necessary. Make sure to explain the equipment, time and effort involved.

Supervision and Interpretation

"S&I" codes describe the supervision and interpretation of a radiological procedure. Common procedures containing a supervision and interpretation component include vascular procedures performed on the veins and arteries. When a procedure requires radiological guidance, a code from the surgery or medicine section may be reported along with the supervision and interpretation code from the radiology section. When the same physician provides both the surgical procedure and the radiological guidance, the physician will report both codes. When a physician performs the surgery, and a radiologist performs the supervision and interpretation, each will report the code for his or her portion of the service.

Administration of Contrast Material(s)

Contrast material is a substance or material that "lights up" the structure being studied so it can be visualized. The phrase "with contrast" represents contrast material administered in three ways:

◖ Intravascularly—using a vein

◖ Intra-articularly—in a joint

◖ Intrathecally—within a sheath, or within the subarachnoid or cerebral spinal fluid

According to CPT® guidelines, "Oral and/or rectal contrast administration alone does not qualify as a study "with contrast." When contrast is given orally or rectally, it is inappropriate to report a "with contrast" code.

Testing Technique
Write a note near the contrast codes reminding you oral and rectal are NOT contrast, and cannot be reported with these codes. Then, make sure you note the codes, such as 74170, for studies without contrast, followed by contrast.

Some studies, such as an MRI or a CT scan, may be performed without contrast, followed by with contrast. In these instances, there often is a single code to report both sets of images.

As you code for contrast imaging, you may need to code an additional procedure. Watch for parenthetical instructions following the imaging codes to see if another procedure—such as the contrast material used for the study or the injection procedure for the contrast—should be reported.

The contrast material is not included in the radiological procedure and can be reported separately, typically with a HCPCS Level II code to identify the substance used.

The Radiology Report

The radiologist's written report is the documentation for the professional component of the radiological procedure, and must be signed.

Types of Radiological Services

The Radiology section in the CPT® codebook is divided into the following subsections:

- Diagnostic Radiology (Diagnostic Imaging) (70010–76499)
- Diagnostic Ultrasound (76506–76999)
- Radiologic Guidance (77001–77032)
- Breast, Mammography (77051–77059)
- Bone/Joint Studies (77071–77084)
- Radiation Oncology (77261–77799)
- Nuclear Medicine (78000–79999)

Diagnostic Radiology (Diagnostic Imaging)

Diagnostic radiology consists of X-rays, MRI, and CT studies.

A plain X-ray is like taking a picture or snapshot of the inside of the body. CT scans use a series of X-rays to produce cross-sectional pictures of the body. MRI produces "slices" of images by using a magnetic field and the protons within your body. The slices can be combined to produce 3-D images that may be viewed from different angles. MRA, or magnetic resonance angiography, is an MRI of the blood vessels.

When coding for diagnostic radiology, a coder will need to determine the anatomic location, the type of radiology used (X-ray, CT, MRI, etc.), the number of views, the type of views taken, and whether contrast material was used.

Testing Technique

A KUB is often referred to on reports and in prep for abdominal surgery. The KUB is also referred to in the CPT® codebook. However, if you try to locate a KUB (or a flat plate abdomen, as they are sometimes called), you will not find the code by looking in the index or reading through the radiology section. A KUB is reported with 74000 *Radiological examination, abdomen; single anteroposterior view.* Make a note in your index where you would naturally look for the code—under K for KUB and under A for abdominal—reminding you of this.

When the anatomic location has been identified, codes for radiologic examination by X-ray often are selected based on the number of views. The number of views is not synonymous with the number of films used. A radiology technician may be required to shoot several films of the same view. The language used in CPT® refers to the number of views, not the number of films.

CPT® Example:

73560	*Radiologic examination, knee; 1 or 2 views*
73562	*3 views*
73564	*complete, 4 or more views*

Sometimes, the code descriptor will state a minimum number of views. When this terminology is used, the code will include any number of views in excess of the number provided in the description. For example, the description for CPT® code 73610 is *Radiologic examination, ankle; complete, minimum of 3 views.* Whether three, four, or more views are taken, 73610 is appropriate.

For some radiologic examinations, the **type** of view taken, instead of the number of views, is the determining factor for code selection. When this is the case, if the physician only documents the number of views, there will be insufficient documentation for code selection.

CPT® Example:

74000 *Radiologic examination, abdomen; single anteroposterior view*

74010   *anteroposterior and additional oblique and cone views*

74020   *complete, including decubitus and/or erect views*

The Components of a Radiology Service

Many codes within diagnostic radiology report the supervision and interpretation of a service. S&I codes contain both a technical and professional component (discussed later in this chapter). Sometimes a procedure is performed by a surgeon and the radiological supervision and interpretation is performed by a radiologist. When this occurs, the surgeon reports the surgery code, and the radiologist reports the supervision and interpretation code.

For example, temporomandibular joint (TMJ) arthrography is a procedure where the patient receives an injection of contrast dye into the TMJ followed by imaging. The two codes for the complete service are:

- 21116 Injection procedure for temporomandibular joint arthrography
- 70332 Temporomandibular joint arthrography, supervision and interpretation

If one physician gives the injection, and another physician provides the imaging supervision and report, each physician should report the service he or she performed. If one physician performs the entire service, he or she should report both codes.

When looking at the surgical procedure, parenthetical instructions guide you to the supervision and interpretation code. For example, a note following 21116 directs the reader to 70332 for the S&I.

Remember: The radiologist billing the supervision and interpretation must be present at the time of the procedure, and there must be a written report.

Diagnostic Ultrasound

Diagnostic ultrasound uses sound waves to visualize internal structures. There are different types of ultrasound scans. Some types include A-mode (A-scan), B-mode (B-scan), M-Mode, and Real-time scan. A-mode (amplitude mode) is a one-dimensional scan typically only seen in ophthalmic ultrasounds. M-Mode (motion mode) is a one-dimensional scan showing the movement of a moving structure (such as the heart). B-mode (brightness mode) is a two-dimensional scan. Real-time scans are B-scans in motion. Three-dimensional scans also are now available; 4-D scans are 3-D ultrasounds in motion.

A coder will need to understand the different types of scans to select the correct code.

A Doppler study is a type of ultrasound that can penetrate solids or liquids. This type of study is useful in imaging the flow of blood. The use of Doppler imaging is separately reportable, except when used alone for anatomic structure identification with real-time ultrasound.

Some anatomic regions have "complete" and "limited" ultrasound codes. Elements comprising a "complete" exam are listed in the code description in parenthesis.

For example, the guidelines in the abdomen and retroperitoneum subsection give the definitions of a complete ultrasound exam for those specific regions.

Sonogram

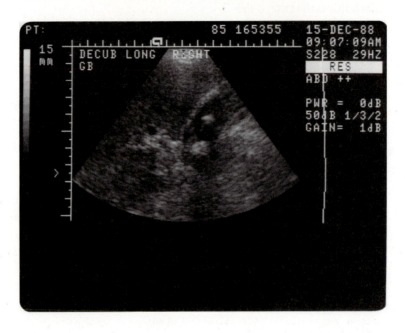

Source: Delmar/Cengage Learning.

The abdomen real-time scan includes the liver, gall-bladder, common bile duct, pancreas, spleen, kidneys, and the upper abdominal aorta and inferior vena cava. If the intent of the procedure is to visualize all of these, but one is obstructed from view, the physician would need to document why he or she was not able to visualize the organ or structure. If less than a complete exam is performed, the coder would need to use the "limited" ultrasound code.

Pelvic ultrasounds are divided further between obstetric and non-obstetric. An obstetric ultrasound either is a pregnant uterus ultrasound or a fetal ultrasound. Non-obstetric ultrasounds include a transvaginal ultrasound, a sonohysterography, and non-obstetric pelvic ultrasounds. A transvaginal (meaning "through the vagina") ultrasound is used to look at the female reproduction organs or in early pregnancy, as it can provide a better view.

A sonohysterography is an ultrasound of the uterus. Saline infusion sonohysterography occurs when sterile saline is put into the uterus through the cervix. The procedure is used to evaluate symptoms such as abnormal uterine bleeding, infertility, or abnormalities of the uterus lining.

Ultrasonic Guidance codes are selected based on what type of procedure is being provided (such as pericardiocentesis, vascular access, needle placement, etc). During an encounter, either a diagnostic ultrasound code or an ultrasound guidance code may be reported, but not both.

Radiologic Guidance

The radiologic guidance codes are organized by the type of radiological guidance used—whether it is fluoroscopic, CT, MR, or other type of guidance—and selected based on the precise procedure performed.

Fluoroscopy is a continuous X-ray displayed onto a screen for monitoring. The continuous image is used in real time to view the movement of a body part, or of an instrument or dye moving through the body. Fluoroscopic guidance codes are used for catheter insertion, needle placement, and localization of a needle or catheter.

CT also allows the physician to view a constant image on a screen to monitor the movements made within the body. CT-guided stereotactic localization is used to make sure the radiation beams are targeting the tumor instead of surrounding tissue or other vital organs. CT also can be used to assist monitoring parenchymal tissue ablation and the placement of radiation therapy fields.

Breast, Mammography

Mammography codes are selected based on the imaging device, procedure performed, whether it is screening or diagnostic, and whether it is unilateral or bilateral.

Screening mammograms are always bilateral. Diagnostic mammograms may be unilateral or bilateral, and focus on a sign or symptom. Diagnostic mammograms also may be combined with software using computer algorithm analysis designed to help the radiologist interpret mammograms. When this software is used, it is considered computer-aided detection (CAD) and an add-on code is reported with the mammogram.

A ductogram, or galactogram (galact is a root word meaning milk), is imaging of the ducts in the breast.

Testing Technique
Make a note in the mammography section of CPT® to indicate mammograms performed on Medicare patients should be coded from HCPCS Level II.

A ductogram, or galactogram ("galact" is a root word meaning milk), is imaging of the ducts in the breast.

Bone/Joint Studies

Bone and joint studies are performed to determine bone or joint abnormalities.

- A bone age study typically is performed on children to estimate the maturity of a child's skeletal system, based on the appearance of the growth plate in the bone.
- A bone length study is used to determine discrepancies in limb length.

- Osseous surveys are radiological procedures used to detect fractures, tumors, or degenerative conditions of the bone. Osseous surveys are coded based on the whether the service is limited or complete, or if the survey was performed on an infant.

Dual-energy X-ray absorptiometry (DXA or DEXA) is a common test performed to determine bone density. This test helps to evaluate risk of bone fractures (which often are the result of osteoporosis). DEXA scans are coded based on the location of the body being scanned.

Radiation Oncology

Radiation oncology is a multi-disciplinary medical specialty involving physicians, physicists and dosimetrists, nurses, biomedical scientists, computer scientists, radiotherapy technologists, nutritionists, and social workers. It is a highly-specialized and complex method for delivering radiation treatment to tumors.

The radiation oncology subsection in the CPT® codebook is divided into:

- consultation
- treatment planning
- radiation physics, dosimetry devices and special services
- radiation treatment management
- treatment deliveries
- hyperthermia
- clinical intracavitary hyperthermia
- clinical brachytherapy

When a patient first visits the radiation oncologist, there is a consultation to determine if radiation will benefit the patient. According to CPT®, this service is coded from the appropriate evaluation and management, medicine, or surgical code.

After the initial consultation, the patient and provider will plan the treatment. According to CPT®, clinical treatment planning involves:

- interpretation of special testing
- tumor localization
- treatment volume determination

- treatment time/dosage determination
- choice of treatment modality
- determination of the number and size of treatment ports
- selection of appropriate treatment devices, and
- other procedures.

The appropriate code is based on the level of planning: simple, intermediate, or complex. Planning levels are defined by the number of treatment areas, ports, and blocks, and also consider special dose time, and if rotational or special beams are required.

A port is the place where radiation enters the body and is often marked with tattooing. Blocks are special pieces of lead designed specifically for each patient to shield healthy normal tissue from receiving the radiation, allowing the radiation to focus solely on the tumor.

During the treatment planning process, the provider and patient will go through simulation. The simulation is selected based on the number of ports, blocks, and the use of contrast material and 3-D simulation.

The information gained in simulation is then sent to medical radiation physicists and medical radiation dosimetrists. Dosimetry is the calculation of the dose of radiation. These highly-trained physicians design and create the blocks that shield the healthy tissue. They also plan the dose delivery. The services of the physicists and dosimetrists are coded using the codes in the subsection for Medical Radiation Physics, Dosimetry, Treatment Devices and Special Planning.

The actual delivery of radiation is reported by the facility. The oversight of the delivery is reported by the physician, including review of the port films, dosimetry, dose delivery, treatment parameters, and treatment setup. This oversight is considered radiation treatment management, and is reported by the number of fractions.

Patients typically receive radiation treatment in "fractions." When the delivery is twice per day, it is considered two fractions.

The treatment delivery sections reported by the facility (technical component only) include the following Radiation Oncology subsections:

- Stereotactic Radiation Treatment Delivery
- Radiation Treatment Delivery (except for the stereoscopic guidance)
- Neutron Beam Treatment Delivery
- Proton Beam Treatment Delivery

Hyperthermia

Hyperthermia (heat) used with radiation therapy currently is under investigation. Some insurance carriers will allow only for deep hyperthermia and some do not allow hyperthermia at all. Review your insurance carrier contracts and guidelines.

Clinical Brachytherapy

Clinical brachytherapy uses radioactive material sealed in needles, seeds, wires, or catheters. The sealed radioactive material then is placed in or near a tumor. Interstitial brachytherapy occurs when the seeds, or other sealed radioactive material, are inserted into tissue at or near the tumor site. Intracavitary brachytherapy is when it is inserted into the body with an applicator.

Nuclear Medicine

Nuclear medicine is the use of small amounts of radioactive material to examine organ function and structure. Therapeutic nuclear medicine also can be used to treat cancer and other medical conditions. The radiopharmaceuticals used in nuclear medicine are not included in the coding of the tests, and should be reported separately (typically using a HCPCS Level II code). Nuclear medicine codes are selected based on the test performed.

HCPCS Level II Coding

HCPCS Level II codes exist for mammography and PET scans. When a Medicare patient receives a PET scan for melanoma without the specified indications covered by Medicare, the service is coded using a HCPCS Level II code (for instance, G0219 *PET imaging whole body; melanoma for non-covered indications*).

When contrast material is used during MRI or CT, a HCPCS Level II code may be coded in addition to the scan.

Modifiers

The two most common modifiers used with radiological services are:

- 26 Professional services
- TC Technical services

The cost of the equipment, overhead of the supplies, and resources, such as the room, electricity, and the salary of the radiology technician, are all included in the technical component. The technical component is reported by the facility or office who owns the equipment. To report the technical component, modifier TC is appended to the CPT® code from the radiology section.

After the radiology has been performed, it has to be read (interpreted) by a physician. The physician can be a radiologist, but this is not required to code the services. The interpretation and report of the radiological service is considered the professional component, indicated by appending modifier 26 to the CPT® code from the radiology section. A facility owning the equipment and employing the radiologist/physcian may bill for both the technical and professional component. Both components together are considered "global." Sometimes, a physician's office will own the equipment, read the X-ray, and provide the report. An example of this might be an orthopaedic office with X-ray equipment. When the office owns the equipment, has the overhead cost of the procedure, reads the X-ray, and provides the report, the office may bill the global procedure. A global procedure is reported using the correct CPT® code without a modifier appended.

Testing Technique

Write a note to yourself to read the problem carefully for hints as to where and how the test was performed. This will help to assure you do not miss the TC *Technical component* and 26 *Professional component* where applicable.

Additional modifiers applicable to radiological procedures include:

- 76 *Repeat procedure or service by same physician*
- 77 *Repeat procedure or service by another physician*

- 79 *Unrelated procedure or service by the same physician during the postoperative period*
- RT *Right*
- LT *Left*

Glossary

Angiography—Radiographic image of the blood vessels using contrast material.

Aortography—Radiographic image of the aorta and branches using contrast material.

Atherectomy—To remove plaque from an artery.

Brachytherapy—Radiation placed in or near a tumor within the body. Catheters, needles, seeds or wires may be used.

Bronchography—Radiographic image of the bronchi of the lungs using contrast material.

Cephalogram—Radiographic image of the head.

Cholangiography—Radiographic image of the bile duct.

Cineradiography—Radiography of an organ in motion (for example, a beating heart).

Colonography—Radiographic image of the (interior) colon.

Computed Tomography (CT)—Using specialized equipment, two-dimensional X-ray images are taken around a single axis of rotation. The images are combined to create a 3-D image or pictures of the inside of the body. These cross-sectional images of the area being studied may be examined on a computer monitor, printed or transferred to a CD.

Corpora Cavernosography—Radiographic image of the corpora cavernosa and draining veins using contrast medium.

Cystography—Radiographic image of the bladder.

Dacryocystography—Radiographic image of the lacrimal drainage system.

Discography—Radiographic image of the spine.

Doppler—A type of ultrasound, especially useful for imaging blood flow. The Doppler can create images either in shades of gray or, when processed by a computer, in color.

Ductogram—Imaging of the ducts in the breast.

Duodenography—Radiographic examination of the duodenum and pancreas.

Echocardiography—Imaging using sound waves to create a moving picture of the heart.

Echoencephalography—Ultrasound image of the brain.

Epidurography—Imaging of the epidural space in the spine.

Fluoroscopy—A continuous X-ray image, used to view the movement of a body part, or of an instrument or dye moving through the body.

Hyperthermia—A type of cancer treatment in which tissue is exposed to high temperatures (up to 113°F).

Hysterosalpingography—Fluoroscopic imaging (with contrast) of a woman's uterus and fallopian tubes.

Intraluminal—Within the lumen.

Laryngography—Radiographic image of the larynx.

Lymphangiography—Diagnostic imaging to view lymphatic circulation and lymph nodes; utilizes X-ray technology and the injection of a contrast agent.

Magnetic Resonance (MR)—Magnetic fields align the protons within the body to produce image "slices," which are combined to produce 3-D images that may be viewed from different angles; performed either with or without contrast.

Myelography—Radiographic image of the spinal cord.

Nephrotomography—CT image of the kidneys.

Orthopantogram—Panoramic, radiographic image of the entire dentition, alveolar bone, and other adjacent structures on a single film; taken extra-orally.

Pachymetry—Measurement of corneal thickness.

Pancreatography—Radiographic image of the pancreatic ducts following injection of radiopaque material.

Pelvimetry—Measurement of the dimensions and capacity of the pelvis.

Portography—X-ray visualization of the portal circulation using radiopaque material.

Pyelography—Radiographic imaging of the renal pelvis of a kidney following injection of a radiopaque substance through the ureter or into a vein.

Shuntogram—Placement of a radioactive isotope in the shunt reservoir in the head to measure the speed with which it moves to the abdomen. Shuntogram is the term used for angiography of an A/V fistula for renal dialysis.

Sialography—Radiographic image of the salivary ducts and glands.

Sonohysterography—Ultrasound imaging of the uterus.

Splenoportography—Radiography of the splenic and portal veins; includes injection of a radiopaque medium.

Teletherapy—Any treatment whereby the source of the therapeutic agent (for instance, radiation) is at a distance from the body.

Transcatheter—Performed via the lumen of a catheter.

Urethrocystography—Radiography of the urethra and bladder using a radiopaque substance.

Urography—Imaging of the kidneys and ureters.

Vasography—Radiographic image of the vas deferens and ejaculatory duct following dye injection.

Velocity Flow Mapping—A non-invasive method to image blood flow through the heart by displaying flow data on the two-dimensional echocardiographic image.

Venography—A radiographic image of the veins following injection of contrast dye.

Xeroradiography—Creation of radiographs by photo-electric process using metal plates coated with a semi-conductor (for instance, selenium).

Chapter Review Questions

1. What is a radiographic image of the blood vessels using contrast material?

    A. Angiography

    B. Venography

    C. Aortography

    D. Vasography

2. What position has the side of the subject next to the film and can be performed as erect or decubitus?

    A. Prone

    B. Lateral

    C. Oblique

    D. Supine

3. A patient presents to the ER after being struck by a car. A frontal and lateral view of the thoracic spine is performed. What is the CPT® code for this procedure?

    A. 72070

    B. 72074

    C. 72100

    D. 72128

4. Multiple axial images are taken through the abdomen and pelvis following the administration of oral and intravenous contrast. What CPT® codes are reported for this service?

    A. 74160, 72193

    B. 74177

    C. 74170, 72194

    D. 74174

5. A physician manages radiation therapy treatments for a patient with small cell lung cancer. The patient met with the radiation oncologist to review the port films and 6 treatments of 18 MeV external beam applications. What CPT® code should be used to report the radiation oncologist's services?

    A. 77404

    B. 77404-26

    C. 77427

    D. 77427-26

6. A two-year-old presents to ED with arm pain. Right humerus anterior/posterior and lateral views are obtained of the right humerus. No fracture, dislocation, or other abnormality is seen. What CPT® and ICD-9-CM codes are reported for the physician's services?

   A. 73060-26, 729.5

   B. 73060, 793.99

   C. 73090, 729.81

   D. 73092-26, 730.2

7. An MRI of the lumbar spine with and without contrast is performed. It includes various echo, axial, and sagittal images taken through the lumbar spine. Which CPT® code is reported for this service?

   A. 72080

   B. 72132

   C. 72158

   D. 72159

8. From a percutaneous right common femoral artery access, a 6-French vascular sheath is placed. An Omni Flush catheter is advanced into the aorta, and serial aortography is performed. The catheter is pulled back to the bifurcation of the aorta, and contrast is injected, for complete bilateral lower extremity angiography. The physician notes in his report the aorta is mildly atherosclerotic, and there is a 50 percent narrowing of the left popliteal artery. What CPT® codes are reported for the physician?

   A. 36200, 75630-26

   B. 36200, 75625-26, 75716-26

   C. 36200, 75625-26, 75710-50-26

   D. 36200, 75716-26

9. **Radiology Report:**

Reason for Exam: Lump in breast, history of breast cancer at age 73.

Ordered: MAMMOGRAPHY, DIGITAL, BILATERAL

Report: Bilateral CC, MLO, and XCCL views were taken.

Impression: The breast tissue is heterogeneously dense. This may lower the sensitivity of mammography. There are no dominant masses or suspicious calcifications. There is architectural distortion and increased density in the upper outer left breast consistent with post-op and post-radiation changes.

Assessment: BIRADS 2: BENIGN FINDINGS

Recommendation: Routine screening mammogram.

What are the procedure and diagnosis codes for this Medicare patient?

10. **Operative Report:**

PREOPERATIVE DIAGNOSIS: Right hydronephrosis. POSTOPERATIVE DIAGNOSIS: Right hydrone-phrosis. OPERATION: Cystoscopy and right retrograde pyelogram. ANESTHESIA: General. FINDINGS: 1. Mild right hydroureteronephrosis. 2. No filling defects. 3. Urine samples taken from the bladder and the right renal pelvis for urine cytology. 4. The bladder is normal. 5. Ureteral orifices laterally located. PROCEDURE IN DETAIL: After informed consent was obtained, the patient was taken to the operating room and general anesthetic was induced. The patient was prepped and draped in the usual sterile manner in the dorsolithotomy position. Female sounds were used to dilate the urethra and then a 23 French cystoscope was passed into the bladder. The bladder was carefully inspected using 30 degree and 70 degree lenses. No tumors or stones were visualized. The first effluxed urine from the bladder was sent for urine cytology. Then a 6-French access catheter was passed into the right ureteral orifice, it was quite snug and it required a 0.35 guidewire to help cannulate the right ureteral orifice because of the angulation. There was some stiffness in the intramural portion of the ureter; then, the catheter popped through into a more dilated ureter. Contrast was injected and there were no filling defects noted. There was a bubble on one image that was saved, but it was very mobile and seen on the other pictures; there was no fixed tumor and no stone. There was mild hydroureteral nephrosis against the bladder. There was obvious narrowing of the ureter at the UVJ, but no other abnormalities. The renal pelvis was barbotaged with saline and the renal pelvis urine was drained and sent to pathology for urine cytology. After the retrograde pyelogram was performed, the access catheter was removed and there was brisk efflux of the contrast and drained very well. The bladder was then drained and the patient was awakened and transferred in stable condition to the recovery room. Blood loss: none. No complications. Specimens to pathology: urine for cytology from the bladder, and the right renal artery and AL pelvis.

What are the appropriate CPT® and ICD-9-CM codes?

Introduction

This chapter discusses CPT®, ICD-9-CM, and HCPCS Level II codes related to pathology and laboratory services. These services apply to all parts of the body and nearly all disease processes. Often they are defined by the process used to perform the service, or by the substance analyzed (the analyte).

The objectives for this chapter include:

◖ Define terms and concepts specific to pathology and laboratory coding

◖ Apply ICD-9-CM guidelines for assigning codes for diagnostic services, and identify specific codes helpful in describing the medical necessity and outcomes of specific lab tests

◖ Select CPT® and HCPCS Level II codes to describe the services and procedures for pathology and Laboratory services

◖ Utilize CPT® and HCPCS Level II modifiers, when appropriate

Anatomy and Medical Terminology

Pathology is study of diseased tissue and cells (path = disease, -logy = study of). Cytopathology is study and diagnosis of diseases on a cellular level (cyto = cell). Cytogenetics studies the genes within cells to determine whether disease have inherited components and to identify the specific genetic components of certain disease processes.

Laboratory, in this context, refers to tests performed primarily in a medical laboratory (also called a clinical laboratory). Tests of clinical specimens provide information for the diagnosis, treatment, and prevention of disease.

Molecular diagnostics is measurement of DNA (deoxyribonucleic acid), RNA (ribonucleic acid), proteins, or metabolites to detect genotypes, mutations, or

biochemical changes. Hematology is study of the components and behavior of blood (hemat = blood). Immunology is study of the immune system and its components and function. Microbiology (micr/o = small, bio = life) includes four subspecialties: bacteriology (study of bacteria), mycology (study of fungi), parasitology (study of parasites), and virology (study of viruses).

Tests may be identified as quantitative or qualitative. Qualitative testing determines the presence or absence of a drug only. Quantitative testing identifies not only the presence of a drug, but the exact amount present (quantitative shares the same root word as quantity). For example, a patient is brought to the emergency department (ED) after having been in an auto accident. If there is a suspicion the individual has been drinking, a qualitative test might be performed to confirm the presence of alcohol in the bloodstream. If alcohol is detected, a separate quantitative test is needed to determine the quantity of alcohol in the bloodstream. Tests also may be semi-quantitative. Semi-quantitative tests describe an amount within a specified range or over a certain threshold, but do not identify a specific quantity.

Gross examination (eg, 88300) is inspection of the entire specimen without sectioning it into slides for examination under a microscope. Microscopy (88302–88309) is examination of a specimen under a microscope. Most codes for microscopic examination include gross examination.

The word forensic refers to studies used or applied in the investigation and establishment of facts or evidence in a court of law. The Latin term *in vivo* refers to an area of pathology where studies are performed "within the living body."

The Clinical Laboratory Improvement Amendments (CLIA) regulations were passed in 1988 to establish quality standards for all laboratory testing, to ensure the accuracy, reliability, and timeliness of patient test results. Diagnostic test systems are placed into one of three CLIA regulatory categories: 1) waived tests; 2) tests of moderate complexity; 3) and tests of high complexity. Any lab or clinic performing any diagnostic test must have a CLIA number. All bills for tests must include the CLIA number of the testing location. Certificates for waived tests can be issued by application, without any inspection. Certificates for more complex testing require inspections, calibration of equipment, and other tests to assure the quality and accuracy of tests performed.

Key Root Words for Pathology and Laboratory Coding

Bacteri/o	bacteria
Bi/o	life
Cyt/o	cell
Gen/o	origin
Hemat/o	blood
Immun/o	immune
Micr/o	small
Myc/o	fungus
Parasit/o	parasite
Path/o	disease
Vir/o	virus

ICD-9-CM Coding

Pathology and laboratory studies identify infectious and parasitic disease, presence and morphology of neoplasms, quantities of various naturally occurring substances in various body fluids and other tissue, pregnancy status, hormonal changes, and many other factors about health and disease. As such, almost any code in any chapter of ICD-9-CM might be appropriate as an indicator for a test or a finding.

ICD-9-CM Codes for Diagnostic Services

Any time a provider orders a laboratory test or pathologic examination, he or she must identify a reason for the order. This reason is the "medical necessity" for the service. Common reasons to order a test include:

◖ Screening

◖ Signs and/or symptoms
◖ Previous abnormal finding
◖ Current disease
◖ Personal or family history of disease

Always code to the highest degree of certainty. Never code "possible," "rule out," or "exclusion" diagnoses; instead, code the sign or symptom indicating the reason the test was ordered. If a more specific diagnosis is confirmed by the test, code for the test result rather than the indications for the test. If test results are inconclusive, code for abnormal findings.

Consider this example: A young man is planning to get married. He and his fiancee have agreed to get HIV tests prior to their wedding. He has no symptoms or reasons to think he has the disease. When the first test is ordered, report V73.89 *Screening for other specified viral diseases*. If the test is negative, this is the only code used. If the test results come back inconclusive, report 795.71 *Inconclusive serologic test for human immunodeficiency virus [HIV]*. If further testing continues to be inconclusive, this is the only code used. If the test results come back positive for HIV exposure without clinical manifestations, report code V08 *Asymptomatic human immunodeficiency virus infection status*. This code is used until the patient develops symptoms of AIDS. Once symptoms develop, the patient is diagnosed with 042 *Human Immunodeficiency Virus [HIV] disease*.

Abnormal Findings

In ICD-9-CM Volume 1, chapter 16: Signs, Symptoms and Ill-Defined Conditions (780–799), codes 790–796 describe abnormal findings for various tests. These codes are not used when a more specific diagnosis is known, but are useful when a test returns an abnormal result without confirmatory clinical findings. For example:

◖ A 50-year-old man has a screening prostate specific antigen (PSA) blood test as part of his annual exam. The results are elevated, but the patient has no clinical indications of prostate cancer. Report 790.93 (elevated PSA).

◖ A 68-year-old woman, status post-hysterectomy for prolapse, has a vaginal Pap smear as part of her annual breast and pelvic exam. Results show low-grade squamous intraepithelial lesion (LGSIL). Report 795.13.

To code a nonspecific abnormal finding, start with the alphabetic index under "Findings/Abnormal."

Supplementary Classification of Factors Influencing Health Status and Contact with Health Services (V Codes)

V codes describe the reason for a test or study, or the outcome of a study when results are negative or normal.

- Contact with or exposure to communicable diseases (V01)
- Carrier or suspected carrier of infectious diseases (V02)
- Infection with drug-resistant organisms (V09)
- Personal history (V10–V15)
- Family history (V16–V19)
- Reproduction and development (V20–V29)
- Organ or tissue replacement (V42–V43)
- Procedures for aftercare (V58)
- Donor (V59)
- Pregnancy testing (V72.4x)
- Screening (V73–V82)

Abbreviations and Acronyms

BAC	blood alcohol content (or concentration)
Cr	creatinine
CSF	cerebrospinal fluid
Hct	hematocrit
Hgb	hemoglobin
MRSA	methicillin-resistant staphylococcus aureus
PSA	prostate specific antigen
UA	urine analysis

CPT® Coding

Codes in the Pathology and Laboratory chapter of CPT® represent a wide diversity and describe the work of performing a test, usually on some body fluid or tissue. All of these services are performed by a physician or by technologists under supervision of a physician. Some

of the tests are simple and can be performed in a physician's office. Some are complex and require special equipment and/or processes in addition to expert handling and interpretation. Some of these services produce only a test result returned to the ordering provider. For others, there is an expectation an expert will interpret test results further to provide more information or a final diagnosis.

Organ or Disease-Oriented Panels (80047–80076)

Codes in this section describe panels of tests often ordered together. These codes are used whenever all of the specific tests listed under the panel heading are performed, whether the panel is described with the title. If one or more of the tests listed is not performed, the panel code may not be used, and the specific tests must be coded separately. If more tests than those listed in the panel are performed, the panel is coded and additional tests are listed separately. The codes for each individual test are listed beside the test under each heading.

Several panels require all of the tests in another panel to be performed in addition to several other tests (eg, 80050 *General health panel* includes a 80053 *Comprehensive metabolic panel* as well as a blood count and thyroid stimulating hormone). To bill for the more extensive panel, **every** test listed in the less comprehensive panel must be performed, in addition to any added tests listed in the more comprehensive panel.

Several panels allow either of two different tests to be performed. These two tests produce the same information, but can be performed in different ways. For example, the Obstetric Panel includes "Blood count, complete (CBC), automated and automated differential WBC count" OR "Blood count, complete (CBC), automated and appropriate manual differential WBC count."

Drug Testing (80100–80104)

The code range 80100–80102 in the Drug Testing subsection of CPT® are for qualitative analysis of blood for certain drugs. Drugs listed in the table of contents for this section are examples of drug tests performed. Tests can be for multiple drug classes with chromatographic method (80100), multiple drug classes other than chromatographic method (80104), or for a single drug class method (80101). Each code can be listed multiple times, as appropriate. All positive findings are confirmed with a second test (80102). Code 80103 describes preparing the material to be tested. After the presence of a drug is confirmed, a further (and separately billable) test may be performed to determine how much of the drug is present.

Drug tests may be CLIA waived.

Therapeutic Drug Assays (80150–80299)

Some drugs must be maintained at a therapeutic level to work effectively, but may have negative side effects, or even be toxic, if levels get too high. These drugs require regular monitoring to confirm the level of drug in the patient's system. Levels may be tested by therapeutic drug assays. The tissue most often examined is blood, but these codes may be used for assays on any source (eg, urine, sputum).

A number of drugs requiring monitoring for therapeutic levels are listed with specific codes in this section. Other drugs may be found in the Chemistry subsection. If there is no code for the drug being tested in either the Therapeutic Drug Assays subsection or the Chemistry subsection, use code 80299 to describe the service. For qualitative analysis of these drugs, use codes from the Drug Testing subsection (80100–80104).

Evocative/Suppression Testing (80400–80440)

Evocative/suppression tests describe how well various endocrine glands are functioning. Each code in the Evocative/Suppression Testing subsection includes several tests. The tests are performed after administration of an evocative or suppressive agent specific to the gland being tested. The administration of the agent is coded separately, as determined by the route of administration.

Each of the tests listed in the panel code must be performed the number of times listed in the code. For example, 80430 *Growth hormone suppression panel (glucose administration)* requires glucose be measured three times and human growth hormone (HGH) be measured four times. If extra tests are performed, they

are coded separately. If fewer than the listed number of tests are performed, the panel code cannot be used and each test must be coded separately.

Consultations (80500–80502)

Consultations (Clinical Pathology) codes are unlike consultation codes in the Evaluation and Management chapter, but are similar to radiologic consultation codes. Pathology consultation codes are used when tissue samples are sent from another lab or pathologist for a second opinion. Code 80500 is used when only the specimen is reviewed. Code 80502 is used when clinical information is sent along with the specimen so the patient's history, treatments, and other medical information can be taken into consideration as part of the review.

Urinalysis (81000–81099)

Urinalysis includes both simple and complex tests and analyses. All tests are performed on urine specimens. Code 81000 is a simple dipstick test checking for common changes in urine indicating disease. Similar, more involved tests are coded with 81001–81003 and require special equipment or evaluation of the specimen under the microscope. Codes 81005–81020 are complex analyses measuring quantities of these changes, or screen for other conditions.

Urine pregnancy test by color comparison (81025) is similar to tests commercially available over the counter. Volume measurement for timed collection (81050) measures the amount of urine produced over a period, usually 24 hours (often called a 24-hour urine). Dipstick urinalysis and urine pregnancy tests are CLIA waived tests.

Molecular Pathology (81200–81408)

This section of CPT® lists procedures involving the analyses of genes. This exciting and developing area of medical testing promises clues to illnesses and possible future treatments. Code selection is typically based on the specific gene(s) being analyzed. The molecular pathology codes include all analytical services performed in the test. This section contains useful definitions. "Genes," "mutations" and other very useful terms are described and should be reviewed.

Tier 1 Molecular Pathology Procedures (81200–81383)

These molecular pathology codes are gene-specific representing genomic procedures. This includes genetic tests for breast cancer (BRCA1 & BRCA2) (81211–81216) and for cystic fibrosis (81220–81224) among others.

Tier 2 Molecular Pathology Procedures (81400–81408)

These molecular pathology procedure codes report codes for procedures not listed in Tier 1 molecular pathology. These codes represent medically useful procedures generally performed less commonly than Tier 1 Molecular Pathology Procedures. These codes are very specific and are listed by level ranging from Level 1 to Level 9.

Chemistry (82000–84999)

Tests in the chemistry section detect substances in the body, including naturally occurring, therapeutic or non-therapeutic drugs, and other substances. All codes in this section describe quantitative analyses, unless otherwise specified. If a quantitative test for a therapeutic drug is performed and not listed here, it may be found in the Therapeutic Drug Assays subsection. The alphabetic index to CPT® can be helpful in locating the correct code if you know what the test is called.

Also included in this section are the molecular diagnostic codes, also known as nucleic acid or genetic tests. These codes describe the various steps in preparing a specimen for genetic analysis. The professional component of these services (eg, interpretation and report) is reported with 83912.

The tests in this section are performed on any body fluids or tissues. If the same test is performed on more than one type of specimen, each specimen is billed separately. Codes in this section describe tests for specific substances by any method. If no code describes the substance for which the test is being performed, four codes exist for description of tests by method. Use 82491–82492 to describe testing by column chromatography (82491 for one analyte at a time and 82492 for multiple analytes at the same time), and 82541–82544 to describe quantitative and qualitative testing by mass spectrometry.

Hematology and Coagulation (85002–85999)

The Hematology and Coagulation section includes complete blood counts (CBCs) (85025–85027) and other counts of blood components. This section does not include blood bank services, which are found in the Immunology section (86077–86079).

Testing Technique
"H and H" on a medical report stands for "hematocrit and hemoglobin." You'll find these at codes 85014 and 85018 in your codebook, along with appropriate abbreviations in parentheses. Make a note; these are VERY common.

Immunology (86000–86849)

Codes in this section identify and quantify antigens, antibodies, and allergens. Antigens may be viruses, bacteria, or other immune triggers the body fights off by creating antibodies. Antibodies are elements the human body creates to deal with antigens. Sometimes, antibodies are created in response to inflammatory changes or other stimuli in the body. Antibodies can be formed to parts of our bodies, called autoantibodies. An example of this is lupus. Allergens are substances causing a histamine response in the body. Identifying and quantifying these elements can tell a physician which disease a patient has, whether someone has been exposed to a disease, has an active immunity, or has other immune issues to be treated.

Most codes in this section are qualitative or semi-quantitative and describe multistep processes. Each substance should be coded as precisely as possible. If there is no code to describe the level of precision identified (eg, the specific class), the more generic code may be used multiple times to describe each separate substance tested.

Blood Banking and Tissue Typing (86077–86079, 86805–86849)

Codes to describe blood banking (86077–86079) and tissue typing (86805–86822) services are found in Immunology. Blood banking services deal specifically with transfusion reactions. Tissue typing studies consider immunologic factors making a specimen appropriate for transplant or not for a transplant candidate.

Blood banking services need not take place in a blood bank. Codes describe specific services, not specific locations. They may be coded any time the described services are performed.

Transfusion Medicine (86850–86999)

The codes in the Transfusion Medicine subsection describe services related to blood typing, screening, preparation, and storage. These codes also can be used to describe the same work when transfusion isn't involved. For example, Rh (D) screening (86901) typically is performed during pregnancy to be sure there will be no Rh incompatibility, although no transfusion is planned. ABO blood typing (86900), identifying whether the individual has type A, B, AB, or O blood, is performed before surgery, even if there is no expectation that blood will be needed during the procedure.

Microbiology (87001–87999)

The Microbiology subsection includes bacteriology (the identification and study of bacteria), mycology (the identification and study of fungi), parasitology (the identification and study of parasites), and virology (the identification and study of viruses).

Identification is performed by one of two methods: presumptive or definitive. Presumptive identification is performed by identifying the characteristics of the microorganism. In other words, the tester looks at growth patterns, color, success in culturing the specimen in certain media, etc. Definitive identification requires other methods identifying the genus and species of the microorganism, and may require DNA analysis (coded separately).

Codes are specific to the source material for the study. Starting with code 87260, the source material must be primary only. In other words, the source is the individual's blood or other tissue for direct examination. Secondary sources, including materials grown on media, are not coded with these codes.

The infectious agent is coded as specifically as possible. Testing of unidentified infectious agents or agents without a specific code may be coded by testing technique using 87300–87301. This section also includes codes for the work of identifying drugs to which the organism may be susceptible or resistant.

Although most of the codes in this section require special equipment and expertise, a few codes describe services performed routinely in a physician office. Most common is the Rapid Strep Test, or RADT. This is a reagent strip test for group A Streptococcus and commonly is performed to test for Strep throat. This is billed with 87880 and is a CLIA-waived test.

Anatomic Pathology (88000–88099)

The Anatomic Pathology subsection includes all of the postmortem pathologic examinations, or necropsies, more commonly called autopsies. Codes in this section vary based on whether the study is gross only, or gross and microscopic. There are further differentiations based on whether the central nervous system (brain and spinal cord) is included in the examination.

Additionally, 88040 is for forensic necropsy examination; 88045 is for a coroner's call. Forensic examinations are detailed exams for legal evidence. Coroner's call is for responses to crime scenes.

Cytopathology (88104–88199)

The most common cytopathologic studies are Papanicolaou (Pap) smears, which are examinations of cervical and/or vaginal cells. Pap smear results are reported by two methods: Bethesda and non-Bethesda. Under the Bethesda system, Pap test samples having no cell abnormalities are reported as "negative for intraepithelial lesion or malignancy." Samples with cell abnormalities are divided into the following categories:

- ASC—atypical squamous cells
- ASC-US—atypical squamous cells of undetermined significance.
- ASC-H—atypical squamous cells cannot exclude a high-grade squamous intraepithelial lesion
- AGC—atypical glandular cells
- AIS—endocervical adenocarcinoma *in situ*

◀ LSIL—low-grade squamous intraepithelial lesion
◀ HSIL—high-grade squamous intraepithelial lesion

Testing Technique

The Pap smear done at the physician's office is usually part of the E/M visit in the Preventive Medicine Visits subsection. It is not separately chargeable. You must read carefully the problem or the medical record to decide if you are coding for the Pap smear evaluation, or collection of the specimen.

Similar studies can also be performed on aspirated fluids or cells obtained by washings or brushings.

Flow cytometry (88182–88189), or FCM, is a technique for counting and examining microscopic particles, such as cells and chromosomes, by suspending them in a stream of fluid and passing them by an electronic detection apparatus. Flow cytometry is used routinely in the diagnosis of health disorders, especially blood cancers, but has many applications.

Cytogenetic Studies (88230–88299)

Cytogenetics includes routine analysis of G-Banded chromosomes, other cytogenetic banding techniques, as well as molecular cytogenetics, such as fluorescent *in situ* hybridization (FISH) and comparative genomic hybridization (CGH). Also in this section are codes for storage and thawing of materials for cytogenic analysis.

Surgical Pathology (88300–88399)

Basic surgical pathology services include accession, examination, and reporting. Documentation of all three components is required to bill the service. Code 88300 is used when only gross examination is needed; all other codes require both gross and microscopic examination. The type of specimen, including how the specimen was obtained, determines the code to be selected. For example, a colon biopsy is assigned to Level IV (88305); a colon segmental resection for a condition other than a tumor is assigned to a Level V (88307); and a colon segmental resection for tumor is assigned to a Level VI (88309).

This section includes codes for special treatment of specimens including special stains and decalcification of specimens.

Intraoperative consultations (88329–88334) are performed during operative sessions.

Two surgical pathology codes are described for the appendix: 88302 *Level II surgical pathology, gross and microscopic examination*; includes Appendix, incidental, (the appendix is being removed during the same operative session of another procedure) and 88304 *Level III surgical pathology, gross and microscopic examination*; includes Appendix, other than incidental (the appendix is the only surgery being performed).

In Vivo Laboratory Procedures (88720–88749)

This subsection of Pathology and Laboratory includes four codes for transcutaneous analysis of blood components.

Other Procedures (89049–89240)

This subsection includes codes for miscellaneous procedures, including analysis of substances found in other body fluids and tissues. A number of tests are specific for conditions and diseases.

Reproductive Medicine Procedures (89250–89398)

All services in the Reproductive Medicine Procedures subsection are related to *in vitro* fertilization and storage of various reproductive tissues. The codes can be used alone to describe a single step in the process, or can be used in combination, when appropriate.

HCPCS Level II Coding

HCPCS Level II codes beginning with P are specifically for pathology services. (P2028–P9615). They are not often used because most pathology and laboratory services are coded from CPT®.

◀ Chemistry and Toxicology Tests (P2028–P2038)
◀ Pathology Screening Tests (P3000–P3001)

◖ Microbiology Tests (P7001)

◖ Miscellaneous Pathology and Lab Tests (P9010–P9615)

Modifiers

CPT® modifier 26 indicates the professional component of the service was performed. The professional component is the interpretation of results with a written report of the interpretation. Quite a few services in the Pathology and Laboratory section of CPT® do not have a professional component because the ordering physician receives the results and makes his or her own interpretation, combined with his or her clinical findings. To bill the professional component of a service, a physician must write an interpretive report based on the test results.

HCPCS Level II modifier TC indicates the technical component of the service was performed. The technical component of any test includes the work of preparing and running the test, as well as the equipment and supplies involved. It also includes the time and skill of the individual who performed the test. When a test is performed in a hospital or other facility setting, the reimbursement for the technical component of the service belongs to the facility. If a physician's office performed only the testing, but sent the results for interpretation, the test code could be billed with modifier TC.

When both the professional and technical components of a test are performed by the same provider (eg, a global service), a modifier is not needed. For instance, if the service is performed in a physician's office and a report is written with the interpretation of the results, the code is billed without a modifier.

Four other modifiers apply specifically to Pathology and Laboratory codes:

◖ Modifier 90 is used when an office or facility is billing for a test performed at an outside reference laboratory. This can be done only when the reference lab has billed the facility for the testing and the facility or physician office then bills the insurer for the test. There are many payer-specific rules about billing for a reference lab; coders need to know the rules for each specific payer.

◖ Modifier 91 is used to indicate a repeat diagnostic test was needed. It is similar to modifiers 76 and 77, but does not specify a provider. This is appropriate for tests not having a separate professional component. This modifier is used when medical necessity dictates another test is needed. If a test is repeated because of an error, or because the specimen was insufficient, this is not a separately billable service.

◖ Modifier 92 describes testing using special single-use transportable equipment. This equipment often is used when tests are performed in other patient locations, but use of the modifier is not limited to other locations. It may be used any time the equipment is used. Modifier 92 is added to the code describing the basic test.

◖ Modifier QW is used when the service provided is a CLIA waived test. The modifier is required for Medicare claims. Third-party payers also may require QW; check with your individual payer.

Glossary

Autopsy—Examination of a dead body to determine the cause(s) of death (also called necropsy).

Bacteriology—Study of bacteria.

Cytopathology—Study of the cellular changes in disease.

Cytogenetics—Study of genes to determine whether disease has inherited components and also to identify the specific genetic components of certain disease processes so they can be better treated.

Clinical Laboratory—Place where tests are performed on clinical specimens in order to get information about the health of a patient as pertaining to the diagnosis, treatment, and prevention of disease.

Clinical Laboratory Improvement Amendments (CLIA)—Quality standards for all laboratory testing to ensure the accuracy, reliability and timeliness of patient test results, CLIA waived tests—simple tests that may be performed in non-laboratory settings.

Definitive Identification—Identification of the genus and species of the microorganism.

Forensics—Studies used or applied in the investigation and establishment of facts or evidence in a court of law.

Gross—Examination of the entire specimen without sectioning of the specimen into thin slides to be examined without the use of a microscope.

Hematology—Study of the components and behavior of blood.

Immunology—Study of the immune system and its components and function.

In Vivo—Studies performed within the living body.

Microbiology—Study of microscopic life.

Microscopy (microscopic)—Examination under a microscope.

Molecular Diagnostics—Measurement of DNA, RNA, proteins or metabolites to detect genotypes, mutations or biochemical changes.

Necropsy—Examination of a dead body to determine cause(s) of death (also called autopsy).

Panel—A group of tests performed together and listed in the code description.

Pathology—Study of diseased tissue and cells.

Presumptive Identification—Identification of a microorganism based on the growth patterns, color, and success in culturing the specimen in certain media, etc.

Mycology—Study of fungi.

Parasitology—Study of parasites.

Qualitative—Test determining the presence or absence of a drug.

Quantitative—Test identifying not only presence of a drug, but the exact amount present.

Semi-quantitative—Test identifying the amount of an analyte within a specified range but does not identify a specific quantity.

Virology—Study of viruses.

Chapter Review Questions

1. **What is the study of disease changes within cells or cell types?**

    A. Cytogenetic studies

    B. Cytopathology

    C. Molecular diagnostics

    D. Cellular composition

2. **Which statement is true regarding coding of surgical pathology specimens?**

    A. Two specimens requiring individual examination and pathologic diagnosis are coded separately.

    B. Two specimens from the same patient cannot be coded separately.

    C. Two specimens from the same organ in a patient should always be coded as one specimen.

    D. Regardless of the location, all specimens from one patient should be coded as one specimen.

3. A 30-year-old female is coming in for a routine gynecological exam. A Pap smear is taken from the cervix and the screening is done by an automated system under physician supervision. What lab code should the physician report?

    A. 88164

    B. 88174

    C. 88147

    D. 88148

4. A 32-year-old patient with a history of illegal drug use arrives at the ER in a coma. The treating physician orders a multiple class drug screen using chromatographic method to detect the presence of drugs. The report comes back positive for opiates. The physician orders a confirmatory test using high performance liquid chromatography (not quantitative). Select the correct CPT® code(s) for the laboratory testing.

    A. 80102 x 2 units

    B. 83925

    C. 80101, 83935

    D. 80100, 80102

5. A physician performs surgical removal of two skin lesions: one being a pigmented nodule measuring 2 cm x 2.5 cm on the left, upper back; the second lesion, an inclusion cyst measuring 2.5 cm x 3 cm in the middle of the back. Both specimens are placed in individual containers and sent to surgical pathology for gross and microscopic examination. Select the correct CPT® code(s) for this service.

    A. 88304 x 2

    B. 88305 x 2

    C. 88304, 88305

    D. 88304 x 2, 88329

6. Dr. Mitchell orders a fibrin degradation test to evaluate for possible DVT. The correct laboratory code is:

    A. 85362

    B. 85378

    C. 85379

    D. 85380

7. An established patient comes in complaining of nausea and vomiting and states she has not had a menstrual period in over a month. A complete CBC and automated differential WBC is ordered. The doctor also orders: Hepatitis B antigen, Rubella, RPR, Antibody Screen, Blood Typing for Rh and ABO, and a urine pregnancy test. Select the correct CPT® code(s) for the laboratory testing.

   A. 80055

   B. 85004, 87340, 86762, 86592, 86850, 86900, 86901, 81025

   C. 80055, 81025

   D. 85025, 87340, 86762, 86592, 86850, 86900, 86901

8. An embryologist is performing a conventional in vitro insemination of oocytes and assisting in the fertilization of four oocytes under microtechnique for an infertile couple using ART. The services of the embryologist are coded as:

   A. 89268, 89280

   B. 58321, 89251

   C. 58322, 89281

   D. 89260, 89280

9. Lab Report #1:

   Surgical Pathology Report Collected: 4/14/2010 **Received:** 4/14/2010

   Clinical Data: Gastric bypass; ventral hernia repair; history of recurrent ventral hernia with mesh

   Gross Description:
   A) Received fresh in a container labeled "skin ulcer" is an 8.0 x 6.0 x 2.0 cm skin ellipse with a centrally-located 5.0 x 1.4 cm ulcer, with multiple blue stitches. The margins of resection are inked black. The specimen is serially sectioned and representative sections are submitted in two cassettes.

   B) Received fresh in a container labeled "old hernia mesh" are two fragments of tan-brown soft tissue and mesh, measuring 10.0 x 6.0 cm and 6.0 x 3.5 cm. The specimen is serially sectioned and representative sections are submitted in one cassette.

   Final Diagnosis:
   A) Skin ulcer, excision: Skin and underlying soft tissues with ulcer, granulation tissue, and chronic active/suppurative inflammation and focal foreign body reaction. No evidence of neoplasm.

   B) Old hernia mesh, excision: Fibrofatty tissue with no evidence of neoplasm.

   What are the CPT® and ICD-9-CM codes for this service?

10. **Lab Report #2:**

R/O MRSA—Central line catheter

Clinical Indications: Patient with fever not responsive to antibiotics		
Collected: 03/30/xx 17:45	Accession Num: TXXXXX	Status: **Authenticated**

Method: Single nucleic acid sequence

Culture:	Methicillin Resistant Staphylococcus Aureus isolated

What are the CPT® and ICD-9-CM codes for this service?

Chapter 17

Evaluation and Management

Introduction and Objectives

Evaluation and management (E/M) services are placed prominently at the front of the CPT® codebook. For many providers, these services represent the bulk of codes reported. Across all medical specialties, correct, consistent E/M service reporting is elemental, but may be achieved only by applying a methodical approach to documentation and code selection.

Specific objectives for this chapter include:

◖ Define E/M services

◖ Summarize CPT® E/M service guidelines

◖ Review common terms (new patient, established patient, transfer of care, etc.)

◖ Explain the key components of history, exam, and medical decision making (MDM), and the factors that comprise each of these

◖ Differentiate between the E/M service categories (office visits, hospital visits, consultations, etc.)

◖ Provide guidance and tools to select an appropriate E/M service level, as determined by the key components

◖ Discuss the importance of time, and how it may factor into E/M service leveling

◖ Alert you to important differences between CPT® and CMS treatment of E/M services

◖ Establish the importance of ICD-9-CM code assignment to support E/M services

◖ Increase your understanding through examples, to demonstrate the above concepts

E/M Services Defined

E/M codes (99201–99499) describe providers' services, including evaluating patient's condition(s) and determining the management of care required to treat that patient. Services based solely on time, such as physician

standby services, also may be defined as E/M services (these will be discussed in detail later in the chapter).

For example, a patient may visit the family physician's office, complaining of sore throat, fever, and body aches lasting over a week. Or, a patient may arrive at the emergency department (ED) with chest pain and shortness of breath. When properly applied, E/M service codes represent the physician's work in evaluating and treating those patients. E/M services may be provided at different "levels," from relatively simple to very complex. Several factors—such as severity of the patient's problem, difficulty of determining a diagnosis, and the number of possible treatment options—play a role in determining the overall level of service. How to select an appropriate E/M service level based on provider documentation will occupy the majority of this chapter.

E/M codes are divided into broad categories representing the type and/or location of service—such as office visits, ED visits, or nursing facility care, etc. Some categories, such as neonatal intensive care, may apply only to patients of a specific age. Categories may be divided further into subcategories to indicate specific details reflecting patient status (for instance, new vs. established patient). We will discuss the categories of E/M service below.

Levels of E/M codes in each category are often referred to as level I, level II, level III, etc., depending on the last number of the code referred to in that category.

Example

New Patient Office or Other Outpatient Visits:

99201 Office visit, new patient: *level I*

99202 Office visit, new patient: *level II*

99203 Office visit, new patient: *level III*

Diagnostic or therapeutic procedures (for instance, taking a throat culture, taking a chest X-ray, or performing emergency surgery to stabilize a trauma patient) are not included as part of the E/M service, and may be reported separately.

In contrast, many diagnostic and therapeutic procedures include an inherent E/M component. Generally, if a diagnostic or therapeutic procedure is performed or ordered as the result of a same-day E/M service, the diagnostic or therapeutic procedure and E/M service may be reported separately. If the diagnostic or therapeutic procedure was scheduled at a previous encounter, an E/M service may *not* be reported separately unless the patient has a new problem, or a significant exacerbation of the current condition requiring the provider to perform a separate E/M service. This concept will be explored in detail when discussing application of modifier 25 *Significant, separately identifiable evaluation and management service by the same physician on the same day of the procedure or other service.*

CPT® E/M Services Guidelines

CPT® provides extensive instruction for E/M service reporting in the E/M Services Guidelines that precede the E/M code listings. Additional instruction for applying specific E/M service codes will be found throughout the CPT® E/M section—in subsection headings, parenthetical notes, and within code descriptors. All coders and providers should read these guidelines and instruction carefully, and review them regularly.

Rather than treat the E/M service guidelines and other CPT® instruction separately, we will introduce individual concepts and terminology as they become relevant throughout our discussion of E/M services.

New vs. Established Patient

Many E/M service categories differentiate between "new" and "established" patients. Presumably, the work of evaluating a patient is less if the provider has seen the patient previously, whereas the work required is greater if the provider is seeing a patient for the first time (for instance, initially gathering and assessing the patient's past medical history).

A patient is new if he or she has not received any *face-to-face* professional services from the physician, or a physician of the exact same specialty/subspecialty within the group practice, within the last three years (36 months). This is the so-called "three-year rule." If a patient is seen by another member of the group within the past three years, but that physician is of a different specialty/subspecialty, the patient may still be new. For example, a patient sees an orthopedist in a group practice to be evaluated for possible hip replacement. The same patient has seen an internist in the same group practice several times over the past three years. The patient is "new" to the orthopedist, but "established" for the internist.

Where the patient is seen is not a factor in determining new vs. established. For example, Mrs. Jones' general practitioner, Dr. Smith, joins a new group practice across town. As long as Dr. Smith has seen Ms. Jones within the past three years, she is an established patient at the new location. Likewise, if a physician has provided services face-to-face with a patient in the hospital, and sees the same patient in his or her office within three years, the patient is established.

Key Components of an E/M Service

There are seven components that make up an E/M service: history, exam, medical decision making (MDM), counseling, coordination of care, nature of presenting problem, and time. Three of these components—history, exam, and MDM—are considered key components to determining the overall level of an E/M service. Under some circumstances, time will be the deciding factor in determining the E/M service level.

Using his or her best clinical judgment, experience, and training, the provider determines the extent of the history (and other key components) based on medical necessity. For instance, the physician could spend one hour documenting an exhaustive medical history for a patient with a splinter in her finger, but this would not be necessary or appropriate to the circumstances. Likewise, if a new patient presents with a wide variety of health problems, such as hypertension, diabetes, and symptoms of stroke, such as slurred speech, a quick five-minute history would not suffice.

Serious problems may arise when the provider documents a history and/or exam at a level not supported by medical necessity. The *Medicare Claims Processing Manual* (chapter 12-30.6.1.A) states, "It would not be medically necessary or appropriate to bill a higher level of evaluation and management service when a lower level of service is warranted. *The volume of documentation should not be the primary influence upon which a specific level of service is billed"* [emphasis added].

Medical necessity is supported, in part, by ICD-9-CM code assignment.

In some cases, to report a given level of service, you must meet all three key components. In other cases, the code descriptor may allow you to report a given level of service by meeting two of the three key components at the specified level. For example, the code descriptor for a level II established patient, outpatient visit specifies that to report the service, at least two of three key components—a problem focused history, a problem focused examination, and straightforward MDM—must be documented.

Testing Technique

In the description of the majority of E/M codes, the number of key components is specified. For example:

99201 Office or other outpatient visit for the evaluation and management of a new patient, *which requires these 3 key components*:

- A problem focused history;
- A problem focused examination;
- Straightforward medical decision making.

99213 Office or other outpatient visit for the evaluation and management of an established patient, *which requires at least 2 of these 3 key components*:

- An expanded problem focused history;
- An expanded problem focused examination;
- Medical decision making of low complexity

Highlight or underline the components required for each code.

We will explain in detail how to distinguish among the various levels of history, exam, and MDM when reviewing provider documentation. For now, a basic understanding of the key components and how they factor into E/M level selection will allow you to appreciate better the review of E/M service categories that follows.

E/M Service Categories

When selecting an E/M service code, the first step is to determine the appropriate E/M category for the service provided. What follows is an overview of the available E/M categories, along with basic coding instruction.

Office or Other Outpatient Services

Office or Other Outpatient Services is divided into subcategories for new and established patients. This category represents visits performed in the physician's office, outpatient hospital, or other ambulatory facility, such as an urgent care center or nursing home.

Hospital Observation Services

When a patient has a condition that needs to be monitored to determine a course of action, he may be admitted to "observation status." For example, a patient presents to the emergency department (ED) with a concussion. In this case, the provider can admit the patient to observation status. After a period of monitoring, the patient may be discharged, or—if the condition worsens—may be admitted to the hospital as an inpatient for additional treatment.

The patient is not required to be in a specific area of the hospital to be deemed in "observation status." There is no distinction between a new or established patient for observations services. When the patient is seen at another site of service (eg, ED), and observation status is initiated at that site of service, all E/M services provided by the admitting physician are considered part of the initial observation care and not reported separately.

Hospital Observation Services includes three types of service: observation care discharge services, observation care, and subsequent observation care.

Initial Observation Care codes are reported only by the physician admitting the patient to observation status. Initial Observation Care codes require three of three key components be met to report the chosen level of service.

Subsequent Observation Care codes are used when the patient is seen on a day other than the date of admission or discharge.

Observation Care Discharge Services are used to report the final exam and discharge of the patient. Typically, a patient is admitted to observation care for less than 24 hours; however, a patient can remain in observation care for up to three days.

The initial observation care and the observation care discharge should be reported separately only if they occur on separate dates of services.

Example

A patient arrives at the hospital and is admitted to observation status at 9:30 p.m., Oct. 1. The patient is discharged from observation status and sent home at 8:30 a.m., Oct. 2. In this case, a code from Initial Observation Care would be reported for Oct. 1, and the observation care discharge services would be reported for Oct. 2.

If the patient is admitted to observation status, and discharged on the same date of service, a code from the Observation or Inpatient Care Services (including Admission and Discharge Services), range 99234–99236, would be reported.

When a patient is admitted to the hospital during an observation stay, the observation services should not be reported separately. The observation services provided on the same date as a hospital admission should be included as part of the admission. An observation discharge should not be reported on the same date as the hospital admission.

Hospital Inpatient Services

Hospital Inpatient Services are subcategorized by Initial Hospital Care and Subsequent Hospital Care.

Initial hospital care should be reported only by the admitting physician, according to CPT® guidelines. Medicare allows the use of Initial Hospital Care codes in place of Inpatient Consultation codes.

Any services performed on the same date of service, when related to the admission, should be included in the Initial Hospital Care code and not reported separately. This includes office visits, observation visits, and nursing facility visits if provided by the same provider on the same date of service. Initial hospital care requires that three of three key components be met to report the chosen level of service.

Subsequent Hospital Care codes are used to report the subsequent visits to the patient, while the patient is in the hospital. These codes include the provider reviewing the medical record, diagnostic test results, and changes in the patient's status since the last physician assessment. Subsequent Hospital Care codes require that two of the three key components be met.

Observation or Inpatient Care Services (including Admission and Discharge Services) codes should be used to report an admission and discharge on the same date of service.

Hospital Discharge Services codes report the total time the physician spent on the date of discharge. Discharge services include the final examination, a discussion of the stay, continuing care instructions, discharge paperwork, prescriptions, and referral forms. This service is reported by the amount of time spent by the physician on the date of discharge, even if the time is not continuous. Visits to the patient on the date of discharge by physicians who are not the attending physician should be reported using Subsequent Hospital Care codes (99231–99233).

Consultations

Consultation codes are divided into two subcategories based on the location of the consult: Office or Other Outpatient Consultations and Inpatient Consultations. All consultation services must meet all three key components.

According to CPT®, a consultation has the following components:

- A physician (or other appropriate source) requests another physician (or appropriate source) to evaluate a patient's specific problem or condition and render an opinion. The request can be written or verbal; if verbal, the request must be documented in the patient's medical record.
- The opinion or advice of the consultant can result in giving requesting physician recommendations for the patient's condition, or in the consultant providing ongoing management of the patient's condition.
- The consultant's written report back to the requesting physician (or other appropriate source).

A consultation differs from a referral. A referral occurs when a patient is sent to another physician for care of a specific problem or condition. The requesting physician is not expecting to receive recommendations back from the referring physician.

Example

Consultation: A patient's family physician requests the patient to see a cardiologist to evaluate a heart murmur found during examination and give recommendations for the patient's care.

Referral: A patient's family physician refers the patient to see a cardiologist to treat a heart murmur found during examination.

If another physician requests an opinion or advice on the same condition, or a new condition, for the same patient in the outpatient setting, the consulting provider can again report a consultation code. If an additional consultation is requested in the inpatient setting, the consulting provider reports a subsequent hospital care code. According to CPT® guidelines, only an inpatient consultation can be reported by a provider during the admission.

When transfer of care has been established, the provider accepting the patient's care bills subsequent visits with the appropriate established patient visit codes based on the location; Office or Other Outpatient Established Patient Visit (99211–99215), Domiciliary or Rest Home (99334–99337), Home Visit (99347–99350), Subsequent Hospital Care Services (99231–99233), or Subsequent Nursing Facility (99307–99310).

Consultations requested by a patient or family member should be reported using the appropriate codes from categories other than consultation; Office or Other Outpatient Visits, Home Service, or Domiciliary or Rest Home. When a consultation is mandated by a third-party payer, or by government, legislative, or regulatory requirement, append modifier 32 Mandated services to the consultation code.

Reporting Consultations for Medicare

As is true with all services, payers may have their own policy regarding the use of consultation codes. Medicare no longer pays for consultation codes (except telehealth consultations), and has provided guidelines on how consultation codes should be reported.

Medicare requires consultations services be billed with the most appropriate (non-consultation) E/M code for that service. Outpatient consultations should be reported by selecting the appropriate level code from the Office or Other Outpatient Services (99201–99215). Report inpatient consultations using an Initial Hospital Care code (99221–99223) for the initial evaluation and a Subsequent Hospital Care code (99231–99233) for the subsequent visits. The physician who admitted the patient as a hospital inpatient (whether that physician is the "consultant" or another physician), should append modifier AI *Principal physician of record* to indicate that he or she is the admitting physician, and to distinguish that physician from others who may provide inpatient services.

Other payers may allow you to continue reporting consultation codes. Check with individual payers for guidelines.

Emergency Department Services

An emergency department (ED) is a section of a hospital organized and designated to treat unscheduled patient visits for immediate medical attention. Emergency departments must be open 24 hours a day, seven days a week. A patient may receive critical care treatment in an emergency department. Report critical care codes when this happens.

Another service found in this category is the physician direction of emergency medical systems (EMS) emergency care, advanced life support (99288). This code reports the services of a physician, located in a facility's emergency department or critical care department, who is in two-way communication with emergency services personnel. The physician directs the personal in performing life-saving procedures.

Critical Care Services

Critical Care Services codes are used to report the direct delivery, by a physician, of medical care to a critically injured or critically ill patient. According to CPT®, "a critical illness or injury acutely impairs one or more vital organ systems, such that there is a high probability of imminent or life-threatening deterioration in the patient's condition."

Critical care is a condition, not a location. A patient does not have to be in an intensive care unit (ICU) or other designated area to meet the requirements of critical care; nor do all patients in an ICU or other designated unit automatically qualify for critical care. Only patients who meet the definition of critically ill or critically injured may qualify for critical care.

Critical care bundles a number of services, such as cardiac output measurements (93561, 93562), that typically may be required for critically ill or critically injured patients. A complete list of services bundled with critical care may be found in the critical care portion of the CPT® codebook.

Testing Technique

To identify included services in critical care codes easily, bracket or highlight the paragraph listing those services in your CPT® codebook. Locate each code included in the critical care codes, and write "included in critical care" next to it.

Critical Care Services codes are reported based on time. The time includes all of the time the physician spent devoted to, and directly available to, that patient. The physician cannot work on any other patient during this time; however, the time is not required to be continuous and the physician is not required to be in the same room as the patient. The physician can only report time spent on the same unit or floor as the patient. All time spent on managing the patient's condition while on the same floor or unit as the patient is totaled throughout the day and reported with 99291 and 99292. When the time is less than 30 minutes, critical care codes are not reported. When the total time is between 30 and 74 minutes, report code 99291. Each additional 30 minutes, or part thereof, is reported with a unit of 99292.

Example

Physician provides 125 minutes of critical care to a patient. These services would be reported as 99291, 99292 x 2:

99291 for the first 74 minutes;

99292 for the next 30 minutes (minutes 75–104); and

99292 for the remaining 21 minutes.

Testing Technique

Use the Critical Care Time Table in the CPT® codebook to calculate critical care time.

For younger patients, specific code ranges may apply when reporting critical care:

- **Neonates (28 days of age or younger)**—Inpatient critical care services are reported with neonatal critical care codes 99468 and 99469.

- **Infants 29 days through 71 months (5 years, 11 months) of age**—Inpatient critical care services are reported with pediatric critical care codes 99471–99476.

- **Neonates and infants up through 71 months (5 years, 11 months) of age**—Outpatient critical care services are reported with critical codes 99291 and 99292.

Testing Technique

Find the above guidelines in the Critical Care Services section and highlight them for easy reference.

Nursing Facility Services

Nursing Facility Services are subcategorized into Initial Nursing Facility Care, Subsequent Nursing Facility Care, Nursing Facility Discharge Services, and Other Nursing Facility Services. E/M services provided to patients in a nursing facility or a psychiatric residential treatment services are reported using codes from this category.

For Medicare, the initial visit can be reported by more than one physician, but the physician of record for an admission to the nursing home should append modifier AI to indicate he or she is the primary physician of record.

Nursing facility discharge codes report the services provided by a physician to discharge the patient. The codes are reported by time, which includes all time spent on the patient for the date of discharge.

The final code in this section is for an annual nursing facility assessment by the provider. Government regulations require nursing facilities to perform Minimum Data Set/Resident Assessment Instrument (MDS/RAI) annually. When a physician completes this information and performs the comprehensive nursing facility code, report 99318.

Domiciliary, Rest Home, or Custodial Care Services

This category includes E/M services provided to patient's residing in domiciliary, rest home, or in custodial care. Domiciliary care refers to care provided in a supervised home setting. Assisted living facilities would be considered domiciliary care. New patient visits require all three key components to be met to report the chosen service level. Established patient visits require two of three key components to be met.

Domiciliary, Rest Home, or Home Care Plan Oversight (CPO) Services

Care plan oversight indicates oversight of the services provided to patients in certain locations. Oversight of patients in a domiciliary, a rest home, or in the patient's own home is reported with codes from this category, based on the physician time.

Home Services

E/M services provided to a patient in a private residence are reported from this category. The codes distinguish between new and established patients. New patient services require all three key components to be met to report the chosen service level; established patient services require two of three key components.

Prolonged Services

Codes in this category are subcategorized based on whether the physician has direct (face-to-face) contact with the patient, and are reported based on location and time.

Prolonged services with direct patient contact are add-on codes that should be reported in addition to one of the designated E/M codes listed in the parenthetical instructions after each code.

Prolonged services without direct patient contact are used to report services for time spent on the patient without direct face-to-face patient contact.

Prolonged services are reported in addition to a primary E/M service. Prolonged services without direct patient contact may be billed on a different date than the primary service. There is a requirement that the service be related to a prior face-to-face service. Prolonged

Services codes should be reported only in addition to other E/M codes having time stated in the description. As an example, the descriptor for level V established patient outpatient service 99215 specifies, "Physicians typically spend 40 minutes face-to-face with the patient and/or family." By contrast, observation services (99234–99236) do not include a stated time component; therefore, prolonged services may not be reported in addition to observation services.

Prolonged services may not be reported for services of fewer than 30 minutes.

Occasionally, a request is made for a physician to be available to perform a procedure. For example, when there is a delivery involving risk to a neonate, the obstetrics/gynecologist (OB/GYN) delivering the neonate may request for a pediatrician to "stand by" in case a surgical procedure is necessary. Standby services must be at least 30 minutes to be reported and cannot be reported if the standby results in performing a procedure with a global package. To report standby services, you would use the standby services code 99360.

Case Management Services

The Case Management Services category includes Anticoagulant Management and Medical Team Conference.

Anticoagulation management codes are used to report this oversight, which includes ordering, review, and interpretation of the international normalized ratio (INR) testing, communication with the patient, and dosage adjustments, as necessary. The initial management must include at least 60 days of therapy and include a minimum of eight reported INR measurements. Each subsequent 90 days of therapy, including at least three INR measurements, may be reported using 99364.

Medical Team Conference codes report meeting or conference time (face-to-face) of at least three qualified health care professionals, with or without the presence of the patient or patient's family member. The health care professionals should be of different specialties, and all should be involved directly in the patient's care. The code is selected based on whether the patient or patient's family is present. If the patient or patient's family is not present, the code is selected based on the type of provider (physician or nonphysician qualified health care professional).

Care Plan Oversight Services

When the care of a patient involves complex and multi-disciplinary care modalities, physician supervision is required to monitor the patient's progress and adjust the care plan, as necessary. These services are reported with the codes from the Care Plan Oversight Services category. The codes are selected based on the location of the patient, and the amount of time spent within a 30-day period to oversee the patient's care.

Preventive Medicine Services

Preventive Medicine Services, also referred to as "well visits," describe E/M services provided to a patient without a sign, symptom, condition, or illness. The comprehensive exam as described here is an age-appropriate examination of the patient, and not the same as the comprehensive exam referred to in other E/M code categories. The preventive medicine codes are determined based on the age of the patient, and whether the patient is new or established.

During preventive medicine exams, a provider may discover an abnormality, or address a condition already in existence. If the abnormality or condition requires the provider to perform a significant amount of work, above normally is performed for a preventive service, the additional work can be reported with a separate E/M service code. The additional E/M code is reported with modifier 25 appended. When determining whether a problem required a significant amount of work, separate the documentation into two distinct separate notes, one to support each service.

The reporting and payment of preventive services and additional E/M codes will depend largely on payer policy. Effective Jan. 1, 2011, Medicare pays for preventive medicine visits. Many commercial policies do not include preventive visits as a benefit.

The Preventive Medicine Services category includes the subcategories Counseling Risk Factor Reduction and Behavior Change Intervention services.

Preventive Medicine, Individual Counseling codes are for services provided to patients to prevent a risky behavior from developing or to prevent injury from happening. The counseling occurs to address issues such as drug abuse, family problems, diet and exercise, etc. These services may not be reported in addition to preventive medicine visits (99381–99397). Codes selection is based on the face-to-face time spent with the patient, and according to whether the counseling is provided to an individual or in a group setting.

Behavior Change Interventions, individual services are provided to patients who have already developed the risky behavior. Smoking cessation (quitting smoking) counseling, and alcohol and substance abuse counseling, are found in the behavior change intervention codes. The codes are selected based on the substance and the amount of time spent with the patient.

Non-Face-to-Face Physician Services

Non-Face-to-Face Physician Services are becoming increasingly popular with the advancement of technology. Services include Telephone Services and Online Medical Evaluations. Not all telephone encounters or online correspondence may be reported using these codes. Telephone services resulting in a visit to the physician within the next 24 hours, or next available urgent appointment, are considered part of that service and are not reported separately. To bill for a telephone service not resulting in a visit, the call must be initiated by an established patient, or established patient's guardian. If the physician calls the patient within seven days of an E/M for something related to that E/M visit, the call is not reported separately.

Online Medical Evaluation codes have similar guidelines. Online evaluations must be permanently stored. Online communications with the patient involving E/M services provided by the physician within seven days prior to the communication are reported separately.

Special Evaluation and Management Services

Obtaining basic life or disability insurance requires a medical evaluation, and that a physician complete some forms on the patient's behalf. In the Basic Life and/or Disability Evaluation Services subcategory, codes exist to report these services. The code is selected based on the type of benefit being sought (basic life or disability).

Newborn Care Services

After the delivery of a newborn, the newborn is evaluated by a pediatrician or other qualified practitioner. Codes in this category are reported based on the location of the delivery and episode of care (initial or subsequent).

Additional critical services may be provided to the newborn immediately after delivery. These services include attendance at the delivery and stabilization of the newborn (99464) and the resuscitation, provision of positive pressure ventilation, and/or chest compressions (99465).

Inpatient Neonatal Intensive Care Services and Pediatric Neonatal Critical Care Services

CPT® includes two age-specific (24 months of age or less) codes for pediatric critical care patient transport (99466, 99467). These services require direct, face-to-face physician care. Physician direction of emergency care using two-way communication does not qualify as pediatric critical care transport, and should be reported 99288 *Physician direction of emergency medical systems (EMS) emergency care, advanced life support.*

Codes 99466 and 99467 are time-dependent. Reporting time begins when the physician assumes primary responsibility of the patient at the referring facility, and ends when the receiving facility accepts responsibility for the patient, according to CPT® guidelines.

Pediatric critical care codes apply only for direct, physician-delivered care to the critically ill or critically injured patient, age 28 days or younger (99468–99469), age 29 days up to 24 months (99471–99472), or 2–5 years of age (99475–99476). CPT® defines a critical illness or injury for all patients, regardless of age, as impairment of one or more vital organ systems, "such that there is a high probability of imminent or life threatening deterioration the patient's condition."

Pediatric critical care codes 99471–99476 include all the same services as adult critical care, plus additional services (such as ventilator management and lumbar puncture) as listed in the Inpatient Neonatal and Pediatric Critical Care services guidelines. Always check your CPT® codebook prior to coding for additional services with critical care, to be sure those additional services are separately reportable.

Only one physician may report pediatric critical care for the same patient, for any calendar day. When physicians from different groups provide same-day services at two separate facilities, the referring physician reports critical care and the receiving physician reports the admission service. If two separate physicians from different groups provide critical care on *different* days, each physician may report the appropriate pediatric critical care code for his or her respective service.

Codes 99477–99480 describe initial (99477) and subsequent (99478–99480) *intensive* care for a child. Intensive care is not the same as critical care. CPT® clarifies that children requiring intensive care are not critically ill, but require "intensive observation, frequent interventions, and other intensive care services."

The initial care code applies only to neonates, age 28 days or less. CPT® provides parenthetical notes to direct coding for services provided to children who do not meet the requirements of 99477. Subsequent care is reported per day, and depends on the infant's body weight: 1500 grams or less (99478), 1500–2500 grams (99479), or 2501–5000 grams (99480).

Other Evaluation and Management Services

The only code in this section is unlisted E/M service code 99499. This code would be reported only if no other available E/M code describes the service provided. When reporting an unlisted service or procedure code, documentation must substantiate the nature of the service. Whenever possible, avoid reporting such an unlisted code.

Choosing the E/M Service Level

As previously described, within each E/M category or subcategory, code descriptors define the specific details of the service, to include place and or type of service; content of the service provided; nature of the presenting problem; and the time generally required to provide the service.

Also as explained, most E/M services are provided at varying levels of intensity. The extent of the patient's

illness or injury will determine the amount of physician work and skill required to evaluate and treat the patient. This physician effort (when documented appropriately and supported by medical necessity) drives the E/M service level.

To review, the example below represents the basic format of an E/M service category.

Example

Office or Other Outpatient Services *(category)*

New Patient *(subcategory)*

99201 *Office or other outpatient visit for the evaluation and management of a new patient, which requires these 3 key components*:

- o A problem focused history
- o A problem focused examination
- o Straightforward medical decision-making

Counseling and/or coordination of care with other providers or agencies are provided consistent with the nature of the problem(s) and the patient's and/or family's needs.

Usually, the presenting problem(s) are self limited or minor. Physicians typically spend 10 minutes face-to-face with the patient and/or family.

The Evaluation and Management (E/M) Services Guidelines in your CPT® codebook outlines six steps to determine the level of an E/M service:

1. Select the category or subcategory of service and review the guidelines.

2. Review the level of E/M service descriptors and examples.

3. Determine the level of history.

4. Determine the level of exam.

5. Determine the level of medical decision making.

6. Select the appropriate level of E/M service.

So far, we have covered steps 1 and 2. Before moving on, we first must discuss essential tools required to complete steps 3 through 6: The 1995 and 1997 Documentation Guidelines for Evaluation and Management Services.

1995 and 1997 E/M Documentation Guidelines

The 1995 and 1997 Documentation Guidelines for Evaluation and Management Services (DGs) were developed to assist providers in determining the level of service provided to a patient. Both sets of guidelines can be found on the CMS website (www.cms.gov/MLNEdWeb-Guide/25_EMDOC.asp).

Either the 1995 or the 1997 guidelines can be used for any particular E/M service. The main difference between the 1995 and 1997 DGs is the leveling of the exam component. The set of guidelines that benefit the provider the most (eg, results in a higher level of code) should be used. There are instances when the insurance carrier or company policy will dictate which guideline is used, or if either set of guidelines can be used. When determining a level of visit, it is important to know company policy, as well as payer policy to determine the correct level of codes.

The 1995 and 1997 DGs, in combination with CPT® instructions, define in specific detail the steps necessary to define the levels of history, exam, and MDM—and the overall level of service—for E/M services.

Testing Technique

Use the 1995 and 1997 DGs to build grids in your CPT® codebook, to help you determine the levels of history, exam, and MDM.

Determine the Level of History

You have decided upon the appropriate E/M service category from which to select a code to represent the documented service, and you have read the descriptors and examples to confirm your category selection. You have your documentation guidelines (1995 and 1997 versions) on hand. Now, you are ready to determine the level of history.

CPT® defines four levels of history, as determined by the amount and depth of information the practitioner collects from the patient. These include:

◀ Problem focused

◀ Expanded problem-focused

◀ Detailed

◀ Comprehensive

The history component of any E/M service is divided further into constituent elements, as defined by 1995 and 1997 DGs. The specific elements that determine the history level include:

◀ History of present illness (HPI)

◀ Review of systems (ROS)

◀ Past family and social history (PFSH)

History of Present Illness (HPI)

The HPI is a chronological description of the patient's present illness development, from the first sign or symptom, or previous encounter, to the present. Under both the 1995 and 1997 DGs, the HPI can be quantified by a patient's statements regarding: location, quality, severity, duration, timing, context, modifying factors, and associated signs and symptoms.

The 1997 guidelines also allow credit in the HPI for patients who are seen for chronic conditions, such as follow up of COPD, HTN, and DM. Statements of this type are not credited specifically under the 1995 guidelines, but may be given credit by the 1997 guidelines as chronic conditions when the status of at least three chronic conditions are the reason for the visit. It is not sufficient, however, simply to document the chronic problem: The status of at least three chronic (or inactive) conditions must be documented to meet the requirements of an extended HPI. Furthermore, this option is available *only* for an extended HPI. If the status of fewer than three chronic (or inactive) conditions is documented, without documentation of any of the eight HPI elements, the documentation guidelines for a brief HPI have *not* been satisfied.

For most payers, you should not "mix and match" 1995 and 1997 DGs. If you select 1997 guidelines for the history component, you should use the same guidelines to determine the exam level and MDM.

There are only two HPI levels. For both 1995 and 1997 E/M Documentation Guidelines, the HPI is brief if at least one of the eight elements that quantify HPI (location, quality, severity, etc.) is documented. For both 1995 and 1997 DGs, the HPI is extended if at least four of the eight elements that quantify HPI are documented.

For 1997 guidelines only, patient statements regarding the status of at least three chronic conditions may also be considered an extended HPI.

Review of Systems (ROS)

Both 1995 and 1997 DGs define the ROS as an account of body systems obtained through questioning to identify patient signs and/or symptoms. The ROS might include verbal questioning by the provider or by a separate patient intake or questionnaire form. The ROS may include the systems directly related to the problems identified in the HPI and/or additional body systems.

The 14 body systems recognized for ROS are:

1. Constitutional
2. Respiratory
3. Integumentary
4. Psychiatric
5. Eyes
6. Gastrointestinal (GI)
7. Neurological
8. Allergic
9. Ears, Nose, and Throat
10. Genitourinary
11. Endocrine
12. Cardiovascular
13. Musculoskeletal
14. Hematologic and Lymphatic

There are only three ROS levels. The least amount of credit defined by the ROS—assuming that at least one system is reviewed and documented—is a problem-pertinent ROS. The second ROS level, an extended ROS, requires a documented review of at least two of the 14 organ systems. The final ROS level, a complete ROS, requires a documented review of at least 10 of the 14 organ systems.

Example

A level IV new patient visit (99204) requires a comprehensive history. To meet the work of a comprehensive history, a complete ROS (review of at least 10 of 14 organ systems) must be documented.

Medical necessity determines the extent of the ROS. For instance, it might be considered necessary to obtain a complete ROS when a new patient presents, but medically unnecessary to repeat that complete review on every follow-up.

For most payers, if there is separate documentation of at least one pertinent positive or negative ROS element, and the provider states the remaining systems are reviewed and negative, credit should be given for a complete ROS. For example, the ROS in a new patient visiting a cardiologist may read, "Denies shortness of breath, pain in chest, or any additional cardiac complaints; the remaining systems were reviewed and otherwise negative."

Past, family and social history (PFSH)

The patient's past history includes previous diseases, illnesses, operations, injuries, treatments, and medications. If a patient presents for follow-up on a chronic condition, both the HPI and past history should be considered. Positive findings of past diagnoses discovered on ROS also should be considered.

Family history is a review of medical events in the patient's family, including the parents and other relatives' age of death, and diseases that may be hereditary or place the patient at an increased risk.

Social history is a review of the patient's past and current activities, such as the patient's occupation, whether he or she smokes or drinks alcohol, engages in sexual activity, and is married. Social history should be age appropriate. For example, it would not be reasonable to document that a 6-year-old is not married.

Inquiries about the patient's PFSH may be made by the provider, obtained by the staff, or gathered via a form completed by the patient.

There are only two PFSH levels. The PFSH is pertinent if at least one of the three constituent categories (past history, family history, or social history) is documented.

The second level of PFSH, a complete PFSH, requires a documented review of two of three constituent categories (past history, family history, and social history) for established patient office or other outpatient services, ED, established patient domiciliary care, and established patient home care; or documented review of all three constituent categories (past history, family history, and social history) for new patient office or other outpatient services, hospital observation services, hospital inpatient services, consultations, comprehensive nursing facility assessments, new patient domiciliary care, and new patient home care.

Example

A level IV new patient visit (99204) requires a comprehensive history. To meet the comprehensive history work, a complete PFSH must be documented.

Totaling the History Component

All three history elements must support the work level to meet the overall history level requirement. The lowest element within the history component will always determine the overall history level. For example, if the HPI and ROS both support a detailed history level, but the PFSH supports only an expanded problem-focused history level, the history level will stay at the expanded problem focused level.

Now, let's use what we've learned and determine the overall history level of a typical office note.

Office Note

CC: sneezing, watery eyes

History: 26-year-old female presents today sneezing, watery eyes, and nasal congestion.

Symptoms started 2 days ago after spending all day working in garden.

Patient's eyes are not watering as much since she started taking a prescription decongestant issued at previous visit, but only has 2 dosages left.

ROS: Eyes—Watery

ENT—Nasal congestion, sneezing

Cardio—No cardio symptoms

Respiratory—No respiratory symptoms

Personal History: Multiple sinus infections over last 3 years

Social History: Smoker

To find out the level of history, mark the HPI, ROS, and PFSH information on the following page.

Table A: History

History		Brief (1–3)	Brief (1–3)	Extended (4 or more)	Extended (4 or more)
HPI Location Severity Timing Modifying Factors Quality Duration Context Assoc Signs & Symptoms		Brief (1–3)	Brief (1–3)	Extended (4 or more)	Extended (4 or more)
ROS Const GI Integ Hem/lymph Eyes GU Neuro All/Immuno Card/Vasc Musculo Psych All other negative Resp ENT, mouth Endo		None	Pertinent to problem (1 system)	Extended (2–9 systems)	Complete
PFSH Past history (current meds, past illnesses, operations, injuries, treatments) Family history (a review of medical events in the patient's family) Social history (an age appropriate review of past and current activities)		None	None	Pertinent (1 history area)	Complete (2 (est) or 3 (new) history areas)
		Problem Focused	Expanded Problem Focused	Detailed	Comprehensive

In the last row, draw a line to the first column selected within the grid (extended review of systems). This will be the level for the history. The level of history detail requires HPI to be extended; ROS to be extended; and PFSH to be pertinent; however, the HPI and PSFH exceeded the requirement, so we must select the column meeting the requirement, equaling the level for history.

Five Key Points to Consider When Selecting History Level

1. A chief complaint is a medically necessary reason for the patient to meet with the physician. Both sets of E/M documentation guidelines require a chief complaint. A chief complaint is the primary reason the patient is seeking medical care. It is part of the history component. If there is no chief complaint, the service is preventive and would need to be reported using a dedicated preventive service code.

   The chief complaint is often stated in the patient's words, for example, "My throat is sore," or "I am having pain in my back."

Occasionally, documentation states the reason for a visit is "follow up." A simple statement of "follow up" is not sufficient for a chief complaint. A provider must document the condition being followed up on. A more concise statement would be "follow up of ankle pain," or "follow up of diabetes."

2. If documentation establishes the provider cannot obtain a history from the patient or other source (for example, if the patient is unconscious), the provider is not penalized, nor are the overall medical necessity level and provider work discounted automatically.

3. Additional history supplied by a family member or a caregiver and documented by the provider can be credited toward the overall E/M service's MDM component.

4. An ROS and/or PFSH taken from a previous encounter may be updated without complete re-documentation for most payers. The provider should indicate the new history status and indicate where the original documentation is stored.

5. There is a fine line between the signs and symptoms the patient shares in the HPI, and those obtained via the ROS. Individual payers have the power to

interpret the documentation guidelines in their own way, and many prohibit using one documented statement to count for two separate history elements. For example, if the documentation reads, "The patient states that her hip has been painful," credit would not be given to both the HPI location and to the musculoskeletal ROS (this is referred to as double-dipping). If, on the other hand, the documentation reads, "The patient states that her hip has been painful. She denies any other musculoskeletal complaint," there is a distinct component of both the HPI (painful hip) and a separate musculoskeletal ROS (no other musculoskeletal complaint).

Correct interpretation requires consistency, verifiable references, a logical argument, and ultimately medical necessity.

Examination

An E/M service's exam component is, as the name implies, the patient's examination by the physician. The 1995 and 1997 DGs, define differently the specific elements that determine the exam level. The downfall of the 1995 guidelines is that specific acknowledgment of the normal work and documentation of many specialists is not included. A critique of the 1997 guidelines is that too many specific documentation elements are required. Consider your specialty's nature, and the typical documentation the physician generates, to determine which guidelines set to use.

Both 1995 and 1997 DGs recognize the same body areas, including:

- Head, including the face
- Neck
- Chest, including the breast and axillae
- Abdomen
- Genitalia, groin, and buttocks
- Back, including spine
- Each extremity

Both DGs recognize the same organ systems, including:

- Constitutional (for example, the patient's general appearance and vital signs)
- Eyes

- Ears nose, mouth, and throat
- Cardiovascular
- Respiratory
- Gastrointestinal
- Genitourinary
- Musculoskeletal
- Skin
- Neurologic
- Psychiatric
- Hematologic, lymphatic, and immunologic

Both 1995 and 1997 DGs require the provider to elaborate on abnormal findings and describe unexpected findings. Both guidelines also allow a brief note of "negative" or "normal" to document normal findings or unaffected areas or systems.

When reading a chart note, it can be difficult to distinguish between elements belonging to the ROS and those elements relevant to the exam. The ROS and exam elements are not interchangeable, and for most payers, you may not count a single element toward both the ROS and the exam.

The ROS is a series of written or verbal "questions and answers" relevant to signs or symptoms the patient is experiencing at the time of service. Often, the ROS is gathered by having the patient complete a history or intake form given to the patient at the front desk during check-in. The form is a list of questions that generally asks the patient to check off and/or briefly explain signs and symptoms the patient currently has or has had in the past, for instance:

Have you now or have you ever had any of the conditions listed below? If yes, please describe.

Respiratory:

- Severe shortness of breath or wheezing
- Had a cough for more than one month
- Chest pain when you cough hard or take a deep breath
- Cough up blood
- Difficulty breathing
- Shortness of breath when exercising

The ROS also may occur verbally with the provider or other staff. For instance, an assistant may ask the patient, "Do you have any problems breathing? Do you have shortness of breath when exercising, walking, or climbing the stairs?" The patient's response might be documented in a note by the provider as briefly as: "Patient states his chest hurts when he coughs but not when he takes a deep breath. No SOB. No complaints of pain in joints. No problems sleeping."

In contrast to ROS elements, the exam elements are actual visual or hands-on findings. For example, the provider uses an otoscope to inspect the middle ear visually, an ophthalmoscope to check the eyes and their reaction to light, and a stethoscope to listen to lung, heart, and bowel sounds. The provider will document what he or she sees with statements such as:

- Pupils are equal and reactive to light
- Chest: Bilateral rales and rhonchi
- Bowels sounds are normal
- Extremities: No cyanosis or edema

When reading the notes, ask yourself if the notation is something the patient answered, or if it is something the provider observed. An answered question belongs to the ROS; whereas something seen, heard, or measured by a provider is an exam element.

The 1995 and 1997 DGs define the four levels of exam (problem-focused, expanded problem focused, detailed, and comprehensive) differently. The 1995 guidelines define the levels of exam as follows:

- **Problem Focused**—Limited examination of the affected body area or organ system (that is, a limited exam on only one affected body area or organ system).

- **Expanded Problem Focused**—Limited examination of the affected body area or organ system and other symptomatic or related organ system(s) (that is, a limited exam of at least two body areas or organ systems).

- **Detailed**—Extended examination of the affected body area(s) and other symptomatic or related organ system(s) (that is, an extended examination of at least two body areas or organ systems).

- **Comprehensive**—General multi-system examination or complete single-organ system examination (The medical record for a general multi-system examination should include findings about eight or more of the 12 organ systems).

Gray Areas in the 1995 Guidelines

The 1995 guidelines, although generally clear, contain two gray areas that may complicate your ability to determine the exam level:

- An expanded problem-focused exam and a detailed exam both require examination of at least two body areas and/or organ systems; the expanded problem-focus level requires these exams to be "limited," whereas the detailed level requires these exams to be "extended." The terms limited and extended are not defined specifically.

- The definition of a comprehensive single system exam is defined only as "complete." The term complete is not defined specifically.

The 1997 guidelines eliminate this subjectivity by exactly specifying—using bulleted items—the exam requirement for a particular body area or organ system. These requirements provide objective, exact criteria against which to measure physician documentation. A detailed list of bulleted exam requirements may be found in the 1997 Documentation Guidelines, as available at www.cms.hhs.gov/MLNProducts/Downloads/MASTER1.pdf.

When using 1997 guidelines, the physician may select from the general multi-system exam or any of the single organ system exams. The coder must review each documented element to determine which single-organ system exam is the most appropriate E/M service level selection. For instance, a problem-focused, general multi-system examination requires the documentation of at least one bullet. For an expanded problem-focused exam, at least six bullets must be documented. For a detailed examination, there should be documentation to support two bullets in at least six organ systems or body areas, or 12 bullets in two or more organ systems or body areas.

Physicians should focus on the medical necessity of an exam, and should never document "just one more bullet" to achieve a higher service level.

"The type (general multi-system or single organ system) and content of examination are selected by the examining physician and are based upon clinical judgment, the patient's history, and the nature of the presenting problem(s)," according to the 1997 guidelines.

For instance, it might be considered necessary to perform a comprehensive exam when a new patient presents, but medically unnecessary to repeat a complete review on every follow-up.

Totaling the Exam Component

Now, let's continue the office note example, focusing on the exam.

Eyes—Irritated, with mild weeping

ENT—Slight yellowish discharge from nose

Respiratory—Normal

Cardiovascular—Normal

Using the examination box below let's mark our history. From the note above, we can identify four organ systems.

Table B: Examination

Examination					
Body Areas: Head, including face Abdomen Genitalia, groin, buttocks Chest, including extremities Neck Back, including spine Breasts and Axilla	1 body area or organ system	2–7 systems—limited exam	2–7 systems—detailed exam	8 or more systems	
Organ Systems: Constitutional Respiratory Musculoskeletal Psych Cardiovascular GI Skin Hem/Lymph/Imm ENT, Mouth GU Neurological Eyes					
	Problem focused	Expanded Problem Focused	Detailed	Comprehensive	

The level of exam from the example is expanded problem focused.

Medical Decision Making (MDM)

MDM is perhaps the most important of the three primary components of E/M code selection. It is also the most subjective. Whether you use the 1995 or 1997 DGs, the nature of the presenting problem and the medical necessity of the encounter are the best MDM indicators. You will choose an overall MDM level based on three factors:

- The number of diagnoses or management options;
- The amount and/or complexity of data to be reviewed; and,
- The risk of complications and morbidity or mortality.

Diagnoses or Management Options

The number of diagnoses or management options is based on the relative difficulty level in making a diagnosis, and the status of the problem. Although audit tools vary, the number of diagnosis and management options is typically determined using a points system. Under this system, points are assigned according to how sick a patient is and the amount of physician work involved.

- Minor problems, such as those that would resolve regardless of whether the patient had sought medical attention, are worth one point. A patient may have four minor, documented problems. For coding purposes, only a maximum of two such problems can be counted.

- Established, stable, or improved conditions are worth one point each.

- Established, worsening conditions are worth two points each.

- A new problem (new to the patient or new to the provider) without any additional workup is worth three points. You may only count such a problem once per encounter, even if there are multiple occurrences in the encounter.

- A new problem with additional workup is counted as four points (a *workup* is defined as anything the physician had to do after making the diagnosis the patient left with on that day. For example, if the physician suspects a particular diagnosis and sends the patient for a diagnostic test to confirm that suspicion, that diagnostic test would count as workup).

There are four levels of MDM defined by CPT®, and four corresponding diagnosis and treatment level options:

- Straightforward MDM requires a minimal number of diagnosis and treatment options that correlate to (at least) a detailed work level. For both the 1995 and 1997 DGs, the number of diagnosis and management options is minimal if the sum is one point.

- Low MDM requires a limited number of diagnosis or treatment options. For both the 1995 and 1997 DGs, the number of diagnosis and management options is low if the sum is two points.

- Moderate MDM requires a moderate number of diagnosis and treatment options. For both the 1995 and 1997 DGs, the number of diagnosis and management options is moderate if the sum is three points.

- High MDM requires an extensive number of diagnoses or treatment options. For both the 1995 and 1997 DGs, the number of diagnosis and management options is high if the sum is four or more points.

Data Amount and Complexity

The amount and complexity of data for review is measured by the need to order and review tests, and the need to gather information and data. Planning, scheduling, and performing clinical labs and tests from the medicine and radiology portions of CPT® are indications of complexity, as is the need to request old records, or to obtain additional history from someone other than the patient (such as a family member, caregiver, teacher, etc.). Documented discussions with the performing physician about unusual or unexpected patient results

also may result in credit. If a physician makes an independent visualization and interpretation, for example, with an magnetic resonance imaging (MRI) film or a Gram stain—and he or she is not billing separately for that service—it is credited in this component of code selection.

A points system is very effective for measuring the amount and complexity of data for review:

- Clinical labs ordered or reviewed are worth one point.

- Any test(s) reviewed/ordered from the medicine section of the CPT® codebook are worth one point.

- Any procedures reviewed/ordered from the radiology section of CPT® are worth one point. Regardless of the number of radiological procedures reviewed/ordered, only one point may be assigned (eg, five radiology reports reviewed count as one point only).

- Discussing patient's results with the performing or consulting physician is worth one point—if it is captured in the documentation.

- Decisions to obtain old records or additional history from someone other than the patient are worth one point.

- Reviewing and summarizing data from old records or additional history gathered from someone other than the patient is worth two points.

- Independent or second interpretation of an image tracing or specimen is worth two points. Note that this means not just the review of the report, but of the actual film image or tracing.

There are four MDM levels defined by CPT®, and four corresponding data amounts and complexity levels:

- Straightforward MDM requires a minimal amount and complexity of data. For both the 1995 and 1997 DGs, the amount and complexity of data is straightforward if the sum of this data is zero or one point.

- Low MDM requires a limited amount and complexity of data. For both the 1995 and 1997 DGs, the amount and complexity of data options is low if the sum is two points.

- Moderate MDM requires a moderate amount and complexity of data. For both the 1995 and 1997 DGs, the amount and complexity of data options is moderate if the sum of this data is three points.

- High MDM requires an extensive amount and complexity of data. For both the 1995 and 1997 DGs, the amount and complexity of data options is high if the sum is four or more points.

Table of Risk

Risk is measured based on the physician's determination of the patient's probability of becoming ill or diseased, having complications, or dying between this encounter and the next planned encounter. Risk indications include the nature of the presenting problem, the urgency of the visit, co-morbid conditions, and the need for diagnostic test for surgery.

Documentation Guidelines determine the risk level using the Table of Risk (Table E). The Table of Risk is divided into three columns; each column correlates with an overall risk level. The three columns list presenting problems, diagnostic procedures ordered, and management options selected.

There are four levels of MDM defined by CPT®, and four corresponding risk levels:

- Straightforward MDM requires a minimal risk level. For both the 1995 and 1997 DGs, a straightforward level of risk corresponds with any of the columns in the Table of Risk that are labeled "minimal risk."

- Low MDM requires a low risk level. For both the 1995 and 1997 DGs, a low level of risk corresponds with any of the columns in the Table of Risk that are labeled "low risk."

- Moderate MDM requires a moderate risk level. For both the 1995 and 1997 DGs, a moderate level of risk corresponds with any of the columns in the Table of Risk that are labeled "moderate risk."

- High MDM requires a high risk level. For both the 1995 and 1997 DGs, a high level of risk corresponds with any of the columns in the Table of Risk that are labeled "high risk."

Totaling the MDM Component

To select an overall MDM level, at least two of three elements (number of diagnoses or management options; amount and/or complexity of data to be reviewed; risk of complications and/or morbidity or mortality) for that level must be met.

Once again, let's continue with the office note example:

Assessment and plan:

1. Allergic rhinitis—Prescription for eye drops. Use over the counter eye drops for itchy eyes. Allergy skin testing ordered.

Return to office in 10 days if symptoms have not improved.

Using the box below, select the number of diagnoses and treatment options.

Note: Use the following four tables to determine the level of MDM.

Table C: Number of Diagnoses or Treatment Options

Number of diagnosis or treatment options			
Problem	Number	Points	Total (number x points)
Self limited or minor (max. 2 points)		1	
Established problem to provider (stable or improved)	1	1	1
Established problem to provider (worsening)		2	
New problem to provider with no additional work up planned		3	
New problem to provider with additional work up planned.		4	
	Total		1

Note: Back in the history section the documentation for this patient states, "Patient's eyes are not watering as much since she stated taking a prescription decongestant issued at previous visit, but only has 2 dosages left." This documentation indicates this is an established problem improving.

Using the box below, select the data reviewed or ordered.

Assessment and plan:

1. Allergic rhinitis—Prescription for eye drops. Use over the counter eye drops for itchy eyes. Allergy skin testing ordered.

Table D: Reviewed/Ordered Data

Reviewed/Ordered Data	Points
Review and/or order lab tests	1
Review and/or order tests in the radiology section of CPT®	1
Review and/or order tests in the medicine section of CPT®	1
Discussion of test results with performing physician	1
Decision to obtain old records and/or obtain history from someone other than the patient	1
Review and summarization of old records and/or obtaining history from someone other than the patient and/or discussion of case with another health care provider.	2
Independent visualization of image, specimen or tracing (NOT simply a review of report, do not use if billing for the interpretation)	2

The provider ordered allergy skin tests, giving us one point for reviewed/ordered data.

Risk of Complications, Morbidity, and/or Mortality

Risk is based on the table of risk chart below. A selection from each column (presenting problem, diagnostic procedures ordered and management options selected) is made.

The column selected that corresponds horizontally with the risk column on the left will be the level of risk. Continuing with our example select the appropriate boxes:

Assessment and plan:

1. Allergic rhinitis—prescription for eye drops. Use over the counter eye drops for itchy eyes. Allergy skin testing ordered.

Table E: Table of Risk

Level of Risk	Presenting Problem(s)	Diagnostic Procedure(s) Ordered	Management Options Selected
Minimal	One self-limited or minor problem, eg, cold, insect bite, tinea corporis	Laboratory tests required: • Venipuncture • Chest X-rays • EKG/EEG • Urinalysis • Ultrasound, eg, echocardiography • KOH prep	• Rest • Gargles • Elastic bandages • Superficial dressings
Low	• Two or more self-limited or minor problems • One stable chronic illness, eg, well controlled hypertension, non-insulin dependent diabetes, cataract, BPH • Acute uncomplicated illness or injury, eg, cystitis, allergic rhinitis, simple sprain	• Physiologic tests not under stress, eg, pulmonary function tests • Non-cardiovascular imaging studies with contrast, eg, barium enema • Superficial needle biopsies • Clinical laboratory tests requiring arterial puncture • Skin biopsies	• Over-the-counter drugs • Minor surgery with no identified risk factors • Physical therapy • Occupational therapy • IV fluids without additives
Moderate	• One or more chronic illnesses with mild exacerbation, progression, or side effects of treatment • Two or more stable chronic illnesses • Undiagnosed new problem with uncertain prognosis, eg, lump in breast • Acute illness with systemic symptoms, eg, pyelonephritis, pneumonitis, colitis • Acute complicated injury, eg, head injury with brief loss of consciousness	• Physiologic tests under stress, eg, cardiac stress test, fetal contraction stress test • Diagnostic endoscopies with no identified risk factors • Deep needle or incisional biopsy • Cardiovascular imaging studies with contrast and no identified risk factors, eg, arteriogram, cardiac catheterization • Obtain fluid from body cavity, eg, lumbar puncture, thoracentesis, culdocentesis	Minor surgery with identified risk factors • Elective major surgery (open, percutaneous, or endoscopic) with no identified risk factors • Prescription drug management • Therapeutic nuclear medicine • IV fluids with additives • Closed treatment of fracture or dislocation without manipulation
High	• One or more chronic illnesses with severe exacerbation, progression, or side effects of treatment • Acute or chronic illnesses or injuries that pose a threat to life or bodily function, eg, multiple trauma, acute MI, pulmonary embolus, severe respiratory distress, progressive severe rheumatoid arthritis, psychiatric illness with potential threat to self or others, peritonitis, acute renal failure • An abrupt change in neurologic status, eg, seizure, TIA, weakness, sensory loss	• Cardiovascular imaging studies with contrast with identified risk factors • Cardiac electrophysiological tests • Diagnostic endoscopies with identified risk factors • Discography	• Elective major surgery (open, percutaneous, or endoscopic) with identified risk factors • Emergency major surgery (open, percutaneous, or endoscopic) • Parenteral controlled substances • Drug therapy requiring intensive monitoring for toxicity • Decision not to resuscitate or to de-escalate care because of poor prognosis

Using the results from Tables C, D, and E, complete the table below to determine the overall MDM level. The column with two items selected or the column in the middle will be the level for the MDM.

Table F: MDM

Final Result of Tables C, D, E = Level of Medical Decision Making (MDM)					
Table C	Number of diagnosis/treatment options	1	2	3	4
Table D	Amount of data reviewed/ordered	1	2	3	4
Table E	Level of risk	Minimal	Low	Moderate	High
MDM Level		Straightforward	Low	Moderate	High

Using the results from the Tables of History, Exam, and MDM, we will complete the table below resulting in the office visit level of our patient.

Table G: Established Patient Office Visit

Established patient office visit table				
History (Table A)	Problem focused	Expanded problem focused	Detailed	Comprehensive
Exam (Table B)	Problem focused	Expanded problem focused	Detailed	Comprehensive
MDM (Table F)	Straightforward	Low	Moderate	High
Level of Visit	99212	99213	99214	99215

Two of three key components are needed to make established patient level visit. The level for the visit is 99213.

Contributory Factors to E/M Service Leveling

Contributory factors include counseling, coordination of care, and nature of the present problem. The first two factors are important in E/M, but are not required for each visit. The nature of the presenting problem is considered as the disease, illness, condition, injury, symptom, signs, finding, complaint, or other problem with or without a diagnosis.

Counseling

Counseling may be included during the visit of a patient and reflect topics such as diet exercise andweight control. The provider may counsel the patient on the adverse effects of a sedentary life style and unhealthy eating habits. He also may prescribe weight loss management and an exercise program.

Nature of Presenting Problems

Nature of a presenting problem includes five types:

◀ **Minimal**—A problem that may not require the presence of the physician; however, services provided are under the physician's supervision.

◀ **Self-limited or minor**—Does not permanently alter health status, and with management and compliance has an outcome of "good."

◀ **Low severity**—Risk of morbidity/mortality without treatment is low and full recovery with no functional impairment is expected.

◀ **Moderate severity**—Risk of morbidity/mortality without treatment is moderate; uncertain prognosis or increased probability of prolonged functional impairment.

High severity—Risk of morbidity/mortality without treatment is highly probable; uncertain prognosis or high probability of severe prolonged functional impairment.

Time

Time may be considered the controlling factor to qualify for a particular E/M service level, "When counseling and/or coordination of care dominates (more than 50 percent) the physician/patient and/or family encounter," according to CPT® guidelines. The E/M category selected must include a time reference. As an example, the descriptor for level V established patient outpatient service 99215 specifies, "Physicians typically spend 40 minutes face-to-face with the patient and/or family." By contrast, observation services 99234–99236 do not include a stated time component, so these services may not be reported with time as the deciding component.

Time includes face-to-face time in the office or other outpatient setting, or floor/unit time in the hospital or nursing facility, and includes time spent with parties who have assumed responsibility for the care of the patient or decision making whether they are family members.

The time the physician spends taking the patient's history or performing an examination does not count as counseling time. The physician must look at the entire patient encounter and decide if he or she spent the majority of time in counseling and/or coordinating care or if the key components of history, exam, and MDM should be the deciding factor when choosing an E/M level.

Counseling and coordinating care could include discussion with the patient (or his or her family) about one or more of the following, according to CPT® guidelines:

- Diagnostic results
- Impressions and/or recommended diagnostic studies
- Prognosis
- Risks and benefits of treatment options
- Instructions for treatment and/or follow-up
- Importance of compliance with chosen treatment options
- Risk-factor reduction
- Patient/family education

The provider's documentation should support the content and extent of the patient counseling. For example, Amy Jo on care to prevent further damage of the weak wrist, including: no lifting of heavy objects and no gymnastic activities involving direct pressure on the wrist (such as hand springs, head stands, etc.). In this case, time is the predominant factor of the E/M visit; not the E/M visit leveling of history, exam, and MDM.

The most important part of coding by time is complete and adequate documentation of the visit—including documentation of the total visit time and the total time the physician spends counseling.

Diagnosis Coding for E/M Services

The primary diagnosis for any E/M service should be the reason the visit was initiated. This can be a symptom, such as a cough, or a disease, such as diabetes. It could also be a preventive care visit, which would require the use of a V code to report the reason for the service. The diagnosis can be considered acute, chronic, or an acute phase of a chronic condition. When the condition is an acute phase of a chronic condition, list the acute code first, then the chronic code if codes for both exist.

Symptoms typically are coded from chapter 16, Signs, Symptoms, and Ill-Defined Conditions (780–799) of the ICD-9-CM codebook. Symptoms should be used only as a diagnosis if no definitive diagnosis is provided. For example, if the patient comes in with cough, congestion, and a headache, but the provider determines the patient to have an upper respiratory infection, only the upper respiratory infection would be used as a diagnosis. Likewise, if a patient is seen for chest pain, but the provider has not yet provided a definitive diagnosis, then "chest pain" would be used for the diagnosis.

Signs and symptoms routinely associated with a disease process should not be coded separately from the definitive diagnosis. Signs and symptoms that are not routinely associated with a disease process should be coded separately. To provide accurate reporting of ICD-9-CM codes, coders need to understand the pathology of diseases to determine if a sign or symptom is part of the disease process or if it should be separately reported. For example, let's look at a patient with a fever and a cough. The provider diagnoses the patient with pneumonia. Fever and cough are part of the disease process for pneumonia, so they would not be coded separately. If the same patient also complains of elbow pain, the elbow pain would be reported separately because it is not part of the disease process for pneumonia.

When a patient is seen who has multiple conditions, only conditions affecting care or requiring care or management by the provider should be coded.

Glossary

Auscultation—Listening to body organs.

Chief Complaint—The reason the patient presents for an encounter.

Critical Care—Care provided for a critical illness or injury which acutely impairs one or more vital organ systems and is an imminent or life threatening condition.

Established Patient—Patient who has seen a provider of the same specialty in the same group within the past three years.

New Patient—Patient who has not been seen by a provider of the same specialty, in the same group, within the past three years.

Medical Necessity—Reasonable and necessary services to bring a cure or a change in the condition for which the patient is being seen.

Observation Status—Patient's condition requires monitoring, but the decision to admit to inpatient status has not been made.

Palpation—Touching the body.

Percussion—Creating sounds from the body by tapping.

Review of Systems—Series of questions regarding signs and symptoms that are associated with the patient's chief complaint.

Chapter Review Questions

1. **Which system is given credit in the exam component when the provider documents "range of motion, strength, and stability are adequate in both legs?"**

   A. Constitutional

   B. Neurologic

   C. Musculoskeletal

   D. Rheumatoid

2. **When a patient complains of epigastric pain. Where is the pain located?**

   A. The upper central region of the abdomen

   B. The lower right quadrant of the abdomen

   C. The right upper quadrant of the abdomen

   D. The lower central region of the abdomen

3. A two-year-old comes in for an initial WCE. Mom doesn't have the child's immunization record. She states the child's last shot was when he was 5 months old. Medical review and documentation of a new patient supports one element of HPI, five elements of the ROS, and a complete PFSH. The examination was 8+ organ systems. The physician orders the immunizations to be given in the office today. Immunizations given: MMR, Varicella. What CPT® codes are reported?

   A. 99391-25, 90471, 90710

   B. 99202-25, 90707, 90716

   C. 99382-25, 90471, 90472, 90707, 90716

   D. 99212-25, 90471, 90472, 90707-51, 90716-51

4. An established 45-year-old woman is seen today at her doctor's office. She is complaining of being dizzy and feels like the room is spinning. She has had palpitations on and off for the past 12 months. She reports chest tightness and dyspnea but denies nausea, edema, or arm pain. She drinks two cups of coffee per day. Her sister has WPW syndrome. An extended five body area examination is performed. This is a new problem for the physician. An EKG is ordered and labs are drawn, and physician documents a moderate complexity MDM. What CPT® code is reported for this visit?

   A. 99203

   B. 99214

   C. 99215

   D. 99204

5. A 33-year-old white male was admitted to the hospital 12/17/xx from the ER, following a motor vehicle accident, to have a splenectomy done. The patient is being discharged from the hospital on 12/20/xx. During his hospitalization, he was experiencing pain and shortness of breath, but with an antibiotic regimen of Levaquin, he improved. The physician performed final examination and reviewed chest X-ray that revealed possible infiltrates and a CT of the abdomen that ruled out any abscess. He was given a prescription of Zosyn. The patient was told to follow up care with PCP or return back to the hospital for any pain or bleeding. The physician spent 20 minutes. What CPT® code is reported for the 12/20 visit?

   A. 99283

   B. 99221

   C. 99231

   D. 99238

6. The physician was notified to go to the hospital floor for medical management of a 56-year-old patient admitted one day ago for aspiration pneumonia and COPD. No chest pain at present, but still SOB and some swelling in his lower extremities. He was tachypenic yesterday; lungs reveal course crackles in both bases, right worse than left. He is continuing with intravenous antibiotic treatment and respiratory support, reviewed chest X-ray and labs. The patient is improving and a pulmonary consultation has been requested. What CPT® code should be reported?

    A. 99221

    B. 99231

    C. 99218

    D. 99232

7. A 25-year-old male is brought in by the EMS to the ER for nausea and vomiting. The patient has elevated blood sugars per EMS. EMS and the physician are unable to get a history due to patient's altered mental status. The ED physician performed an eight organ system exam and a high level MDM. Patient was transferred to ICU in stable condition. Total critical care time 25 minutes. What CPT® code is reported?

    A. 99285

    B. 99291

    C. 99236

    D. 99223

8. A physician makes a home care visit on a 63-year-old patient that is a hemiplegic having insomnia for the last two weeks. The patient has been home bound for the last year. The last visit from this physician was four months ago to control his DM. The physician performs an expanded problem-focused examination and low MDM. The physician then speaks with the spouse about the possibility of placing the patient in a nursing facility. What CPT® code is reported?

    A. 99213

    B. 99342

    C. 99348

    D. 99335

9. **History and Physical**

Patient: SP

Date: 2/4/xx

Referring Physician: SK, M.D.

Chief Complaint: Chronic UTIs

HPI: Ms. P is a 29-year-old young lady referred to us by Dr. K for evaluation of the above. She states that she underwent a C-section in 20xx. This was complicated by a reaction to the epidural as well as a post-op hematoma. It has resulted in decreased sensation of her bladder filling. She has had some predominant urge incontinence and urgency, which was preceded by a stress incontinence that she has not been treated for. This has also resulted in a UTI about once a month. She seemed to be doing timed voiding on her own to decrease the amount of urine and to have fewer accidents. She says she has good stream when she voids. She feels like she does not completely empty. She has had no dysuria, frequency, or hematuria, but does have nocturia three times a night. Thus Dr. K referred her to us for evaluation of the infections and urinary incontinence. She has no history of stones, sexually transmitted disease, or family history of any urologic problems.

Past Medical History: Significant for depression

Past Surgical History: Tonsillectomy, adenoidectomy, C-section, and myringotomy tubes

Medications: Zoloft

Allergies: STADOL, MORPHINE, LATEX, RELPAX

Social History: She is married and is a medical assistant at Max's Dermatology. She does not smoke. Drinks occasionally. No history of alcohol abuse. Exercises regularly.

Family History: Significant for hypertension.

Physical Exam: Constitutional: Well-nourished, well-developed white female who looks her stated age, in no acute distress, pleasant, and cooperative.

HEENT: Within normal limits Neck: Supple, no masses. Respiratory: Clear to auscultation. Cardiovascular: Regular rate and rhythm. GI: Abdomen is mildly obese, benign. No CVA tenderness, back without deformity. Extremities: No clubbing, cyanosis, or edema Neuro: Nonfocal. Genitourinary: Pelvic exam was essentially unremarkable.

Labs: Urinalysis specific gravity 1.010, pH 5, otherwise negative. PVR of 60 cc.

Assessment/Plan: We will have her obtain a MESA symptom score, voiding diary, and a local cystourethroscopy. We will obtain her records from Dr. M. for further evaluation and review.

DB, M.D., F.A.C.S
Urology
Board Certified Urologist

February 4, 20xx

Official CPC® Certification Study Guide   **301**

SK, M.D.
29 Mountain Trail
Colorado Springs, CO 29192

Dear Dr. K:

I appreciate your asking me to evaluate SP for her chronic UTIs and urinary incontinence. She was seen today in my office. A brief summary and recommendations are as follows:

We will have her undergo some routine testing including a cystourethroscopy. We will obtain her records from her gynecologist and make further recommendations at that time.

Thank you again for your kind referral. I appreciate your gesture and will keep you updated regarding her urological progress.

Sincerely,

DB, M.D., F.A.C.S.

What are CPT® and diagnosis codes to report?

10. **Chief Complaint:** Left knee pain.

HPI: A 67-year-old female is seen today as a new patient with left knee pain for approximately one month. She offers a catching sensation. Pain is primarily through the medial joint line. There is no significant instability. She is currently taking Celebrex for pain. She offers prior history of automobile accident in the 1980s. She is currently not performing any home exercises, nor has she undergone any recent injections.

Current Medications: Metformin, metoprolol, Lipitor, glipizide, Synthroid, Altace, ranitidine, Celebrex.

Allergies: Sulfa, penicillin, and IVP dye.

Past Medical History: Significant for hypertension, diabetes, thyroid disorder, previous history of a stroke, cardiac disease.

ROS: She currently denies any unstable angina, no pulmonary disorders or productive coughs. No history of renal dysfunction. Denies gastric ulcer. She was without any unexpected weight loss or constitutional signs of infection. She has no known coagulopathies.

Social History: She denies tobacco and alcohol use. She is retired.

Family History: Diabetes, heart disease, and cancer.

Physical Examination: She has pronounced retropatellar crepitation. There is bogginess of the synovium, tenderness through the medial joint line. Ligamentous evaluation is stable. She has varus alignment of the knee. She is intact to sensation, has palpable pulses.

Ancillary Studies: AP, lateral and sunrise views ordered and interpreted today, May 3, 20xx. They reveal calcification within the vascular structures. There is decreased joint space through the medial compartment where she has near bone-on-bone contact, flattening of the femoral condyles, no fractures noted.

Impression: Left knee pain secondary to underlying degenerative arthritis.

Plan: We will proceed with a course of joint lubrication therapy and physical therapy. Injection series has been ordered. In the interim, she may continue activities as comfort allows, limiting repetitive stair climbing and kneeling.

What are the CPT® and diagnoses codes to report?

This chapter will introduce a diverse group of noninvasive or minimally invasive services, including:

- Immunizations
- Vaccines, Toxoids
- Psychiatry
- Biofeedback
- Dialysis
- Gastroenterology
- Ophthalmology
- Otorhinolaryngology
- Cardiovascular
- Non-invasive Diagnostic Vascular Studies
- Pulmonary
- Allergy & Clinical Immunology
- Endocrinology
- Neurology/Neuromuscular Procedures
- Medical Genetics & Genetic Counseling Services
- Central Nervous System Assessments/Tests
- Health & Behavior Assessment/Intervention
- Hydration, Therapeutic, Prophylactic, Infusions & Injections
- Photodynamic Therapy
- Special Dermatological Procedures
- Physical Medicine & Rehabilitation
- Nutritional Therapy
- Acupuncture
- Osteopathic & Chiropractic Manipulative Treatment
- Education & Training for Patient Self-Management
- Non-Face-To-Face Nonphysician Services
- Qualifying Circumstances for Anesthesia
- Moderate Sedation
- Home Health Procedures/Services
- Medication Therapy Management Services

Anti-infective Immunizations

Codes 90281–90399 describe anti-infective immunizations derived from human blood or recombinant immune globulin products created in a laboratory. Each code is specific to the type of anti-infective administered, with 90399 reserved for an immune globulin that is not described in a code.

Do not report modifier 51 if these services are performed with another procedure.

The administration of these products must be reported in addition to the product. Codes 96365–96368, 96372, 96374, 96375 are the codes reported for administration of immune globulin. When the delivery is by infusion (96365–96371), adhere to times stated in the code descriptor. A minimum time of 31 minutes is required to report the add-on code for an additional hour.

Procedure coding tip: The coder must refer to the nurse's notes for the delivery technique and start and stop infusion times of each drug/substance administered to report the service correctly. These codes also may describe addition of sequential substances as an add-on to the base code. Generally included in the service are local anesthesia, IV start, vascular access, flush at conclusion of an infusion, standard tubing, syringes, and supplies. When fluids are used for delivery of the substance/drug, the fluid administration is incidental to the administration and is not separately reported. Codes 96365–96371 are not reported for chemotherapy administration.

Physician work for these services usually includes development of the treatment plan and direct supervision of staff. If a significant, separately identifiable E/M service is performed at the same encounter, the appropriate E/M code is reported with modifier 25.

Diagnosis coding tip: If the substance is ordered due to exposure to infection, report a "V" code as the diagnosis. Example: V01.71 *Varicella* (90396).

Vaccines and Toxoids

Codes 90476–90748 describe vaccines and toxoids and are reported for the product only.

The administration codes are 90460–90474. Report codes 90460–90461 only if the physician counsels the patient/family face-to-face during the administration of the vaccine/toxoid to a child younger than 18 years of age. Report codes 90471–90474 if no counseling is provided for a child under 18 years of age and for the administration of vaccines/toxoids to patients over 18 years of age.

Do not report modifier 51 with these services.

If a significant, separately identifiable E/M service is provided at the same encounter, the appropriate E/M service may also be reported with modifier 25.

Subcutaneous injections (Sub-Q) are delivered into the subcutaneous layer of skin. Intramuscular injections (IM) are administered directly into a muscle.

Diagnosis coding tip: Review V codes for need for prophylactic vaccination and innoculation. Example: V03.1 *Typhoid-paratyphoid alone [TAB]* (90691).

Psychiatry

Codes 90801–90899 are reported for psychiatric services, which may include psychotherapy, behavior modification, and addictive disease therapy. The correct code is chosen based on whether interactive tools are used during the evaluation.

The remaining psychotherapy codes are used to report therapeutic services provided to the patient. Code selection is based on location of therapy (inpatient or in an office), type of psychotherapy, and time spent with the patient.

Whether medical E/M services were provided also affects code selection. Specific psychotherapy codes include E/M; codes from the E/M section should not be reported in addition to psychotherapy services.

Example:

90804	Individual psychotherapy, insight oriented, behavior modifying and/or supportive, in an office or outpatient facility, approximately 20 to 30 minutes face-to-face with the patient
90805	with medical evaluation and management services

HCPCS Level II coding tip: If the payer is Medicare and the encounter is a brief office visit for the sole purpose of monitoring or changing pschycoactive prescription drugs, report M0064.

Diagnosis coding tip: If a definitive condition has been documented, it is reported as the diagnosis. If the patient is being observed for behavior patterns pending diagnosis, it may be appropriate to report a V code for observation of certain conditions.

Biofeedback

Codes 90901–90911 are reported for biofeedback, during which patients learn to improve their health by using their own body signals, such as re-education of muscle groups to improve spasticity or weakness.

Diagnosis coding tip: Conditions may include stages of paralysis, muscle spasms, and urinary incontinence.

Dialysis and End Stage Renal Disease Services

Codes 90935–90940 are reported for hemodialysis, or direct removal of toxins from blood: Report 90935 for one physician evaluation and 90937 for repeat evaluations. Report 90940 for evaluation of blood flow through the graft or AV fistula during hemodialysis.

Codes 90945–90947 are reported for dialysis other than hemodialysis, such as peritoneal or hemofiltration.

Codes 90951–90962 are reported once per month for end-stage renal disease services. Codes are selected based on the age of the patient and on the number of face-to-face physician visits.

If a complete assessment has been provided, but the patient had less than one month of treatment, report codes 90967–90970 per day. Home dialysis patients admitted as inpatients will have a break in their home dialysis. In this case, report codes 90967–90970 for each day outside of inpatient hospitalization.

Report as appropriate, codes 90935–90937, 90945, or 90947 for dialysis during an inpatient stay.

Codes 90989–90993 are reported for patient and helper dialysis training. If a complete training course has been accomplished, report 90989. If the training course has not been completed, report 90993 per training session.

Significant, separately identifiable E/M services provided at the encounter, unrelated to dialysis and cannot be performed during the dialysis session may be reported separately using modifier 25.

Procedure coding tip: For declotting of an A/V fistula, report: 36831, 36833, 36860, 36861 or 36870 (percutaneous thrombectomy and intra-graft thrombolysis). Report 36861 when an external cannula is declotted and the thrombus is removed with a balloon catheter. Report 36833 if a revision is made to the graft after removing the clot.

Diagnosis coding tip: Patients requiring dialysis often have other chronic disease processes relating to dialysis. Specifically, when the patient has hypertension, renal failure, and heart failure, the coder should report a combination code in lieu of reporting each condition separately. Report a code from category 403 for hypertensive renal failure and report a code from category 404 for hypertensive heart and chronic kidney disease.

HCPCS Level II code tip: Dialysis patients often experience fatigue and anemia. Procrit® (erythropoietin) is a drug often administered to dialysis patients to encourage production of red blood cells. Report this drug with J0886 for dialysis patients.

Gastroenterology

Medicine codes for gastroenterology are covered in chapter 9: Digestive System.

Ophthalmological Services & Special Otorhinolaryngologic Services

Medicine codes for the eye and ocular adnexa are covered in chapter 13: Eye and Ocular Andexa, Auditory Systems.

Cardiovascular Services

Medicine codes for the cardiovascular system are covered in chapter 8: The Cardiovascular System.

Noninvasive Vascular Diagnostic Studies

Noninvasive vascular diagnostic studies are reported for investigation of blood flow in the head, extremities, viscera, and penis.

Duplex scans are ultrasonic scanning procedures confirming patterns and direction of blood flow. The scan produces real-time, two-dimensional images of arteries and veins.

Cerebrovascular arterial studies evaluate right and left anterior and posterior circulation territories (including both the vertebral and basilar arteries) using ultrasound technology. If two or fewer territories are evaluated, report the code for a limited study.

Diagnosis coding tip: Indications for these studies include occlusion and stenosis of an artery, with or without infarction, arterial syndromes, transient ischemic attack (TIA), atherosclerosis, aneurysm, embolism, thrombosis, and arterial injury.

Pulmonary Studies

These services are covered in chapter 17: Respiratory, Hemic, Lymphatic, Mediastinum, and Diaphragm.

Allergy and Immunology

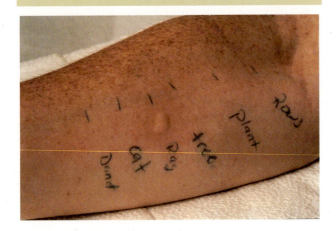

Scratch Test

Source: Delmar/Cengage Learning.

Codes 95004–95075 are reported for the testing of persons who exhibit hypersensitivity to certain materials, and include test interpretation and report by the physician. If the provider does not issue a report, append modifier 52 for reduced services.

Codes 95115–95199 describe professional services of allergen immunotherapy. Code 95180 is reported for rapid desensitization, which involves injecting an extract of allergen in gradually increasing doses.

Endocrinology & Neurology and Neuromuscular Procedures

These services are covered in chapter 12: Endocrine and Nervous System.

Medical Genetics and Genetic Counseling Services

Code 96040 describes services provided by a qualified genetic counselor to determine genetic risk of hereditary diseases. It is a time-based code to be reported for each 30 minutes face-to-face time with the patient and/or family.

Coding tip: Coders who work in molecular laboratories involved in genetic testing should refer to Genetic

Testing modifiers located in Appendix I of the CPT® codebook.

Central Nervous System Assessments/Tests

Psychological services (96101–96125) include psychological testing for neurocognitive and mental status. Health and behavior assessment interventions (96150–96155) focus on cognitive, social, and behavior factors, with a goal of prevention or improvement of the patient's physical health problems. Coding for these services is determined by time documented by the provider and whether the session is individual, group, or in the presence of family.

Coding tip: Payers may require modifier AH be appended to the claim to indicate a clinical psychologist, or modifier AJ to indicate a clinical social worker as the service provider.

Hydration, Therapeutic, Prophylactic, Diagnostic Injections/Infusions and Chemotherapy, Highly Complex Drugs or Highly Complex Biologic Agent Administration

Hydration

Codes 96360–96361 are reported for hydration administration. These are time-based codes. The infusion consists of pre-packaged fluid and electrolytes. These codes are not used for infusion of other substances.

Hydration codes are not reported separately if the fluid is used solely to facilitate administration of other drugs, such as chemotherapy. The coder should review the record to determine if the fluids were delivered to a dehydrated patient needing hydration therapy.

Start and stop times for the infusion, as well as the agent, will be recorded. If the administration occurs in the facility, these codes are not reported by the physician. The solution should be reported in addition to the administration charge using a HCPCS Level II code.

Non-Chemotherapy Complex Drugs and Substances

Codes 96365–96371 are reported for injection and infusion of complex nonchemotherapy drugs and substances. These codes are specific to time, technique, substances added during the infusion time, and additional setup and establishment of a new infusion. They are not reported by a physician when performed in a facility setting.

If a different type of administration is used, report it as subsequent, even if it is the first service from the infusion group.

Example:

Initial infusion of 1 hour, different drug administered by IV push; report the IV push as a subsequent service.

When several techniques or drugs are given, always determine the primary service. Chemotherapy is primary to nonchemotherapy infusion, which is primary to hydration.

Do not report the add-on code for additional hour of time unless at least 31 additional minutes are utilized.

If multiple drugs are infusing at the same time through the same IV line, they are "concurrent." Concurrent infusions may be reported only once per patient encounter unless protocol dictates two separate IV lines must be used. If infusion of a different drug through the same access site begins after the completion of the initial infusion, a sequential infusion is reported. Clinical justification for subsequent rather than concurrent should be clearly stated in the documentation.

Chemotherapy

Codes 96401–96425 are reported for chemotherapy administration by infusion, IV push, or injection. Codes are specific to time, technique, and additional substances added during administration. The substance is reported in addition to administration using the appropriate HCPCS Level II code(s). Chemotherapy drugs are located in the J9XXX range.

Codes 96440–96549 are reported for services other than standard infusion/injection techniques.

When thoracentesis is performed and the chemotherapy is delivered into the pleural cavity, code 96440 is reported. Thoracentesis is included.

Report 96446 when peritoneocentesis is performed and chemotherapy is delivered into the peritoneal cavity. Peritoneocentesis is included.

Report 96450 when chemotherapy is delivered into the central nervous system (for example, by intrathecal technique). Spinal puncture is included.

If a ventricular reservoir has been implanted for chemotherapy administration into the subarachnoid or intraventricular areas, report 96542.

Report 96549 for an unlisted chemotherapy procedure.

For refilling or maintenance of the implanted reservoir, report 96522. For irrigation of an access device implanted for the purpose of drug delivery, report 96523 if no other services are performed on the same day.

Coding tips: If infusion time is 15 minutes or less, IV push is reported. These infusion services include local anesthesia, start of the IV, access to indwelling IV, access to port or catheter, end of procedure flush and standard tubing, supplies, and syringes.

When multiple substances are delivered, only one initial administration code is reported unless a separate IV site is required. For example, an ICU patient requires two lines. A central line is placed for a Dopamine drip for hypotension and another line is required for antibiotics. Do not report the add-on code for an additional hour of time unless at least 31 additional minutes are utilized. If multiple drugs are mixed in the same bag, report one administration code unless the time extends to at least 1 hour, 31 minutes. Drugs are reported separately.

When multiple types of infusions are reported, an established hierarchy is utilized. For physician reporting, report the initial service as the primary reason for the encounter. For facility reporting, chemotherapy is reported primary to therapeutic, prophylactic, and diagnostic delivery, which is primary to hydration. Infusions are primary to IV push, which is primary to injections.

Patients receiving chemotherapy have a malignancy. Utilize the Neoplasm Table in ICD-9-CM for the correct site to report a neoplasm. The primary site is the origin of the cancer. Cancers metastasized to secondary sites are reported with the secondary category. There may be more than one secondary site. If the physician clinically is unable to determine the origin of the cancer, report 199.1 as the primary site. Blood cancers, such as leukemia and lymphoma, are located in the index instead of the Neoplasm Table.

Photodynamic Therapy & Special Dermatological Procedures

These CPT® codes describe special dermatology procedures frequently rendered on a consultative basis.

Actinotherapy involves exposing the patient's skin to ultraviolet light to treat skin disease, such as acne. Photochemotherapy combines light (photo) and chemicals to deliver an effective treatment. Goeckerman treatment involves topical application of tar (which makes lesions more sensitive to ultraviolet B light) or petrolatum and increasingly strong doses of ultraviolet B light. This form of therapy is used to treat psoriasis, eczema, or mycosis. Psoralens and ultraviolet A light help prevent the accelerated growth of immature skin cells characterizing psoriasis.

Code 96913 describes an aggressive form of photochemotherapy used to treat severe psoriasis and is usually an inpatient procedure.

Laser treatment for inflammatory skin disease (psoriasis) involves use of a beam of laser light concentrated on active psoriatic skin plaques. Codes are selected based on size in square centimeters of the area treated.

Physical Medicine and Rehabilitation

Codes 97001–97546 are reported for this service. The physician develops an initial treatment plan outlining the problem(s), goals, modalities to be used and projected time to reach the goal.

Procedures are performed by qualified physical, occupational, and speech therapists. The referring physician should review progress each 30 days. Medicare rules for billing and payment of therapy services may be different from CPT® information. Refer to the CMS website under therapy services for CMS guidelines.

Evaluation and Re-evaluation

Codes 97001–97006 are reported by the therapist for the initial evaluation and re-evaluation of a patient for physical therapy, occupational therapy, or athletic training.

Modalities

Codes 97010–97028 are modalities not requiring one-on-one contact by the therapist. These modalities include hot or cold packs, traction, vasopneumatic devices, paraffin bath, whirlpool, diathermy, infrared, ultraviolet, and some types of electric stimulation. More than one modality may be utilized during the therapy session. Modifier 51 is not appended for codes 97001–97755.

Codes 97032–97039 are modalities requiring one-on-one (constant attendance) patient contact by the therapist. These modalities include contrast baths, Hubbard tank, ultrasound, manual electric stimulation, and iontophoresis (introduction of ions into the tissue by electricity). These codes are reported for each 15-minute increment and require provider documentation of time for correct reporting of units.

Codes 97110–97546 are reported for therapeutic procedures performed to improve function and require one-on-one interaction by the provider. Code 97542 is reported for fitting and training of wheelchair use. Codes 97545 and 97546 are reported for work conditioning. Code 97150 is reported for group therapy of two or more patients.

Codes 97597–97606 are reported for wound care management. The provider must document the technique used to remove the tissue and the surface area of the wound. Services are reported for each session and require one-on-one interaction by the provider. Removal by debridement is reported with codes 97597–97602. Tissue removal by vacuum (negative pressure therapy) is reported with 97605–97606. Nonphysicians usually perform these procedures. Surgical debridement services are reported with 11040–11047 and should not be reported with 97597–97602.

Code 97750 is for reporting of performance measurement. When assistive technology is used to improve patient functionality, report 97755.

Codes 97760–97762 are reported for management of prosthetics and orthotics. Report 97761 for patient training in use of an extremity prosthesis.

Coding tip: Orthotic and prosthetic products are custom-made for the patient and reported separately using HCPCS Level II codes L0112–L9900. Modifiers used in therapy are: GN *Services delivered under an outpatient speech-language pathology plan of care*, GO *Services delivered under an outpatient occupational therapy plan of care*, and GP *Services delivered under an outpatient physical therapy plan of care*.

Medical Nutritional Therapy

Codes 97802–97804 are reported for special dietary assessments for patients requiring special dietary management. Codes 97802 and 97803 are reported for face-to-face interaction with the patient and are reported in 15-minute increments. Code 97804 is reported for a group session with two or more participants and is reported in 30-minute increments.

HCPCS Level II coding tip: Enteral and parenteral therapy products are reported separately with HCPCS Level II codes B4034–B9999.

Acupuncture

Codes 97810–97814 are reported for acupuncture services, with or without electric stimulation. The provider is face-to-face with the patient. Services are reported in 15-minute increments.

Coding tip: If a separate E/M service is provided at the same encounter, and is significantly outside the normal pre and post procedure work, it may be additionally reported using modifier 25. Do not include the time of the acupuncture service in the E/M service.

Osteopathic Manipulative Treatment

This service involves the provider (osteopathic physician, DO) using hands to move muscles and joints and includes stretching, gentle pressure, and resistance. Codes 98925–98929 are reported for application of

manual manipulation to improve somatic and related disorders. Code selection is based on the number of body regions manipulated.

Coding tip: If a separate E/M service is provided at the same encounter, and is significantly outside the normal pre- and post-procedure work, it may be additionally reported using modifier 25. Services may be related to symptoms for which osteopathic manipulative treatment (OMT) was provided.

Chiropractic Manipulative Treatment

Codes 98940–98943 are reported for chiropractic services (CMT). Codes are reported per number of regions manipulated, with 98940–98942 reported specifically for spinal manipulation. Code 98943 is reported for extraspinal manipulation.

Coding tip: Diagnosis codes will be related to neuropathy, spinal lesions, osteoarthrosis, spondylosis, inflammation, intervertebral disc disorders, spinal stenosis, scoliosis, injuries and muscle spasms. If the diagnosis describes an acute condition, include modifier AT *Acute treatment* on the service line. Medicare rules governing chiropractic services may be found at www.cms.hhs.gov.

Education and Training for Patient Self-Management

Codes 98960–98962 are reported for patient self-management training and education when prescribed by a physician. A nonphysician practitioner (NPP) provides the service. Training and education are applicable to the condition(s) identified by the appropriate diagnosis code(s). Codes are selected based on the number of patients. Codes will be selected based on the number of patients. Caregivers may be included in the sessions.

The codes are reportable in 30-minute increments and require the provider to document the time of the encounter.

Non-Face-to-Face Nonphysician Services

Telephone Services

Codes 98966–98968 are reported by qualified NPPs for telephone services provided to an established patient, parent, or guardian. If the telephone discussion results in a determination to see the patient within 24 hours or at the next available urgent appointment, the telephone service is considered part of the pre-work for the upcoming encounter, and should not be reported as a telephone service. These codes may be billed only if the call does not result in an urgent appointment and does not relate to an assessment and/or management service within the past seven days.

Codes are selected by time, which must be documented by the provider.

Coding tip: Coverage and reimbursement for codes 98966–98968 is payer-specific. Discuss with your payer the circumstances of coverage. Report codes 99441–99443 if a physician provides the telephone service.

Online Medical Evaluation

Code 98969 is reported for online medical evaluation using the internet or other electronic communication modes to answer an established patient's online inquiry. Service may include parent or guardian inquiry. The service is reported by a qualified NPP once per seven-day period, per provider, for the same episode of care. The response must be timely and the ability to store the communication is required. If services are provided within seven days or within the post-operative period of a previously completed procedure, the service is considered covered by the previous encounter. It is expected that the communication will include a total of telephone calls, laboratory orders, and prescription management that relate to the online patient encounter.

Coding tip: Coverage and reimbursement for code 98969 is payer-specific. Discuss with your payer the circumstances of coverage. Report code 99444 (found in E/M section at the beginning of CPT®) if a physician provides the online service.

Special Services, Procedures, and Reports

Codes 99000–99091 are miscellaneous codes involving special services, procedures, and reports.

Physicians often contract with an independent laboratory to test specimens and provide reports. Code 99000 is reported for transfer of a laboratory specimen from a physician office to a laboratory. Code 99001 is reported for transfer of a specimen from the patient in a site other than a physician's office.

When a physician order involves a service related to custom-made devices, report 99002. These items need to be fitted and adjusted by the physician and require delivery to the physician office.

Report code 99024 for a related post-operative visit during the global period of a procedure to indicate the E/M service provided. This code is not separately payable, but is considered a component of the procedure.

Report codes 99026 and 99027 for mandated hospital on-call personnel. These codes typically are not reimbursed, but are required by certain hospital personnel. Do not report codes 99026 and 99027 for physician standby services.

Codes 99050–99060 are reported for patient encounters outside normal posted business hours or for special circumstances at the request of the patient. These codes are reported in addition to the basic service.

Coding tip: Coverage and reimbursement for codes 99050–99060 are payer specific. Discuss the circumstances of coverage with your payer.

Code 99070 is reported for supplies provided by the physician not usually included in an office visit. Items may include sterile trays, drugs, vaccines, and immune globulins; and may be reported separately if not considered integral to a procedure. Reimbursement may be on an acquisition cost basis.

Coding tip: Eyeglasses are not included in 99070. Refer to HCPCS Level II codes for specific eyeglass codes. Some payers (Medicare and possibly others) require individual listing of the items/drugs using HCPCS Level II codes instead of 99070.

Code 99071 is reported for physician cost of educational materials dispensed to the patient for specific educational information.

Code 99075 is reported for time the physician spends providing medical testimony.

Code 99078 is reported for group educational sessions when conducted by a physician.

Code 99080 is reported for completion of forms and reports exceeding usual and standard information.

Code 99082 is reported for unusual travel by a physician (for example, accompanying a patient).

Code 99090 is reported for analyzing stored data in a computerized mode.

Code 99091 is reported for interpretation of data that has been stored digitally and transmitted to the physician or qualified health care professional. Transmission may be by the patient or caregiver. The provider must spend at least 30 minutes to report this code.

Coding tip: Coverage and reimbursement for codes 99071–99091 is payer-specific. Discuss with your payer the circumstances of coverage.

Qualifying Circumstances for Anesthesia & Moderate (Conscious) Sedation

These services are covered in chapter 14: Anesthesia.

Other Services and Procedures

Code 99170 is reported for an anogenital colposcopic examination of a child when there is suspicion of trauma.

Coding tip: Diagnosis codes may be related to injuries in the rectal and/or genital area and suspected child abuse. If an examination is performed with no confirmation of diagnosis, report codes V65.5 *Person with feared complaint in whom no diagnosis was made* or V70.4 *Examination for medicolegal reasons.*

Code 99172 is reported for determination of visual acuity, ocular alignment, color vision, and visual field.

The service must use graduated visual acuity stimuli allowing a quantitative estimate of visual acuity (sharpness of vision). Code 99173 is reported for a screening test of visual acuity.

Coding tip: Do not report codes 99172 and 99173 if a general ophthalmological service or an E/M of the eye is performed. If an additional E/M service is performed and is unrelated to these tests, it may be reported separately using modifier 25.

Code 99174 is reported for bilateral ocular photoscreening with interpretation and report.

Coding tip: Do not report 99174 with 92002–92014, 99172, and 99173. Diagnosis codes supporting this service are in categories 367–378.

Code 99175 is reported for administration of ipecac or similar material for initiation of emesis. The provider observes the patient until the stomach has emptied.

Coding tip: Refer to the Table of Drugs and Chemicals in the ICD-9-CM book for diagnosis code information.

Code 99183 is reported for hyperbaric oxygen therapy when supervised and attended by a physician. Procedures such as wound debridement and/or E/M services may be reported separately when provided during a hyperbaric oxygen therapy session in a dedicated treatment facility.

Code 99190–99192 is reported for operation of a pump with oxygenator or heat exchanger, and includes assembly and operation of the unit. Codes are selected based on time.

Coding tip: Appropriate diagnosis codes are related to cardiac failure in category 428. They also may be reported for cardiogenic shock.

Home Health Procedures and Services

Codes 99500–99602 are reported by nonphysician practitioners providing services in a home setting (the environment in which the patient resides, including assisted living facilities, group homes, and custodial care facilities).

Code 99500 is reported for a home visit for prenatal services including monitoring of gestational diabetes, fetal assessment, and uterine monitoring.

Coding tip: Diagnosis codes are in categories 641, 642, 643, 644 and 648 if a condition has been confirmed. If the encounter is for supervision or examination, report the diagnosis from category V22 or category V24.

Code 99501 is reported for a home visit for postnatal follow-up care.

Coding tip: Diagnosis codes are reported from category V24.

Code 99502 is reported for home care assessment of a newborn.

Coding tip: Diagnosis code from range V20.31–V20.32 is reported for this service.

Code 99503 is reported for home care management of respiratory conditions, including evaluation of apnea, oxygen management, and changes in medication such as bronchodilators.

Coding tip: Review diagnosis codes related to respiratory neoplasms, cystic fibrosis, obstructive bronchitis, asthma, pneumonia, and other pulmonary conditions.

Code 99504 is reported for home care management of a ventilator.

Coding tip: Diagnosis codes are reported from category 518 or categories 768–769 for newborns.

Code 99505 is reported for home care of ostomies and stomas.

Coding tip: The diagnosis code should be reported from category V55 range, along with the condition requiring the ostomy/stoma.

Code 99506 is reported for a home visit for intramuscular injections. Diagnosis codes are determined by the condition as stated by the physician plan of care. Medications may be reported with appropriate HCPCS Level II codes, in addition to the injection administration code.

Code 99507 is reported for a home care visit for catheter maintenance. The service varies depending on the type, location, and reason for the catheter.

Coding tip: The diagnosis code is V58.82, plus the condition that required the catheter.

Code 99509 is reported for a home visit for assistance with activities of daily living. The patient must be unable to perform two or more activities of daily living, such as: eating, toileting, transferring, bathing, dressing, and continence.

Coding tip: Diagnosis codes are reported to describe the impairment preventing independent daily activities. Do not report this code for speech therapy (92507–92508), nutrition assessment (97802–97804), or self-management training (97535).

Code 99510 is reported for a home visit for counseling sessions including marriage counseling. Participants may be an individual or family.

Coding tip: Diagnosis codes to report are in category V62 and category V65, including any specific problems addressed in the physician order for services.

Code 99511 is reported for a home visit for management of fecal impaction and/or administration of enema.

Coding tip: Refer to diagnosis codes 560.30, 560.39, or 564.00–564.09.

Code 99512 is reported for home visits for hemodialysis.

Coding tip: The diagnosis code is V56.0 *Encounter for renal dialysis*. Other diagnosis codes may include categories 403 and 404 and 585.1–585.9. Do not report this code for peritoneal dialysis (90945–90947).

Home Infusion Procedures

Peritoneal Dialysis

- Fresh dialysate solution
- Tenchkoff peritoneal catheter
- Peritoneal cavity
- Adapter
- Used dialysate solution

Source: Delmar/Cengage Learning.

Codes 99601 and 99602 are reported for home visits for infusion of specialty drug administration, and are reported per visit.

Coding tip: These codes may be reported for peritoneal dialysis and other therapeutic and prophylactic agents. Medications given are reported separately.

Medication Therapy Management Services

A pharmacist may report codes 99605–99607 for patient assessment, intervention, or management of medication interaction/complications. Code selection is determined on whether the patient is new or established, and time reported for the management service.

Coding tip: Report a diagnosis code from category V65.

Glossary

Allergy—Hypersensitivity caused by exposure to an antigen (or allergen).

Artery—Vessel carrying blood from the heart to the tissues.

Autonomic—Involuntary, relating to the autonomic nervous system.

Biofeedback—Training technique for development of a person's ability to control his or her autonomic nervous system.

Bipolar Disorder—Affective disorder with alternating mood swings from euphoria to depression.

Catheterization—Insertion of a catheter into a body structure.

Chemotherapy—Treatment of disease by means of chemical substances or drugs; usually cancers.

Chiropractic—Treatment predominately using manipulation of spinal and musculoskeletal structures and recuperative powers of the body.

Cognitive—Thoughts or thinking, learning, or memory processes.

Comorbidity—Presence of two or more illnesses at the same time. There may or may not be an association between the illnesses.

Compulsion—Repetitive behavior with ritualistic characteristics; uncontrolled impulse.

Debridement—Removal of dead or damaged tissue to promote healing.

Decompensation—Deterioration; exacerbation of an illness or condition.

Desensitize—Lessening of sensitivity by administration of a specific antigen in low doses.

Dialysis—Removal of toxins from the blood by diffusion over a membrane or filter in patients with renal impairment or failure.

Disorientation—Inability to estimate direction or location.

Doppler Study—Use of an ultrasound probe to determine blood flow.

Enteral Nutrition—Nutrients for patients with impaired ability to chew/swallow or ingest food, typically delivered by gastric or nasogastric tube.

Extracranial—Outside the skull.

Extraspinal—Outside the spine.

Gait Training—Method of restoration of balance, extremity swings, stance.

Gastroenterology—Study of the stomach, intestine, esophagus, liver, gallbladder, and pancreas.

Genetics—Study of heredity.

Grandiosity—Unrealistic concept of self importance.

Hallucination—False sense of perception or reality.

Home Care—Prescribed medical care provided in a patient's home.

Hydration—Replenishment of fluids.

Immune Globulin—Antibodies derived from blood plasma providing short term protection against certain infections.

Infusion—Therapeutic agent (liquid) introduced into the body by a vein.

Injection—Fluid introduced into tissue, cavity or vessel, usually by needle.

Loosening of Association—Frequent change of subject, often with minimal relationship.

Manipulation—Thrusting movement to achieve realignment of joints or spine.

Modality—A therapeutic agent or application.

Neuropsychology—Study and treatment of psychiatric and neurological disorders.

On Call—Medical personnel with special training and skills available to provide services when summoned.

Orientation—Awareness; ability to comprehend and to adjust in an environment.

Orthotic—Custom made mechanical appliance used in orthopaedics.

Panic Attack—Intense anxiety; feels like a loss of control.

Parenteral Nutrition—Nutrients delivered intravenously to patients who are postoperative, in shock, or otherwise unresponsive.

Prosthetic—Artificial body part.

Psychology—Study of behavior, thoughts, feelings.

Psychotherapy—Method of treating mental disorders. Treatment may involve education, pharmacology, suggestion, psychoanalysis.

Range of Motion—Natural movement; usually referring to movement of a joint.

Reflux—Backward flow.

Rehabilitation—Effort to restore to optimal function.

Short Term Memory—Ability to recall recent events.

Therapeutic—To promote healing; treatment.

Toxoid—Substance no longer toxic but is capable of stimulating antibody production.

Vaccine—Preparation of (bacteria or virus) nonpathogenic material, induces immunity to prevent disease.

Vein—Blood vessel carrying blood toward the heart.

Venom—Poisonous fluid secreted by bites or stings from snakes, spiders, etc.

Chapter Review Questions

1. PAD rehabilitative physical exercises are used for what disease/disorder?

    A. Pernicious anemia disorder

    B. Peripheral artery disease

    C. Peroneal muscular atrophy disease

    D. Psychologically defeated disorder

2. Nerve conduction, amplitude and latency study of the median sensory nerve to the first digit is coded with what CPT® code?

    A. 95900

    B. 95903

    C. 95904

    D. 95905

3. A pregnant 35-year-old established patient with thoracic and low back pain, requests osteopathic manipulative treatment to her back. Osteopathic manipulative therapy is done on one to two body regions for somatic dysfunction. Therapy is performed by high velocity, low amplitude. Muscle spasm is not present. What CPT® and diagnoses codes are reported for this encounter?

    A. 98925, 724.1, 724.2

    B. 98926, 724.1, 724.5

    C. 98940, 724.4, 724.2

    D. 98943, 723.1, 724.2

4. Patient presented in clinic today for asthma exacerbation. Spirometry was done prior to albuterol. Albuterol 1 mg was given via nebulizer, and then two out of three attempts were obtained for spirometry and showed an obstructive pattern. After nebulizer use, most of her wheezing resolved with slightly increased air movement, but there was still restricted flow. What CPT® code is reported for this service?

    A. 94010

    B. 94060

    C. 94012

    D. 94070

5. A 10-year-old, established patient has a high fever and sore throat. The mother contacts the office at closing time and is told to bring the child to the office for treatment. The office remained open until they arrived. The physician performs a problem focused history, expanded problem focused exam, and the medical decision making is of low complexity. What CPT® codes are reported for this service?

    A. 99213, 99058

    B. 99212, 99056

    C. 99213, 99050

    D. 99212, 99051

6. Today in the office, a 53-year-old receives two allergy injections IM in her left upper arm for ragweed and cat dander. The doctor administers the allergen extract brought in by the patient. What is the CPT® code for this service?

    A. 95144

    B. 95117

    C. 95165 x 2

    D. 95125

7. A 65-year-old stumbles and trips in her home, landing on her side and injuring her left hip. The ER physician gets the X-ray back showing an anterior dislocation of the left hip. Consent is given for sedation for the reduction of the hip. The ER physician administers Ketamine (IV) and a nurse is there to assist in the monitoring of the patient for 15 minutes. Abduction is performed on the right hip and reduction is successful by the ER physician. Upon recovery from sedation, the patient states she feels better. What CPT® code(s) are reported by the ER physician?

    A. 27252-54, 99149

    B. 27266-54

    C. 27250-54, 99144

    D. 27257-54

8. A 6-year-old patient comes in for a preventive medicine service. Along with the exam, the physician does visual acuity screening using the Rosenbaum Test and a hearing screening test. The patient only responds to tones of different pitches and intensities. What CPT® codes are reported for the visual acuity and hearing screening?

    A. 99170, 92550

    B. 99172, 92551

    C. 99173, 92551

    D. 99174, 92550

9. **Medical Record Documentation #1:**

Chief Complaints/Concerns

1. Established patient with back pain, requests OMT to back, is pregnant about 35 weeks.

2. Depression. Has been feeling more stressed and depressed the last few weeks. Has been treated for depression in the past, but not since she has been pregnant. Has been having some bad thoughts but no intent or any kind of planning.

Procedures

Osteopathic manipulation therapy (OMT).
Osteopathic manipulative therapy done on one to two body regions for somatic dysfunction. Therapy performed by the following method: high velocity low amplitude. Muscle spasm is not present.

Exam

VS—T98, RR -20, BP 120/78

Appearance: healthy appearing female at 35 weeks, nutrition good, hair disheveled

Psychiatric: Speech—quiet, slow; asked pt. several times to speak up

Thought processes—reasoning okay, somewhat slow response time, distracted

Associations—loose thinking, wanders from one topic to another

Abnormal or psychotic thoughts—no suicidal ideation; delusions; or hallucinations

Judgment—insight intact regarding current difficult situation

Abdomen—soft, non-tender, S + 35 cm, FH—136

Reflexes—2 +, normal

Extremities—1+ edema, normal

Pelvic exam—not done

Back—no obvious lesions, intact. No redness or swelling

No CVAT

Assessment/Plan

Low back pain (LBP), acute

Pain in thoracic spine, acute

Depression,

Medication prescribed, medications reviewed, side effects reviewed, discussed treatment plan with patient

Somatic dysfunction, thoracic, acute

Somatic dysfunction, lumbar, acute

Encounter for therapeutic drug monitoring, severe

Medications ordered, renewed, and stopped this visit:

Brand Name	Dose	Sig Desc
Zoloft	50mg	One by mouth daily x 3 Days then 2 POQD

Start Date	Stop Date
02/29/20xx	

Follow-up:

Status	Follow-up	Time Frame	Reason/Comment
Ordered	Office visit	in 3 Days	Recheck

What are the CPT® and ICD-9-CM codes for this dictation?

10. **Medical Record Documentation #2:**

Chief Complaints/Concerns: 1. New patient; 2-year-old WCE (well child exam). Mom doesn't have immunization record. States child's last shot was given when he was 5 months old.

Past Medical History & Family History—Reviewed.

Pediatric Interval Social History
Sleep: There are no sleep concerns.

Activity Level: There are no activity or exercise concerns.

Developmental History—All areas of development are appropriate for age.

Review of Systems

Constitutional: No fever, irritability or lethargy; good appetite.

HEENT: Sees and hears well; no eye, ear or nasal discharge.

Respiratory: No cough, no audible wheeze, respirations normal.

Cardiovascular: No color changes.

Gastrointestinal: No vomiting, diarrhea or constipation.

Bowel elimination history: There are no bowel concerns.

Nutrition history:
Patient drinks milk from a cup; on demand; of 2% milk daily.

Patient drinks juice from a cup on demand; of varied juice daily.

Patient drinks water from a cup; on demand; of well water daily.

Genitourinary: Normal urine output.

Bladder elimination history: There are no bladder concerns.

Dermatologic: No unusual rashes.

Musculoskeletal: Moving all extremities as usual; normal gait.

Vital Signs: Height 37.50 in, Weight 35.50 lb

Physical Exam

General/Constitutional: No apparent distress. Well nourished and well developed.

Ears: TM's gray. Landmarks normal. Positive light reflex.

Nose/Throat: Nose and throat clear; palate intact; no lesions.

Lymphatic: No palpable cervical, supraclavicular or axillary adenopathy.

Respiratory: Normal to inspection. Lungs clear to auscultation.

Cardiovascular: RRR without murmurs.

Abdomen: Non-distended, non-tender. Soft, no organomegaly, no masses.

Integumentary: No unusual rashes or lesions.

Musculoskeletal: Good strength; no deformities. Full ROM all extremities.

Extremities: Extremities appear normal.

Assessment/Plan

Routine Infant/Child Health Visit
Immunizations given: MMR, IPV, DTaP, Comvax-HIB, Varicella

What are the CPT® and ICD-9-CM codes for this dictation?

CPC® Exam

The CPC® exam is a 150-question, timed exam. The exam tests coding skills for professional services. The categories include:

- Integumentary Surgical Coding
- Respiratory Surgical Coding
- Nervous System Surgical Coding
- Endocrine System Surgical Coding
- Digestive System Surgical Coding
- Urinary System Surgical Coding
- Musculoskeletal System Surgical Coding
- Mediastinum & Diaphragm Surgical Coding
- Male/Female Genital Surgical Coding
- Hemic & Lymphatic Surgical Coding
- Maternity & Delivery
- Eye & Ocular Adnexa Surgical Coding
- ICD-9-CM
- HCPCS Level II
- Radiology
- Pathology
- Laboratory
- Medicine
- Anesthesia
- Evaluation and Management
- Anatomy and Physiology
- Medical Terminology
- Coding Guidelines
- Practice Management

Preparing for Your Exam

The CPC® exam is open book. The codebooks allowed during the exam include CPT® (Professional or Standard edition), HCPCS Level II, and ICD-9-CM codebooks. You must use the current year version of all codebooks.

Please visit AAPC's website for the list of approved codebooks.

The best strategy to prepare for the exam is reading your codebooks cover to cover. Examinees should review all coding guidelines found within each section and subsection of the CPT® codebook, the Official Coding Guidelines in the ICD-9-CM codebook, and all coding guidelines in the HCPCS Level II codebook. This study guide should be used along with your codebooks as you prepare for the exam.

Successful examinees have well-thumbed codebooks. Become familiar with all parts of your CPT®, ICD-9-CM, and HCPCS Level II codebooks, and know how to locate the codes, guidelines, tables, and instructions within them quickly. This may be the most important tip we can give you: We recommend going through your books to mark them, tab and label them, and make notes in them for easy reference.

Anything with which you feel you might need some extra help is something we would suggest tabbing or marking. For the exam, you can write helpful notes in your books and tab them for easy reference, but you may not glue, tape, staple, or add anything to the books. You also may wish to highlight certain guidelines in your codebooks. Keep in mind, all notes in your codebooks should be relevant to work performed daily by a coder.

Examples of items to highlight or add:

ICD-9-CM codebook in the tabular list:

- Code first notes
- Use additional code notes
- Codes that are excluded from a category
- Note under Fractures category (800–829) that tells you what is considered a closed and opened fracture.

CPT® codebook:

- Key words in the subsection guidelines (eg, new and established patient definition in the E/M section)
- Draw an E/M table in your CPT® if you think it will better assist you in determining E/M services.
- Key words in the Repair (Closure) guideline section defining simple, intermediate, or complex repairs.
- Guidelines for the services included with Adjacent Tissue Transfer or Rearrangement procedures.
- Key words in the Musculoskeletal System guidelines defining surgical procedures, such as closed, opened, percutaneous skeletal fixation, or manipulation.
- All parenthetical notes found in the code description or following the code.
- Make note of any symbols placed before a procedure code indicating the procedure is an add-on code (+13122), modifier 51 exempt (⊘ 31500), or includes moderate sedation (⊙ 35471).
- Make note of procedures performed percutaneously, with any type of scope (endoscope, laparoscope, etc.), or by open technique (meaning the doctor had to cut into the patient to perform the procedure).

If you need additional coding practice, AAPC's online practice tests are excellent test simulation tools. The practice tests follow the same format as the CPC® exam, and have been developed by AAPC's exam content team. The practice tests are available at www.aapc.com/training/practice-exams.aspx.

Exam Registration

CPC® exam registration can be completed on AAPC's website (www.aapc.com). When your examination application has been processed, you will receive a confirmation email regarding the date and location of your exam. You may view the proctor's name and telephone number as well as the exam location and start time on AAPC's website under the "My AAPC" section.

Be sure to arrive to the exam on time. If the exam location is unfamiliar to you, get directions from www.googlemaps.com or www.mapquest.com. Verify the start time and examination address at least two days before your test date.

Day of the Exam

Try to arrive 10–15 minutes early. Take into consideration any construction, traffic, or possible inclement weather during your commute that may affect your drive time.

In addition to your codebooks, you must bring a photo ID, plenty of #2 pencils, and an eraser. Do not bring scrap paper—it is not allowed during the exam.

You will perform better when you get a good night's sleep before the examination. We do not believe staying up all night studying for the exam is very useful. It will not matter how "prepared" you are if you fall asleep during the exam.

We recommend you eat a healthy breakfast (nothing too heavy) and bring light snacks and water to keep you energized during the exam. Peppermint or lemon candy generally keeps you alert. We request that you avoid anything loud or crunchy (eg, soda cans or potato chips) because this could be distracting for other examinees.

If you are sensitive to noise, bring earplugs to eliminate distractions during the exam.

Layer your clothing in case the room temperature fluctuates. A light jacket is always a good idea.

During the Test

Be comfortable but alert. Choose a good spot in the room and make sure you have enough space to work. Maintain comfortable posture in your seat, but do not "slouch."

Listen carefully while the proctor reads the instructions. Ask questions before the examination begins if you do not understand the instructions given.

Stay relaxed and confident. Keep a good attitude. Remind yourself you are well prepared and are going to do well. If you find yourself anxious, take several slow, deep breaths to relax. It is probably best not to talk about the test to other students just before entering the room: Their anxiety can be contagious.

Scan the entire test when you are instructed to begin.

Answer the easiest, shortest questions first. Do not stay on a problem on which you are stuck, especially when time is a factor. Keep moving: This will build confidence and allow you to score points and mentally orient yourself to vocabulary, concepts, and your studies. It also helps you make associations with more difficult questions.

Read all the choices before choosing your answer. First, eliminate those answers you know to be wrong, are likely to be wrong, or do not seem to fit. If you do not know an answer, skip it. Go on with the rest of the test and come back to it later. Other parts of the test may have information that will help you with that question. Make sure if you skip a question you do not accidently fill in the bubble on the grid until you go back to the question.

Remember to pace yourself. Read the entire question and look for key words. You have an average of 2 minutes and 15 seconds to answer each question. Stay relaxed and do not panic.

Read each question slowly and carefully. This may seem obvious, but it helps you avoid careless errors. Note such words in the question as "not," "except," "most," "least" and "greatest," or "add together, code each." These words are often crucial in determining the correct answer. There are no "trick" questions on the exam, so do not worry about hidden words or meanings.

Remember to use the guidelines in your codebooks. Often they will help you select the correct answer. Also, check for any parenthetical statements that may influence your answer.

Answer every question. If you do not know the right answer, eliminate as many wrong answers as possible, then select among the remaining answers. If you do not have a clue, make your best guess. Narrow down the answer options by eliminating answers you know are not correct. A guess is better than a blank response.

Don't worry about how fast other people finish their test; just concentrate on your own test. Be especially careful about marking your answer sheet. Make sure to fill in your selected bubble on the test grid correctly. Try to avoid making any other marking on the answer grid. Exams are machine graded and to ensure an accurate score, bubbles must be filled out as shown on the

example provided on your test grid. Stray marks could be misread. If you must mark your place, you may mark in your test booklet, but be sure to erase any stray marks later on.

If you finish with additional time, use that time to go back and review any questions of which you were unsure. Use the codebooks again to confirm.

Make sure you answer all questions. Only change an answer if you misread or misinterpreted the question; the first answer you choose usually is correct. Watch out for careless mistakes. Double-check to make sure you have filled in the exam grid properly with your first name, last name, and ID number.

Exam Completion

Exam results are usually released within five to seven business days after AAPC receives the exam package back from the proctor. Results will be accessible in the My AAPC area on AAPC's website, www.aapc.com. Official result documents will be mailed within two weeks of their receipt at the national office. Please do not call AAPC for your test results. Exam results may not be released over the telephone.

The following 35 questions will test your comprehension of the information covered in this study guide. You should be able to complete this exercise in approximately 80 minutes. Answers are found in Appendix B.

Important Note: Although this exercise is a useful assessment tool, the best means to gauge your preparedness to pass the CPC exam is to take our online practice exams (found at www.aapc.com/cpcpractice) which mirror the actual test format and difficulty level. The practice exams are timed and are created by the CPC exam development team.

1. **Two malignant lesions on the scalp measuring 1.1 cm and 2.0 cm, and one malignant lesion on the neck measuring 2.2 cm were destroyed. Electrocautery was used for the first two lesions and laser was used for the third lesion.**

    What procedure codes are reported?

    A. 17276

    B. 17273, 17272-51

    C. 17273, 17272-51, 17272-51

    D. 17274, 17273-51

2. **Operative Report**

Preoperative Diagnosis: Possible basal cell carcinoma.

Postoperative Diagnosis: Basal cell carcinoma.

Procedure Performed: Excision lesion 4.3 cm x 2 cm left thigh; FTSG from calf to thigh.

Anesthesia: General by LMA.

Description of Procedure: After undergoing adequate general anesthesia and DuraPrep prepping the left thigh and draping with cloth towels and drapes, 0.25 percent Marcaine with epinephrine, total of 30 cc, was used to anesthetize the skin.

A lesion slightly over 4 cm was observed on the patient's left thigh. A small portion was removed and sent for frozen section analysis. This returned basal cell carcinoma. Per prior consent, we removed the remaining lesion with a .75 surrounding margin. Due to size and location of this lesion, the decision was made to harvest a full thickness skin graft from his left lower leg.

Lower leg was prepped and draped and 0.25 percent Marcaine was injected. Excision of 5 cm x 5 cm full thickness graft was obtained and placed on back table for prep. We returned to the thigh area. All edges were trimmed and the graft was placed into the defect and sewn with a running #3-0 Vicryl. The skin edges were approximated with a running subcuticular #4-0 Vicryl, and further sealed with Dermabond. Hemostasis was well controlled. The wound was irrigated with normal saline.

What procedure and diagnosis code(s) are reported?

A. 11406, 15770, 12032, 173.71

B. 11606, 15220, 15221, 173.71

C. 11402, 15220, 195.5

D. 11602, 15220, 15221, 195.5

3. **Operative Report**

    Preoperative Diagnosis: Lipoma of right back.

    Postoperative Diagnosis: Lipoma of right back.

    Procedure Performed: Excision of lipoma, right back (6 cm diameter).

    Description of Procedure: The patient was placed on the operating table in the lateral position with the right side elevated. The location of the lipoma had been marked in the preoperative area. It was at the superior edge of the right iliac crest. The area was prepped with Betadine and sterile drapes were applied.

    A transverse incision was made directly over the lipoma. Subcutaneous tissues were incised. The lipoma was identified and found to be smooth, multilobulated, yellow, and discrete. It was completely excised down to the muscle overlying the iliac crest. Bleeding was controlled with electrocautery. The subcutaneous tissues were approximated with a continuous subcuticular 3-0 plain catgut suture. Benzoin, Steri-Strips, and dry gauze dressings were applied.

    Blood loss was negligible and the final sponge count was reported as correct. The patient was sent to the recovery room in stable condition.

    What CPT® and ICD-9-CM codes are reported?

    A. 27047, 214.1

    B. 21931, 214.1

    C. 21930, 173.50

    D. 11606, 173.50

4. **A 55-year-old patient complains of an injury to his right hip leading to a probable dislocation that occurred 1 hour prior to arrival. The patient states he was sleeping in bed, fell off, and landed on his right side. Patient denies numbness or tingling. Patient denies any further injury. No additional complaints or treatments prior to arrival.**

    Intervention:

    IV: normal saline; Pulse Ox: 98 percent on room air X-ray right hip: Positive hip dislocation. Dr. Thompson was notified of the patient's physical exam findings and test results. The patient was prepared and agreed to conscious sedation to include placement on continuous EKG monitoring, O2, suction and bag-valve-mask ready, pulse oximetry in place. Fentanyl 50 mg IV and Versed 2 mg IV was given by Dr. Miller who supervised the MCS for 30 minutes. The patient's right hip was easily reduced using gentle traction by Dr. Thompson. Post reduction X-ray showed right hip in good location with no obvious fracture. The patient tolerated the procedure very well.

    What procedure codes are reported by both physicians?

    A. 27257-RT, 99149

    B. 27257-RT

    C. 27250-RT, 01200

    D. 27250-RT, 99149

5. At the patient hospital bedside using Xylocaine local anesthesia, aseptic technique, and ultrasound guidance, a 21-gauge needle was used to aspirate the right cephalic vein of a 72-year-old patient. Ultrasound demonstrated vascular needle entry and vessel patency of the cephalic and subclavian veins. When blood was obtained, a 0.018 inch platinum tip guidewire was advanced to the central venous circulation. A 6 French dual lumen PICC was introduced through a 6 French peel-away sheath to the SVA RA junction; and, after removal of the sheath, the catheter was attached to the skin with a STAT-LOCK device and flushed with 500 units of Heparin in each lumen. Permanent ultrasound recordings were placed in the record. A sterile dressing was applied and the patient was discharged in improved condition.

What CPT® code(s) are reported for the physician?

    A. 36569, 76937-26

    B. 36568, 76942-26

    C. 36569, 76942-26

    D. 36556, 76942-26

6. **Operative Report**

Preoperative Diagnosis: Symptomatic bradycardia

Postoperative Diagnosis: Symptomatic bradycardia

Operative Procedure: Implantation of cardiac pacemaker

Indications: The patient is an 83-year-old white male who presented with spells of being lightheaded and near syncopal. Evaluation showed him to be in first-degree AV block with symptomatic bradycardia and rates in the 40s. For this reason, consideration was given regarding implantation of a dual chamber pacemaker. I reviewed the risks, rationale, expected outcome, typical postoperative course of implantation of a cardiac pacemaker. He appears to understand and is willing to proceed.

Procedure: The patient was placed on the operating room table in the supine position under satisfactory intravenous sedation. The skin of the anterior chest wall and base of the neck was prepped and draped in the usual sterile fashion. Following this, the infraclavicular space was thoroughly anesthetized with a 50:50 mixture of 1 percent Lidocaine with epinephrine and 0.5 percent Marcaine.

Following this, two separate needle sticks in the subclavian vein were made and two guide wires inserted. Over the first or more proximal guide wire, an introducer sheath was passed and the ventricular lead was introduced. The ventricular lead was taken down into what appeared to be the ventricle. Placement was very difficult as there were a lot of surfaces in the right ventricle, which were nonconductive. Eventually we were able to find an area near the tip of the ventricle with R waves in the 7–10 range and capture at 0.5 volt. This being an acceptable parameter, we passed a split sheath introducer over the other wire and an atrial lead slipped into place. It was positioned relatively easily into the atrial appendage. The lead was screwed into position and it returned P waves in the 1.5 range and capture down to 1.1 volt. Overall this was, considering the circumstances and his advanced age, felt to be a reasonable implant site.

The leads were secured at the pectoralis major muscle with suture of 2-0 silk, and the pacemaker attached without incident. The pacemaker was placed in its pocket. The wound was closed in layers of 2-0 Vicryl subcutaneous and 3-0 Monocryl for a subcuticular skin closure. Tegaderm dressing was applied. The patient tolerated the procedure well, and was transported to the recovery area in stable condition.

What procedure code is reported?

    A. 33208

    B. 33206

    C. 33207

    D. 33212

7. Mildred was seen by the surgeon for a right parotid mass measuring 1.7 x 1.1 cm. She complained of pain, and did not get relief from antibiotics. A right lateral lobe parotidectomy, with dissection and preservation of the facial nerve, was completed.

   What procedure code is reported?

   A. 42410-RT

   B. 42415-RT

   C. 42420

   D. 42330

8. **Operative Report**

   Preoperative Diagnosis: Carcinoma of the colon: colonic polyps

   Postoperative Diagnosis: Carcinoma of the colon: colonic polyps

   Operative Procedure: Colonoscopy

   Indications: The patient is a 75-year-old white male patient of Dr. Smith whom I have followed for a number of years for colon polyps. About three years ago he underwent a radical right hemicolectomy for carcinoma of the hepatic flexure of the colon. His postoperative course has been uneventful to date. He returns now for his routine recommended screening colonoscopy. He appears to understand the risks, rationale, expected outcome, typical postoperative course, and is willing to proceed.

   Procedure:

   The patient was placed on the table in the left lateral decubitus position, given intravenous Demerol and propofol for sedation. Following this, a digital rectal exam was performed which was essentially unremarkable. This was followed by introduction of the Olympus video colonoscope, which was advanced through a relatively normal appearing rectum, sigmoid colon, descending colon, and transverse to the level of the ileocolic anastomosis. This was unremarkable in its appearance and widely patent. The scope was then withdrawn. There were no polyps, telangiectasias, angiodysplasias, or other endoluminal abnormalities encountered. The scope was removed. The patient tolerated the procedure well and was transferred to the recovery area in stable condition.

   What are the diagnosis and procedure codes for this Medicare patient?

   A. G0121, V76.51

   B. 45378, 154.0

   C. G0105, V10.05, V12.72

   D. 45380, 154.0, 211.3

9. After the patient was placed in the left lateral decubitus position, five needle biopsies were obtained from each prostate lobe under ultrasound guidance. No suspicious areas were noted on the US evaluation of the prostate, which demonstrated a prostate the size of approximately 68 grams. Procedure was performed in the outpatient facility.

   What procedure code(s) are reported?

   A. 55700, 76942-26

   B. 55706

   C. 55700, 10021, 76942-26

   D. 55705, 76942

10. A 36-year-old who is 37 weeks pregnant with twins goes into labor. Twin A is delivered vaginally with no complications. Twin B is delivered via cesarean section because the cord is wrapped around the infant's neck. The obstetrician performing the deliveries performed the prenatal care and will follow the patient throughout the postpartum period. This is the patient's first pregnancy.

   What procedure code(s) are reported?

   A. 59400 x 2

   B. 59610

   C. 59510, 59409-51

   D. 59400, 59514-51

11. **Operative Report**

   Preoperative Diagnosis: Bilateral serous otitis media

   Postoperative Diagnosis: Bilateral serous otitis media

   Operative Technique: The patient has a history of persistent serous otitis media, unimproved with aggressive antibiotic therapy over the past six months, with recurrent acute otitis and failure on maintenance antibiotics.

   The patient was brought to the operating room, given a general anesthetic by mask. The ear canals were inspected. A tympanostomy incision was made in the anterior inferior quadrant in a radial incision. A small amount of serous fluid was found in the middle ear space on both sides. An Armstrong grommet ventilation tube was placed in both ears with alligator forceps and suctioned clear. TobraDex drops were placed through the PE tube in each ear.

   The patient was sent to the recovery room in good condition, discharged with TobraDex drop prescription for two days, and will follow up in the office in two weeks.

   What procedure code is reported?

   A. 69631-50

   B. 69433-50

   C. 69641-50

   D. 69436-50

12. Using fluoroscopic guidance, the anesthesiologist injects an analgesic and steroid mixture into the para-vertebral facet joint on both the right and left side at L2–L3 and L3–L4 for persistent pain secondary to spondylosis with myelopathy.

    What procedure codes are reported?

    A. 64493 x 2, 77003-26

    B. 64490, 64491

    C. 64493-50, 64494-50

    D. 64493-50, 64494-50, 77003-26

13. A 28-day-old male child is brought into the emergency room in respiratory arrest with suspected SIDS. The emergency room physician performs critical care for 45 minutes. In addition to the critical care time, CPR, placement of a central venous line, and emergency endotracheal intubation are performed. What procedure codes are reported for this encounter?

    A. 99291-25, 36555, 92950, 31500

    B. 36568, 92950, 31500

    C. 99466-25, 92950

    D. 99284-25, 36555, 92950, 31500

14. Emily, age 23 months, has severe diarrhea and vomiting. She is extremely dehydrated. She is brought to the outpatient clinic to see her pediatrician. The patient's pediatrician performs a history including 4 elements for HPI, and 5 elements for ROS. He performs an eight-organ-system exam. The physician orders labs to be performed in the office including carbon dioxide, chloride, potassium, and sodium. The nurse performs venipuncture to obtain the blood sample. The physician instructs the mother to increase fluid intake to hydrate the baby. The MDM is moderate.

    What procedure and diagnosis(es) codes are reported for this encounter?

    A. 99213-25, 36415, 80051, 276.51, 787.01, 787.91

    B. 99204-25, 82374, 82435, 84132, 84295, 276.51

    C. 99203-25, 36415, 80051, 276.51

    D. 99214-25, 36415, 80051, 276.51, 787.03, 787.91

15. The physician inserted a ventriculoperitoneal shunt for the purpose of draining a cerebrospinal fluid shunt in a 10-year-old male patient with secondary hydrocephalus resulting from bacterial meningitis. Anesthesia was started at 11:00 AM and ended at 11:50 AM. The procedure was performed from 11:05 AM to 11:45 AM.

What CPT® code is reported for the anesthesia and what anesthesia time is reported?

   A. 00211; 40 minutes

   B. 00210; 45 minutes

   C. 00220; 50 minutes

   D. 00215; 50 minutes

16. What CPT® code(s) is/are reported for anesthesia for a patient having a cystoscopy for fulguration of a bladder tumor and biopsy with the cystoscope being inserted through the urethra into the bladder?

   A. 00912

   B. 00910

   C. 00910, 00912

   D. 00400

17. An MRI is taken to confirm the diagnosis of a subperiosteal abscess (SPA) between the orbital bones and periorbital caused by a Staphylococcus infection. The MRI is performed first without contrast material and then followed by contrast materials and further sections. An independent radiologist reads the MRI confirming the diagnosis. What are the CPT® and ICD-9-CM codes for the radiologist's services?

   A. 70542-26, 730.88, 041.49

   B. 70540-26, 70481-26, 730.89, 041.19

   C. 70543-26, 376.03, 041.10

   D. 70546-26, 70545-26, 730.89, 379.63

18. A patient with recurrent bladder infections presents today for a voiding urethrocystogram. The urologist performs the injection procedure and four views under radiological supervision and interpretation in his office.

What codes are reported by the urologist?

   A. 51600, 74430

   B. 51605, 74430

   C. 51605, 74455

   D. 51600, 74455

19. **Pathology Report**

   Preoperative Diagnosis: Abdominal pain

   Tissues Submitted: Gallbladder, NOS

   Gross Description: The specimen is received in formalin in a container labeled "gallbladder." The specimen consists of an unopened gallbladder measuring 6.0 cm in length by up to 2.5 cm in diameter at the tip. The light purple-tan serosal surface is glistening and the duct at the margin measures 0.2 cm. The gallbladder contains a small amount of thick, dark green-brown fluid. The dark pink-tan mucosa is velvety and free of ulceration, erosion, and cholesterolosis. The wall appears slightly thickened. No stones are noted within the gallbladder or loose within the container. Representative sections from the tip, midportion, and neck region are submitted along with a section demonstrating the duct adjacent to the margin.

   Microscopic Description: A microscopic examination has been performed.

   Clinical Diagnosis: Gallbladder: mild chronic cholecystitis.

   What code does the pathologist report?

   A. 88304

   B. 88329

   C. 88348

   D. 88333

20. A patient presents to the ER with crushing chest pain radiating down the left arm and up under the chin. There are elevated S-T segments on EKG. The cardiologist orders three serial CPK enzyme levels with instructions that the tests are also to be performed with isoenzymes when the initial tests are elevated for that date of service. The CPK enzyme levels were elevated; therefore, the lab codes would be:

   A. 82550, 82552, 82550-76 x 2 units, 82552-76 x 2 units

   B. 82550, 82552, 82552-91 x 2 units

   C. 82550, 82550-91 x 2 units, 82552, 82552-91 x 2 units

   D. 82550 x 3 units, 82554 x 3 units

21. The patient was brought to the physician's office in a severely dehydrated condition. She received one hour and 32 minutes of hydration therapy with 1,000 cc of normal saline.

   What codes are reported?

   A. 96360, J7030

   B. 96360, 96361 x 2, J7030

   C. 96360, 96361, J7030

   D. 96365, 96366, J7030

22. **Operative Report**

Preoperative Diagnosis: Atrial fibrillation.

Operation: Direct current cardioversion.

Procedure: After obtaining informed consent, a direct current cardioversion was performed. The patient was given sedation by a member of the anesthesia department. A 120 J of synchronized shock was delivered but atrial fibrillation appeared to persist after a few sinus beats. A 200 J of synchronized biphasic shock was delivered. Once again, sinus rhythm was restored but only for 50 seconds. Then, delivered a second 200 J of synchronized biphasic shock, and this time sinus rhythm was restored and persisted.

Conclusions: Successful direct current cardioversion after a few attempts with restoration of normal sinus rhythm.

What are the diagnosis and procedure codes?

    A.   92960, 427.31

    B.   92961, 427.31

    C.   92971, 427.41

    D.   92950, 427.41

23. **What is an ureteropyelogram?**

    A.   A radiographic study of the renal pelvis and ureter

    B.   A test for transplant compatibility

    C.   An abdominal computed tomographic study

    D.   A radiographic study of the kidney and bladder

24. **An IOL would be inserted in which of the following surgeries?**

    A.   Cataract surgery

    B.   Tubal ligation

    C.   Ankle arthroplasty

    D.   Lap-band procedure

25. **Which of the following best describes an acetabulum?**

    A.   A flat, bony component of the shoulder joint

    B.   A bone in the middle ear

    C.   The hip joint

    D.   The base of the spine

26. Which of the following vessels is in the third order branch of the celiac trunk?

    A. Gastroepiploic

    B. Left ulnar

    C. Left cerebral

    D. Right subscapular

27. The site of the patient's cellulitis is within the fold of redundant skin in his apron of fat. It covers approximately 20 cm of skin. A swab from the site was cultured and found to be methicillin resistant Staphylococcus aureus. What code(s) are reported for the diagnosis?

    A. 041.11

    B. 682.9, 041.12

    C. 682.2, 041.12

    D. 680.2, 041.12

28. The MRI shows a full-thickness tear of the rotator cuff that is consistent with Mr. John's acute symptoms. The symptoms began when he slipped on the ice Thursday. What code(s) are reported for the diagnosis?

    A. 840.0

    B. 727.60

    C. 727.61

    D. 840.4

29. The patient's dense breast tissue made the mammogram unreadable, and she is here today for a breast ultrasound. Her mother and sister both have history of breast cancer. What codes are reported for the diagnosis?

    A. 610.8, V16.3

    B. V76.19, 611.79, V16.3

    C. V76.19, 793.82, V16.3

    D. V76.10, 793.82, V16.3

30. What is the code for supplies for a two-way silicone Foley catheter?

    A. A4311

    B. A4312

    C. A4314

    D. A4316

31. **What is the code to report 1,000 units of epoetin alfa for a patient on dialysis with ESRD?**

    A. J0881

    B. J0882

    C. J0885

    D. J0886

32. **Which of the following is true regarding ICD-9-CM codes with the statement "in diseases classified elsewhere" in their descriptions?**

    A. They can never be the first listed code.

    B. They should always be the first listed code.

    C. They are unspecified codes and should be used only when more specific diagnoses cannot be found.

    D. None of the above.

33. **What is the correct code to select when a patient is given oral contrast to complete a CT scan?**

    A. Select the code that includes "with contrast" in the description.

    B. Select the code that includes "without contrast" in the description.

    C. Select the code that includes "without and with" in the description.

    D. Select the code for the scan without contrast and a code for oral administration.

34. **Which of the following is an example of fraud?**

    A. Reporting services with codes supported by medical documentation

    B. Storing orders for radiology services in the film jacket

    C. Coding for an intermediate closure whenever a simple closure is performed

    D. Having patients sign an ABN prior to a procedure that may not be covered

35. **When should a provider have a patient sign an ABN?**

    A. An ABN should be signed when a service is statutorily excluded from coverage under Medicare.

    B. An ABN should include the items that may be denied and should be signed prior to performing the service.

    C. An ABN should be signed when the service is covered under Part B fee schedule.

    D. An ABN should be signed prior to treating a patient who requires emergency services that might not be covered.

Chapter 1

1. D. Part D

RATIONALE: Medicare Part D is for prescription drug coverage. The patient's prescription for the pain medication would be billed to Medicare Part D.

2. B. Translating medical documentation into codes

RATIONALE: Coding is the process of translating written or dictated medical records into numeric or alpha-numeric codes.

3. A. $221.04

RATIONALE:

Work RVU x Work GPCI	3.17 x 1.000 = 3.170
+ Transitioned Non-Facility PE	
RVU x PE GPCI	2.36 x 1.072 = 2.52992
+ MP RVU x MP GPCI)] x CF	0.27x 2.984 = 0.80568
= Sum of geographic adjustment	6.5056

6.5056 (Geographically-adjusted RVUs) x $33.9764 (Conversion Factor) = $221.04

4. C. LCD

RATIONALE: National Coverage Determinations (NCDs) explain when Medicare will pay for items or services. Each Medicare Administrative Contractor (MAC) is responsible for interpreting national policies into regional policies, called Local Coverage Determinations (LCDs).

5. B. When a service is not expected to be covered by Medicare

RATIONALE: The Advance Beneficiary Notice (ABN) is a standardized form that explains to the patient why Medicare may deny the particular service or procedure. The ABN form should be completed for services potentially non-covered by Medicare to advise the patient of potential financial responsibility.

6. B. $100 or 25% of cost

RATIONALE: CMS instructions stipulate, "Notifiers must make a good faith effort to insert a reasonable esti-mate…the estimate should be within $100 or 25 percent of the actual costs, whichever is greater."

7. C. Clearinghouse

RATIONALE: A Health Care Clearinghouse is an entity that processes nonstandard health information they receive from another entity into a standard (such as standard electronic format, or data content), or vice versa.

8. D. Protected Health Information

RATIONALE: PHI is defined under HIPAA as Protected Health Information.

9. B. Fraud

RATIONALE: The definition of fraud is to purposely bill for services that were never given or to bill for a service that has a higher reimbursement than the service produced. Abuse consists of payment for items or services that are billed by providers in error that should not be paid for by Medicare.

10. D. OIG Work Plan

RATIONALE: Each year in October, the OIG releases a Work Plan outlining its priorities for the fiscal year ahead.

Chapter 2

1. C. Leg

RATIONALE: The great saphenous vein carries blood from the great toe up the leg to the thigh, where it drains into the femoral vein. The great saphenous vein is sometimes harvested for use in multiple coronary artery bypass or peripheral artery bypass surgeries. Any confusion regarding venous anatomy can be cleared up by consulting the anatomy chart at the front of your *CPT® Professional* codebook.

2. A. Supplies digestive enzymes

RATIONALE: The pancreas is part of the endocrine system, producing insulin that helps control blood sugars. But it is an exocrine gland, producing digestive enzymes that are carried by ducts to the small intestine to aid in the digestion of food. The pineal gland manufactures melatonin, and thyroxine and triiodothyronine are secreted by the thyroid gland to stimulate growth. The pituitary gland produces vasopressin, which raises the blood pressure. The answer to this question can be inferred by discovering that pancreatitis and other pancreas disorders are indexed in ICD-9-CM to the digestive system chapter.

3. D. Integumentary

RATIONALE: Sebaceous glands are small oil-producing glands in the hair follicles and skin. As such, they are part of the integumentary system. The oil, called sebum, produced by these glands lubricates the skin and hair to protect it from dryness and irritation. Hormones can affect the secretion of sebum, and poor hygiene can result in its build-up. Either of these circumstances can lead to acne.

4. C. Lens

RATIONALE: Refraction is the bending of light to focus the image. This can be artificially accomplished with eyeglasses, contact lenses, corneal surgery, or intraocular lenses. In the natural eye, all transparent elements on the pathway to the retina help in refraction: the cornea, aqueous, lens, and vitreous. Therefore, C is correct. The macula supplies nutrients to the retina. The retina is the receptor for the image cast onto the back of the eye. The iris regulates the amount of light coming into the eye.

5. D. Left ventricle

RATIONALE: Myocardium is heart muscle. The heart consists of four chambers. Deoxygenated blood enters into right atrium through superior or inferior vena cava to begin the cycle. From here, the tricuspid valve opens and blood drops into the right ventricle. Next, the pulmonary valve opens, and deoxygenated blood moves through it into the pulmonary artery. The pulmonary artery carries the blood into the lungs, where it picks up oxygen from the capillary beds. Next, the pulmonary vein brings oxygenated blood back to the left atrium. The mitral valve opens and blood flows into left ventricle. The left ventricle is responsible for pushing the oxygenated blood out into the body, and has a muscle mass that is much greater than any other chamber in the heart.

6. A. Male reproductive

RATIONALE: The tunica vaginalis is part of the male reproductive system, securing the testes, which are suspended by a rope-like structure called the spermatic cord. This cord is composed of a number of parts including arteries, veins, nerves, lymphatics and connective tissue. Surrounding the testes is the tunica vaginalis, which keeps the testes from twisting or otherwise dislocating. Tunica vaginalis is indexed in the CPT® codebook. All codes classified under this entry reference the Male Reproductive System subsection of the Surgery section of CPT®.

7. D. Malleus

RATIONALE: The middle ear contains three ossicles, or small bones, commonly called the hammer (malleus), anvil (incus), and stirrup (stapes). Vibrations on the tympanic membrane are carried through these three interconnected bones to the oval window and the labyrinth of the inner ear. Illustrations of the ear can be found in your *CPT® Professional* and ICD-9-CM codebooks.

8. B. Nervous

RATIONALE: Hemiplegia may cause problems with other body systems, but has its roots in the nervous system. Hemiplegia is a paralysis or reduced movement of one side of the body. The underlying cause of any hemiplegia is going to be damage to the brain, which is part of the nervous system.

9. A. Urine will not be able to flow from the kidney to the bladder

RATIONALE: The body has two ureters, each about a foot long. One extends from each of the kidneys to the bladder. A block in the ureter would prevent urine from traveling from the kidney to the bladder. This type of blockage can be caused by ureteral stones; inflammation due to underlying disease; kinks or fibrosis; or neoplastic growth.

10. C. Nephrolithiasis

RATIONALE: Renal calculus is a synonym for kidney stone, or nephrolithiasis. Pyel(o)- is a Greek root relating to the pelvis of the kidney, and nephr(o)- is a Greek root relating the kidney, so all of these terms relate to the kidney. The suffix -ectasia refers to dilation or expansion; hydro- refers to the accumulation of fluid, and pyo- refers to pus. The right answer includes the root -litho, a Greek form identifying a stone or calculus.

Chapter 3

1. D. V20.2

RATIONALE: In the *ICD-9-CM Official Guidelines for Coding and Reporting*, there is a list of V codes that can be reported as first-listed diagnosis codes.

2. A. When no further treatment is provided and there is no evidence of any existing primary malignancy, code V10.87.

RATIONALE: According to the *ICD-9-CM Official Guidelines for Coding and Reporting*, when the patient has completed treatment for cancer and there is not an existing malignancy, select a personal history of malignancy by site. From the ICD-9-CM index, look up History/malignant neoplasm (of)/thyroid.

3. D. 463

RATIONALE: There is no need for a second code for gangrene. In the index, gangrenous appears as a nonessential modifier (eg, in parentheses) with the term Tonsillitis, and gangrenous is an acceptable component of code 463. Similarly, in the index under Gangrene, tonsillitis is classified to 463. The documentation indicates that the tonsillitis is acute, so 463 is the appropriate code.

4. B. 042

RATIONALE: Always pause to consider the meaning of "history" when you see it in a note. Physician documentation does not always dovetail with the language of ICD-9-CM. History is a good example of this. A physician may document that the patient has a history of a disease, and this usually will mean that the disease has been eradicated. But it may mean that the disease is not a diagnosis new at this encounter, but something ongoing in the patient's care. It may also mean that this is a problem that the patient has had and resolved in the past, and that it has recurred. In the case of "history of symptomatic HIV," we all know this is not a disease that resolves. Once a patient has symptomatic HIV, regardless of whether the patient exhibits symptoms, the diagnosis is coded as 042. According to *ICD-9-CM Official Guidelines for Coding and Reporting*, once a patient with HIV develops symptoms or an opportunistic disease, report code 042.

5. **C. 786.51**

RATIONALE: Keep in mind that codes describing symptoms and signs, as opposed to diagnoses, are acceptable for reporting purposes when a diagnosis has not been confirmed by the physician. Coders should select an ICD-9-CM code to describe the diagnosis, symptom, complaint, condition, or problem, indicating why the service was performed if a final diagnosis is not available. In this case, angina was ruled out by the physician, so 413.9 is incorrect. The costochondritis, 733.6, has not been confirmed. The guidelines tell us we cannot report "rule out" or "probable" diagnoses in an outpatient setting; all we can code is the precordial pain, 786.51. Code 786.50 is unspecified, and because we know the pain is behind the sternum, 786.51 is a better choice. See Pain/substernal, which takes us to 786.51.

6. **C. 428.0, 174.9, E930.7**

RATIONALE: Congestive heart failure has many codes, but without more information, we must choose 428.0 (Failure/heart/congestive). The heart failure is an adverse effect of the drug trastuzumab, an antineoplastic antibiotic agent. The adverse affect in therapeutic use is reported with E930.7 (in therapeutic use), according to the Table of Drugs and Chemicals. Report the breast cancer, as suspension of therapy for the breast cancer will need to be addressed at some point in this patient's plan of care, but we don't have enough information on the breast cancer to report anything other than 174.9. Because the patient is still being treated with trastumumab and the physician notes that treatment is being discontinued for contraindications, she is still considered to have active cancer, and a history code would be inappropriate. Note that separate codes exist for antineoplastic drugs versus antineoplastic antibiotics. Answers B and D mix up the two types of drugs and are in error. Only answer C captures the clinical situation correctly.

7. **A. 338.3, 197.0**

RATIONALE: The reason for this encounter is pain management; pain in neoplastic disease (338.3) should be the first listed diagnosis. The patient has metastatic cancer of the lung, which is reported with 197.0 as a secondary diagnosis.

8. **A. 996.82, 199.2, 155.0**

RATIONALE: This situation requires three codes. Notations at 199.2 direct the coder to report a code from 996.8x, and to code also the site of the malignancy. When a transplanted organ is compromised, this complication is the first code reported, in this case, 996.82 *Complications of transplanted liver*. Report 199.2 for malignancy in the transplanted organ and 155.0 for the nature of the malignancy itself. Appendix A, Morphology of Neoplasms, will tell us that the patient's condition is a malignancy because it is categorized with a /3 in ICD-9-CM. Also, looking up Cholangiocarcinoma/and hepatocellular carcinoma, combined, we are directed by the index to 155.0. Code V45.87 reports status in which the transplanted organ has been removed; there is no notation that this is the case here, so reporting V45.87 would be an error.

9. B. 783.0, 276.51

RATIONALE: Although "anorexia" is often a short way of describing "anorexia nervosa," in this case, there is no documentation of an eating disorder as a psychological disorder, so simple anorexia, 783.0, is the correct diagnosis. Dehydration is reported with 276.51. Each of these terms requires a simple look-up in the index and reference to the tabular section to confirm selection. Guidelines tell us not to report an unsubstantiated "probable" or "rule out" diagnosis, so a diagnosis of dementia would not be appropriate at this time.

10. A. 250.11, 488.12

RATIONALE: The reason for this patient's hospitalization is the DKA, which is also the main concern of the endocrinologist, so the diabetes is sequenced first. This patient has had diabetes since age 2, so the patient has type I diabetes, reported with a fifth digit 1 or 3. Although the patient has DKA, there is no mention that the diabetes is uncontrolled, so a fifth digit 1 is appropriate. If there is any ambiguity regarding the type of diabetes the patient has, confirm with the physician before coding. In this instance, A is the only viable choice because of sequencing and the lack of documentation for "uncontrolled."

The patient is also diagnosed with the H1N1 flu. From the index, look up Influenza, due to, novel H1N1. You are referred to 488.12.

Chapter 4

1. D. Trachea

RATIONALE: To find this code in the CPT® index, it is important to know the carina is part of the trachea. Look in the index under Trachea/Reconstruction/Carina.

2. C. Third Order Branch

RATIONALE: In Appendix L, the vascular families are given based on the assumption the aorta is the starting point for the catheterization. The R. Brachial is a third order branch to the Innominate.

3. C. 11200, 11201 x 2

RATIONALE: CPT® code 11200 is reported for the first 15 lesions; 11201 is an add-on code, used in addition to 11200. Code 11201 reports each additional 10 lesions, or part thereof. After reporting 11200, we have 15 skin tags remaining to report. Code 11201 reports another 10 lesions, leaving 5 lesions remaining. The "part thereof" statement tells us we do not have to have a full count of 10 remaining in order to report it. Code 11201 is reported twice. Modifier 51 is not appropriate when using an add-on code.

4. D. Comprehensive/Component; a modifier will bypass the edit

RATIONALE: Refer to the NCCI edit example provided in this chapter. The edit for 11042 and 10060 is is found in the Comprehensive/Component edits for NCCI. There is a modifier indicator of 1 listed next to the edit, indicating a modifier is allowed if supported by the documentation and will bypass the edit.

5. **A. 58**

RATIONALE: The second operation performed was more extensive than the first. Modifier 58 reports a procedure is staged or related to a prior procedure and is more extensive than the prior procedure.

6. **B. General Anesthesia**

RATIONALE: A digital block or topical anesthesia, talking with the family and other physicians, and the E/M prior to a major surgery and during the postoperative care are all considered included in a CPT® surgical code. General anesthesia would be reported separately.

7. **B. Quarterly**

RATIONALE: HCPCS Level II codes are maintained by CMS and are released quarterly on the CMS website.

8. **A. 26**

RATIONALE: When a service having both a technical and professional component is performed in the hospital, the physician may bill for the professional component only. Modifier 26 represents the professional component.

9. **D. 30999**

RATIONALE: According to the parenthetical instruction listed below CPT® code 30130, excision of superior or middle turbinate should be reported with CPT® code 30999.

10. **C. 49560**

RATIONALE: According to the CPT® guidelines for Hernioplasty, Herniorrhaphy, and Herniotomy, the use of mesh or other prostheses is separately reportable with incisional hernia repairs.

Chapter 5

1. **D. Stratum Basale (Stratum Germinativum)**

RATIONALE: The stratum germinativum is the deepest layer of the skin and contains melanocytes. Melanocytes produce pigment called melanin which is responsible for skin pigmentation.

2. **C. A chronic condition characterized by lesions that are red, dry, elevated, and covered by silvery scales.**

RATIONALE: Psoriasis is a common chronic, autoimmune condition characterized by the eruption of reddish, silvery-scaled maculopapules.

3. A. 10060

RATIONALE: Incision and drainage is performed on a skin abscess located on the upper arm. In the CPT® index, look up Incision and Drainage/Abscess/Skin. You are referred to 10060–10061. Review the codes to choose the appropriate service. The correct code is 10060, because there was one abscess that did not need closure, packing, or a drain placed to allow continued drainage.

4. C. 17311, 15240

RATIONALE: Skin cancer on the neck was removed with the Mohs surgery technique. In the CPT® index, look up Mohs Micrographic Surgery. You are referred to 17311–17315. Review codes to choose the appropriate service. The correct code is 17311, because this technique was performed on the neck with two tissue blocks. For the second procedure, a full thickness graft is used where skin from the left axillae is used to repair the neck. In the CPT® index, look up Full Thickness Graft. You are referred to 15200–15261. The correct code is 15240, because the graft measured 5 sq cm.

5. A. 11042, 97597-59

RATIONALE: The patient is coming in for a follow-up debridement of severe dragging injury wounds sustained on both hands. Debridement for the right palm was performed to the depth of the epidermis. The use of a scalpel indicates it is selective debridement. Debridement of the epidermis is considered wound management. In the CPT® index, look up Debridement/Skin/Wound, selective. You are directed to 97597–97598. Code 97597 is the correct code. The left palm was debrided to the depth of the subcutaneous layer. In CPT®, look up Debridement/Skin/Subcutaneous Tissue. You are referred to 11042–11047. Review the codes to choose the appropriate service. The correct code is 11042. According to CPT® guidelines: When reporting debridement of more than one site, the physician reports the secondary code (eg, the second code listed) with modifier 59 appended to indicate the different areas that were given attention.

6. B. 11100, 11101, 11200-59

RATIONALE: Two lesions were punch biopsied. In the CPT® codebook look up Skin/Biopsy. You are referred to 11100–11101. Review the codes to choose the appropriate service. The correct code is 11100 for one back lesion biopsied and 11101 is the correct code for the second additional lesion that was biopsied. A skin tag also was removed. In the CPT® book, look up Skin/Tags/Removal. You are referred to 11200–11201. Review the codes to choose the appropriate service. The correct code is 11200, because only one tag was removed. Modifier 59 is used to indicate the skin tag removal was performed on a separate lesion. If a biopsy and removal are performed on the same lesion, only the removal is coded. In this case there are separate lesions so all services are coded.

7.   D.   16030, 16000-59, 943.20, 941.10, E924.0

RATIONALE: In the scenario there are two different types of burns. The most severe is the second-degree burn to both arms. In the CPT® index, look up Burns/Dressing. You are referred to codes 16020–16030. Review the codes to choose the appropriate service. The correct code is 16030, because the code descriptor gives an example of "more than one extremity" needs to be involved to assign this code. For the first-degree burn on the face, look up Burns/Initial Treatment. You are referred to 16000. Review the code to verify accuracy. Modifier 59 is required to show the different sites of the burns. According to ICD-9-CM guidelines: Sequence first the code with highest degree of burn in cases of multiple burns. In the ICD-9-CM index, look up Burn/arm(s)/second degree. You are referred to 943.20. Review the code in the Tabular List to verify accuracy. In the ICD-9-CM index, look up Burn/head/first degree. You are referred 941.10. Review the code in the Tabular List to verify accuracy. In the ICD-9-CM index, go to External Causes. Look up Burning/hot/liquid. You are referred to E924.0. Review the code in the tabular section to verify accuracy.

8.   C.   11606, 15220-51, 15221

RATIONALE: In the CPT® index, look up Excision/Skin/Lesion/Malignant. You are referred to 11600–11646. Review the codes to choose the appropriate service. The correct code is 11606, because the malignancy was on the thigh and an excised diameter was over 4 cm. In the CPT® index, look up Integumentary System/Repair/Free Skin Grafts. You are referred to 15050–15136, 15200–15261. Review the codes to choose the appropriate service. The total size of the graft is 25 sq cm. Code 15220 is used to report the first 20 sq cm. Code 15221 is used to report the additional 5 sq cm.

9.   11602, 12031-51, 17261-59, 172.6, 173.71

RATIONALE: The first lesion is basal cell carcinoma right lower leg and is excised with a layered closure. Basal cell carcinoma is a malignant lesion, so you will begin by looking in the CPT® codebook at the range for excision of malignant lesion (11600–11646). The range is narrowed by the location of the excision—right lower leg (11600–11606). The size of the lesion is determined by the excised diameter which is 1.9 cm, further defining the code to be 11602. This was closed with an intermediate layered closure. When an excision is closed with an intermediate closure, the closure can be coded separately. The wound is 2.5 cm in length and reported with 12031. The diagnosis is for a basal cell carcinoma of the right lower leg. To find the diagnosis code, look at the neoplasm table in the ICD-9-CM index. Find Skin/thigh, there is a note to "*see also* Neoplasm, skin, limb lower." In the Neoplasm Table, find Skin/Limb/Lower/Basal Cell Carcinoma. The correct diagnosis code is 173.71.

The second lesion is melanoma *in situ*, left dorsal forearm and is used using electrodissection indicating it was destroyed. To find the CPT® code, you would look for Destruction/Lesion/Skin/Malignant which directs you to 17260–17286, 96567. Code range 17260–17286 is for destruction, malignant lesion, any method. Code range 17260–17266 is further narrowed to lesions of the trunk, arms or legs. The lesion measures .9 cm, so CPT® code 17261 is appropriate. The diagnosis is for malignant neoplasm of the arm. From the ICD-9-CM index, go to Melanoma/arm. The correct code is 172.6.

Modifier 59 is appended to 17261, indicating it was performed on a different site than 11602. Code 11602 and 17261 are mutually exclusive according to NCCI edits, but a modifier is allowed to report the services.

10. 12032, 11402-51, 11402-51, 706.2

RATIONALE: The first procedure is an excision of a cyst of the midline upper back. Excision of a cystic lesion is coded from the section for excision of benign lesions (11400–11471). A lesion of the back is further defined as code range 11400–11406. The lesion measures 1.1 cm with no documentation of the margins. Code 11402 represents excision of a benign lesion for the trunk for an excised diameter of 1.1 to 2.0 cm.

The second procedure is an excision of a cyst left upper back. Coded from the same code range as the first procedure, CPT® code 11402 is selected based on the size of the lesion, 1.5 cm.

An intermediate repair was performed on both lesions and would be coded separately from the excision. Although lesion excisions are reported separately, the repairs are added together and reported with one code. The sum of both repairs totals 5.4 cm (2.5 cm + 2.9 cm = 5.4 cm), coded with 12032.

Lesion excisions are reported separately. So modifier 59 is not required. Modifier 51 would be used to indicate multiple procedures.

Both cysts are documented as epidermoid cysts. From the ICD-9-CM index, go to Cyst, epidermod. You are referred to 706.2. Review the code description in the Tabular List to verify code accuracy.

Chapter 6

1. C. Tendons, aponeuroses and directly to bone

RATIONALE: Tendons are white bands attaching muscle to bone. Aponeuroses are flat, wide bands holding muscle to the bone covering. Muscle is attached directly to bone. Ligaments attach bones to bones.

2. A. Neuromuscular junction

RATIONALE: Myasthenia gravis is characterized by weakness and muscle fatigue of muscles under voluntary control. It is an autoimmune disorder caused by abnormal destruction of the acetycholine receptors at the neuromuscular junction.

3. B. 20206

RATIONALE: In the CPT® index, look up Biopsy/Muscle. You are referred to 20200–20206. The biopsy is taken through the skin, or percutaneously. Although the biopsy is deep, it is performed percutaneously, which is reported with 20206.

4. **A. 23076-RT**

RATIONALE: A 4 cm mass was removed from the soft tissue of the shoulder. To access the mass, the provider had to go thru the proximal aspect of the teres minor (muscle). The mass was located distal to the inferior glenohumeral ligament (IGHL). Masses that are removed from joint areas as opposed to masses removed close to the skin require special knowledge and become more of an orthopaedic concern due to the joint involvement. It is coded from codes within the orthopaedic section. Code 23076 is used because the mass was deep (distal to the IGHL).

5. **D. 29881**

RATIONALE: In the CPT® index, look up Arthroscopy/Surgical/Knee. You are referred to 29871–29889. Review the codes to choose the appropriate service. The correct code is 29881 since the tear was in the "medial meniscus" and a meniscectomy was performed. Shaving and debridement of the patellofemoral joint is included in the primary procedure, as indicated by the code descriptor, even though they were different compartments of the knee. The surgery had started out as a "diagnostic procedure," but that changed when the physician decided to perform surgical procedures on the knee, rather than only examining the knee for diagnostic purposes.

6. **A. 24640-54, 832.2, E927.0**

RATIONALE: In the CPT® index, look up Elbow/Dislocation/Closed Treatment. You are referred to 24600–24605, and 24640. Review the codes to choose the appropriate service. The correct code is 24640 to report a child with a dislocated nursemaid's elbow and the physician manipulated (reduced) it successfully. In the ICD-9-CM index, look up Nursemaid's/elbow. You are referred to 832.2. Review the code in the tabular list to verify accuracy. According to ICD-9-CM guidelines: A dislocation not indicated as closed or open should be classified as closed. In the ICD-9-CM alphabetic Index to External Causes, look up Pulling, injury/due to/sudden strenuous movement. You are referred to code E927.0. Review the code in tabular section to verify accuracy. Modifier 54 is used to report that the physician performed the surgical portion of the service. The patient is referred to an orthopedist for follow-up care.

7. **D. 27301-78, 998.12**

RATIONALE: In the CPT® index, look up Hematoma/Leg, Upper. You are referred to 27301. Verify the code in the tabular list for accuracy. Modifier 78 is appended to 27301 to indicate that an unplanned procedure related to the initial procedure was performed during the postoperative period. In the ICD-9-CM index, look up Hematoma/postoperative. You are referred to 998.12. Review the code in the tabular list for accuracy.

8. **C. 26055-F6, 20610-51-LT**

RATIONALE: In the CPT® index, look up Trigger Finger Repair. You are referred to 26055. Review the code to verify accuracy. In the CPT® index look up Injection/Joint. You are referred to 20600–20610. Review the codes to choose appropriate service. The correct code is 20610, because the shoulder is getting the injection. Modifier F6 is used to report the finger that was repaired. Modifier LT is used to indicate the side of the body the joint injection was performed. Modifier 51 is used to indicate a multiple procedure was performed.

9.   25606-LT, 813.42

RATIONALE: The physician manipulated fracture, then placed a K-wire percutaneously to stabilize the fracture. To find the CPT® code, look in the index under Fracture/Radius/Percutaneous Fixation and you are guided directly to code 25606. LT is used to indicate the fracture is of the left wrist. Manipulation and reduction is included in this code and not reported separately. For the ICD-9-CM code, look in the index under Fracture/Radius/Distal End. You are told to see Fracture/Radius/Lower End. Fracture/Radius/Lower End or Extremity takes you to ICD-9-CM code 813.42.

10.   20680-RT, 996.78

RATIONALE: The procedure indicates removal of previously implanted hardware in the clavicle. To find the CPT® code, look in the index for Removal/Implantation. Under Implantation, there is no further index for the shoulder. Implantation guides you to CPT® codes 20670 and 20680. The difference between the two CPT® codes is whether the implant is superficial or deep. In this case, both a plate and screws were removed. There is also indication the hardware was deep. The correct procedure code is 20680, with an RT modifier to indicate the right clavicle. For the diagnosis, look in the ICD-9-CM index under Complications/Orthopaedic device, implant, or graft/internal (fixation)(nail)(plate)(rode) NEC, which directs you to code 996.78. Verification of code 996.78 in the Tabular List confirms codes selection.

Chapter 7

1.   D.   The presence of air in the mediastinum

RATIONALE: The prefix "pneumo-" means air. Pneumomediastinum is air in the mediastinum.

2.   C.   Emphysema

RATIONALE: Emphysema is the loss of lung function due to overexpansion and destruction of the alveoli. Since alveoli are the primary units for the exchange of oxygen and carbon dioxide in the lungs, breathing becomes increasingly rapid, shallow and difficult.

3.   A.   38525

RATIONALE: In the CPT® index, look up Lymph Nodes/Excision. You are referred to 38500, 38510–38530. Review the codes to choose appropriate service. The correct code is 38525. The patient had an incision made (open surgery) to remove (dissected free and excision) the lymph node and axillary nodes.

4.   B.   32608, 042, 136.3

RATIONALE: In the CPT® index, look up Thoracoscopy/Diagnostic/with Biopsy. You are referred to 32604, 32606, and 32607–32609. Review the codes and choose the appropriate service. The correct code is 32608 because the lung nodules were biopsied. According to ICD-9-CM guidelines: If a patient is admitted for an HIV-related condition, the principal diagnosis should be 042, followed by additional diagnosis codes for all reported HIV-related conditions. Patients previously diagnosed with any HIV illness (042) should never be assigned to 795.71 or V08.

For this scenario Pneumocystis carinii fungus causes pneumonia in AIDS patients, meeting the guidelines of it being an AIDS- or HIV-related condition. In the ICD-9-CM index, look up AIDS.

You are referred to 042. Review the code to verify accuracy. In the ICD-9-CM index, look up Pneumocystis carinii pneumonia. You are referred to 136.3. Review the code to verify accuracy.

5. D. 38510

RATIONALE: In the CPT® index, look up Biopsy/Lymph Nodes/Open. You are referred to 38500, 38510–38530. Review the codes to choose the appropriate service. The correct code is 38510. The physician is removing only cervical nodes deep in the neck, not muscles, glands, arteries, and/or veins (cervical lymphadenectomy).

6. D. 31256

RATIONALE: In the CPT® index, look up Antrostomy/Sinus/Maxillary. You are referred to 31256–31267. Review the codes to choose the appropriate service. The correct code is 31256. An endoscope is used to perform a maxillary antrostomy, and diseases tissue is removed.

7. C. 30520

RATIONALE: The physician performs a septoplasty using a graft. In the CPT® index, look up Septoplasty. You are referred to 30520. This code includes replacement with a graft. Read the code description to verify code accuracy.

8. D. 39561

RATIONALE: In the CPT® index, look up Diaphragm/Resection. You are referred to codes 39560–39561. Review the codes to choose the appropriate service. Code 39561 reports a resection of the diaphragm performed with a complex repair using prosthetic material.

9. 30520, 30801-59, 470, 478.0

RATIONALE: The first procedure is to reshape the nasal septum due to a deviation of a bone causing airway obstruction. In otorhinolaryngology, submucous resection is cutting out or removing a portion of a deviated nasal septum after first laying back a flap of mucous membrane, which is replaced or repositioned after the operation. The procedure code is found in the index under Nasal Septum/Submucous Resection or Septoplasty, guiding you to code 30520. The reduction of the inferior turbinates is inclusive to the septoplasty.

The second procedure performed is to remove an inferior hypertrophic nasal turbinates, which are also obstructing the nasal airway. The correct code is 30801 because the procedure was performed using cautery. Modifier 59 is appended to show both services were for different purposes. 30801 would be inclusive to 30520 if the 30801 is performed to control bleeding.

The first diagnosis is found in the alphabetical index of the ICD-9-CM codebook, under Deviation/septum (acquired) (nasal), guiding you to code 470.

The second diagnosis is indexed under Hypertrophy/turbinate (mucous membrane), guiding you to code 478.0.

10. 31267, 30920-51, 784.7

RATIONALE: For reporting the first procedure code, the operative note documents that an endoscope was placed in the nose to the maxillary sinus. This is indexed under Endoscopy/Nose. You will see two sets of codes one for diagnostic, meaning the physician only looked in the nose and did not perform any surgical procedures during the exam. The operative note documents that tissue was removed from the maxillary sinus, making this procedure a surgical one, guiding you to codes 31237–31294.

The codes that deal with the maxillary sinus are 31256 and 31267. Because tissue was removed within the maxillary sinus, report code 31267.

For reporting the second procedure code, the operative note documents that the right internal maxillary artery was isolated and ligated (tied or binded) with three clips to stop the nose bleed. This is indexed under Ligation/Artery/Maxillary, guiding you to code 30920. Modifier 51 is appended to this code because there was more than one procedure being performed during the same surgery session.

For the diagnosis code, a look in the alphabetical index in the ICD-9-CM codebook under Epistaxis guides you to code 784.7.

Chapter 8

1. B. Subclavian vein

RATIONALE: A central venous catheter is placed into a vein, not an artery. CPT® guidelines for Central Venous Access procedures state, "To qualify as a central venous access catheter or device, the tip of the catheter/device must terminate in the subclavian, brachiocephalic (innominate) or iliac veins, the superior or inferior vena cava, or the right atrium."

2. D. Left ventricle

RATIONALE: The left ventricle, which forces oxygen-rich blood into the body, is the most muscular chamber of the heart.

3. D. 402.00

The Hypertension Table indexes "cardiovascular disease" to 402.00 in the malignant column. Guidelines in Sec. I.C.7. a.2 state that code 402 is used when a casual relationship is stated or implied. Vol. 1 confirms that code 402.00 is correct, as heart failure is not specified.

4. D. 33228

RATIONALE: In the CPT® index, look up Pacemaker, Heart/Replacement/Pulse Generator Only. You are referred to 33227–33229. Review the codes to choose the appropriate service. The correct code is 33228 to report the removal and replacement of a dual chamber pulse generator. According to the parenthetical note following 33229, "Do not report 33227–33229 in conjunction with 33233."

5. B. 36556, 36620

RATIONALE: In the CPT® index, look up Central Venous Catheter Placement/Insertion/Central. You are referred to 36555–36558. Review the codes to choose the appropriate service. The correct code is 36556 because a non-tunneled catheter was inserted into the subclavian vein (central vein, not a peripheral vein) of a patient over 5 years of age. In the CPT® index, look up Catheterization/Arterial/Percutaneous. You are referred to 36620. Review the code to verify accuracy. A needle punctured the skin (percutaneous) to place the catheter in the radial artery. This service is reported with 36620. Code 36620 is modifier 51 exempt.

6. C. 33206

RATIONALE: The pacemaker is a single chamber pacemaker. The documentation states that a pacing wire (lead) is placed into the right atrium using fluoroscopic guidance. Before threading the lead into the heart, a venogram is taken through the IV that was placed in the antecubital fossa, which is the depression at the bend of the elbow. Radiological supervision and interpretation related to the pacemaker procedure is included in 33206 as noted in the CPT® Pacemaker or Pacing Cardioverter-Defibrillator notes; therefore 75820, *Venography, extremity, unilateral, radiological supervision and interpretation*, is not reported. Venography can be reported separately if the patient has symptomology to indicate stenosis, such as a swollen arm. In such instances, modifier 59 is required to show that the venography was truly separate. Do not report venography when performed to determine vein patency. Insertion of pacemakers is not a procedure that is performed in an office and the report indicates she was taken to a procedure room.

7. D. 36569

RATIONALE: PICC is the acronym for peripherally inserted central venous catheter. In the CPT® index, look up Central Venous Catheter Placement/Insertion/Peripheral; the code range for PICC placement is 36568–33569, depending on age. Documentation states the patient is 72, so the correct code is 36569. The last note of the guidelines for Central Venous Access Procedures indicates that codes 76937 or 77001 are to be used for the imaging. Documentation indicates the procedure was performed with ultrasound, 76937. According to the description of 76937, there must be documentation of selected vessel patency, and concurrent realtime ultrasound visualization of vascular needle entry, with permanent recording and reporting. The documentation to support 76937 is not evident; therefore, it is not reported.

8. B. 34802

RATIONALE: Endovascular repair codes are selected based on the vessel and type of prosthesis. In the CPT® Index, look up Aneurysm/Abdominal Aorta and check the range of codes. The abdominal aortic aneurysm repair is represented by code range 34800–34805. Documentation states that a "modular bifurcated prosthesis with one docking limb" was used. This corresponds to the description of 34802 *Endovascular repair of infrarenal abdominal aortic aneurysm or dissection; using modular bifurcated prosthesis (one docking limb)*.

9. 33208, 427.81

RATIONALE: The operative note documents the patient is coming in for an insertion of a permanent pace-maker. In the CPT® index, look under Pacemaker, Heart/Insertion. This guides you to codes 33206–33208. The three codes are different based on where the pacemaker wires (leads) are placed. In the operative note it is documented that a lead was placed in the right ventricle and an atrial lead was positioned in the right atrial appendage. This information guides you to code 33208.

Fluoroscopic guidance was used to guide the leads in to position. According to the notes for Pacemaker or Pacing Cardioverter-Defibrillator the radiological supervision and interpretation related to the pacemaker or pacing cardioverter-defibrillator is included in 33206–33249.

The diagnosis for this procedure is in the alphabetical index in the ICD-9-CM codebook under Syndrome/Sick/Sinus, guiding you to code 427.81. Or the code can be indexed under Bradycardia/sinus/with paroxysmal tachyarrhythmia or tachycardia, also guiding you to code 427.81.

10. 33533, 33517, 413.9

RATIONALE: The operative note documents the patient is having a coronary artery bypass. In the CPT® index, look under Bypass/Coronary Artery, which guides you to three sets of codes: Angiography (93556), Arterial (33533–33536), Venous Graft (33510–33516). There is no documentation of an angiogram being performed so this eliminates code 93556.

To decipher between an arterial or venous graft being used, you will need to turn to those codes and the guide-lines. The first paragraph in the guidelines under Arterial Grafting for Coronary Artery Bypass gives examples of the different arteries that are used for these codes. In the operative note it is documented the bypass graft is the internal mammary artery (single arterial graft), guiding you to code 33533.

The guidelines for this section indicate, "To report combined arterial-venous grafts it is necessary to report two codes: (1) the appropriate arterial graft code (33533–33536); and (2) the appropriate combined arterial-venous graft code (33517–33523)." The operative note documents that a saphenous vein was also harvested, indicating that a venous graft was also performed along with the arterial graft, for which you will report an add-on-code taken from 33517–33523. Code 33517 is the correct code because only one venous graft is performed.

The diagnosis is in the alphabetical index in the ICD-9-CM codebook under Angina, guiding you to code 413.9.

Chapter 9

1. C. The transverse and descending colon

RATIONALE: The Splenic (left colic) flexure lies in between the transverse and descending colon. It is where the colon bends sharply near the spleen.

2. D. Jejunostomy

RATIONALE: Jejun/o is the root word for Jejunum; and -stomy is the prefix meaning surgical creation of an opening. Jejunostomy is a surgical procedure that creates an opening into the jejunum.

3. C. 43770

RATIONALE: In the CPT® index, look up Laparoscopy/Gastric Restrictive Procedures. You are referred to 43644–43645 and 43770–43775. Review the codes to choose the appropriate service. The correct code is 43770. The patient is having gastric banding done, not a gastric bypass or removal of any part of the stomach.

4. D. 49560

RATIONALE: In the CPT® index, look up Hernia Repair/Abdomen/Incisional. You are referred to 49560. This is the correct code. The hernia is not mentioned as being recurrent and the repair was performed by an incisional surgery not by laparoscopy.

5. D. 46221

RATIONALE: In the CPT® index, look up Hemorrhoidectomty/Ligation. You are referred to 46221. This is the correct code. The hemorrhoid was removed (ligated) using a rubber band.

6. A. 45378-53

RATIONALE: In the CPT® index, look up Colon/Exploration/Endoscopy. You are referred to 44388, 45378, 45381, and 45386. The correct code is 45378. A scope without ultrasound imaging was inserted into the anus, not through the mouth or an abdominal incision. Modifier 53 is correct since the physician elected to terminate the procedure due to the patient's blood pressure dropping, threatening the well-being of the patient.

7. A. 47564

RATIONALE: In the CPT® index, look up Cholecystectomy/Any Method/with Exploration Common Duct. You are referred to 47564, 47610. Review the codes to choose the appropriate service. The correct code is 47564. There was laparoscopic removal of the gallbladder with exploration of the common duct. This procedure includes incision of the common duct to extract stones and the insertion of a T-tube that is brought out through the abdominal wall.

8. C. 44120

RATIONALE: In the CPT® index, look up Intestines, Small/Excision. You are referred to 44120–44128. Review the codes to choose the appropriate service. The correct code is 44120 because a single section of small bowel (intestine) was resected with anastomosis. CPT® code 44005 is not coded because it is designated as a separate procedure and is considered an integral component (part of or included with) when another intestinal surgical procedure is performed at the same time.

9. 45378, 558.9, V10.06

RATIONALE: The patient received a diagnostic colonoscopy to see if there are any further problems after a history of rectal cancer. The colonoscopy was advanced to the cecum. In the CPT® index, look up Colon/Endoscopy/Exploration. You are referred to 44388, 45378, 45381, 45386. Review the codes for the appropriate service. The CPT® 45378 is correct. The patient is diagnosed as having diffuse colitis. Diffuse colitis means the inflammation is through the entire colon. Look in the Index to Diseases for Colitis, 558.9. Look in the index for History of/ malignant neoplasm/rectum. Code V10.06 reports the personal history of rectal cancer. Check the codes in the Tabular List.

10. 43235, 530.81

RATIONALE: The patient received an upper gastrointestinal endoscopy. The documentation shows the esophagus, gastroesophageal junction, stomach, and small bowel were all examined. The small intestines (small bowel) consists of the duodenum, jejunum, and the ileum. In the CPT® index, look up Colon/Endoscopy/Exploration. You are referred to 43234–43235. Check the range of codes. This is a diagnostic endoscopy which is coded with 43235. The reason for the endoscopy is GERD. GERD is gastroesophageal reflux disease. To find this in the ICD-9-CM codebook, look in the Index to Diseases for Diseased/gastroesophageal reflux (GERD), which refers you to 530.81. Verify the code in the Tabular List.

Chapter 10

1. B. Ureter

RATIONALE: Urine passes through the ureters and flows into the bladder, where it is stored.

2. B. Kidney

RATIONALE: The loop of Henle is a long, U-shaped portion of the tubule in each nephron of the kidney that conducts urine.

3. B. 54670-LT

RATIONALE: Exploration and repair of a laceration/wound of the testicle tissue is more involved than a closure of the integumentary. The service provided by the urologist is most accurately reported by code and modifier LT explains which testicle was repaired.

4. A. 52005, 74420-26

RATIONALE: A cystourethroscope passed through the urethra into the bladder to examine the urethra, bladder and ureteric opening into the bladder. Then a catheter was inserted (catheterization) in the ureter to inject contrast for a radiological study of the renal pelvis and ureter (ureterophyelography, retrograde pyelogram). In the CPT® index, look up Cystourethroscopy/Catheterization/Ureteral. Review the code to verify accuracy. The correct code is 52005. The note also indicates a retrograde pyelogram was performed. Look in the CPT® index under Pyelography and you are directed to 74400 or 74425. In the same section, you will see 74420 is for the retrograde. Modifier 26 is used to indicate the professional component of the radiology service.

5. C. 50688, V55.6

RATIONALE: In the CPT® index, look up Ureterostomy Stent/Change. You are referred to 50688. Review the code to verify accuracy. The correct code is 50688 to report a ureteral stent that is being changed via ileal conduit. An ileal conduit is an isolated loop of ileum to which the ureter has been anastomosed at one end with the opposite end exiting through the skin and attached to an ostomy bag. In the ICD-9-CM index, look up Attention to/ureterostomy. You are referred to V55.6. Review the code in the tabular section to verify accuracy. According to ICD-9-CM guidelines: V codes are sequenced depending on the circumstance or problem being coded. Some V codes are sequenced first to describe the reason for the encounter, while others are sequenced second. The aftercare codes are generally first listed to explain the specific reason for the encounter.

6. D. 55700, 52235-51, 76942-26

RATIONALE: In the CPT® index, look up Prostate/Biopsy. You are referred to 55700–55706. Review the codes to choose the appropriate service. The correct code is 55700. Multiple needle biopsies were taken under ultrasound guidance. The procedure was not done by a stereotactic template-guided saturation sampling to map prostate cancer. In the CPT® index, look up Bladder/Excision/Tumor. You are referred to 52234–52240. Review the codes to choose the appropriate service. The correct code is 52235. A medium-size tumor was removed (resection). The parenthetical note under code 55700 states, "If imaging guidance is performed use 76942." Because the service is performed in an ASC, modifier 26 is used to report that only the professional component was performed by the physician.

7. D. 52234

RATIONALE: In the CPT® index, look up Bladder/Cystourethroscope. You are referred to 52204 — the correct code because tissue samples were taken (biopsies) from the bladder. In the CPT® index, look up Tumor/Bladder. You are referred to 52234–52240. Review the codes to choose the appropriate service. The correct code is 52234 to report the 1.5 cm mass that was destroyed by fulguration. 52204 *Cystourethroscopy, with biopsy(s)* is an inclusive procedure to 52234.

8. A. 54150

RATIONALE: In the CPT® index, look up Circumcision/Surgical Excision/Newborn. You are referred to 54150, 54160. Review the codes to choose the appropriate service. The correct code is 54150 because the circumcision was performed with a penile nerve block (ring block) and a clamp for the procedure. According to CPT® guidelines: The neonatal period pertains to the period immediately following birth and continuing through the first 28 days of life. From a CPT® coding perspective, either CPT® code 54160 or 54150 would be used to report a circumcision performed within the first 28 days. The appropriate code would be selected based on the technique employed (eg, using a clamp or other device or by surgical excision other than clamp, device or dorsal slit).

9. 52353, 74420-26, 592.1

RATIONALE: The physician examines the urinary collecting system with endoscopes passed through the urethra into the bladder (cystourethroscope) and ureter (ureteroscope) to destroy the ureteral stone by smashing it into small particles to be washed or taken out (lithotripsy). This is indexed in the CPT® codebook under Ureter/Lithotripsy, guiding you to 52353.

The operative report documents a pyeloureterogram was done for radiographic imaging. This is indexed under X-ray/Urinary Tract, guiding you to codes 74420–74425. Code 74420 is the correct code since it was retrograde (moving against the usual direction of flow) to show the flow of contrast as it moves through the urethra and into the upper urinary tract. Radiology codes have two components in which a modifier (26 or TC) needs to be appended. Modifier 26 (professional component) is appended since the physician performed the diagnostic service (radiological supervision and interpretation). The hospital or outpatient facility where the surgery took place will bill the same radiological code, but will append modifier TC (technical component) indicating that they owned the equipment that was used for that procedure.

The diagnosis is found in the ICD-9-CM index under Stone/ureter or Calculus/ureter, guiding you to code 592.1.

10. 55041, 54840-50-51, 55250-51, 603.9, 608.1, V25.2

RATIONALE: The operative note documents the removal of the hydrocele (a sac of fluid in the tunica vaginalis or along the spermatic cord). This procedure is indexed in the CPT® codebook under Hydrocele/Excision. You then have to choose if the procedure was performed bilaterally or unilaterally. The operative note documents that a bilateral excision of the hydrocele was performed and the body of the note supports this. Modifier 50 is not appended to this code because the code description includes the hydrocele removal being performed bilaterally.

The second procedure documented is the removal of spermatocele (which is a small cyst, filled with fluid and spermatozoa between the body of the testis and the epididymis). This is indexed under Spermatocele, guiding you to code 54840. Modifier 50 is appended to this code because spermatocele were excised bilaterally, which the operative note supports. Modifier 51 is appended because this was an additional procedure performed in the same surgery session.

The last procedure documented is a vasectomy. This is indexed under Vasectomy, guiding you to code 55250. Modifier 51 is appended because this was an additional procedure performed in the same surgery session.

For the diagnoses codes, the first one that is reported needs to support the reason for the hydrocele removal procedure. In the ICD-9-CM codebook, look up Hydrocele in the alphabetical index to be directed to code 603.9. The second diagnosis needs to support the reason for the removal of the spermatocele. In the alphabetical index, look for Spermatocele to find code 608.1. The last diagnosis needs to support the reason for the vasectomy; under Vasectomy, admission in the index, you'll find V25.2.

Chapter 11

1. A. An incision made in the perineum to enlarge the passage for the fetus during delivery

RATIONALE: An episiotomy is cutting the skin between the vagina and the anus (the perineum). This is usually done to enlarge the passage for a fetus during delivery.

2. A. Cervix

RATIONALE: A Pap smear is typically taken from the cervix.

3. A. 59614

RATIONALE: We are asked to code only for physician B, who performed the vaginal delivery and postpartum care. The correct code for a vaginal delivery and postpartum care following a previous caesarean section is 59614. The antepartum services were supplied by physician A; physician B cannot bill for the prenatal visits.

4. D. 56632, 184.4

RATIONALE: According to the CPT® instructional paragraphs for the Vulva, Perineum and Introitus, the procedure performed is described as a radical partial vulvectomy along with bilateral inguinofemoral lymphadenectomy. The correct code is 56632. Because the description of 56632 includes "bilateral," it is inappropriate to append modifier 50. The patient is diagnosed with a vulvar malignancy. From the neoplasm table, look up vulva and refer to the code in the primary malignancy column. The correct code is 184.4. Verify the code accuracy in the Tabular List.

5. B. 58301, 996.76, 626.2, V25.12

RATIONALE: In the CPT® index, look up Intrauterine Device (IUD)/Removal. You are referred to 58301. Review the code to verify accuracy. In the ICD-9-CM index, look up Complications/contraceptive device, intrauterine NEC. You are referred to 996.76. Review the code in the tabular list to verify accuracy. Under the subheading, 996.7 lists "Hemorrhage" as an "Other complication." For this scenario, the patient is having menorrhagia (hemorrhage) due to the IUD. It also states: Use additional code to identify complication. In the ICD-9-CM index, look up Menorrhagia. You are referred to 626.2. Review the code in the tabular list to verify accuracy. In the ICD-9-CM index, look up Removal (of)/device/contraceptive. You are referred to V25.12. Review the code in the Tabular List to verify accuracy.

6. B. 57100

RATIONALE: In the CPT® index, look up Biopsy/Vagina. You are referred to 57100–57105, 57421. Review the codes to choose the appropriate service. The correct code is 57100 to report a biopsy (small amount of tissue is obtained) from the vaginal wall.

7.   B.   58925, 58720-51

RATIONALE: The physician performs a cystectomy on the right ovary but does not remove it. From the CPT® index, look up Cystectomy/Ovarian. You are referred to 58925, which is the correct code. The physician also performs a salpingo-oophorectomy on the left side. From the CPT® index, look up Salpingo-oophorectomy; you are referred to 58720, which is the correct code. Modifier 51 is appended to indicate multiple procedures were performed.

8.   B.   59510, 59409-51, 651.01, 652.31, V27.2

RATIONALE: When coding for the delivery of twins, the codes are selected based on method of delivery. When one baby is delivered via caesarean and the other is delivered vaginally, you select 59510 or 59618 to report the cesarean delivery and 59409 or 59612 for the vaginal delivery. You would not report the prenatal and postpartum care with both delivery codes only on the cesarean. Modifier 51 is reported to indicate a multiple procedure was performed. To report the diagnosis codes, look up Delivery/multiple gestation/twins NEC. You are referred to 651.0x. When you refer to the tabular list, the fifth digit is "1" delivered, with or without mention of antepartum condition. The transverse position indexed, Delivery/complicated/transverse/presentation or lie, of the second baby is reported with 652.31. The outcome of healthy twins is reported with V27.2, indexed Outcome of delivery/twins/both live born.

9.   58558, 626.2, 621.8

RATIONALE: CPT® code: The physician is inspecting the uterus with a hysterscope, removing uterine tissue for a biopsy, and also performing a cervical dilation and uterine curettage (D&C). This is found in the CPT® index, under Hysterscopy/Surgical with Biopsy, guiding you to code 58558.

ICD-9-CM code 626.2 is reported for the diagnosis menometrorrhagia. This diagnosis is listed in the ICD-9-CM alphabetical index under Menometrorrhagia.

Code 621.8 is reported for the irregular endometrium. The pre-operative diagnosis was uterine mass, but in the op note the physician documents there was no mass seen in the endocervix. It continues in the op note that there was an irregularity of the endometrium. This diagnosis is listed in the ICD-9-CM index under Disease/uterus/noninflammatory/specified NEC, guiding you to code 621.8.

10. 58262, 57240-51, 618.2

RATIONALE: The physician is performing a vaginal hysterectomy, removing a uterus weighing less than 250 grams, and also removing the tubes and ovaries. This is indexed in the CPT® codebook under Hysterectomy/Vaginal/Removal Tubes/Ovaries. There are many codes from which to select. When reviewing the codes, 58262 is the correct code because the procedure was not performed with a laparoscope, the uterus weighed less than 250 grams, and an enterocele was not performed.

The physician is also repairing a herniation of the bladder into the anterior vaginal wall (cystocele) which is causing it to bulge downward. A colporrhaphy is performed by reconstructing the vagina by suturing the vaginal wall and surrounding fibrous tissue. This is indexed in CPT® under Colporrhaphy/Anterior, guiding you to codes 57240, 57289. The correct code is 57240 because there is no mention of a Pereyra procedure being performed.

Modifier 51 is appended to this code to indicate that this was an additional surgical procedure performed on the same date of service by the same provider.

There is only one code to report for the two diagnoses documented in the findings of the op note. The first diagnosis listed is indexed in the ICD-9-CM index under Prolapse/uterus, guiding you to code 618.1. The second diagnosis listed is indexed in the ICD-9-CM index under Cystocele/female/with uterine prolapse/incomplete, guiding you to code 618.2. This code covers both the prolapse uterus and the cystocele together as a combination code.

Chapter 12

1. **B. Pancreatic islets**

RATIONALE: The pancreatic islets (also known as the islets of Langerhans) have alpha cells which produce glucogon and beta cells which produce insulin, both used to help regulate blood sugar.

2. **A. Neurotransmitters**

RATIONALE: Neurons communicate with the cells they control by releasing neurotransmitters across synapses.

3. **B. 64719**

RATIONALE: In the CPT® index, look up Ulnar Nerve/Neuroplasty. You are referred to 64718–64719. Review the codes to choose the appropriate service. The correct code is 64719. The ulnar nerve in the wrist was released for carpal tunnel syndrome.

4. **B. 64635, 64636**

RATIONALE: In the CPT® index, look up Destruction/Nerve. You are referred to codes 64600–64640, 64680–64681. Review the codes to choose the appropriate service. The nerves are destructed by a neurolytic agent in two facet joints. The correct code is 64635 for the first facet joint and 64636 for the second facet joint. Modifier 51 is never appended to an add-on code. Modifier 50 would have been appended if the injection was also given on the left side.

5. **A. 63047, 63048**

RATIONALE: In the CPT® Index, look for Laminectomy/with Facetectomy and you are referred to 0202T, 63045–63048. The correct primary procedure code is 63047. A laminectomy was performed with facetectomy and foraminotomy, along with decompression of the spinal cord. Code 63048 is also reported. The physician performed the procedure on an additional lumbar segment (L4–L5).

6. D. 62223

RATIONALE: In the CPT® index, look up Cerebrospinal Fluid Shunt/Creation. You are referred to 62180–62192, 62200–62223. Review the codes to choose the appropriate service. The correct code is 62223. The creation of the shunt was performed to drain the cerebrospinal fluid from the lateral ventricle into the peritoneum (ventriculo-peritoneal cavity).

7. B. 60252

RATIONALE: In the CPT® index, look up Thyroidectomy/Total/for Malignancy/Limited Neck Dissection. You are referred to 60252. Review the code to verify accuracy. The patient has cancer (malignancy) of the thyroid and a total removal of both lobes was performed, and several large lymph nodes were removed (limited neck dissection).

8. D. 60650

RATIONALE: In the CPT® index, look for Excision/Adrenal Gland/Laparoscopic and you are referred to 60650. The patient had the adrenal gland removed (adrenalectomy) under a laparoscopy.

9. 64493-50, 64494-50, 722.52

RATIONALE: The provider performed two bilateral facet joint injections: one at the L4–L5 level, and another at the L5–S1 level. Look in the CPT® index under Injection, Paravertebral Facet Joint/Nerve/with Image Guidance and you are guided to code range 64490–64495. The codes are distinguished by location, then by level. Codes 64493–64495 are for injections performed at the lumbar or sacral level. Code 64493 is for the first level and 64494 is for the second level. Injections were performed bilaterally at both levels, so modifier 50 is appended to both codes. Modifier 51 is not required because 64494 is an add-on code. The diagnosis is low back pain and degenerative lumbar disc. Low back pain is a symptom of degenerative disc. To find the diagnosis code, look in the ICD-9-CM codebook under Degeneration, degenerative/disc disease, which tells you to see Degeneration/invertebral disc/lumbar. Looking at Degeneration/invertebral disc, you will find the location (lumbar). ICD-9-CM code 722.52 is the correct code.

10. 60225, 241.1

RATIONALE: The provider removed all of one lobe, including the isthmus and a contralateral subtotal lobectomy. To find this in the CPT® codebook, look in the index under Lobectomy/Thyroid Gland/total and you have the CPT® range 60220–60225. Code 60225 is correct because a contralateral subtotal lobectomy was performed. The diagnosis is multinodular goiter of the thyroid. In the ICD-9-CM index, look for Goiter/multinodular and you are directed to diagnosis code 241.1.

Chapter 13

1. B. Eye

RATIONALE: Retro- is a Latin adverb meaning behind, and –bulbar is Latin for onion. In this case, that's not enough information because all of the selections are roughly onion-shaped. A retrobulbar injection is an injection into the back of the eye from an anterior approach. A review of the CPT® index could lead you to the correct answer. In the CPT® index, look up Injection/Orbit and you will see two entries for Retrobulbar.

2. B. Opacities or other defects in the lens of the eye

RATIONALE: Cataracts are opacities or other defects in the lens of the eye, disrupting the visual pathway. Surgeons can remove the defective lenses and replace them with clear, artificial lenses in an outpatient procedure. When the intraocular pressure within the eye rises, it can damage vision by cutting off the blood supply to eye tissues. The high pressure is called glaucoma and can be treated with medications or surgery. Retinopathy is the proliferation of abnormal vessels at the back of the eye, and a droopy eyelid that occurs with age is called blepharoptosis. All of these terms can be understood by studying your ICD-9-CM codebook.

3. B. 367.20

RATIONALE: Always read the notes associated with categories before selecting your code. Under category 369 Blindness and low vision, it states "Excludes correctable impaired vision due to refractive errors." Because the note tells us that the astigmatism is "corrected with glasses," a code from 369 would not be reported. Instead, report the astigmatism, which hasn't been further specified by type.

4. C. 69631, 69990, 384.20

RATIONALE: During the procedure, a tympanoplasty is performed without mention of a mastoidectomy. From the CPT® index, look up Tympanoplasty/without Mastoidectomy. Although CPT® does not have 69990 as inclusive to 69631, according to NCCI, the use of an operating microscope is included in 69631. According to CPT® coding guidelines, which are followed for test purposes, report 69990 separately. Most payers will consider the service included and will not pay separately for the use of the operating microscope. To find tympanic membrane tear in the ICD-9-CM codebook, look in the index under Perforation, perforative/tympanum to find 384.20.

5. C. 69200

RATIONALE: In the CPT® index, look for Removal/Foreign Body/Auditory Canal, External. Removal of a foreign object from the external auditory canal can be coded with 69200 or 69205, depending on whether general anesthesia was used. In this case, there is no mention of general anesthesia so this service is reported with 69200.

6. C. 67343

RATIONALE: In the CPT® index, look for Eye Muscles/Repair/Strabismus/Release of Scar Tissue without Detaching Extraocular Muscle. During this procedure, extensive scar tissue is released. There are no additional services performed during this case. The release of scar tissue is reported with 67343.

7. D. 69436-50

RATIONALE: A typanostomy is performed bilaterally. A ventilation tube is placed in both ears. Modifier 50 is used to report the bilateral procedure. The procedure is reported with 69436. From the CPT® index, look up Tympanostomy. You are referred to codes 69433–69436. Review the codes to choose the appropriate service.

8. D. 67904-E1, 67904-E3, 15823-E1, 15823-E3

RATIONALE: The blepharoptosis repair is performed using an external approach and levator resection (67904). Look in the CPT® index for Blepharoptosis/Repari/Tarso Levator Resection/Advancement/External Approach. The procedure is performed on both of the upper eyelids, reported with modifiers E1 and E3. For the second procedure, look in the CPT® index for Blepharoplasty and you are referred to 15820–15823. In the description of the blepharoplasties, the physician removes herniating fat, which qualifies for code 15823. This procedure also is performed on both of the upper eyelids and also reported with modifiers E1 and E3.

9. 65280-RT, 871.0, 871.4

RATIONALE: In this case, the surgeon performs a corneal laceration repair. From the CPT® index, look up Cornea/Repair/Wound. You have two choices: nonperforating or perforating. Because this is a full thickness injury, it is coded as perforating. You are referred to 65280–65285. The difference between the codes is whether the uveal tissue is involved. The uveal tissue is the vascular layer of the sclera. In this case, the uveal tissue is not involved, which makes 65280 the correct code. Modifier RT is appended to indicate the procedure is performed on the right eye. The patient has a ruptured globe and full thickness corneal laceration. From the ICD-9-CM index, look up Rupture/globe and you are referred to Rupture/eye. There is no documentation of intraocular tissue involvement. You are referred to 871.0. The next code is found in the index under Laceration/cornea, which refers you to Laceration/eyeball. You are referred to 871.4. When you look up the code description, it is "unspecified laceration of the eye." The documentation provided is specific but we do not have an "other specified" option.

10. 69436-50, 381.10

RATIONALE: The surgeon performs a tympanostomy with insertion of ventilating tubes in both ears. From the CPT® index, look up Tympanostomy. You are referred to 69433–69436. When selecting the proper tympanostomy code, you need to know what type of anesthesia was required. In this case, general anesthesia was required, which supports 69436. There is a parenthetical note that instructs the coder to append modifier 50 if the procedure is performed on both ears. The patient has chronic serous otitis media. From the ICD-9-CM index, look up Media/chronic/serous. You are referred to 381.10. Verify the code description for accuracy.

Chapter 14

1. C. Regional

RATIONALE: Epidural anesthesia provides decreased sensation to the lower half of the body and is considered regional anesthesia.

2.   D.   **Introduction of an arterial line**

RATIONALE: Anesthesia guidelines at the end of the second paragraph state, "Unusual forms of monitoring (eg, intra-arterial, central venous, and Swan-Ganz) are not included." They may be billed separately.

3.   A.   **00220-P1, 99100**

RATIONALE: The patient undergoes a ventriculo-peritoneal shunt procedure. From the CPT® index, see Anesthesia/Shunt/Spinal Fluid. You are referred to 00220. Refer to the code description to verify code accuracy. The patient is healthy, which is reported with P1. The patient is 79-years-old, which is reported with qualifying circumstance 99100.

4.   C.   **00862-P2, 189.1, 250.00**

RATIONALE: The patient receives anesthesia for a laparoscopic radical nephrectomy. From the CPT® index, see Anesthesia/Nephrectomy. You are referred to 00862. Review the code description to verify accuracy. The patient has controlled type II diabetes which supports use of P2. The patient has renal pelvis cancer. The distinction of secondary cancer is not made, the cancer is coded as a primary neoplasm. In the neoplasm table go to the kidney/pelvis row and the primary column. You are referred to 189.1. The patient also has controlled type II diabetes. Look up diabetes to be referred to 250.0x. A fifth digit is required. The scenario stated the patient is controlled with type II, which is reported with a fifth digit of "0."

5.   C.   **01830-QS-P1**

RATIONALE: The patient receives monitored anesthesia care (MAC), which is reported with HCPCS Level II modifier QS. There is no indication the patient has a history of a cardiopulmonary condition, so G9 is not appropriate. From the CPT® index, look up Anesthesia/Forearm. You are referred to multiple codes (00400, 01810–01820, 01830–01860). Read the descriptions for these codes to determine the correct code. The procedure was open and performed on the distal radius. The appropriate code is 01830.

6.   B.   **00326**

RATIONALE: The patient receives general anesthesia for the removal of a laryngeal mass. From the CPT® index, see Anesthesia/Larynx. You are referred to 00320 and 00326. Review code descriptions. Code 00326 is reported to indicate the procedure was performed on a patient younger than one year. Code 99100 is not reported because the patient's age range is included in the description of the anesthesia code. There is a parenthetical note following 00326 stating the code should not be reported with 99100.

7.   A.   **01922**

RATIONALE: The anesthesia is administered for radiation therapy. From the CPT® index, see Anesthesia/Radiological Procedures. You are referred to 01905–01922. Code 01922 is correct.

8.   B.   00402

RATIONALE: The patient had a previous mastectomy. For this encounter, mastopexy and reconstruction are performed. From the CPT® index, see Anesthesia/Breast. You are referred to 00402–00406. Check the code descriptions to determine 00402 is the correct code for anesthesia administered for breast reconstruction.

9.   00567-AA-P5, 99140, 36556-59, 93503, 996.09, 414.00

RATIONALE: General anesthesia is performed for coronary artery bypass graft surgery (CABG). From the CPT® index, see Anesthesia/Heart/Coronary Artery Bypass Grafting. You are referred to 00566 and 00567. When you refer to both of these codes, the determining factor is whether a pump oxygenator is used. In this case, it is documented pulmonary bypass is used, which makes 00567 the correct code. Modifier AA is used to identify the anesthesiologist performed the anesthesia. The anesthesiologist also documents that the physical status modifier is P5. The qualifying circumstance code 99140 is reported because emergency surgery is performed. In addition to the anesthesia code, the anesthesiologist performs an insertion of a central access line, which is coded based on whether the catheter is non-tunneled versus tunneled and the age of the patient. For anes-thesia, the catheters are non-tunneled and the age of our patient is 58, which makes 36556 the correct code. Modifier 59 is required because 36556 is a component code of 93503. In this case, insertion of the Swan-Ganz is reported because it is inserted in a separate vessel than the central access line. If the same vessel was involved, you would only report 93503. Insertion of the central access line is included with the insertion of the Swan-Ganz catheter inserted into the same vessel.

The indication for the surgery is a failed stent, which is reported as a complication. From the ICD-9-CM index, see Complications/due to any device, implant or graft/arterial/coronary. You are referred to 996.03, which is for a coronary bypass graft and not the complication for this case. There is not a diagnosis code specific to a stent, which leads to the selection of 996.09 other. The patient has coronary artery occlusive disease, which is coded as arteriosclerosis. From the index, see Artertiosclerosis/coronary. You are referred to 414.00. Verify code's accu-racy in the tabular section.

10.   Anesthesiologist: 00794-QK-P3, 36556, 36620

        CRNA: 00794-QX-P3

        ICD-9-CM codes for both the CRNA and Anesthesiologist: 157.0, 571.5, 577.0

RATIONALE: A Whipple procedure is performed, which is a pancreatectomy with duodenectomy; partial gastrectomy; choledochoenterostomy and gastrojejunostomy; with pancreatojejunostomy. To determine the anesthesia code, see Anesthesia/Pancreatectomy. You are referred to 00794, which is the correct code. Because there are two anesthesia providers in this case, you need to report the anesthesia code for each and the correct modifiers to indicate the types of providers involved. The anesthesiologist is providing medical direction for up to four concurrent cases, which is reported with QK. The CRNA is medically directed, which is reported with QX. The physical status modifier is reported with P3. The anesthesiologist performed the insertion of an arterial line and insertion of central venous access line. The central venous access line is reported with 36556 for this 56-year-old patient. The arterial line is reported with 36620.

The patient is diagnosed with adenocarcinoma of the uncinate process of the pancreas. From the index, see Adenocarcinoma. There is not a subterm for pancreas. There is an instruction following adenocarcinoma stateing, "see also Neoplasm, by site, malignant." Go to the Neoplasm Table and see pancreas. The uncinate process is in the head of the pancreas, which is reported with 157.0. The patient is also diagnosed with liver cirrhosis and pancreatitis. See Cirrhosis/liver. We have no additional information. The correct code is 571.5. Next, see Pancreatitis, which is reported with 577.0. Verify all codes in the Tabular List for accuracy.

Chapter 15

1. **A. Angiography**

RATIONALE: Angi/o means vessel. An angiography is a radiographic image of the blood vessels using contrast material.

2. **B. Lateral**

RATIONALE: Lateral position is when the side of the subject is next to the film and can be performed as erect lateral (standing side) or lateral decubitus (lying down side).

3. **A. 72070**

RATIONALE: From the CPT® index, look up X-ray/Spine/Thoracic. You are referred to 72070–72074. The proper code for two views is 72070.

4. **B. 74177**

RATIONALE: Axial images are created using CT scan. In this case, the patient is administered contrast. A CT is performed of the abdomen and pelvis. There is no indication that scans were performed without contrast prior to the scans with contrast. From the CPT® index, look up CT Scan/with Contrast and note the codes for both Abdomen (74160) and Pelvis (74193). Refer to the code descriptions to verify accuracy. Below code 74160 is a parenthetical instruction directing you to 74176–74178 for a combined CT Pelvic and Abdomen study. Code 74177 is the correct code. According to CPT® coding guidelines, you do not report the IV administration of the contrast because the service is bundled with the CT scan.

5. **C. 77427**

RATIONALE: When coding for radiation treatments, you need to know the number of treatments delivered. The actual treatment is a technical component that is only billed by the hospital. The radiation oncologist bills for the treatment management. From the CPT® index, look up Radiation Therapy/Treatment Management/Weekly. Review the code descriptions. Modifier 26 is not appropriate. These codes are for professional services only and do not have a technical component. There were six treatments. The guidelines tell us one or two fractions beyond the five are not reported separately.

6. A. 73060-26, 729.5

RATIONALE: The results of the X-ray are normal. In this case we code the symptom the patient had, which is arm pain. From the ICD-9-CM index, look up Pain/arm. You are referred to 729.5. Verify code accuracy in the tabular section. The X-ray of the humerus includes two views (A/P and lateral). This service is reported with 73060. Modifier 26 is appended to identify that the physician performed the professional service only. The hospital will bill for the technical component.

7. C. 72158

RATIONALE: The MRI is performed with and without contrast. From the CPT® index, look up Magnetic Resonance Imaging/Spine/Lumbar. You are referred to 72148–72158. Select the code that includes "performed without contrast followed by with contrast," which is 72158.

8. B. 36200, 75625-26, 75716-26

RATIONALE: The catheter was advanced into the aorta 36200 (nonselective) and aortography was performed, 75625. Next, the catheter was pulled back to the level of the aortic bifurcation, and angiography was performed for both extremities, 75716. The radiologic professional services are reported with modifier 26. Code 75630 is reported when the catheter is advanced to one location in the aorta, and contrast is injected for aortography with bilateral runoff to the legs. In this case, the catheter was moved to another location in the aorta, and contrast was again injected for bilateral extremity angiography.

9. G0204, 611.72, V10.3

RATIONALE: The patient is covered by Medicare. She presents for a bilateral diagnostic mammogram. Code G0204 is used to report a digitally imaged bilateral diagnostic mammogram. If a HCPCS Level II code describes a service provided to a Medicare patient, it should be used. Although the exam was normal, it was ordered for diagnostic purposes. Select the diagnosis codes for why the mammogram was ordered because the results were normal. The test was ordered because she had a lump on her breast and a history of breast cancer. From the ICD-9-CM index, look up Lump/breast, you are referred to 611.72. Also look up History of/malignant/breast. You are referred to V10.3. Verify both codes in the tabular section.

10. 52005, 74420, 591

RATIONALE: The physician performs a cystoscopy and retrogram pyelogram. Cystoscopy is a common term used for cystourethroscopy. The provider documents dilation of the ureter and instillation of dye, which is reported with 52005. This technique is used so the pyelogram can be performed. From the CPT® index, look up Pyelogram, you are referred to Urography. Under Urography, look up Retrograde. You are referred to 74420. There is no indication for the location of service, so modifier 26 is not required for this question. If the procedure was performed in an outpatient hospital setting, modifier 26 would be appended to 74420.

Chapter 16

1. **B. Cytopathology**

RATIONALE: Cytopathology is the study and diagnosis of diseases on a cellular level (cyto = cell).

2. **A. Two specimens requiring individual examination and pathologic diagnosis are coded separately.**

RATIONALE: According to CPT®, two or more specimens submitted for individual and separate attention requiring individual examination and pathologic diagnosis are coded separately.

3. **C. 88147**

RATIONALE: In the CPT® index, see Pap Smears. You are referred to codes 88141–88155; 88164–88167; 88174–88175. Review the codes to choose the appropriate service. Code 88147 correctly reports the smear/cytopathology was taken from the cervix and was screened by an automated system under the physician's supervision.

4. **D. 80100, 80102**

RATIONALE: In the CPT® index, see Drug Screen. You are referred to codes 80100–80101; 82486; 99408–99409. Review the codes to choose the appropriate service. Code 80100 is correct. According to CPT® guidelines, "Chromatography, which can identify multiple drug classes, is coded using 80100 (when used in drug screening)." In the CPT® index, see Drug/Confirmation. You are referred to 80102. Review the code to verify accuracy.

5. **C. 88304, 88305**

RATIONALE: In the CPT® index, see Pathology/Gross and Micro Exam. You are referred to a list of Level II–Level VI; 88302–88305, 88307, 88309. Review the codes to choose appropriate services. For this encounter, two lesions were removed. The first one a pigmented nodule falling under code 88305 (Skin-other than cyst/tag/debridement/plastic repair). The second excision was an inclusion cyst, falling under code 88304 (Skin-cyst/tag/debridement).

6. **D. 85380**

RATIONALE: In the CPT® index, see Fibrin Degradation Products. You are referred to codes 85362–85380. Review the codes to choose the appropriate service. Code 85380 correctly reports testing for a possible deep vein thrombosis (venous thromboembolism).

7. **C. 80055, 81025**

RATIONALE: In the CPT® index, see Blood Tests/Panels/Obstetric Panel. You are referred to 80055. Review the code to verify accuracy. According to CPT® guidelines, "In order to report a code for a panel, all of the tests listed in the panel definition must be performed. If tests are performed in addition to those listed in the panel definition, they should be reported in addition to the panel code." For this encounter, an additional test, urine pregnancy test, was ordered. In the CPT® index, see Pregnancy Test/Urinalysis. You are referred to 81025. Review the code to verify accuracy.

8. **A. 89268, 89280**

RATIONALE: In the CPT® index, see Insemination/Artificial. You are referred to codes 58321–58322, 89268. Review the codes to choose the appropriate service. Code 89268 is the correct code because the embryologist is inseminating a sperm cell to an egg (oocyte) for fertilization. In the CPT® index, look up Fertilization/Assisted Oocyte/ Microtechnique. You are referred to 89280–89281. Review the codes to choose the appropriate service. Code 89280 is correct because 4 oocytes (less than 10) were fertilized. According to CPT® guidelines, "Code 89268, Insemination of oocytes, includes the work involved in conventional in vitro insemination of oocytes and is not included in assisted oocyte fertilization (89280, 89281) and both should be reported if both are performed."

9. **Lab Report #1: 88305, 88302, 553.21, 707.9**

RATIONALE: Two separate specimens were received and analyzed: Although the first specimen is received in two cassettes, it is in one container and analyzed as one diagnosis; therefore, it is coded as one unit. The skin ulcer is found under surgical pathology code 88305 (Skin, other than cyst/tag/debridement/plastic repair) and the old hernia mesh is found under surgical pathology code 88302 (Hernia sac, any location). Although this is not a hernia sac, according to CPT® guidelines for Surgical Pathology, "any unlisted specimen should be assigned to the code which most closely reflects the physician work involved when compared to other specimens assigned to that code." For the diagnosis, a recurrent ventral hernia is coded as an incisional hernia (553.21). The second diagnosis is for a skin ulcer, site unspecified. In the ICD-9-CM index, see Ulcer/skin, you are directed to 707.9.

10. **Lab Report #2: 87641,: 041.12**

RATIONALE: In the CPT® index, see under Nucleic Acid Probe/Staphylococcus Aureus, and you are directed to 87640–87641. The codes differ based on whether it is methicillin resistant. Code 87641 defines the MRSA. Below 87641 there is a parenthetical instruction confirming this selection which states, "For assays that detect methicillin resistance and identify Staphylococcus aureus using a single nucleic acid sequence, use 87641." The diagnosis confirms MRSA, which can be found in the ICD-9-CM index under Methicillin/resistant Staphylococcus aureus, code 041.12.

Chapter 17

1. **C. Musculoskeletal**

RATIONALE: Range of motion, strength, and stability indicate the provider examined the patient's musculoskeletal system.

2. **A. The upper central region of the abdomen**

RATIONALE: The abdomen is divided into quadrants. The epigastric region is located in the upper central (middle) portion of the abdomen.

3. **C. 99382-25, 90471, 90472, 90707, 90716**

RATIONALE: The patient is coming in for a well child exam (WCE), which is considered a preventative medicine E/M service. Look up Evaluation and Management/Preventative Services. You are referred to codes 99381–99429. Review the codes to select the appropriate level of service. The patient is new and 2-years-old, which is reported with 99382. Modifier 25 is appended to the E/M service because additional services (vaccines) are performed during the same encounter.

According to CPT® guidelines: "For immunization administration of any vaccine that is not accompanied by face-to-face physician counseling to the patient/family, report codes 90471–90474." Two shots were given. In the CPT® index, look up Administration/Immunization/One Vaccine/Toxoid. You are referred to 90471 or 90473. The vaccine is administered intramuscularly, which is reported with 90471. Two vaccines are administered. The second intramuscular administration is reported with 90472. In addition to reporting the administration, you must also select the codes for the vaccine product. In the CPT® index, look up Vaccines/Measles, Mumps, and Rubella (MMR). You are referred to 90707. Look up Vaccines/Varicella (Chicken Pox). You are referred to 90716. Review the codes to verify accuracy.

4. **B. 99214**

RATIONALE: The answer is B. This patient is an established patient being seen in a doctor's office. The provider performs a detailed history (extended HPI, extended ROS, and pertinent PFSH) + detailed exam ('95 guidelines extended exam of 2–7 body areas) + moderate MDM, as stated in the scenario. An established office visit requires two out of three key components, which is 99214.

5. **D. 99238**

RATIONALE: The answer is D. The patient is being discharged from the hospital. Hospital discharge codes are determined based on the time documented that the physician spent providing services to discharge the patient. The provider documented 20 minutes, which is reported with 99238.

6. **D. 99232**

RATIONALE: The physician is providing subsequent hospital care to an inpatient. The physician performed an expanded problem focused interval history (brief HPI, pertinent ROS since last assessment) + problem focused exam (1 system) + moderate MDM (uncertain prognosis [pulmonary consult], three data points and established diagnosis that is improving). Subsequent hospital codes require two out of three key components. The code documented is a 99232.

7. A. 99285

RATIONALE: According to CPT® guidelines: "99291 is used to report the first 30–74 minutes of critical care on a given date. Critical care of less than 30 minutes of total duration on a given date should be reported with the appropriate E/M code". For this encounter, the physician is short 5 minutes of 30 minutes needed to bill the critical care code. The encounter takes place in the emergency department. In the CPT® book, look up Evaluation and Management/Emergency Department. You are referred to 99281–99285. Review the codes to choose the appropriate level of service. Code 99285 is correct. For emergency room services, three out of three key components are required. In this case, the provider is unable to obtain a history due to the patient's condition. According to CMS documentation guidelines, the provider must indicate the reason why a history could not be obtained. The level is determined by the exam and MDM. The exam is comprehensive (eight organ systems) and MDM is moderate (new problem to the examiner, 0 data points and high level of risk). The proper code is 99285.

8. C. 99348

RATIONALE: For this encounter, a physician is visiting this patient in his home. According to CPT® guidelines, Home Services codes (99341–99353), found in the Evaluation and Management (E/M) section, are used to report E/M services provided in a private residence. This is an established patient. Established patient home care codes require two of three key components. The correct code is 99348. The provider performed an expanded, problem-focused exam and low MDM.

9. 99242, 599.0, 788.30

RATIONALE: The patient is presenting to the office at the request of another physician for an evaluation of the patient's condition. The physician provides a written report back to the referring physician providing his recommendations. This service qualifies for a consultation because there is no indication that the patient is covered by Medicare. If this was a Medicare patient, the service would be reported with a new patient office code (99211–99215). The provider performs an expanded, problem-focused history (extended HPI, problem pertinent ROS and complete PFSH). The provider performs an eight-system exam, which is a comprehensive exam. The provider performs low medical decision making. This is a new problem to the examiner, which requires additional workup, 1 data point for requesting prior records and low risk for the cystourethroscopy. For office consultation services, three of the three key components are required. With an expanded, problem-focused history, comprehensive exam and low MDM, the code is 99242.

The patient is diagnosed with chronic UTIs and urinary incontinence. From the ICD-9-CM index, look up Infection/urinary. There is not a sub term for chronic. The code you are referred to is 599.0. For the next code, look up Urinary/incontinence/female. You are referred to 788.30. Check the accuracy of both codes in the Tabular List.

10. 99202-25, 73562-LT, 715.96

RATIONALE: The note indicates this is a new patient. The provider performs a detailed history which includes an extended HPI, extended ROS and a complete PFSH. The provider performs an extended, problem-focused exam (limited exam of at least two body areas and/or systems). The provider performs low complexity medical decision making. This is a new problem to the examiner which does not require additional workup to diagnosis the patient. The provider orders an X-ray, which is worth one data point. The provider also interprets the X-ray; however, because he bills for the X-ray, the data points for the interpretation cannot be credited. The work involved with interpreting the X-ray is reimbursed using the radiology code. If the provider was not billing for the interpretation (eg, a radiologist was billing the interpretation), then two points could be given. In this case, only one point is given. For a new patient with a detailed history, expanded, problem-focused exam and low MDM, the proper code is 99202. Modifier 25 is appended because another service (X-ray) is performed during the same encounter.

An X-ray of the knee is performed in the office. Modifier 26 is not appropriate because when the service is performed in the physician's office, he can bill for the technical and professional component. The X-ray includes three views, reported with 73562. Modifier LT is reported to indicate the X-ray was performed on the left knee.

The patient has left knee pain, the result of underlying degenerative arthritis. From the ICD-9-CM index, look up Arthritis/degenerative. You are referred to "see also Osteoarthritis," which is reported with 715.9. There is a symbol alerting that a fifth digit is required. Turn to category 715 in the tabular section. The lower leg is classified with the fifth digit "6," making the correct code 715.96.

Chapter 18

1.   B.   Peripheral artery disease

RATIONALE: Peripheral arterial (or artery) rehabilitation uses physical exercises to help reduce symptoms of PAD and is reported with CPT® code 93668.

2.   C.   95904

RATIONALE: In the index of the CPT® codebook, nerve conduction is determined based on whether the nerve being tested is a motor nerve, sensory nerve or mixed nerve. To see what type of nerve, see Appendix J in the CPT® codebook. The Median sensory nerve to the first digit is assigned to code 95904.

3.   A.   98925, 724.1, 724.2

RATIONALE: In the CPT® index, see Manipulation/Osteopathic. You are referred to code 98925–98929. Review the codes to choose the appropriate service. The correct code is 98925 because only two regions were involved. In the ICD-9-CM index, see Pain(s)/thoracic spine. You are referred to 724.1. Verify the code in the tabular section for accuracy. In the ICD-9-CM index, see Pain(s)/low back. You are referred to 724.2. Verify the code in the tabular section for accuracy.

4. B. 94060

RATIONALE: In the CPT® index, see Spirometry. You are referred to 94010–94070. Review the codes to choose the appropriate service. The correct code is 94060. According to CPT® guidelines: 94060 Bronchospasm evaluation: spirometry as in 94010, before and after bronchodilator (aerosol or parenteral). For this encounter, spirometry was done before and after a nebulizer treatment.

5. C. 99213, 99050

RATIONALE: In the CPT® index, see Office Medical Services/After Hours. You are referred to 99050. Review the code to verify accuracy. 99050 states it is billed in addition to the primary service, which is a level 3 office visit. Two out of three components are required to be met for an established patient.

6. B. 95117

RATIONALE: In the CPT® index, see Allergen Immunotherapy/Allergen/Injection. You are referred to codes 95115–95117. The correct code is 95117 because two injections were given and the physician did not prepare or provide the allergenic extract.

7. C. 27250-54, 99144

RATIONALE: In the CPT® index, see Hip Joint/Dislocation. You are referred to 27250–27252. Review the codes to choose the appropriate service. The correct code is 27250 because it was not a hip replacement being reduced and the technique to reduce the hip was by abduction. In the CPT® index, look up Sedation/Moderate. You are referred to 99143–99150. The correct code is 99144 because sedation was given by the same physician doing the reduction and the patient is over 5 years of age. Coding the dislocation requiring anesthesia is incorrect when a patient is under moderate sedation. According to CPT® guidelines: Moderate sedation does not include minimal sedation (anxiolysis), deep sedation or monitored anesthesia care (00100–01999).

8. C. 99173, 92551

RATIONALE: In the CPT® index, see Visual Acuity Screening. You are referred to codes 99172–99173. Review the codes to choose the appropriate service. According to CPT® guidelines: Code 99172 is intended to describe services performed on adult patients in an occupational field where optimal vision is crucial and safety standards for vision exist (eg, firefighter, heavy equipment controller, nuclear power plant operator), as opposed to code 99173, which is intended to be used primarily in the pediatric age group and tests visual acuity only. The correct code is 99173 because under the code descriptor in the parenthetical note it states: Other identifiable service unrelated to this screening test provided at the time may be reported separately [eg, preventative medicine services]. In the CPT® index, see Audiologic Function Tests/Screening. You are referred to 92551. Review the code to verify accuracy.

9.   99213-25, 98925, 724.2, 724.1, 311, 739.2, 739.3

RATIONALE: The patient had both an office visit for depression, and OMT separate from the office visit, so both are coded. The office visit is a level three office visit with a problem-focused history, expanded problem-focused exam and moderate medical decision making. OMT is reported separately. The patient's treatment was for low back pain (724.2), thoracic spine pain (724.1) depression (311), acute thoracic somatic dysfunction (739.2), and acute lumbar somatic dysfunction (739.3). The code for the encounter for therapeutic drug monitoring is not reported because V58.83 is reported when a blood test is performed to measure the level of the medication in the blood or the effectiveness of the drug.

10. CPT® codes: 99382, 90471, 90472x4, 90700 (DTaP), 90713 (IPV), 90707 (MMR), 90748 (HepB-Hib), 90716 (Varicella)

     ICD-9-CM codes: V20.2 (WCE), V04.0 (IPV), V03.81 (HepB-Hib), V06.4 (MMR), V06.1 (DTaP), V05.4 (Vericella)

RATIONALE: The patient arrived for a 2-year-old well child visit. This is a new patient identified by the office; patient does not have a shot record. The preventive visit is coded with 99382. The immunizations given were listed individually. The diagnoses are for the well child visit as well as the immunizations.

1. **C. 17273, 17272-51, 17272-51**

RATIONALE: Codes are selected for the destruction of malignant lesions based on the location and size of the lesion. When multiple malignant lesions are destroyed, a code is selected for each lesion. Destruction can be accomplished by multiple methods including electrocautery, cryosurgery, chemosurgery, laser and curettement. The malignant lesion of the neck is 2.2 cm, which is reported with 17273. The 1.1 cm malignant lesion on the scalp is reported with 17272. The 2.0 cm of the scalp is also reported with 17272. Modifier 51 is appended to indicate multiple procedures were performed. To locate the codes in the CPT® Index, look for Destruction/Lesion/Skin /Malignant, which refers you to codes 17260–17286, 96567.

2. **B. 11606, 15220, 15221, 173.71**

RATIONALE: An excision is performed of a malignant lesion. Look in the CPT® Index for Excision/Skin/Lesion/Malignant and you are referred to codes 11600–11646. The code is selected based on the site and size of the malignant lesion removal. The largest diameter of the lesion is 4.3 cm. The margins are .75 cm. The excised diameter (4.3 + .75 + .75) is 5.80 cm. The excision is reported with 11606. The repair is performed using a full thickness skin graft. Look in the CPT® Index for Full Thickness Graft and you are referred to codes 15200–15261. The code is selected according to the sq cm of the graft. The measurement is 5 cm x 5 cm, which is a total of 25 sq cm, reported with 15220 for the first 20 sq cm, and 15221 reported for the additional 5 sq cm. The patient is diagnosed with basal cell carcinoma. From the ICD-9-CM index, look up Carcinoma/basal cell. You are referred to "*see also* neoplasm, skin, malignant." From the Neoplasm Table, go to Skin/limb/lower/basal cell carcinoma and refer to the Primary column. The correct code is 173.71.

3. **B. 21931, 214.1**

RATIONALE: A lipoma measuring 6 cm is excised from the patient's back. From the CPT® index, look up Excision/Tumor/Back/Flank and you are referred to 21930–21936. The code is selected based on the size of the lipoma. The correct code is 21931. From the operative report, we see the lipoma is removed from the subcutaneous tissue of the patient's back. From the ICD-9-CM index, look up Lipoma/subcutaneous tissue. You are referred to 214.1. Verify the code accuracy in the Tabular List.

4. **D. 27250-RT, 99149**

RATIONALE: A closed treatment repair of a traumatic hip dislocation was performed. From the CPT® index, look up Dislocation/Hip Joint/Closed. You are referred to 27250–27252 and 27265–27266. The dislocation was the result of a fall, which is considered traumatic. Although moderate conscious sedation is performed, it is not general anesthesia, making 27250 the correct code. Modifier RT is appended to report the procedure was performed on the right hip. Moderate conscious sedation is performed by a physician other than the physician performing the procedure. The code is selected based on the patient's age and total sedation time. The patient is 55 years old and Dr. Miller performed MCS for 30 minutes, which is reported with 99149. From the CPT® index, look up Sedation/Moderate. You are referred to 99143–99150.

5. A. 36569, 76937-26

RATIONALE: Using ultrasound guidance, a PICC (peripherally inserted central catheter) line is inserted. A port or pump has not been inserted. Look in the CPT® Index for Central Venous Catheter Placement/Insertion/Peripheral, and you are referred to codes 36568–36569. The code is selected based on the patient's age. In this scenario, the patient is 72-years-old. The correct code is 36569. The ultrasound guidance is reported with 76937. From the CPT® index, look for Ultrasound/Vascular Access. The procedure is performed in a facility setting (patient hospital bedside). Modifier 26 is appended to report the professional component.

6. A. 33208

RATIONALE: Pacemaker insertion codes are selected based on the type of pacemaker and number of leads, also known as electrodes. A dual pacemaker system, which consists of a pulse generator and two leads (electrode), is inserted; one lead in the atrium, and one lead (electrode) is inserted into the right ventricle. Look in the CPT® Index for Pacemaker, Heart/Insertion and you are referred to codes 33206–33208. The procedure is reported with 33208.

7. B. 42415-RT

RATIONALE: The procedure performed is a right lateral lobe parotidectomy. From the CPT® index, look up Parotid Gland/Excision/Partial. You are referred to 42410–42415. Review the code descriptions to select the correct code. Modifier RT is appended to indicate the procedure was performed on the right parotid gland.

8. C. G0105, V10.05, V12.72

RATIONALE: When coding for a screening colonoscopy for a Medicare patient, a HCPCS Level II code is required. It is extremely important when coding from operative reports that you do not code from the preoperative and postoperative diagnosis headings and the procedure heading. From the indication, we know the patient has a history of colon cancer that has been treated. In the description of the procedure we see that the there are no polyps or other abnormalities. In this case, the indication and description of the procedure provide information that is lacking in the procedure and diagnosis headings of the report. The patient has a history of colon cancer, which qualifies as a high-risk screening. The procedure is reported with G0105. Look in the HCPCS index for Colorectal, screening, cancer and you are referred to G0104–G0106, G0120–G0122, G0328, and S3890. The patient has a history of colon cancer. From the Index to Diseases, go to History/malignant/colon. You are referred to V10.05. The patient also has a history of polyps. From the Index to Diseases, look up History/polyps, colonic. You are referred to V12.72. Refer to both codes in the Tabular List to verify accuracy.

9. A. 55700, 76942-26

RATIONALE: Using ultrasound guidance, five needle biopsies from the prostate are collected. Look in the CPT® index for Biopsy/Prostate. You are referred to 55700–55706. The biopsies are reported with 55700. The CPT® code description includes single or multiple, so the code is only reported once. Below 55700, in parentheses, you will see—If imaging guidance is performed, use 76942. Code 76942 is reported for the ultrasound guidance. Modifier 26 is appended to indicate the professional component, because the provider performs the service in an outpatient facility.

10. C. 59510, 59409-51

RATIONALE: The guidelines in the Maternity Care and Delivery section explain that antepartum care is prior to delivery and postpartum care follows delivery. The physician delivers one baby by vaginal delivery and one by cesarean delivery. Although there are two deliveries, the antepartum and postpartum care is the same and should not be included in the delivery codes for both deliveries. A cesarean is a more complex delivery and would have a higher value assigned to it, so it is listed first as a global code with the antepartum and post-partum care included. The vaginal delivery is coded as delivery only with modifier 51 Multiple procedures. This is referenced in *CPT® Assistant,* August 2002, page 1.

11. D. 69436-50

RATIONALE: A tympanostomy is performed bilaterally under general anesthesia. A ventilation tube is placed in both ears. Modifier 50 is used to report the bilateral procedure. The procedure is reported with 69436. From the CPT® index, look up Tympanostomy. You are referred to codes 69433–69436. Review the codes to choose the appropriate service.

12. C. 64493-50, 64494-50

RATIONALE: In this scenario, facet joint injections are performed bilaterally on two lumbar levels. In the CPT® index, look for Injection/Paravertebral Facet Joint/Nerve/with Image Guidance, and you are referred to codes 64490–644945. The first lumbar level is reported with 64493, and the second lumbar level is reported with add-on code 64494. Modifier 50 is appended to both codes to indicate the procedures were performed bilater-ally. Fluoroscopic guidance is included in the code description and cannot be reported separately.

13. A. 99291-25, 36555, 92950, 31500

RATIONALE: In the scenario, the physician performed 45 minutes of critical care. The critical care is performed in the emergency room, which is considered an outpatient setting. Critical care in the outpatient setting is reported with 99291–99292, regardless of the age of the child. Modifier 25 is required because additional proce-dures were performed during the encounter. Insertion of central venous line codes are determined by the age of the patient. From the CPT® index, the patient is 28 days old; therefore, the central line is reported with 36555. CPR is reported with 92950, and is found in the CPT® index under Cardiopulmonary Resuscitation. Look in the CPT® index under Intubation/Endotracheal Tube, for code 31500, which is modifier 51 exempt. The additional procedures performed are not bundled with critical care codes 99291–99292.

14. D. 99214-25, 36415, 80051, 276.51, 787.03, 787.91

RATIONALE: The patient is seen by her pediatrician, which is an indication she is an established patient. The physician performs an expanded problem focused history (4 HPI and 5 ROS). Because a PSFH is not performed, the highest level for history is expanded problem focused. The provider performs an eight-organ-system exam, which is a comprehensive exam. The MDM is moderate. For an established patient with expanded problem focused history, comprehensive exam, and moderate MDM, the E/M level is 99214. Modifier 25 is appended, because venipuncture is performed in the office. Venipuncture is reported with 36415. The labs are reported with an electrolyte panel, which is reported with 80051. The patient is diagnosed with dehydration, vomiting and diarrhea. From the Index to Diseases, look up Dehydration. You are referred to 276.51. Look up Vomiting. You are referred to 787.03. Look up Diarrhea. You are referred to 787.91. Verify the codes In the Tabular List.

15. C. 00220; 50 minutes

RATIONALE: From the CPT® codebook, look up Anesthesia/Shunt/Spinal Fluid. You are referred to code 00220. Anesthesia time is determined by the anesthesia start and stop times. In this case, the anesthesia lasted 50 minutes. Surgical start and stop times are not relevant when determining anesthesia time.

16. B. 00910

RATIONALE: Anesthesia codes are selected based on the anatomical site of the surgery performed. When more than one procedure is performed, the anesthesia code for the most labor-intensive procedure is reported. From the CPT® index, look up Urethrocystoscopy. You are referred to 00910. In the code description for 00910 , you will see urethroscopy.

17. C. 70543-26, 376.03, 041.10

RATIONALE: Magnetic imaging codes are selected based on the area being imaged, whether contrast is used, and in what sequence. Documentation shows the MRI was performed to confirm a diagnosis pertaining to the orbital bones. Look in the CPT® index for Magnetic Resonance Imaging (MRI)/Orbit, and you are referred to code sequence 70540–70543. Because the MRI was performed without contrast, and then repeated with contrast, the correct code is 70543. The physician provided only the professional component, reported with modifier 26.

In the ICD-9-CM alphabetic index, Abscess/subperiosteal refers you to *see* Abscess, bone. Periosteum is the membrane covering bones, so subperiosteal is referring to bone, reported with 730.0x. There is also a note to "*see also* Osteomyelitis." Osteomyeliltis is an infection in the bone, and indexed under it is orbital, 376.03. According to Vol. 1, code 730.0x is used for "abscess any bone except accessory sinus." The orbital bones, in part, define the accessory sinus, so this is not the correct code. Go next to 376.03, described as "orbital osteomy-elitis," to find the correct code. Also code the infectious organism, identified as Staphylococcus, 041.10. This is found in the Index to Disease under Infection/staphylococcal NEC.

18. D. 51600, 74455

RATIONALE: Look in the CPT® lindex for Urethrocystography/Voiding and you are referred to 51600. Injection for a voiding urethrocystogram is described by code 51600. Under the code is a parenthetical note to see 74430 or 74455 for the S&I. Code 74455 is for the procedure S&I, as documented. No modifier is used on the radiology code, because the procedure was performed in the urologist's office.

19. A. 88304

RATIONALE: Surgical pathology examinations are reported based on the type of tissue examined. The description of the pathology includes both a gross description and a microscopic description of the gallbladder. In this case, the surgical specimen is the gallbladder, reported with 88304. This is found in the CPT® index under Pathology/Surgical/Gross and Micro Exam.

20. C. 82550, 82550-91 x 2 units, 82552, 82552-91 x 2 units

RATIONALE: CPK enzymes levels are reported with 82550, which is a total creatinine kinase. The physician orders a series of three. When lab tests are repeated as a result of a physician order, and not due to an error in the test, modifier 91 is reported on the lab codes to indicate the services were repeated. The second and third CPK test is reported with 2 units of 82550 with modifier 91. In the order, the physician also requests that should the tests be elevated, which they were, that the isoenzyme CPK be performed as well. This is reported with 82552 for the initial test and two units of 82552 with modifier 91 for the second and third tests. This is found in the CPT® index under CPK/Blood. You are referred to 82550–82552. The CPK is report with 82550, and the isoenzym study is reported with 82552.

21. C. 96360, 96361, J7030

RATIONALE: Look in the CPT® index for Hydration, which is reported with codes 96360 through 96361. Code 96360 is reported for the first hour. Code 96361 is reported for each additional hour. There is a parenthetical note following 96361 which states that 96361 is reported for intervals of greater than 30 minutes. Because an additional 32 minutes was performed, 96361 is also reported. The 1,000 cc of normal saline is reported with J7030, which can be found in the HCPCS index under Saline/infusion.

22. A. 92960, 427.31

RATIONALE: The procedure performed is an elective cardioversion. From the CPT® index, look up Cardioversion. You are referred to 92960–92961. The procedure performed is external, reported with 92960. The patient is diagnosed with atrial fibrillation. From the Index to Diseases, look up Fibrillation/atrial. You are referred to 427.31. Verify code accuracy in the Tabular List.

23. A. A radiographic study of the renal pelvis and ureter

RATIONALE: Pyelo- refers to the renal pelvis, and -gram indicates a written record or graph. In ureteropyelo-gram, an X-ray study of the renal pelvis and ureters is performed. This examination may reveal any abnormalities within the renal pelvis or ureters.

24. A. Cataract surgery

RATIONALE: IOL is an acronym for intraocular lens. This is an artificial lens that replaces the crystalline lens following cataract surgery. Insertion of IOLs in cataract surgery is the most commonly performed procedure in ophthalmology.

25. C. The hip joint

RATIONALE: The acetabulum is composed of three bones: the ischium, ilium, and pubis. With these three bones, the acetabulum forms the socket for the femoral head.

26. A. Gastroepiploic

RATIONALE: This may seem like a very tough question, and without your codebook resources, it would be. Very few coders who aren't coding vascular procedures on a daily basis would know this answer. But the job as coders is to be resourceful, and to be able to find answers to our questions quickly. In this case, Appendix L of your CPT® codebook contains charts with the vascular families, and the answer is easily found by turning to the section for First Order, Celiac trunk.

27. C. 682.2, 041.12

RATIONALE: The "apron of fat" is belly fat that creates a redundancy of skin along the hip line of an obese person's front torso, part of the "trunk." This scenario requires two codes: one to report the cellulitis, and one to report the infective agent causing the cellulitis. Code 682.2 reports cellulitis of that region, and 041.12 reports methicillin resistant Staphylococcus aureus (MRSA). MRSA is more difficult to treat than methicillin susceptible staph (MSSA), and this differentiation is clinically significant.

28. D. 840.4

RATIONALE: The key to this one is the presence of a new injury, versus a chronic condition. If you read the section at the beginning of Sprains and Strains, it says that laceration or rupture of joint capsule, ligament, muscle, or tendon is reported with these codes. That makes 840.4 the right choice here. The codes in the 727.6x series are for use when the rotator cuff is fraying over time. There is no overt injury precipitating the pain. Keep in mind: In some cases two codes may be required, as some patients experience acute injuries on chronic conditions. In this case, no chronic condition was documented, and under Tear/rotator cuff/current injury, we are directed to 840.4.

29. C. V76.19, 793.82, V16.3

RATIONALE: Code the special screening as a reason for the encounter, along with a code to report the patient's breast density, which provides medical necessity for a more extensive test. Dense breast tissue occurs in many premenopausal women, and can interfere with reading a mammogram and mask abnormalities in the image. Look in the Index to Diseases for Screening/malignant neoplasm/breast/specified type NEC, and you are referred to V76.19 for the screening ultrasound. Code V76.19 reports a known alternative method (ultrasound). Code 793.82 was introduced to ICD-9-CM to capture breast density and provide a way to report the medical necessity of an ultrasound. Code 793.82 is found in the Index to Diseases under Breast/dense. The family history of breast cancer is found in the Index to Diseases under History/family/malignant neoplasm/breast, and is report with V16.3.

30. B. A4312

RATIONALE: In the HCPCS Level II codebook, look up Foley catheter. Review the code range to which you are referred. A two-way silicone Foley catheter insertion tray is reported with A4312.

31. D. J0886

RATIONALE: In the HCPCS Level II codebook, look in the Table of Drugs for Epoetin alfa. There are two code options to report 1,000 units. Code J0886 is used for a patient with ESRD who is on dialysis.

32. A. They can never be the first listed code

RATIONALE: According to the ICD-9-CM coding guidelines, in most cases manifestation codes will have in the code title, "in diseases classified elsewhere." Codes with this title are a component of the etiology/ manifestation convention. The code title indicates that it is a manifestation code. "In diseases classified elsewhere" codes are never permitted to be used as first-listed or principal diagnosis codes. They must be used in conjunction with an underlying condition code, and they must be listed following the underlying condition.

33. B. Select the code that includes "without contrast" in the description

RATIONALE: According to the CPT® coding guidelines, the phrase "with contrast" is used when contrast is administered intravascularly, intra-articularly or intrathecally. Oral or rectal contrast does not qualify for "with contrast."

34. C. Coding for an intermediate closure whenever a simple closure is performed

RATIONALE: The only example of fraud in the answers provided is reporting an intermediate closure instead of a simple closure. This is an example of upcoding services rendered.

35. B. An ABN should include the items that may be denied and should be signed prior to performing the service

RATIONALE: An Advance Beneficiary Notice (ABN) must be signed prior to performing the service. The ABN must include the amount for which the patient will be responsible if the service is denied by Medicare and the reason for the potential denial.

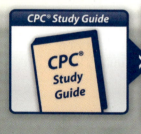